CHAMOUN

THE ART AND LIFE OF
CHAOUKI CHAMOUN

SAQI

Acknowledgements

To my colleague, Dr Nazik Yared, for her diligent work in conducting and eloquently transcribing hours of taped interviews covering historic data about my life, up to the year 2000.

To the renowned art critics and journalists: May Menassa, Akl Awit, Abdo Wazin, Jack Aswad, Nicole Harfouche, Maha Sultan, Faisal Sultan, Ivana Marchalian, Nazih Khater, Lore Ghorayeb and Joseph Tarrab, among others, for their published interviews and reviews in several Lebanese papers and magazines since 1985. They were instrumental in recalling facts, ideas, philosophical and aesthetic issues I raised and discussed at the time, which I conveniently incorporated into my story, as I was reflecting on my earlier works and exhibits.

And finally, to my colleague Brian Prescott-Decie, for his invaluable first reading and editing of the text.

ISBN 978-0-86356-791-9

First published 2013 by Saqi Books

www.chaoukichamoun.com

A full CIP record for this book is available from the British Library.

A full CIP record for this book is available from the Library of Congress.

Printed in Lebanon by Calligraph
Bound by Fouad Baayno Bookbindery

SAQI

26 Westbourne Grove, London W2 5RH
www.saqibooks.com

Contents

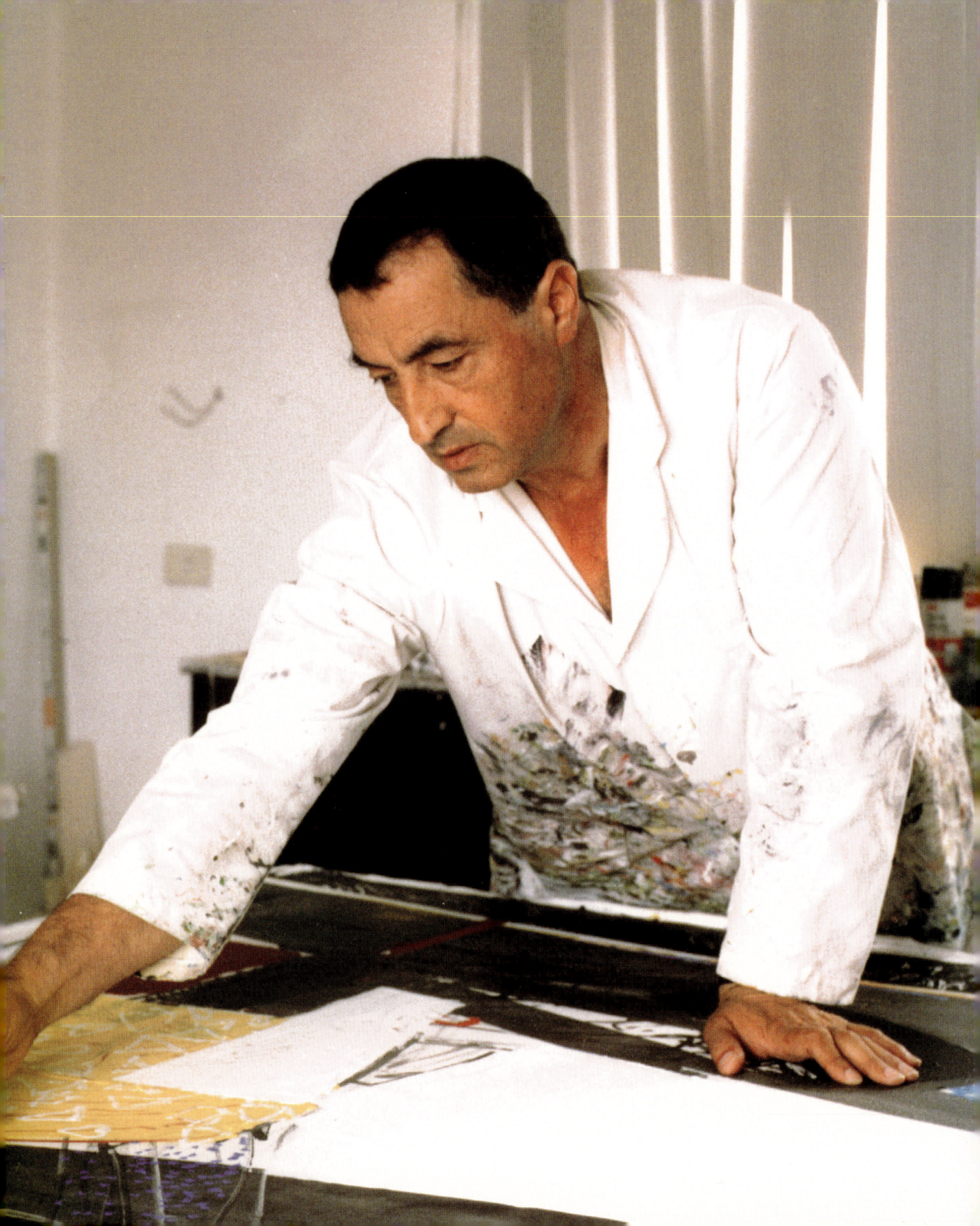

Late on a hot summer afternoon in 1952, I nibbled on breadcrumbs scavenged from the bottom of my backpack as I wandered along with our newly purchased cow. My father, whom I had left behind working on his land, had asked me to lead her home to rest for the day. It was a long and lonely walk.

The mountains surrounding the Bekaa Valley were the limit of my world. I did not question what might be behind them, for I knew that the sun had risen over one side and was on its way to set behind the other. I knew my mother would be waiting for me impatiently: a few days ago, as she was stuffing my backpack with food, I had heard her cursing the day my father had bought that cow and wishing that it would never yield the fresh milk my father hoped to provide for the family. She was adamantly opposed to letting me care for a cow. I was the oldest and the closest to her heart, and she did not want me to be a cowboy even for a day.

Unexpectedly, the cow started hopping, jumping and chasing her tail. An insect had stung her. Then she galloped off at top speed towards the nearby town where we had bought her from my aunt. I ran after her but soon I was way behind; out of breath, frightened and tired, struggling to keep her in view. Crossing a field of wheat that was taller than me, a large bird flew out of hiding into the air, scaring me so witless that I fell onto my back. I had lost sight of the cow. I got up and kept going towards my aunt's house. Luckily, I found the cow there. 'We told his father the kid wouldn't be able to handle this cow,' my aunt told her husband angrily. Only after she had washed and fed me did she let me walk back home. This time I was alone.

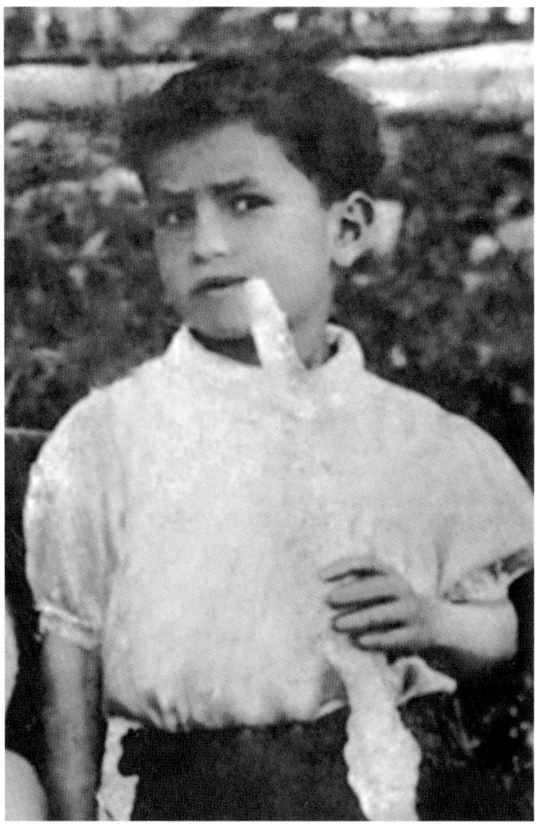

Just as it was getting dark, I saw my mom and dad from a distance, standing in front of our house. I began wondering what my father would do. I expected a beating, but how long would it last and what would he use? My worried mother started running towards me, screaming as soon as she saw me: 'What has happened to you? Where have you been? Are you well?' She picked me up, kissing and wiping my face, checking my body to make sure I had not been harmed.

'What happened to Arouss?' my father asked.

'To hell with Arouss,' my mother replied. 'I hope she's lost. I hope she's dead. I won't have her back. My son ought to be in a good school, not caring for a cow.'

1
Palm Sunday, 1947

Facing page
2
DAD, 1972
Watercolor
39 x 45.5 cm

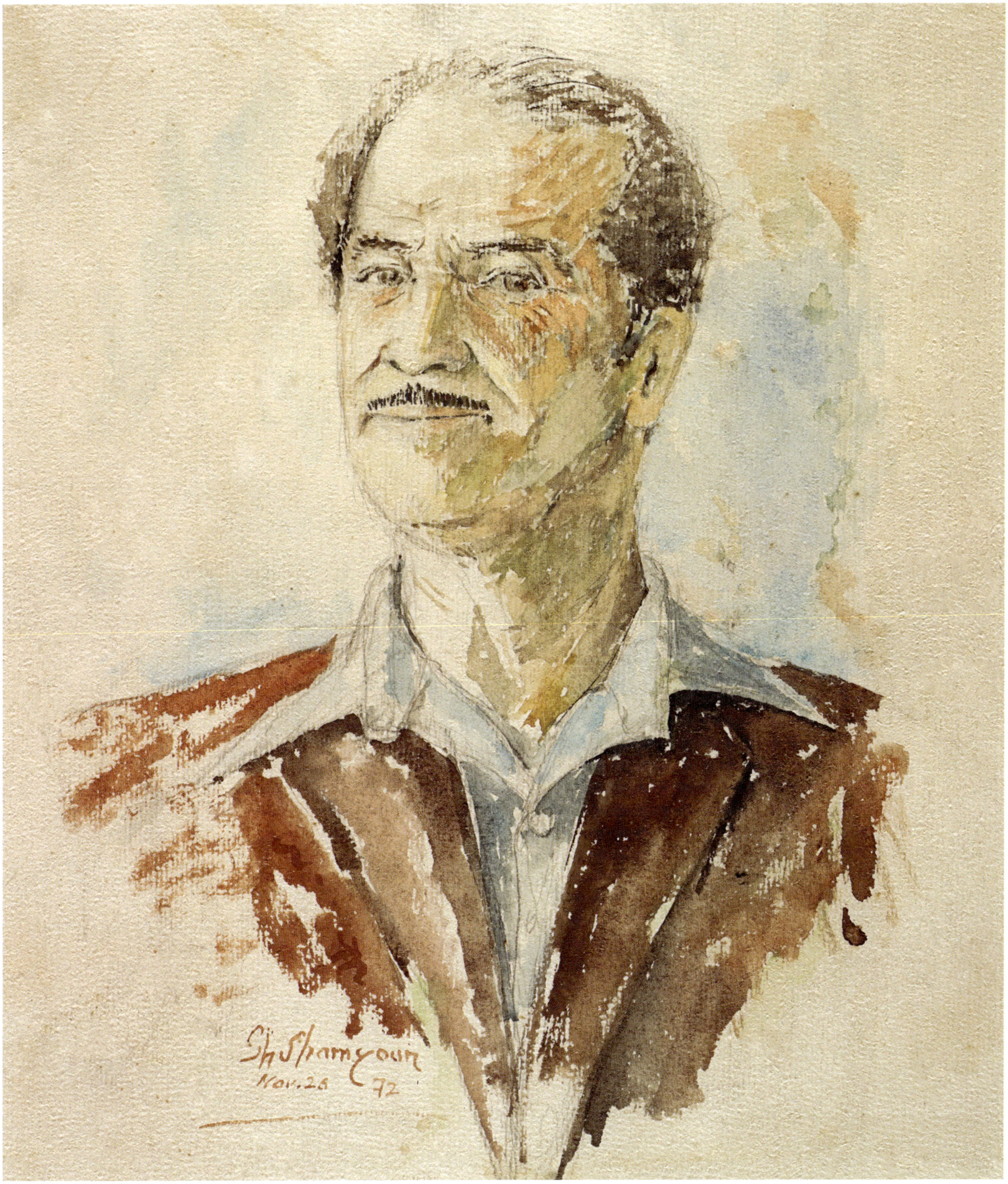
Sh Shamyoun
Nov. 26 72

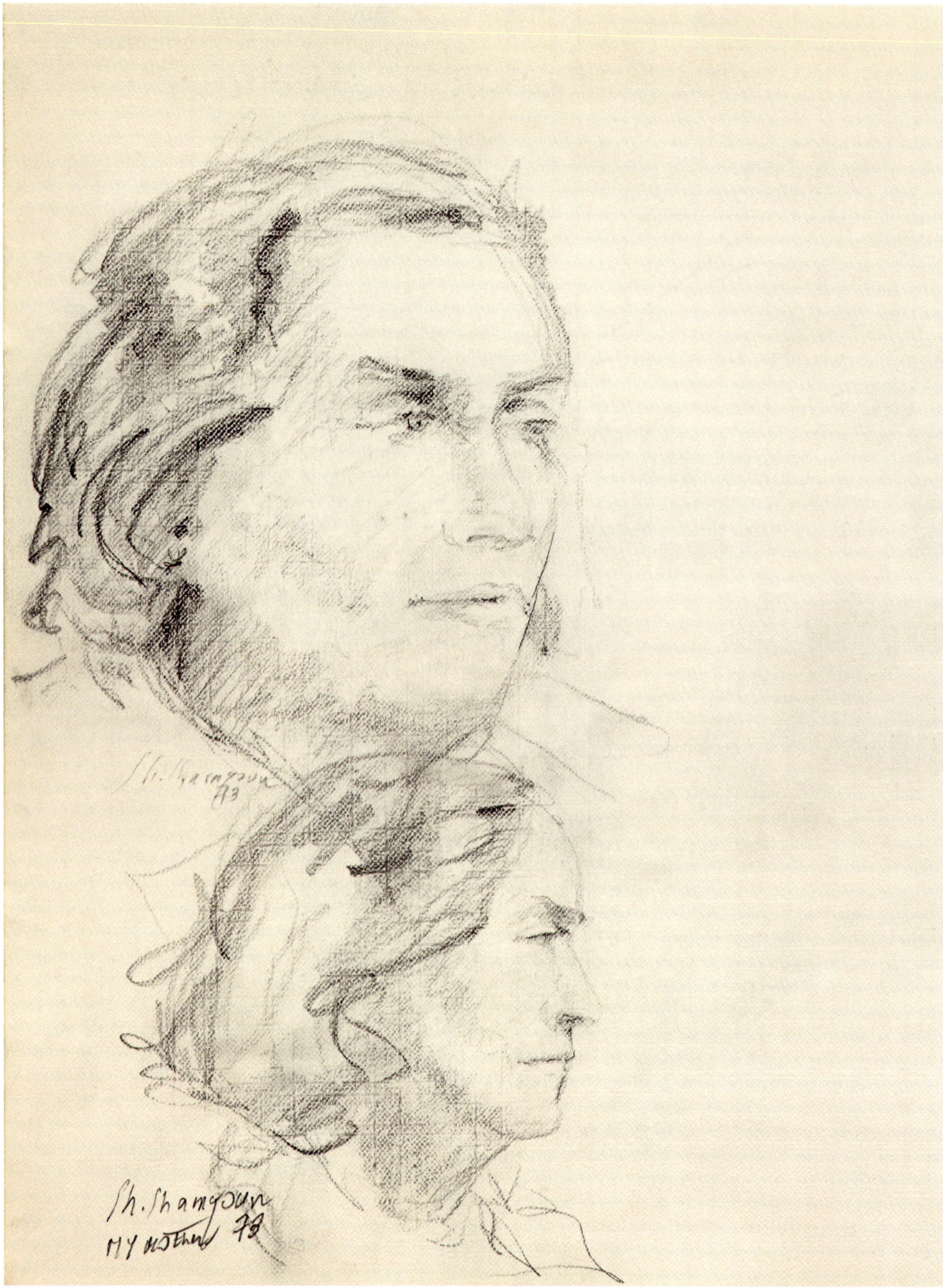

The Beginning and Years of Self-Discovery

I was born in Lebanon on 19 January 1942 in Sariine Tahta near
Baalbeck in the Bekaa Valley, the eldest of four brothers and
2 two sisters. My father, who was born in 1911, was the youngest
of four. He was raised by his mother Mariam and her brother
Youssef, who helped move the family from Zahle to Sariine
after his father died in the early days of World War I. My
3 father did not recall having met him. My mother was born in
1925. Her parents both died when she was still an infant, so she
was unable to describe them to me.

At the age of seventeen, my father joined the army as a soldier. Thereafter, our family had to move whenever he was reassigned. Thus, when I was around three and a half years old, we moved to Shiyah. I remember the ground floor of the small two-level house we lived in and the orange trees surrounding it. Another picture I retain from childhood is of a second floor apartment, with an external staircase that seemed to
extend beyond what I could see. That was in Achrafieh, in the
4 Siyyar area. Across from us lived my uncle Dib and his family,
who had raised my mother.

Our next move was to the Fayadiyeh army barracks. We lived in a big one-room home with a tin roof: the bathroom

Facing page
3
MY MOTHER, 1973
Pencil on paper
25 x 35.5 cm

and drinking water, both outside the house, were shared with
the neighbours. I must have been around five years old when 1
we went there, because I remember my parents taking me to a private school in the upper section of the old town. I was given candy that day, and I later wondered why they did not keep on giving me candy. It was a very windy day, and the wind kept blowing sand onto the naked skin below my shorts. I can still feel the itch in my legs. And I also recall being on the sidewalk of the nearby Damascus highway on my way home from school when I was hit by a car. My mother and two young men rushed to take me to a nearby doctor's clinic.

When I was about seven, the family returned to the one-
room house in Sariine where I had been born. It was a typical 5, 9
peasant house with clay walls, roof and floor. There was a *maw'adeh* (fireplace), and a *leyouk* (hollow) for storing the mattresses and blankets in the thick wall which separated the living area from the *mouneh* (storage area). We had one brass bed, which my parents had brought back with them from Fayadiyeh; a wooden linen chest with decorative engravings by the northern wall; and two three-seater benches with arms. I loved caressing the engravings on the wooden box, once spreading a piece of paper over them and rubbing my pencil over it to create a printed image of it.

I was sent to a one-room school nearby in the village, which was run by a distant relative. I had to take a pomegranate branch with me to school, so that the teacher, Uncle Wadih,

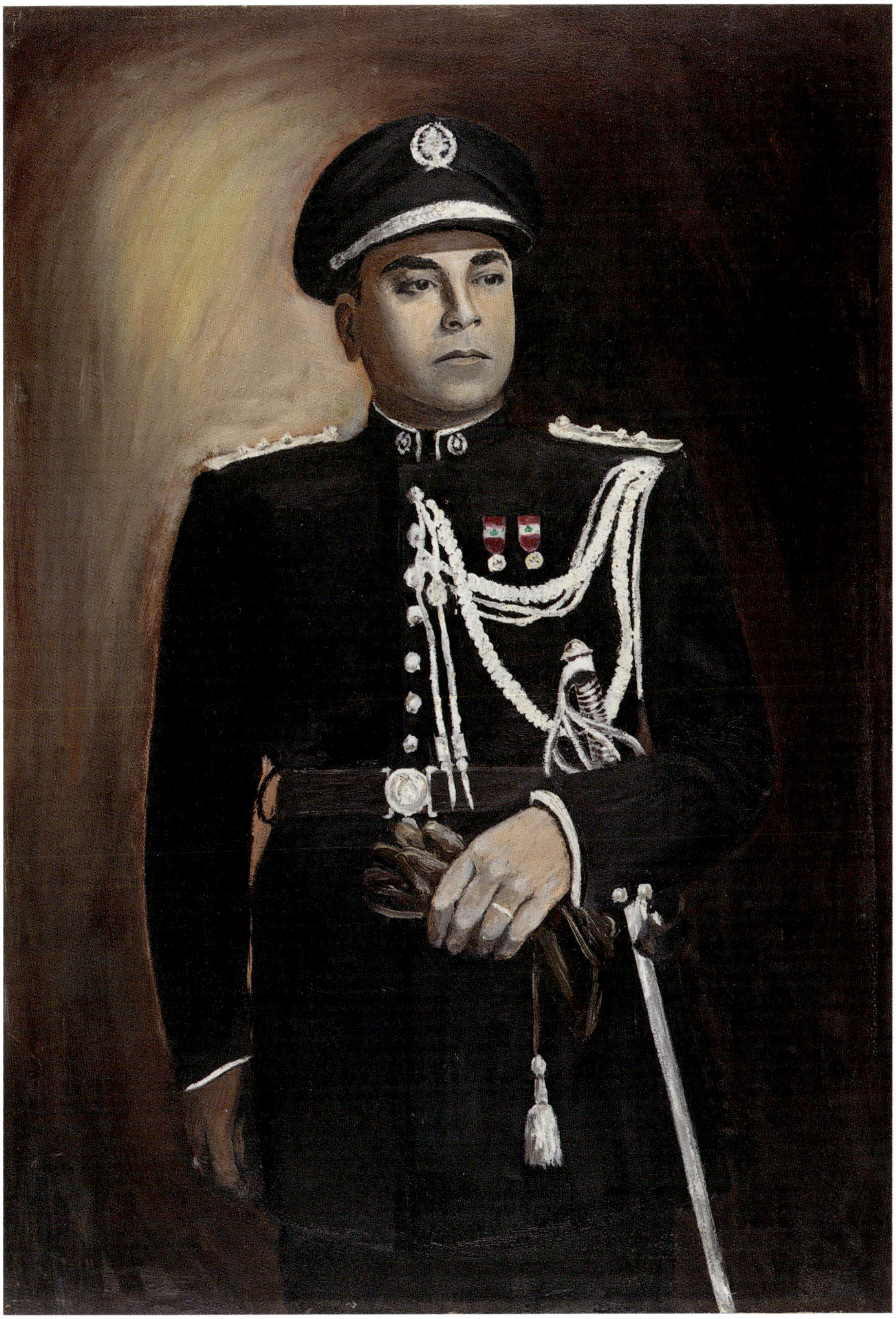

4
UNCLE DIB, 1963
Oil on canvas
54.5 x 80 cm

Until autumn 1968, 'Uncle Dib' was the only painting from the self-taught era that remained with the family. Paintings were given away, lost, or bought by collectors whom I could not locate.

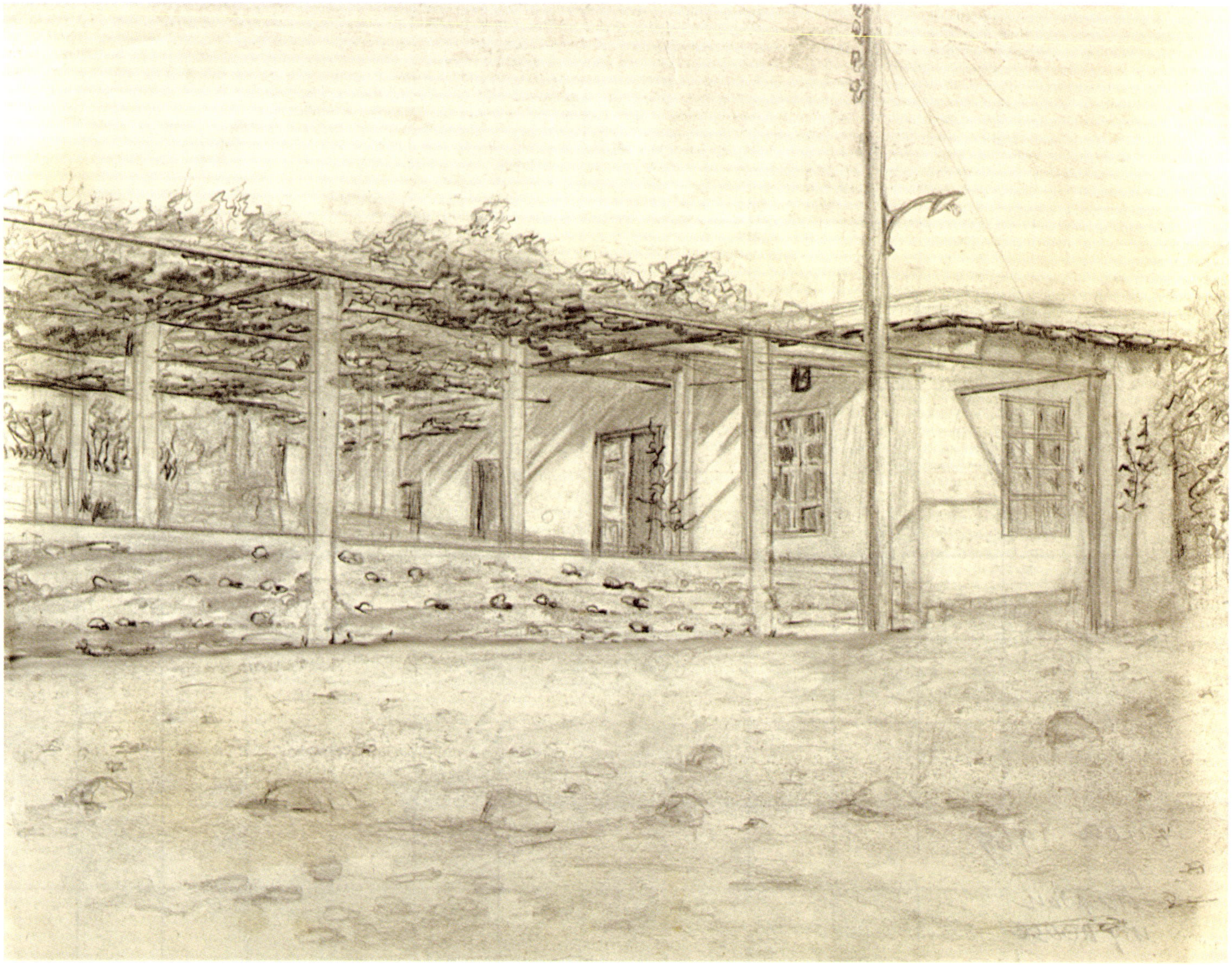

5
MY BIRTH PLACE, 1967
Pencil on paper
28 x 22 cm

could hit me and the other children with it when necessary. The longer the stick, the better it was for him; he could hit the children farthest away from him without moving. Such were the pedagogical methods in the Bekaa schools in the middle of the last century.

Later on, I went to another one-room school run by another relative, Khalil, who was considered to be better educated than most. In the summer, classes would convene in the open air under the only pistachio tree in the village. At school, I was taught Arabic, French, arithmetic and drawing. Drawing was considered to be a relaxing activity, designed to give the pupils a break. Nothing was more pleasurable for me: I often extended my drawing time through other lessons, even though I was punished or beaten for it.

There were several benches in the public school my parents sent me to next, into which the pupils were divided according to age or reading level. Mr Antoine, who always held a three-sided ruler ready to smack the palms of our hands, was the only teacher. When he wrote on the blackboard I would try to imitate his beautiful calligraphy. On my way to and from school, I drew other students' faces on the whitewashed walls of the village.

I enjoyed growing up in a loving and supportive family who never asked me not to draw, despite the fact that my mother was illiterate and my father had never gone to school but managed to learn to read and write in the army. He

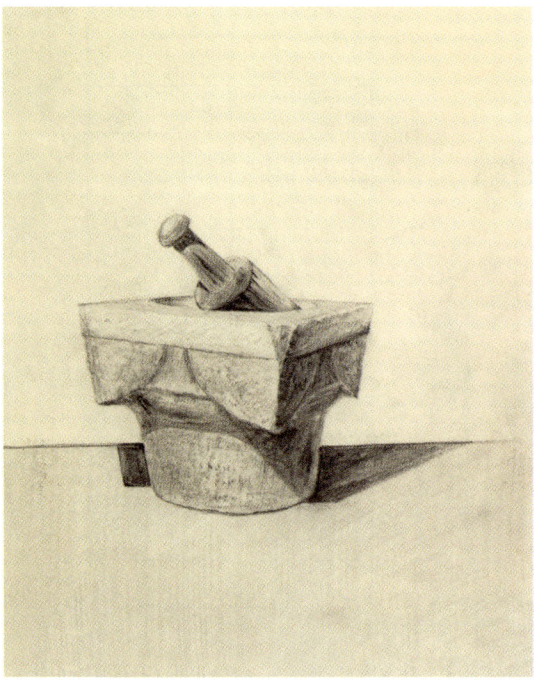

6
MOM'S JURN EL KIBBI II, 1966
Pencil on paper
22 x 28 cm

benefitted from the help of those soldiers who had some knowledge of writing and reading to send letters to his mother back home. Much later, I learned that he had gone to an old friend of the family for advice about me.

Our friend was a very respectable and well thought of young man, one of the lucky few to have received a formal education in a good school out of town. When he saw my childhood drawings, he told my father: 'Your son's work will be among the very few things that will remain of Sariine and maybe of the country.' The young man, Moussa Kallas, who was five or six years older than me, later became a highly successful lawyer and an eminent judge. His words were enough to convince my father to encourage me and never question why I was drawing. I had to wait sixty years to thank Moussa, who proudly told me the story when we met again outside the town church in 2011.

In June 1953 my cousin Nazih, just back from his boarding school, took me to his house in Upper Sariine. On our way there, I showed him my new charcoal drawings of the other kids' faces on the white walls along the road, and Nazih sang me his new school anthem and song. I was enchanted but felt ignorant. Nazih told me about his school, what they were studying, how many teachers they had, their Boy Scout adventures, and all the fun he was having. There was no comparison with the village school, where all the students were crammed into a single room with one angry teacher.

'I will ask my dad to send me to Nazih's school in Houmal,' I thought to myself. Just the name of the town was starting to take over my imagination. When I got home, I waited impatiently for my father's return from work to tell him all the good stories about the boarding school in Houmal. I was devastated by his adamant refusal.

I cried for days. As expected, my mother came to my rescue, trying to talk my father into sending me to Houmal. I overheard her telling him that no other child deserved a better school than me, and that it was in my best interests to attend a better school. Nothing good came out of this argument, but my mother went on nagging my father in every possible way and I became ever more eager to take on the adventure.

That summer, as was his habit, Mr Sabeh Feghali, the owner of the Renaissance College in Houmal, came to Sariine to collect overdue fees and recruit new students. When Mr Sabeh heard from Nazih that I wanted to join him in school, he came to visit my parents. I was thrilled to see him stepping into my house. While we were waiting for my father to return from work in the field, I tried to impress Mr Sabeh with my pencil drawings. I well remember the smile on that legendary face as he scanned the drawings in his hands with his shuttling eyes.

When my father arrived, it turned out that he already knew Mr Sabeh. It took him no time at all to explain that he did not have the money to pay for my tuition. Mr Sabeh tried

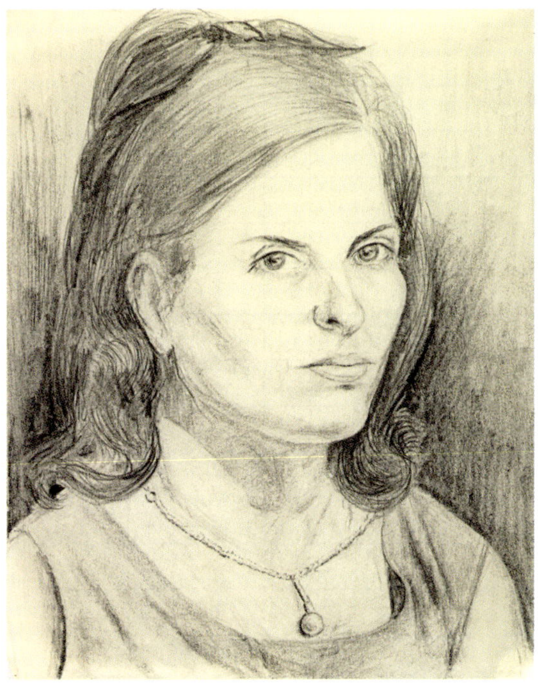

7
THE SUPERVISOR, 1966
Pencil on paper
22 x 28 cm

to make it easy for him by offering to accept beans, corn and other crops in return for my education. 'I have a boarding school, remember, and I have many mouths to feed,' he laughed.

My mother quickly stepped in, asking, 'What else are you waiting for?'

In the end, my father, who had a family of nine and was barely making enough money from his land and his small retirement salary to make ends meet, worriedly agreed.

Uncle Toufic, a self-taught artist and poet, and my father's best-respected friend, was the first to hear about the family's decision. Uncle Toufic was a man I always felt close to. He was a terrific story-teller and I used to spend hours listening to his exciting and never-ending tales. His family and friends always gathered around the stove to hear them on winter evenings. But what I enjoyed most was having him look at my drawings, offering approval and new tips.

'Gerges! Sending Chaouki to a better school is the best decision you've ever made!' I remember Uncle Toufic saying to my father, humming and nodding his head in total agreement with his own words. On that day he was helping us paint and decorate the door of the new extension to our house. I was watching his steady hand draw the final lines separating the different colours of his design attentively and eagerly. Yet I was thinking of his portraits of Saint Challita and Saint George in the churches of Sariine, and his paintings

Facing page
8
LODY, MY DEAR SISTER, 1967
Pencil on paper (detail)
22 x 28 cm

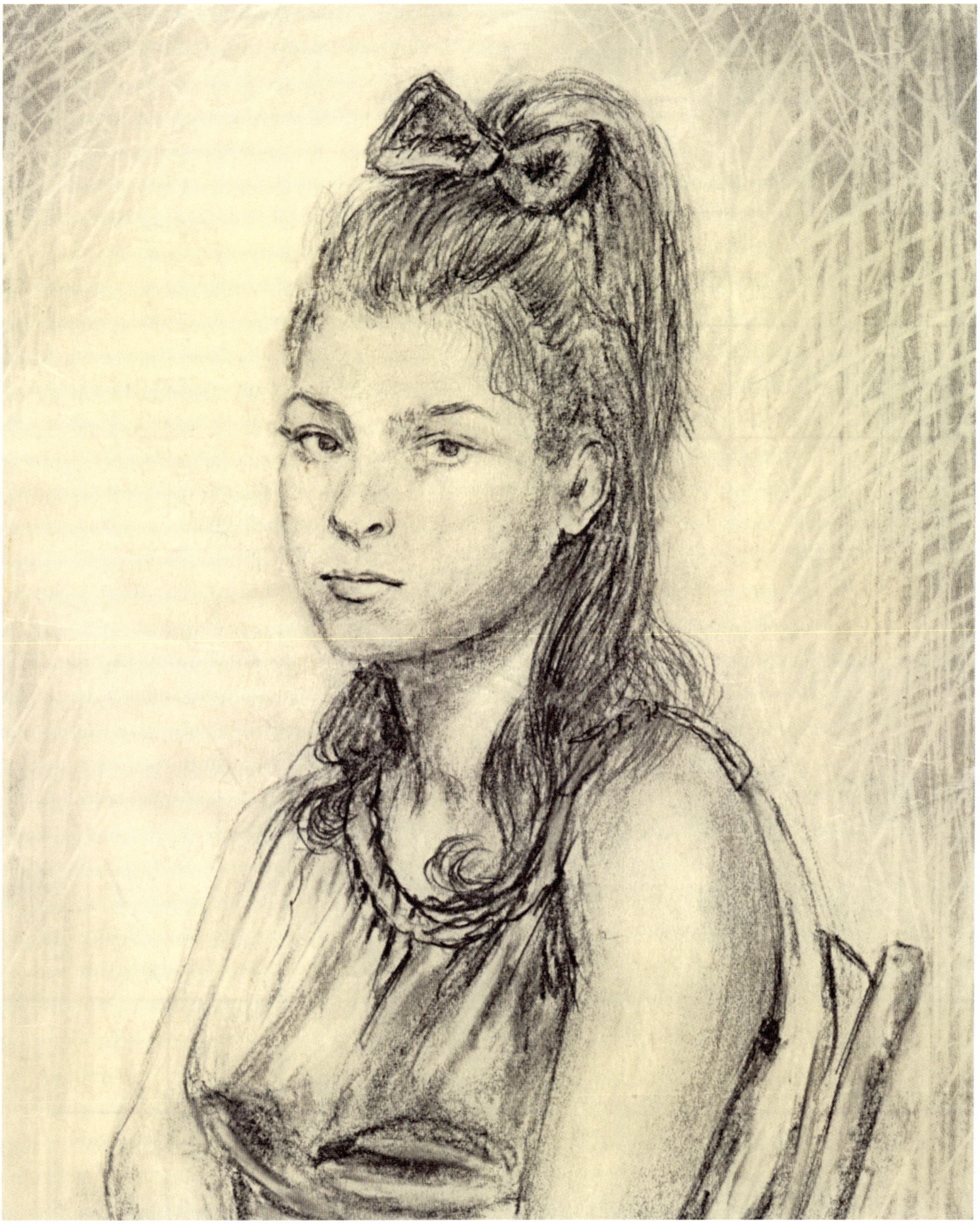

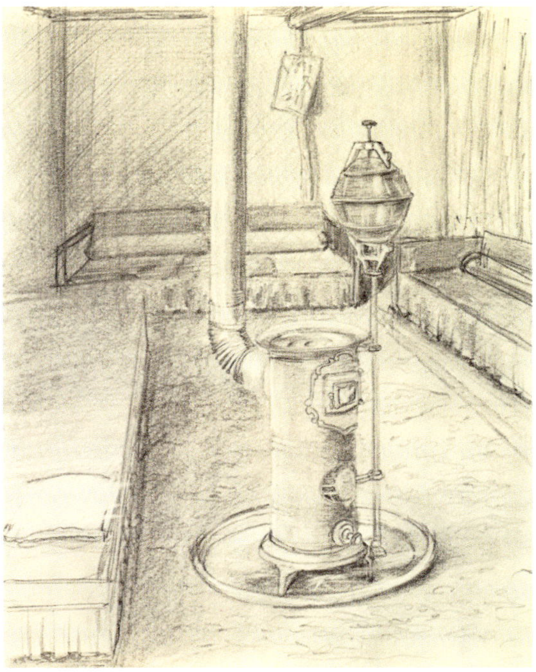

9
STOVE IN MY BIRTH ROOM, 1965
Pencil on paper
22 x 28 cm

of the majestic ruins of nearby Baalbeck, as I watched him finishing the door.

The summer was coming to an end and October, the magic month I had been waiting for, had finally arrived. My mother had already bought me new clothes; she and my grandma were now busy making a wool-stuffed mattress and bed coverings for me to take to the new boarding school.

'This should help keep him comfortable and warm,' I heard Grandma tell my mother confidently once it was finished.

'Najib will be here soon. I hope he will leave enough room in his car to fit all of this ...' my mother replied. 'There he is!' she went on as she saw Najib's car turning into the driveway.

All our neighbours gathered for a farewell party when they saw the car arrive. My mother's eyes filled with tears as my father and Najib loaded my luggage into the trunk and laid the mattress on the top of the car. Then Najib wrapped the mattress with a rope and tied it to the open trunk door to secure the luggage.

First Najib collected Nazih and his older brother George, along with Adel, another cousin. They all seemed anxious and ready to set out. 'Time to go!' Najib commented as he climbed into the driver's seat. 'It's a long trip and I'd like to be back before sunset.' I found myself in my mother's arms; an embrace which stayed with me for life.

Nazih, Adel and I took the back seat, while George chose to sit in the front. The last thing I saw from the car window on my first journey to Houmal was the heart-breaking image of my mother crying as my father stood among all our neighbours, waving goodbye.

When I arrived at the Renaissance High School, I had to take an entry exam, based on which they decided to place me in the third grade. During my years at the school, I advanced through two elementary and another two intermediate classes, skipping one grade altogether.

In spring 1958, following the outbreak of civil unrest in the country, I was relocated to a school in the nearby town of Rayak. At the end of the next academic year, I failed the government Brevet exam.

Since my father could not afford to have me pursue my high school studies, I decided to look for a job. I went back to Houmal and asked if the school had anything available for me. Mr Sabeh was happy to see me back and offered me a job as an overseer, in addition to asking me to teach drawing to the elementary classes. Had he not always called me 'Chaouki the Artist' during the four years I had spent with him? Teaching drawing was a mere pastime in those days, filling in the curriculum requirements, but to me it was a most challenging and serious undertaking.

Meanwhile, Mr Sabeh was giving me the chance to

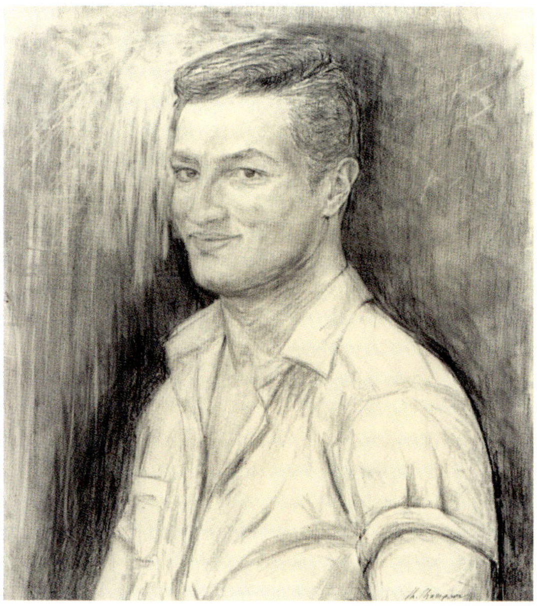

10
SELF-PORTRAIT, 1967
Pencil on paper (detail)
50 x 65 cm

complete my high school studies whilst working. The school also accepted two of my younger brothers as students. However, I was offered a very low salary, twenty pounds a month, and this hurt my pride. One of the other teachers, Mr Farhat, reasoned with me that I was not getting such a bad deal after all, since my two brothers were being educated as well. This convinced me to accept the situation.

Naturally, with all my chores as supervisor and teacher, I could not follow all the courses, the lack of which I felt all along. Years later, when I was at New York University, a great teacher there, Professor Janice Gorn, commenting on my participation in her interdisciplinary studies class and praising the proposal I had completed for my dissertation, told me that I must have come from a great high school. I smiled to myself, but her comment really boosted my self-confidence, although the feeling of having missed out has never left me.

The school also asked me to draw portraits of historical figures from Lebanon's history, and these were posted on the walls in the classrooms. These drawings, along with the many pictures I was making of the students' and teachers' faces, further enhanced my reputation – both in the school and beyond, in the nearby town.

A Twist of Fate

One autumn day in 1959, while I was waiting in Debbas Square in Beirut for the service taxi to fill with passengers, a middle-aged man who was also waiting saluted me as 'Chaouki the Artist'. He asked me if I would draw the faces of two Lebanese political leaders, one of whom was ex-President Camille Chamoun, for them. He wanted them in colour and in oil, something I had never done before. I explained that I could not afford the paints: in response, the man drew a thick wad of notes from his pocket and peeled off three hundred pounds. As he offered it to me, he told me he would pay more if need be.

This was close to a year's salary for most people: I had never seen such a sum in my life. So I went immediately to the art supply store in the Al Azarrieh building in Beirut, where I bought charcoal pencils, and asked for oil paints. When the salesman asked me what colour I wanted, I answered confidently: 'The colour of flesh, I mean the colour of the face.' Laughing, he said there was no such thing and explained to me how different paints could be mixed to obtain the colour I wanted. He suggested that I should start with watercolours but ended sad and baffled when I insisted on buying a big Rembrandt box full of tubes of oil paint. After

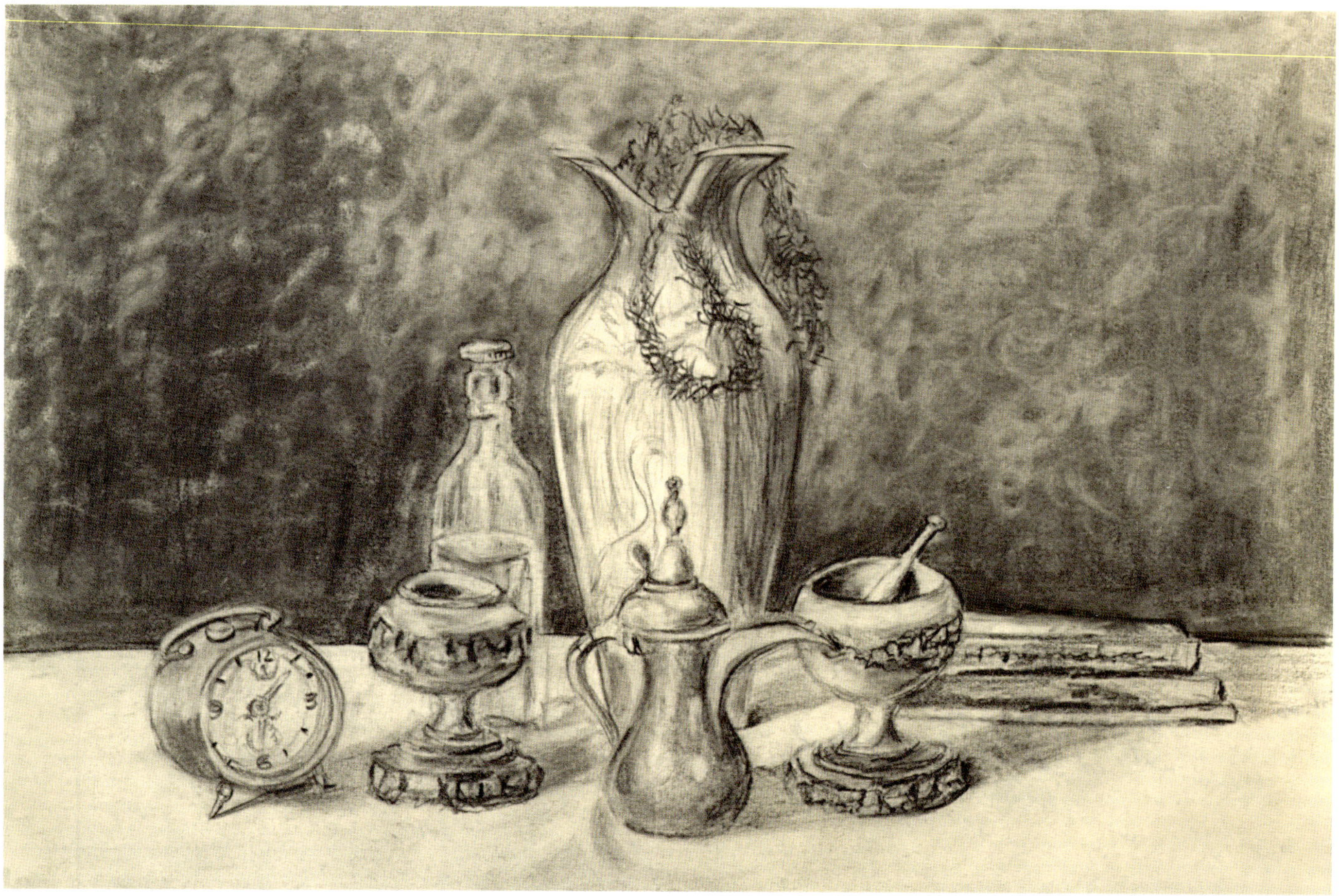

11
STILL LIFE WITH COFFEE POT, 1967
Pencil on paper
28 x 22 cm

further questioning and discussion, I also bought brushes, bottles of linseed oil, turpentine, a palette, and two pre-stretched canvases on board. I paid about fifty pounds and left with my new treasures.

It was then that my real worries began. How would I be able to repay such a huge sum if something went wrong? How would I face the world if I failed? I practised mixing colours, painting them on my hands and face to obtain the colour of skin. At night I would dream of colours, of mixing colours for the first time in my life; the memory is still vivid with me now. It was then that I realised that my dreams were all in colours. I practised drawing the faces the man had asked for from colour pictures that I collected while waiting for him to bring me the portraits he wanted to have painted.

When he finally came, he told me that he had changed his mind and wanted me to paint his own portrait instead. He took a picture of himself out of his wallet. I was going to have to make do with a small faded black and white passport photograph. I froze when I saw it, but I knew that I had to do what the man wanted, as I was unable to give him back his money. So I set to work. When he came to collect his portrait, he showed neither pleasure nor displeasure, but murmured a question about how much I would charge him. Thinking to myself that the price of the paint box and the valuable opportunity he had afforded me were enough, I gave him back the money left over from what he had paid me in advance. I have never forgotten the faded smile on his face as he walked away with his oil portrait, my first ever.

No matter what the painting might have been worth, my success in painting in oil boosted my confidence. As a result, the headmaster of the school asked me to redo all the historical portraits I had done for the school in oil, on top of following whatever courses I could, as well as teaching and supervising. I was working eighteen hours a day.

For the next few years, I concentrated on improving my painting skills. My father loved Gibran's *The Prophet*, and encouraged me to see him as a role model. I was more attracted by the paintings and drawings in the book, and I began to imitate the artist's style by standing naked in front of a mirror and sketching myself.

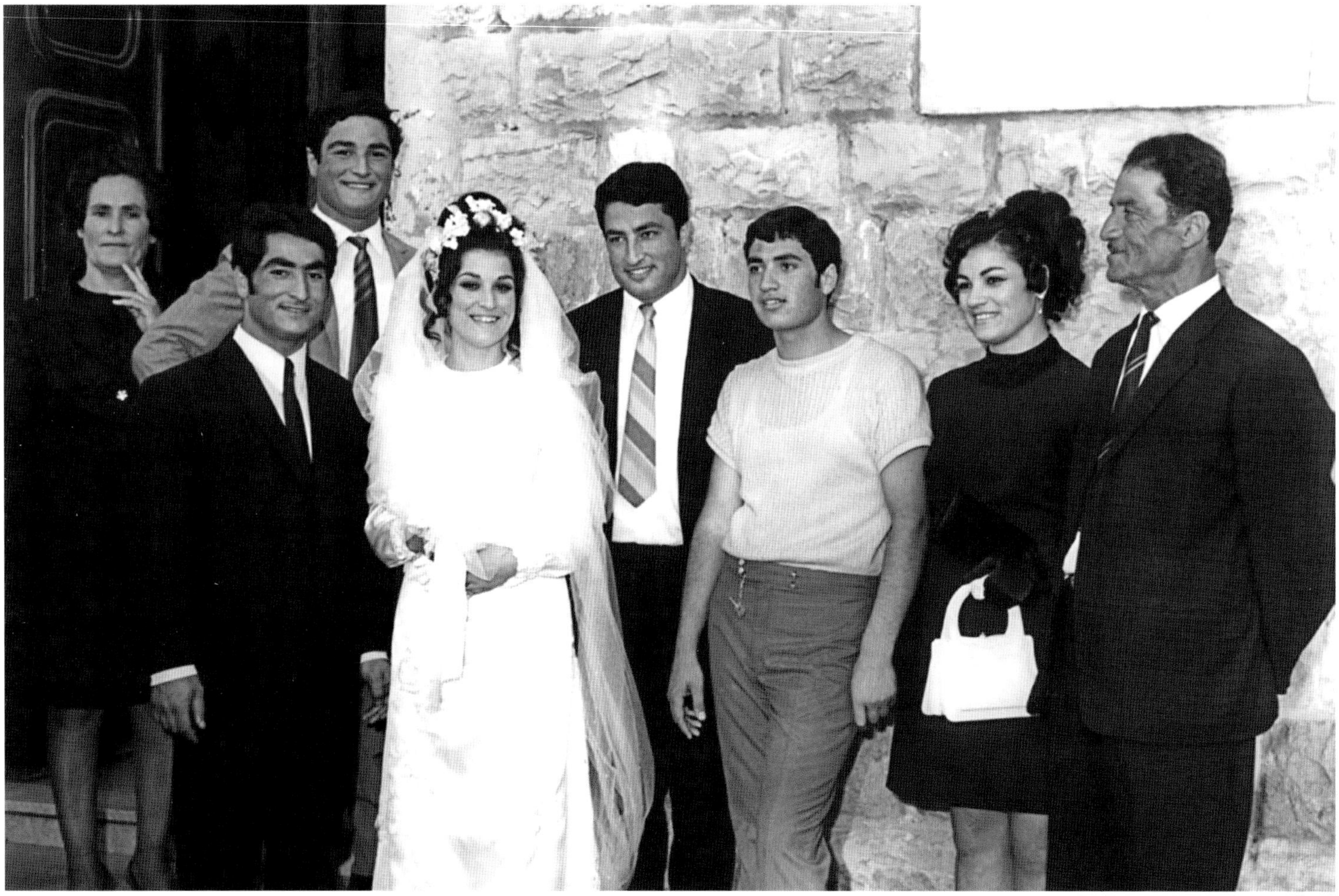

Lody's wedding, 1970
Left to right: my mother Afifi, my brothers Ghassan and Kozhaya, my sister Lody, myself, my brother Rachid, my sister Ahsaan and my father Gerges

Hopes and Setbacks

In autumn 1961 I heard that the Ministry of Education was offering art students scholarships to Italy and France. I put together my original paintings and drawings and headed to the ministry. Mr Joseph Abou Rizk, then head of the art department, looked at my work with full attention and a very encouraging attitude. 'Nice work,' he commented, but he was quick to tell me that the ministry had already sent art scholars to Europe for that year. However, he advised me to enrol in the Lebanese Academy of Fine Arts (ALBA), where I could improve my skills and prepare for a possible future scholarship.

The late painter Jean Khalifeh, whom I had never before seen or heard of, was at the ministry that day. He took me by the hand and walked with me to ALBA, in Mseitby. When we entered the painting class taught by Cezar Gemayel, a name to remember, I saw the students painting a naked female model, Mariam. I would work with her at the Fine Arts Institute seven years later, but this was the first time in my life that I had seen a naked woman modelling, and it presented a very different challenge to my own nude self-portraits. Unfortunately, I could not afford the four-hundred Lebanese pound tuition fee, nor could I afford to stay in Beirut, so I went back to the school in Houmal, where I continued drawing on my own.

With the encouragement of Elie Saadeh, the general supervisor at the school, I had the good fortune to get to know the calligrapher of the newspaper *al Nahar*. He generously provided me with tips and instruction, as well as samples of different styles, to improve my Arabic calligraphy skills. I practised enthusiastically for hours every day. An Egyptian lady who was working for the school brought me the special Egyptian bamboo sticks used by professional calligraphers. I trained in the Naskh, Tulut, Rouq'i, Rouq'i Masri, Diwani, Kufic and Farsi scripts. Overall, however, I was always drawn more towards drawing and painting.

In the summer I would paint the scenery in the mountains and the Bekaa Valley, or pictures of saints. I built an *'erzal* (straw tent) on the roof of our house, where I would paint or carve small stone sculptures.

I met Nasri Daou, a native of Houmal and the owner of Delcaribi Bank in Caracas, in Houmal when he was honoured by the school owner for his achievements. He came to my village in summer 1962 to visit his brother Malik, who always spent his summers in Sariine, and I invited him to look at my paintings. I was overjoyed when Mr Daou offered to take me with him to Venezuela, to work with him and go to an art school. Two months later, instead of a job offer and a visa, I received an apology and a note of regret; the plan had had to be cancelled due to political events and a change of regime in Venezuela.

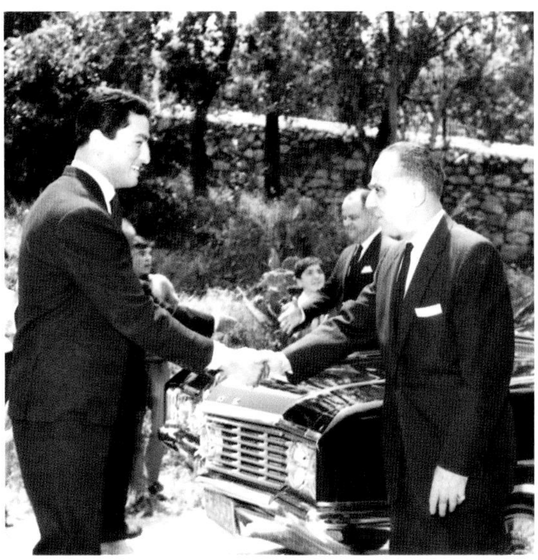

With Nasri Daou in Houmal, 1962

In autumn 1962 I was offered some work drawing furniture for Nicori, a wood-working company in Shiyah. I thought this would give me the opportunity to save some money to go to ALBA. Shortly after I started at the company, I discovered that they wished to use me as a concierge. I was also asked by the owner to help his son with his Arabic. In addition, the manager, the famous wrestler Assad Srour, used to bring me prints of paintings by Monet and other Impressionists to copy in oil on canvas. I was never paid for any of my copies. It was a very disappointing experience, and eventually I quit.

My father had started working in a tile factory in Kafarshima, the owner of which offered me a job in their sales office in the city. I worked there for a short time, making the outdoor signs for the factory in addition to doing some office work as a salesman, but again, I felt that the job was not for me. Then in the summer of 1963 my cousin Nazih introduced me to Yumna Malek Secondary School in Choueifat. I was given a job as the general supervisor of the school, and that is where I stayed for the next five years.

This started a new era in my life. It was a good, respectable school with well-qualified teachers and successful results in the official exams. As well as doing my supervisor's duties, I also taught drawing and Arabic calligraphy. But I had not given up my desire to improve academically. I looked around for night schools, but could find only technical

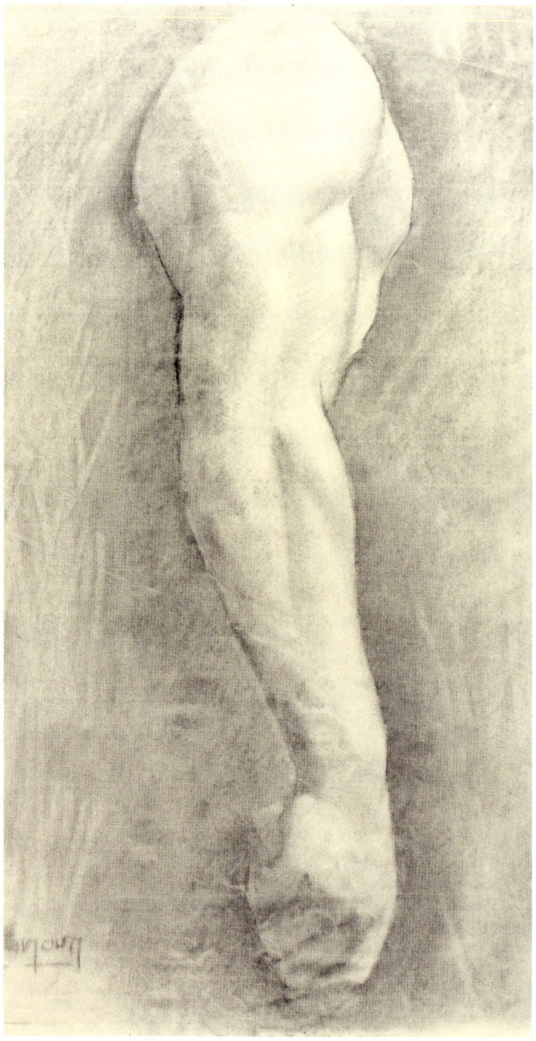

12
ARM, 1968
Charcoal on paper
50 x 65 cm

schools, so I enrolled in one that taught English and in another to study architectural drawing, which I took for two years. Since I excelled in technical drawing, my teacher Asaad Feghali, an architect at the Teknik night school, advised me to go in for architecture. Of course, my lack of time or money meant that this was out of the question, even more so now that my three brothers were with me and I was spending on them as well. Moreover, I had rented a house in Choueifat so that the family could be united again.

Then I heard of a school in London, the ICS, where I could study cartoons and take drawing lessons by correspondence. I studied with them for about three years. This was the best learning experience I ever had in my study of drawing. I would read the books they sent, do the assigned work, and send it for correction. 6–11

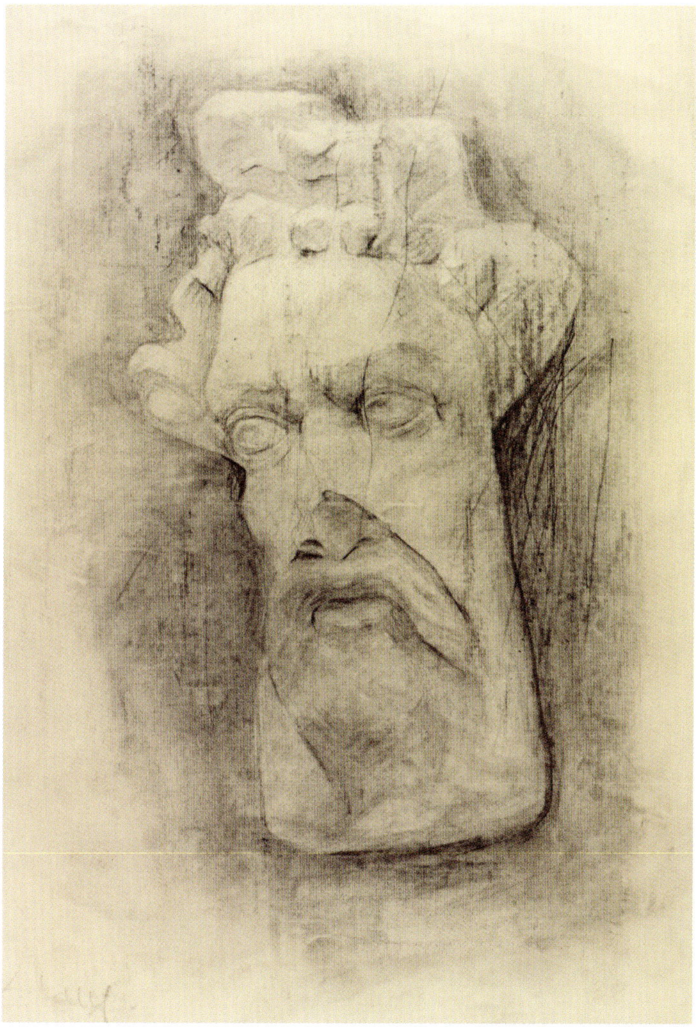

13
FOREST LORD, 1968
Charcoal on paper
50 x 65 cm

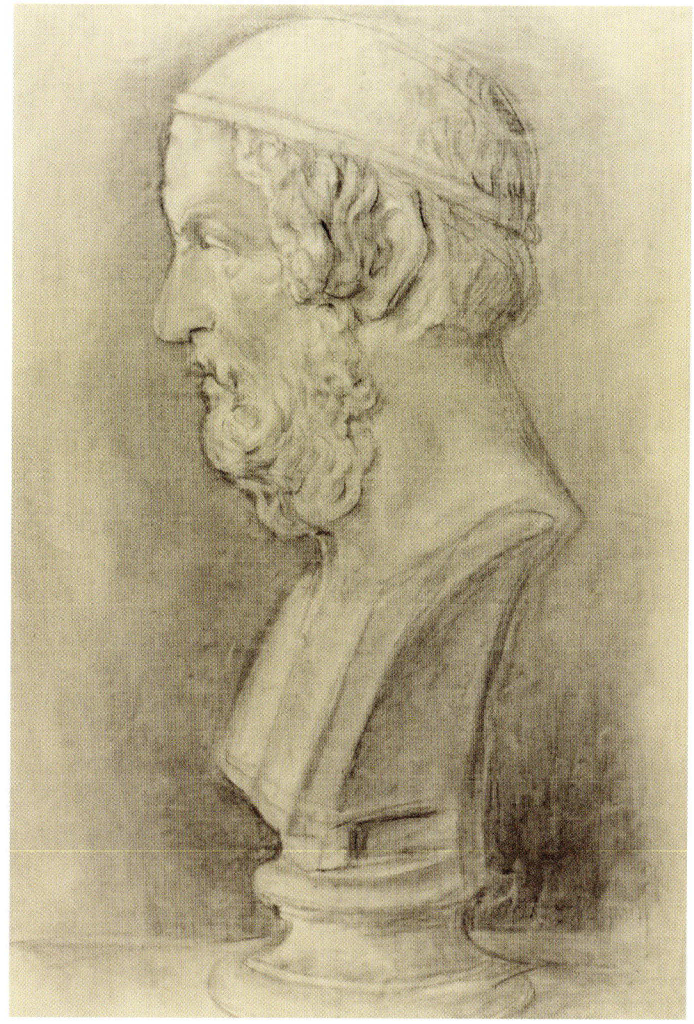

14
HOMER, 1969
Charcoal on paper
50 x 65 cm

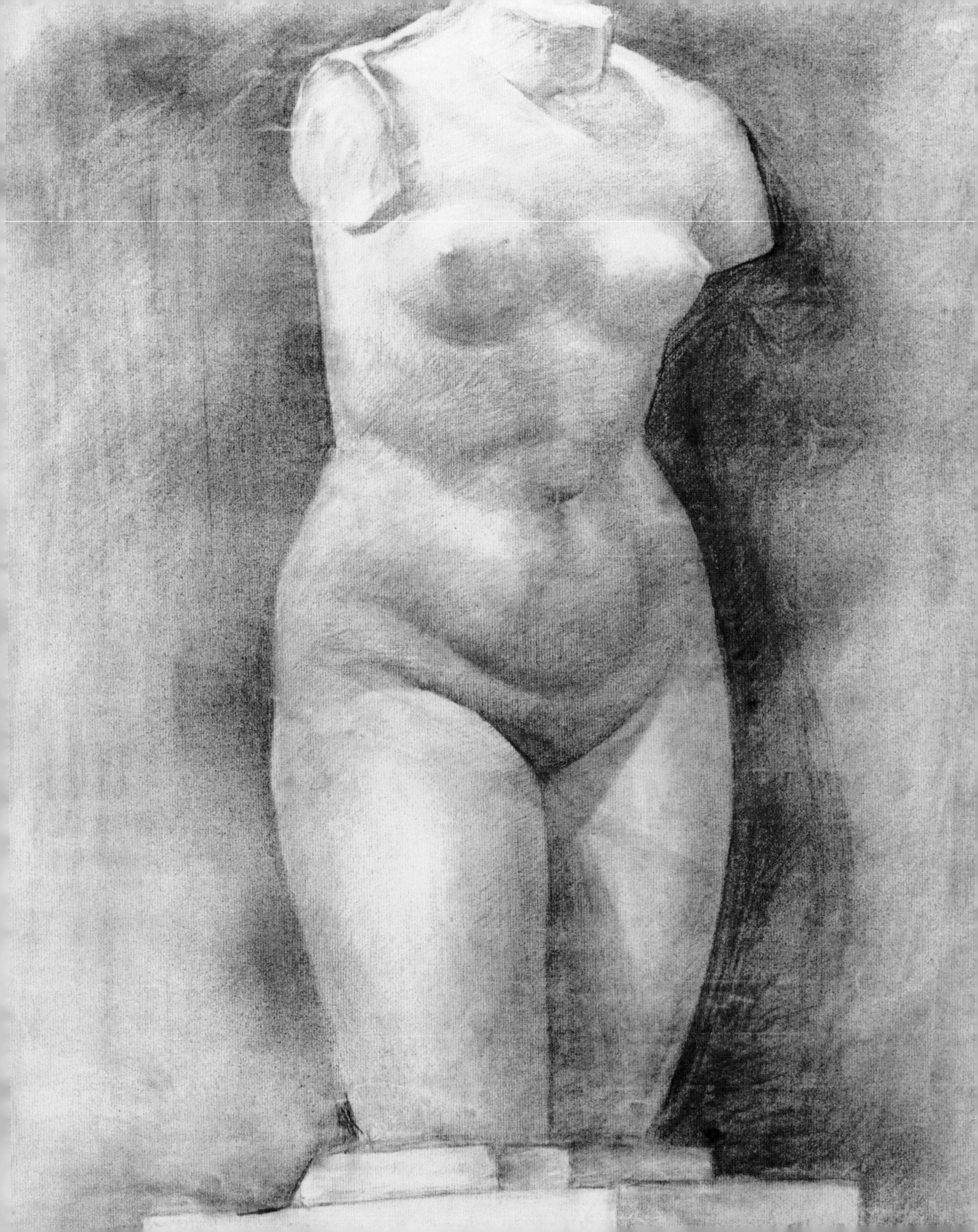

A Dream Come True!

Leaving Choueifat in summer 1968 turned out to be to my advantage: I was offered a job as general supervisor at the Evangelical School in Dbayyeh, which was a far better and more highly reputed school than that of Choueifat, and where classes broke up at 2 p.m. In the meantime, in order to encourage the study of fine arts, the Lebanese University had passed a bylaw dispensing art students from having the Baccalaureate I and II, provided they had finished high school and passed an entrance exam. There had been a fine arts institute in the university since 1965, but I had not known about it. I applied immediately, passed the entry exams, and finally saw the dream of my life come true: I was a university student! The Evangelical School increased my salary and gave me a good discount on my brothers' tuition, and with my half-day job there I was able to work and study. I was in heaven.

The principal appointed me director and vice principal of the school. Later, when I won a scholarship to pursue my education in the United States, he offered me a three-year leave of absence without pay, and took over my job for a symbolic one pound a year, preserving my position if and when I might choose to return to the Evangelical School. Of course that never happened; my life was to take a new path.

Facing page
15
VENUS, 1969
Charcoal on paper
50 x 65 cm

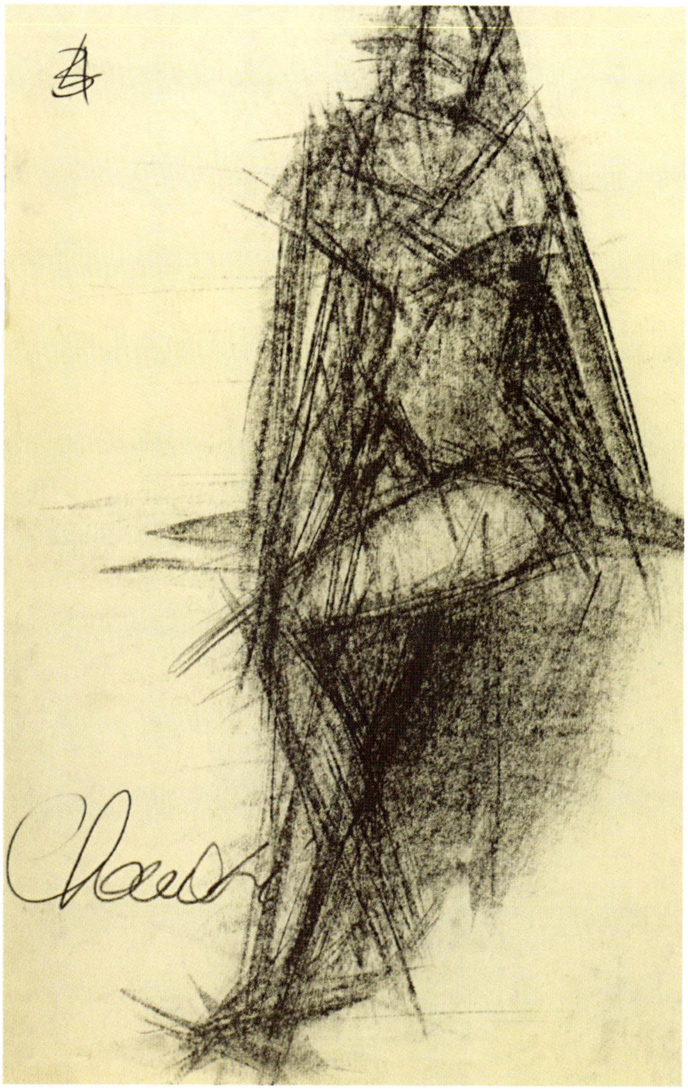

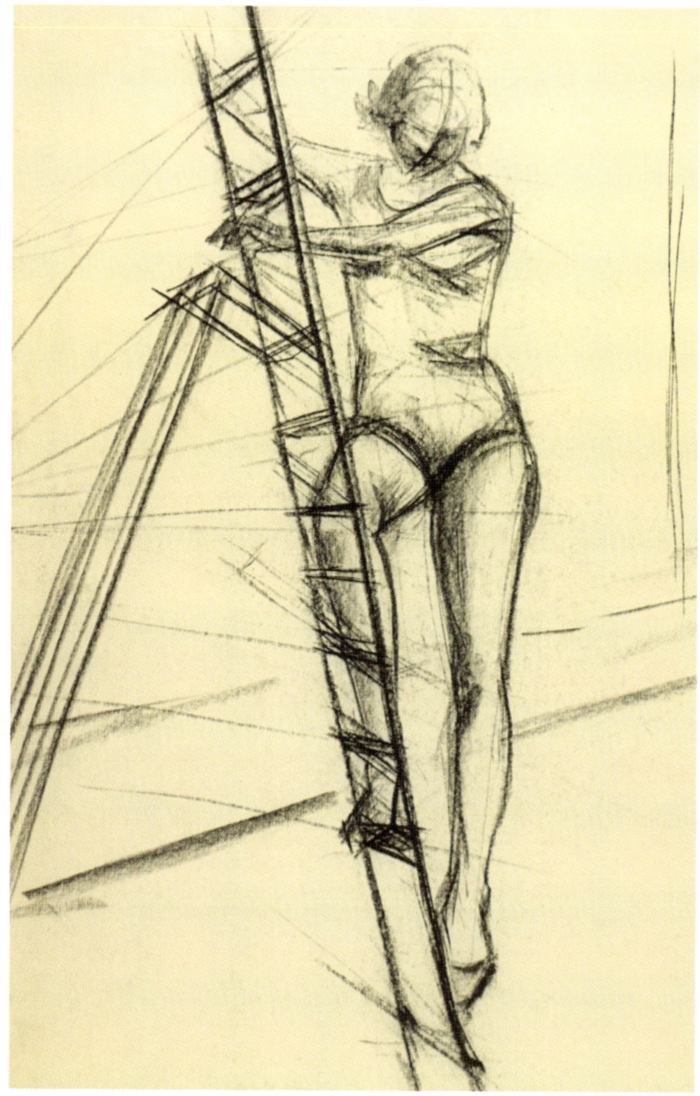

16
MARIAM, SEATED, 1970
Crayon Conté on paper
37.5 x 57 cm

17
MARIAM ON LADDER, 1970
Charcoal on paper
41 x 55.5 cm

Facing page
18
STILL LIFE WITH LAMP, 1970
Oil on Masonite board
50 x 60 cm

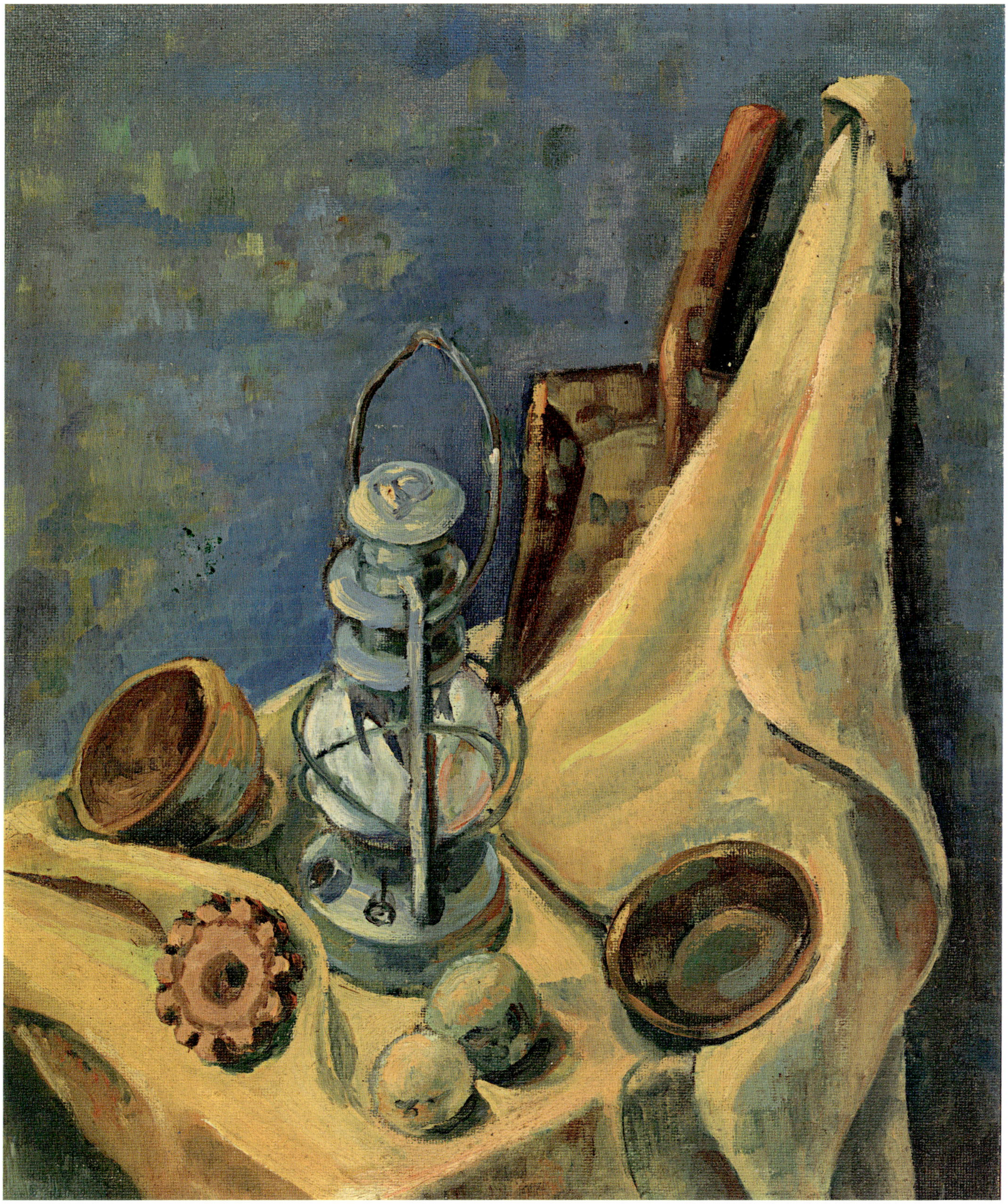

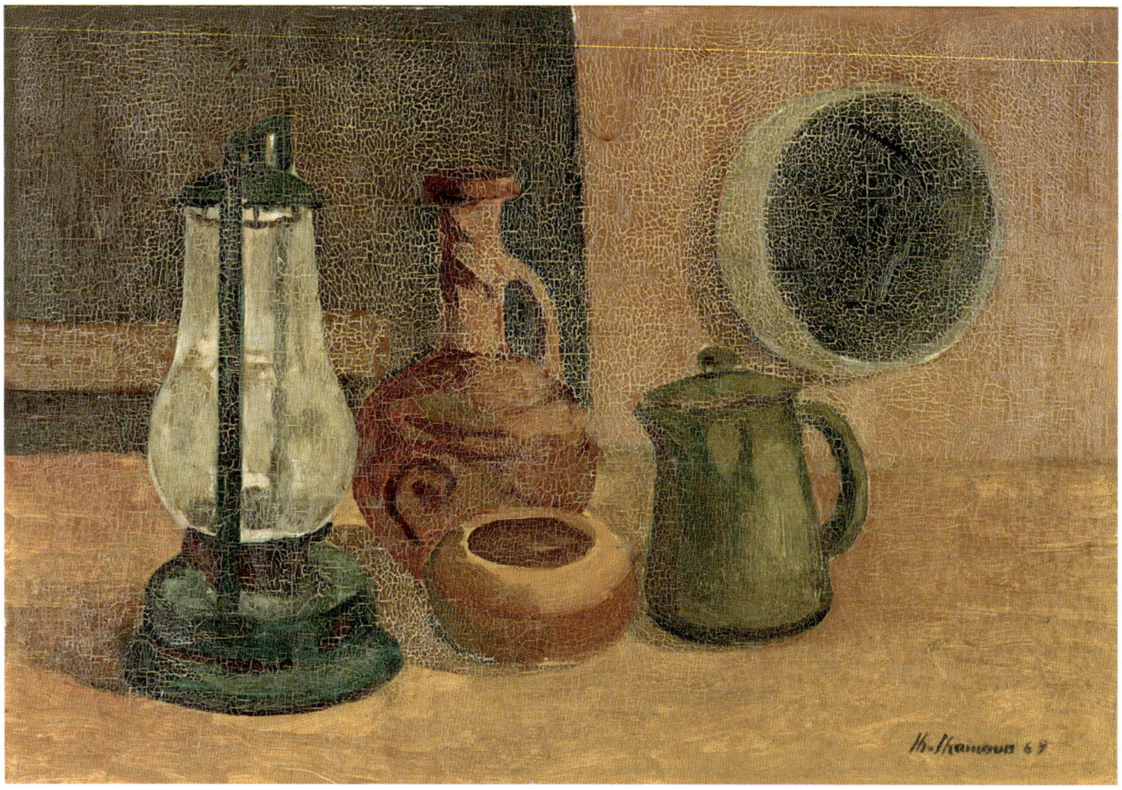

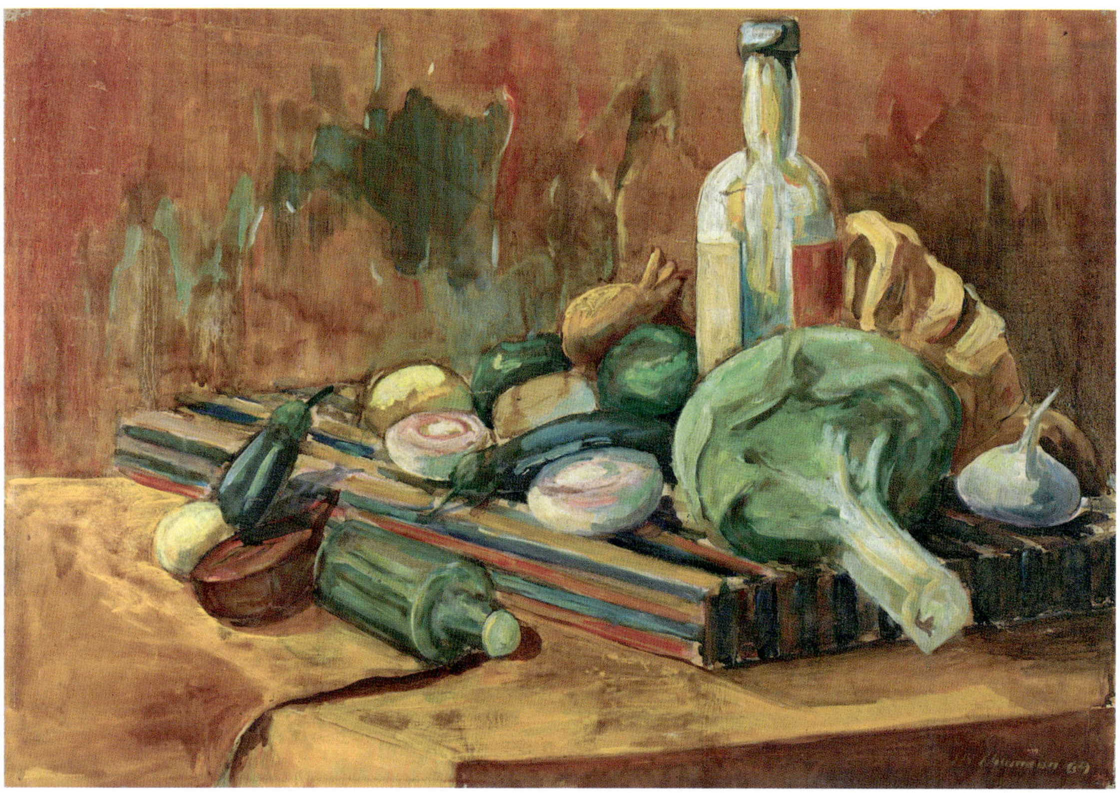

The Cradle of My Art

When I joined the Fine Arts Institute in the Lebanese University, art, to me, meant drawing and painting in the academic sense; knowing how to draw and paint; and the ability to portray nature, man and the world around me in the most representative way. Issues of modern art were not debated until the second year, when we were introduced to Modernism and artists of the modern era by professors such as Nicola Nammar, Munir Najm, Nadia Saikali, Said Akl, Jean Khalify, Aref Rayes, Ivette Achkar, Rafic Charaf and Chafic Abboud, all of whom used to join as visiting artists.

Every now and then, a major modern artist or the name of an art school would be mentioned, in particular when a student's work resembled one of them. Whenever a new artist was mentioned, I would rush to the modest art library we had at the university and try to find as much information as I could. I had no real information or appreciation of Modernism, or of the artists who had created the modern era and the new trends of Cubism and beyond. My appreciation of art had stopped with the Impressionists whose works I was sometimes asked to copy.

Beirut in the sixties and early seventies was the Mecca of Arab art and culture. Several art galleries were

Facing page, top
19
STILL LIFE WITH COFFEE POT, 1969
Oil on canvas
64 x 45 cm

Facing page, bottom
20
LIVE VEGETABLES AND BOTTLE, 1969
Oil on canvas
75 x 53 cm

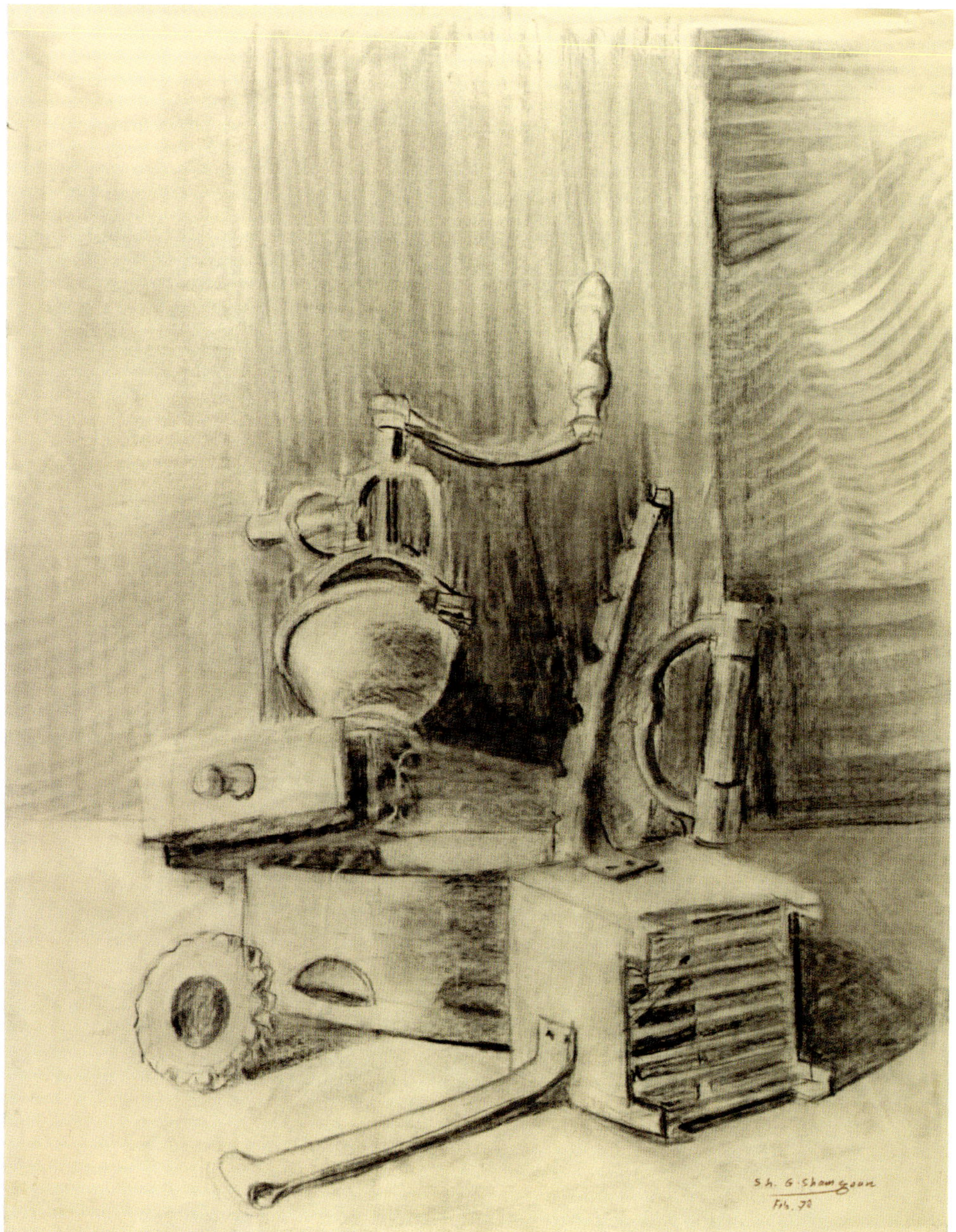

21
STILL LIFE WITH CHARCOAL IRON, 1970
Charcoal on paper
50 x 65 cm

Facing page
22
THE BREAK, 1970
Oil on Masonite board
60 x 83 cm

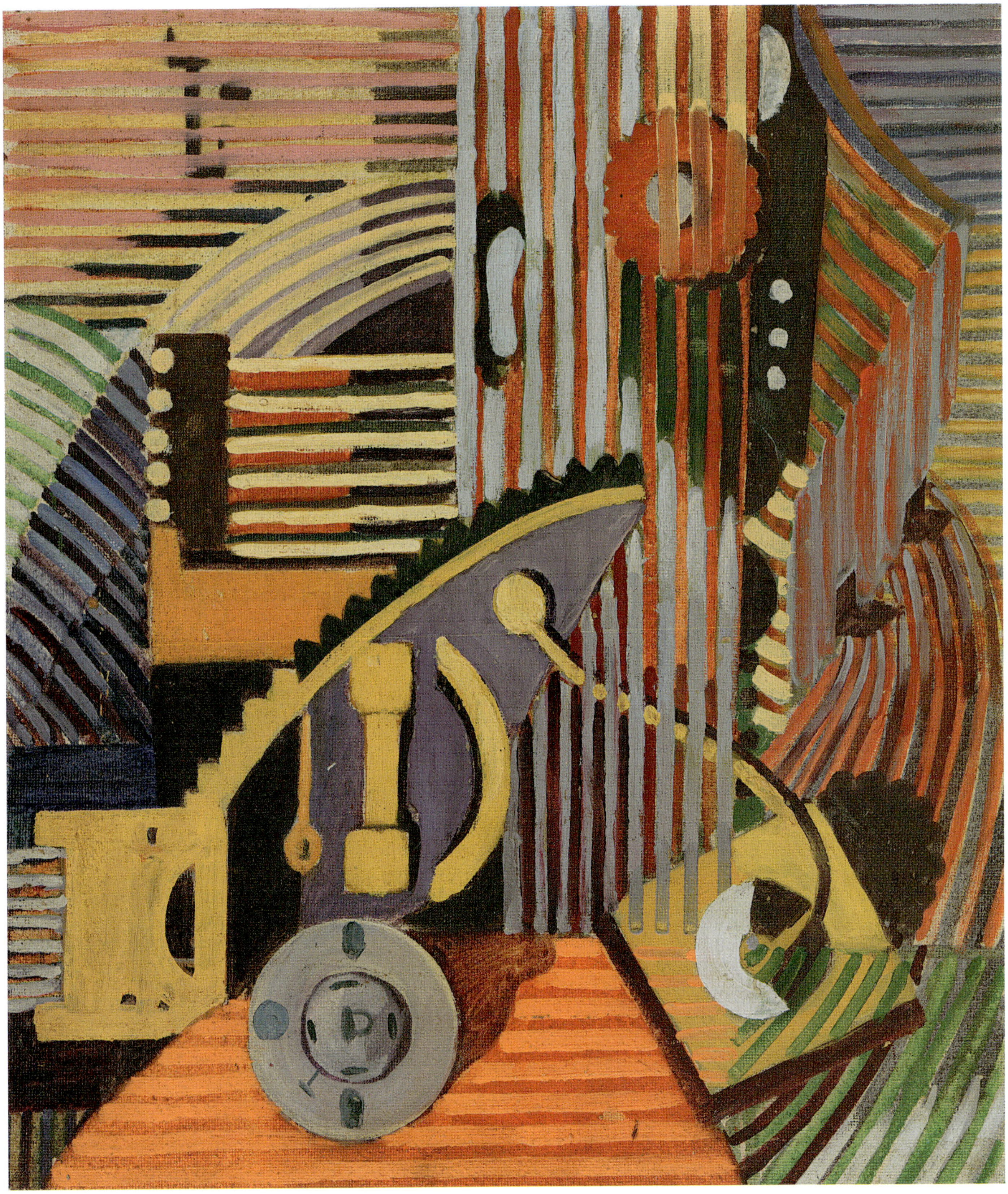

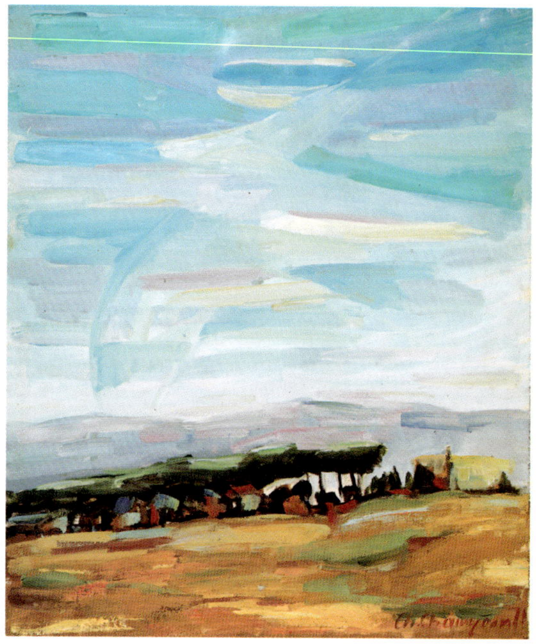

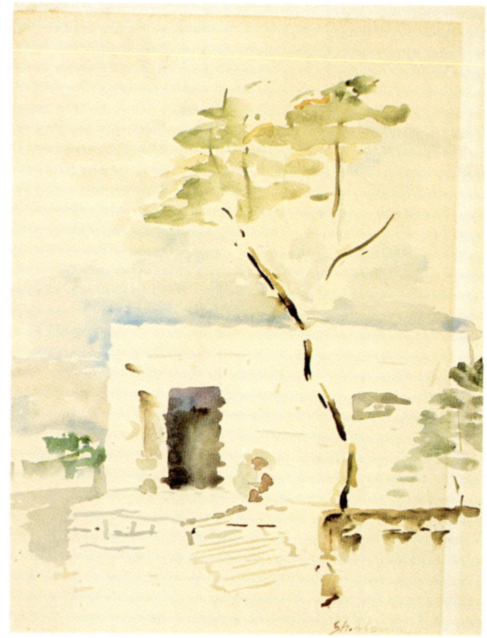

Left
23
CHATILA CAMP, 1971
Oil on canvas
65.5 x 81.5 cm

Right
24
KOURA HOUSE,
1971
Watercolour on paper
27 x 37 cm

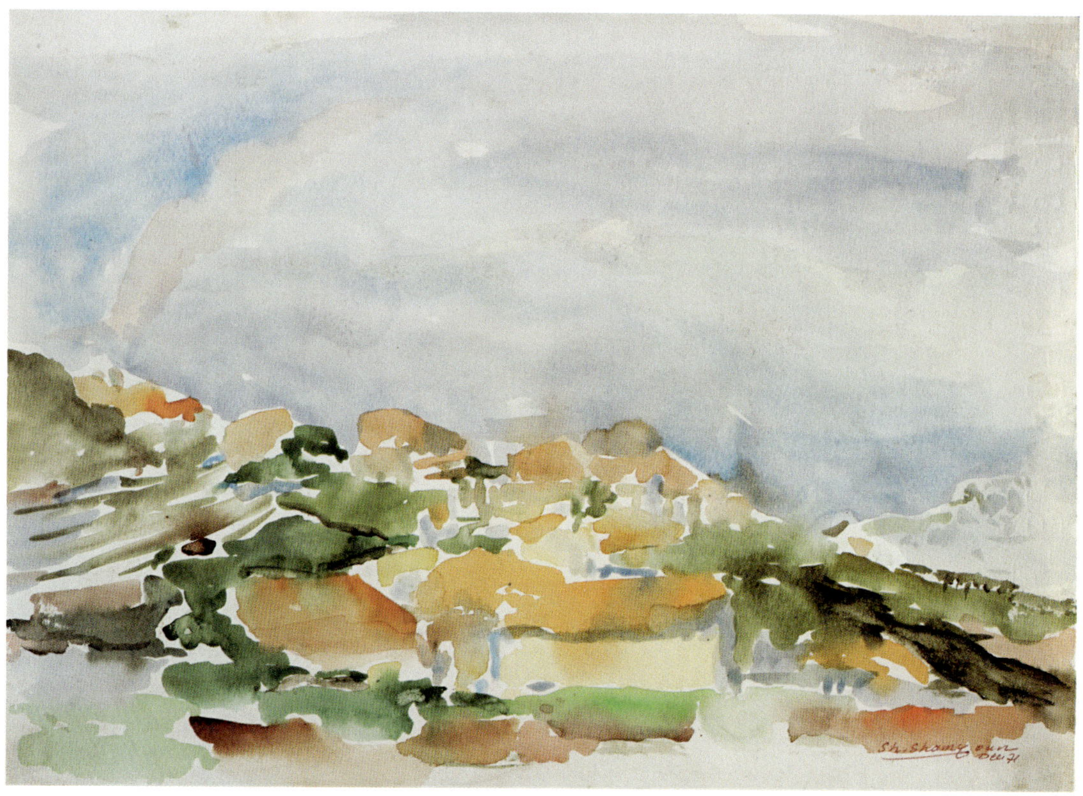

25
ON THE WAY
TO DHOUR, 1971
Watercolour on paper
36.5 x 26.5 cm

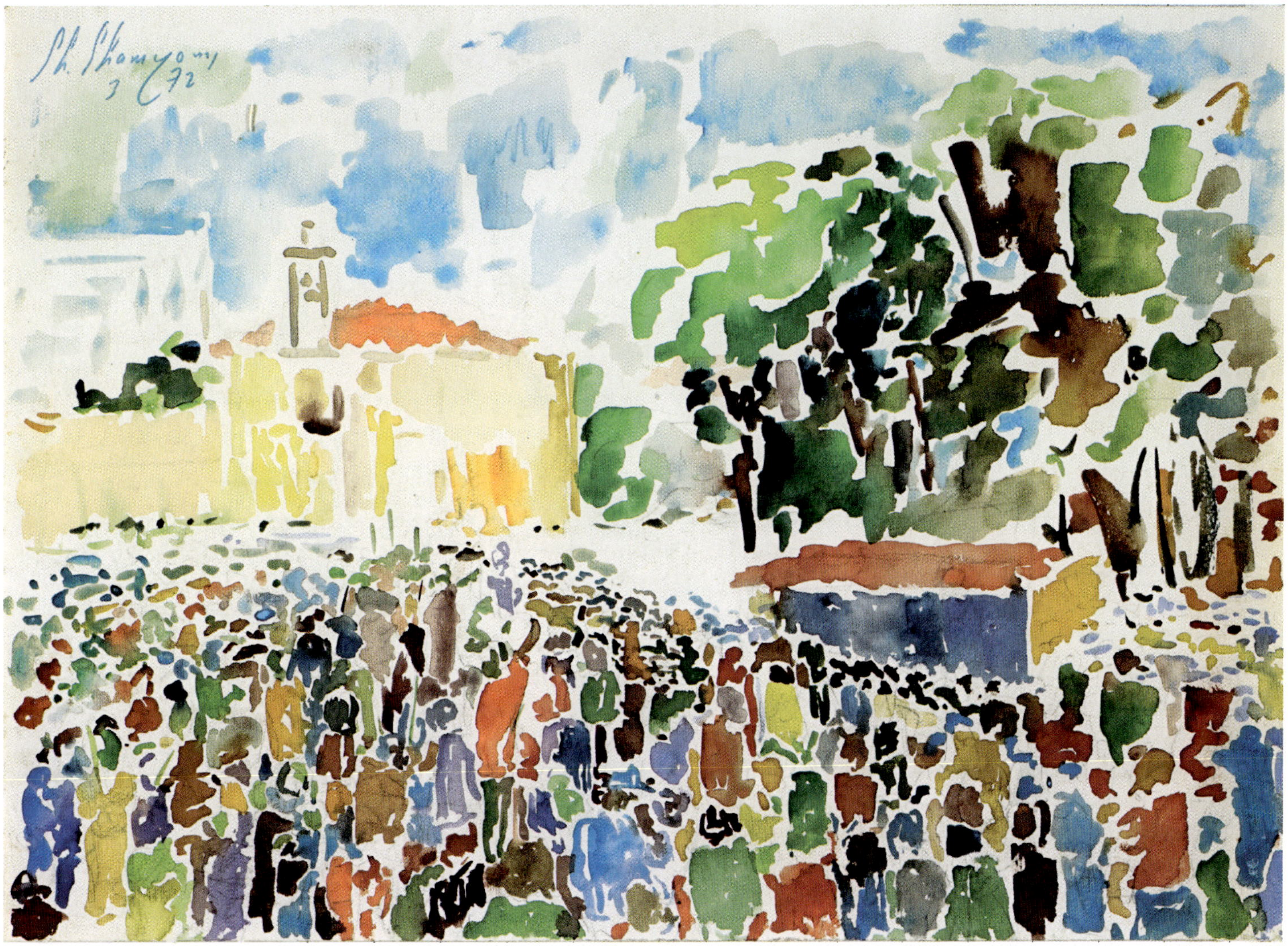

26
PALM SUNDAY ANTELIAS, 1972
Watercolour on paper
37 x 27 cm

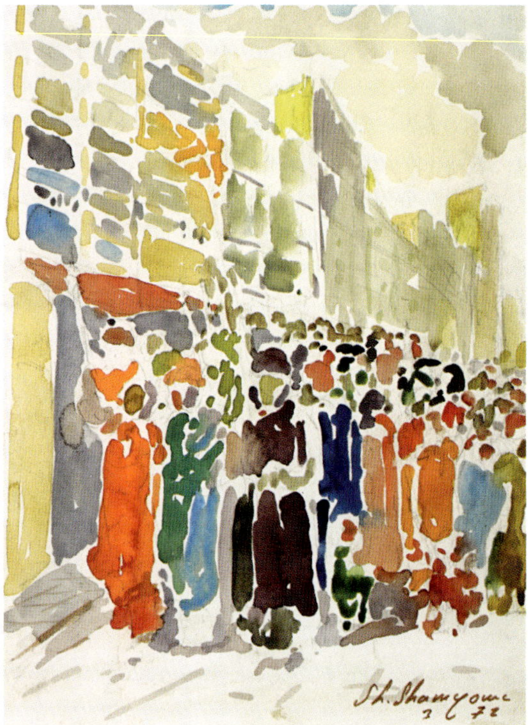

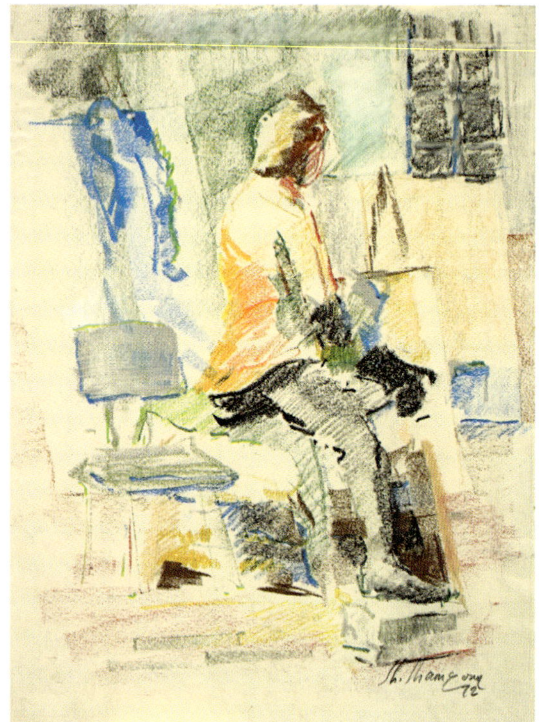

Left
27
PALM SUNDAY 4, 1972
Watercolour on paper
21 x 31 cm

Right
28
STUDY AFTER MARIAM 1, 1972
Pastel on paper
35 x 25 cm

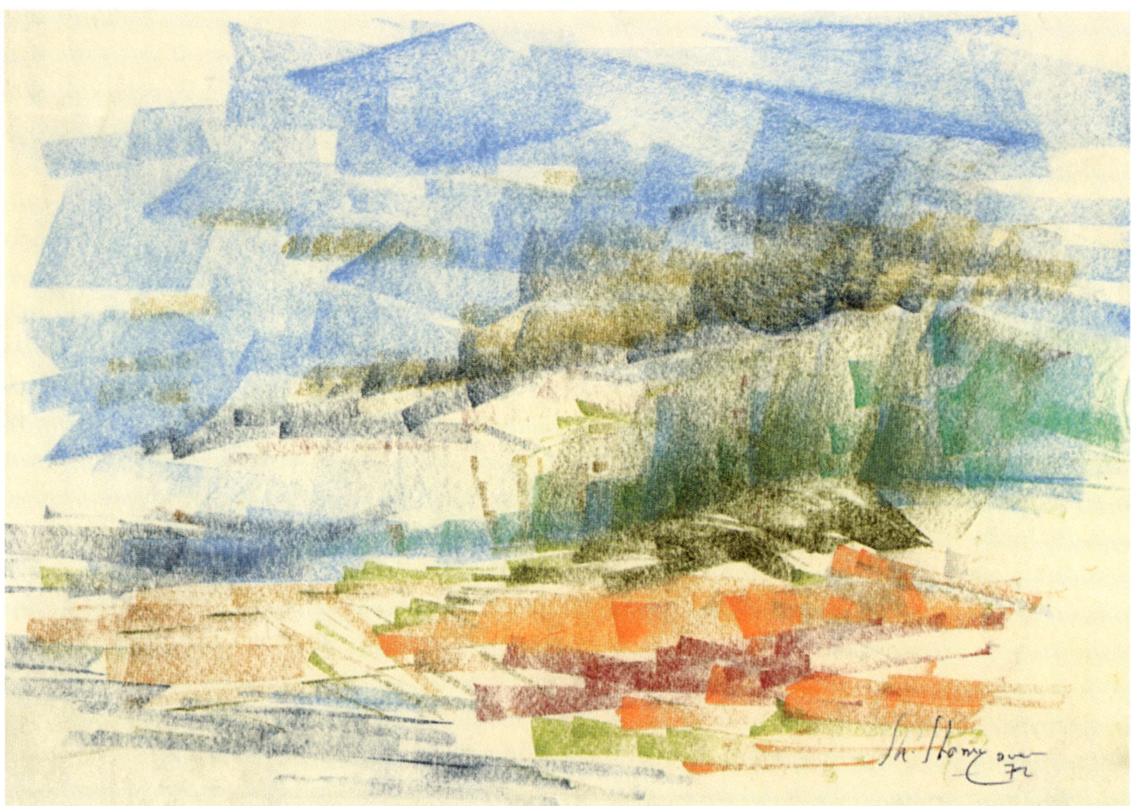

29
ON MY WAY HOME 3, 1972
Pastel on paper
35 x 25 cm

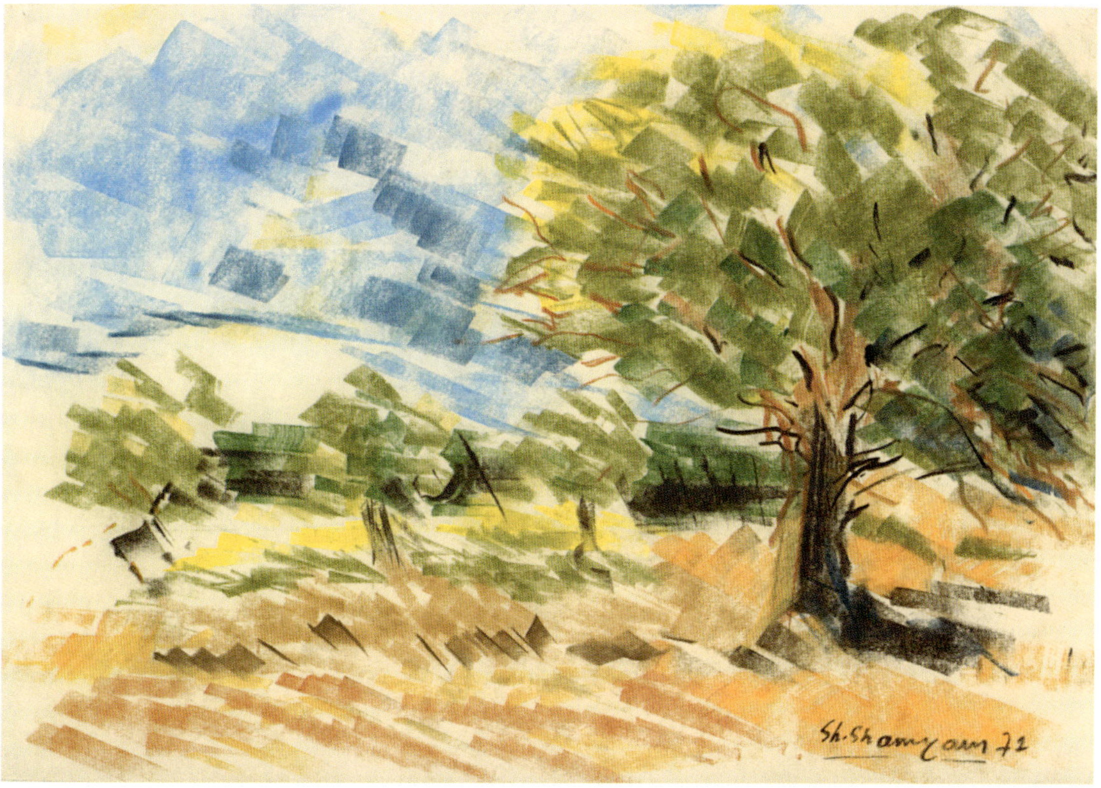

30
ABLAH FIG TREE,
1972
Pastel on paper
35 x 27cm

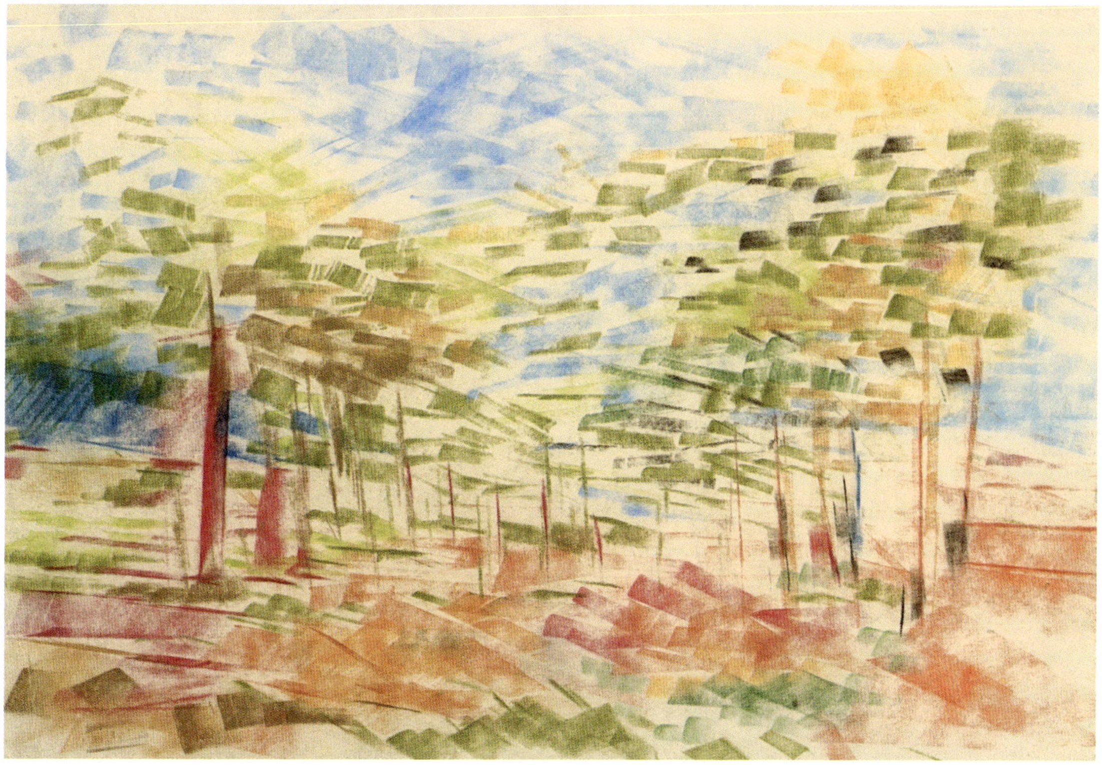

31
ABLAH, 1972
Pastel on paper
35 x 25 cm

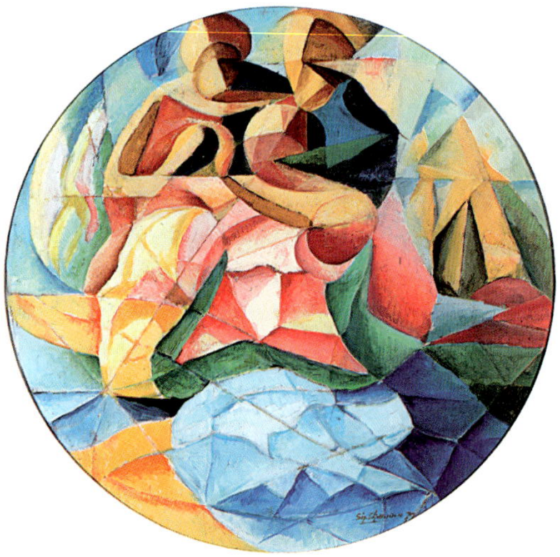

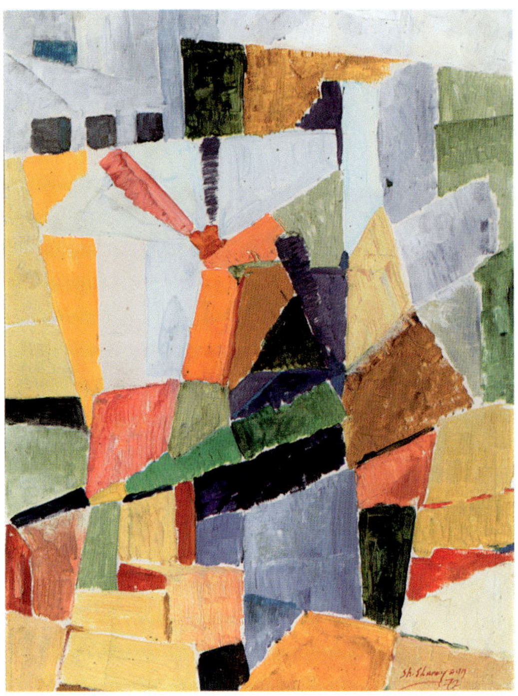

Top
32
MICHELANGELO'S HOLY FAMILY, 1972
Oil on canvas
99.5 x 99.5 cm

Bottom
33
STUDY FOR MEN AND ROCKS, 1972
Oil on canvas
54 x 77 cm

exhibiting Lebanese, Arab and European artists. American contemporary artists were also introduced at the Kennedy Center. What was important for me, as a student was to know how these artists had managed to do what they did, and how
painting had evolved in the modern sense. Rachid Wehbeh 12–15
was the artist I learned most from when it came to the basic academic drawing rules and techniques that enhanced what I had learned on my correspondence course with the ICS
in London. With Munir Najm and Nadia Saikaly, we had 16–20
basic instruction on the use of colour in achieving three-dimensional renderings of still life and figurative subjects.

Awareness of the difficulties inherent in the making of modern painting, sculpture and prints began with the start of the second year. I recall Aref Rayyes coming one evening to the painting studio and finding me working late, struggling
to make sense of a composition based on a still life model 21, 22
of various objects I had found. 'Take these objects apart, dissect them into meaningful small parts, then reassemble them so as to create a new composition merely hinting at the original,' Rayyes suggested to me, before going on to lecture me on Cubism, Mondrian, Kandinsky and so on. After he left, I stayed up all night experimenting with what I had gathered from an artist with whom I was not even taking courses, although I always enjoyed the discussions on art he shared with his students in the institute courtyard. I spent that night and the days that followed analysing the objects and

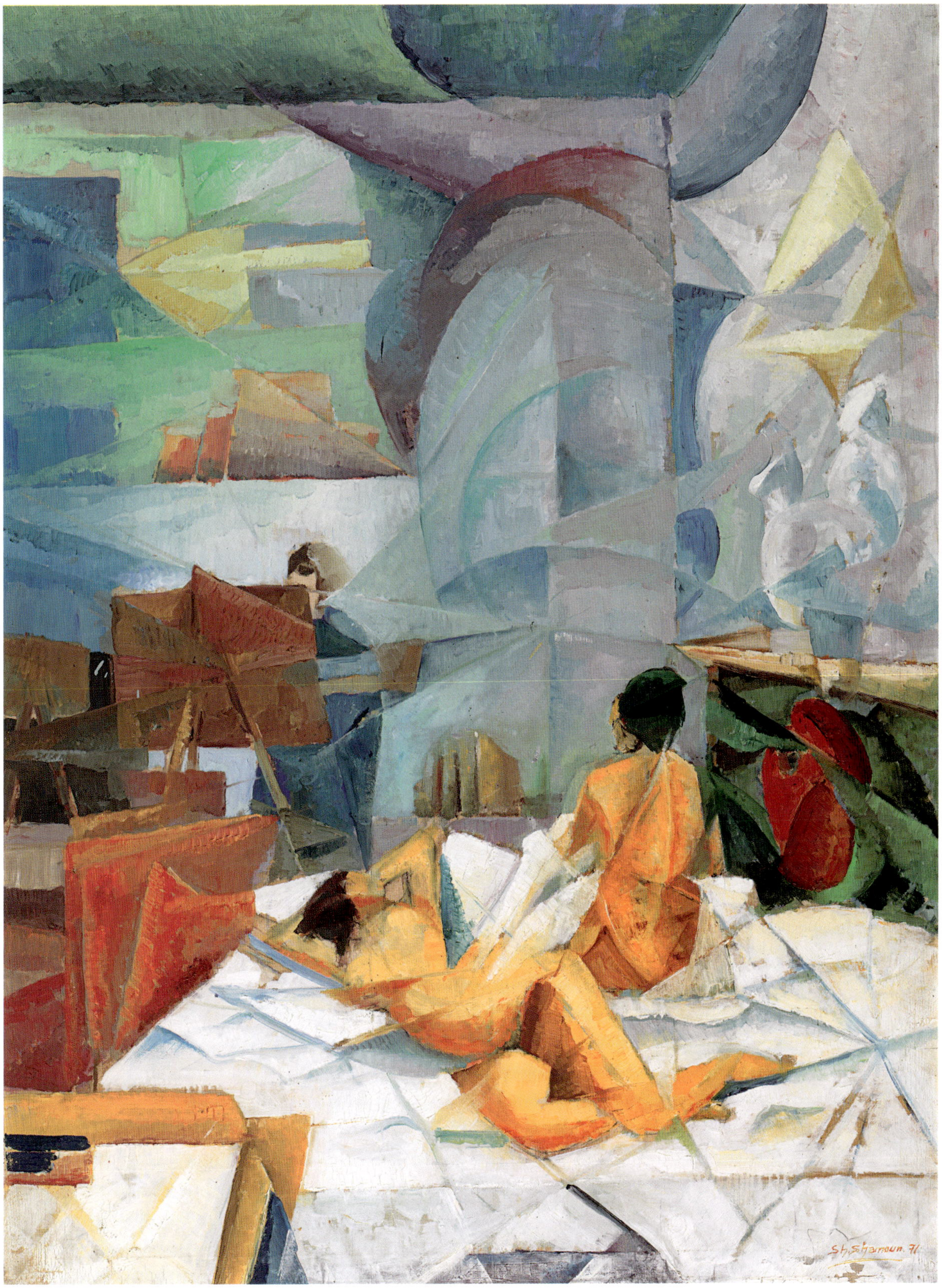

34
L'ATELIER, 1971
Oil on canvas
85 x 131 cm

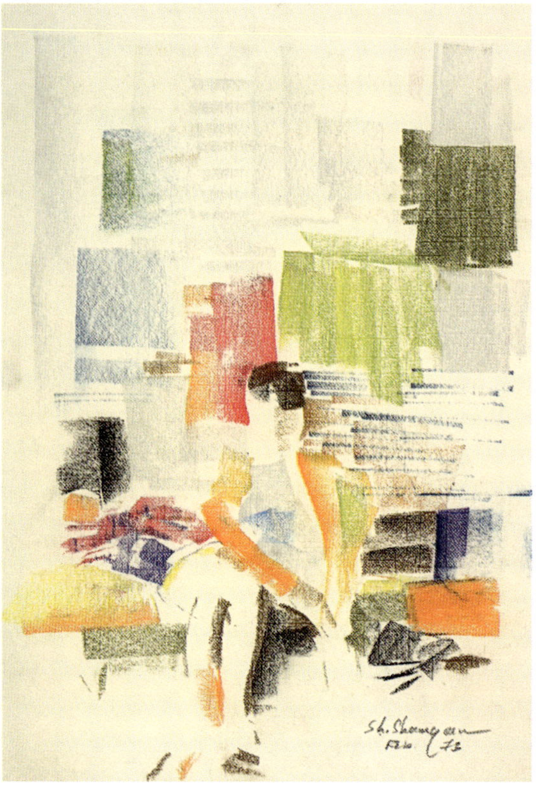

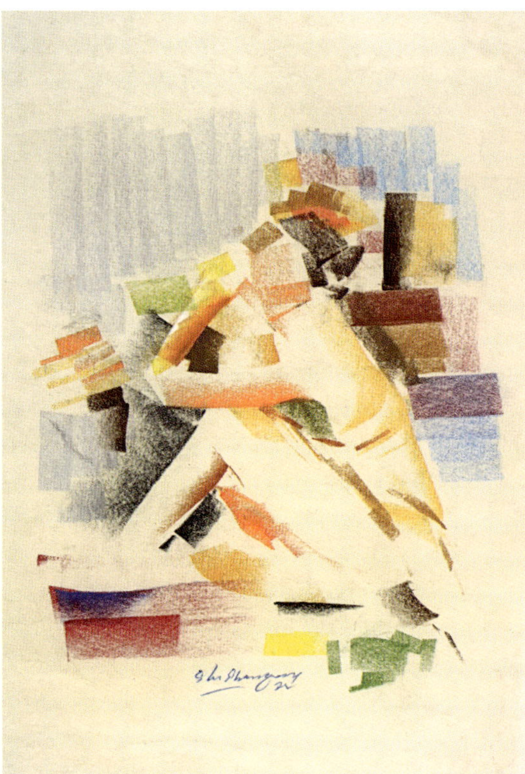

reassembling their new-found facets, a process in line with that of the Cubists. The challenge was that I began to feel the weight of real creation, not the mere depiction of things: a shift from seeking traditional techniques of perspective, modelling and foreshortening to a free play with shapes, colours and lines stressing the two-dimensionality of the painting. The result not only pleased me but brought another level of satisfaction to my creative curiosity. It was the modest beginning of a new intellectual journey. This challenge opened my eyes and interests to a whole new artistic venture.

During the last academic year at the institute, students
were given the liberty to follow whatever style or school of
art they felt closest to. I experimented with various styles 23–31
and techniques, and became strongly attracted to Analytic
Cubism because of the freedom it afforded me. I quickly 32–39
realised the influence of Cubism on modern art and its infinite
possibilities to open new creative ventures. Picasso and
Braque were my heroes. My final thesis for my diploma was
titled 'Cubism between Picasso and Braque'. Unfortunately,
the final painting in this series, 'Men and Rocks', inspired by 40
the inscriptions of invaders on the rock walls of Nahr el Kalb,
was burnt in 1975 in one of the Fine Arts Institutes, at the
beginning of the Lebanese civil war.

Upon graduation, it became clear to me that although the revolutionary ideas of Cubism as conceived and created

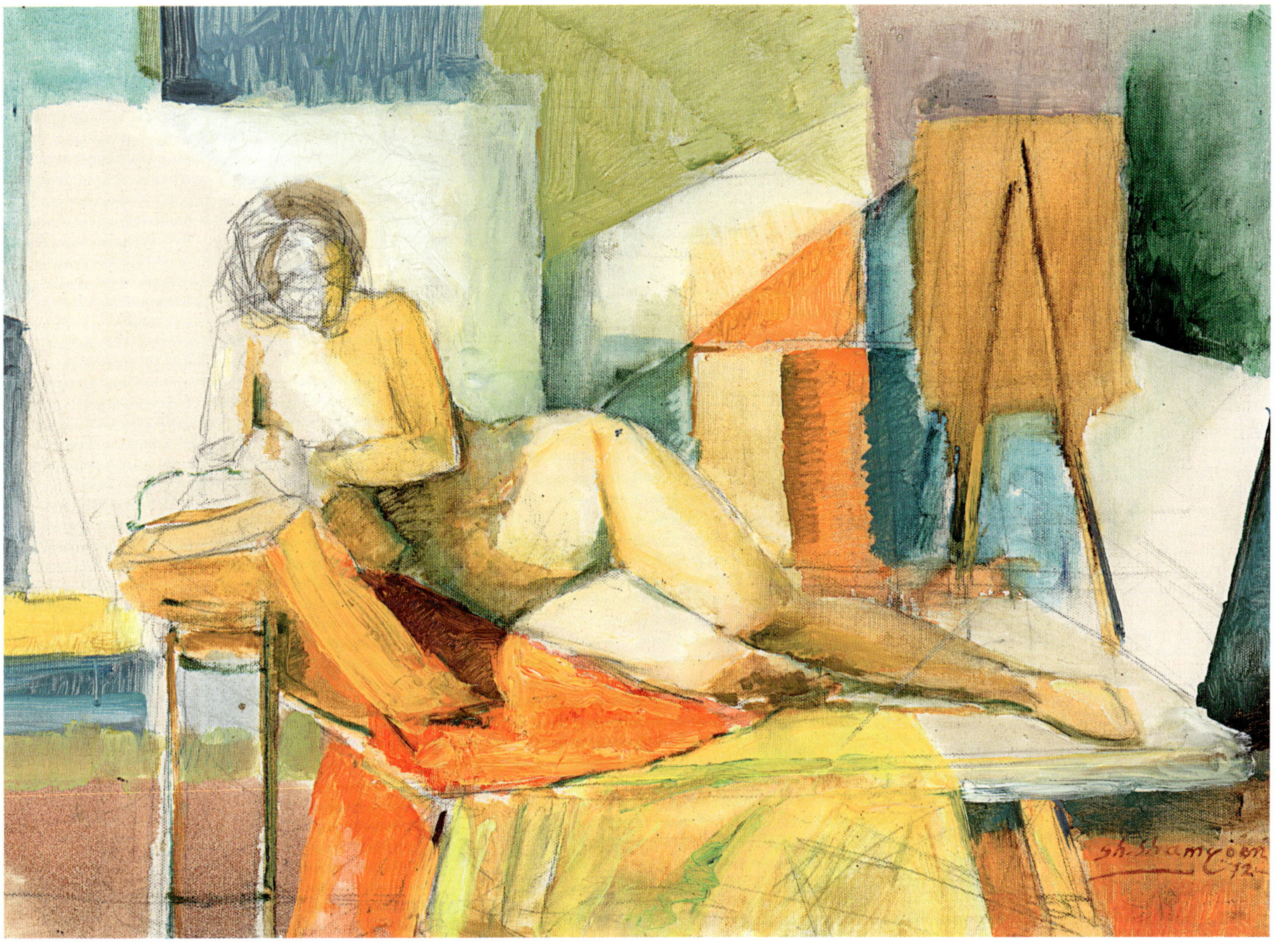

had brought about a full break with the past all the way back to the Renaissance, the movement had in its turn now become part of the past of the modern era it had helped galvanise. In the months following my graduation, I went back to painting free from the Cubists' influence, regaining control of a direct and more expressionistic approach. New trends in modern art, in particular in American art, with which I came into contact for the first time in 1969 at the Kennedy Center in Beirut, had puzzled me. I had seen a fascinating exhibition of several contemporary American artists, including, among others, Larry Rivers and Louise

35
MARIAM AND AN EASEL, 1972
Oil on canvas
56.5 x 40 cm

Facing page, top
36
STUDY AFTER MARIAM 6, 1972
Pastel on paper
35 x 25 cm

Facing page, bottom
37
STUDY AFTER MARIAM S2, 1972
Pastel on paper
35 x 25 cm

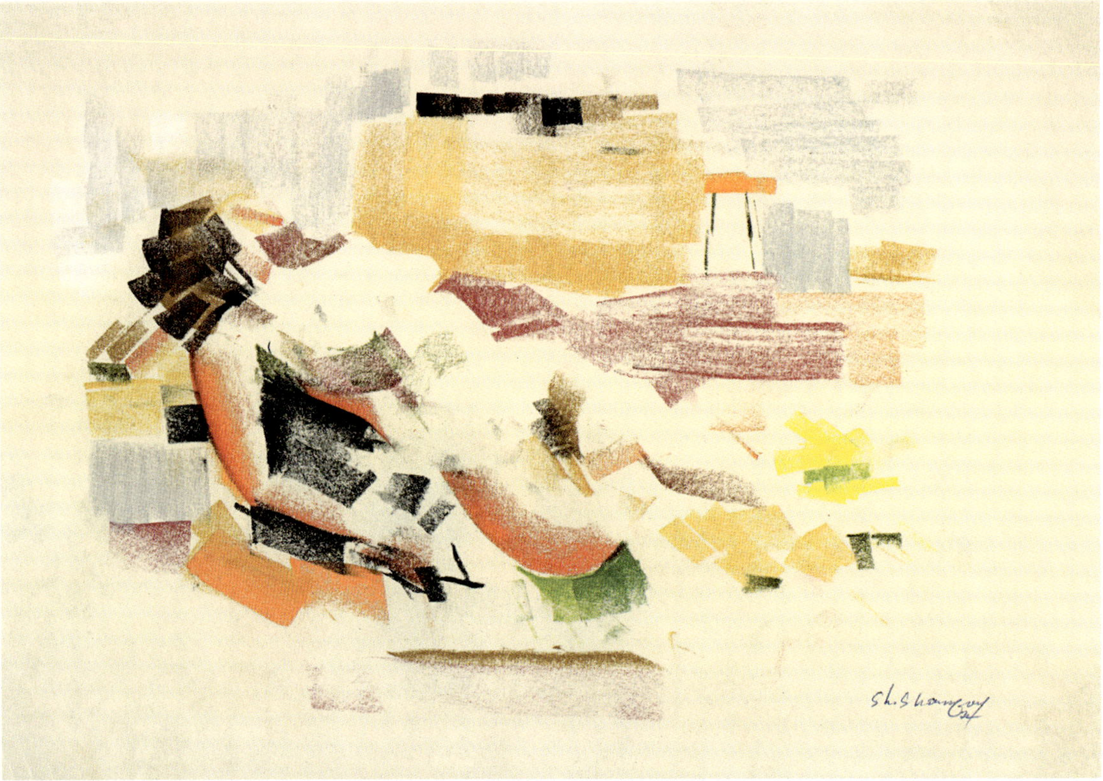

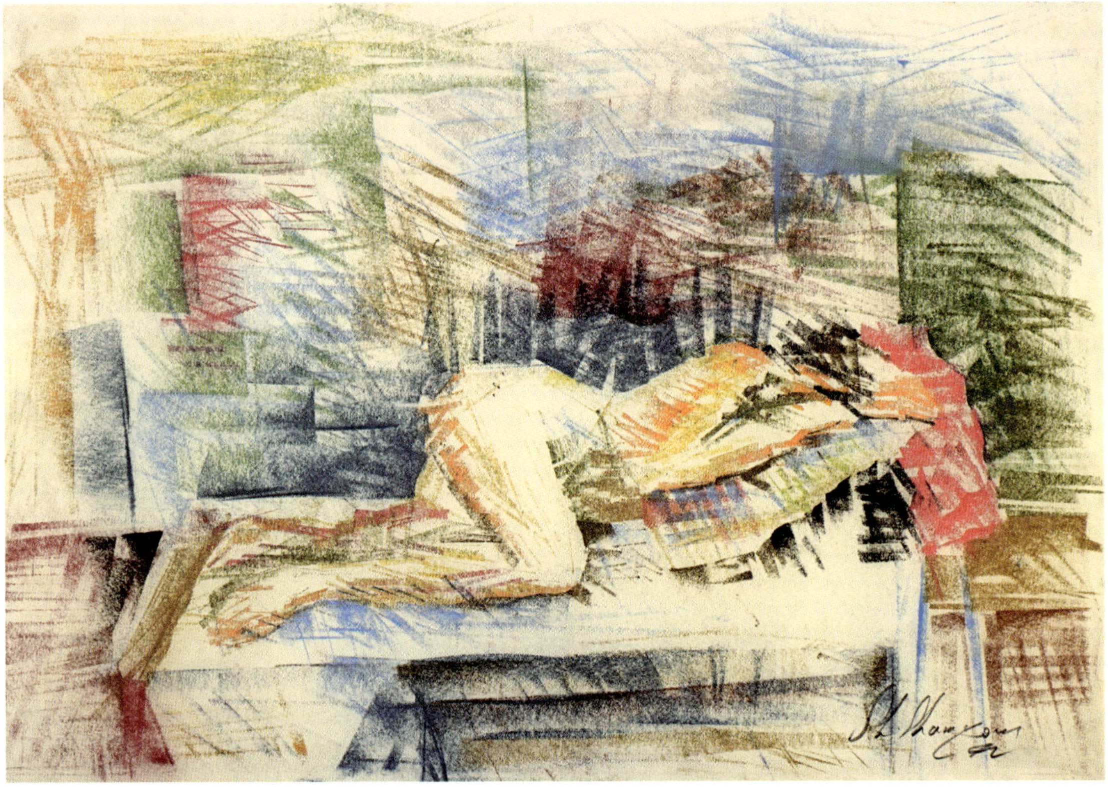

Top
38
STUDY AFTER
MARIAM S3, 1972
Pastel on paper
35 x 25 cm

Bottom
39
STUDY AFTER
MARIAM S1, 1972
Pastel on paper
35 x 25 cm

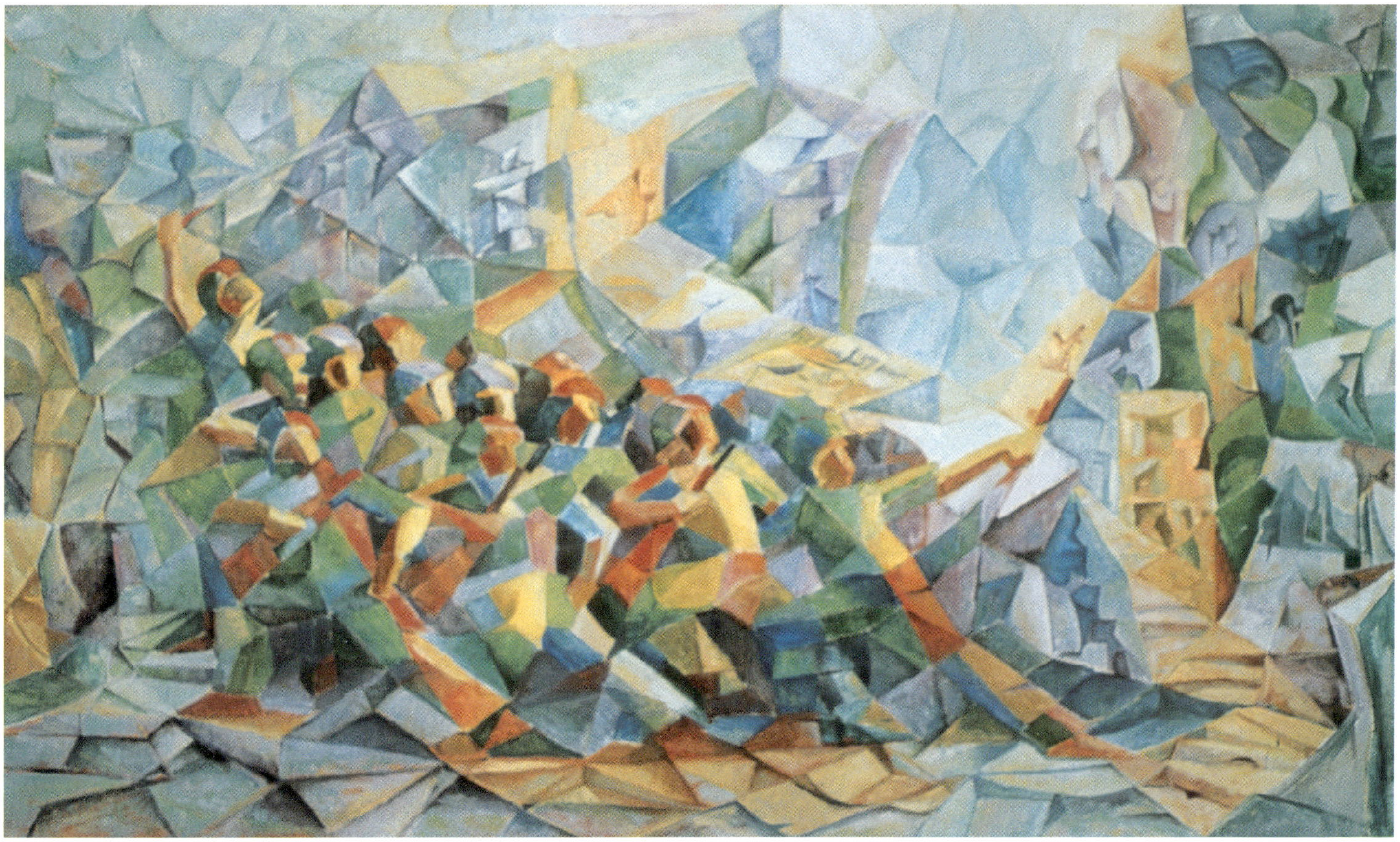

40
MEN AND ROCKS, 1972
Oil on canvas
230 x 166 cm

Nevelson; this drove me to question the new directions art was taking in the New World.

I graduated with the highest average in my class, among the highest ever at the institute. This should have given me the right to a scholarship for higher education abroad, but that year the university decided to cancel the scholarships for the Fine Arts Institute. After a series of objections and arguments that lasted for a whole year, the head of the university, Dr Edmond Naem, signed for my scholarship with the agreement of the University Council. I was off to the US.

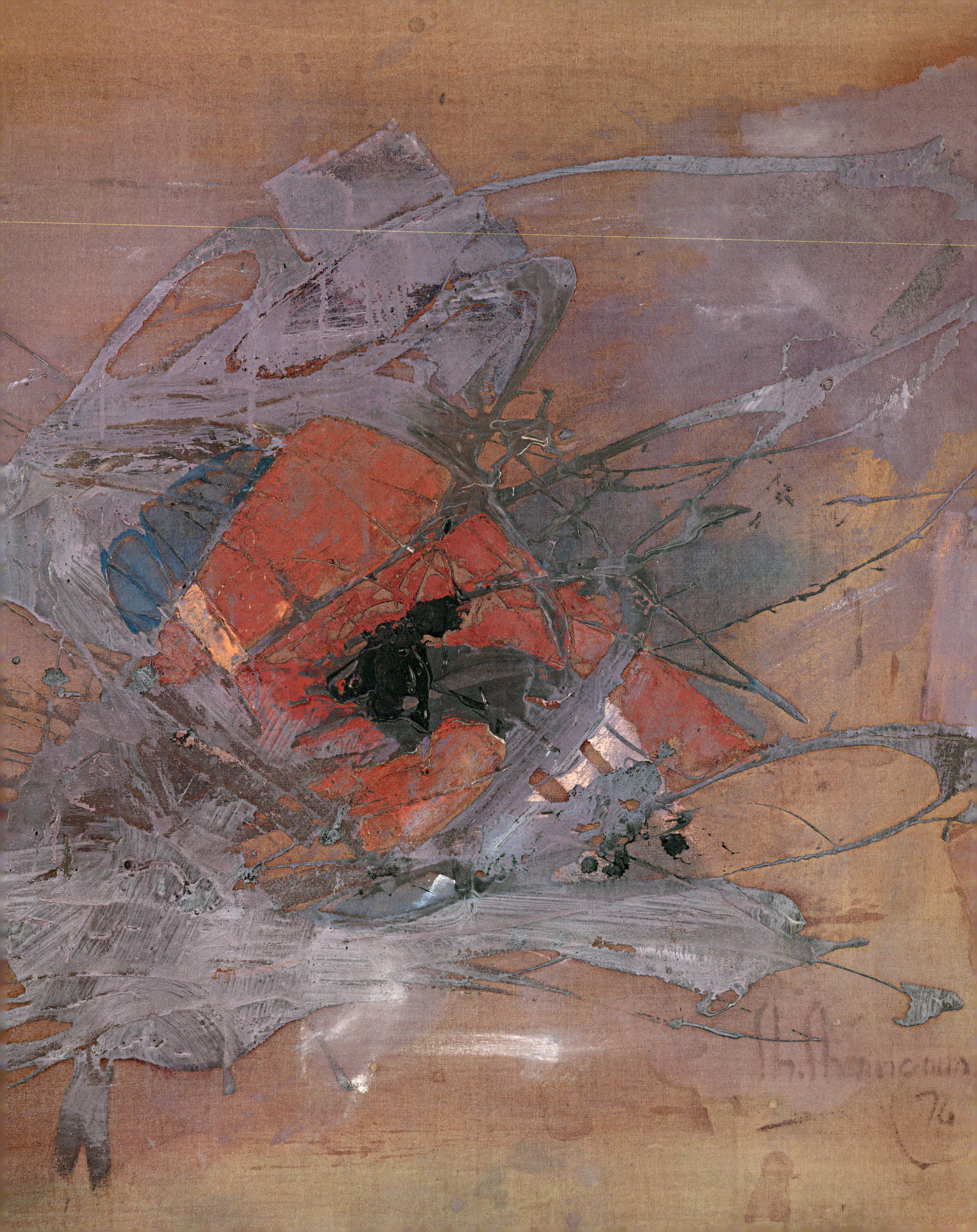

In the United States

In autumn 1973, I was accepted in the undergraduate senior class at the School of Visual and Performance Arts, Syracuse University, Syracuse, New York. I was put into the undergraduate programme because the art curriculum at the Lebanese University was not evaluated to the level of BFA. Determined to continue my education in America, I had accepted the offer because I did not want to waste another year waiting for a graduate offer from other American universities. But after a review of my work at the end of the fall semester, the painting department changed its decision and accepted me in the graduate programme.

That first semester, however, was an important transitional period, which helped me adapt to the new working environment with regular visits to New York galleries and museums. I took a New Material Sculpture course with James Ridlon, and two courses of advanced painting: one with Frank Goodnow, a veteran artist who had spent years at the École des Beaux-Arts in Paris; and another with Darryl Hughto, a younger artist who had been fully educated in the USA and who Clement Greenburg classified as one of the Third Generation of American Abstract Expressionists.

Facing page
41
THE MEETING PLACE, 1974
Oil on acrylic on canvas (detail)
128 x 101 cm

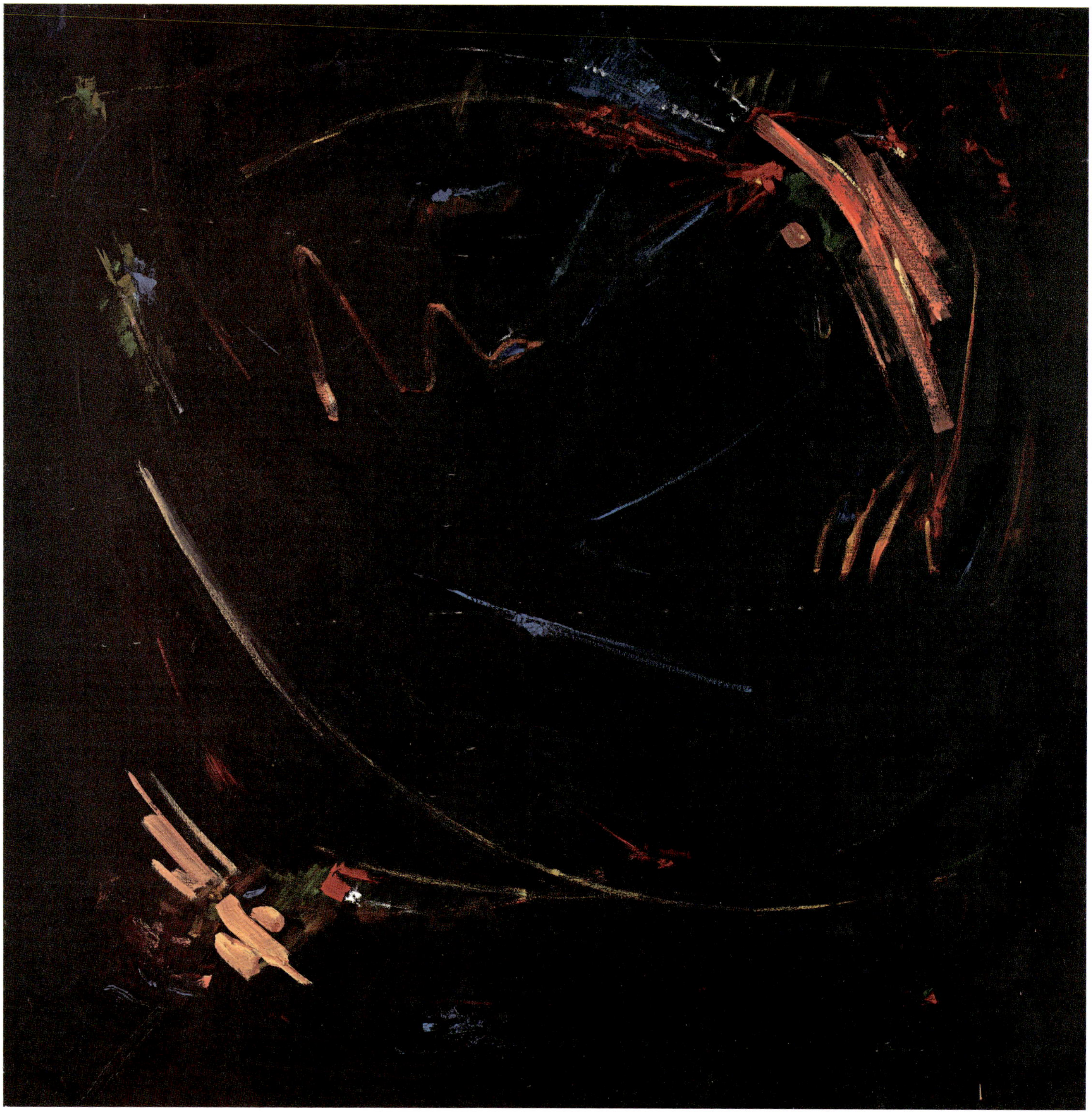

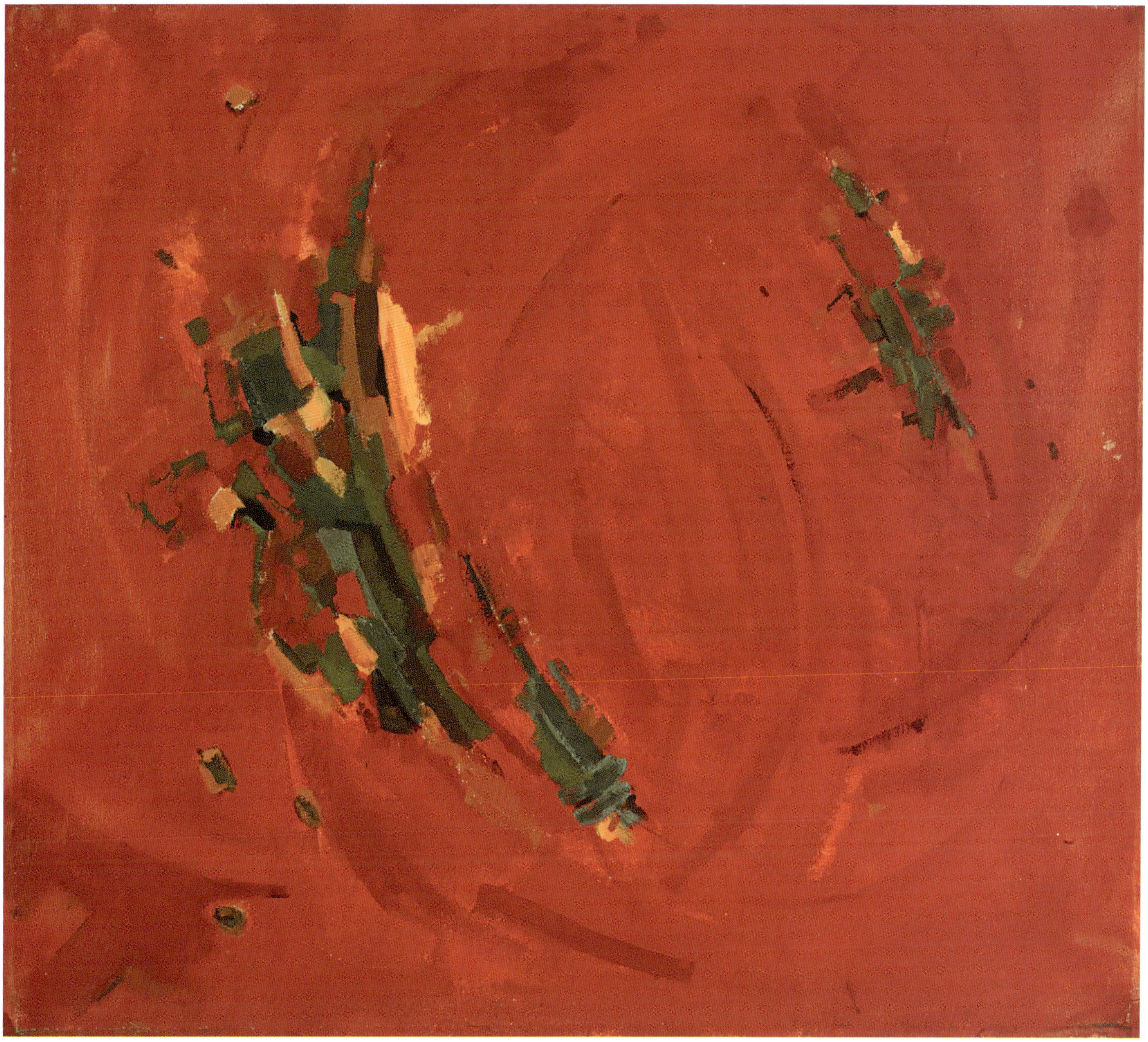

42
POLARITY III, 1973
Oil on acrylic on canvas
132 x 112 cm

Facing page
43
THE HAPPY BLACK, 1973
Oil on canvas
158 x 162 cm

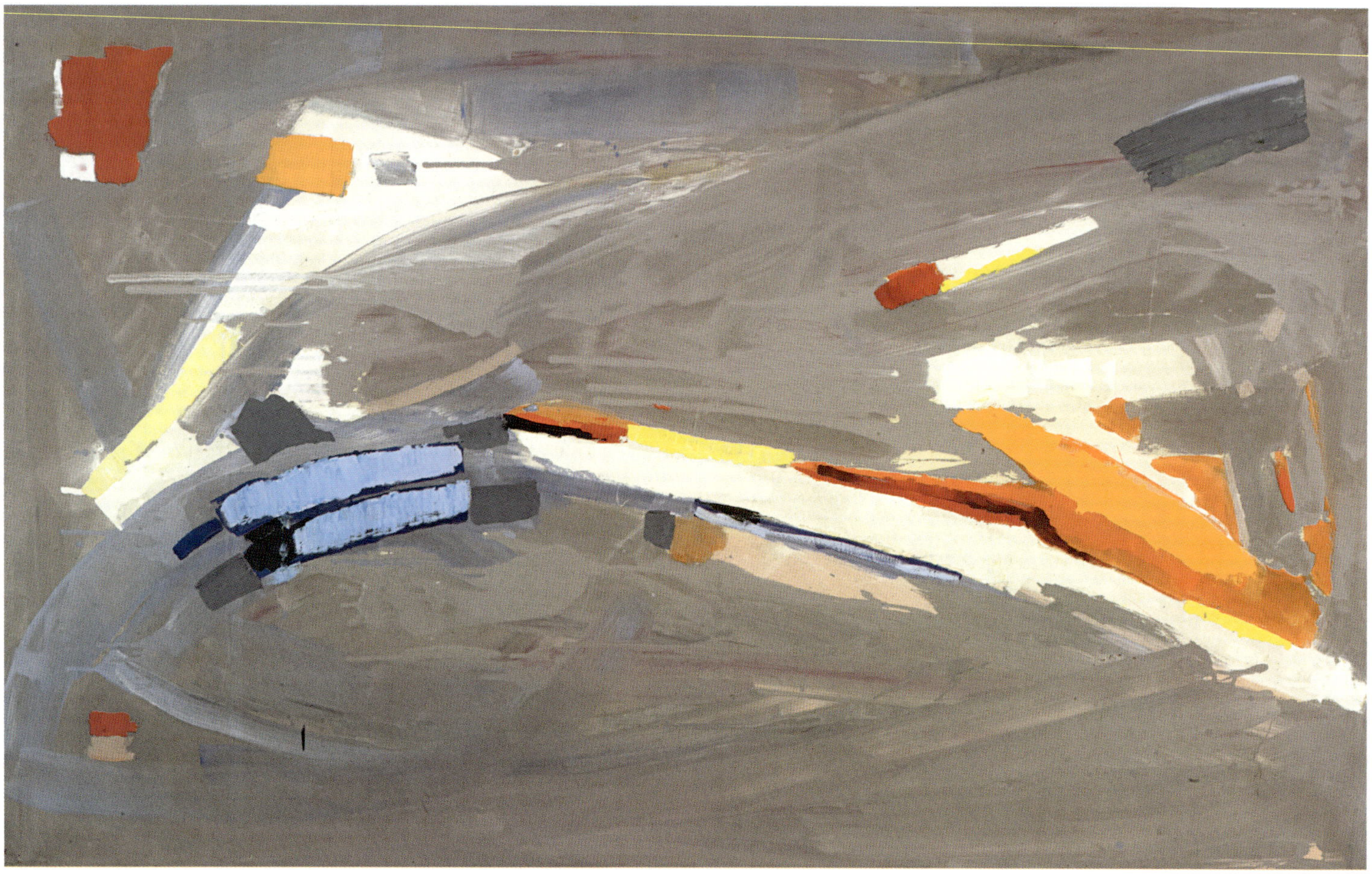

44
FALL 73, 1973
Acrylic on canvas
236 x 150 cm

Facing page
45
333 DAYS IN THE USA (R), 1974
Oil on acrylic on canvas
98 x 167 cm

These two polarising aesthetic forces symbolised my struggle. I was no longer under the direct influence of Analytic Cubism. I realised that even for Picasso, Analytic Cubism, despite its spell and everlasting influence on him and others, was a stage; a springboard for other artistic adventures. I found myself struggling to make aesthetically and technically convincing painting, trying to find a niche for myself in the real world of competitive artistic creation and self-realisation. 41–44, 46

At this point, I received two great boosts to my morale. First, on becoming a graduate student I moved to my own private studio space in Callandale, a building on the periphery of SU Campus. I was also asked to take full responsibility for teaching a drawing course in the Core Programme. Members

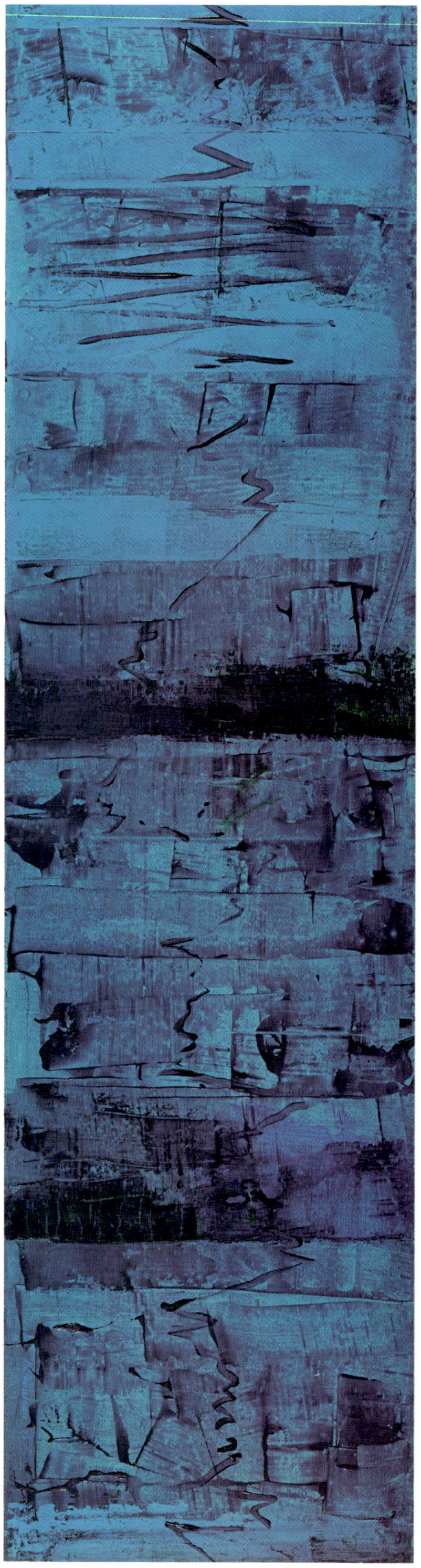

of the faculty started coming to me for one-on-one critical discussions of my work, instead of me running around from one class to another. The exception was a seminar in the office of Dean August Freundlich for all graduate art students. In this forum, we held lively aesthetic discussions centred on the contemporary art scene around the country. Our discussions, based as they were at times on term papers submitted by members of the group, and at others on articles selected from major art magazines, promoted a high level of intellectual engagement.

At my new studio, I felt more independent, and the urge to find my aesthetic path grew stronger. There were eight graduate students occupying the studios. Each seemed to have a single style, echoing an artist or a school of art of his preference. My alignment with Cubism was no different, I thought, but my desperate need to reach beyond and move ahead was unyielding. I went on experimenting with new imageries and techniques, reflecting new observations and direct contacts with works in galleries and museums. This was a continuation of the experiments I had been making during the previous fall, a process of self-finding wonder that would lead to more enduring and sustainable aesthetic discoveries in the months to come.

A large canvas by Helen Frankenthaler in the nearby Everson Museum – itself a masterpiece by architect M. I. Pie – was the first to read differently. So, I discovered, did other abstract expressionists' works. Falling or rising to another human experience is not a reward in itself; the gain is in finding my own ways and adding to that experience, I always reminded myself. Of course, in the beginning, I was never sure what the end results would be ... All I could be sure of was that the experience itself and the creative process were what mattered most.

Frankenthaler's mural looked like a picture of a large earthworks; whether for nostalgic or purely aesthetic reasons, it carried me back into memories of the riverbed at Nahr al Kalb. I seemed to be looking from the top of the surrounding hills into the murky water and the dry land surrounding it. In winter and spring, water gushed through the river; while in the summer and autumn, the riverbed would be almost dry, moving shapes and colours shoved back and forth and arranged by nature's almighty creative hands.

To emulate nature's work was an exciting and challenging experience. Having the space, the necessary materials and the aesthetic backing, I decided to make my own attempt. I tacked a large canvas to the floor of my studio and mixed copious quantities of paint in different tonalities. Then, I took a piece of plywood and began shoving the paint back and forth across the canvas, imitating the flow of the murky water in Al Kalb River. The result was a pool of mud! A 45
disappointment? Not really, I comforted myself the following day. I had already been granted free licence on American

Facing page
46
MOM'S HEART SCAN, 1974
Acrylic on a window shade
196 x 46 cm

47
239 DAYS IN THE USA, 1974
Oil on acrylic on canvas
166 x 170 cm

Facing page, top
48
217 DAYS IN THE USA, 1974
Oil on acrylic on canvas
272 x145 cm

Facing page, bottom
49
THE RIVERBED, 1974
Oil on acrylic on canvas
267 x 167 cm

soil and like many artists I was in the process of abandoning traditional techniques, methods and tools, and beginning a 46–49
new venture.

In my last semester at SU, I continued to work at what seemed to be a difficult aesthetic problem: to maintain a simple and easy-looking painting whilst incorporating subtle changes and variations of colour and texture. It would be 50, 51 54, 55
better described as a one-colour field painting with subtle variation of textures, forms and lines. Towards my graduation date, the painting began to take on a long narrow horizontal format, which was more like a model for a riverbed but far from having any resemblance to the natural make-up of a riverbed. Rather, it emulated the American Abstract Expressionist painting which had inhibited my thinking since the exhibition at the Kennedy Cultural Center in 1969.

What is of special interest, and what served my intention, was my use of the subject as a pretext to reach out to capture the very essence of the aesthetic experience. My paintings were emotionally laden; some were named for the number of days I had spent in the US.

The paintings could be hung vertically or horizontally, or even laid on the floor, and could be read top to bottom, left to right, or vice versa, regardless of position. Reading through the subtle linear texture of the surface allowed for rhythmic observance of the surface, interrupted only by intended imperfections as interval linkages. Music for the

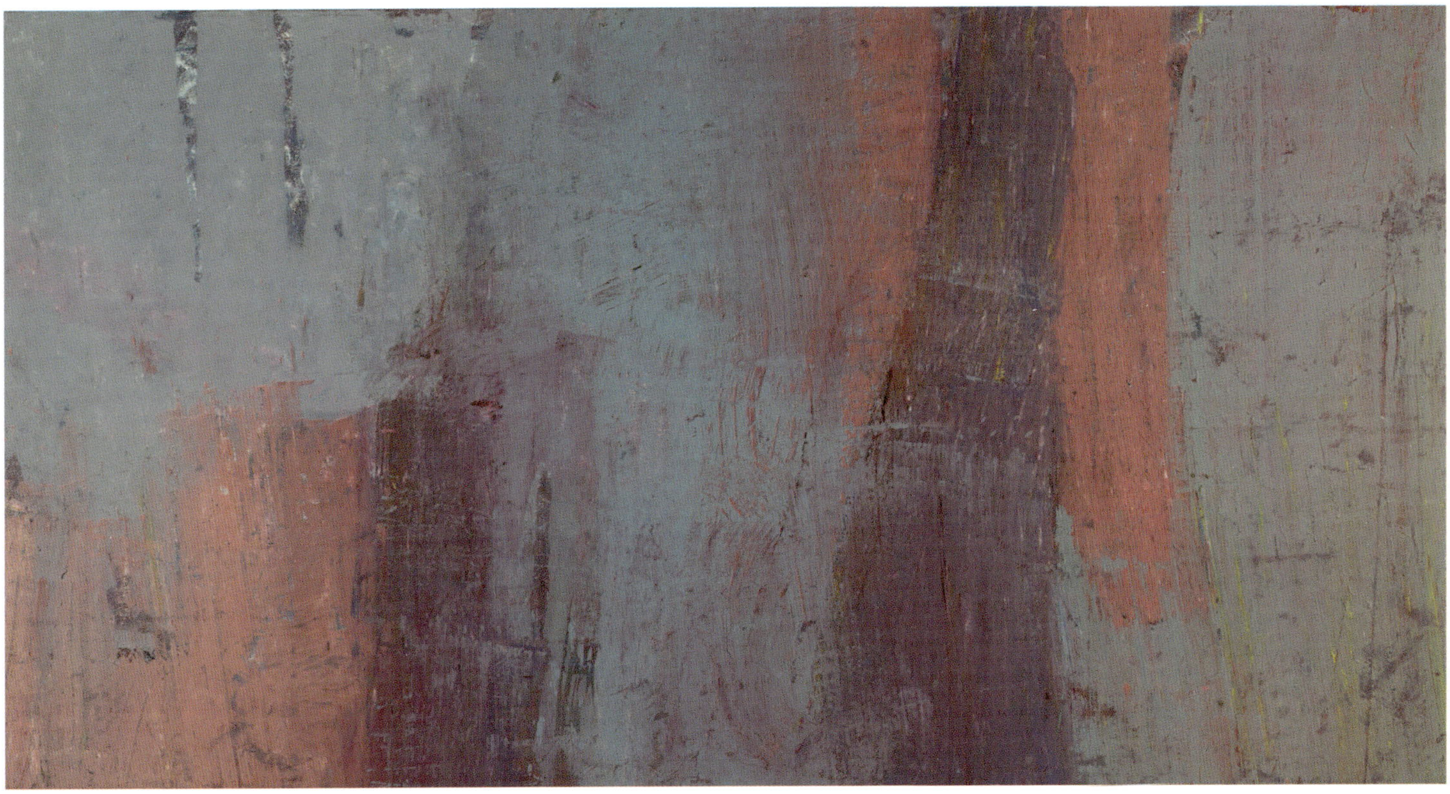

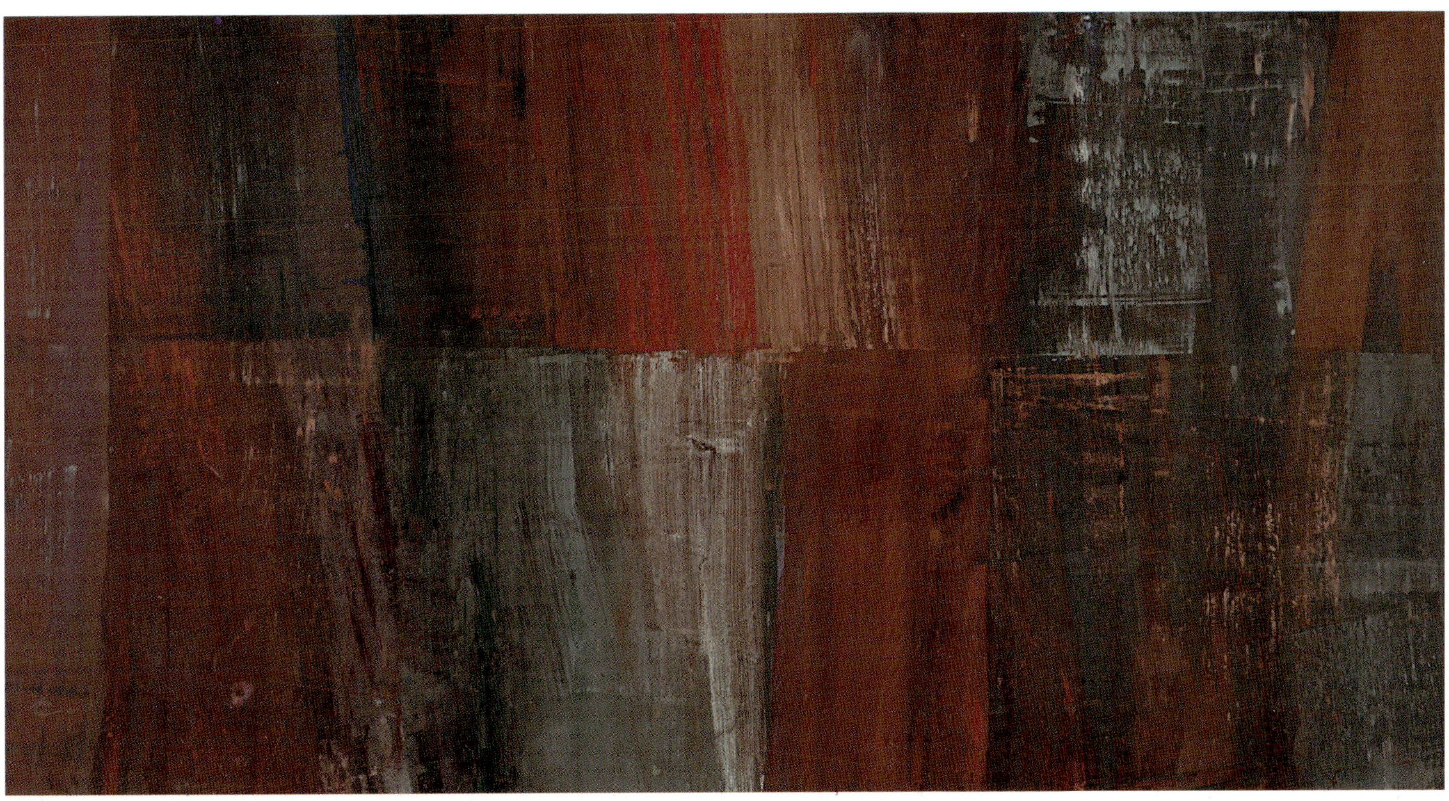

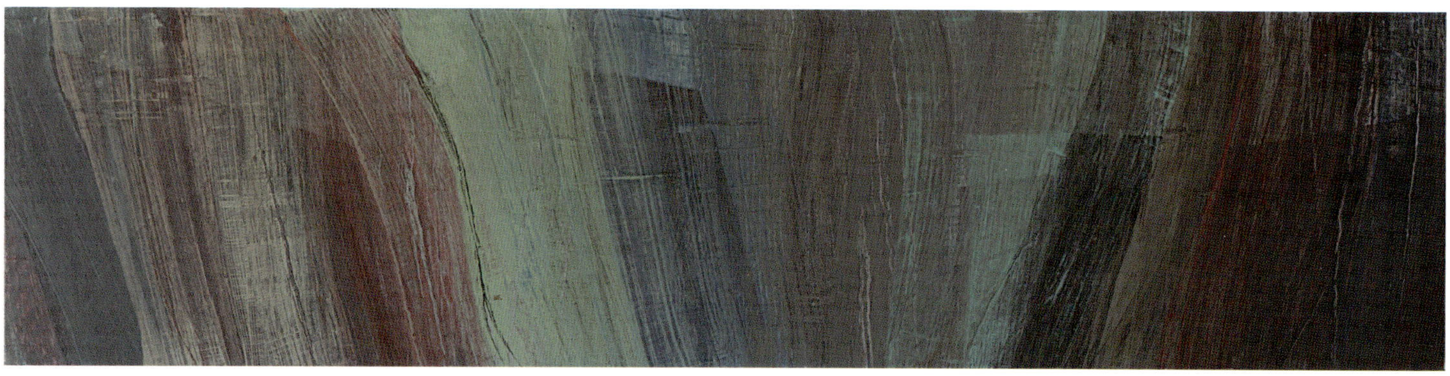

50
RIVERBED 4, 1975
Acrylic on canvas
280 x 70 cm

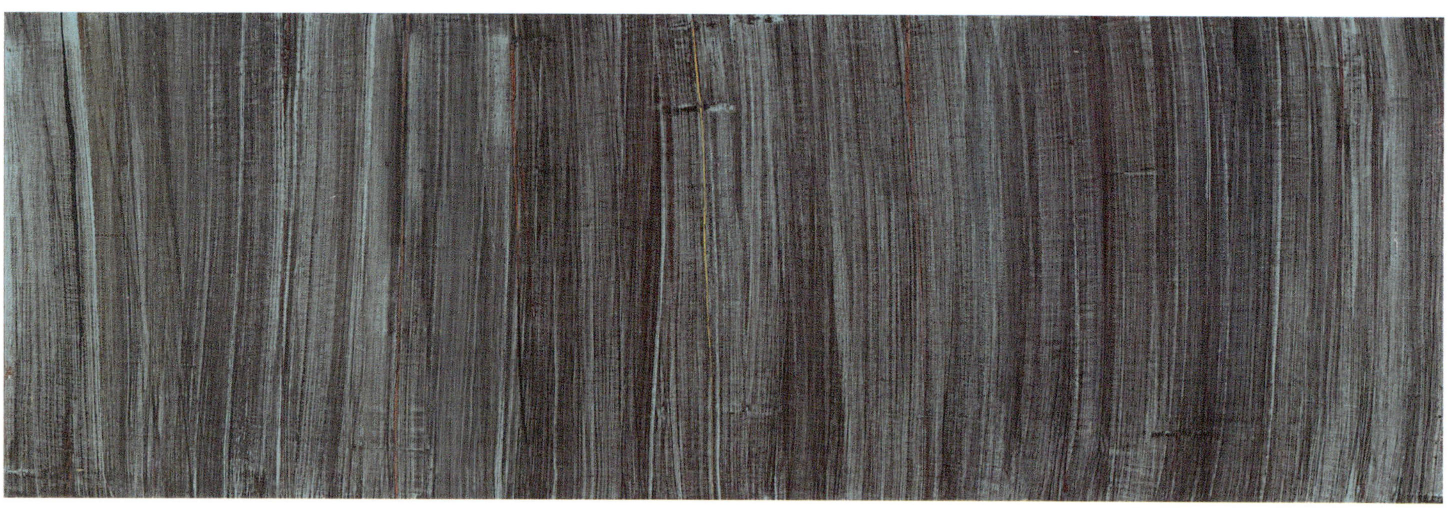

51
RIVERBED 2, 1975
Acrylic on canvas
220 x 75 cm

Facing page
52
RIVERBED II #14, 1976
Acrylic on canvas
55 x 195 cm

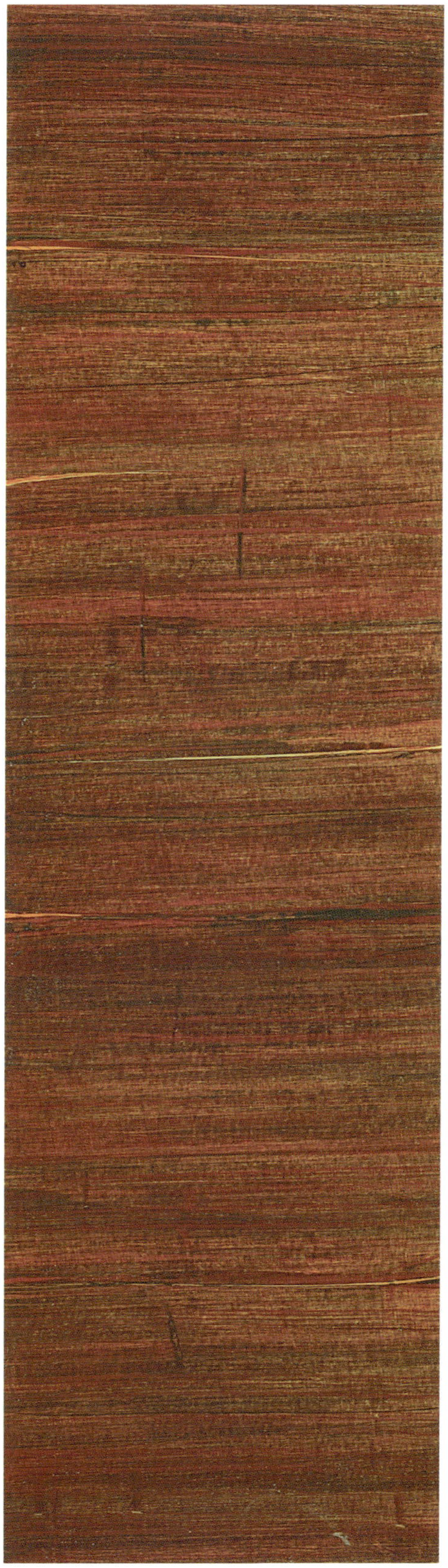

eye, one might think: a possible interpretation of the natural formations of the riverbed flow. The complete absence of linear perspective, despite its references to landscape and the natural, freed the painting from a sense of natural containment. It allowed for infinite continuation of the visual experience beyond the limited longitudinal boundaries of the canvas. The eye and the mind were set free. These paintings were exhibited in May 1975 at the International Living Center at Syracuse University.

I had finished my MFA with honours within two years and still had three years before my fellowship would come to an end. I therefore considered studying a PhD at New York University. Dean Freundlich, who had taught at NYU before he joined SU, strongly endorsed my application and I was accepted as of the autumn of 1975. Living and studying in New York City was another dream come true.

Days before my graduation from SU, on 13 April 1975, civil war erupted in Lebanon. Worried about my family and looking forward to my brother's graduation from the Military Academy, I returned home to spend the summer among family and friends. The Fine Arts Institute was among the first buildings to be burnt and looted. All that was left of 'Men and Rocks' was the black trace of a large frame on a wall.

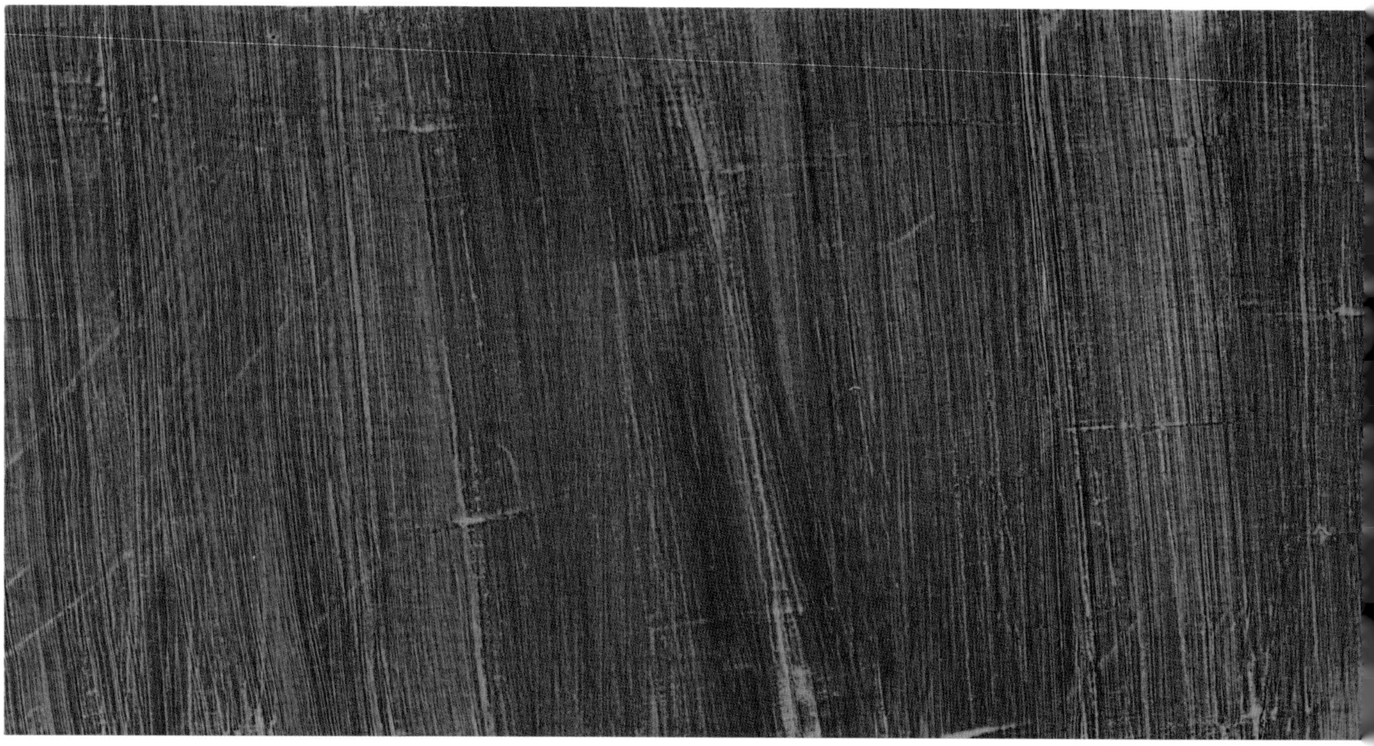

Bottom
53
RIVERBED II, #12, 1977
Acrylic on canvas
229 x 44 cm

Top
54
RIVERBED I, 1975
Acrylic on canvas
260 x 70 cm

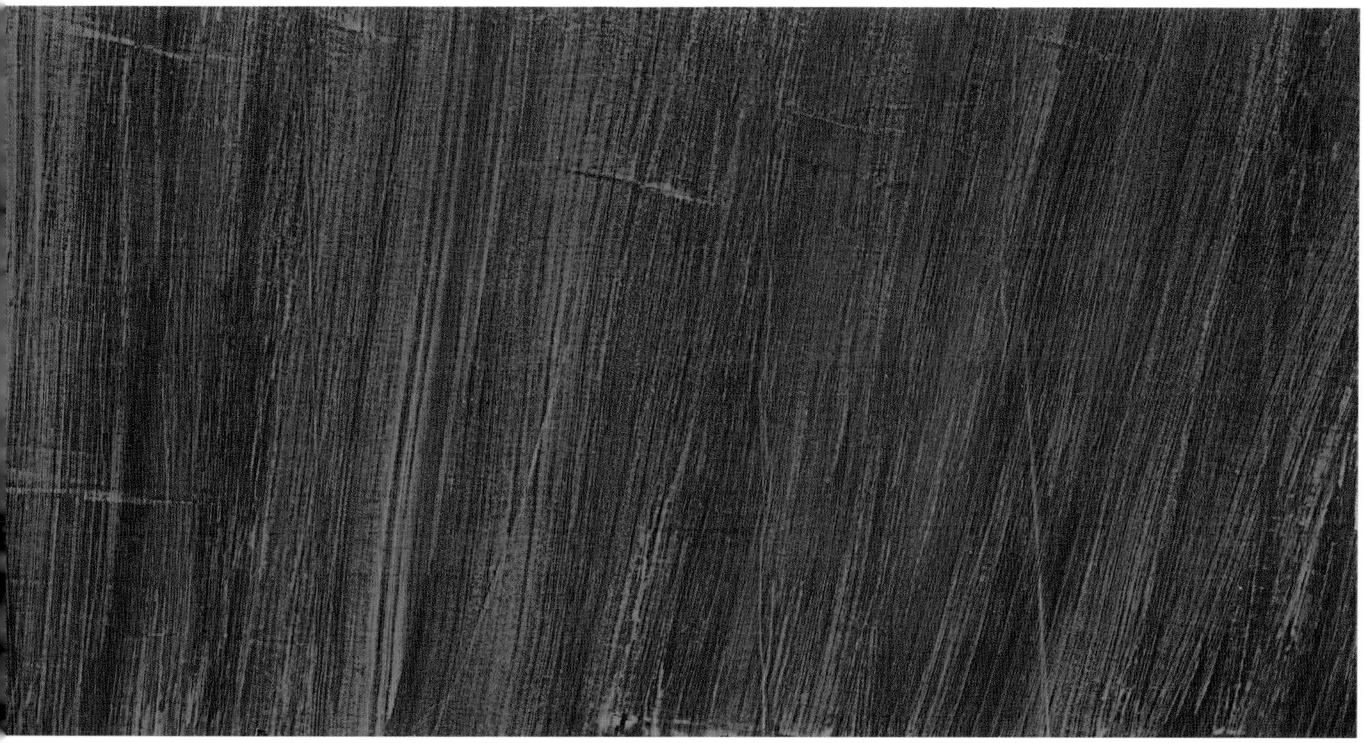

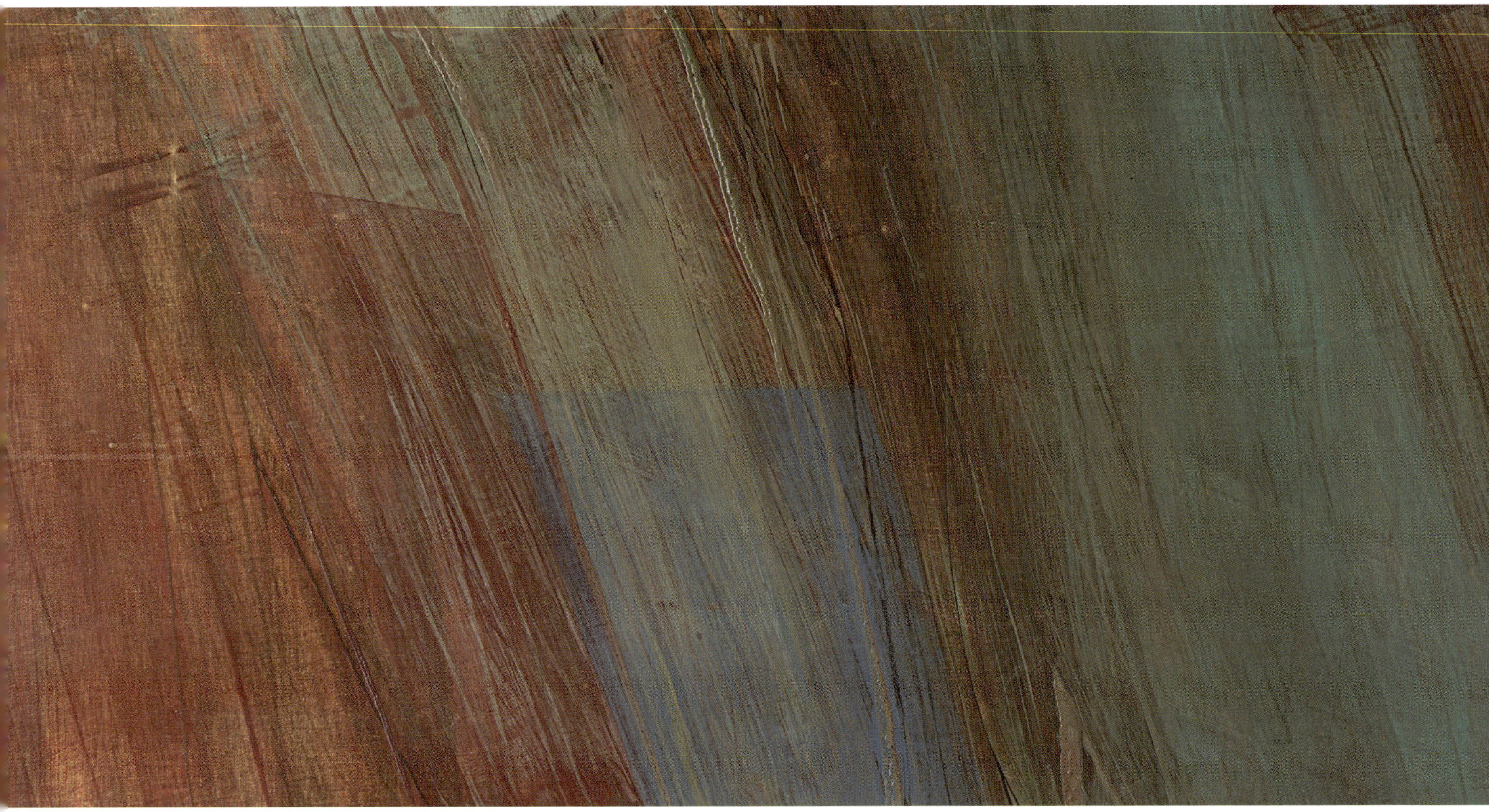

55
RIVERBED XI, 1975
Acrylic on canvas
270 x 72 cm

Back in New York in September 1975, I moved into a one-
bedroom apartment on Twenty-Third Street and Eighth
Avenue, where I turned most of the living room into a painting
area. Angela Churchill, the painting professor and chairwoman
of the art education department, was pleased to see me working
on a continuation of the 'Riverbed' series. I also took courses 52, 53
in print making and was introduced to viscosity printing
techniques using etched zinc plates. The riverbed concept was
the subject of most of the prints I produced up to autumn 1976. 56–58
Then came another series of pastel drawings: 'Bandages for the
War in Lebanon', a conceptual pastel series of infinite questions 59–65
about infinite possibilities, which portrayed my state of mind at
that critical time.

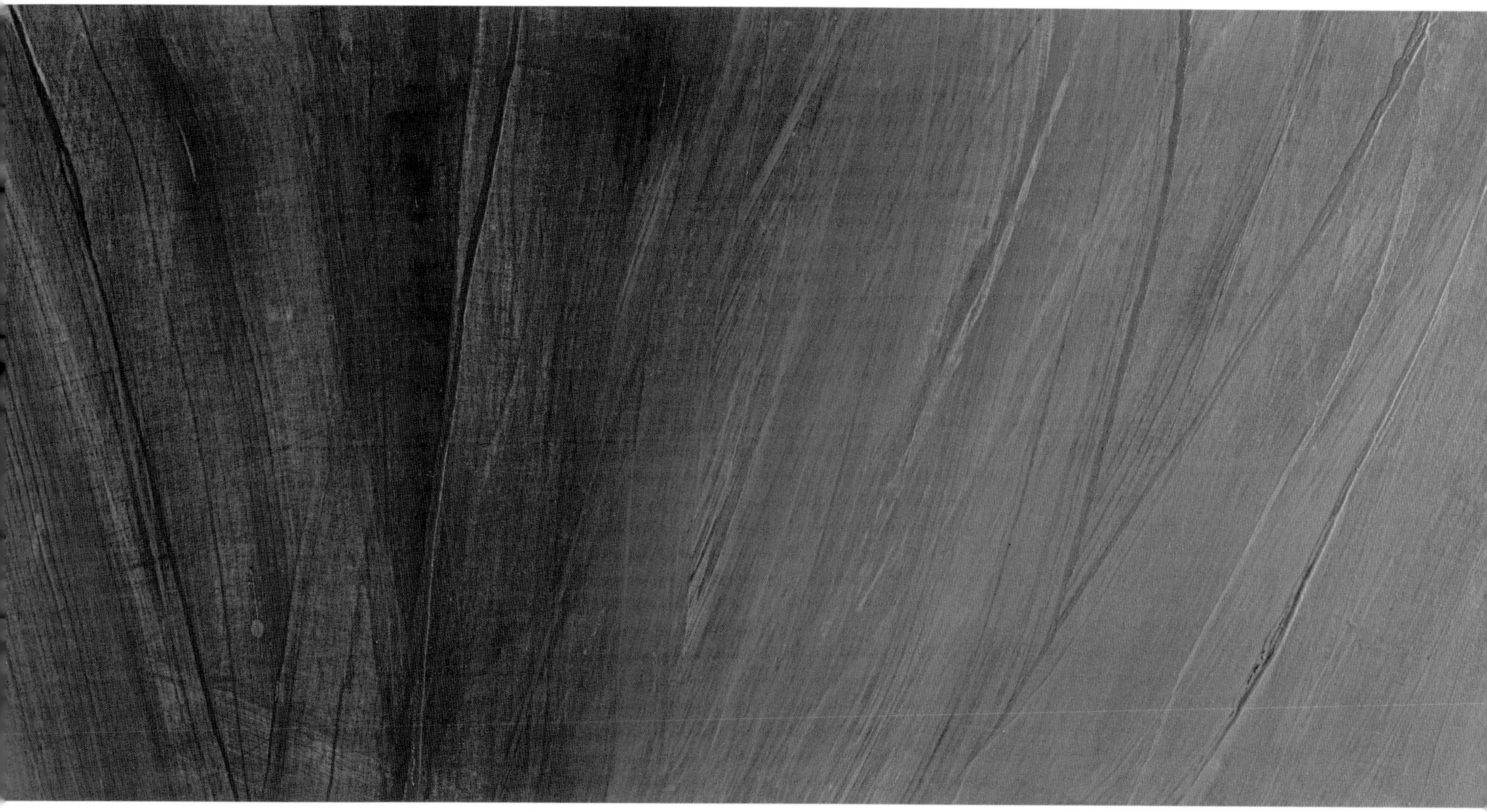

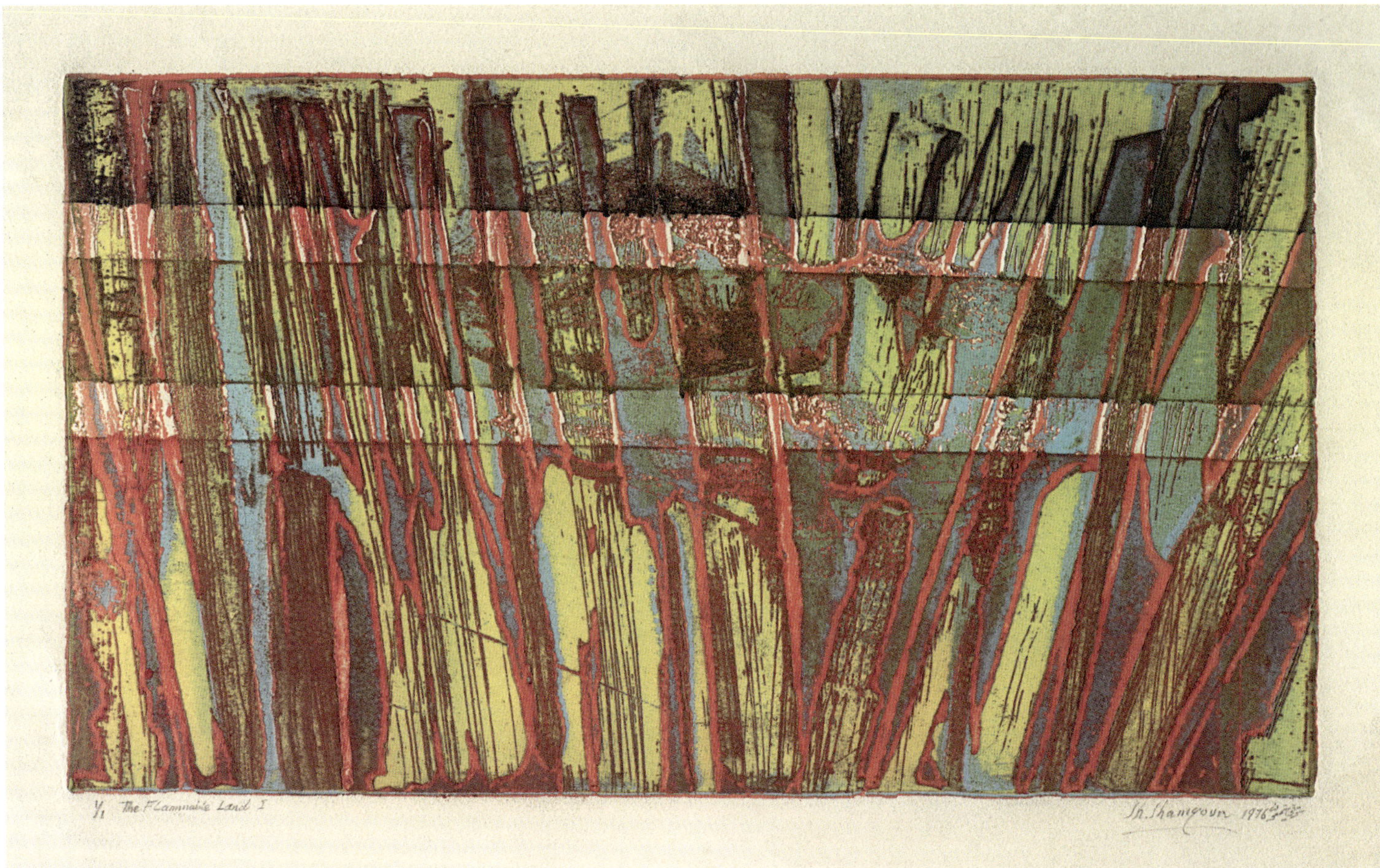

56
RVP-10, 1976
Viscocity print on paper
73.5 x 50.5 cm

Facing page, top
57
VP-VI, 1976
Viscocity print on paper
31.5 x 25.5 cm

Facing page, bottom
58
RVP-6, 1976
Viscocity print on paper
73.5 x 50.5 cm

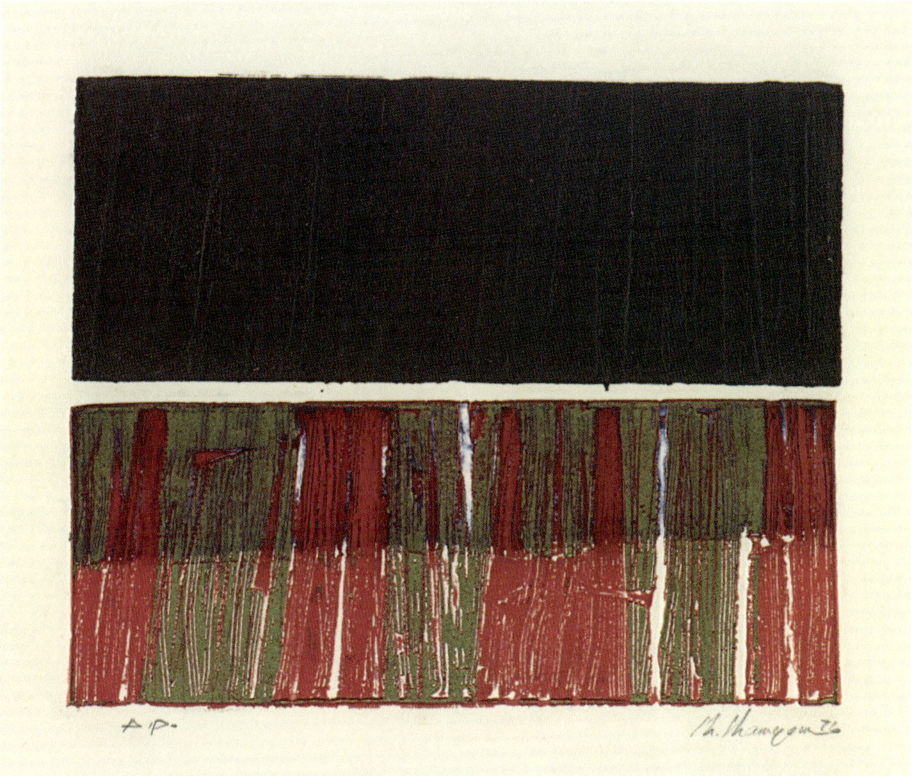

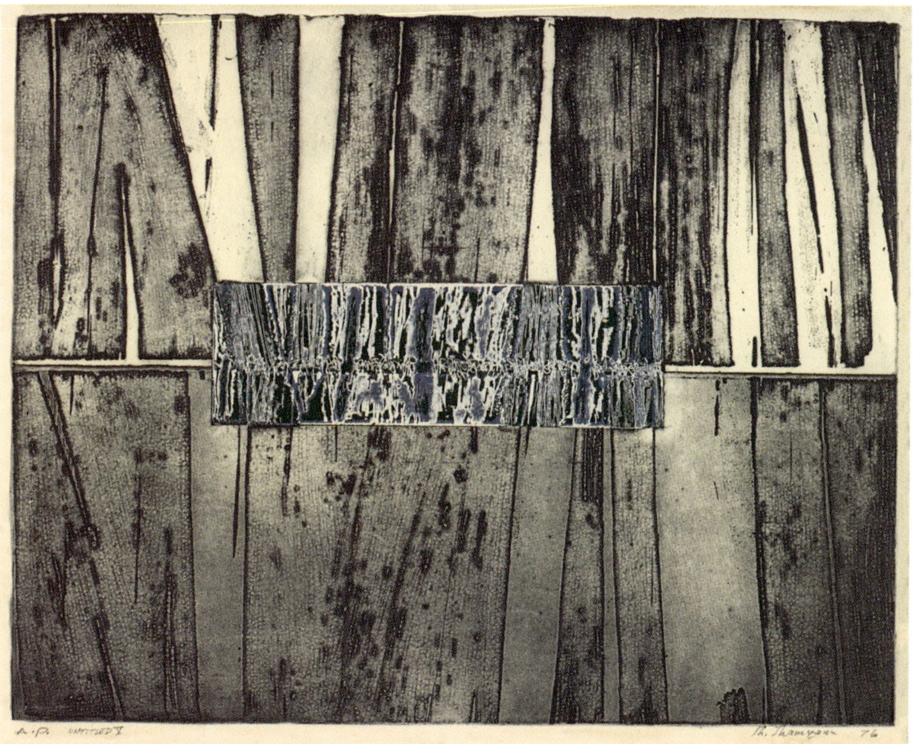

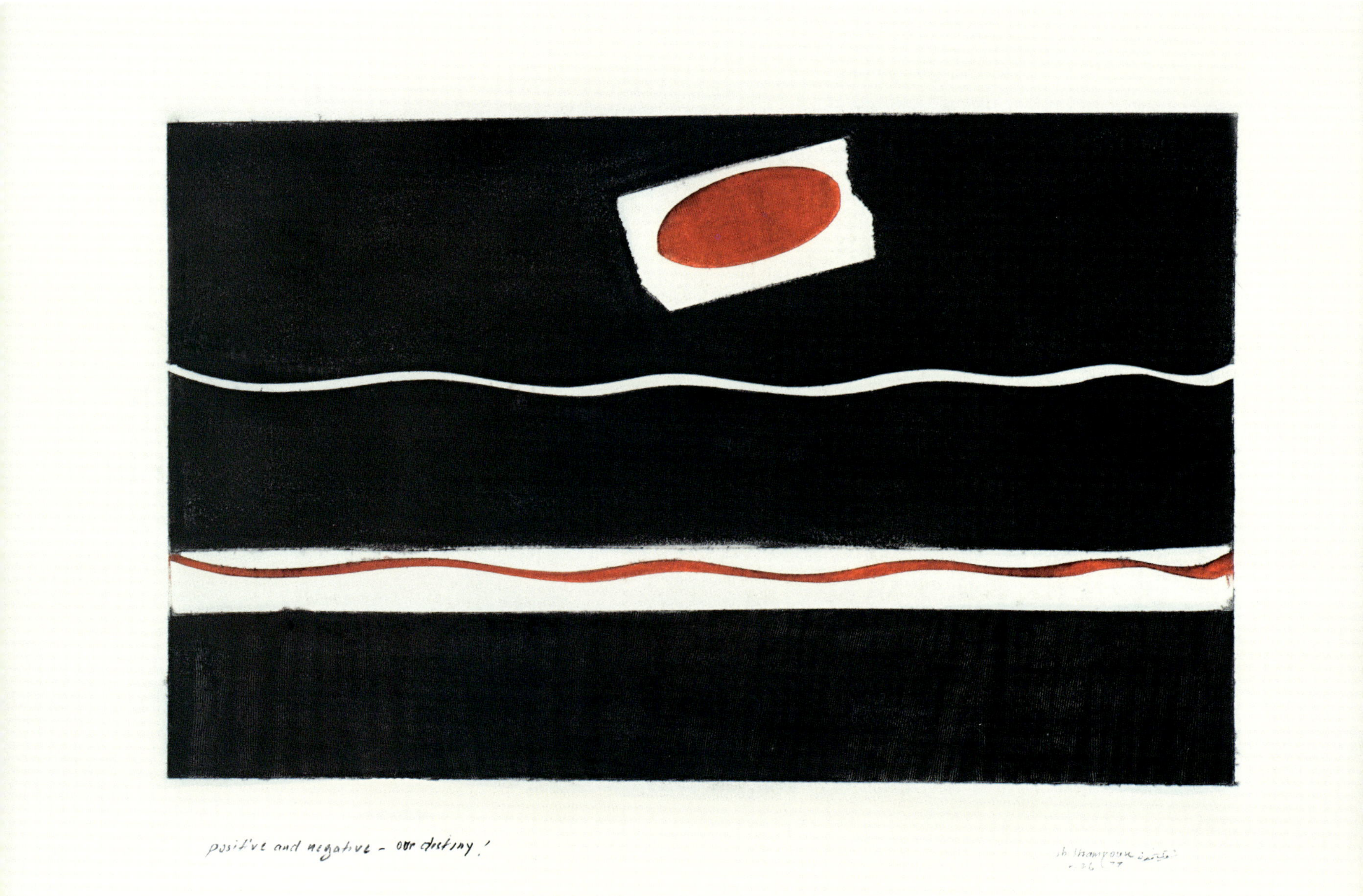

59
POSITIVES AND NEGATIVES: OUR DESTINY, 1977
Pastel on paper
43 x 35.5 cm

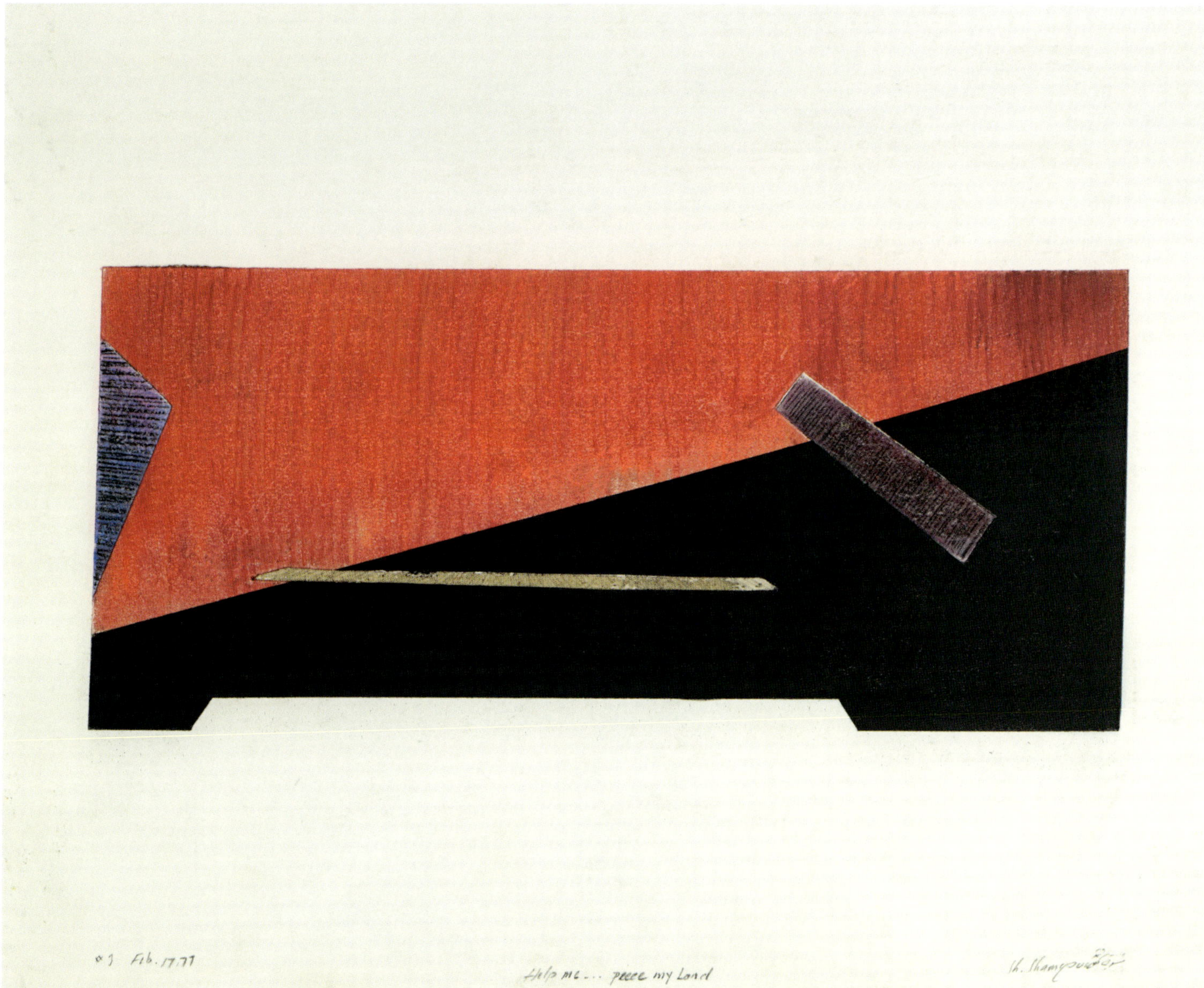

60
HELP ME PIECE MY LAND, 1977
Pastel on paper
35.3 x 27.7 cm

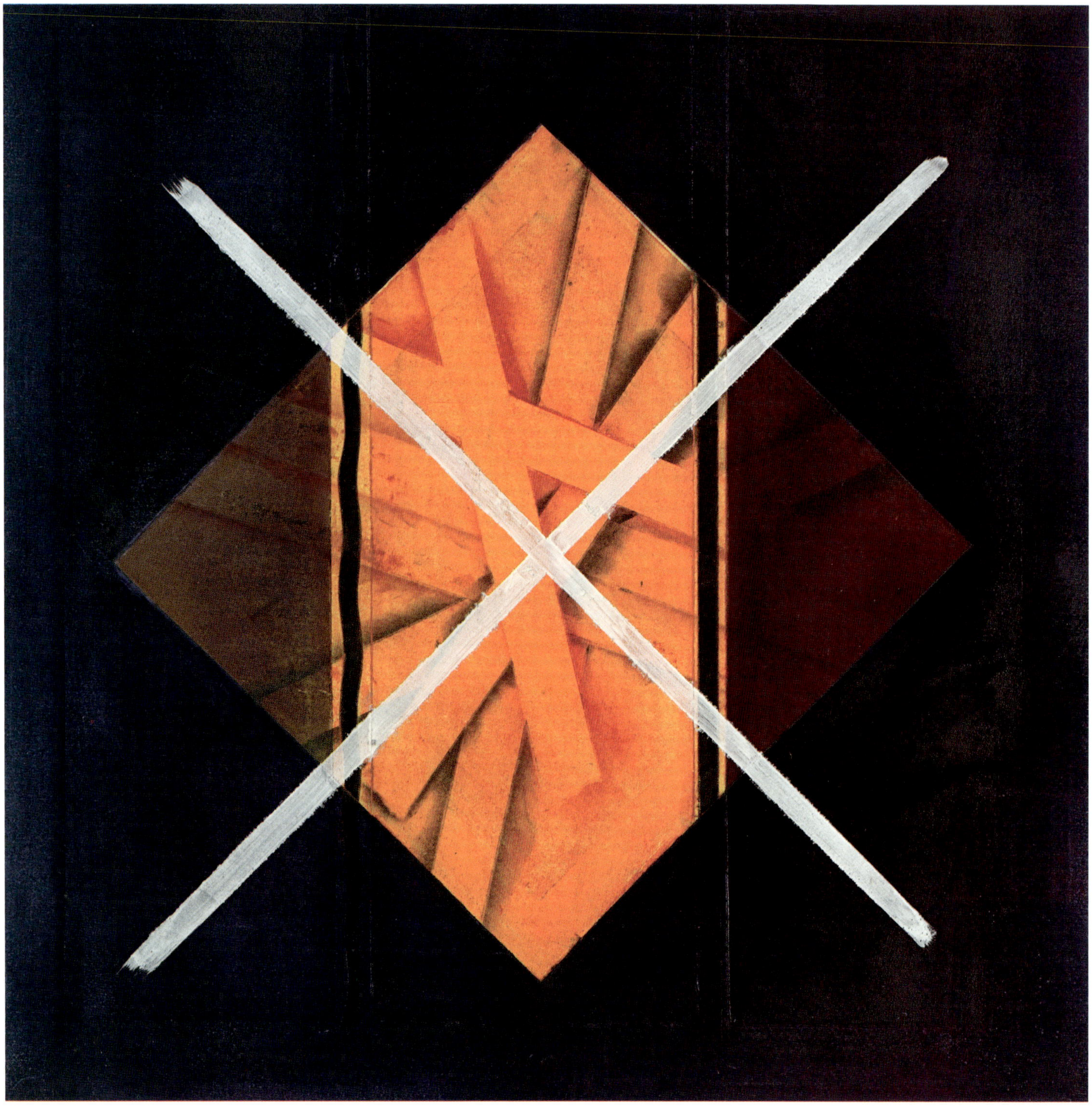

61
BANDAGES IN DIAMOND, 1977
Pastel on paper
35.9 x 35.5 cm

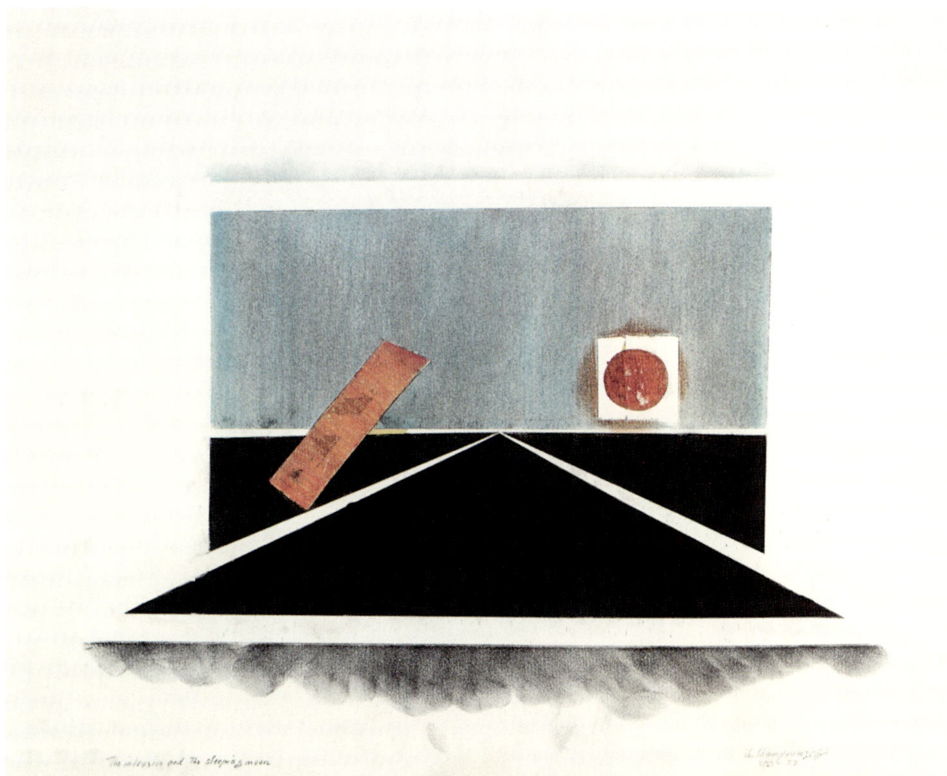

62
THE INTRUSION AND THE SLEEPING MOON, 1977
Pastel on paper
43 x 35.5 cm

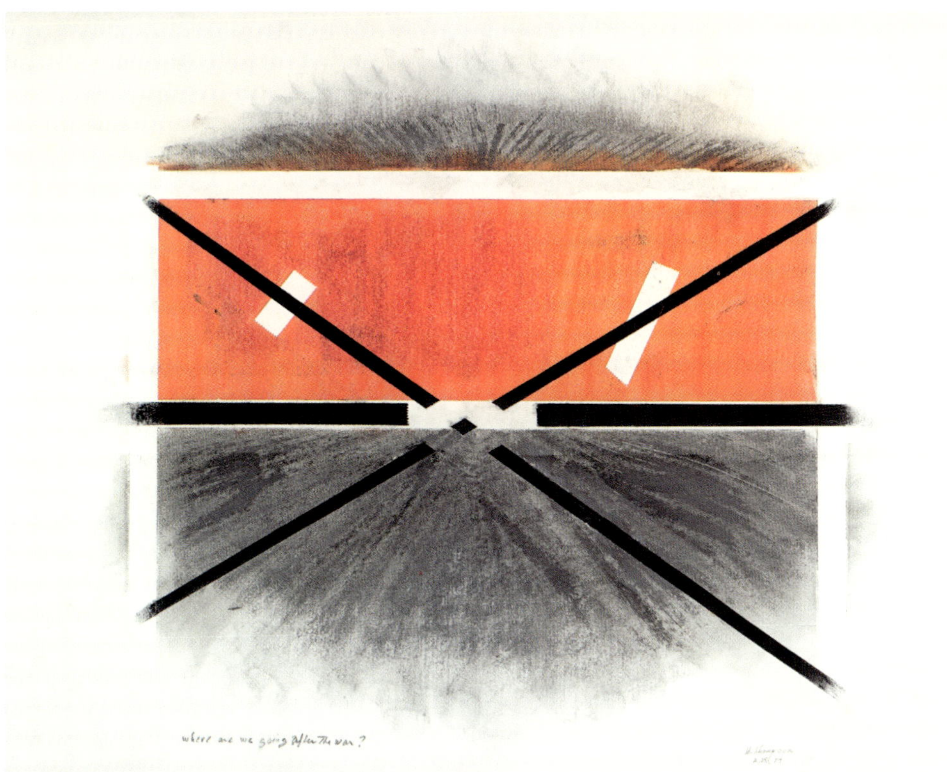

63
WHERE ARE WE GOING AFTER THE WAR, 1977
Pastel on paper
43 x 35.5 cm

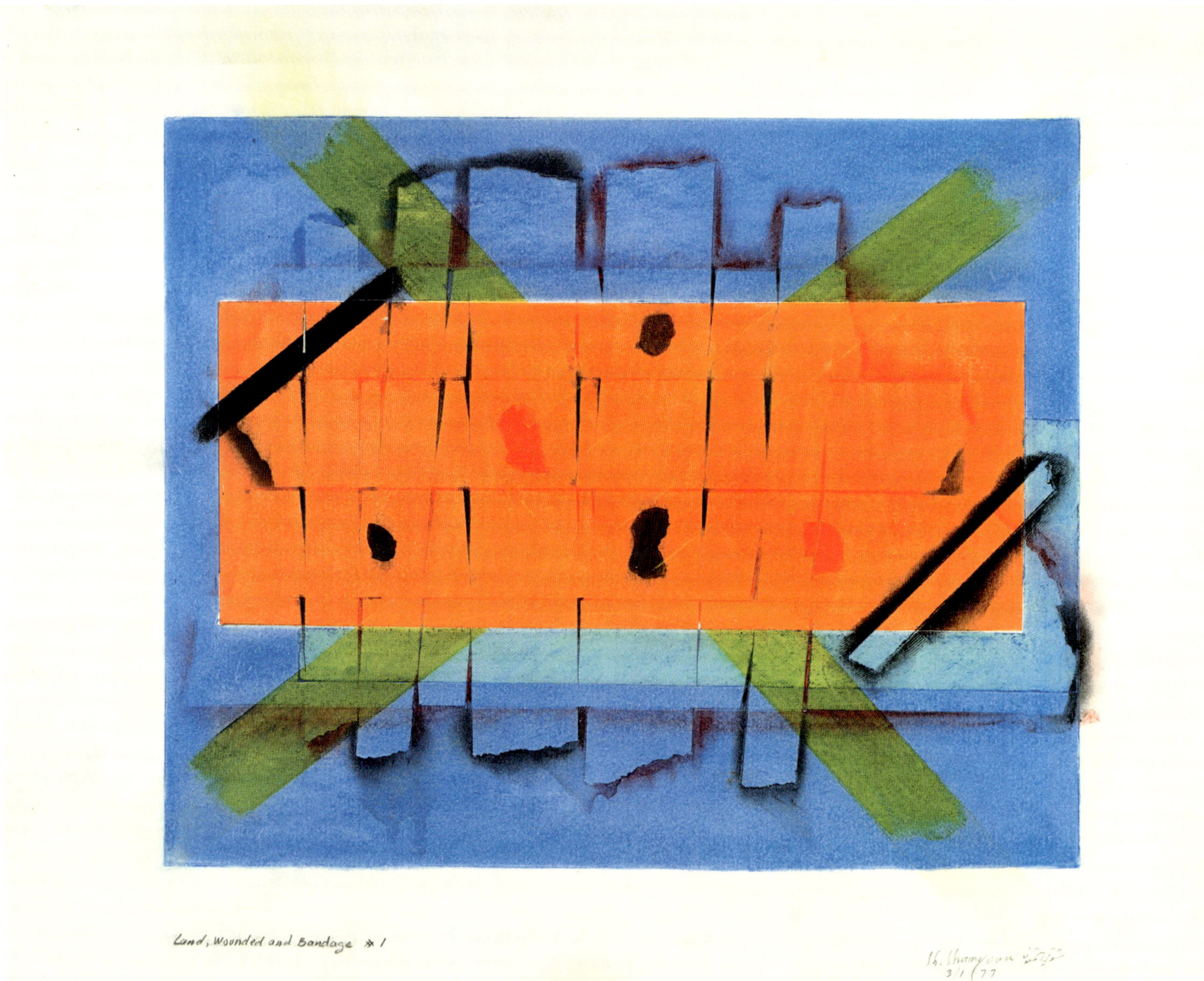

64
THE LAND, THE WOUNDED AND BANDAGES, 1977
Pastel on paper
43 x 35.5 cm

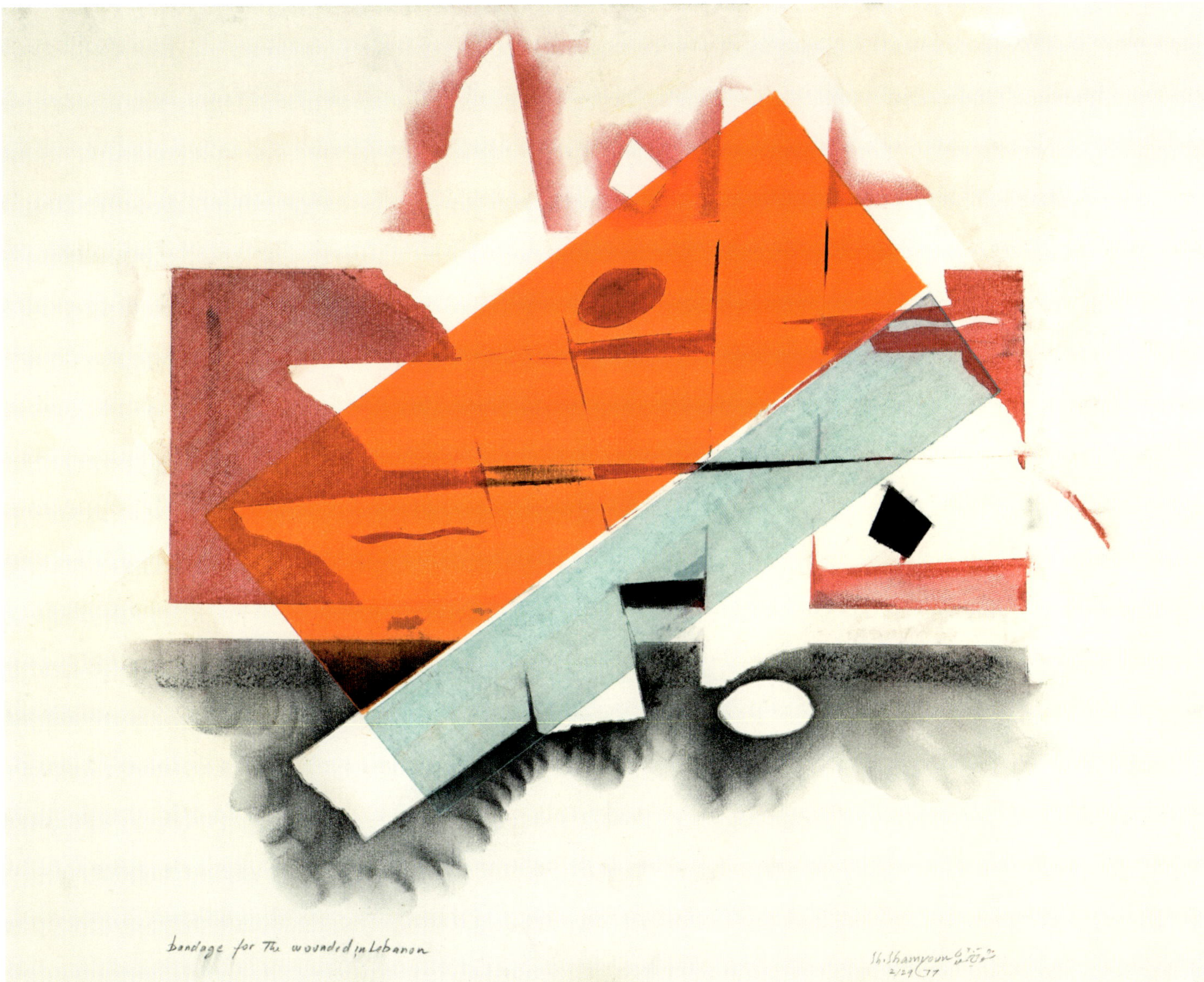

65
BANDAGES FOR THE WOUNDED, 1977
Pastel on paper
43 x 35.5 cm

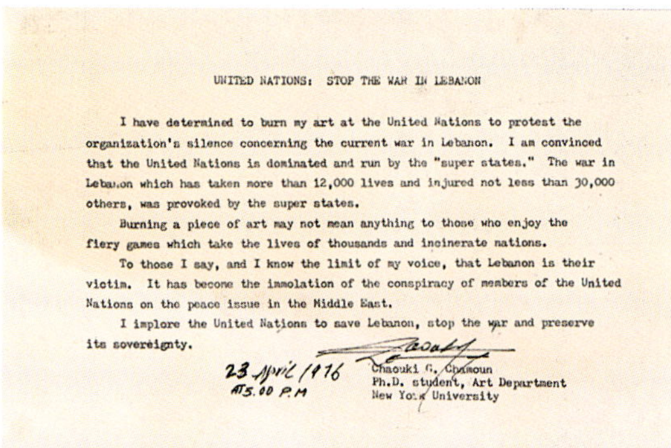

UNITED NATIONS: STOP THE WAR IN LEBANON

I have determined to burn my art at the United Nations to protest the organization's silence concerning the current war in Lebanon. I am convinced that the United Nations is dominated and run by the "super states." The war in Lebanon which has taken more than 12,000 lives and injured not less than 30,000 others, was provoked by the super states.

Burning a piece of art may not mean anything to those who enjoy the fiery games which take the lives of thousands and incinerate nations.

To those I say, and I know the limit of my voice, that Lebanon is their victim. It has become the immolation of the conspiracy of members of the United Nations on the peace issue in the Middle East.

I implore the United Nations to save Lebanon, stop the war and preserve its sovereignty.

23 April 1976
AT 5.00 P.M

Chaouki G. Chamoun
Ph.D. student, Art Department
New York University

Top
66
UN, NY, War Protest Statement, 1976

Facing Page, top
67
FENCES AND LINES XX, 1977
Pastel on paper
70.5 x 50 cm

Facing Page, middle
68
FENCES AND LINES I, 1977
Pastel on paper
55 x 37.5 cm

Facing Page, bottom
69
FENCES AND LINES XXII, 1977
Pastel on paper
70.5 x 50 cm

Parallel to my involvement with studio art, I had very enriching and enlightening courses and discussions on the aesthetics and philosophy of art with Professors David Ecker and Haward Conant, both top-notch academics in a great educational institution. Best of all, I was on the edge of SoHo, the hub of the avant-garde galleries of New York. I could not have had it better. Only the ongoing war in Lebanon was poisoning this special environment for me.

In May 1976 I called on my colleagues in the Aesthetic Inquiries class and other friends in New York to join me in a demonstration at the United Nations headquarters to protest against the war in Lebanon. On one painting I wrote 'UN STOP THE WAR IN LEBANON'. I also wanted to burn a painting as a symbol of the incineration of my beloved country, in protest at the involvement of the superpowers in the extended Lebanese civil war. Because of the city's fire regulations, the New York Police Department would not allow me to set fire to my work. Instead, I tore up drawings and prints, and distributed statements protesting the UN's silence and its failure to act to put an end to Lebanon's civil war; a war of outsiders on Lebanese soil with the Lebanese men and women as its tools. 66

My theoretical involvement as a full-time PhD student for two years – taking courses in aesthetics, philosophy of art and art education, with other courses in printmaking and documentary video, video art and studio art, in addition to collecting data and writing my dissertation – was an aim in itself. The satisfaction I got from the intellectual engagement and enchantment of the New York art scene was fulfilling my thirst for knowledge and helping me to mature artistically. Besides my contribution to some group exhibitions at the universities and other institutions, I was happily preparing myself to go back to Lebanon to fulfil the five-year teaching obligation to the Lebanese University that would pay for my higher education.

Between August 1977 and September 1978 I came back to Lebanon as a PhD candidate collecting data from the Lebanese press and interviewing artists, art critics and educators for my approved proposal on 'Tendencies of Contemporary Painting in Lebanon 1953–1975'. As I crossed from the west to the east side of Beirut, the devastation around me struck me to the heart. 'A giant foot has smashed my city,' I thought, recalling our childhood bullies smashing our sandcastles. My riverbed, my joy, the inspirational piece of Lebanon which I had tried to live with peacefully away from home despite the unbelievable news, began to take on newly
67–71 added fingerprints of war.

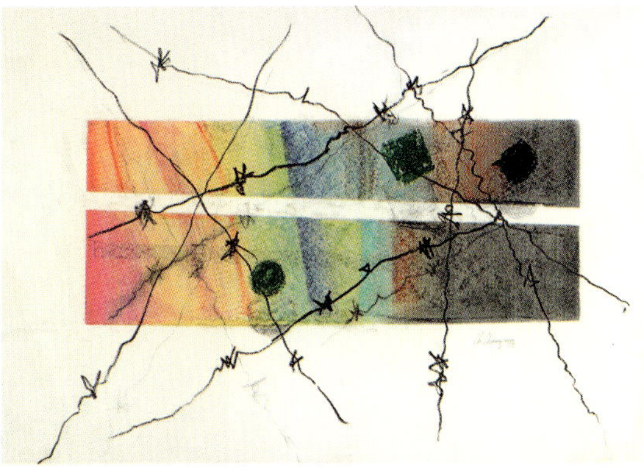

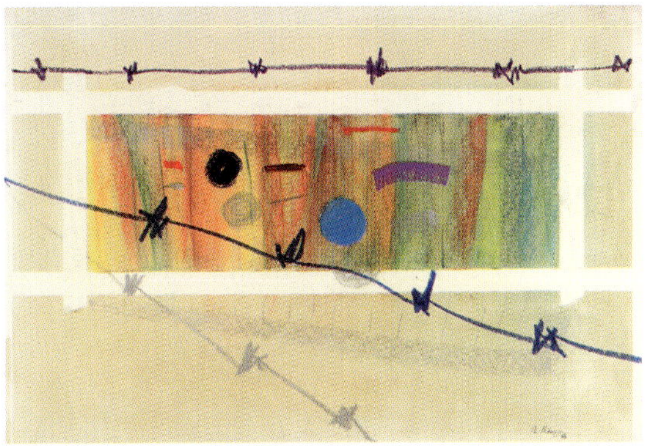

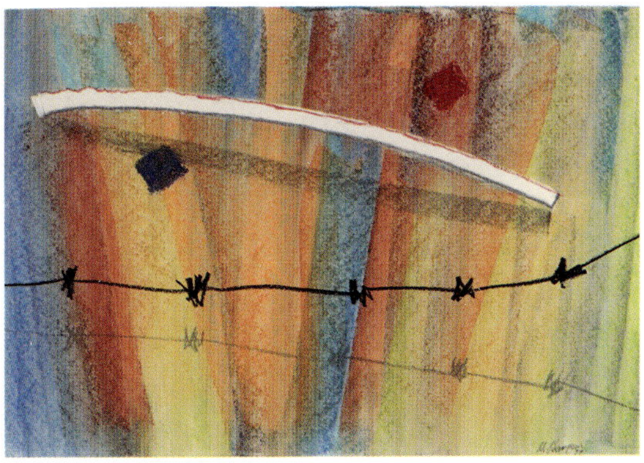

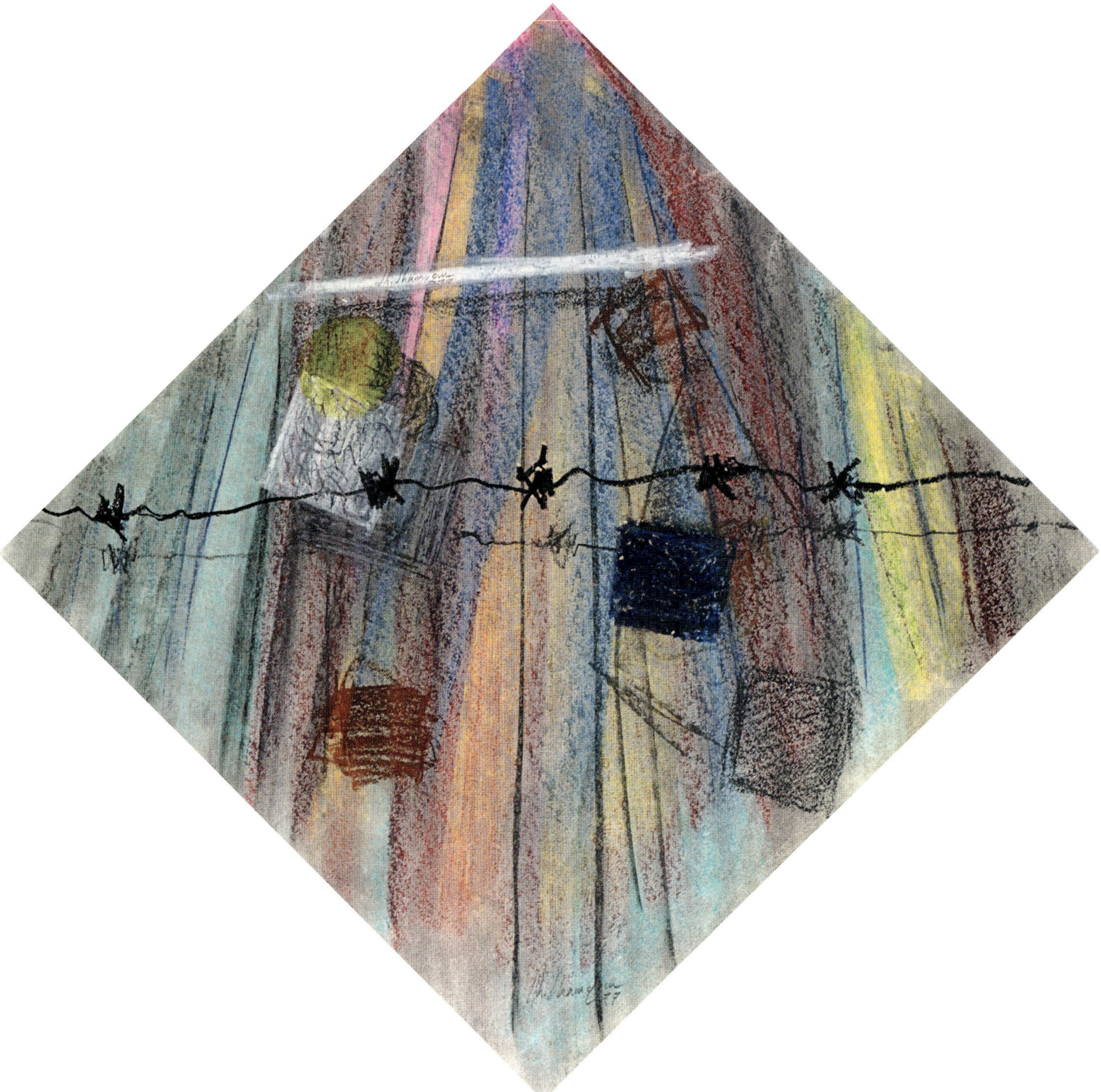

70
FENCES AND LINES XVII, 1977
Pastel on paper
46 x 46 cm

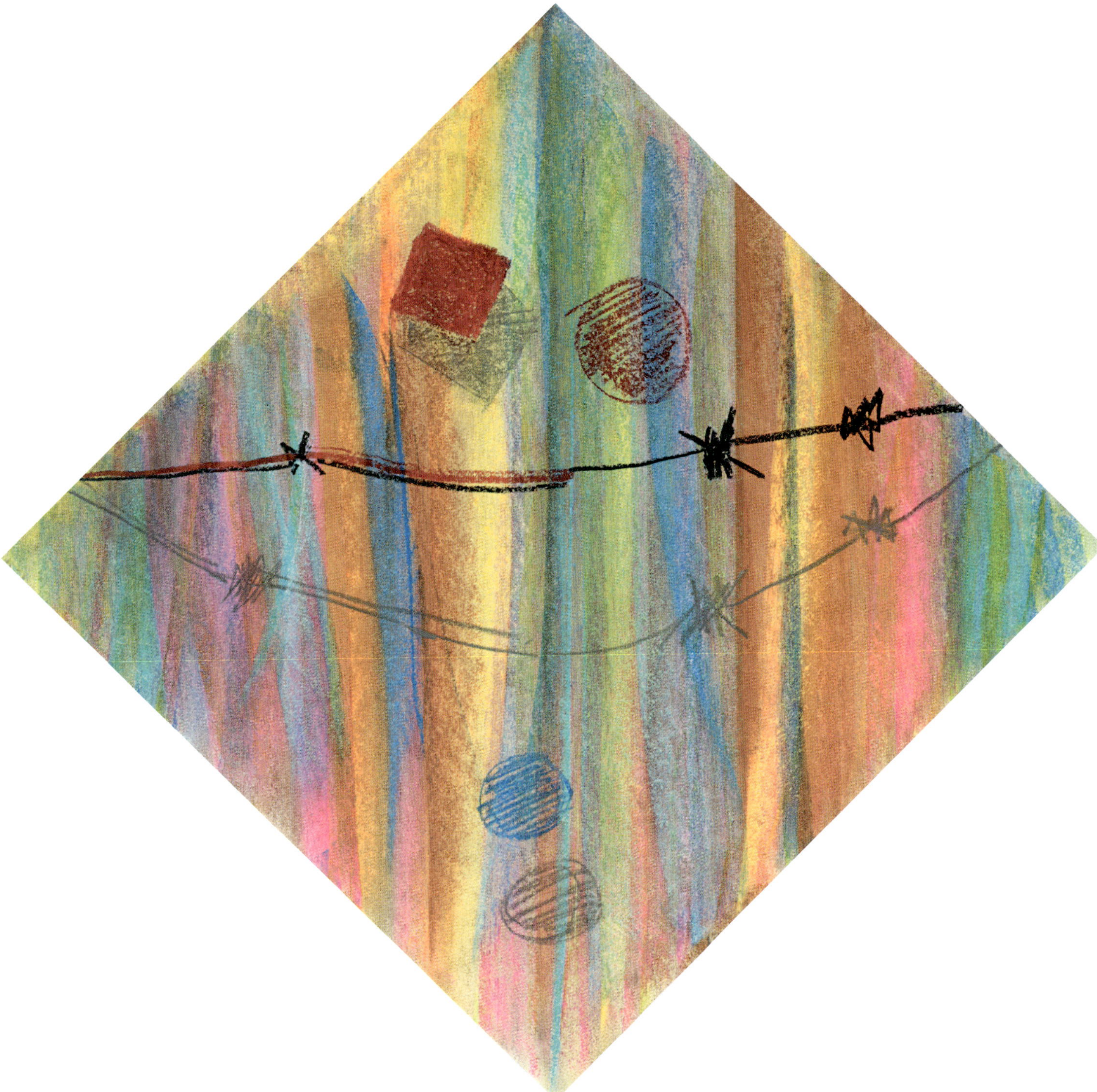

71
FENCES AND LINES XVIII, 1977
Pastel on paper
46 x 46 cm

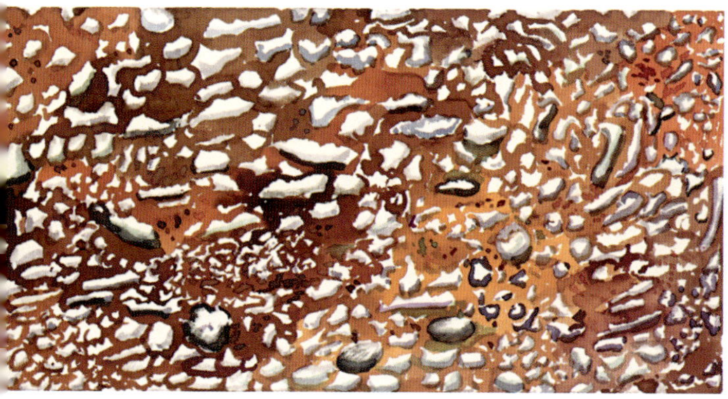

72
SEABED XXV, 1978
Watercolour on paper (detail)
34 x 27.7 cm

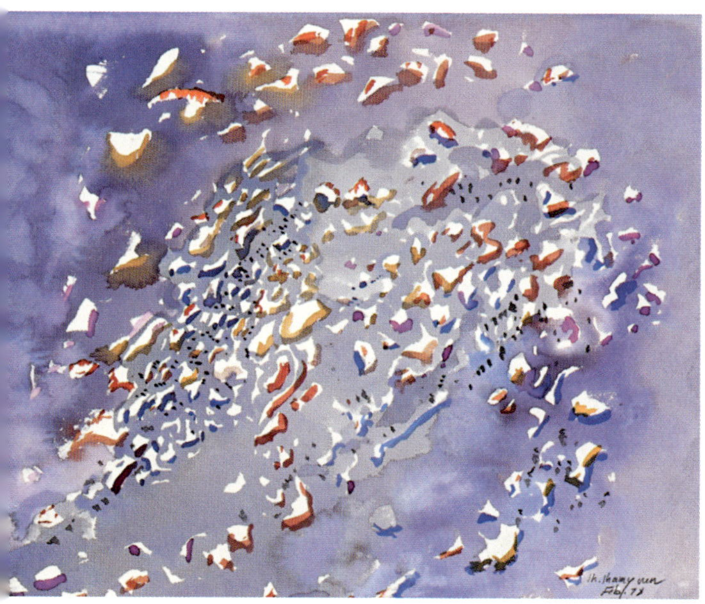

73
SEABED XXIV, 1978
Watercolour on paper (detail)
34 x 27.7 cm

Regaining my usual positive attitude, I experimented with a new series of paintings and drawings based on seaside pebbles, rendered realistically rather than developed into two-dimensional elements in search of a coherent formal structure to reveal their essence. The spirit of the Cubist experience remained a living model for formal and spiritual liberation; a demanding investigative need for new aesthetic findings. The very naturalistic relationship between gravel, stones and pebbles was of great interest to me. As with the riverbed, this very humble subject was strongly enticing, intellectually as well as visually stimulating. I did not need to look for a socially or politically appealing pretext for aesthetic research and visual pleasure in time of war. Nothing at that time looked more harmonious than pure visual experience. It was to be another challenge. 72–78

My stay in Lebanon was very productive. In addition to undertaking laborious research of the press, I conducted interviews with people of the arts. I taught a drawing course at USEK, and contributed to an art exhibition in Zouk, where I also gave a lecture. The poet Henry Zougheib was the curator and organiser of the exhibition and lectures series, in which both established artists and most of the important poets, politicians and thinkers of Lebanon took part. In September 1978, with my research materials packed into two suitcases, I headed back to the States to sort the new data and finish writing my dissertation.

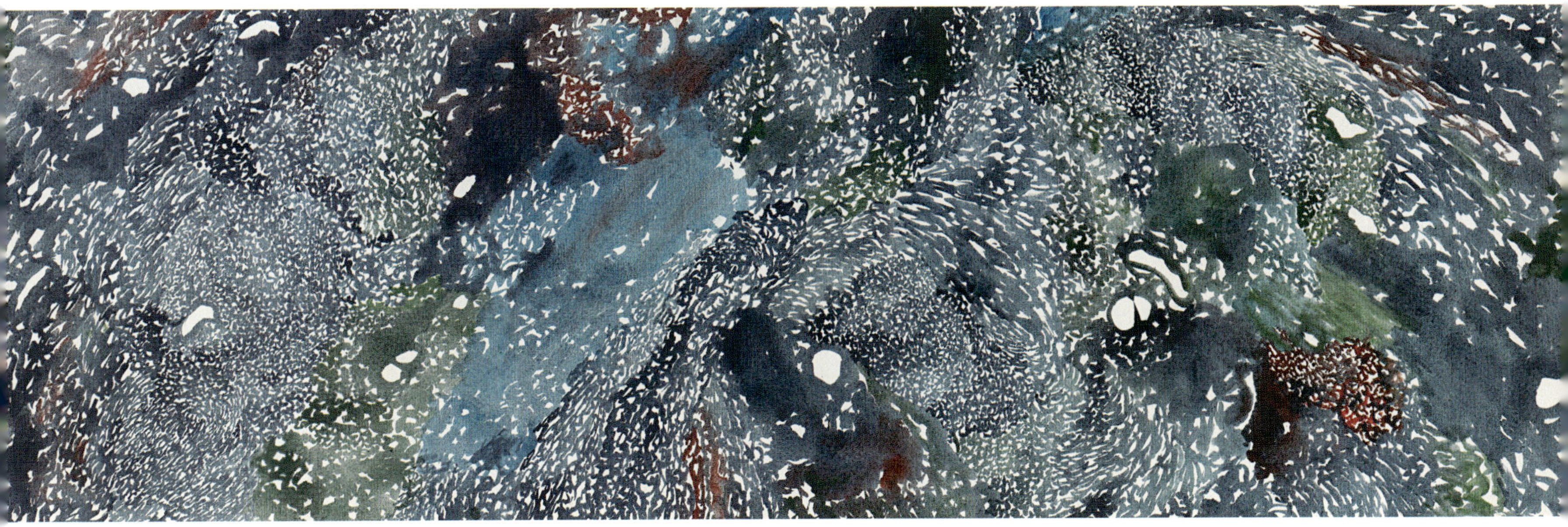

74
SEABED V, 1977
Acrylic on canvas
177 x 60 cm

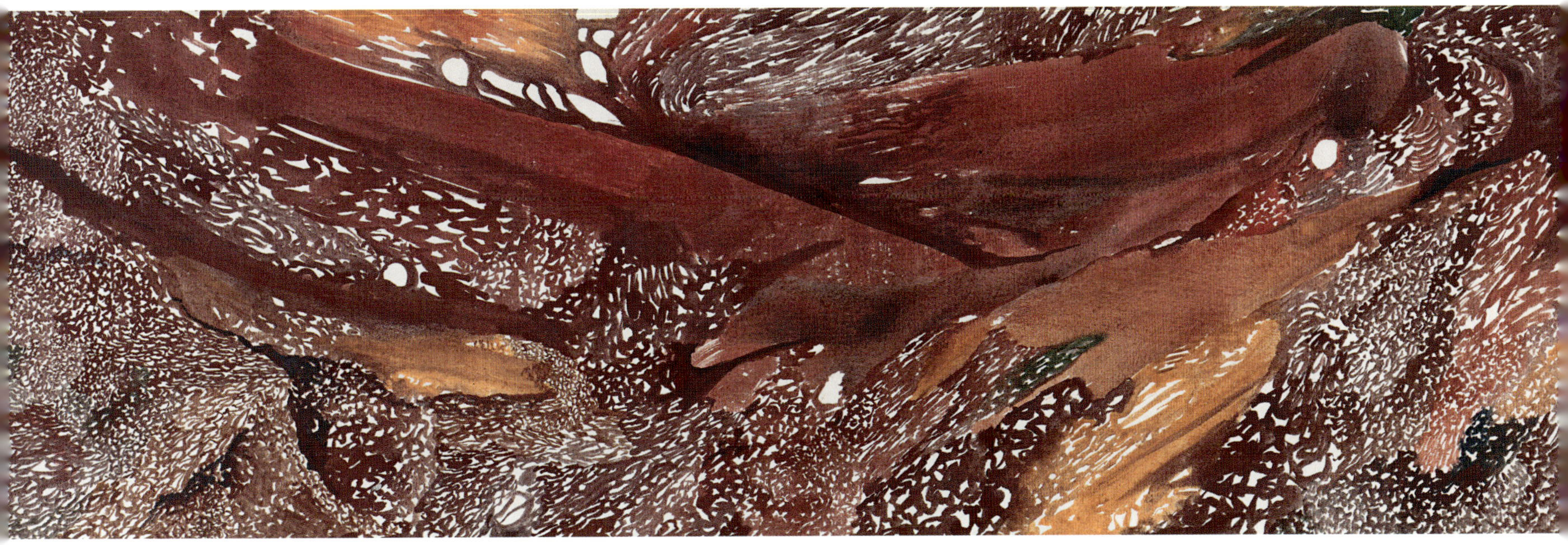

75
SEABED IV 1977
Acrylic on canvas
177 x 60 cm

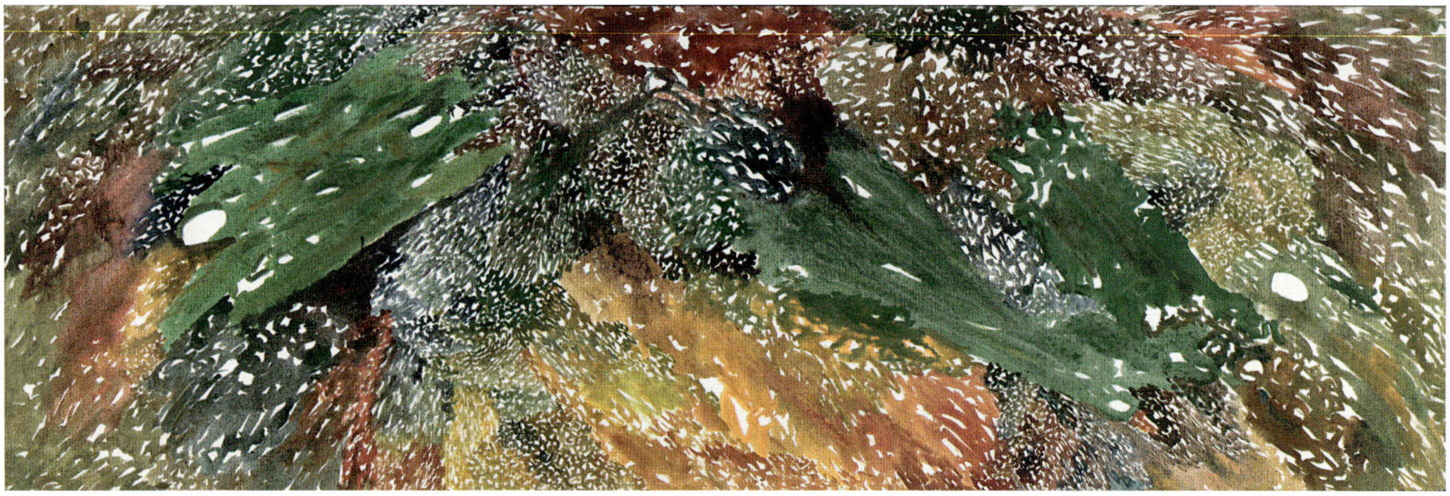

76
SEABED III, 1977
Acrylic on canvas
177 x 60 cm

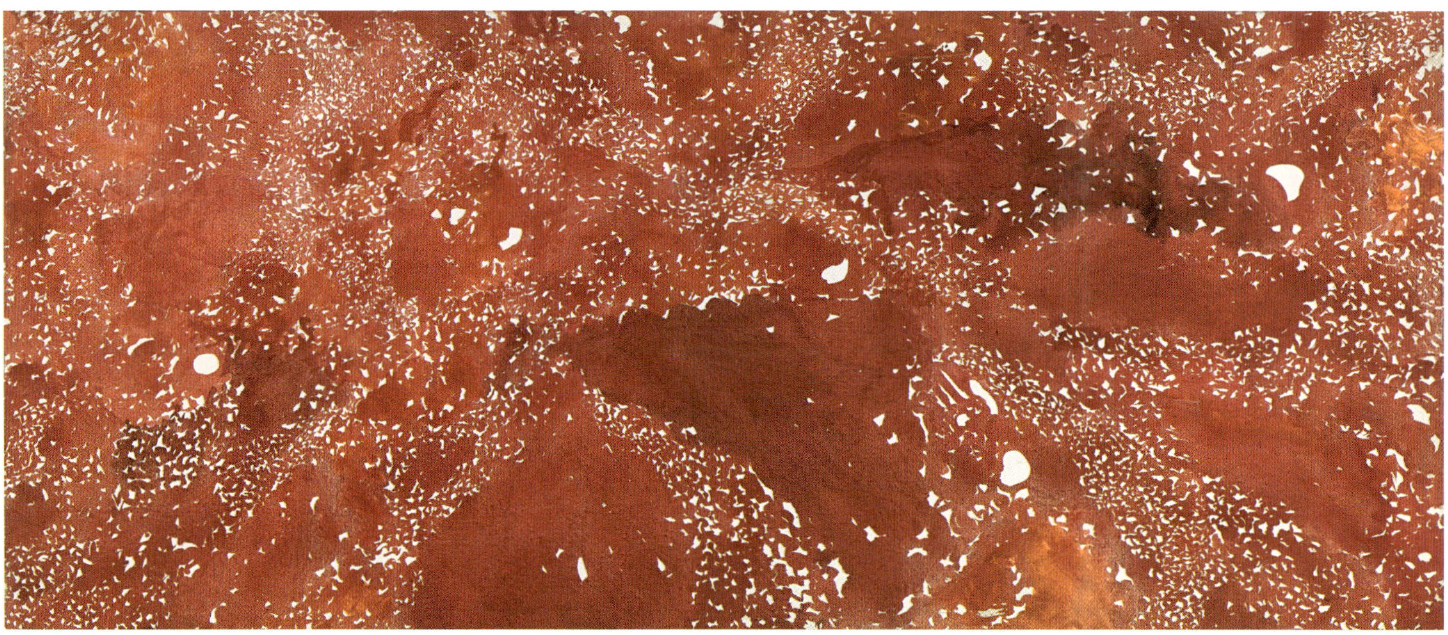

77
SEABED 2 #X-I, 1978
Acrylic on canvas
196 x 85 cm

Facing page
78
SEABED #7, 1978
Acrylic on canvas
196 x 84.5 cm

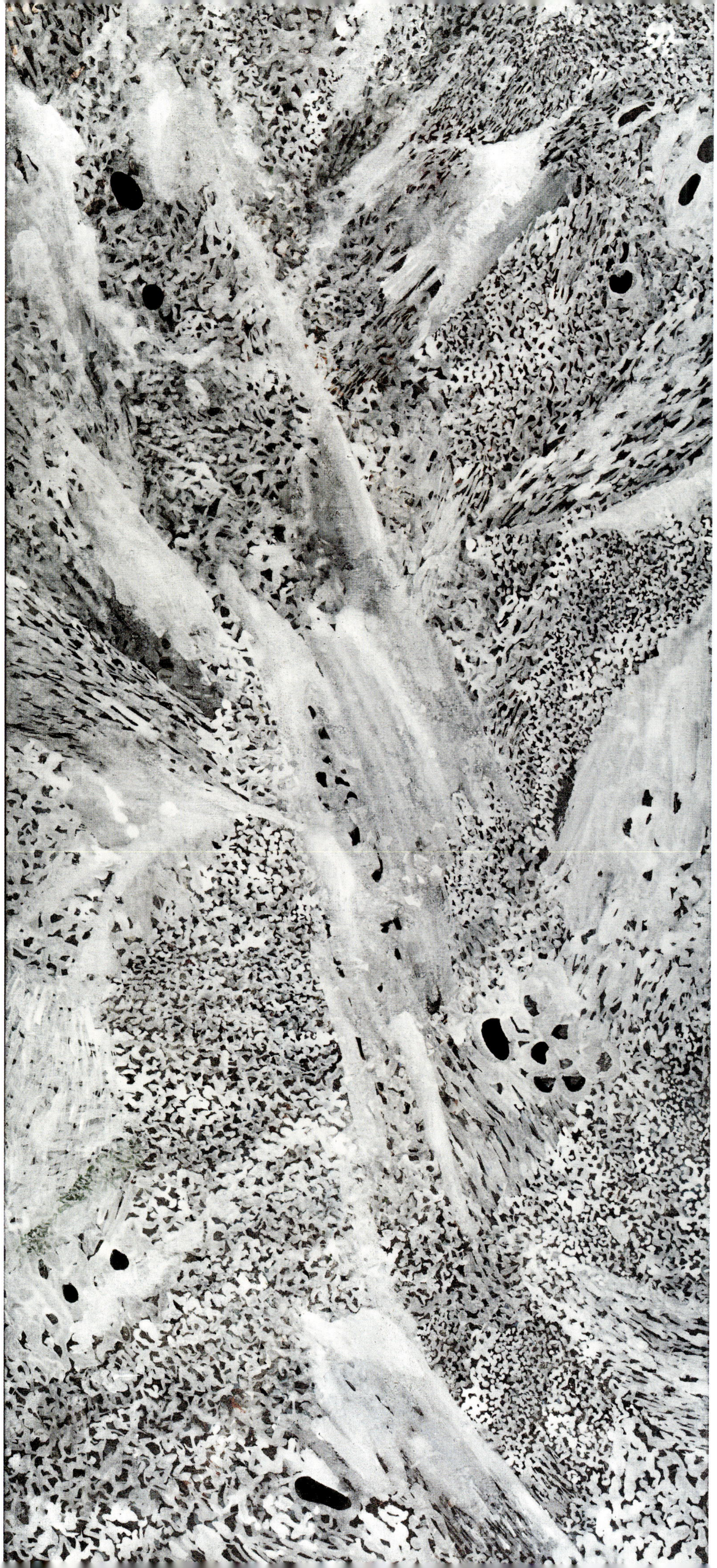

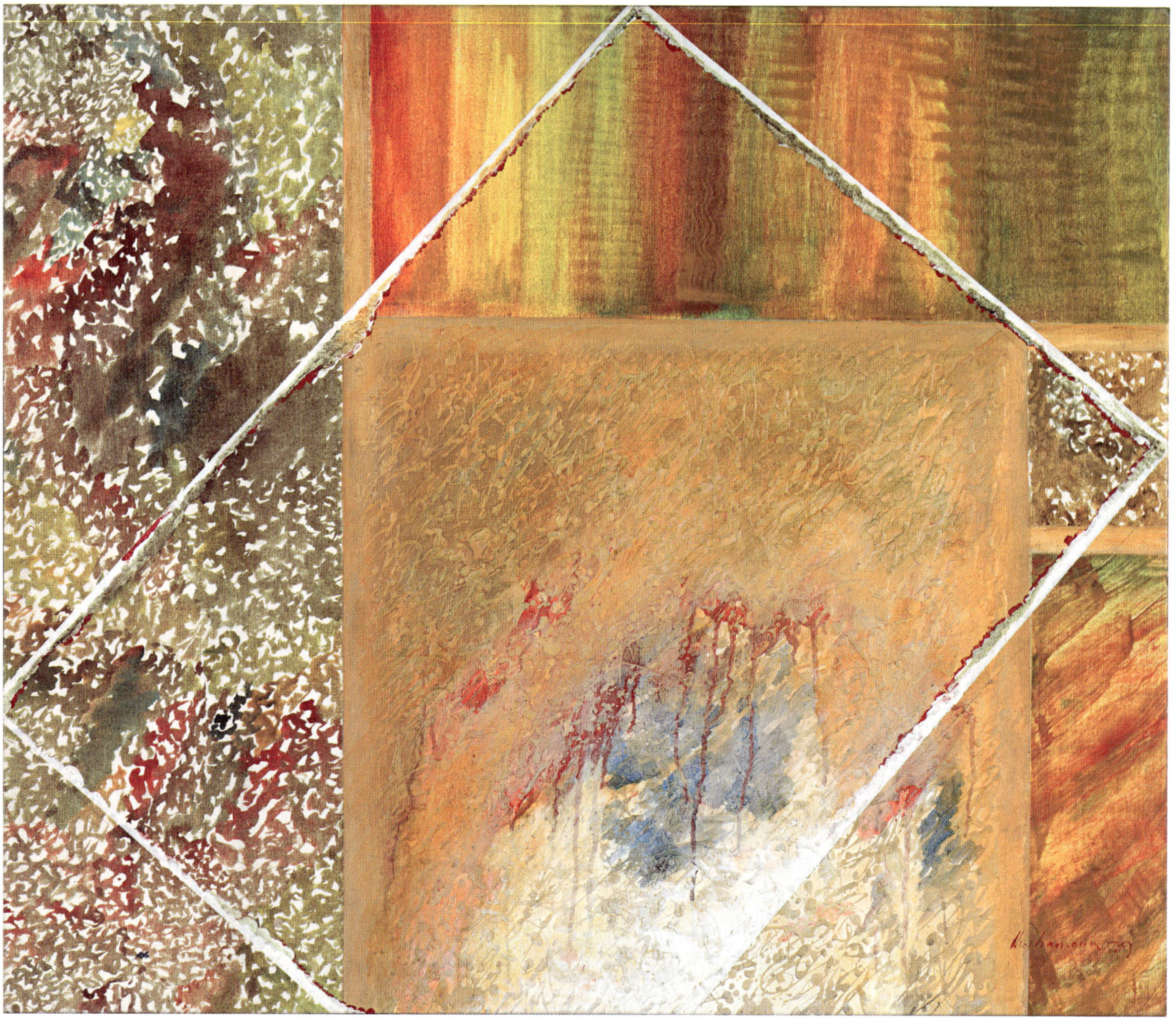

79
ART AND THE CRIMINAL ACT, 1979
Acrylic on canvas
107.8 x 93.8 cm

Years of Agony

Shortly after I left Lebanon for New York, I was informed of the abduction and disappearance of my brother Kozhaya. A highly respected and revered officer in the Lebanese army, he was ambushed and abducted by the Christian militia in Achrafieh, Beirut while on a mission with the Minister of Foreign Affairs on 2 November 1978. The cowardly political and military leadership failed to act in time, instead continuing to fabricate lies and false hopes. The warlords of the criminal militia denied any involvement. All of them refrained from telling me and my family where Kozhaya was, or what had really happened to him. For months and years we searched for him in vain. The truth was suspended forever.

With rumours abounding that my brother had been killed and dumped into the sea, I returned to New York broken-hearted. I was losing faith in my humanist and nationalist beliefs, questioning the value of all that I was and had worked for. My dissertation came to a halt. I became helpless and very depressed, squeezing paint joylessly onto
79, 80 canvas. 'I will not let anyone live off my pain,' I told myself after a series of painful and aimless attempts to overcome my sadness and hopelessness, sorrow and tears.

One day, I received an invitation from my friend Steve

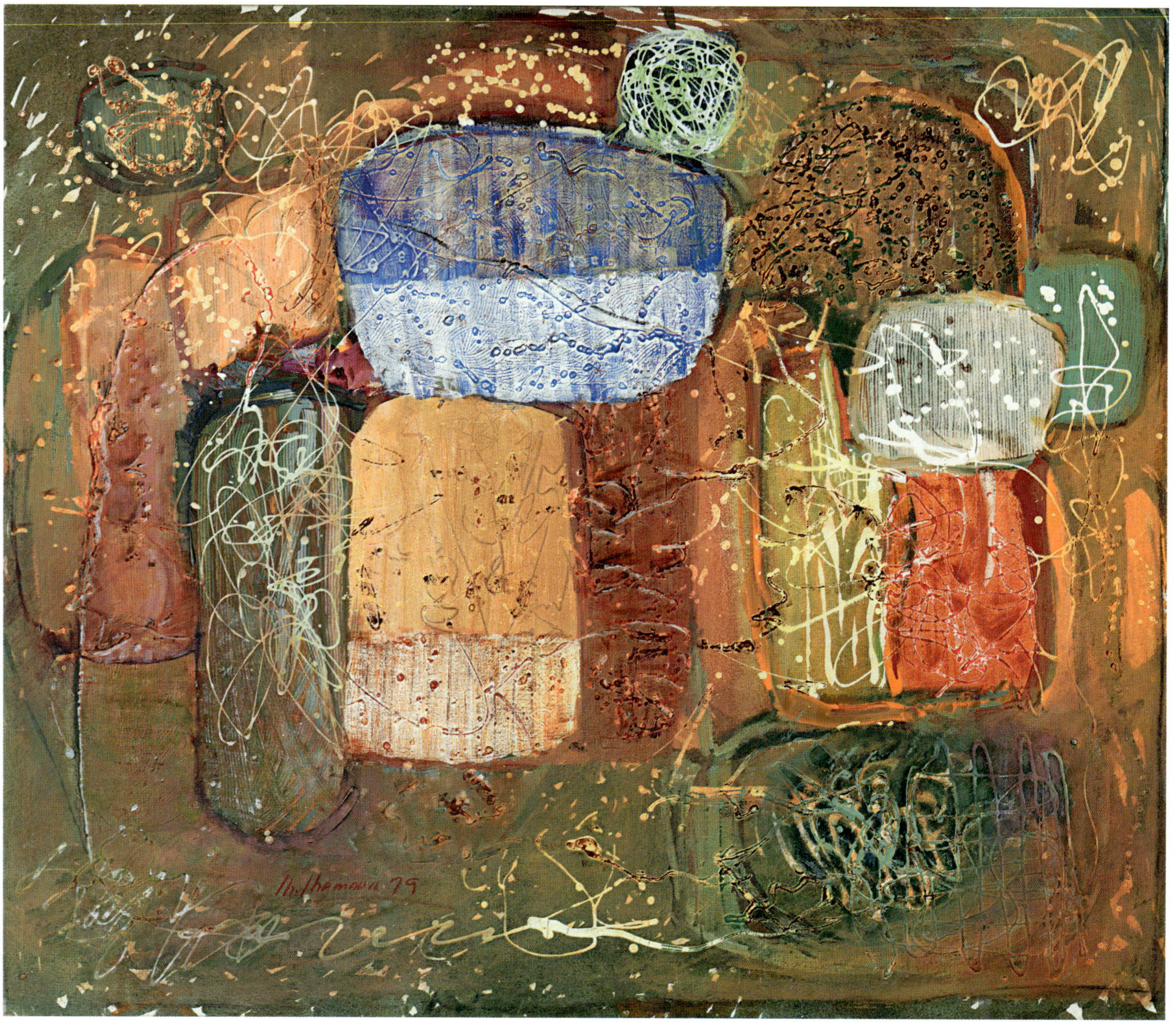

80
WORDS, 1979
Acrylic on canvas
107.8 x 93.8 cm

Duffy, who was an artist and a designer. He was unhappy to see me so depressed, wasting my time driving taxi cabs for a living, wandering aimlessly in the streets of New York while awaiting the cancellation of my scholarship, which had been frozen because of the war. I joined him at Harvey Weston and Associates, an architectural design firm that specialised in department stores. Benefiting from what I had learnt in my architectural drawing courses back at the El Technic night school in Beirut, I started to produce drawings for Steve and Roger Legat, another brilliant designer.

My talent for design was quickly recognised. After working on the design of Alexander's Department Store at the World Trade Center in New York, I was given a full second floor of a Scarborough's Department Store in Austin, Texas, to design. My design was fully accepted by the client, and so another creative venture began. Again on the recommendation of Steve Duffy, who had left to work for Allied Stores Corporation, I was hired as a fully fledged designer to design a Jordan March Department Store in Miami, Florida, and another in Wellington, New Hampshire. My involvement in design and the many working hours required in the creative process helped relieve my depression and brought me solace.

This new peace of mind did not last long. In May 1982 I came to the end of a very troubled on and off marriage (1977–1982). Answering the Lebanese University's call to fulfil

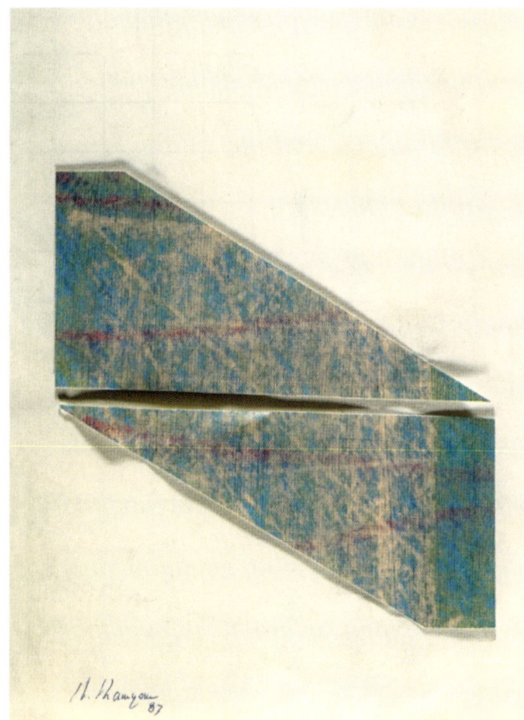

81
COMPOSITION EXP-V, 1983
Pastel and collage on paper
35 x 25 cm

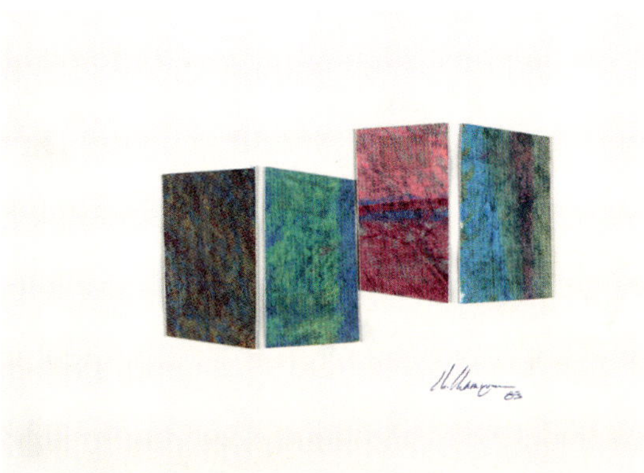

82
COMPOSITION EXP-II, 1983
Pastel and collage on paper
35 x 25 cm

my contract, I brought my one-year-old son George with me to Lebanon, to start a new teaching career and escape another chain of agonies.

Between 1979 and 1982, although I became very successful as a designer, adding many high-end design projects to my CV, my painting had no direction. My emotional incapacity left my art on hold. My art was always associated with my love of my country, a love that had been wounded to the heart, killed in revenge for my brother. But I had only myself to harm. The only thing that could have hurt me more than the savage death of my brother was the deferral of my art. The family that gave a brave and honourable martyr could not produce criminals. I had lost the aim of becoming what I had worked for so hard all my life.

These were disorienting, painfully and silently dormant years. Upon my return to Lebanon in May 1982, many old and new friends came to my support. The sculptor Naim Doumit and the designer Jean Ghorayeb were in the forefront. In addition to my teaching load at the Fine Arts Institute, I was offered teaching hours at Université Saint-Esprit De Kaslik (USEK). I felt that I was again on my feet; a part of the Lebanese artscape anew. I used this time to try to regain full control of my life as an artist. I managed to rent a studio in 1983 at the Saint Georges Center in Adonis, sharing a building with professionals of many fields. With my hands still fettered by my agonising memories and unidentified directions,

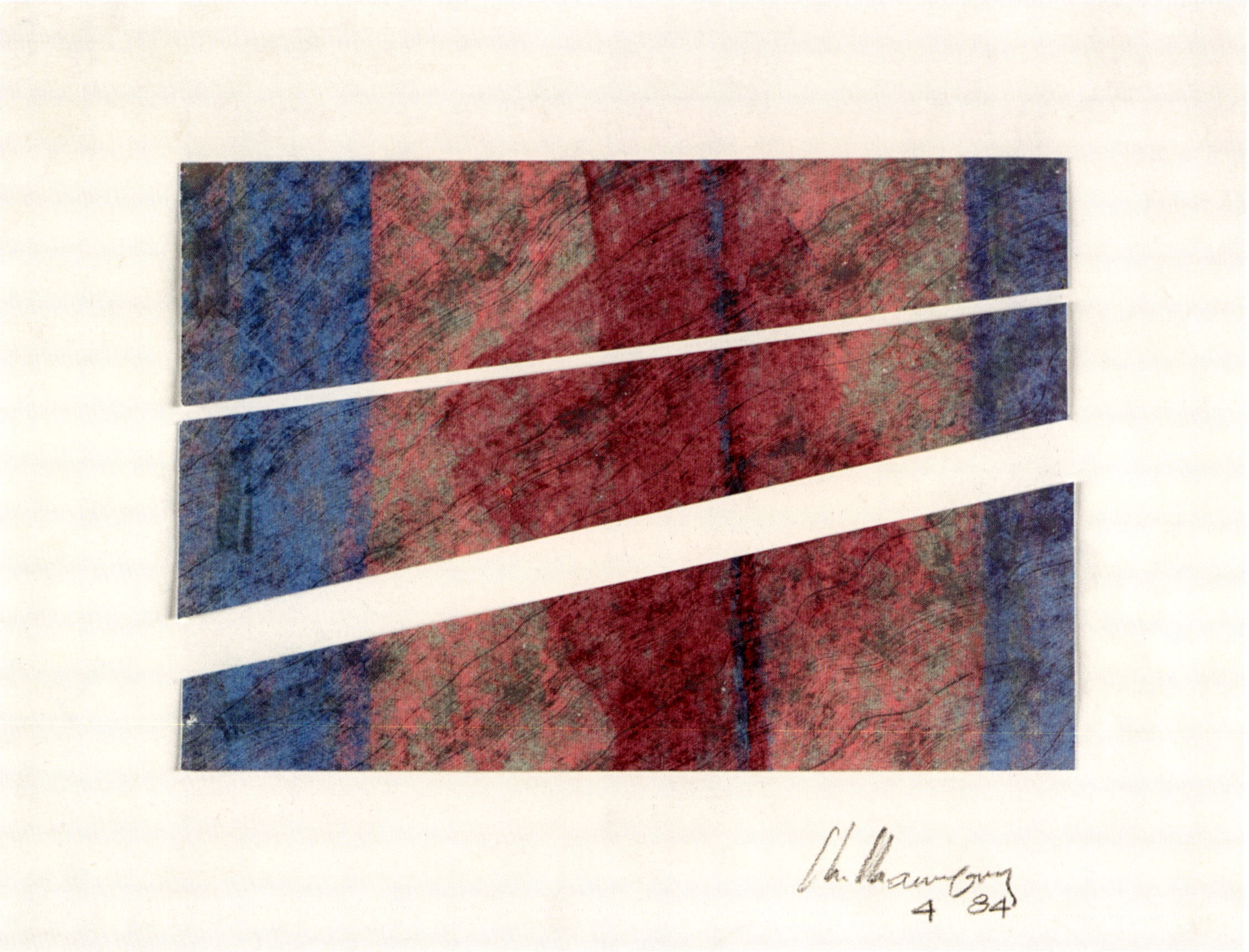

81–83 I tried to move on with some ideas stemming from early experiments. 'Bandage for the War' was a possible start, with which I aimed to creating a composite artwork of multiple frame canvases. I started to make studies in that direction but a sense of dryness held me back.

83
COMPOSITION EXP-III, 1983
Pastel and collage on paper
35 x 25 cm

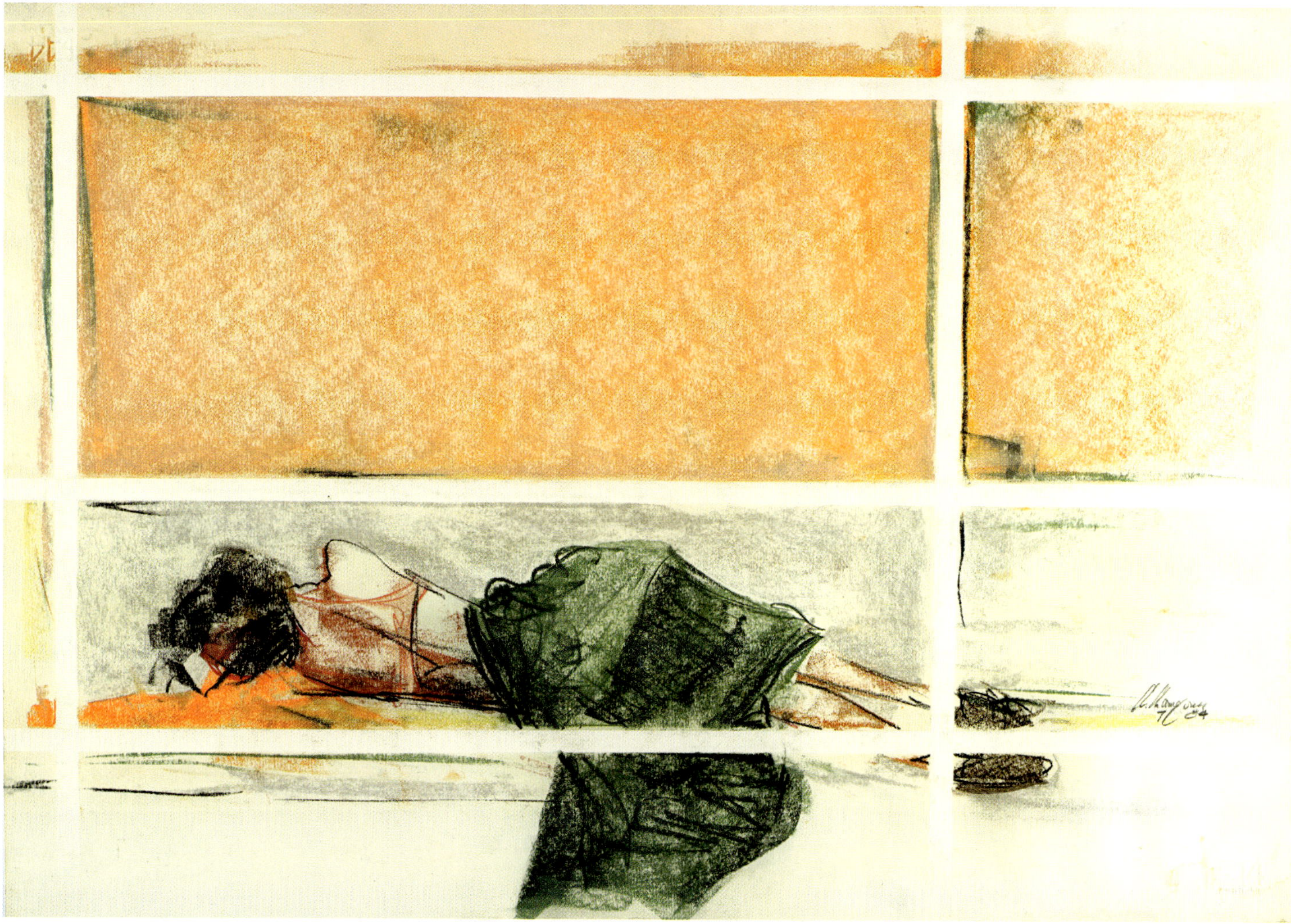

84
LEILA 84-7, 1984
Pastel on paper
70 x 50 cm

A New Beginning: A New Direction

Professor Elia Hawi was a distinguished writer and professor of aesthetics at the Fine Arts Institute. He and I used to exchange our ideas and opinions, as well as books on art and the philosophy of art. Professor Hawi was one of the few people with whom I was able to enjoy discussing these subjects. At that time, he was writing his important book *Al-Fan as-Safi* (Pure Art). One day, while I was visiting him, he asked me if I would care to see his daughter Leila's paintings. I had never met her, nor did I even remember seeing her; probably because she had spent five years as a graduate student at Lyons University. She was now a professor of linguistics at the Lebanese University. The impression I got as she walked in with her paintings has never left me. It was love at first sight!

Shortly thereafter Leila and I started going out together, driving in the mountains, drawing scenery ... Sometimes, when she asked me to, I drew her, too.

Our feelings for each other soon became serious and it did not take me long to decide I wanted to marry her. She accepted my engagement ring, and we got married a year later on 3 February 1985. We have been blessed with three loving and successful children: George, Owana and Oriane.

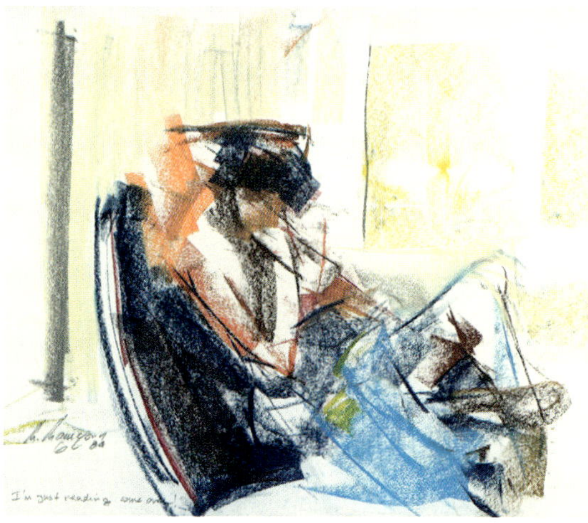

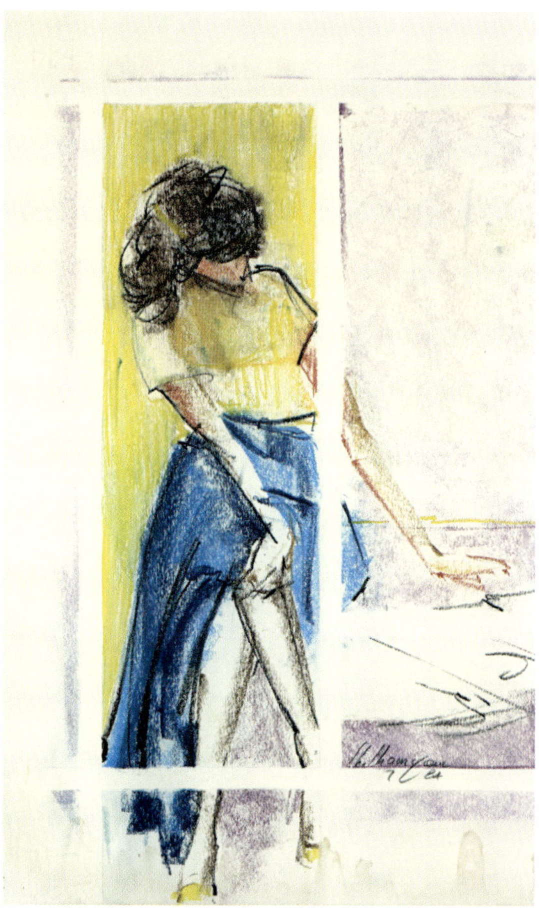

When I started drawing Leila and went back to drawing things in nature, I began to feel I was heading in a different direction. Leila would be reading, writing, crocheting, lying down, and I would be drawing her. I started using masking tape to separate one image from the other, adapting to her movements continuously, and this revealed another way to consider new approaches towards the composition and restructuring of my drawings, in line with the series I had done in New York in 1977, 'Bandages for the Wounded Land'.

A multitude of sketches and cut-out images made up the new colour drawings. My early college experiments came back handily, giving me a student's licence to do whatever I felt was right, as long as I was doing it with value. The most important thing in making art is to be free, for freedom alone can bring about new values. All my appreciation and knowledge of art is always there; I carry it with me. It is there to help me find my way. My experience in art is one that takes me deep into things; it is an experience of depth rather than of looking at someone who is higher or lower than me, or who has gone far beyond what I have achieved. I am always probing for new depth, a new aesthetic vocabulary, recreating not just another painting or another work, but another idea, a thought, a contribution to our knowledge and understanding of art.

It was after meeting Leila that I realised that all the past agonising years had not been lost completely; they had been

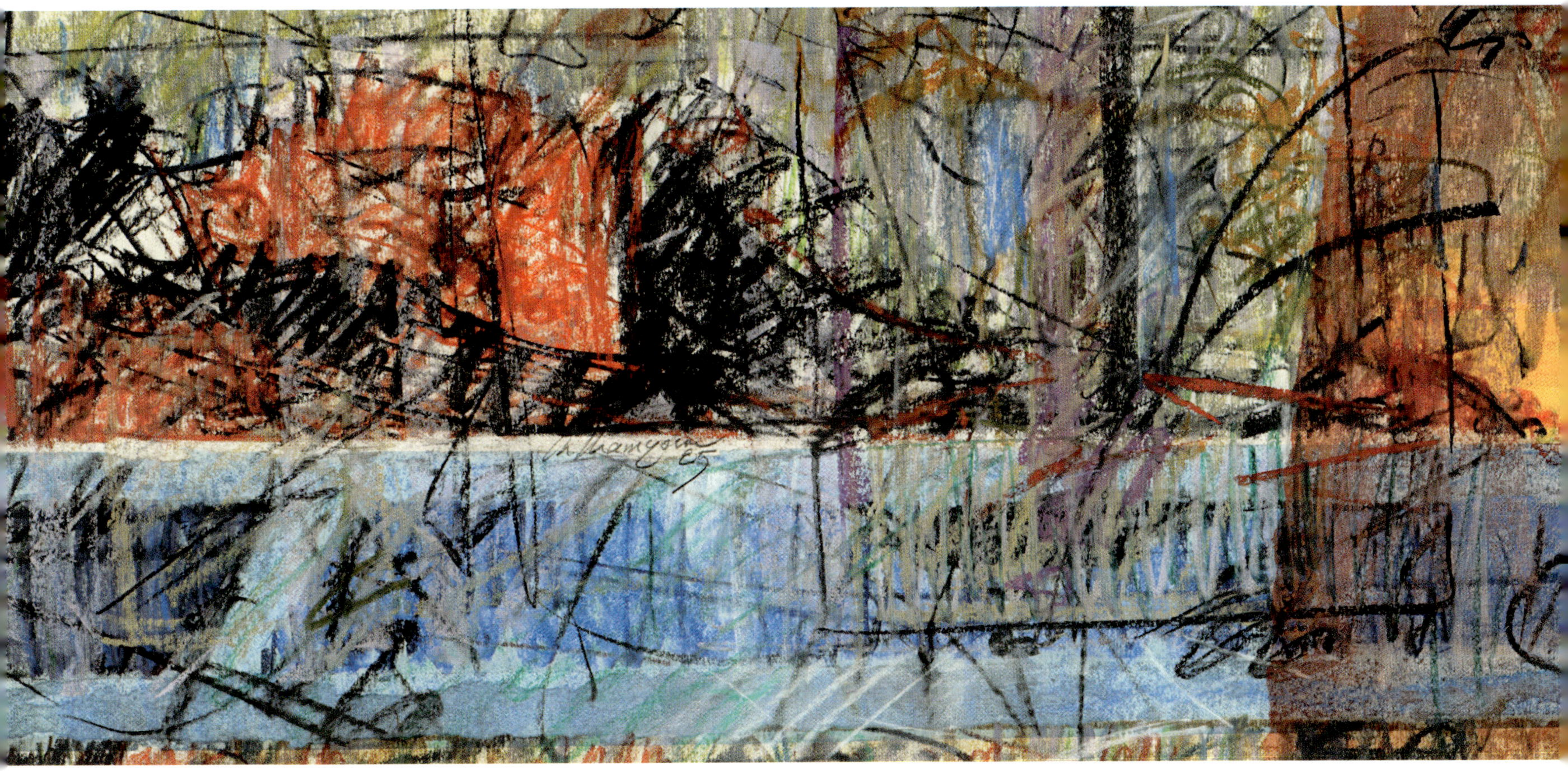

years of accumulating emotions as well as added knowledge. Even when I had more or less stopped painting, I never stopped visiting museums and art galleries, my best refuge and only therapy. All this now came to light while I was working, and every work became an important issue in itself. I wanted to put everything in my artworks, and then alter, remove or cover one thing after the other, following the freedom of the lines, using tapes, choosing the paper and making use of every single accidental thing on it. Doing and redoing things all over again, the one thing I did not lose sight of was that I must not betray my experience of 'Riverbed'. This is evident in the long rectangular shapes of the drawings I did. Sometimes I would scribble in that space or have a figure in it, and 'the Riverbed' became the bed of my new art.

85
STUDY D4, 1985
Pastel on paper
35.5 x 24.5 cm

Facing page, top
86
STUDY LIX, 1984
Pastel on paper
48 x 34 cm

Facing page, bottom
87
LEILA 84-4A, 1984
Pastel on paper (detail)
47.5 x 34 cm

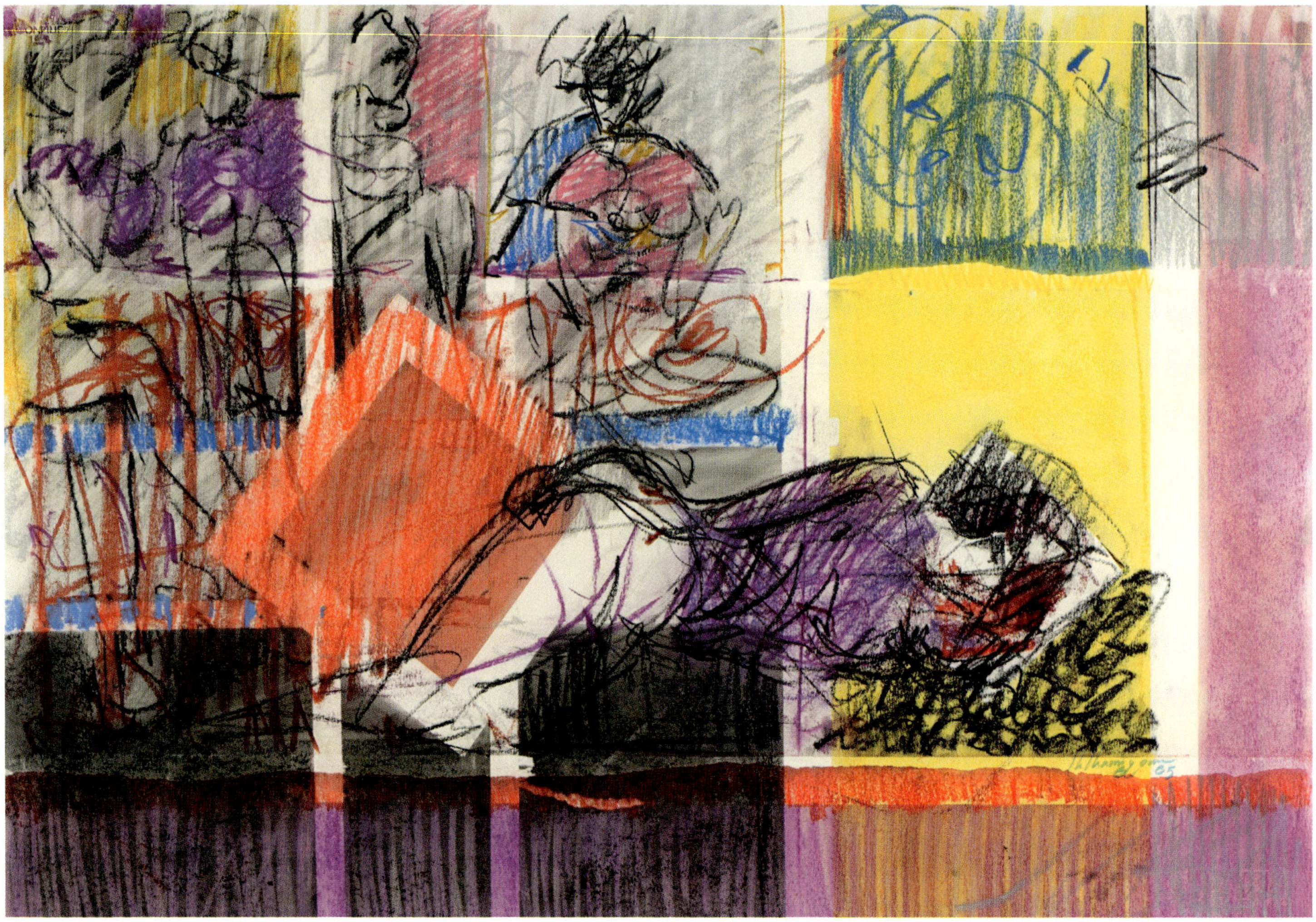

88
LEILA 85-1B, 1985
Pastel on paper
70 x 50 cm

For over a year I enjoyed drawing with pastels and mixed media, charcoal, pencils and any other soft materials I could use: I had used them before, but now they were my preferred materials. I still remember the excitement I felt every time I came to start a new drawing, feeling that a new alphabet was developing under my hands; that I was now able to say things I never thought I would be encouraged to say. Then there was that exhilarating feeling of freedom, of being able to do whatever you feel like doing, to put in whatever you feel like, not being blocked by schools or trends or anything else.

I had been fully devoted to experimentation, study and research, trying to develop an artwork worth offering to the

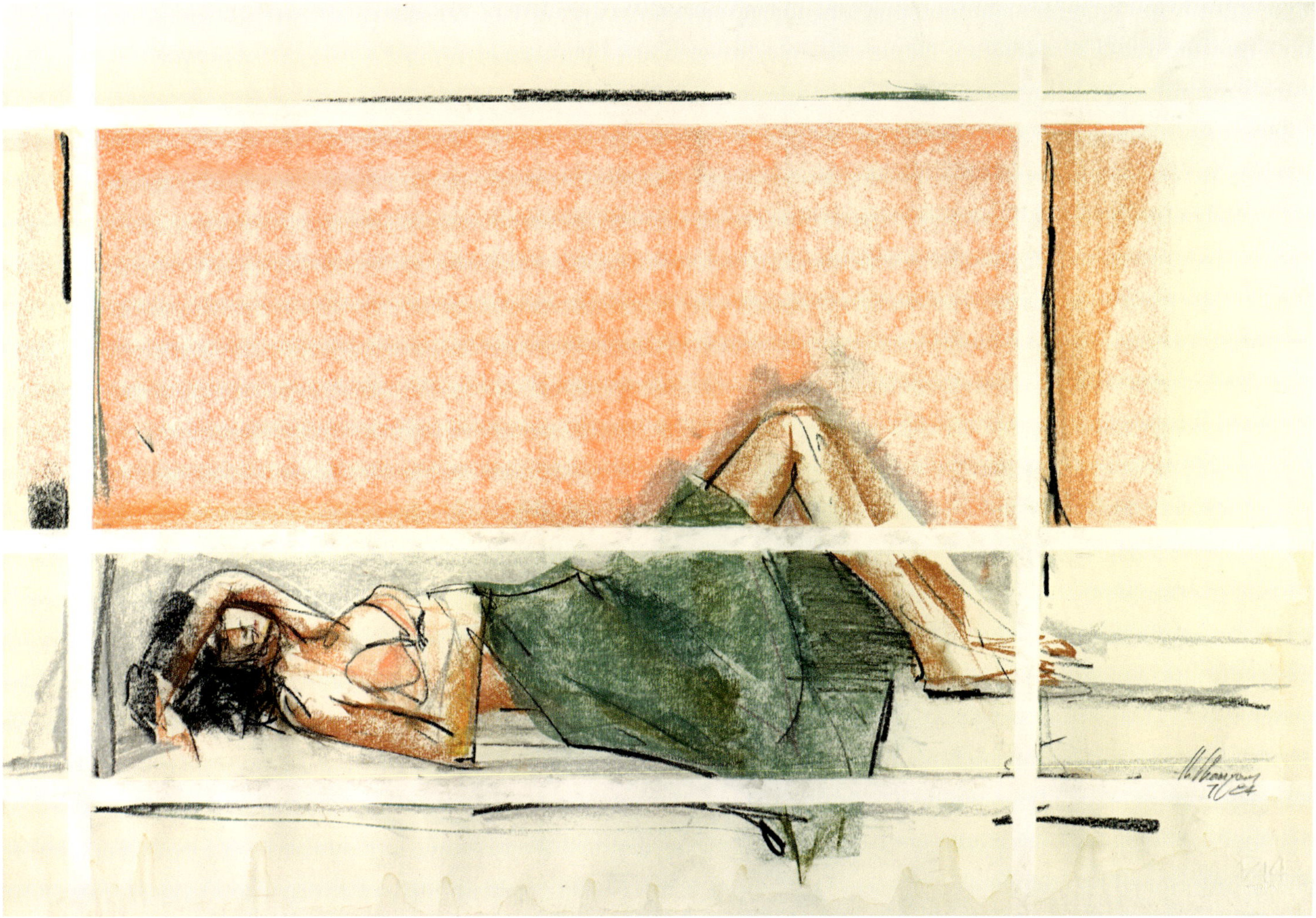

89
LEILA 84-8, 1984
Pastel on paper
70 x 50 cm

viewer; a small step in my long journey of self-realisation. Many prior attempts and experiments were stocked or shelved away. I saw in those works a modest addition to my knowledge of art and to others', the beginning of a long and creative journey. A woman in her daily acts, movement and postures was present in every painting. In reality, one single woman inspired all the works.

Yet I hoped that the viewer would enter my painting through its formal aesthetic components, not merely through its subject – despite the fact that the subject was the most seductive on the level of human relationships, instincts and poetry. The woman holds the same importance to me as the

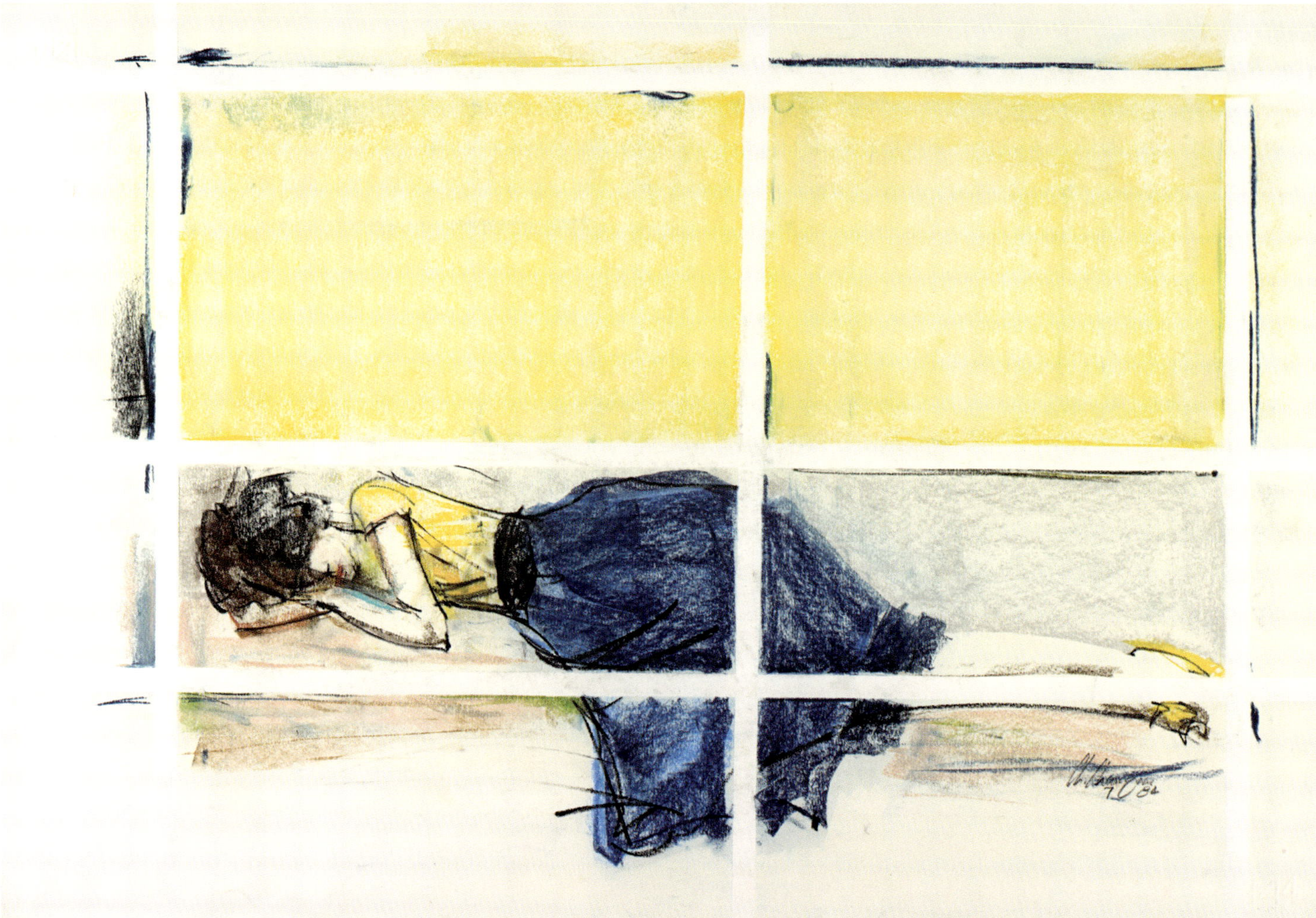

90
LEILA 84-7A, 1984
Pastel on paper
70 x 50 cm

blue adjacent space or the forms that contain or overlap her. Aesthetically, the woman on a level with all the elements that make up the painting, and there is no difference to me between the human and the setting. The absence of one element is the death of the other. Woman, in my works, is an inseparable part of this aesthetic climate, a basic component as much as these lines without which woman, image, or spaces cannot exist. I loved that meeting between my woman and the blue space next to her.

I intended that my experiment should take place in a defined aesthetic climate, with clear aesthetic components. There were three givens: the subject, the format and the

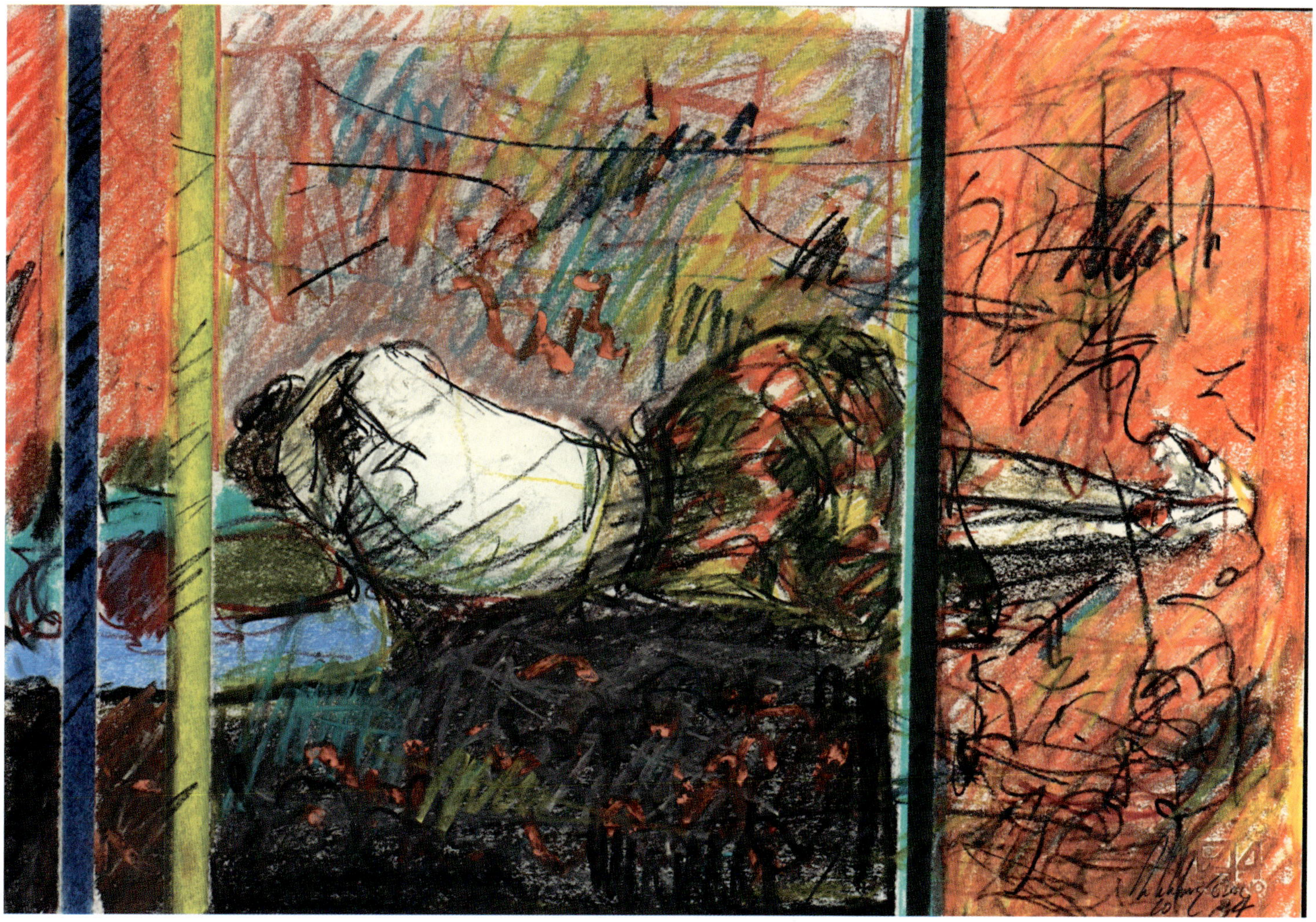

91
LEILA 84-3A, 1984
Pastel on paper
47.5 x 34 cm

materials. The problem was what to do with these elements without adding to them or detracting from other elements. I had no fear of apparent repetition or the failure of the experience. As much as the painting stood on its own, it was there for the unity of the whole.

There is no separation between the techniques of a work of art and its formal structure. One cannot read a form without colour. If we say 'red square', then it is a red square, not simply a square. And if we say a square with a mishmash of red pastel lines, it is so and not of other elements. I was fully aware that all the aesthetic elements I introduced and the materials I used were inseparable. The success of my artwork was and

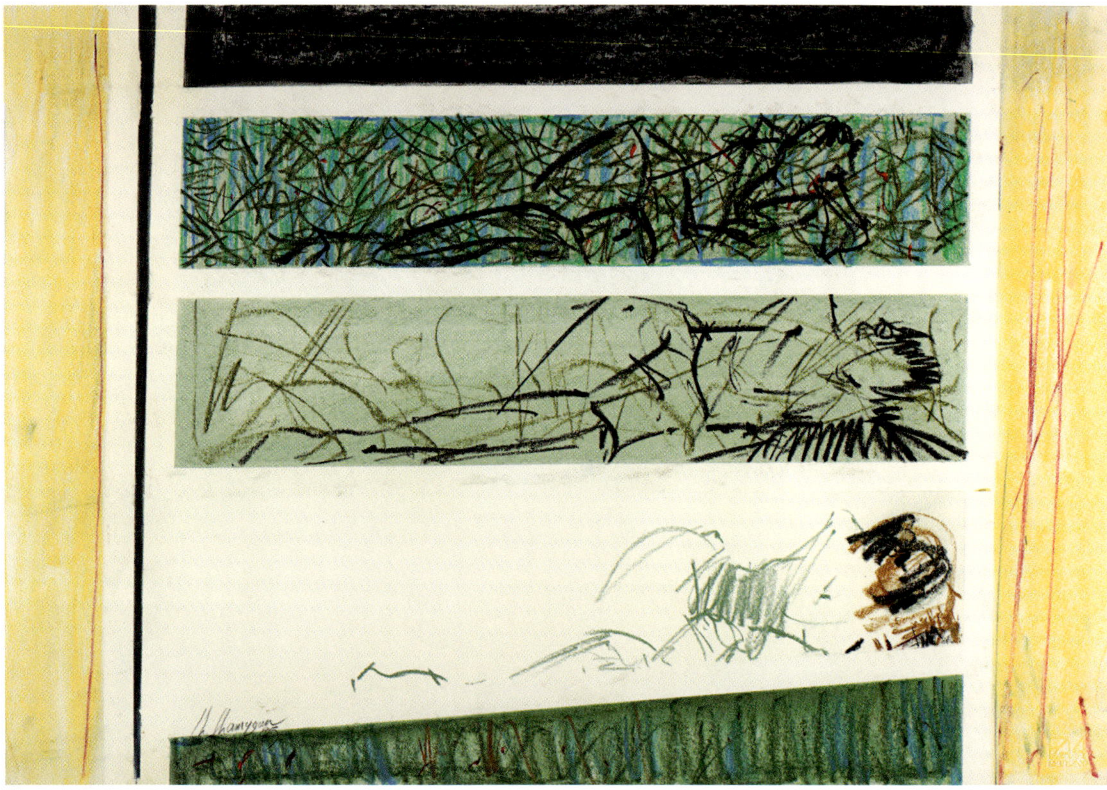

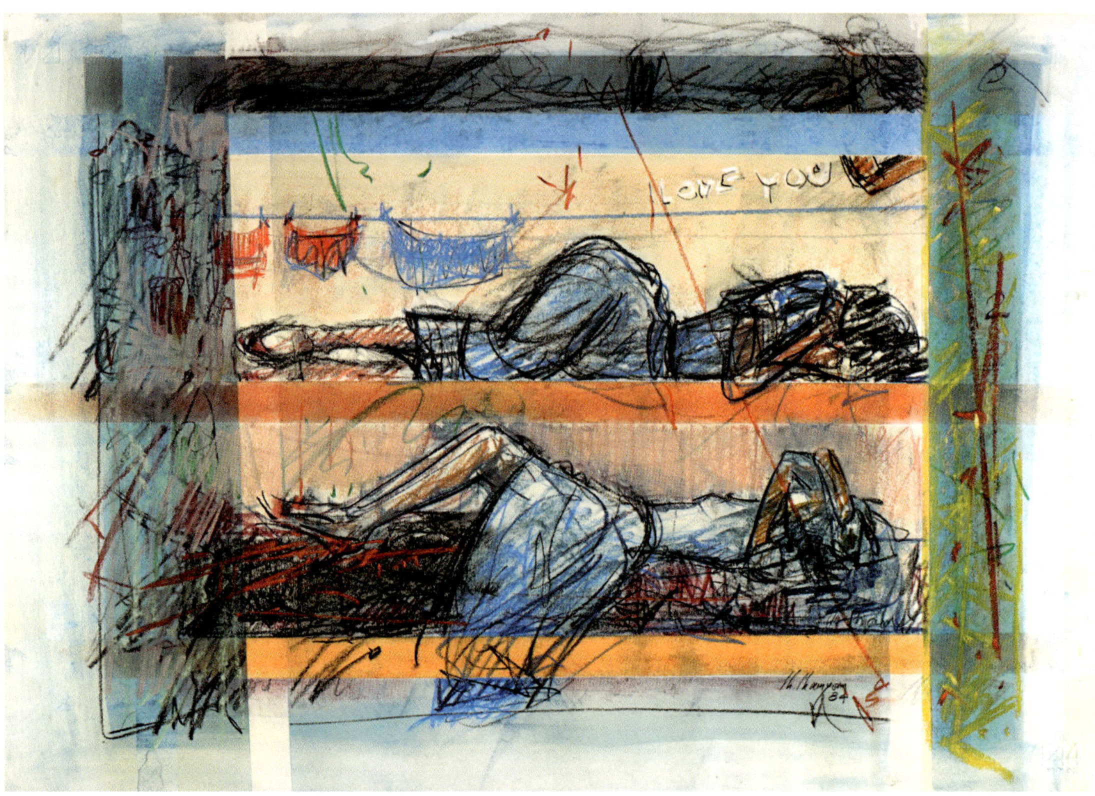

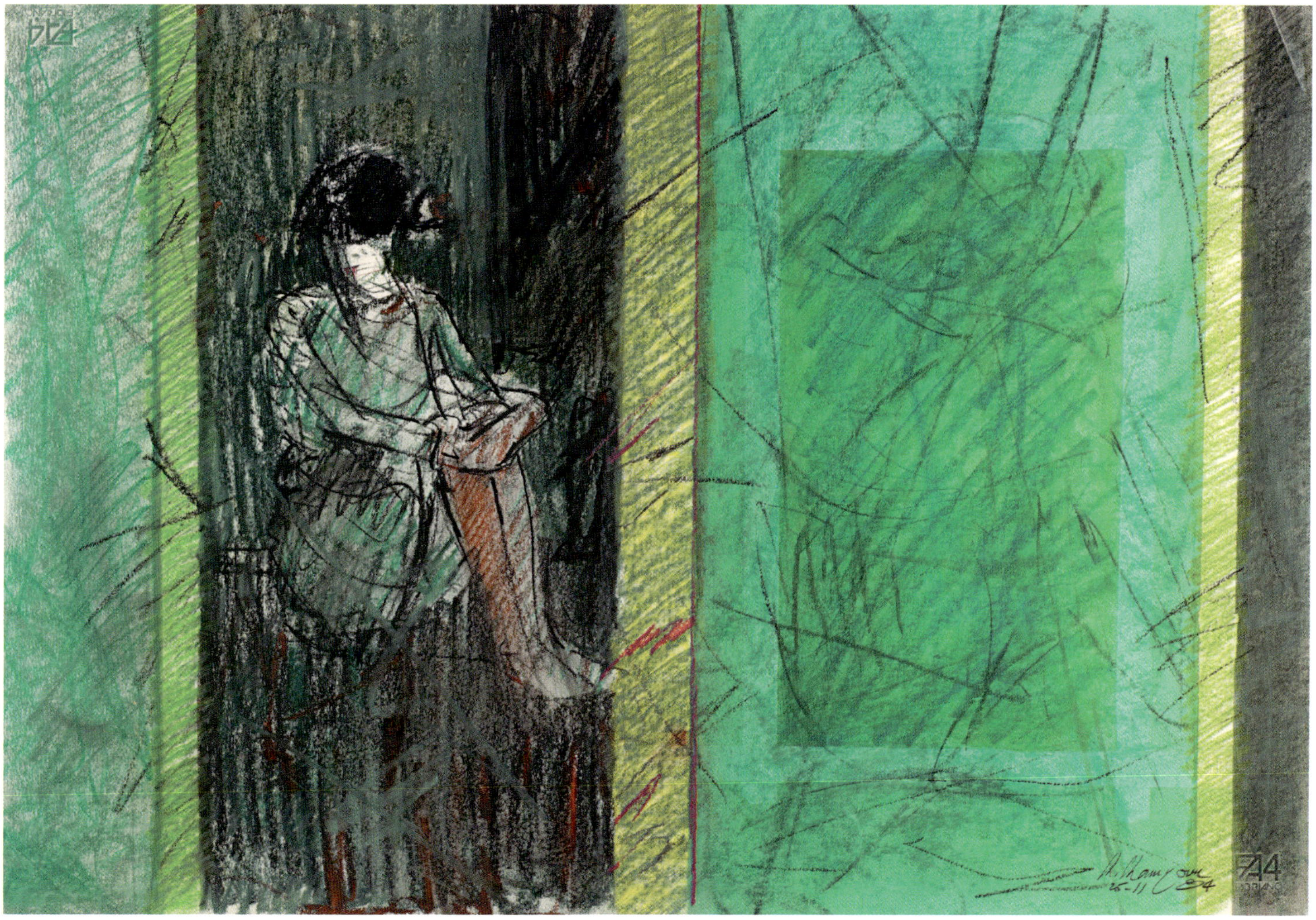

is achievable through an understanding of that awareness. The better I understand the nature of the materials, the more I benefit from their limitless possibilities. There was nothing metaphysical about them.

The line I envisaged leading to a new work of art sometimes scared me. I set it aside, but was always happy to see it reappearing. I did not plan future happenings. My experience walked me there. I had no way back.

The drawings I compiled between 1984 and 1985 made up my first solo exhibition in Lebanon at La Toile Art Gallery, in Rimal, Zouk Mosbeh. The gallery was owned and run by Alexa Burgy. The first time I met Alexa was with Michel

92
LEILA 84-7B, 1984
Pastel on paper
70 x 50 cm

Facing page, top
93
LEILA 85-5B, 1985
Pastel on paper
70 x 50 cm

Facing page, bottom
94
LEILA 84-5, 1984
Pastel on paper
70 x 50 cm

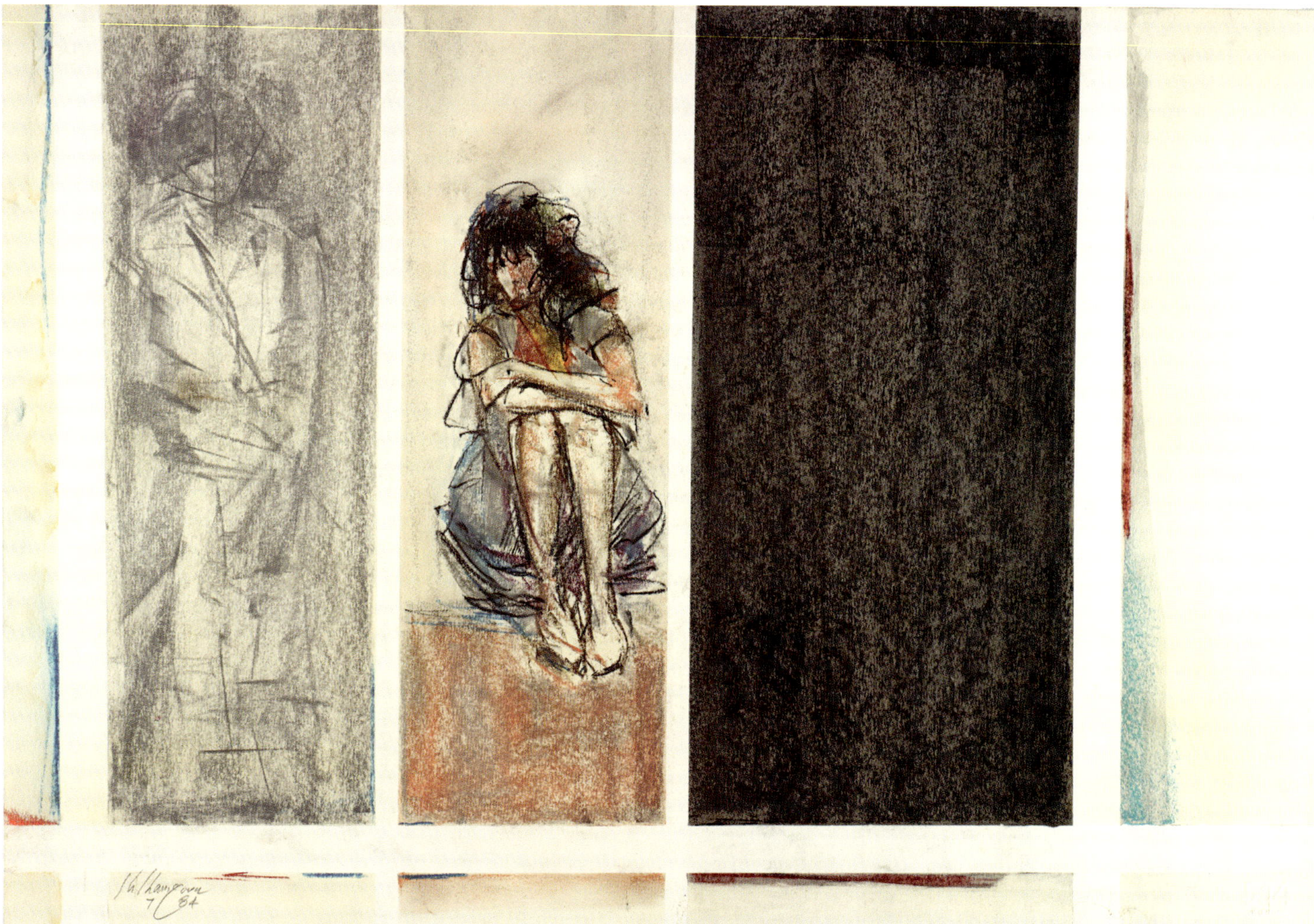

95
LEILA 84-6, 1984
Pastel on paper
70 x 50 cm

Meaiky of TeleLiban, who had interviewed me on TV and wanted to introduce her to me. Mr Meaiky brought Alexa and her late sister to my studio. At the time I had several drawings quickly sketched with chalk pastels, pencil and charcoal, intricately composed and expressively portraying iconic images of women of that time. When Alexa saw my drawings of Leila, although not highly realistic, she told me: 'You know, I think you are drawing all of us.'

Through Leila, I was trying to draw woman as woman sees herself, and Alexa's words touched me to the core. The opening night of the exhibition was like a big wedding, with a buffet and a very warm reception. Despite the fighting

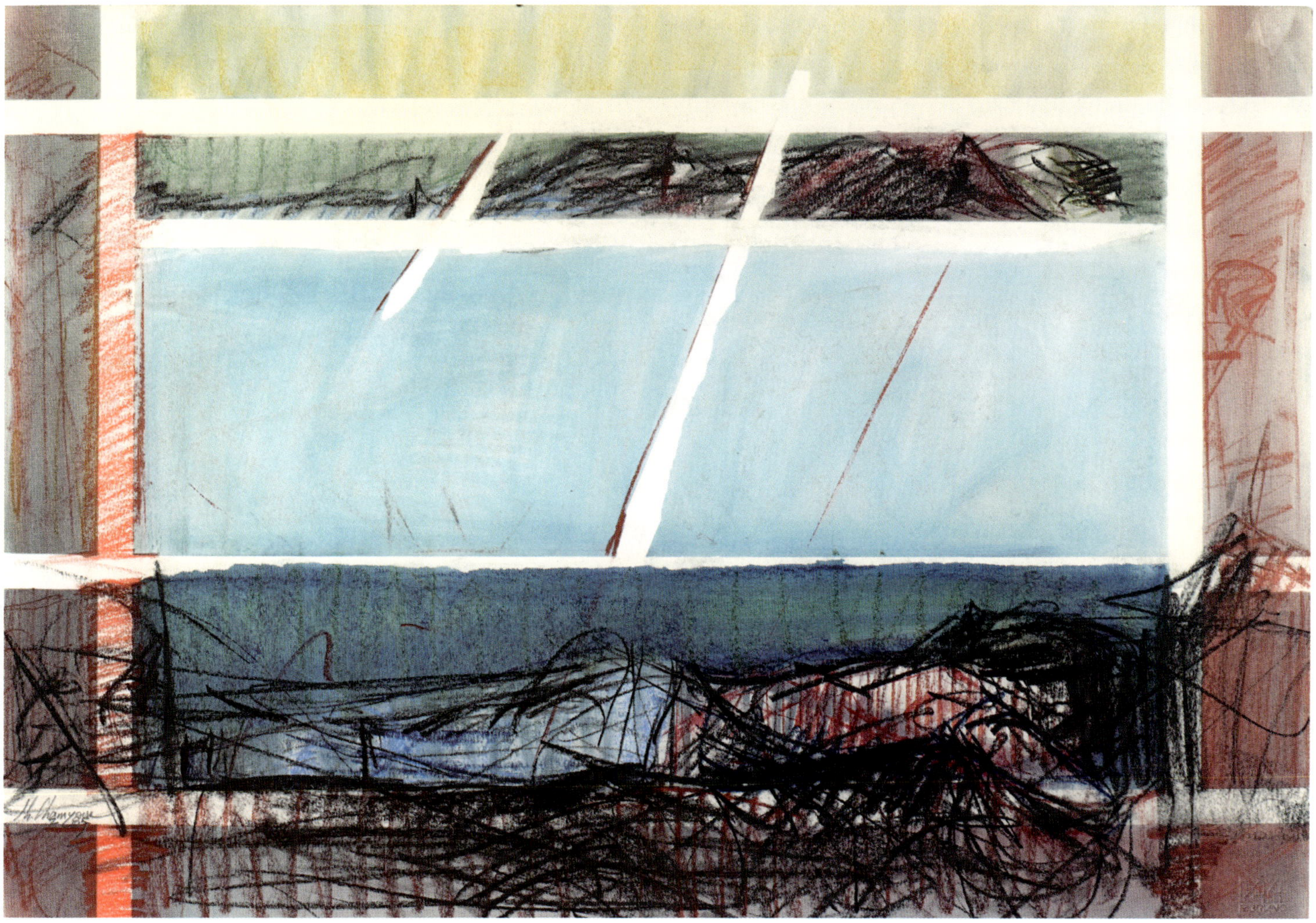

96
LEILA 85-3, 1985
Pastel on paper
70 x 50 cm

that was going on in many areas along the Green Line, a huge number of people showed up. On seeing that so many people had gathered, Alexa ordered her piano to be moved from her chalet to the gallery, where she played to the joy of an amazed crowd. I was so touched and overwhelmed that
88–97, 99, 100 tears came to my eyes. Unexpected encouragement came when many of the exhibited works were sold.

101 'Mother to Be' was the first acrylic painting I had done since 1979. I made it immediately after the La Toile exhibition. The painting was the culmination of the last two years' experiments, with soft materials as its driving influence. It also reflects several basic elements of my previous paintings

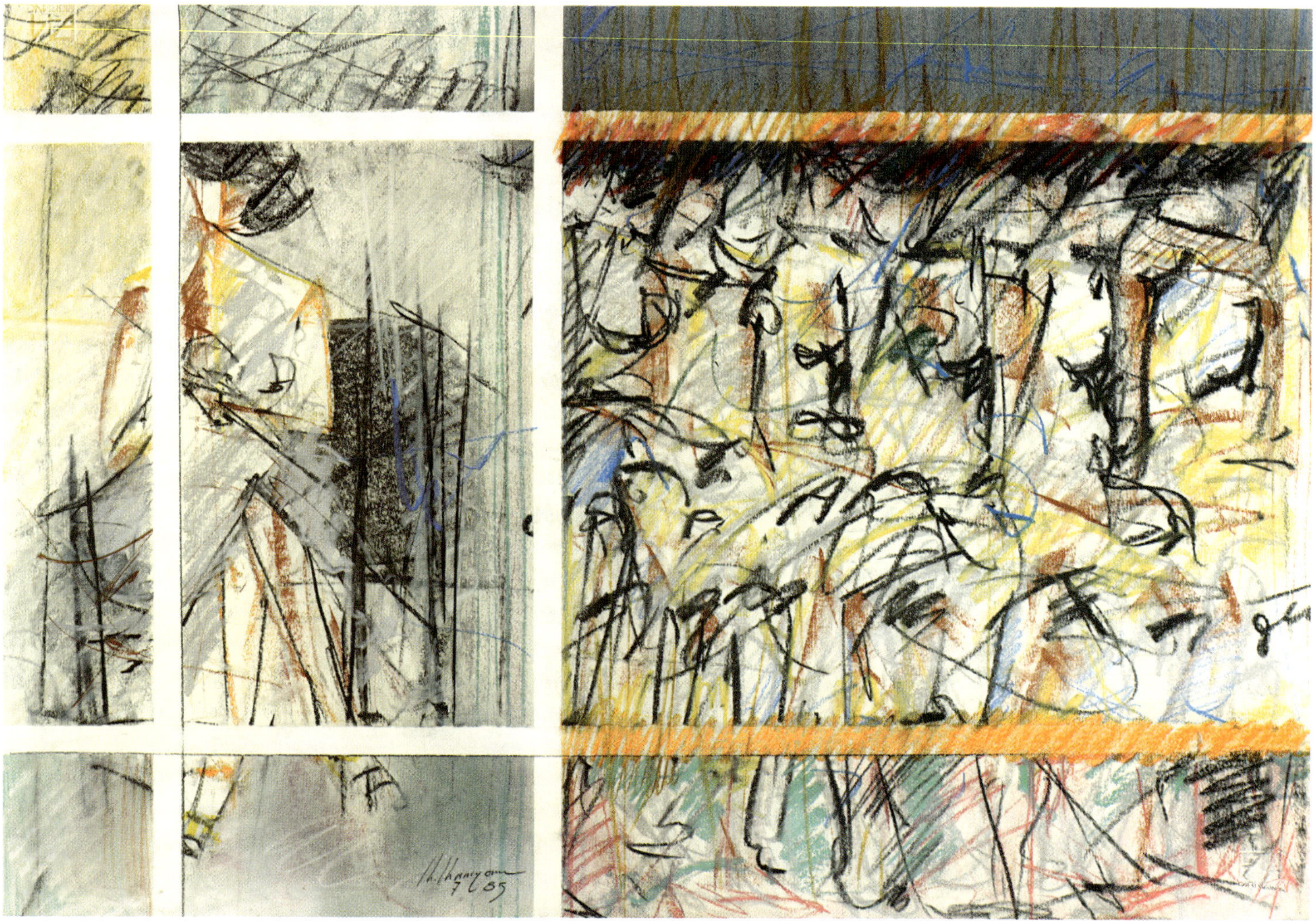

97
LEILA 85-2A , 1985
Pastel on paper
70 x 50 cm

and drawings of the seventies: a combination of brushwork, paint dripping and slashing, transparency, and shoving techniques.

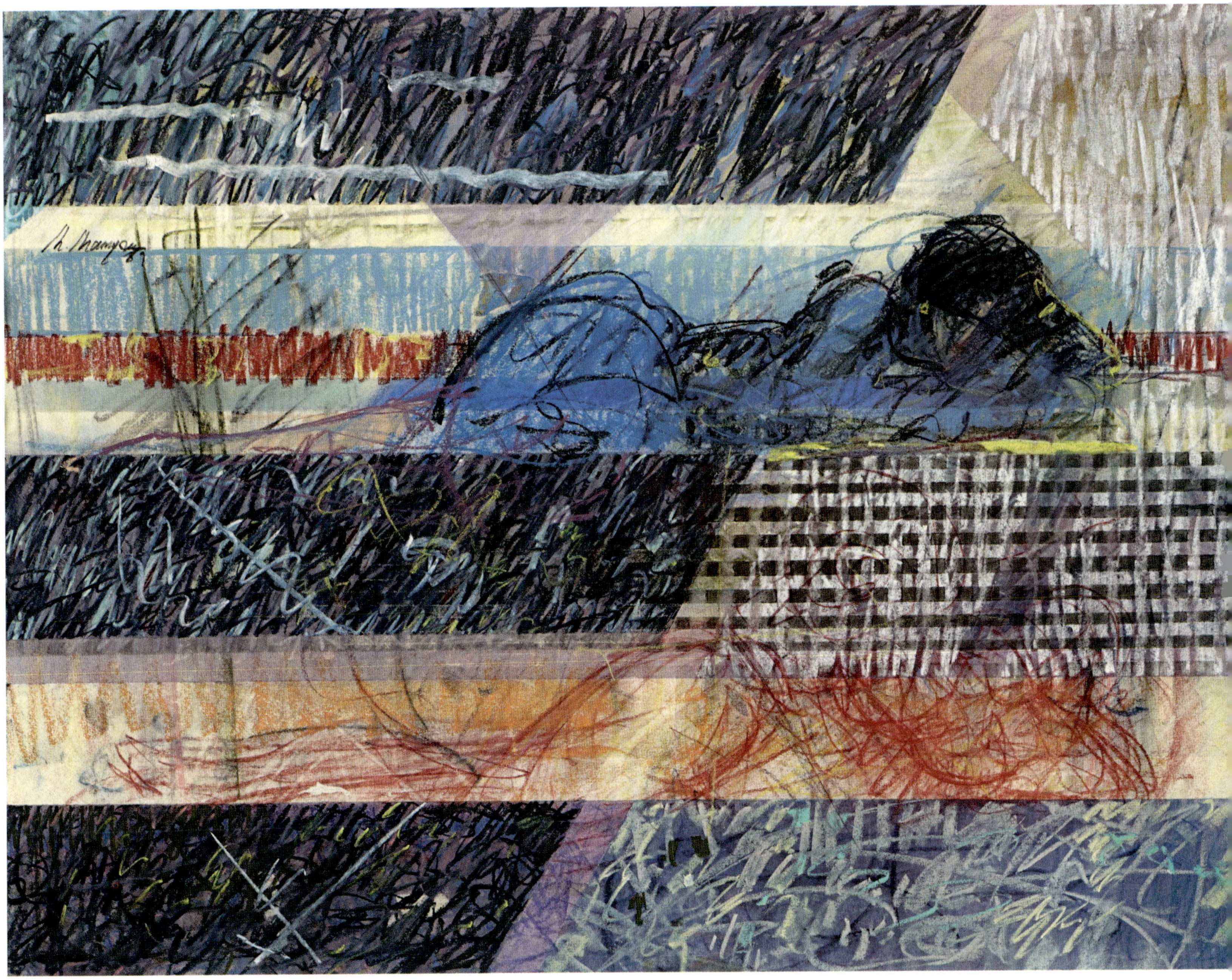

98
LEILA-86-8, 1986
Pastel on paper
60.5 x 45 cm

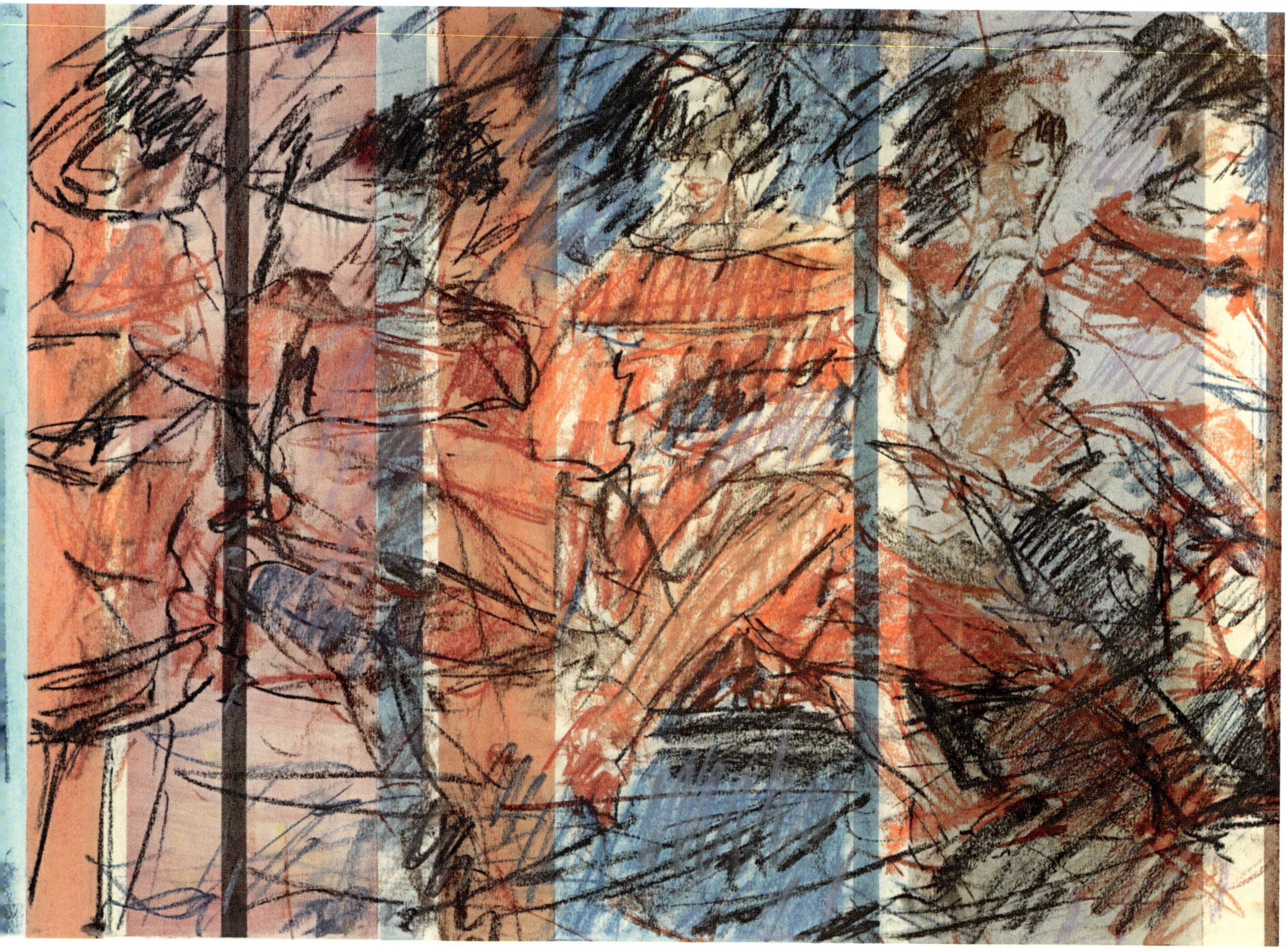

99
LEILA 84-6B, 1984
Pastel on paper (detail)
70 x 50 cm

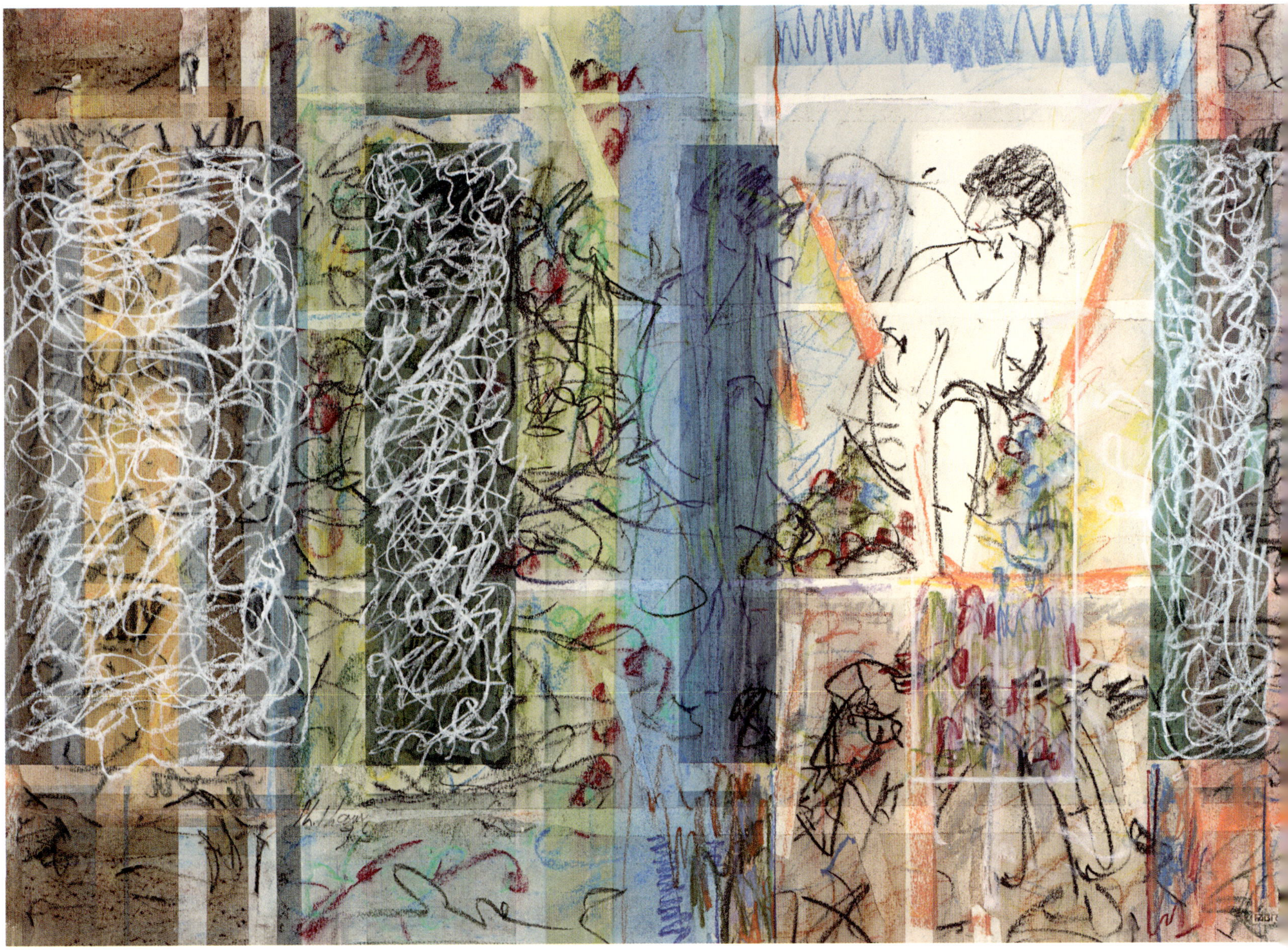

100
LEILA 84-4, 1984
Pastel on paper
70 x 50 cm

Following spread
101
MOTHER TO BE, 1985
Acrylic on canvas (detail)
166 x 156.3 cm

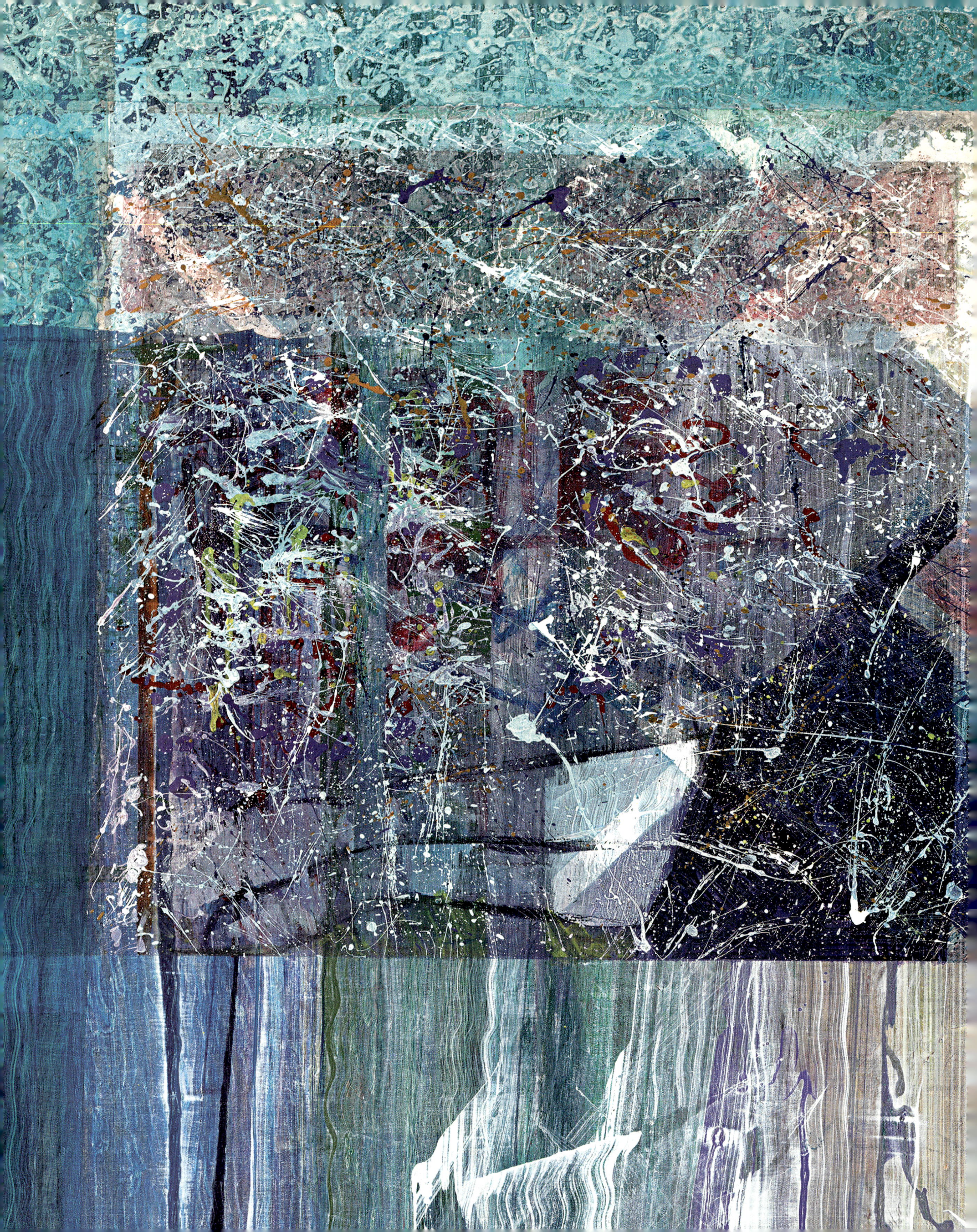

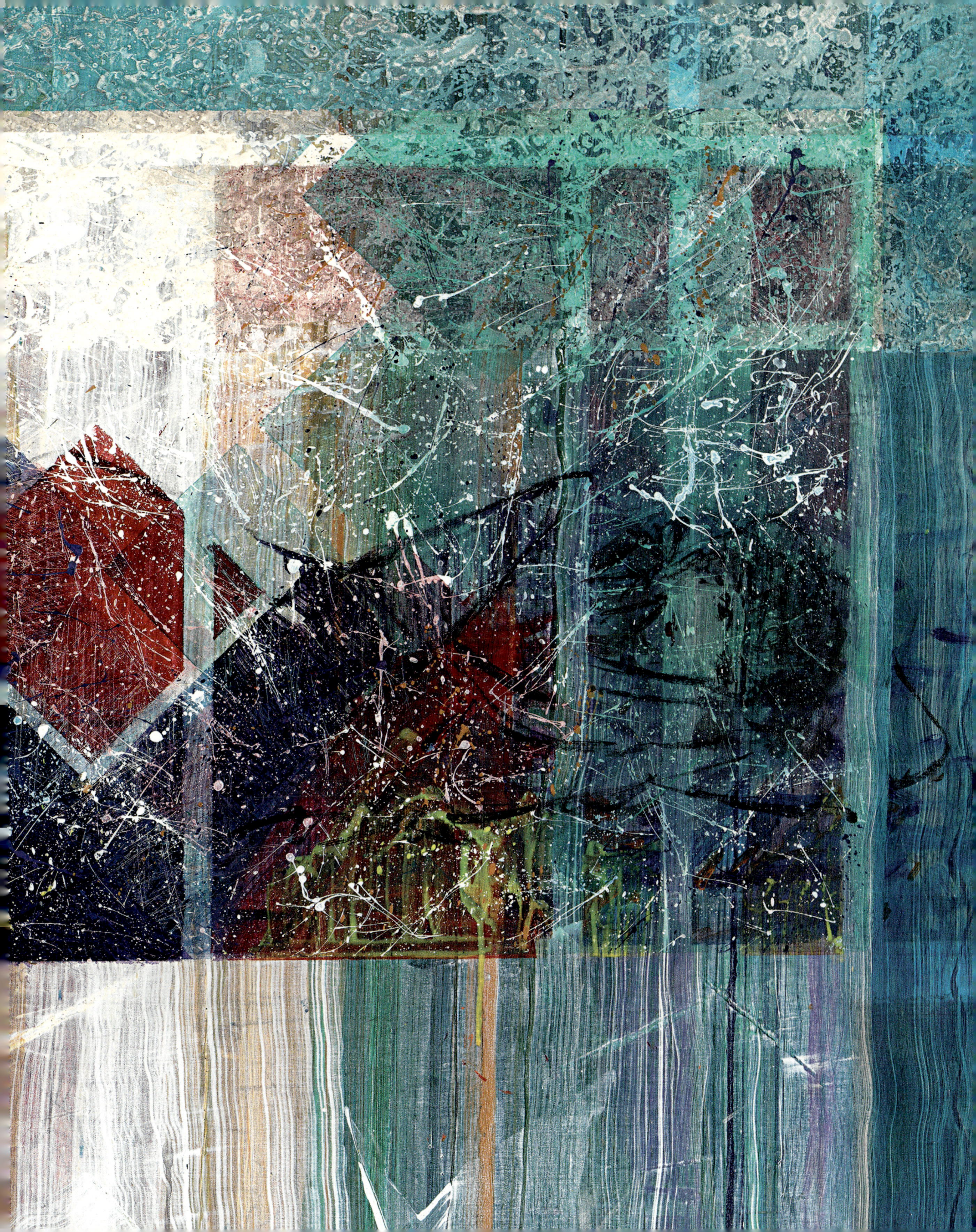

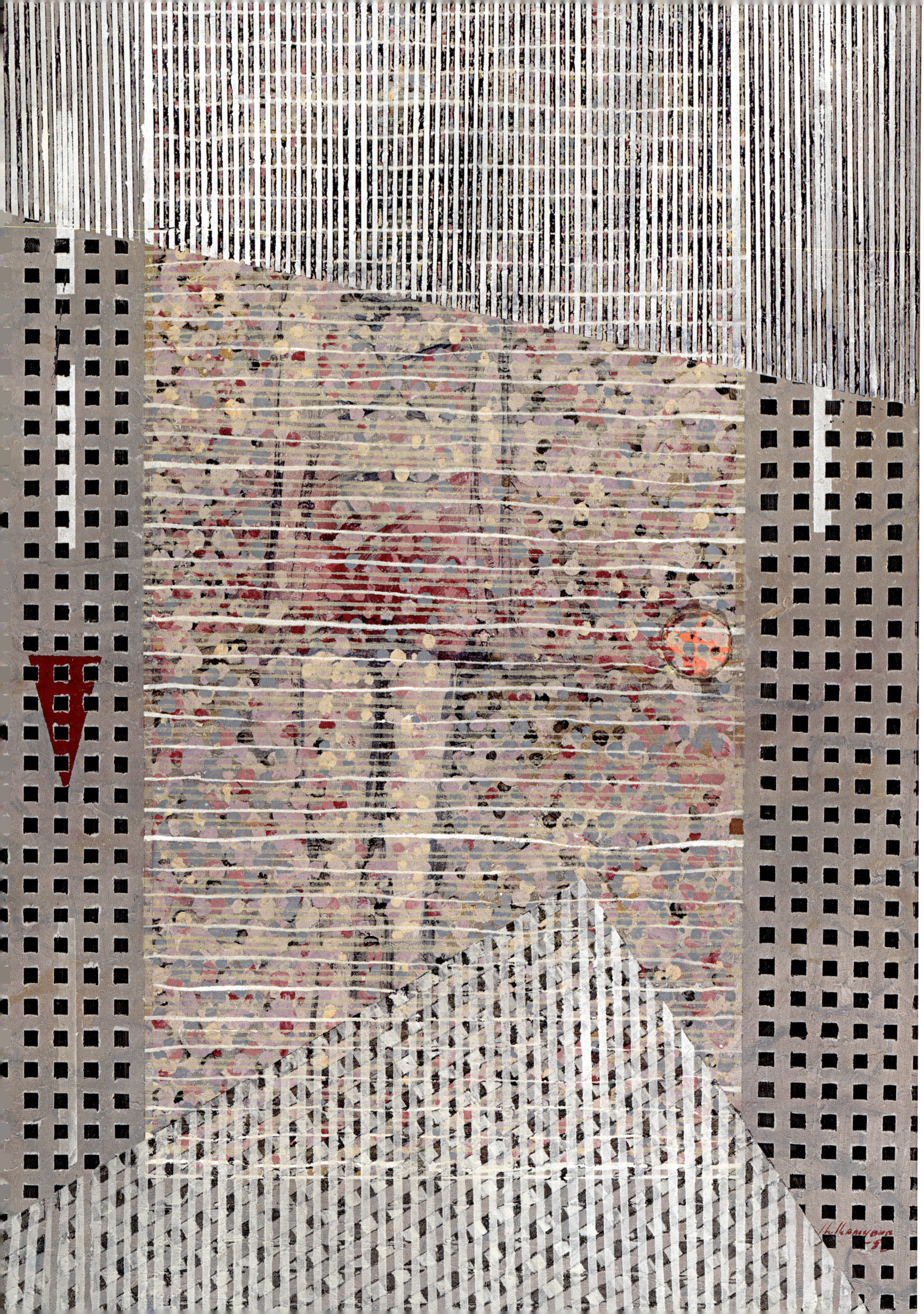

Between Lebanon and the States

By the summer of 1986 the situation in Lebanon was becoming worse every day. Salaries at the Lebanese University, like everywhere else in Lebanon, were deteriorating in value, and no matter how much I had made from selling my paintings, my income was not enough to support my family. So I decided to go back to the States, sell my paintings and try to do some design work. I had asked the university to cram my teaching sessions into a few weeks per semester, using after hours and weekends when necessary, so that I could travel without depriving my students. My time would now be split between New York and Lebanon.

My brother Rachid was still in New York. He and a friend of his had opened a gallery called Woodex, partly to display the furniture he designed and partly for art exhibitions. I exhibited my art there and at the Fine Arts Gallery on Fifth Avenue. I also contacted the firm with which I had worked before leaving for Lebanon, and was both surprised and happy when they told me that my drawing desk was still there waiting for me.

I settled myself into a reasonable working environment by turning my brother's two-door garage into a studio, where I continued to develop the aesthetic concepts I had established for myself in the 1985 exhibition and beyond. 'Mother to Be' led

Facing page
102
THE DATE II, 1986
Acrylic on ccnvas
110 x 160 cm

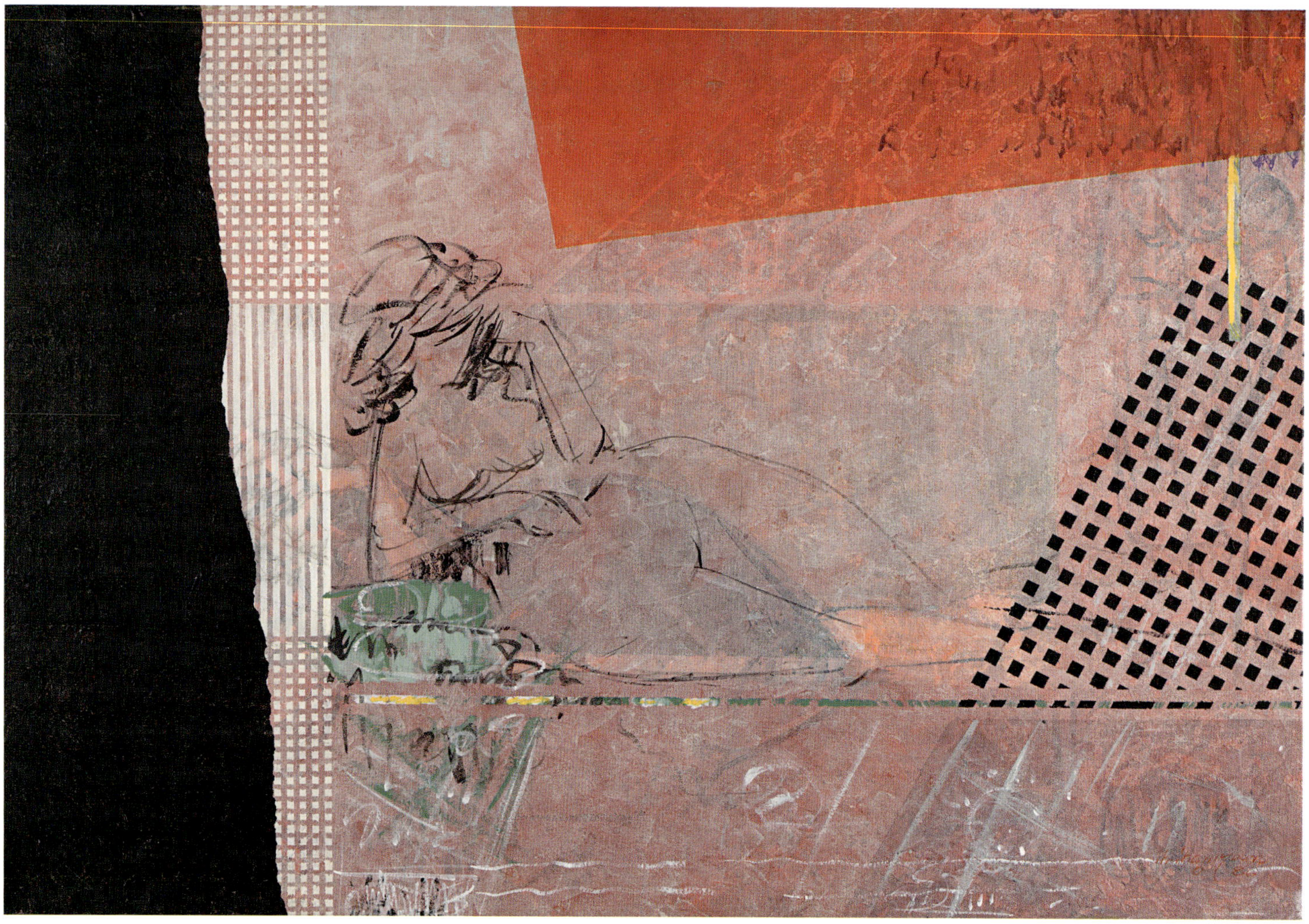

103
A REFLECTION OF HER, 1987
Acrylic on canvas
201 x 140 cm

to several large new acrylic paintings, but charcoal, pencil and pastel remained the materials for my preliminary work. I did several paintings, some of which were exhibited at Woodex. 98, 102, 104–109

La Toile Gallery gave me another exhibition in November of 1987. The paintings and drawings I produced between New York and Adonis were a continuation of my previous experience. They had denser vertical and diagonal lines, with images of the same woman coming through, giving warmth to the architectural structure of the overall painting surface. The sharply delineated divisions created by the vertical/horizontal composition became the overlapping organised fields of veiled squares and lines. 103, 110–114

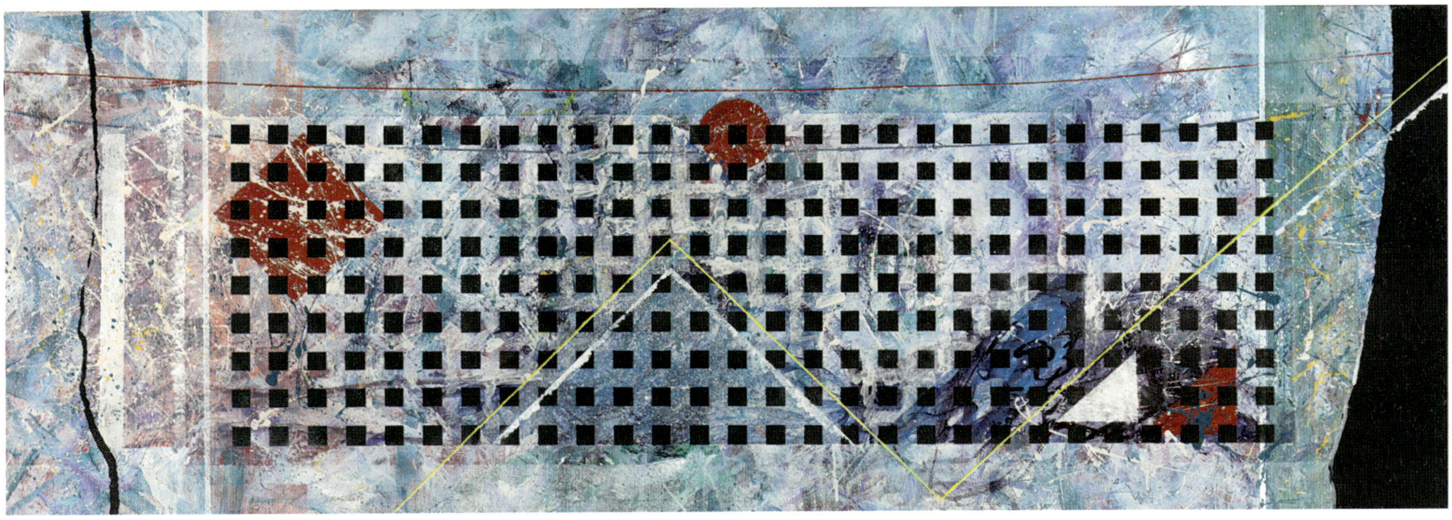

104
SLEEPING BEAUTY, 1986
Acrylic on canvas
191 x 67 cm

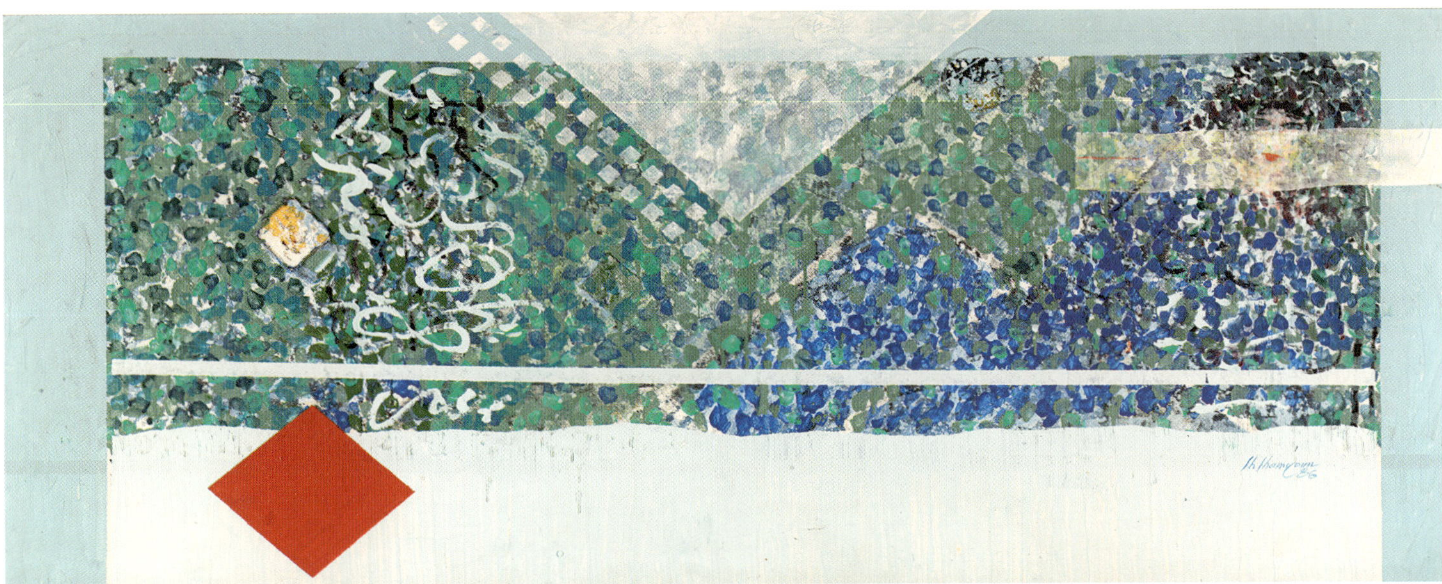

105
QUEEN OF THE NIGHT, 1986
Acrylic on canvas
169.5 x 79 cm

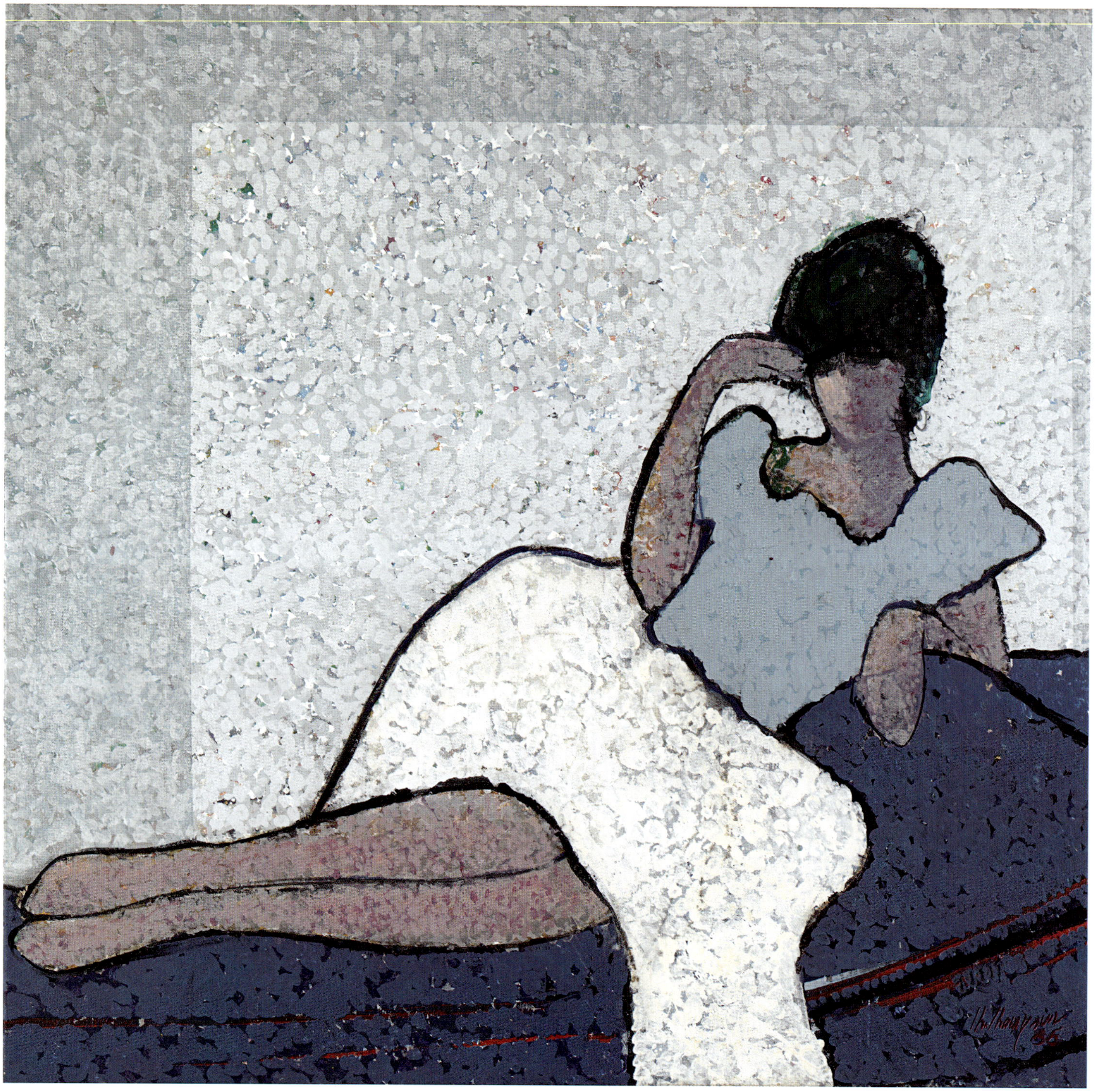

106
LEILA, 1986
Acrylic on canvas
131 x124 cm

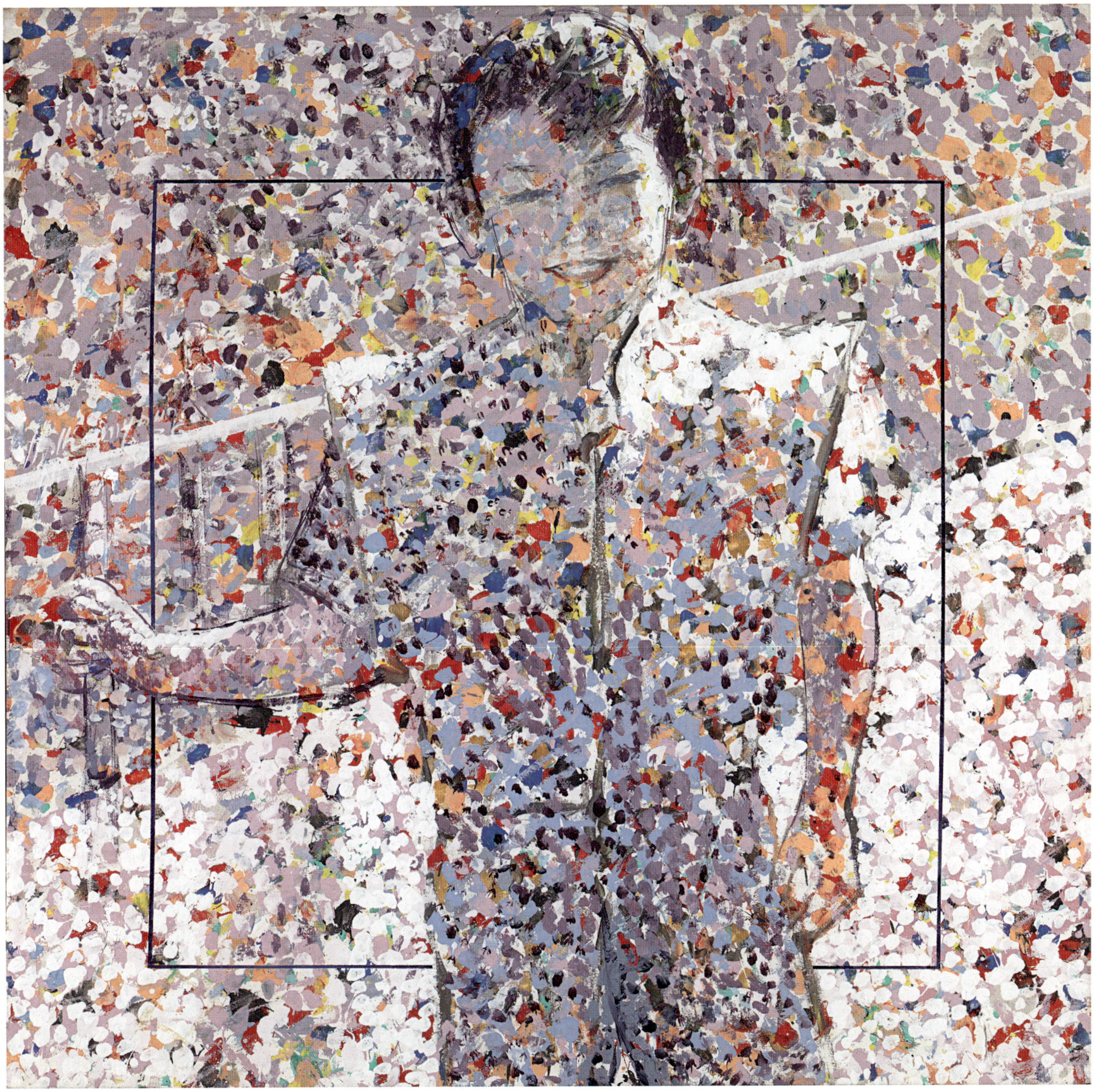

107
GEORGE ON HARISSA STAIRS, 1986
Acrylic on canvas
143 x 143 cm

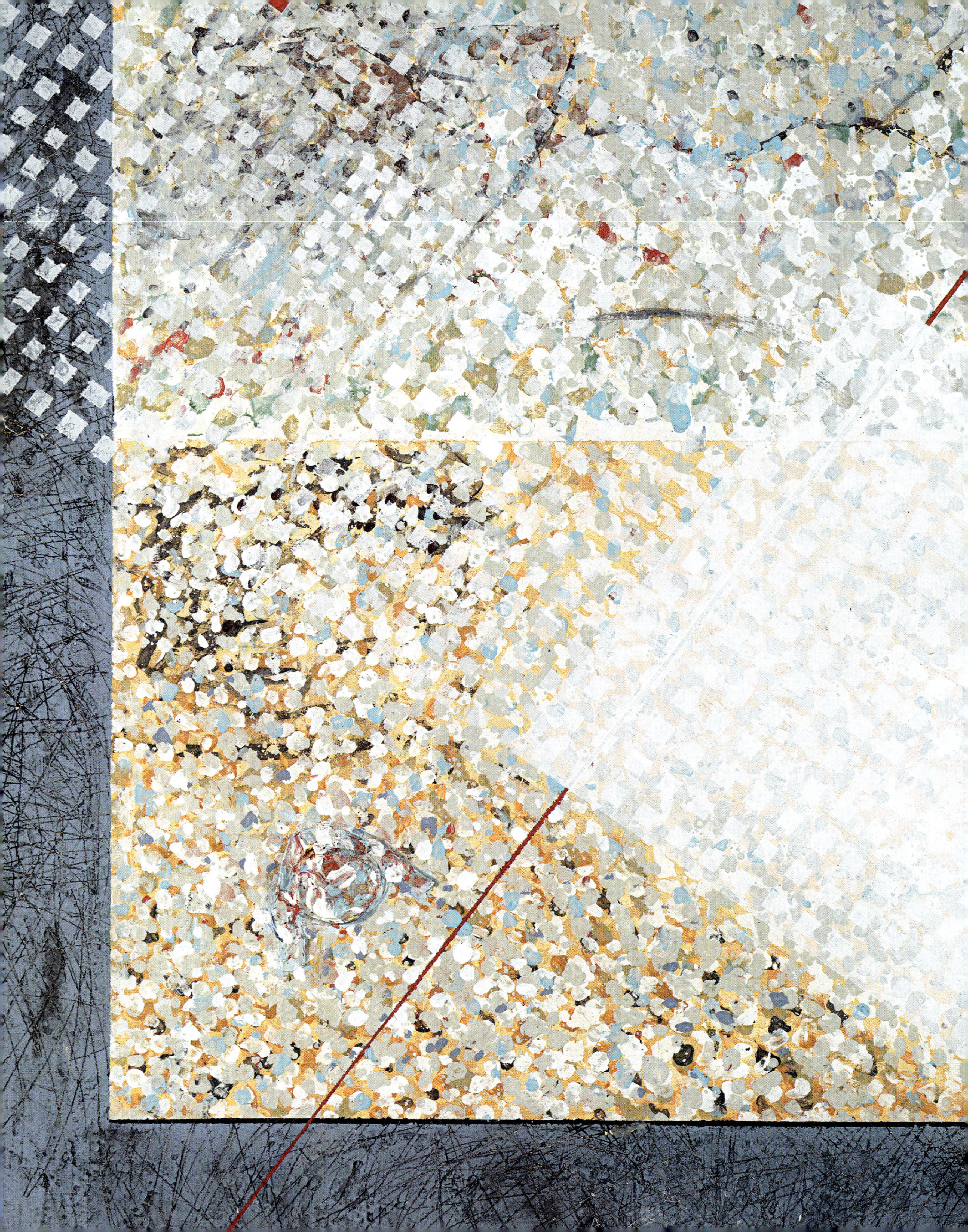

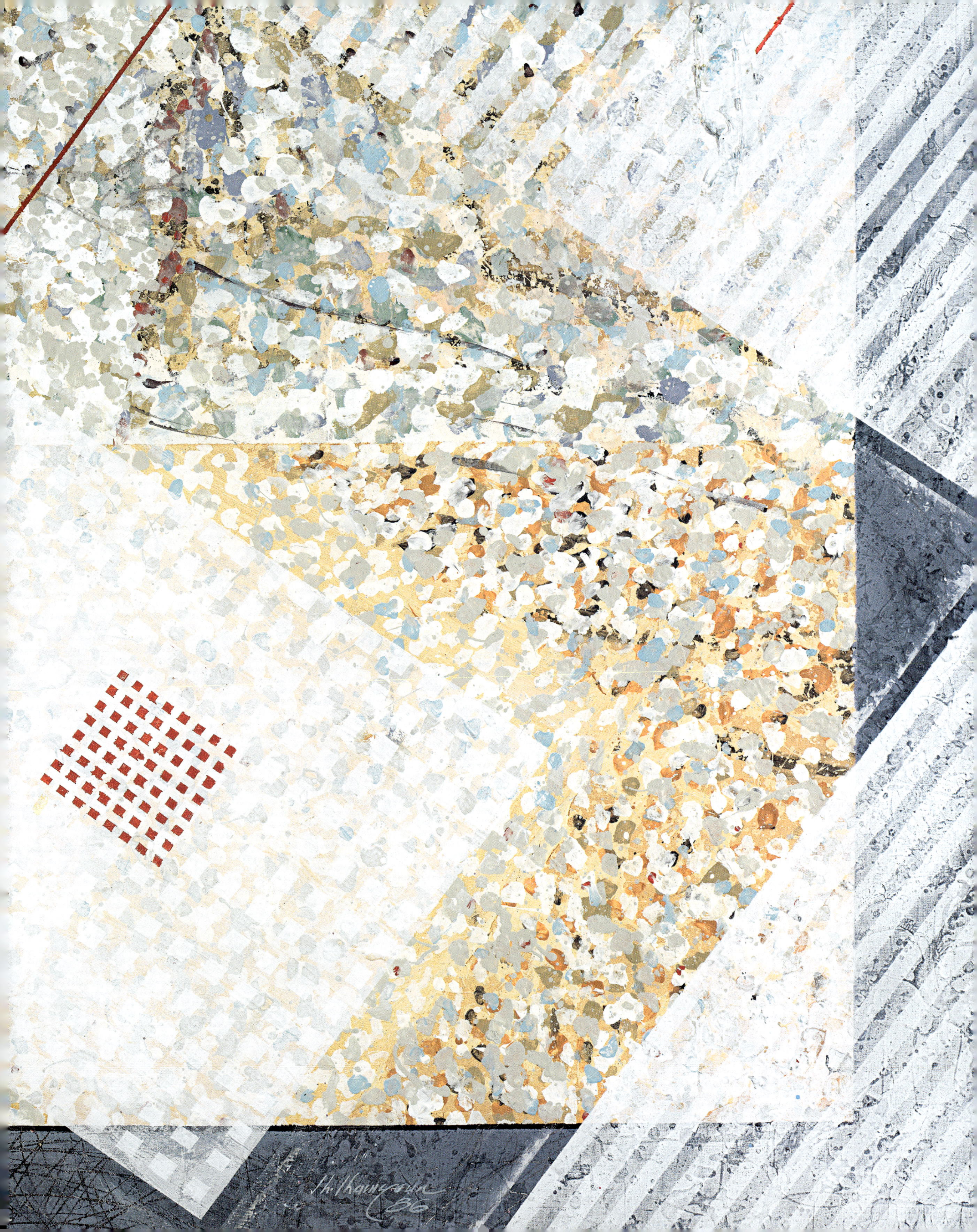

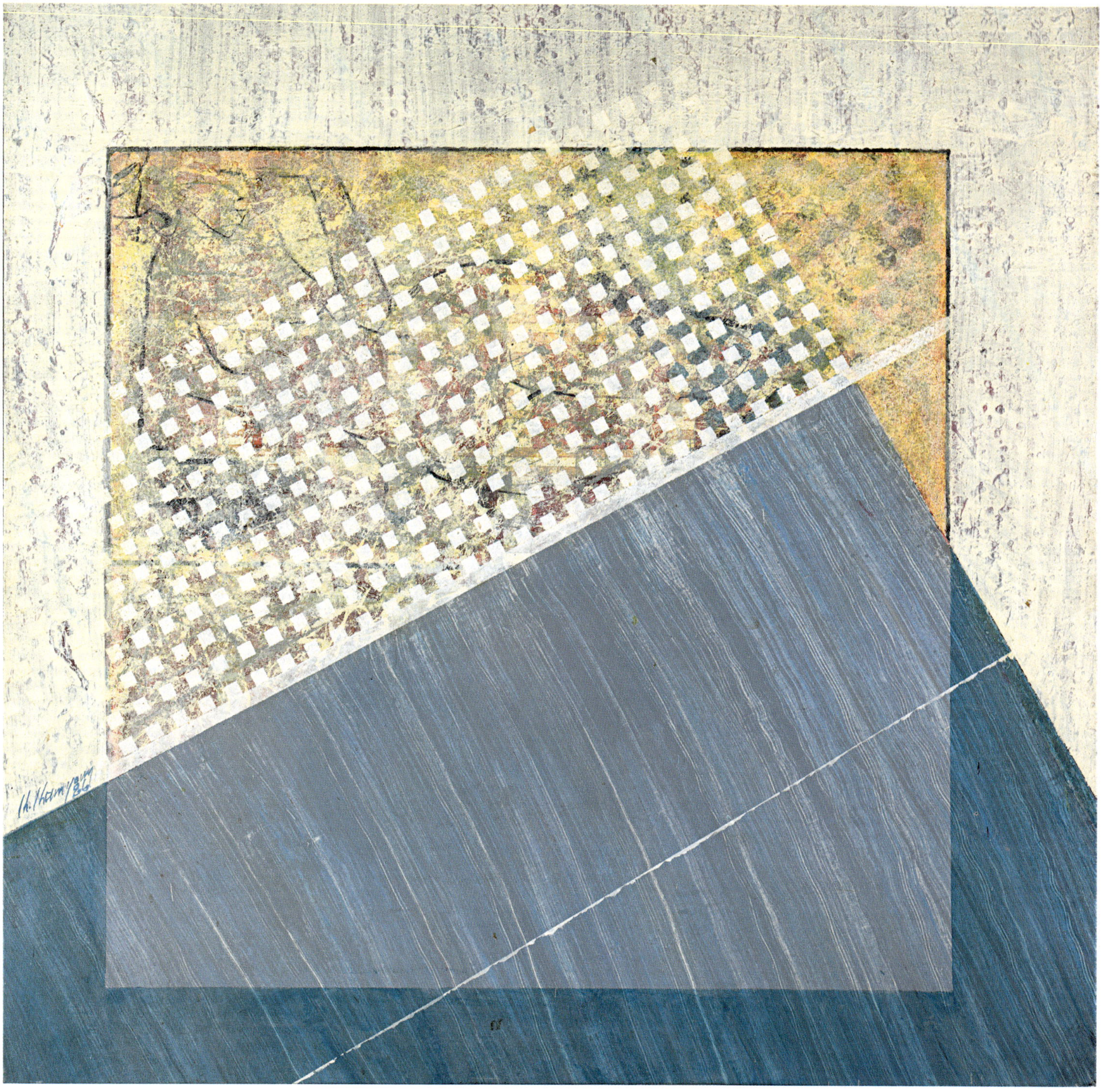

108
READING BEYOND, 1986
Acrylic on canvas
140 x 40 cm

Previous spread
109
AN AFTERNOON NAP, 1986
Acrylic on canvas
201 x 140 cm

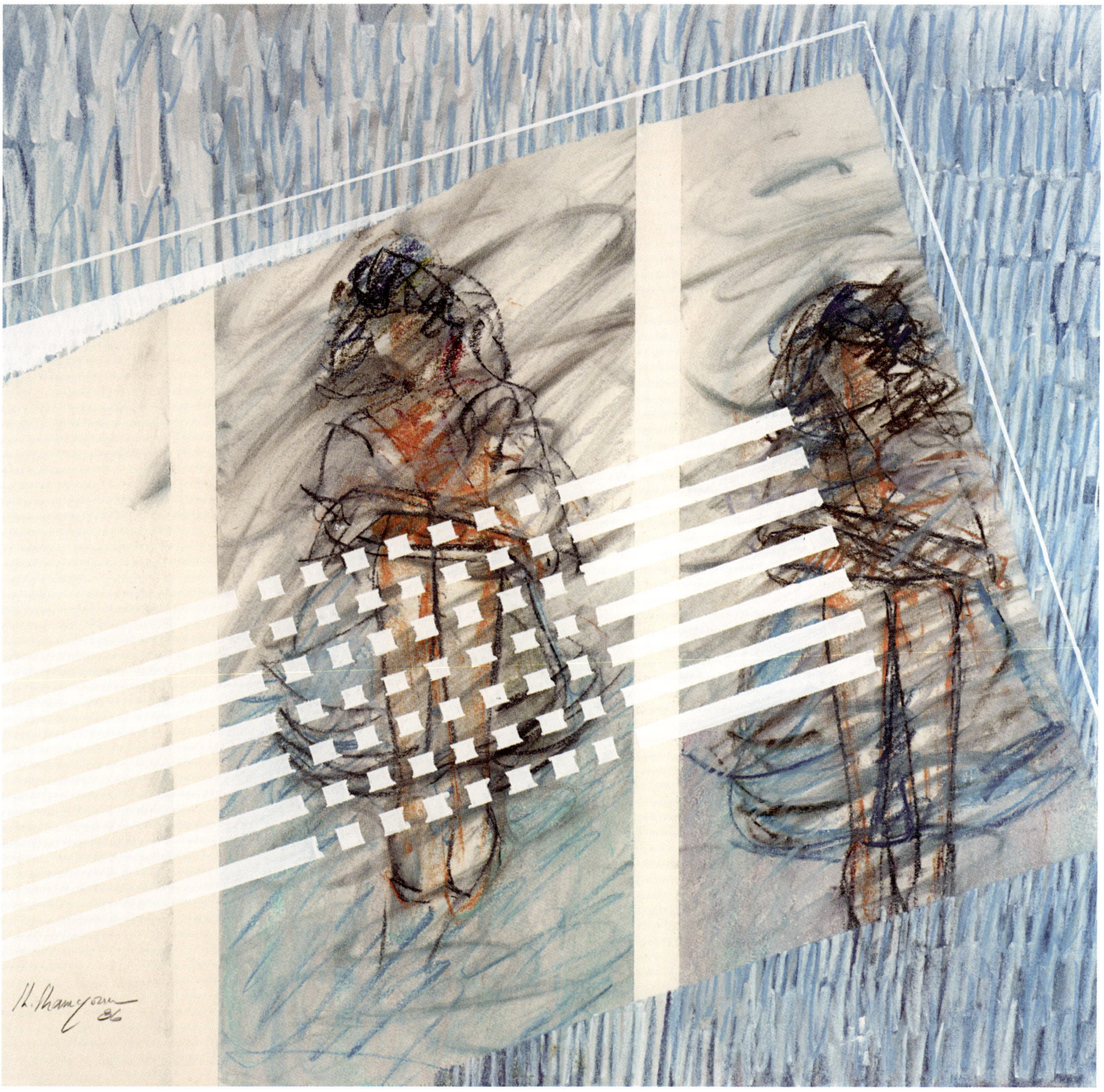

110
LEILA-86-1A, 1986
Pastel on paper (detail)
61 x 46 cm

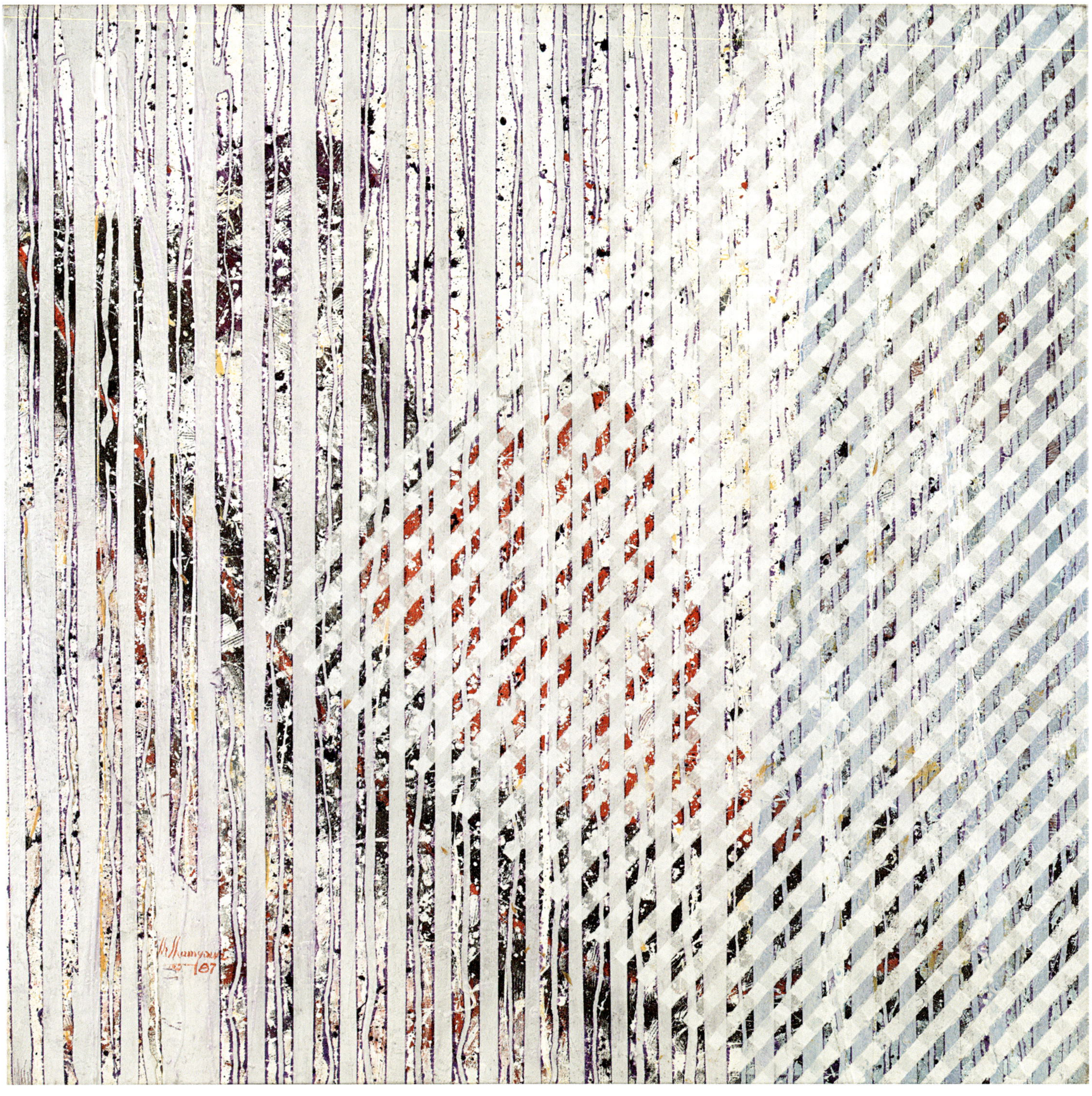

111
READING ALONE, 1987
Acrylic on canvas
124 x 124 cm

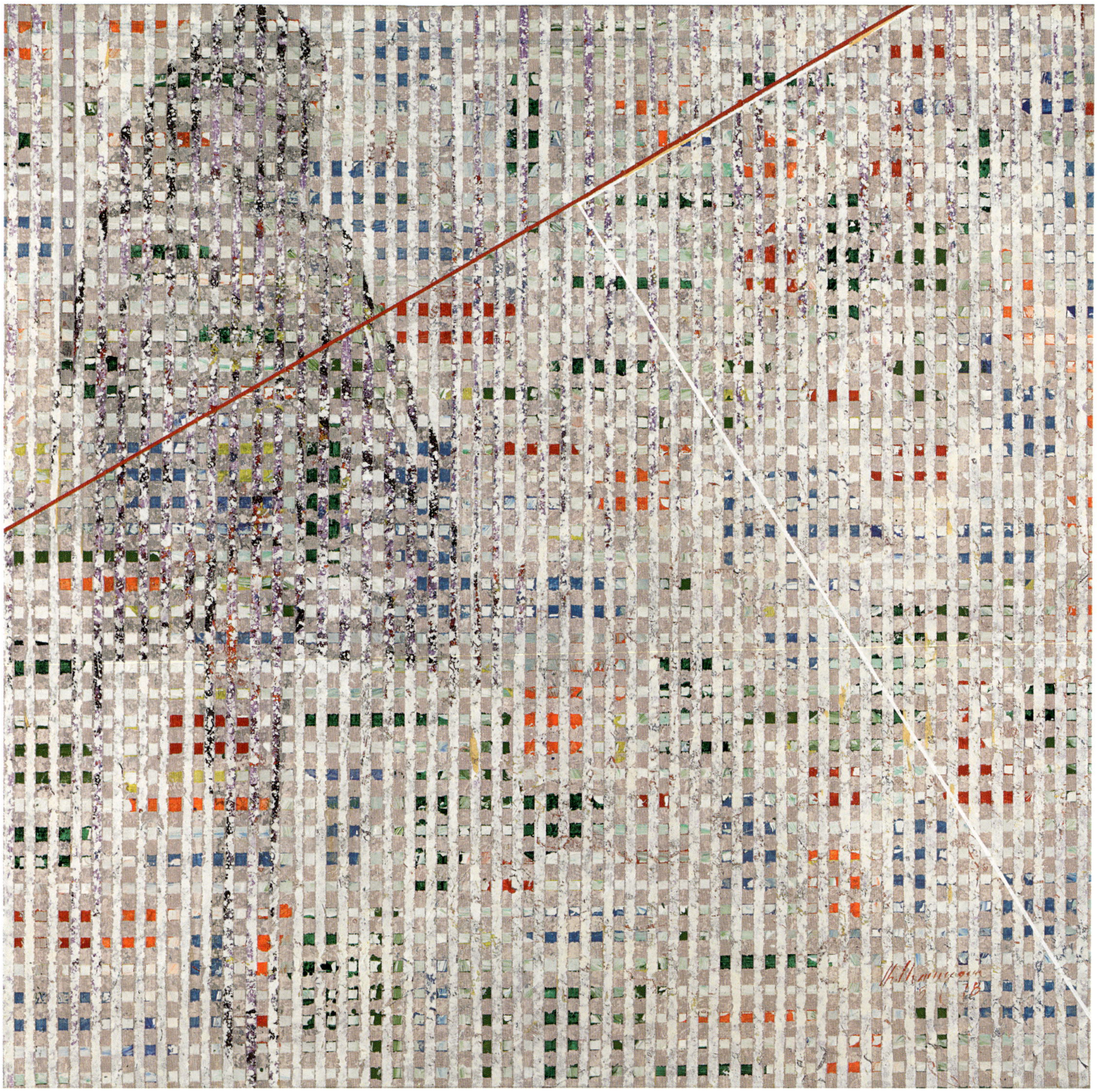

112
HER SHADOW NEVER LEFT, 1987
Acrylic on canvas
124 x 124 cm

113
THE TWINS I, 1987
Acrylic on canvas
89 x 143 cm

114
THE TWINS II, 1987
Acrylic on canvas
89 x 143 cm

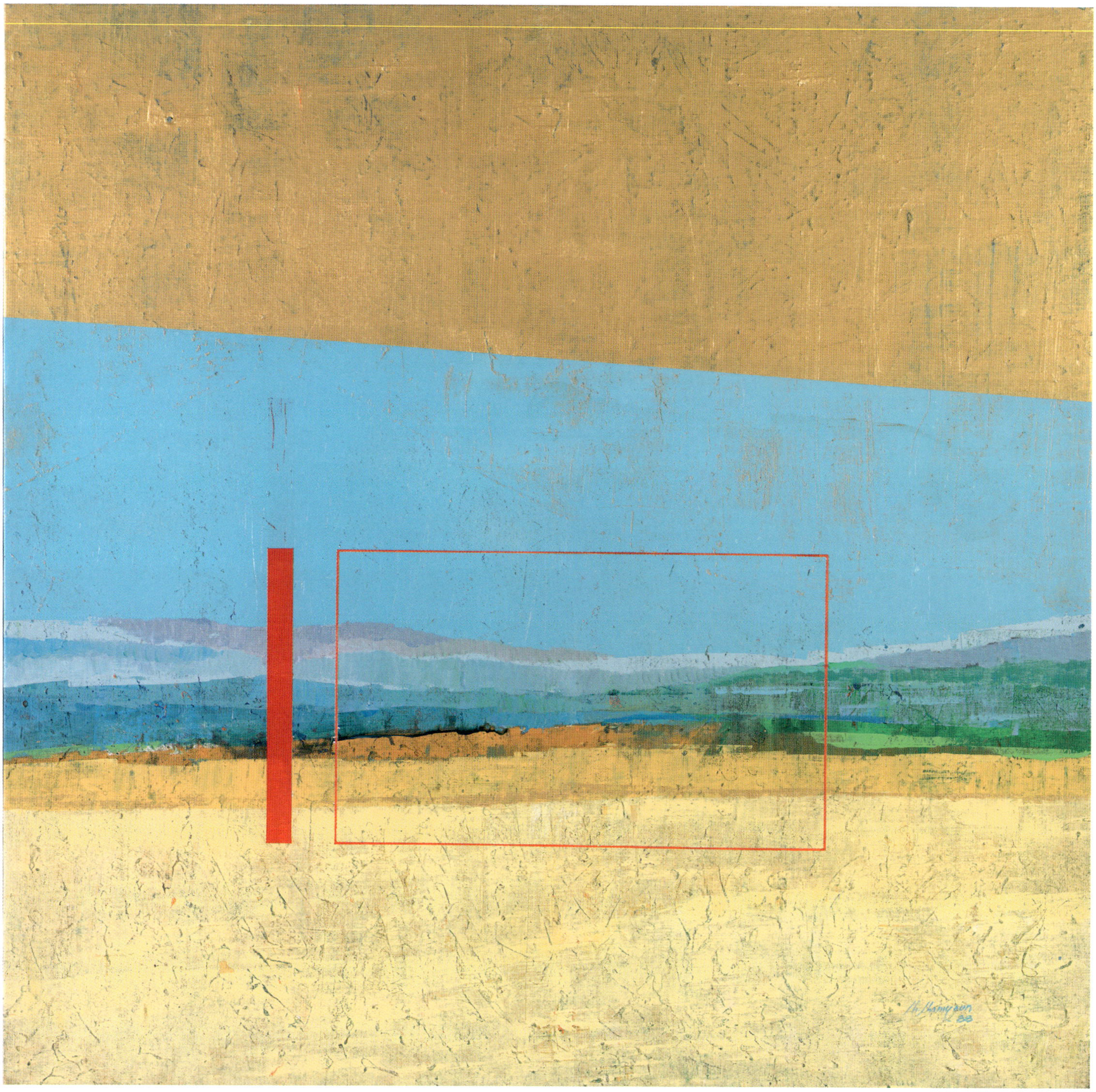

115
THE GOLDEN GATE, 1988
Acrylic on canvas
112 x 112 cm

A Landscape Prelude

After the arrival of Leila, drawing brought me to another, deeper level of sincerity in combining emotions, intellectual and technical knowledge in a search for new aesthetic values.

As of late spring 1988 I had to do a great deal of travelling and driving throughout the US. This is when I became conscious of the majesty of nature in America: vast, flat, varied and gigantic. Nature started revealing itself to me in a different way. In contrast to the busy, scribbling, nervous, linear gestures of the very expressionistic and calculated painting I had been doing, I began to develop flat paintings. I went more for plain flat surfaces and colours. I would sit
116, 117 on the bank of the Hudson River, admiring the lush green or the autumnal woods, contemplating a space beyond the space along the beaches of Long Island, where distant strips of land separated sea from sky in a very linear way. This was nature's graphic creation at its best. The highways and their surroundings were no less powerful. Driven by that enriching aesthetic interaction, I started implanting imaginary sculptural geometric forms, creating virtual installations
115, 118–121 possible only on canvas.

Mrs Amal Traboulsi of the Epreuve d'Artiste Gallery in Kaslik had seen and admired my work in past exhibitions.

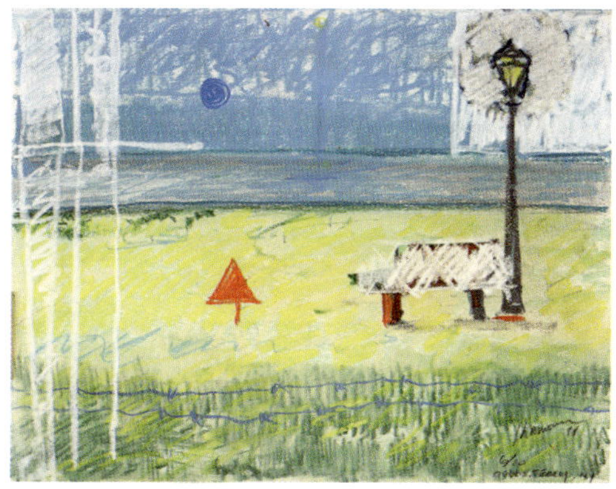

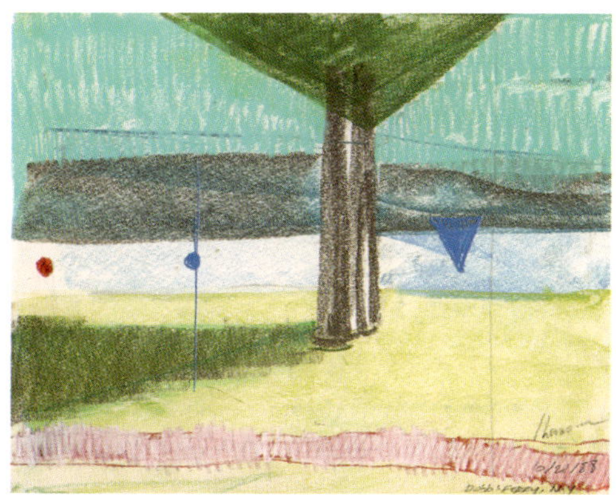

top
116
DOBSFERRY HUDSON SIDE, 1988
Pastel on paper
35.5 x 28 cm

Bottom
117
DOBSFERRY AT THE HUDSON, 1988
Pastel on paper
35.5 x 28 cm

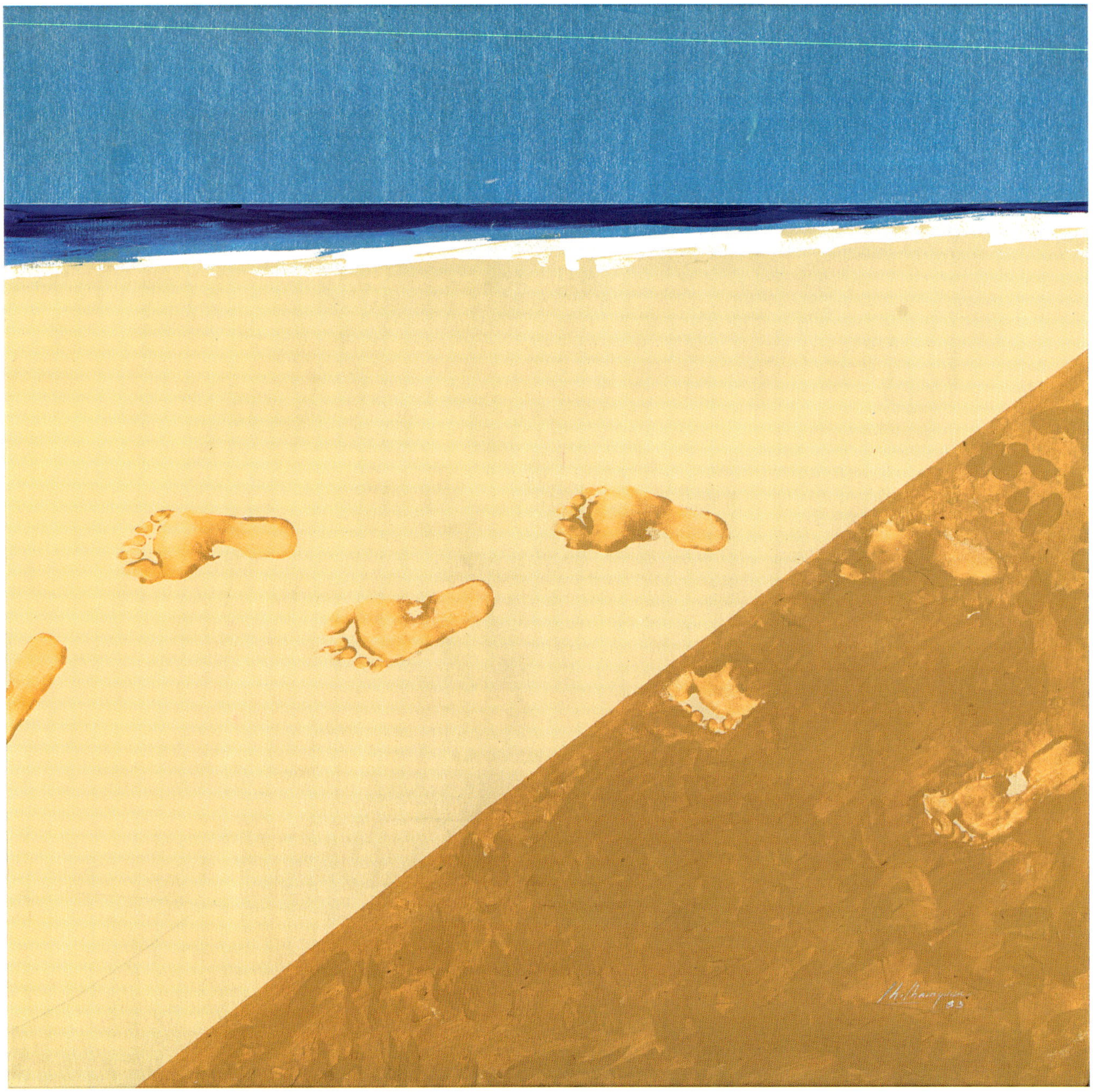

118
FOOTSTEPPING, 1988
Acrylic on canvas
112 x 112 cm

When I met her she offered to give me a six-day show, fitted between two other exhibitions that she had already booked in for December 1988. This exhibition was very successful, and Amal later moved it to the prestigious ski resort at Faqra.

All these successful exhibitions meant that people got to know my work and appreciate it better. In Amal, I saw a

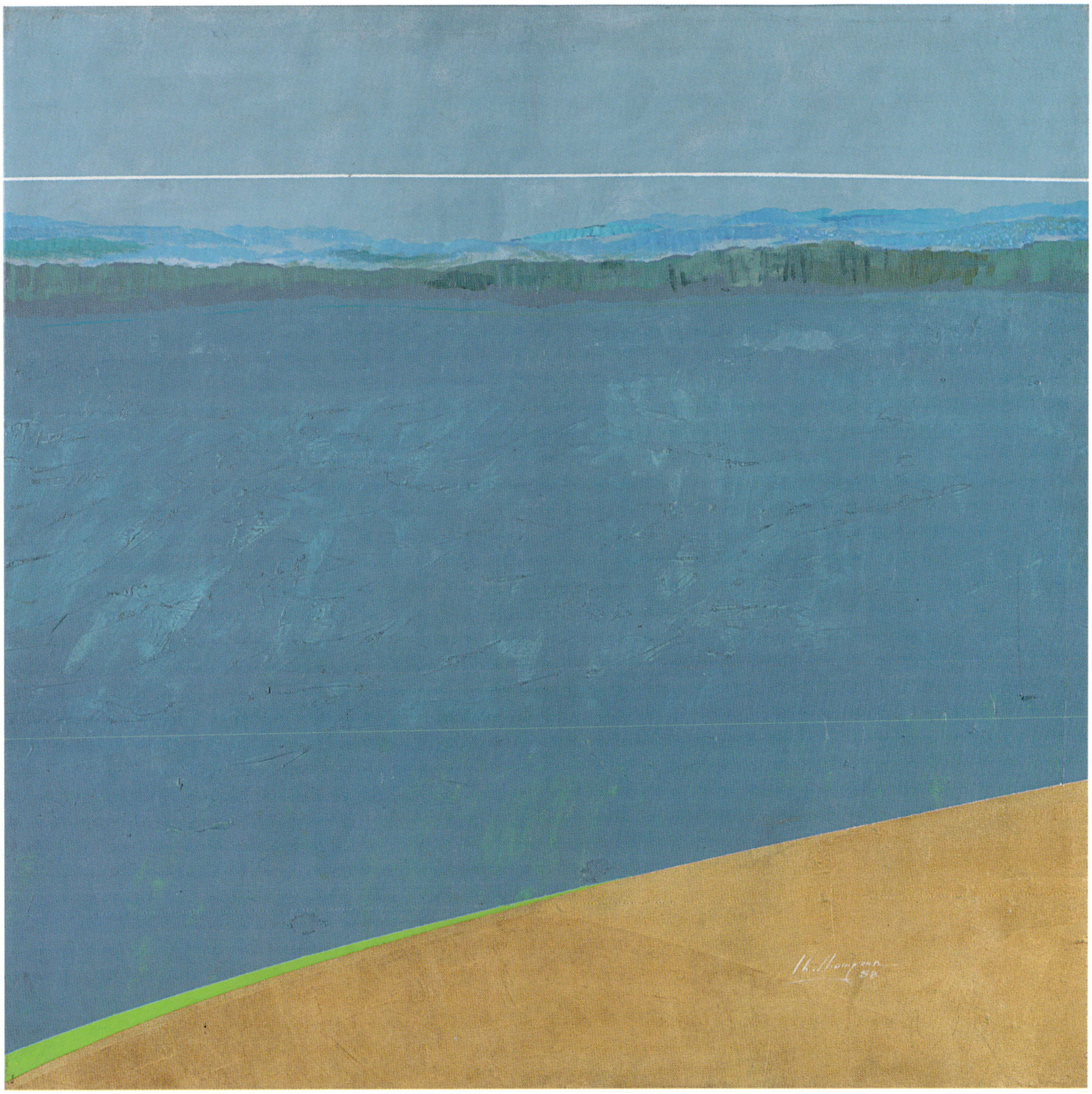

towering figure of the art scene in Lebanon and indeed I still do. Her love of my work, her unlimited and unwavering faith and encouragement, were well pronounced when she told people towards the end of the show: 'A day will come when I will work with no one else but Chaouki.'

119
REMEMBERING SILENTLY, 1988
Acrylic on canvas
112 x 112 cm

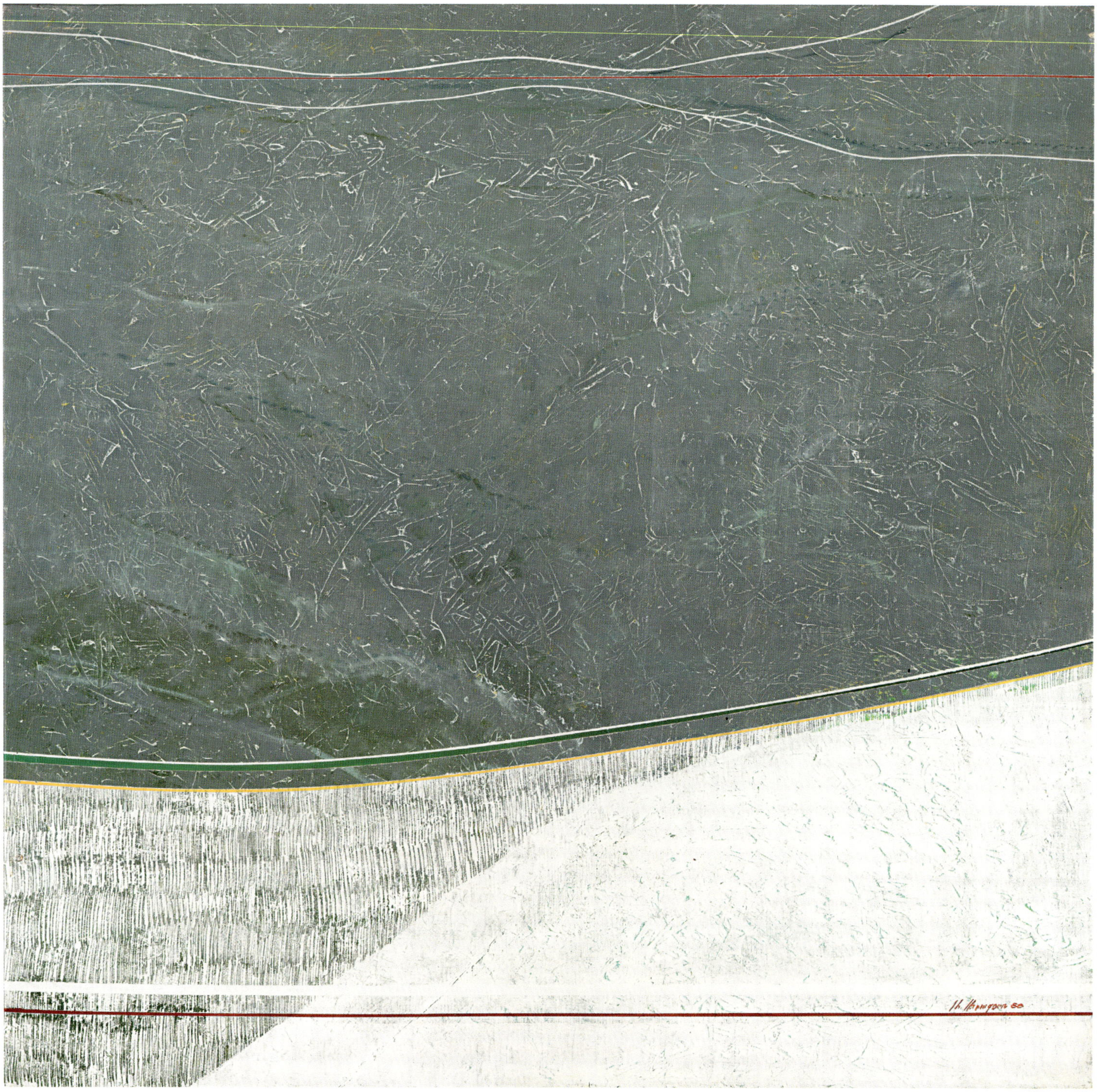

120
THE GREY SLOPE, 1988
Acrylic on canvas
112 x 112 cm

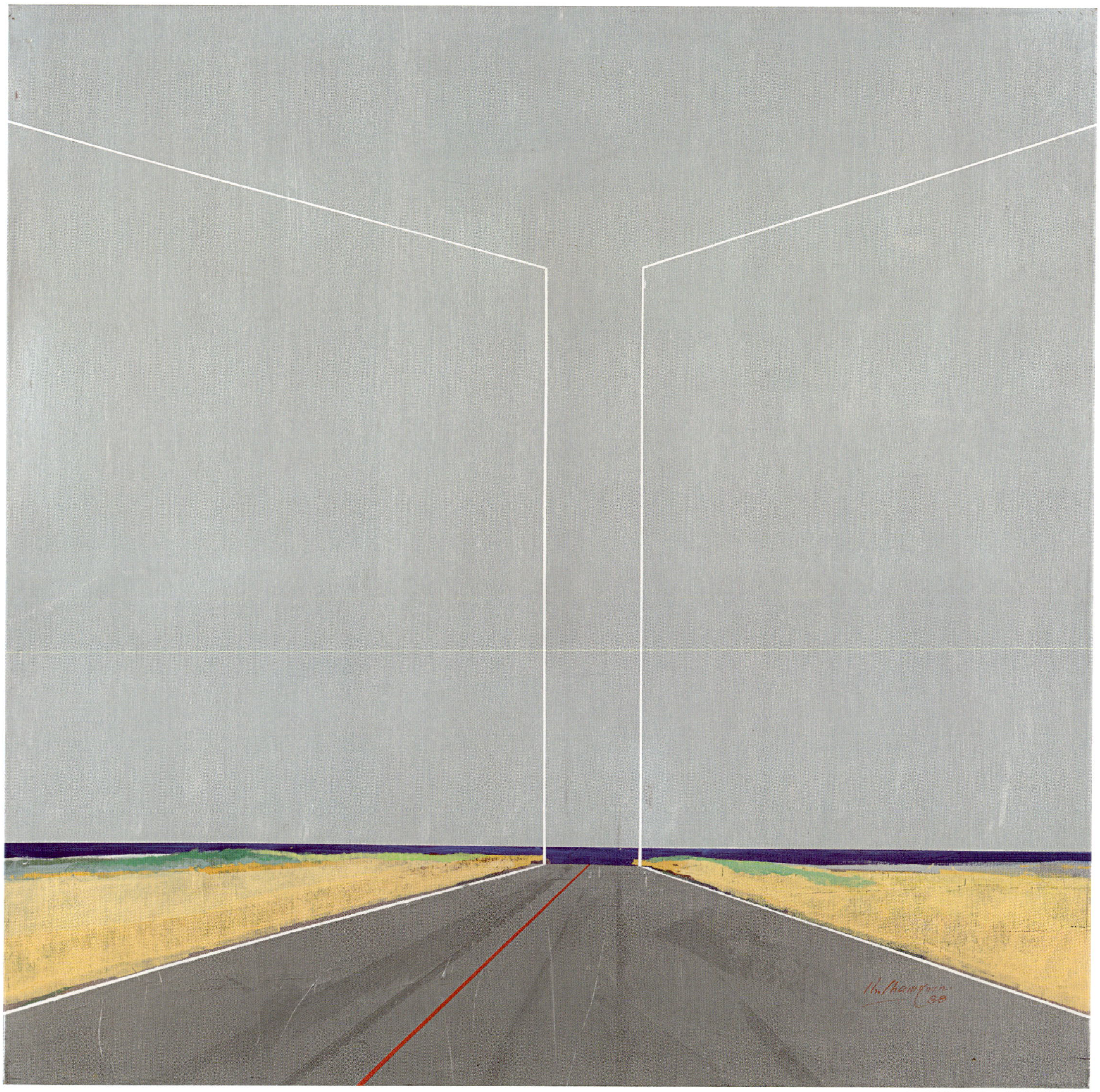

121
THE OTHER HORIZON, 1988
Acrylic on canvas
112 x 112 cm

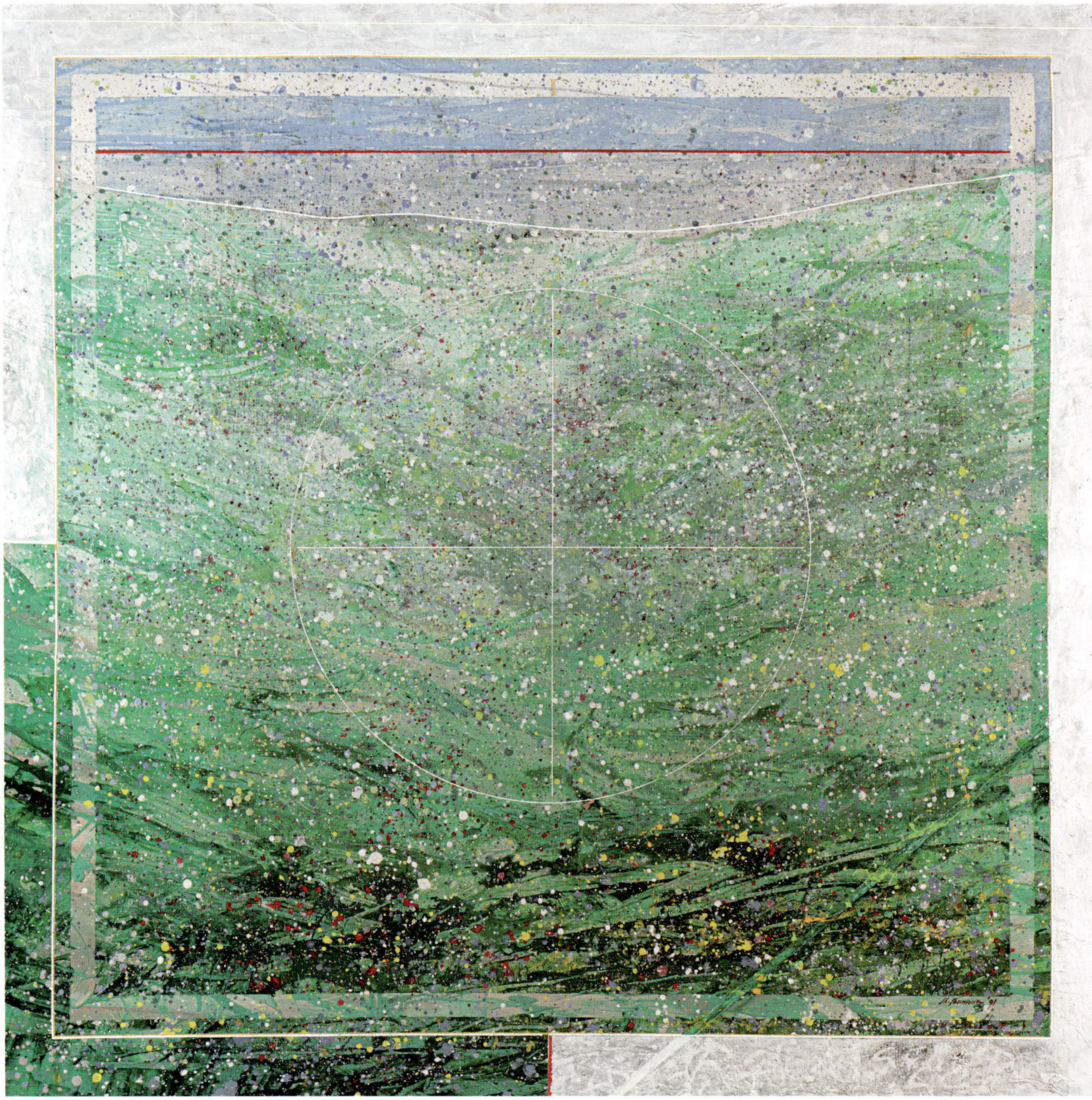

122
ON A SPRING DAY OF 1975, 1991
Acrylic on canvas
224 x 224 cm

Another Experimental Venture

By June 1989 the political situation in Lebanon had deteriorated even more, and the Syrian attacks on the Christian area were becoming fiercer. The office of the President of the Republic had come to an end. The present and future were vague. Now that our children – George, Owana, and our newborn Oriane – were being forced into the bomb shelters with insects, rats, caterpillars and other poisonous little creatures, I decided to take with my family to the States. By now I had obtained a green card, thanks to my sister Lody, but I had to go through Cyprus to get my papers for my family. We crossed to Cyprus by boat, and learned that the Syrians were shelling even the boats heading to Larnaca.

After spending the summer in Cyprus, I finally got my family to New York on Friday 13 September 1989. Shortly thereafter I returned to Lebanon to collect the paintings left over from the Fakra show together with a few more: these would all be used for an exhibition at Opus Gallery in Nicosia, which I had arranged during our stay there.

With the chances dim that fighting in Lebanon would subside any time soon, and my children already started in school, I established myself in a new studio on East Thirteenth Street in Manhattan. I was in a state of self-imposed exile; yet

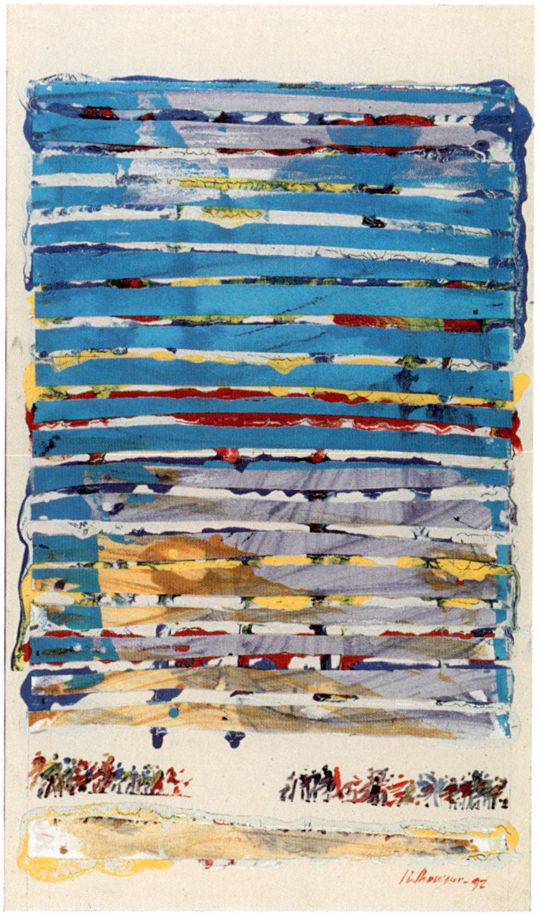

123
WAITING IX, 1992
Acrylic and collage on canvas
65 x 112 cm

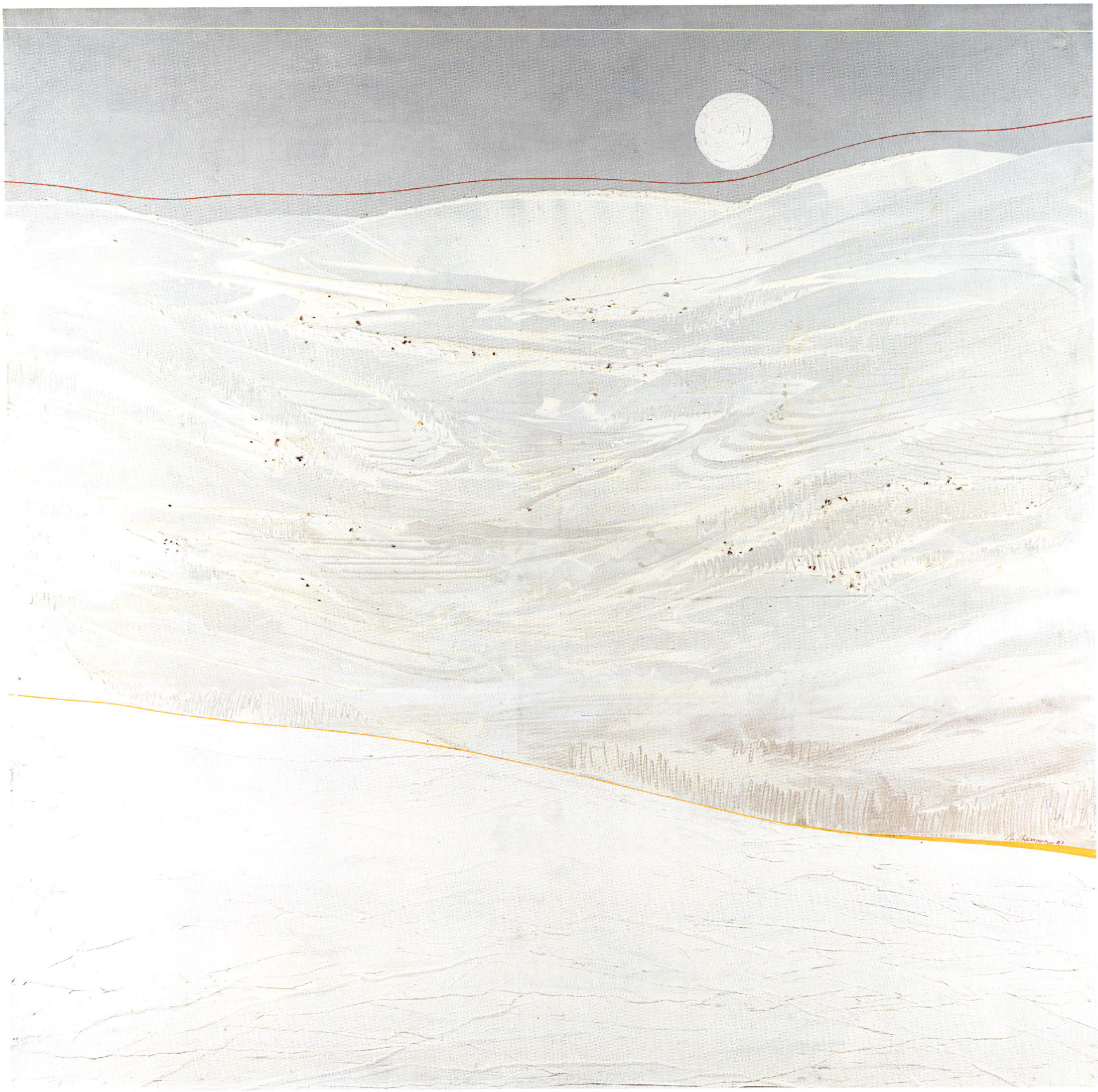

124
RETURNING PEACE AND THE WHITE MOON, 1991
Acrylic on canvas
224 x 224 cm

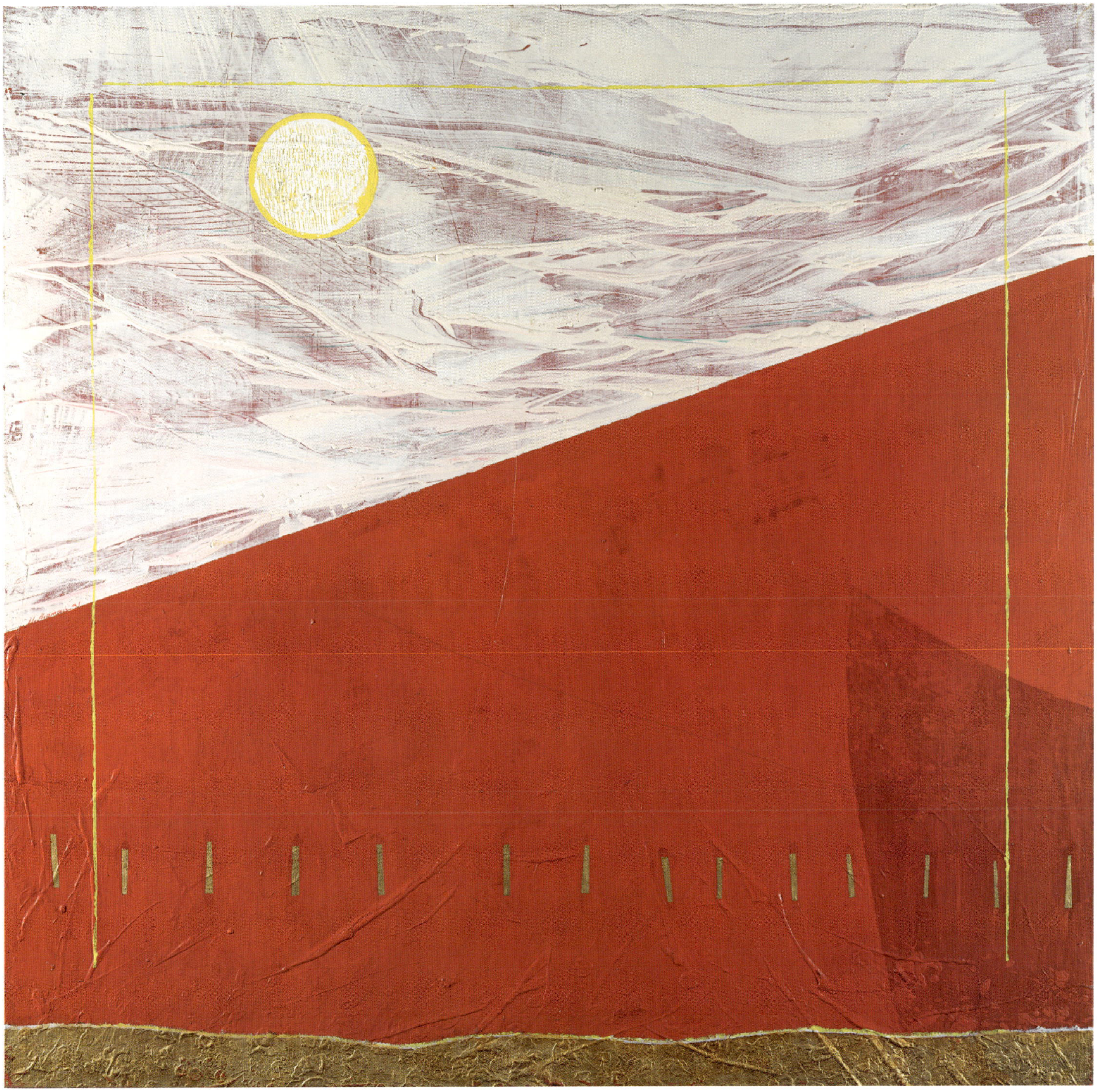

125
THE RED SEASON, 1991
Acrylic on canvas
224 x 224 cm

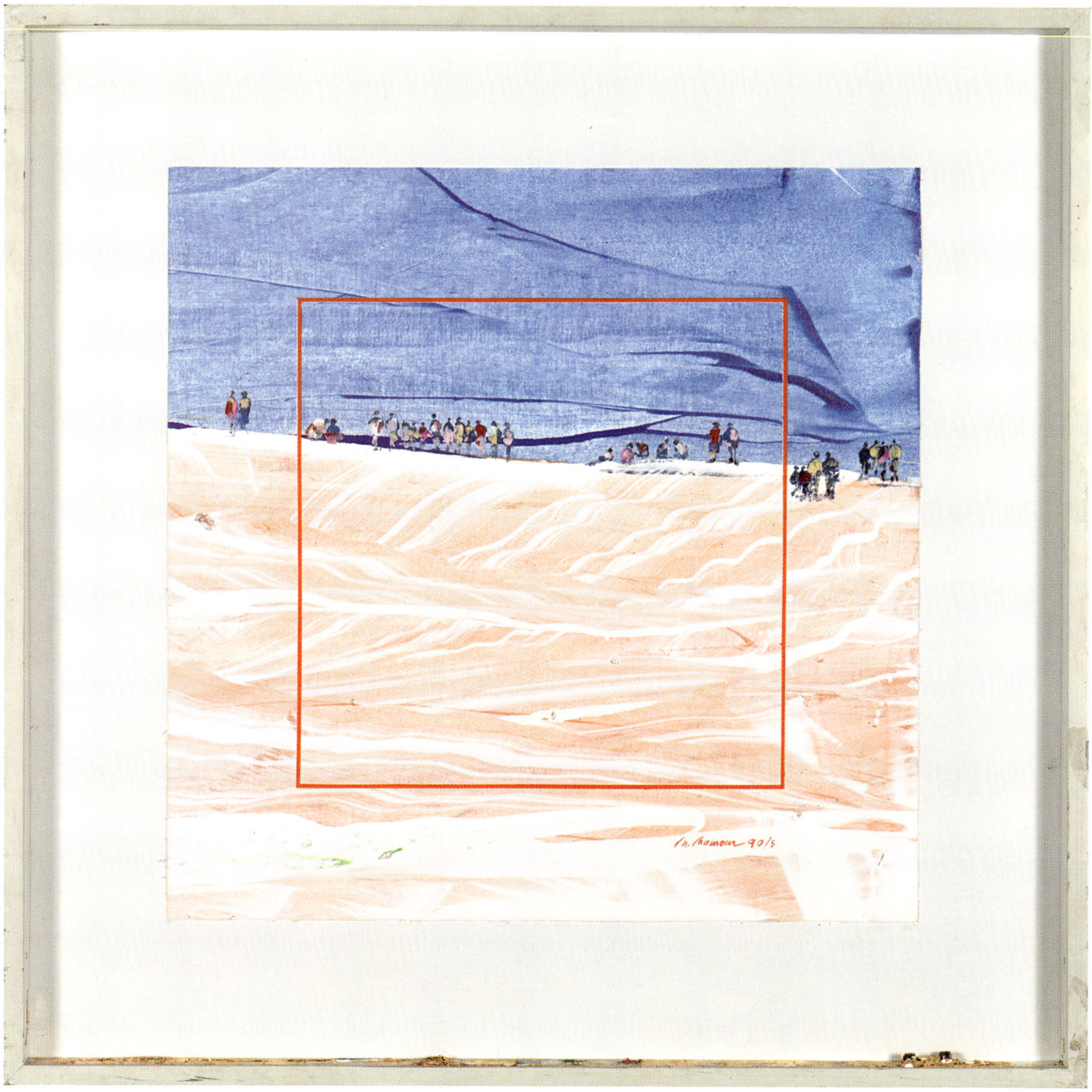

126
A WINDOW TO THE DESERT, 1990
Mixed media
82 x 82 cm

another story of yet another family seeking refuge in the land of the free and the brave. Yet I was still painting Lebanese landscapes – or rather, Lebanese geography and its state of being. Memories travel with us wherever we go, no matter how far.

At first, I thought I was attracted to the natural scenery wherever I was. But I gradually realised that the scenery in memory belongs to no one. It is a land that is trodden by no one. It was the nature that lived only in my memory that made

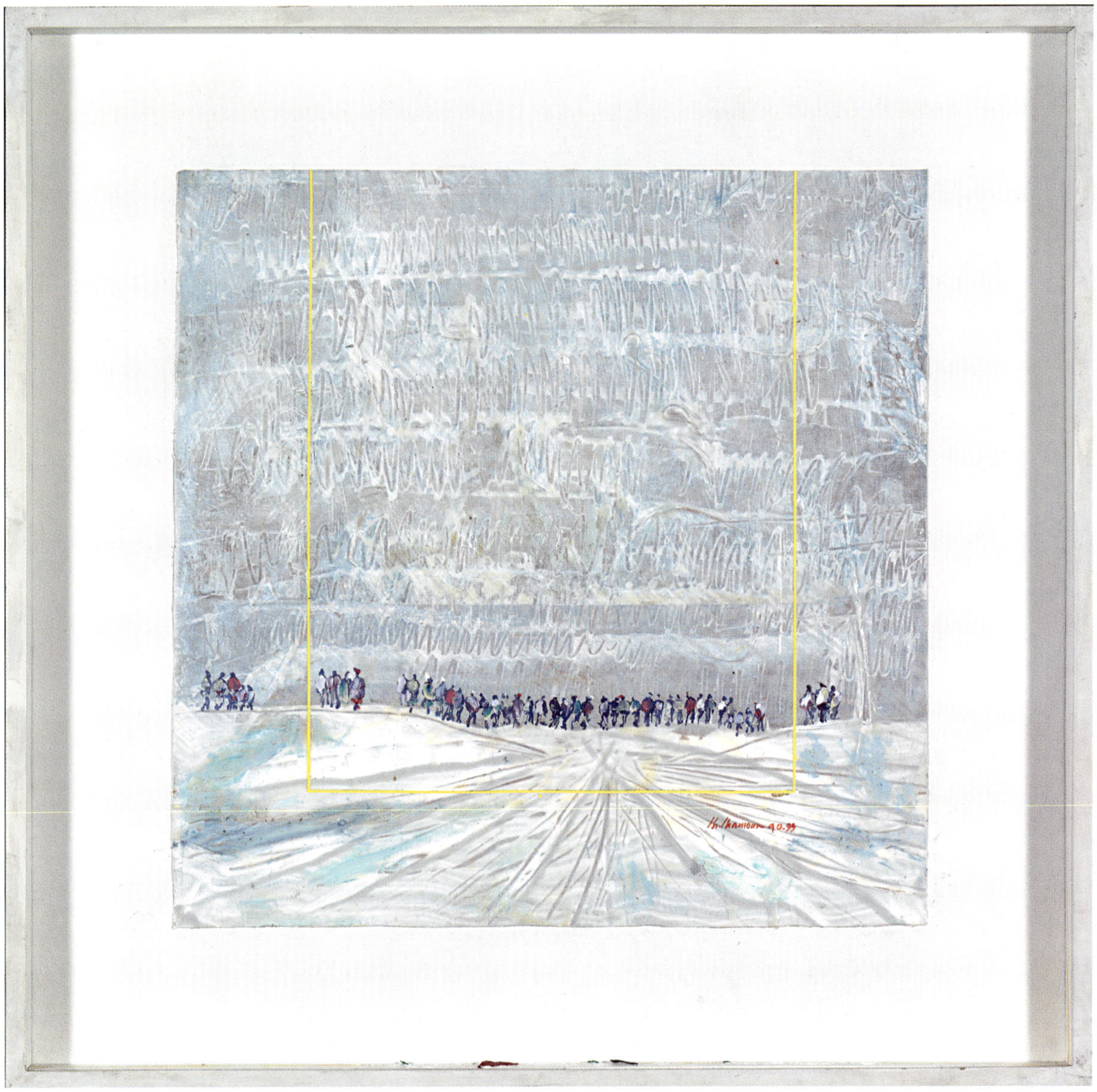

127
THE VALLEY OF THE FOG,
1990
Mixed media
82 x 82 cm

me reborn, and which still recalls my childhood. The past and the present are thus bound together. Most importantly, we no longer distinguish the details of things when we are far away. Only the land remains: everything else vanishes and ceases to exist.

From afar, people's features and names fade away, leaving only comforting thoughts of the land. Lines have a dimension of their own. They perhaps represent the state we are in. Red, yellow, and green lines are intertwined with our fate and the

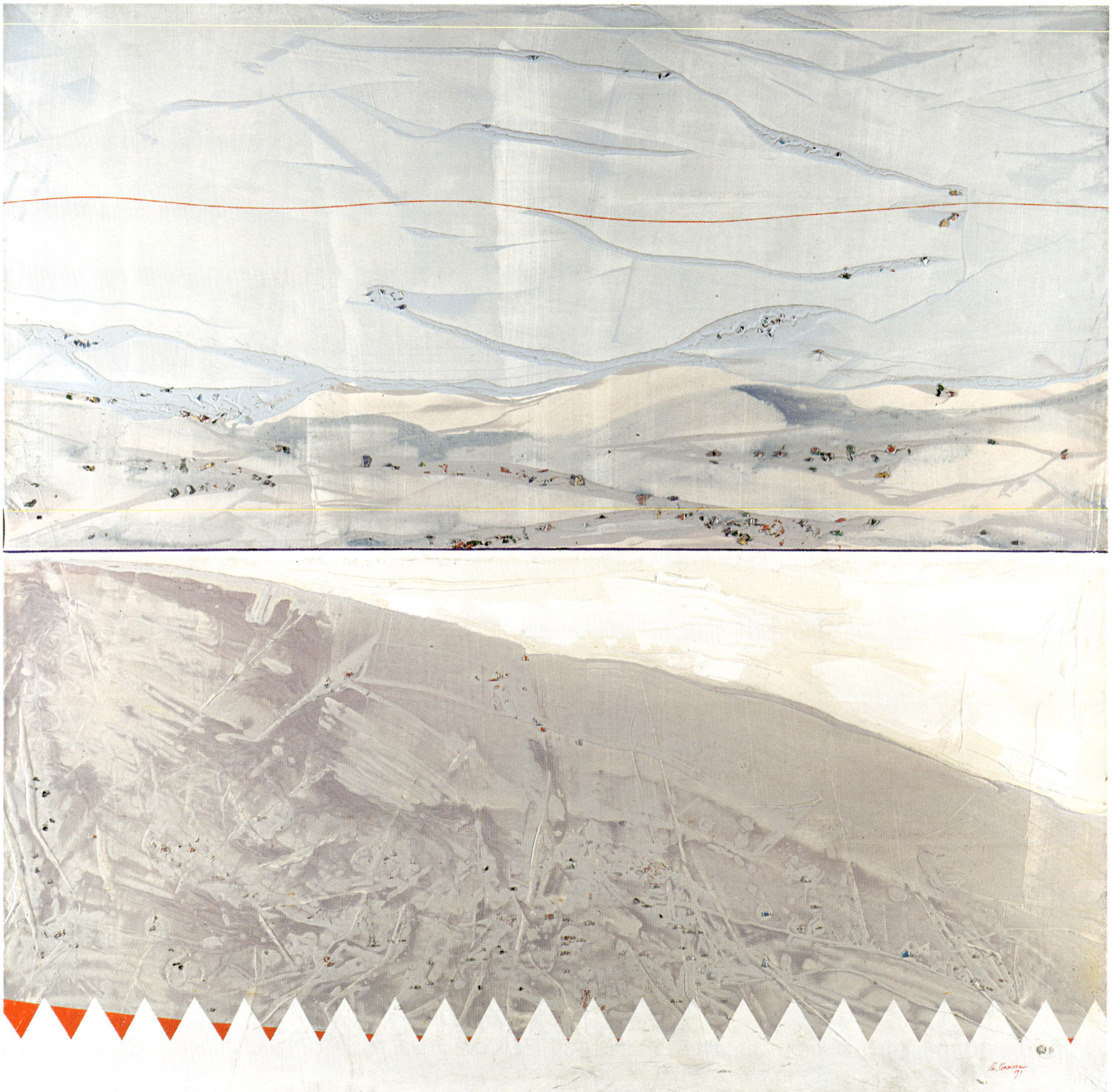

128
MY HOME IS BEHIND THE LINES, 1991
Acrylic on canvas
224 x 224 cm

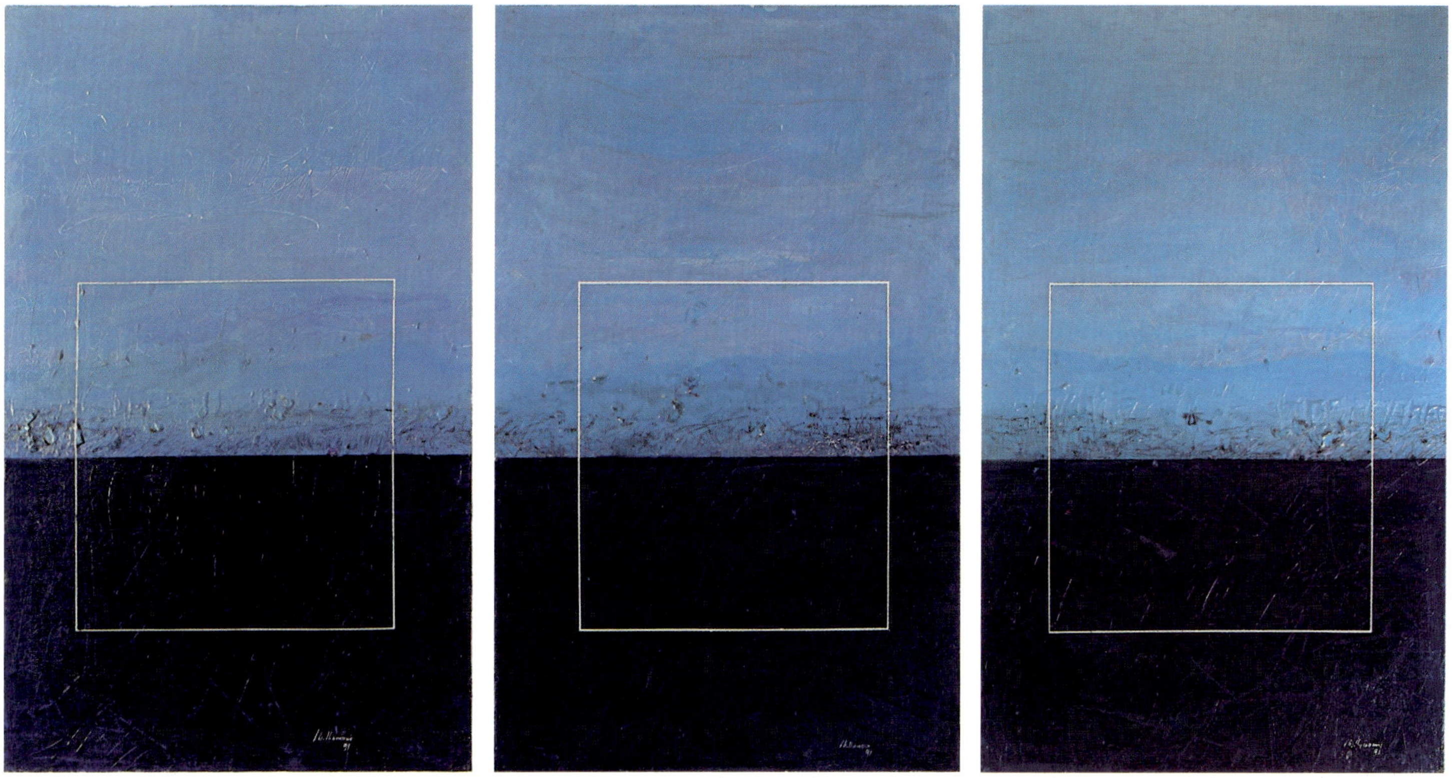

129
LEBANON FROM LARNACA, 1991
Acrylic on canvas
294 x 137 cm
(Triptych)

fate of the painting's ground. In a previous stage of my work, I used to introduce lines into my paintings but did not dare to validate them. I kept them quiet, but the silence concealed real elements: I now thought that the viewer of the painting was entitled to know its essential meaning.

Two important elements came together in my work: the childhood that never grows old in my memory; and the art experience that dips its brush into each event until it obtains it. The childhood is ever-present because we refuse to grow; we refuse to see things in their real magnitude. In my memory, there is an immense plain. I used to shout out in the Beqaa plain, and no one used to hear me. I also used to believe that the mountains were the limit of the world. There was a kind of fog between me and the scenery, so I never saw its true face. When I dipped my brush in this substance, I did not create a foggy scene so much as I painted a foggy reality – perhaps because I was away from Lebanon and started to see it burning

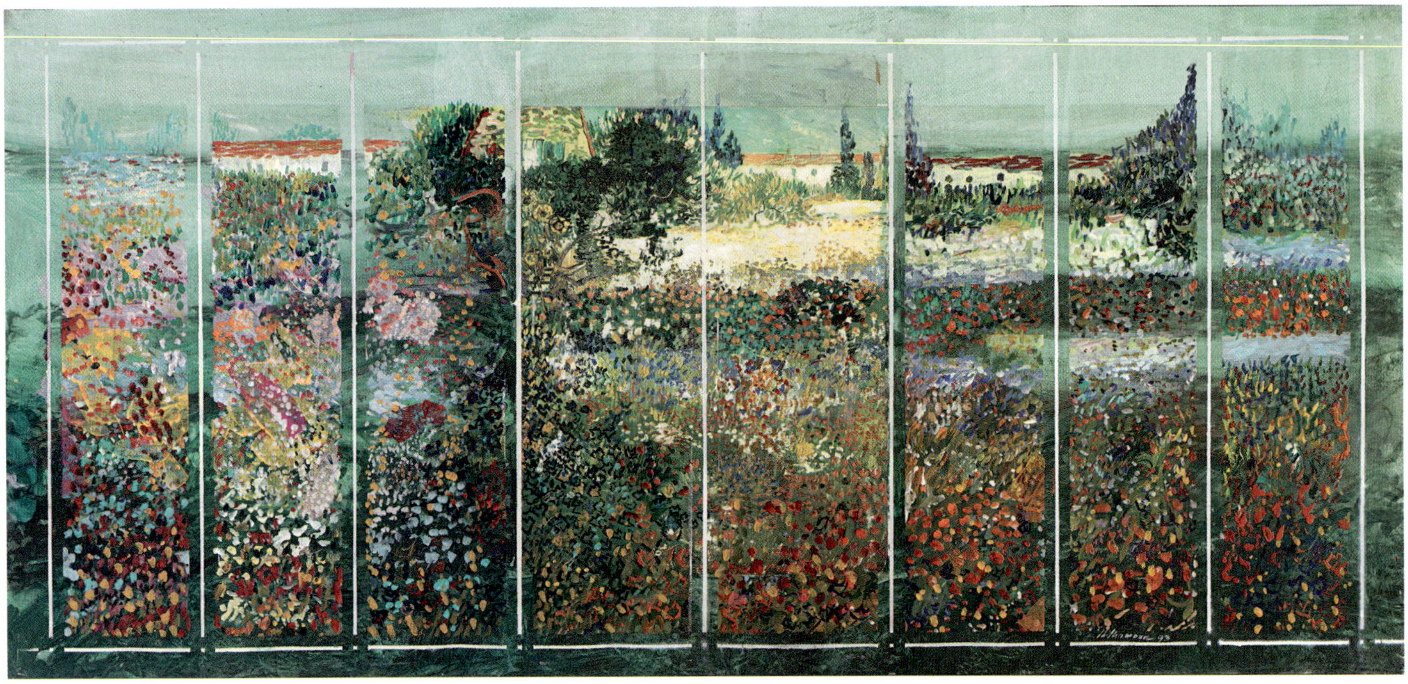

130
TRIBUTE TO VAN GOGH, 1993
Acrylic on image transfer on canvas
233 x 112 cm

on TV. The scenery somehow validated this reality, hence my return to the scenes of my childhood.

A person cannot breathe without history. This is our history, and it is essential that we return. As a child, I was delighted every time I went back to the village. I used to write passionate poetry about the wooden ceilings, the vast plain before me, and so on. But there is a second phase that takes a person away from the simple things that are within his grasp, and he becomes a slave to his ambitions. With every step that takes him further away from his borders, he feels that he becomes more important. We believe that our movement is ascension, while in fact it is nothing but distance. Going back to childhood requires reconciliation with this reality. The fear that accompanied childhood was just an escape from it: we return with joy, and we benefit from this return.

Indeed, I was nostalgic during my first two years in New York. I was afraid of my past, until my aim in life became my art and my culture. This time I felt true exile. My first painting about Lebanon was created in Larnaca; it was

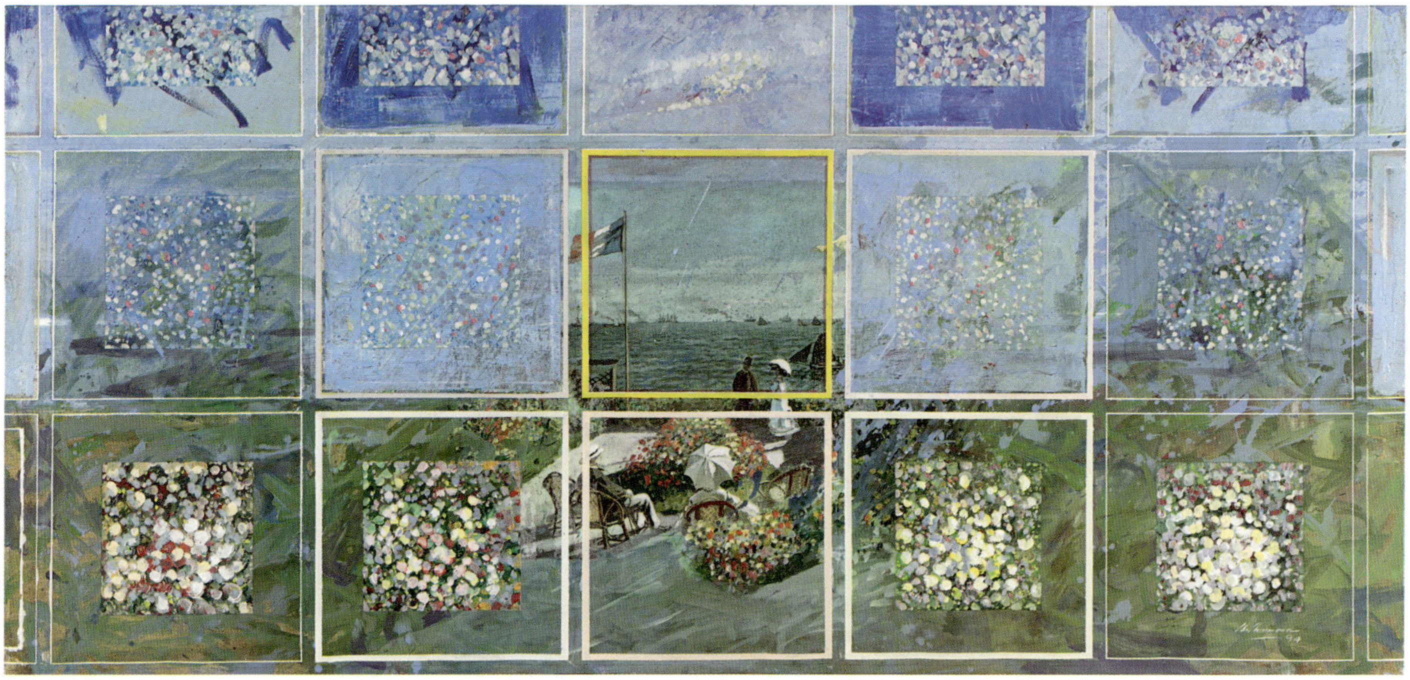

131
TRIBUTF TO MANET, 1994
Acrylic on image transfer on canvas
233 x 112 cm

as if Larnaca had become a gate at which we Lebanese stood, wondering if we could enter. We were scared for our country, afraid it was going to be taken away. In 'Men and Rocks,' my final project at the Lebanese University, my focus was on Nahr el Kalb, which had been the field of my activities during my last two years at the Fine Arts Institute. In parallel, I used to reminisce about my childhood; the days I spent visiting the site, listening to my teacher tell stories about it, even hearing the sound of the invaders' chisels chipping away at the rocks and leaving their names in it. Twenty years later, the grown-up child painted something for the glory of the land and the glory of men.

Images from the first Gulf War served to enhance my melancholia, and the search for an added value to my aesthetic research became an ever more onerous burden. I bought toy tanks, planes and cannons and broke them like children do. I used them along with golden paper on some of the painting's
126, 127 horizontal edges, representing the war of oil and gold.

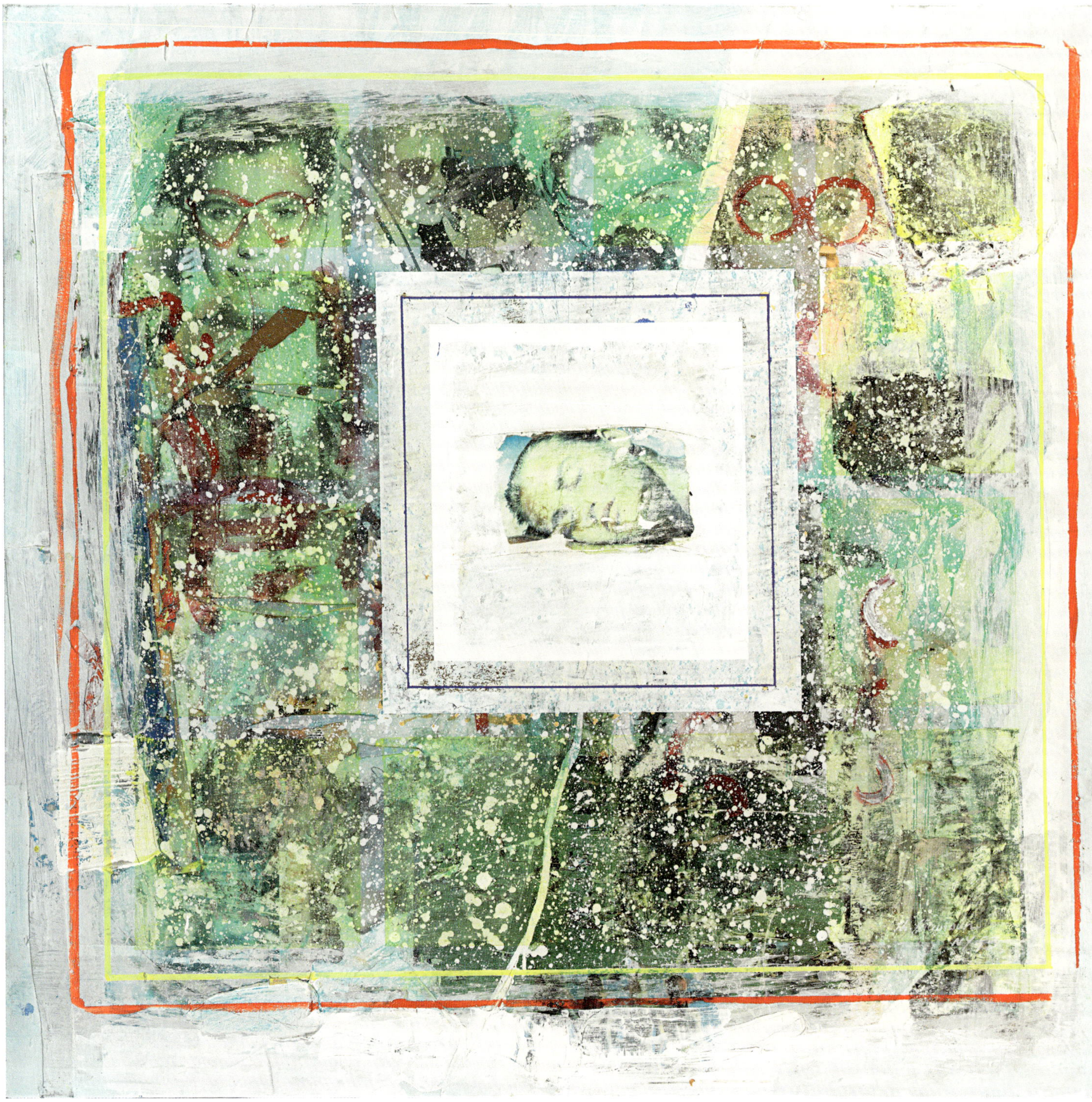

132
UNIDENTIFIED ICON, 1993
Acrylic on image transfer on canvas
112 x 112 cm

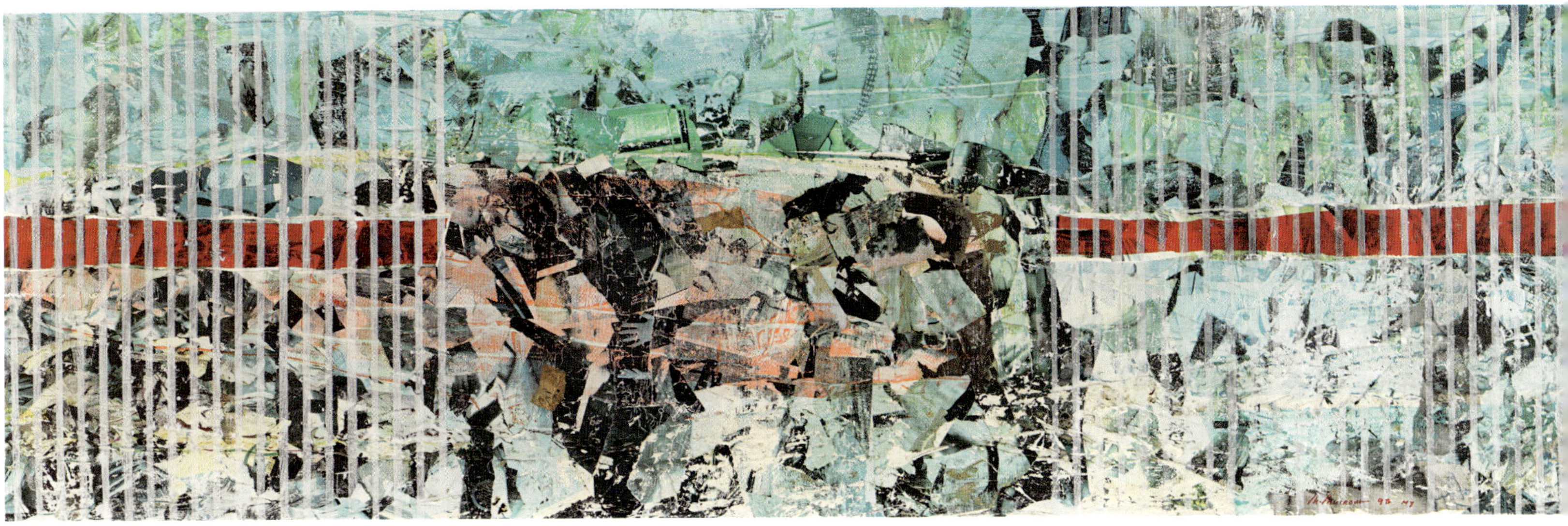

133
MEMORIES, 1992
Acrylic on image transfer on canvas
234 x 88 cm

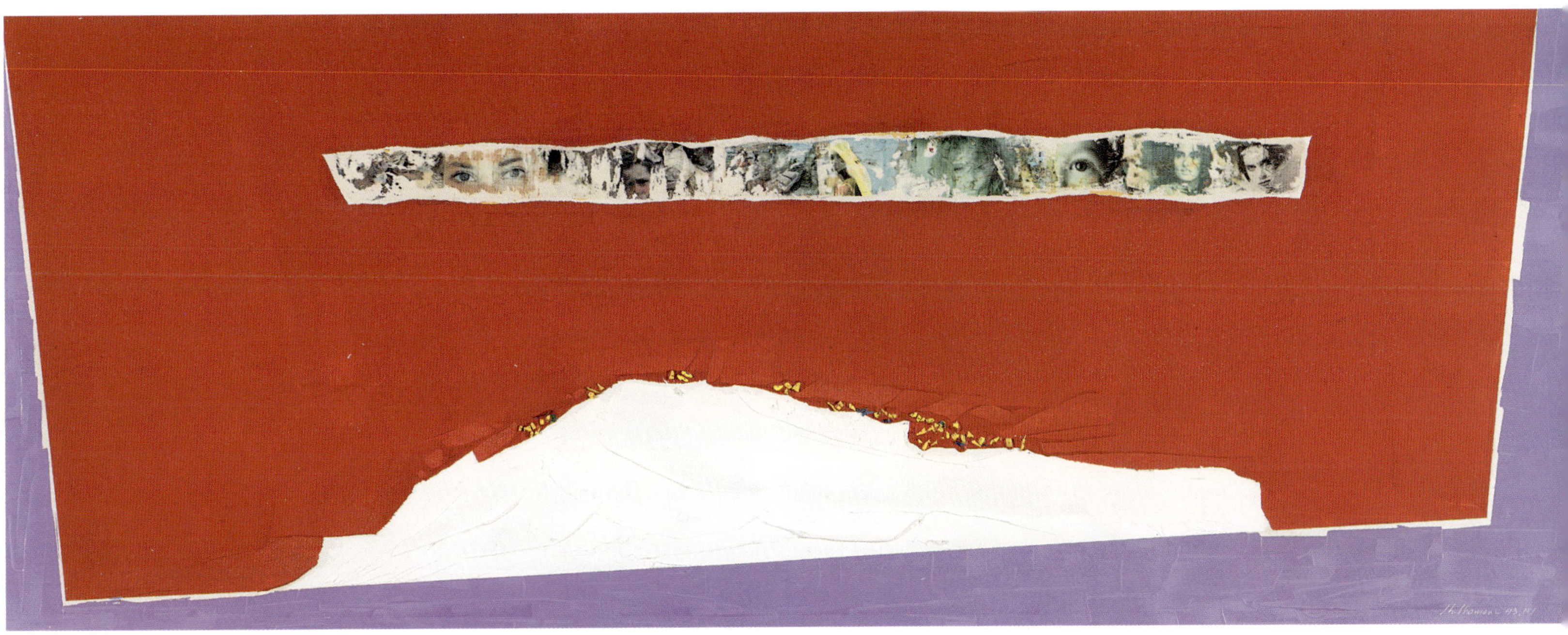

134
EYES IN THE RED, 1993
Acrylic on image transfer on canvas
233 x 112 cm

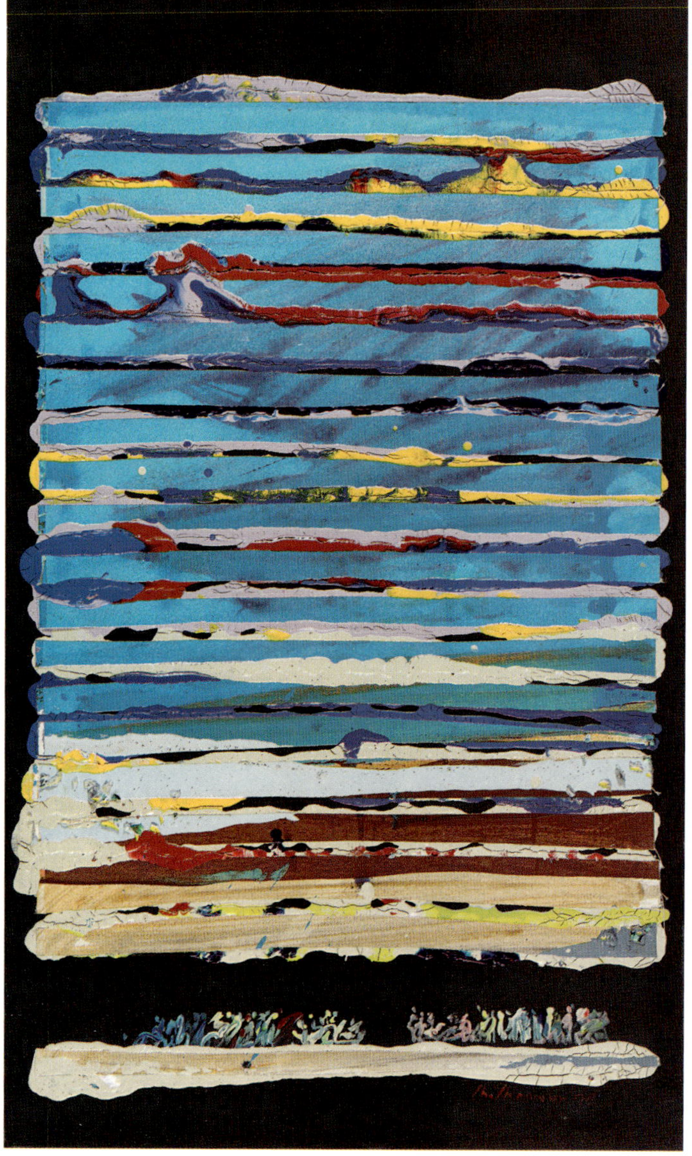

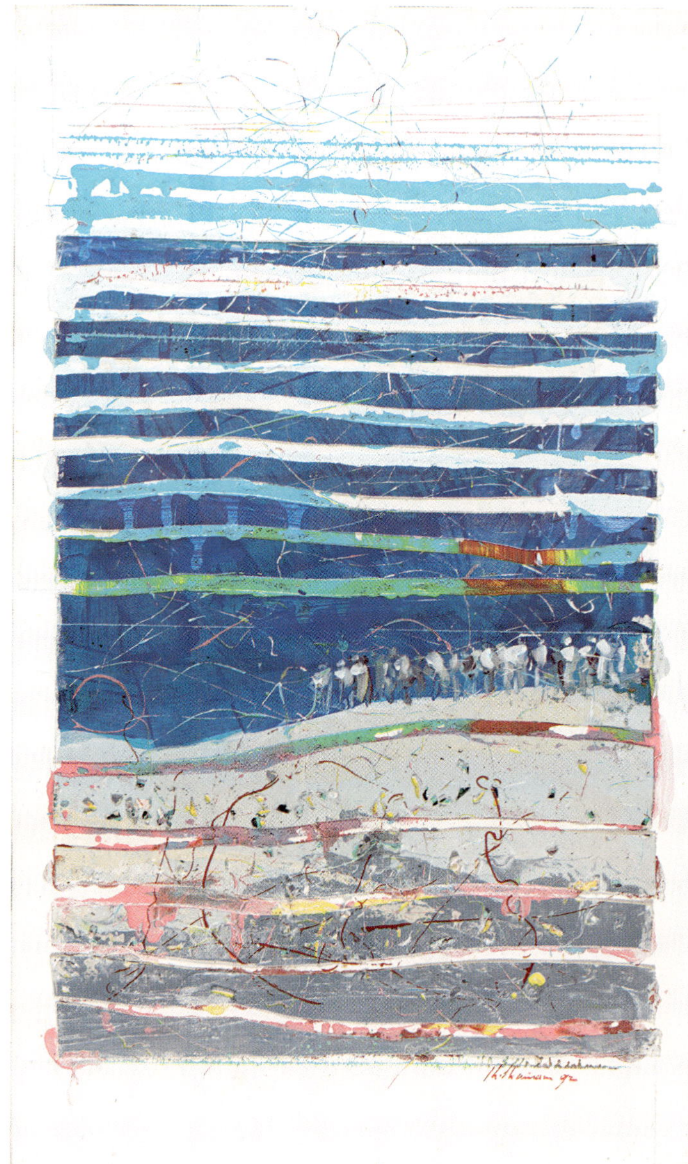

135
WAITING IB, 1992
Acrylic and collage on canvas
65 x 112 cm

136
WAITING IV, 1992
Acrylic and collage on canvas
65 x 112 cm

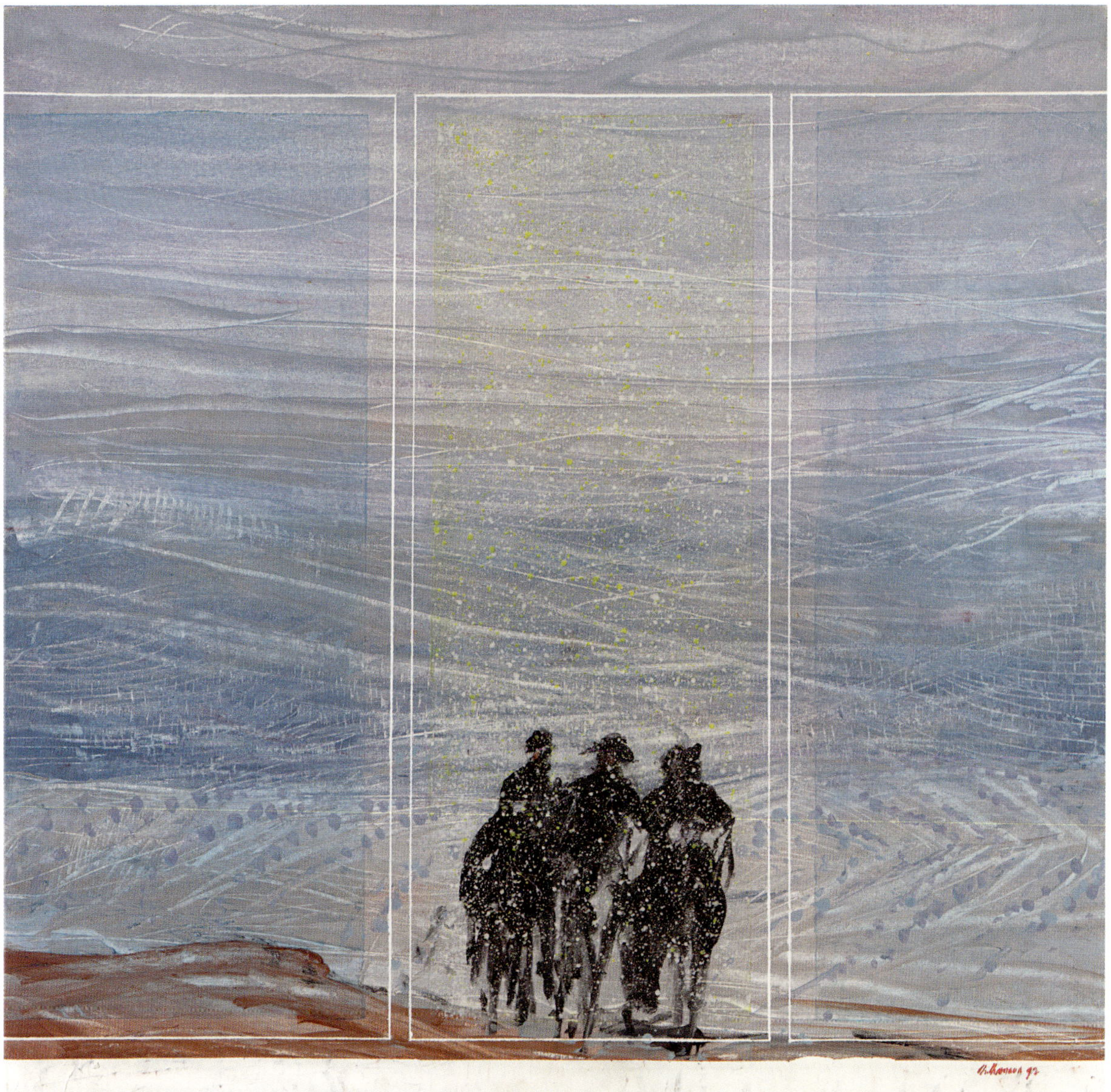

137
WAITING FOR THE HERO, 1992
Acrylic on canvas
112 x 112 cm

Like war machines, their presence was not celebratory but rather ironic and caricaturist. I found it difficult to add these elements to my painting. I had to break toys in order to convey my message. And yet entire countries were broken and no one lifted a finger. I wonder if I disfigured the bare scenery with this, but the truth is that the general situation was disfigured first.

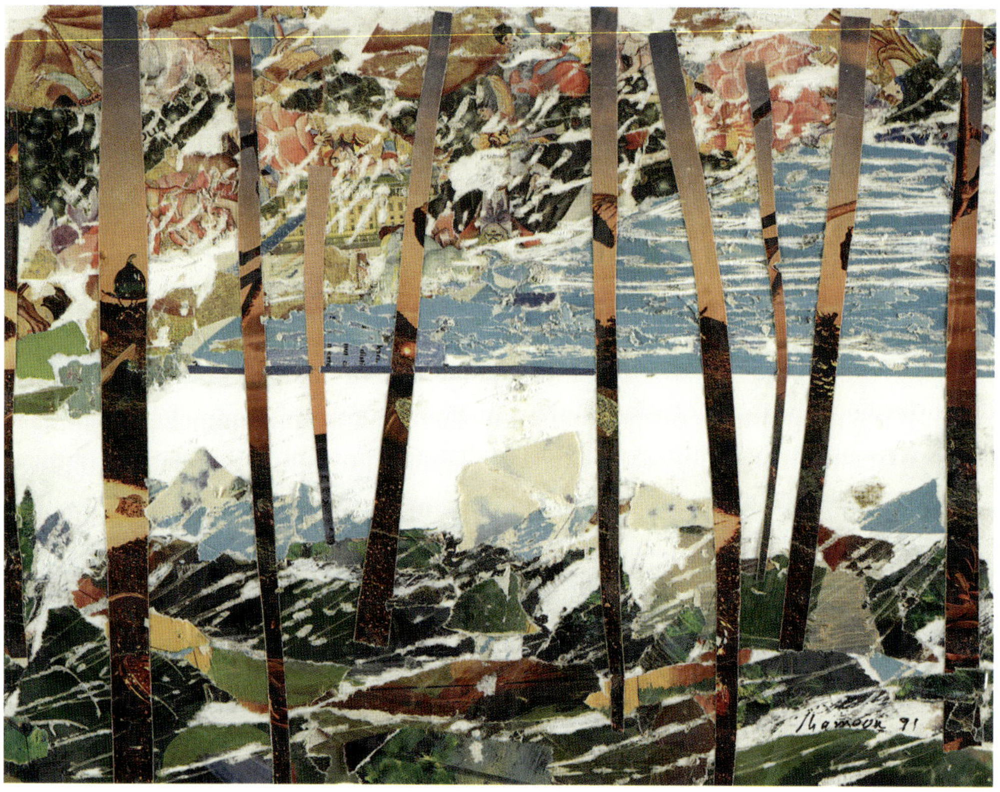

138
MOSTLY LEBANESE, COLLASCAPE XIV,
1991
Paper collage on paper
73 x 28 cm

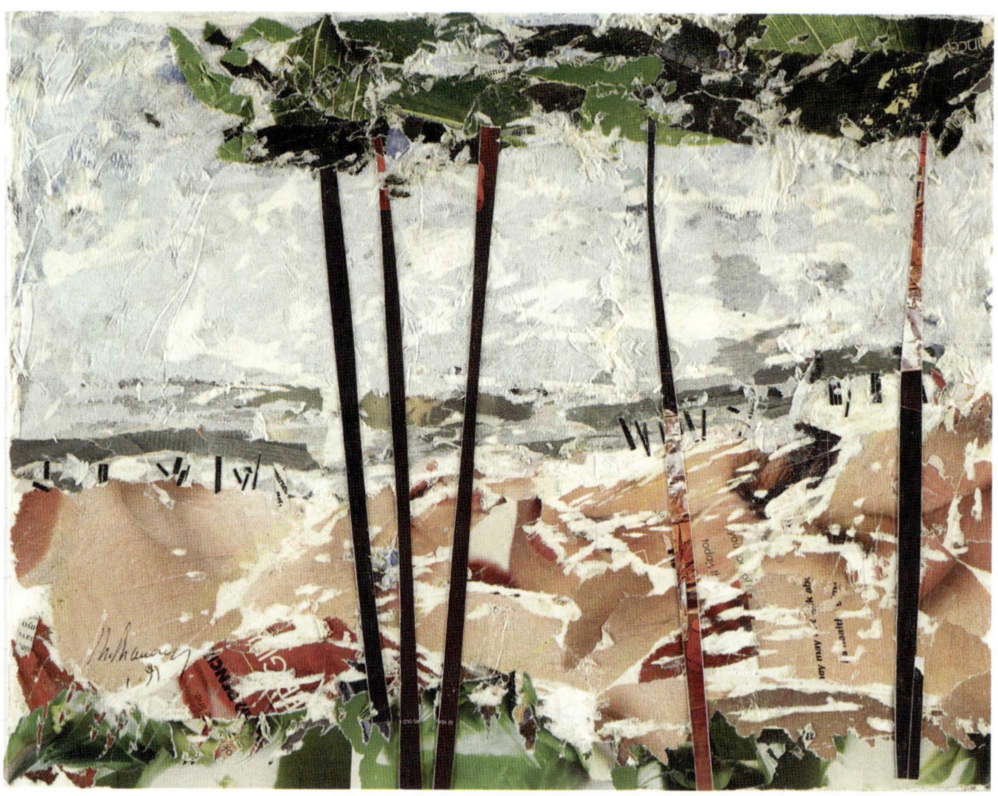

139
MOSTLY LEBANESE, COLLASCAPE I,
1991
Paper collage on paper
73 x 28 cm

122, 124 'On a Spring Day of 1975', 'Lost Peace ... Found Peace',
125, 128 'The Red Season', and 'My Home Behind the Lines'. These paintings among many others portray the Lebanon I was trying to recreate in the East Thirteenth Street studio. They were first shown as part of the 'Lebanese Artists in Diaspora' exhibition staged by the Rihanys' Platform International Gallery in Washington in 1991. They were also exhibited at the Marriott Hotel, New York, at the invitation of the American Friends of Lebanon Group. Soon a new note of peace came from Lebanon, so I wrapped my paintings and hurried back to Beirut for an exhibition at the Epreuve d'Artiste Gallery in Kaslik, another at The Carlton Hotel Exhibit Hall.

In 1991 I started to experiment with calligraphic expressionistic direction using ink on paper. I did this in parallel with a series of collage-on-paper works using
138–141 colour images from magazines portraying 'mostly Lebanese'
142–144 landscape scenery and some abstract compositions with word fragments as titles. The calligraphic experiment would have to wait another twenty years before I addressed it seriously: I became heavily involved in developing collage concepts using different materials and techniques. The arbitrarily torn images that I pasted to each other and then onto drawing paper recalled synthetic Cubism to some extent: they also gave the impression of colour pasting in the building of a landscape.

When I moved on to canvas-on-canvas collage, a

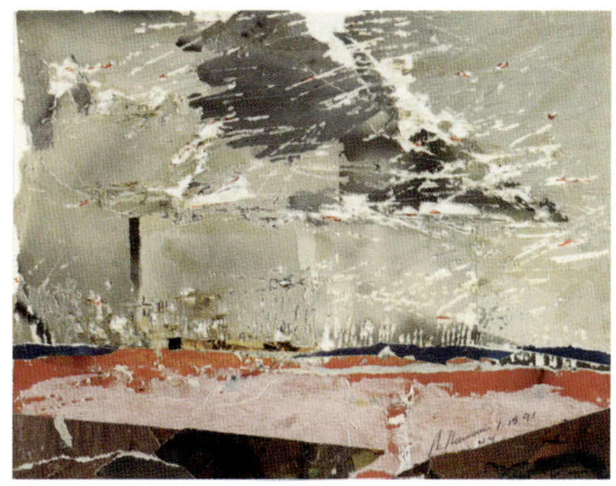

140
MOSTLY LEBANESE, COLLASCAPE III, 1991
Paper collage on paper
73 x 28 cm

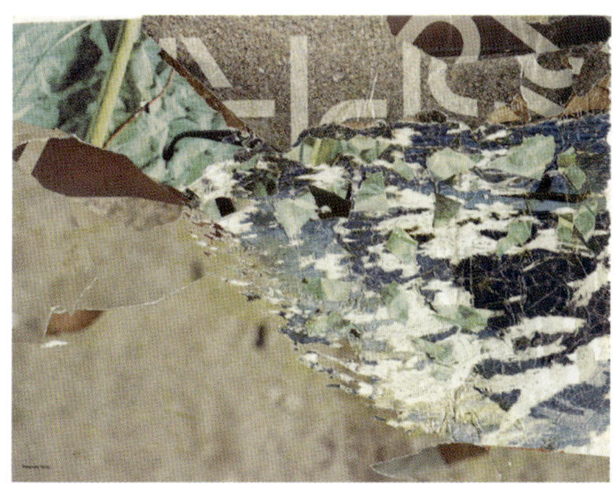

141
MOSTLY LEBANESE, COLLASCAPE II, 1991
Paper collage on paper
73 x 28 cm

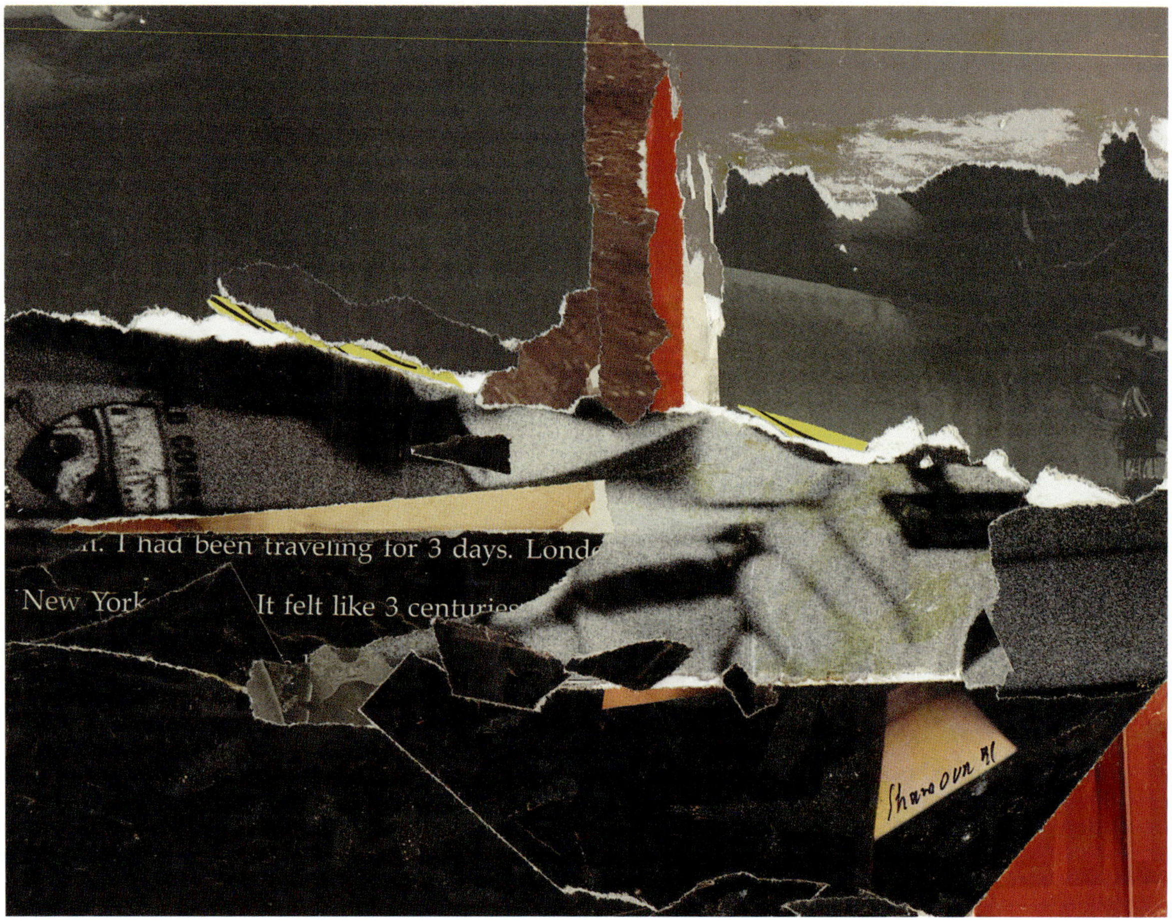

142
I HAD BEEN TRAVELLING FOR 3 DAYS, 1991
Paper collage on paper
73 x 28 cm

new group of artworks allowed me to push beyond these initial possibilities. The queues of people at the bottom of the canvas, reminiscent of all the queues the Lebanese were subjected to, were indicative of the waiting mood that inhabited me in the shadow of growing obscurity. Meanwhile, the vertical strata of the painting of pre-cut tinted canvases dipped into contrasting colours allowed for breathing avenues
in an aesthetically built environment. 123, 135, 136

The other development was a combination of acrylic, collage and print transfer on canvas. This series culminated
in 'Tribute to Van Gogh' and another, 'Tribute to Manet'; 130, 131
each work presented a new iconic image, a record of in-print
materials transferred onto canvas and speaking for their times. 132–134

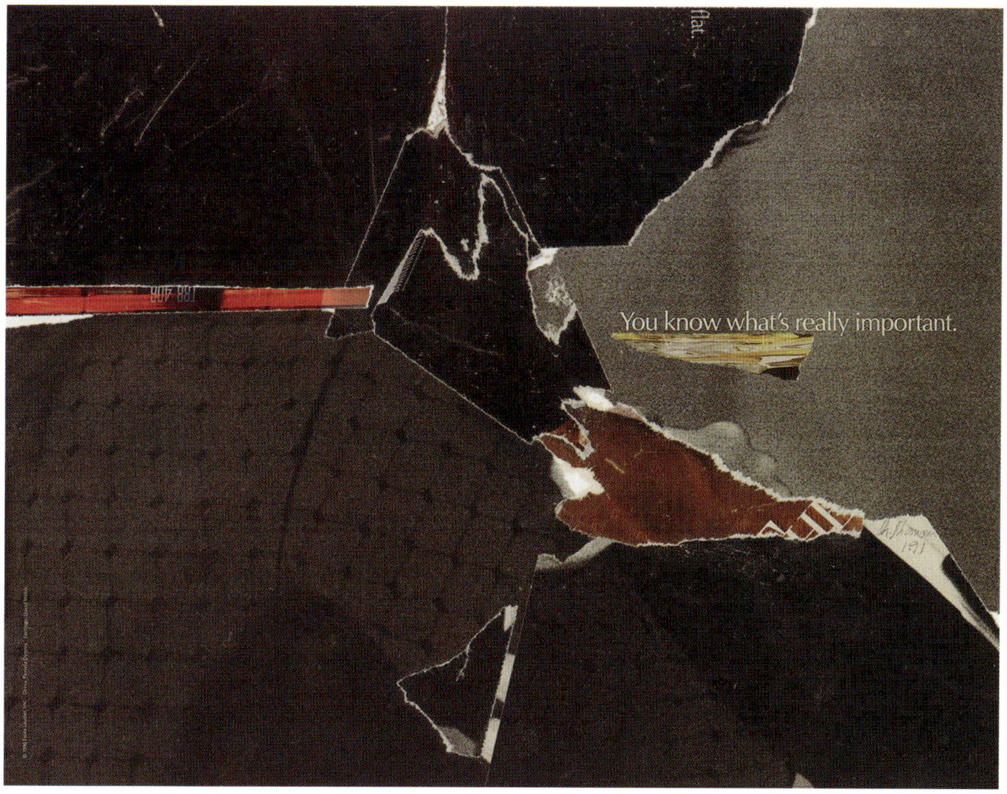

143
YOU KNOW WHAT'S REALLY IMPORTANT, 1991
Paper collage on paper
73 x 28 cm

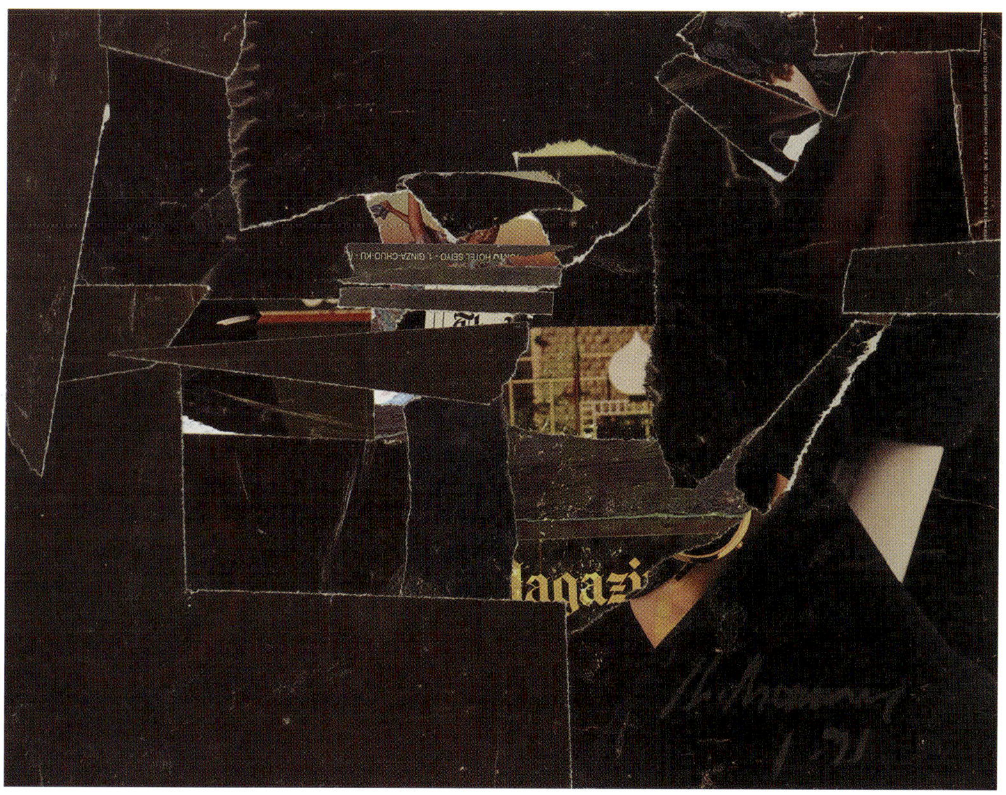

144
HOTEL SEIYO, 1991
Paper collage on paper
73 x 28 cm

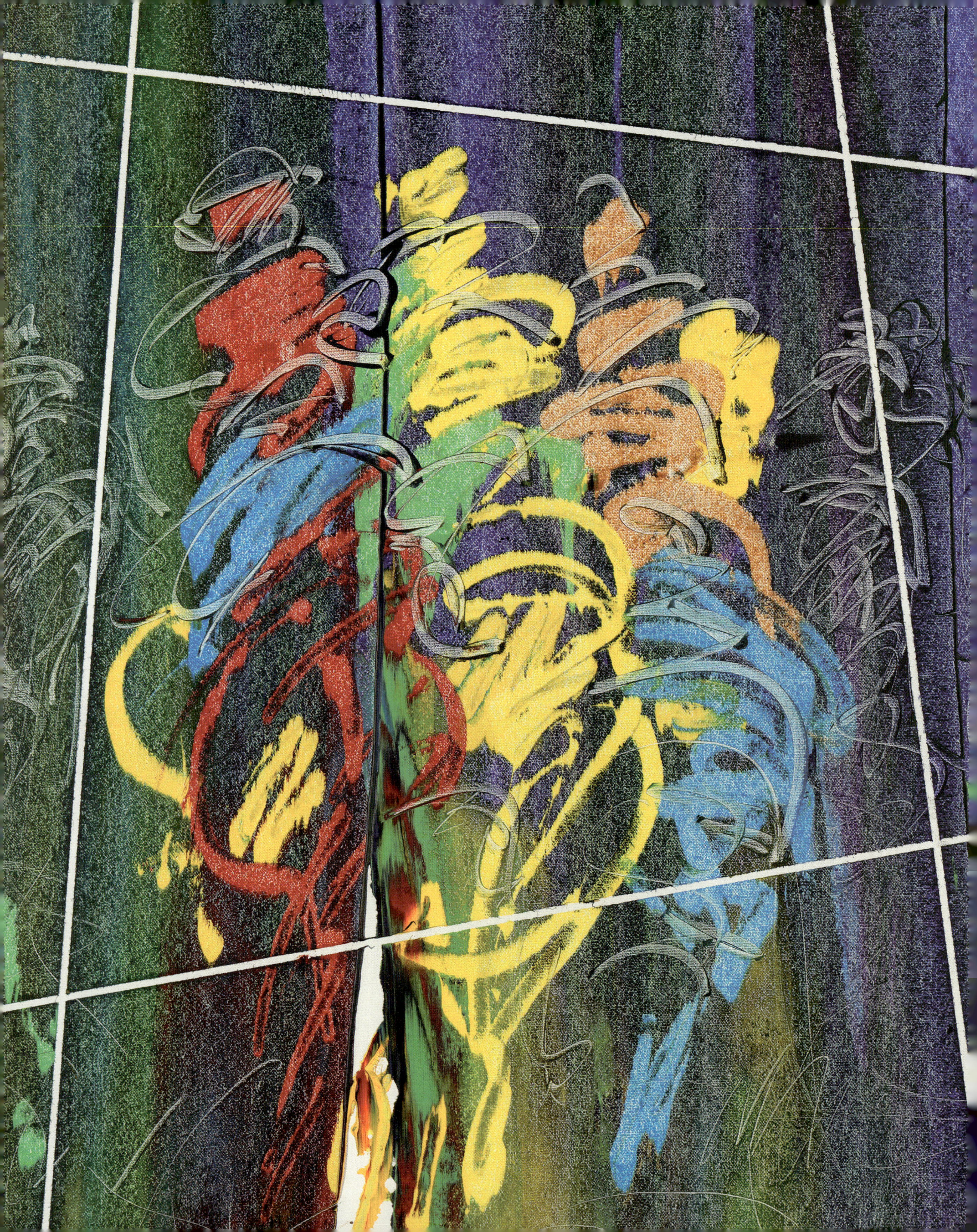

Shuttling Again Between New York and Adonis

In 1994 the situation started to stabilise in Lebanon, so Leila and I decided to return home to resume our teaching positions at the Lebanese University. I resigned from my job as director of store planning and design with Dress Barn, a post I had occupied since 1992. Mr Jaffe, the chairman of the board, with whom I had worked directly to reshape the corporate image and who was a collector of my art, rejected my resignation and offered to keep me on as design consultant. Between semesters and in the summer vacation I would travel to the US to design new prototypes and supervise implementations of the stores I had designed via the Internet.

At the end of May 1995 I accompanied my son to Belmont racetrack. This trip triggered a new involvement with painting horses in motion and I did a series of
146, 147 watercolour paintings on the subject. I had the urge to explore this concept further, as there was a real potential to turn this experience into a major aesthetic development. But nature, the centre of my love affair with art, was again my refuge, my
145, 148, 149 sanctuary. The horses had to run unwatched until 1996.

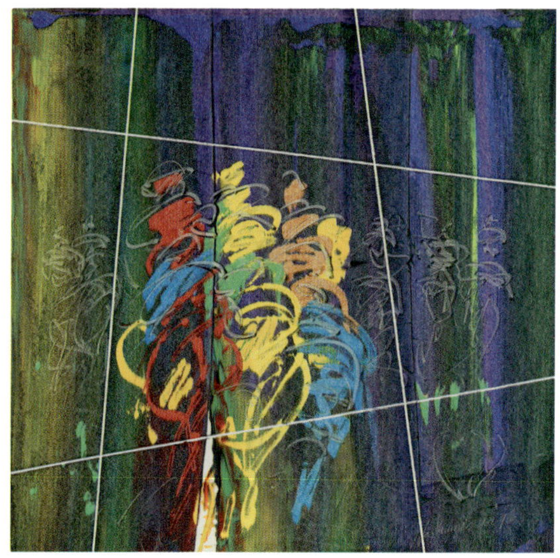

145
IN THE RACE, 1996
Acrylic on canvas
76 x 76 cm

Facing page
(detail)

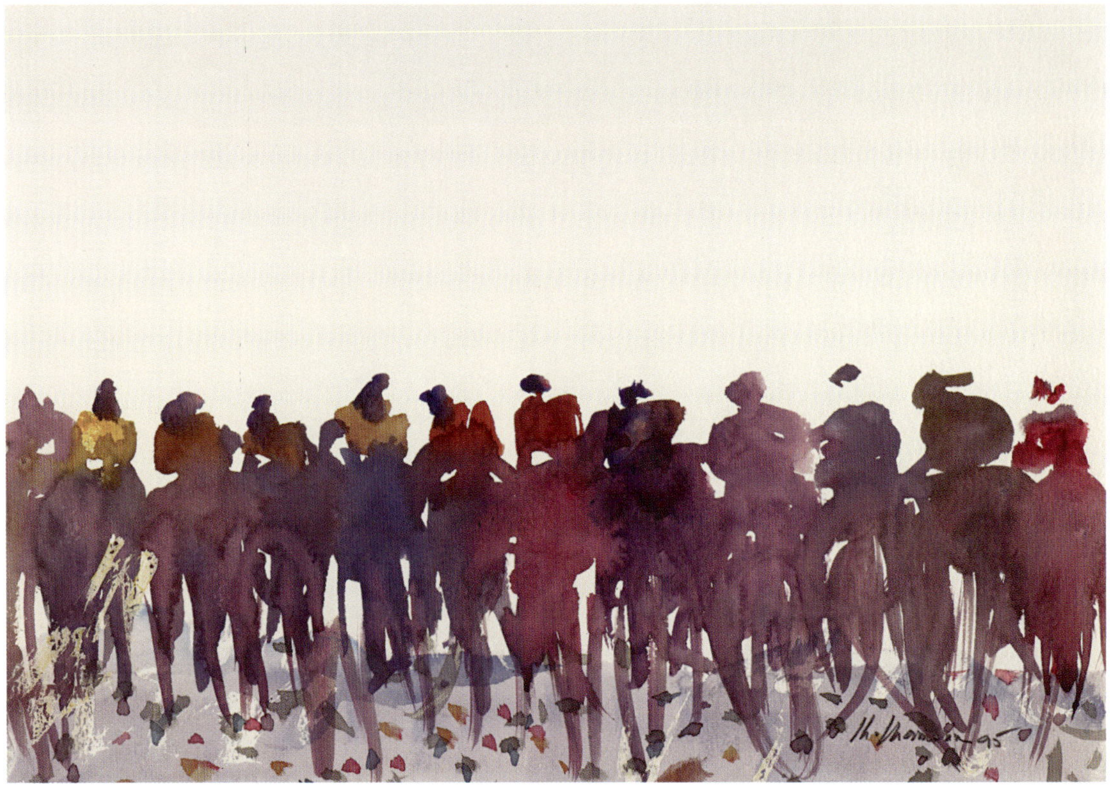

146
RACING IN
BELMONT III,
1995
Watercolour on
paper
35.5 x 25.3 cm

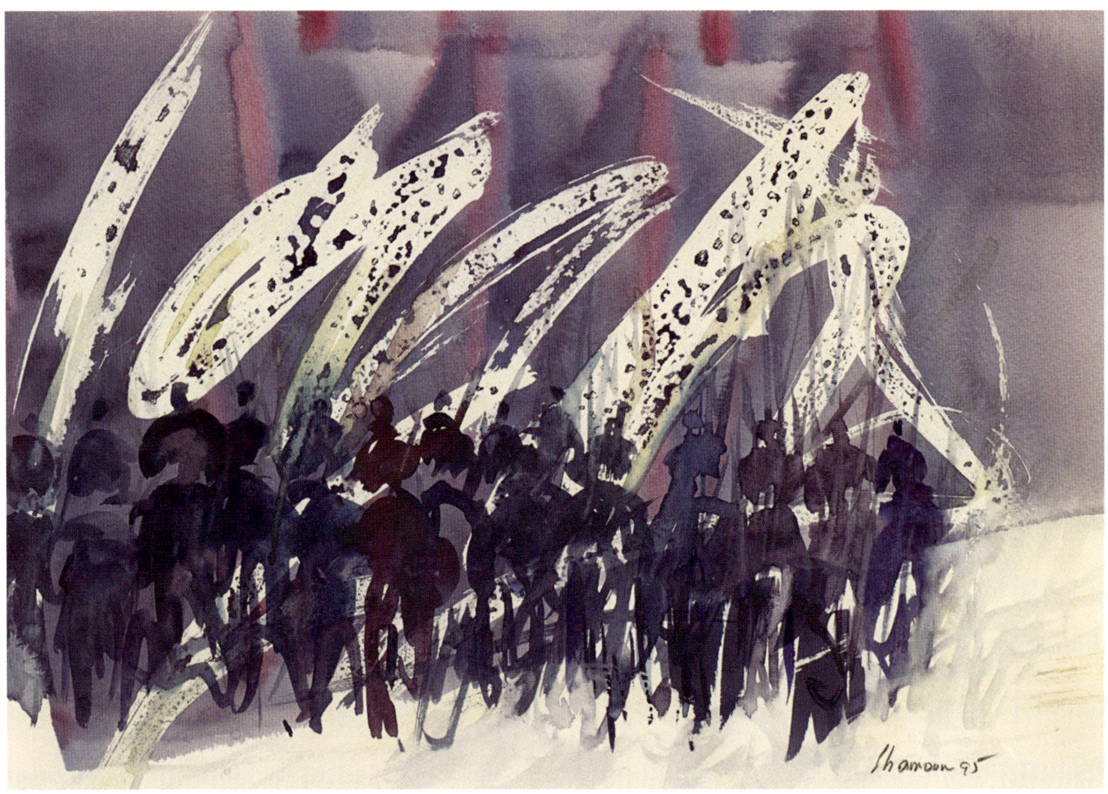

147
RACING IN
BELMONT IX, 1995
Watercolour on
paper
40 x 30 cm

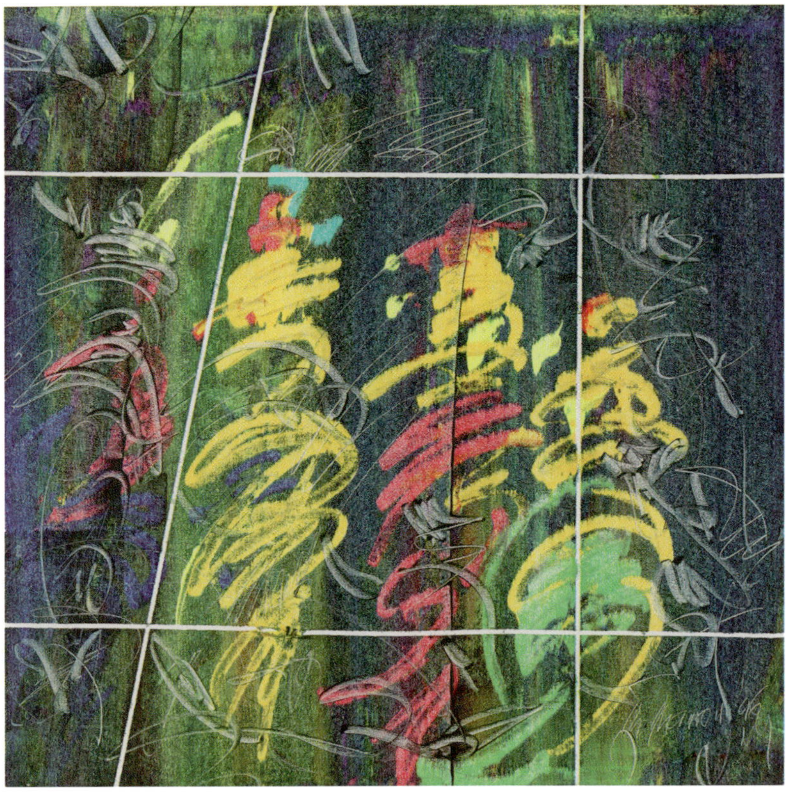

148
RACING #1, 1996
Acrylic on canvas
56 x 56 cm

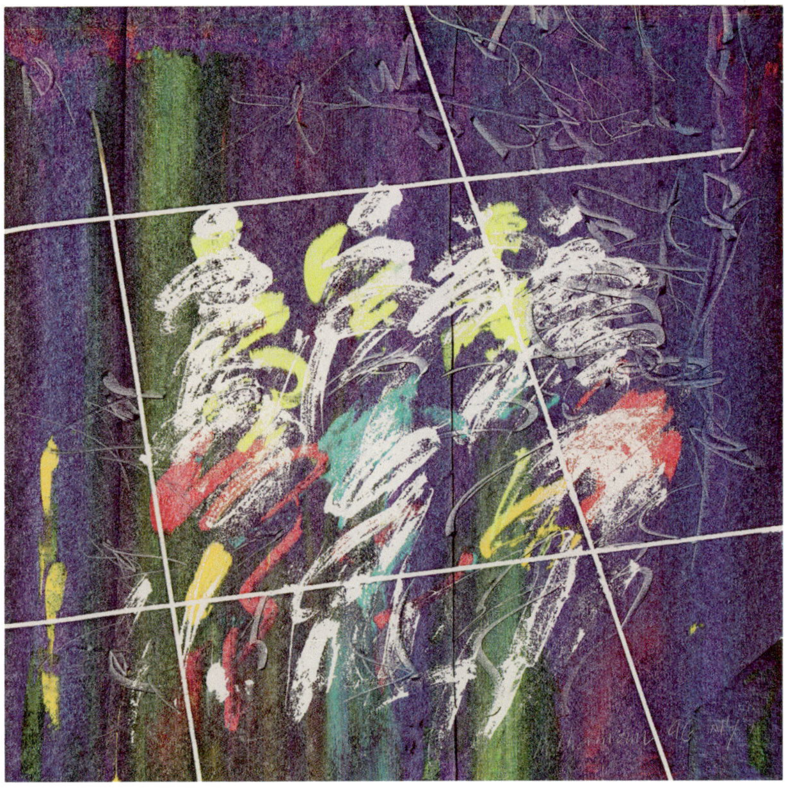

149
RACING #12, 1996
Acrylic on canvas
56 x 56 cm

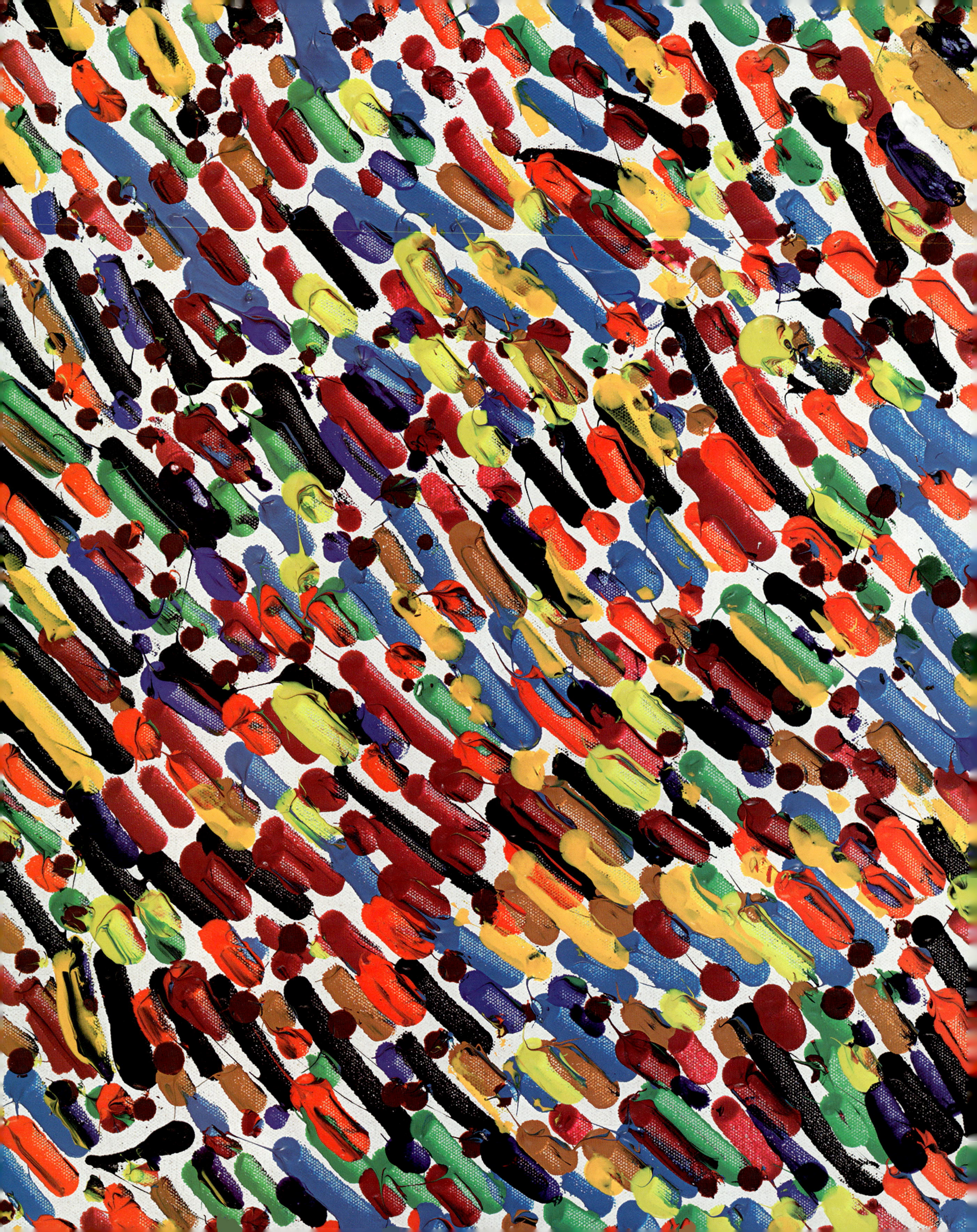

In nearby Suffern, New York, there were two large hilly green parks, Harriman Park and Tuxedo Park. In both, I found some of the most beautiful lakes engulfed by huge trees in dense forests, one following after another as I went up and down the vast and charming hills. In a few of those lakes there were fields of water lilies, which made me imagine Monet sitting painting on the other side of the lake. What a great discovery. What great company. I saw nothing there but transparent surfaces reflecting trees and skies in incredible depth, with water lilies floating over them.
151 I put off an abstract experiment I had started on taking up residence in Steve Duffy's apartment on West 104th Street in Manhattan and began experimenting with my memory-filled images of the lakes. I visited the lakes at different times every day, reading the different surface textures and changing reflections.

I wondered whether I was just echoing Monet. 'Why not? Don't artists always maintain dialogues with their predecessors throughout history on the conceptual level? Don't I also sketch and paint other subjects, as do all other artists?' So I reasoned with myself as I quickly transferred my learning experiences onto the canvas. I used no brushes, just spatulas and paint applied directly from the tubes.

These paintings were exhibited at Epreuve d'Artiste in
150, 152–167 autumn 1995. Some people wondered what had happened to me, and why I was borrowing Monet's best-cherished

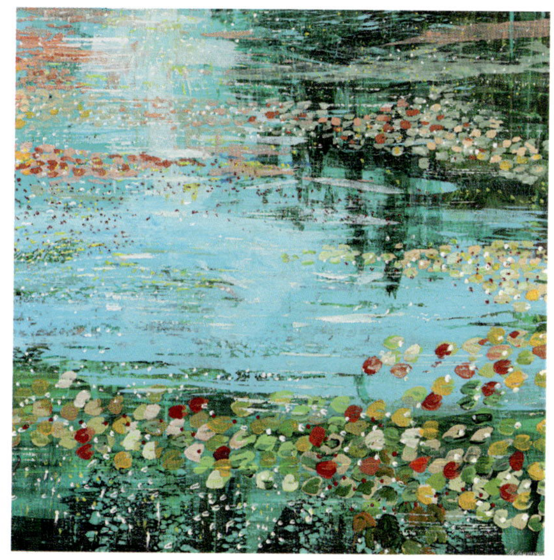

150
TUXEDO PARK II, 1995
Acrylic on canvas
82 x 82 cm

Facing page
151
RACING IN THE OTHER PEACE TIME II, 1995
Acrylic on canvas (detail)
82 x 82 cm

Following spread
152
LAKE WELCH V, 1995
Acrylic on canvas
142 x 82 cm

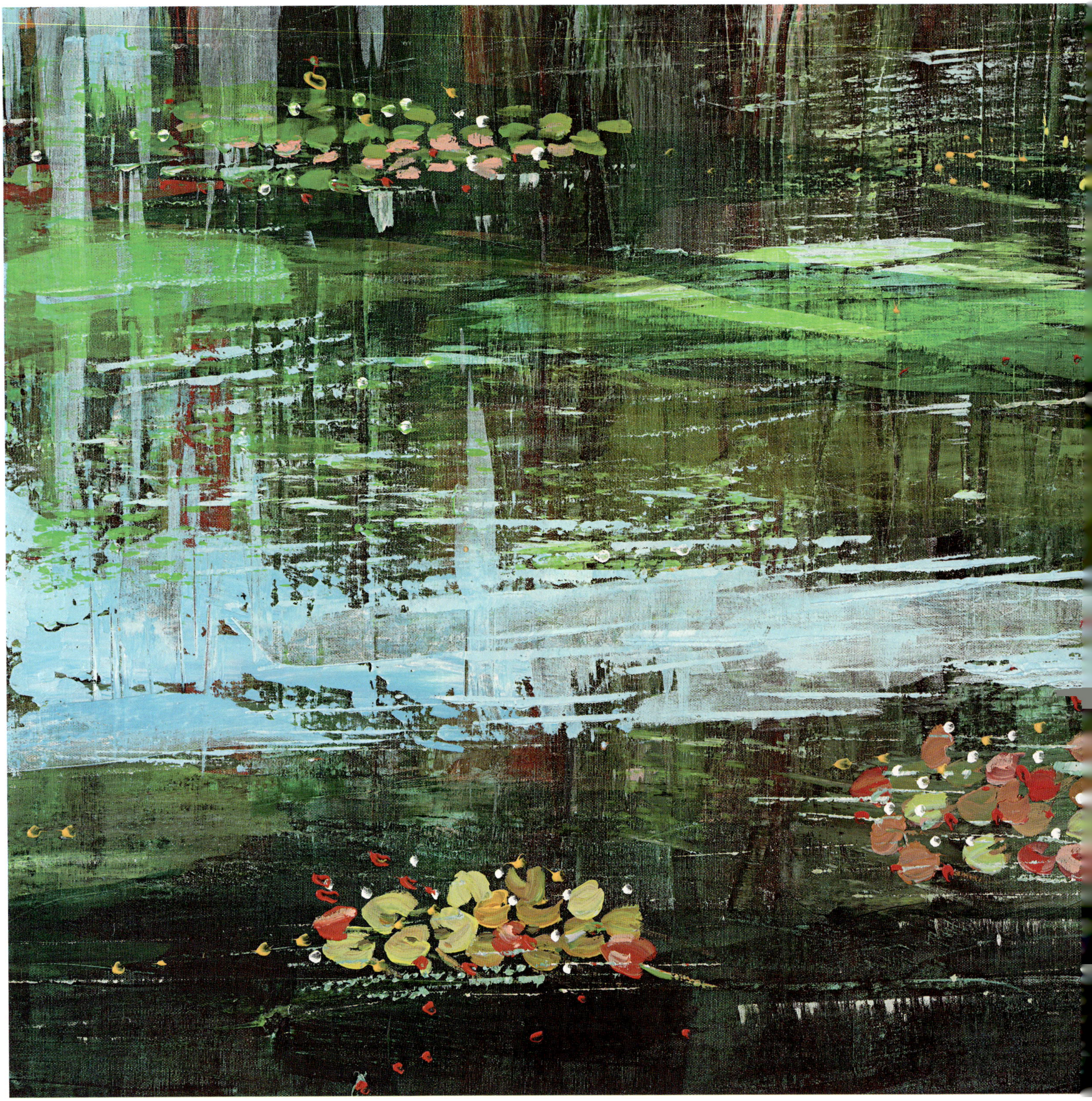

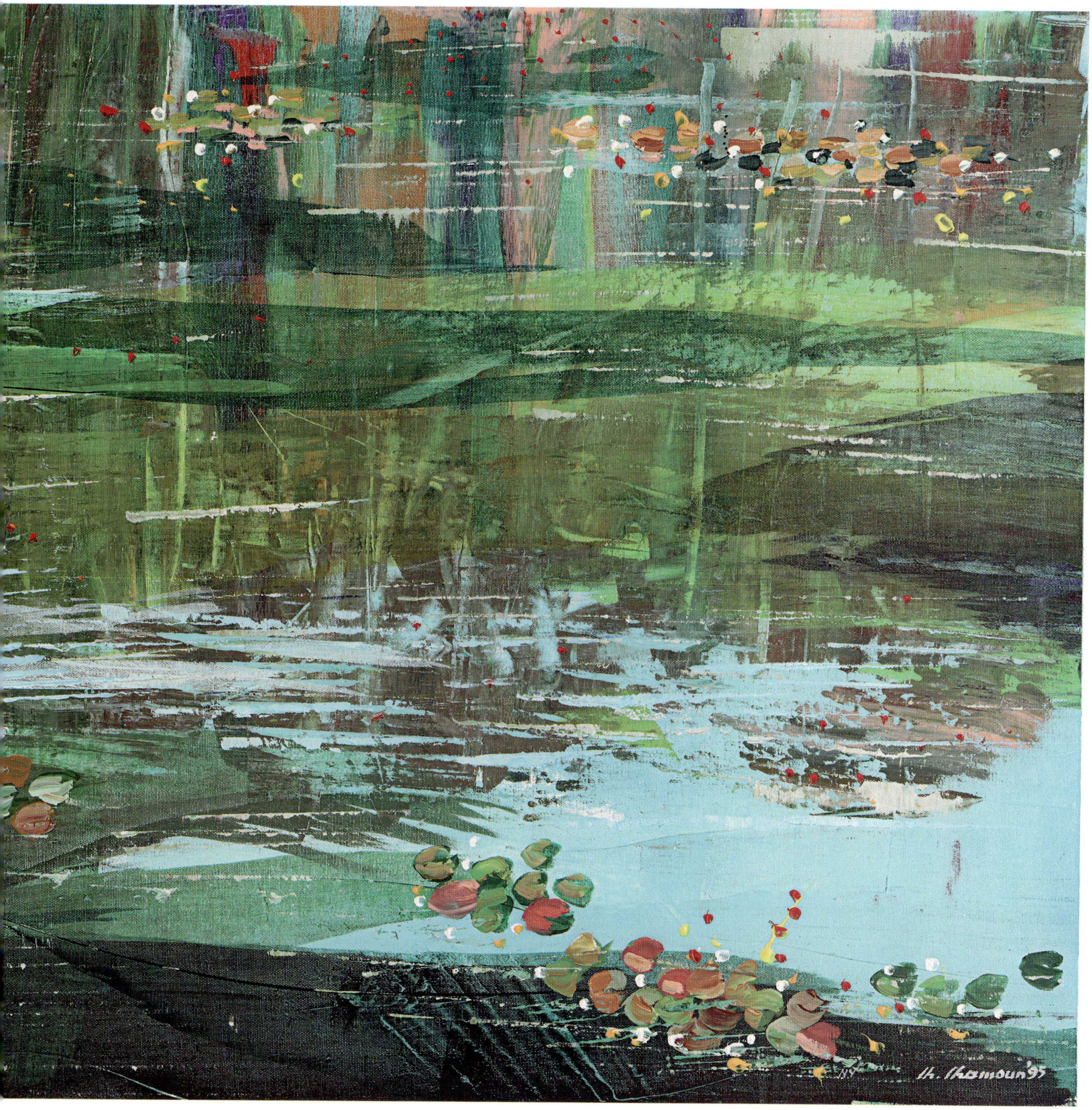

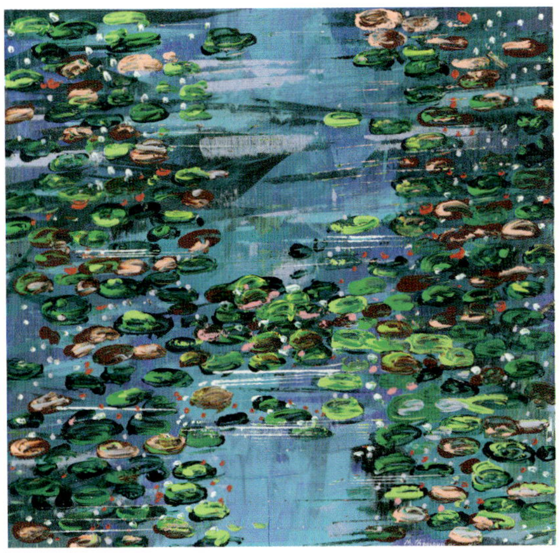

153
LILIES OF HARIMAN PARK, 1995
Acrylic on canvas
81.5 x 81.5 cm

subject. Contrary to those opinions, the prominent art critic Joseph Tarrab wrote:

> Who said that the thirsty does not seek water, but it is rather water that seeks him? The lake needed an artist who was ready to sacrifice his inhibitions and preconceived ideas. Chamoun had the courage of this transformation.
>
> It was partial; it is true, since he kept his way of painting, his taste for acrylic, and his manner of spreading a thin and flat layer of colors, which reveals the granulated canvas. They are neutral layers, without vibrations or the trace of a personal touch, and are often transparent or translucent to convey the fluidity of water. He then adds by juxtaposition and atomisation, without using the brush, colored touches and circles directly from the acrylic tube or with his fingers, in order to restore through visual metaphor the exuberance and landscape of the flowers.
>
> They are simple yet efficient processes, as he masters them perfectly. He always liked action painting: here, the structure of visual reality corresponds to a previous pictorial structure he has.
>
> (Joseph Tarrab, 'Jusqu'au Bout', *L'Orient-le Jour*, N.8446, 20 October 1995)

Of course, others would not understand my need and could not envisage what this experience was leading to or what it was adding to my work. They could not see the differences between stylistic characteristics – the new approach, technique, surface manipulation and the aesthetic

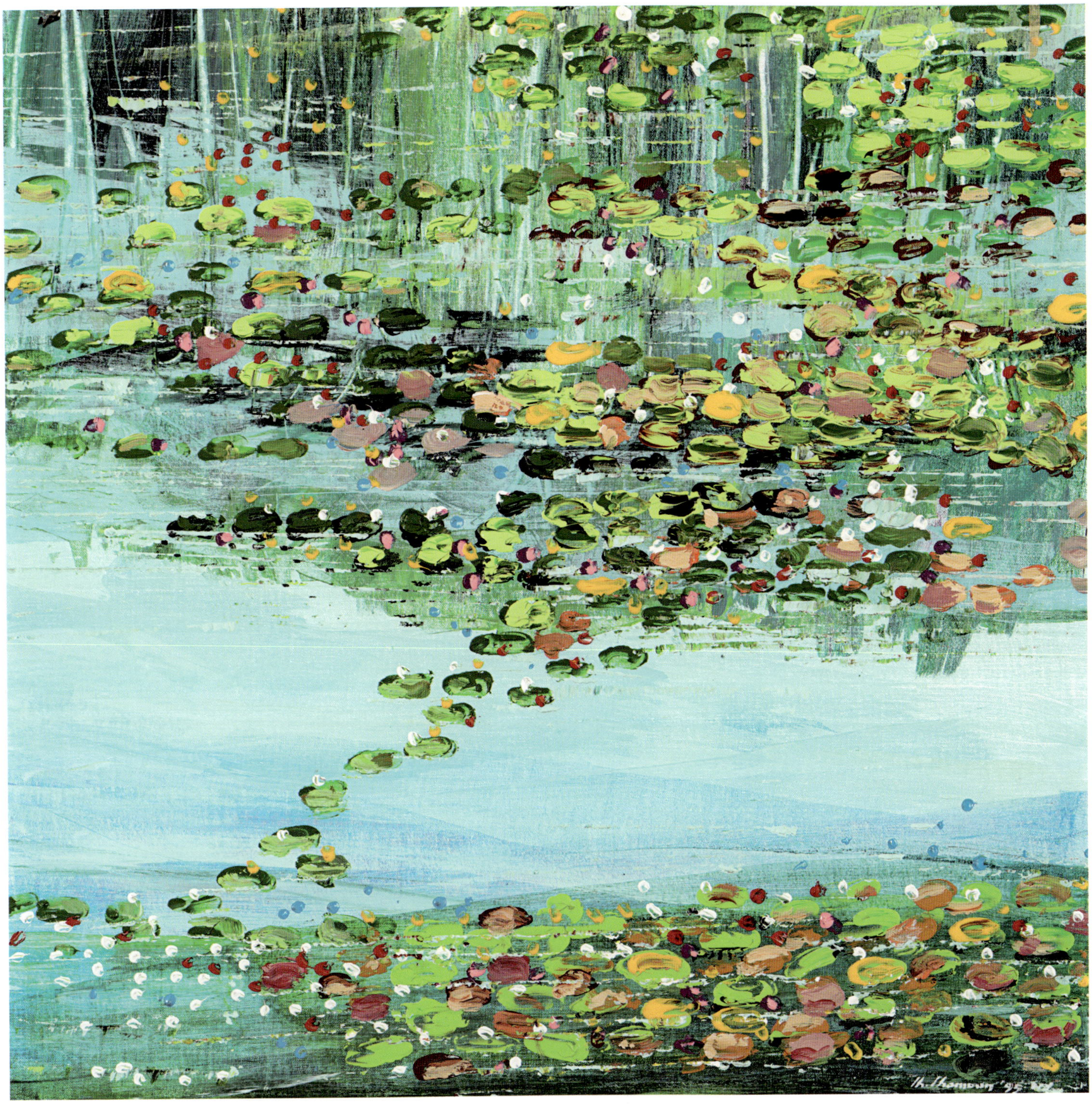

154
LILIES OF HARRIMAN PARK LAKES VII, 1995
Acrylic on canvas
81.5 x 81.5 cm

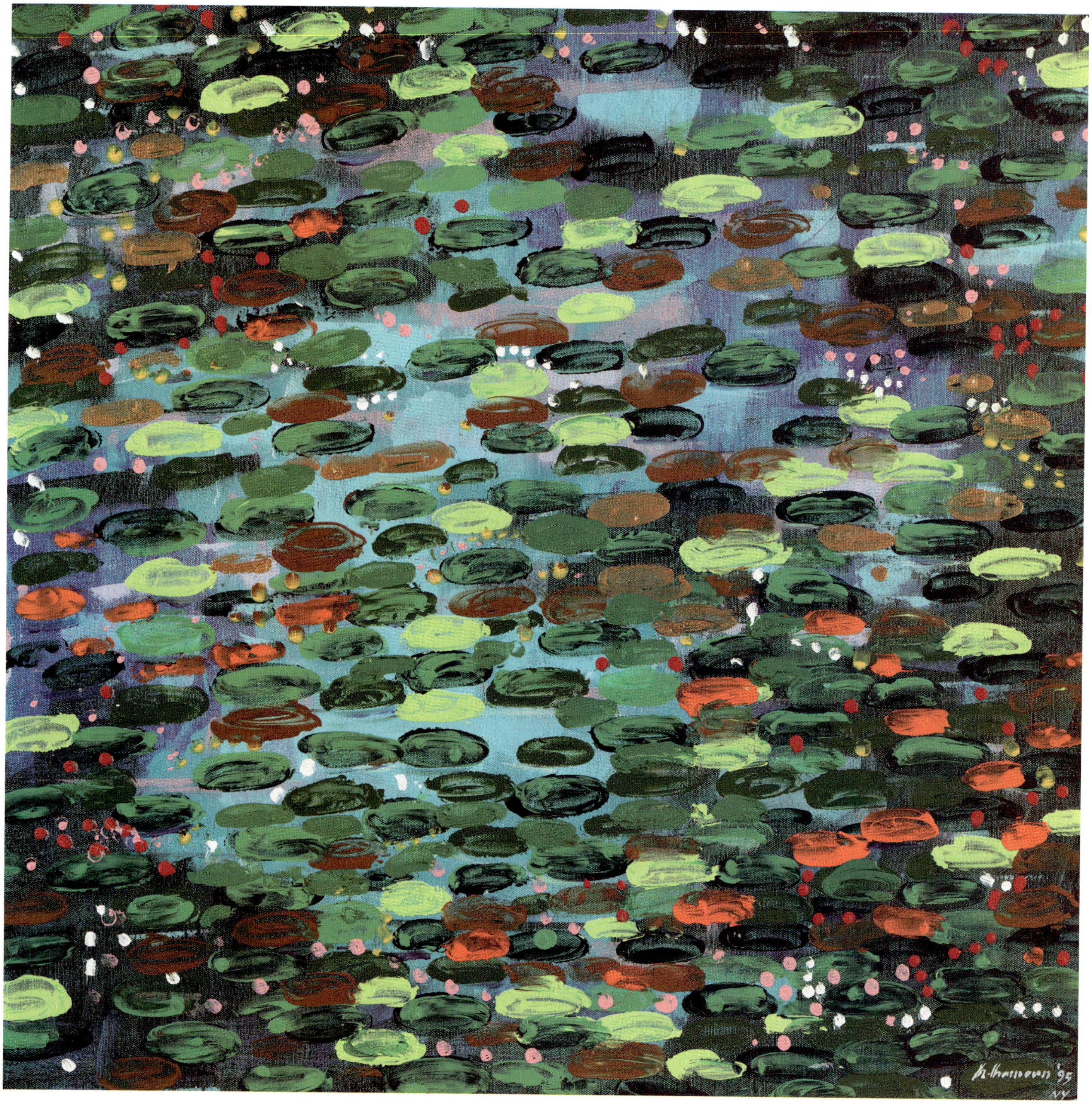

155
TUXEDO PARK I, 1995
Acrylic on canvas
82 x 82 cm

dissimilarity – of my 'Water Reflections' and those of Monet. They could not go beyond the seemingly impressionistic end result.

It is true that it takes some people time to catch up with things. Yet I do not believe that artists are ahead of their time. Rather, artists are a reflection of their time, because they live in their time. It is others who are sometimes behind the times. It is also true that when I look at things simply and unconditionally, with an old eye, I get stuck. I believe that art feeds on art as science feeds on science when it comes to re-examining natural phenomena. Knowledge in both takes one to a deeper and more meaningful experience.

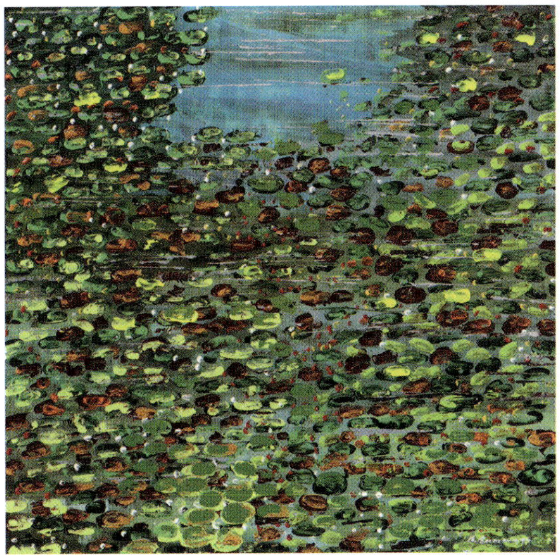

156
WAITING FOR THE FALL, 1995
Acrylic on canvas
82 x 82 cm

To me what was important was to paint things as I saw them, with the hope of finding my way to a solid understanding and appreciation of their inner aesthetic structure. No paintings sold during the 'Water Reflections' exhibition, but in the following months, most were bought; all except the ones I gave my children. The *Conseil de la Pensée* (Council for Thought) paid me tribute at the gallery by inviting the art critics Maha Sultan, Ahmad Bazzoun, and Chawki Dalal, with lawyer George Chamoun as moderator, to join me in a panel discussion of the new works.

In our discussion, I concluded that the most important thing in a painting is its surface; you either see it all in the surface or you see nothing. The surface is the carrier of all the aesthetic elements of a work, including its deeper meaning.

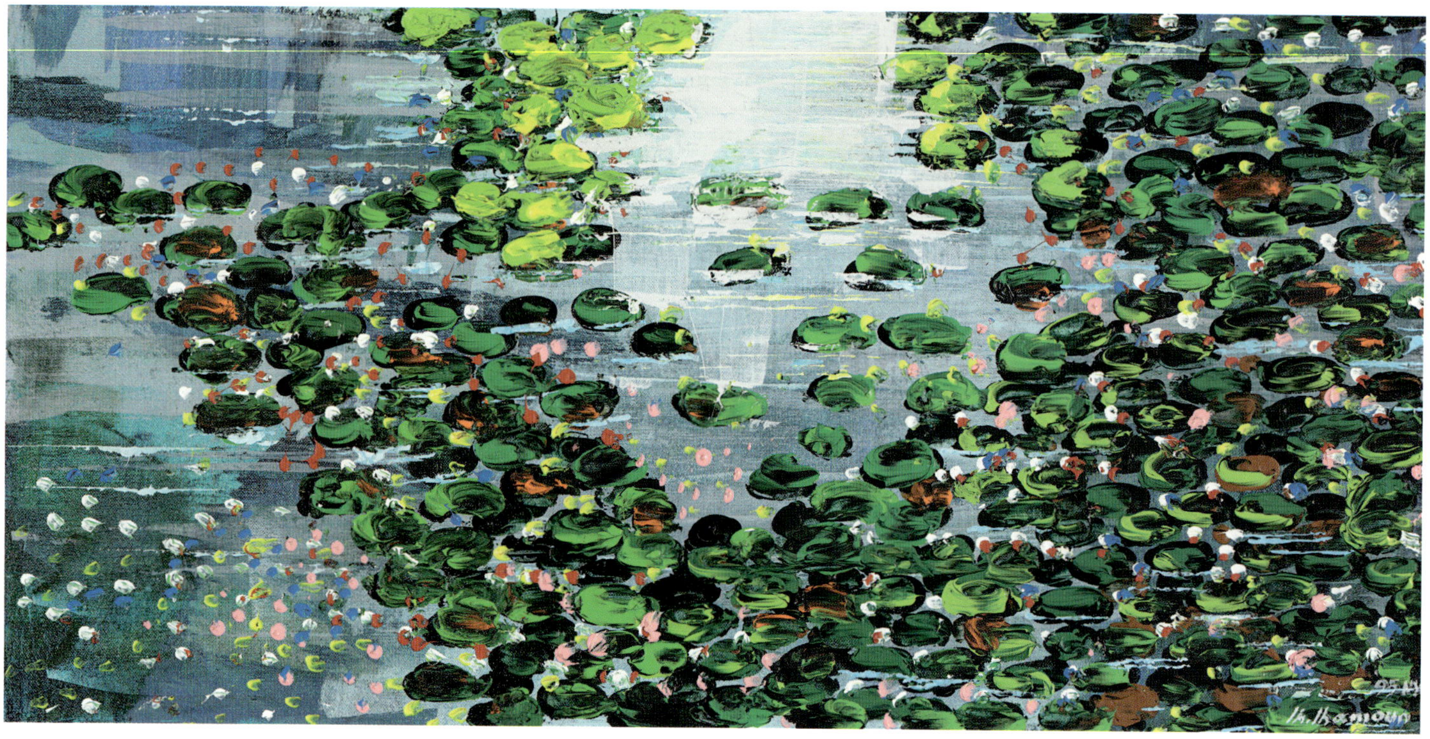

157
TUXEDO PARK, 1995
Acrylic on canvas
82 x 51 cm

We do not look at a painting and use it as a mere window or vehicle that invites or leads us to other ideas, be they religious, social, political or whatever. The surface of a painting is the invitation as well as the event. It is not there to be bypassed, forgotten or used to recall another experience; it is there because it is the most important thing in a painting. No single aesthetic element of a painting, its intended meaning included, has any independent value of its own if it does not add to the value of the whole. Of course, a personally lived experience is different from an experience lived by another artist. But being influenced by another artist gives one materials that offer the possibility to progress and help one find one's way and materialise one's own findings.

My development of the 'Water Reflections' (November 1995 through June 1996) ended with a few large landscape paintings: 'Nature Revisited'. I had to wait until the spring of 1997 to exhibit this series at Noura Joumblat's 50x70 Gallery. 168–175

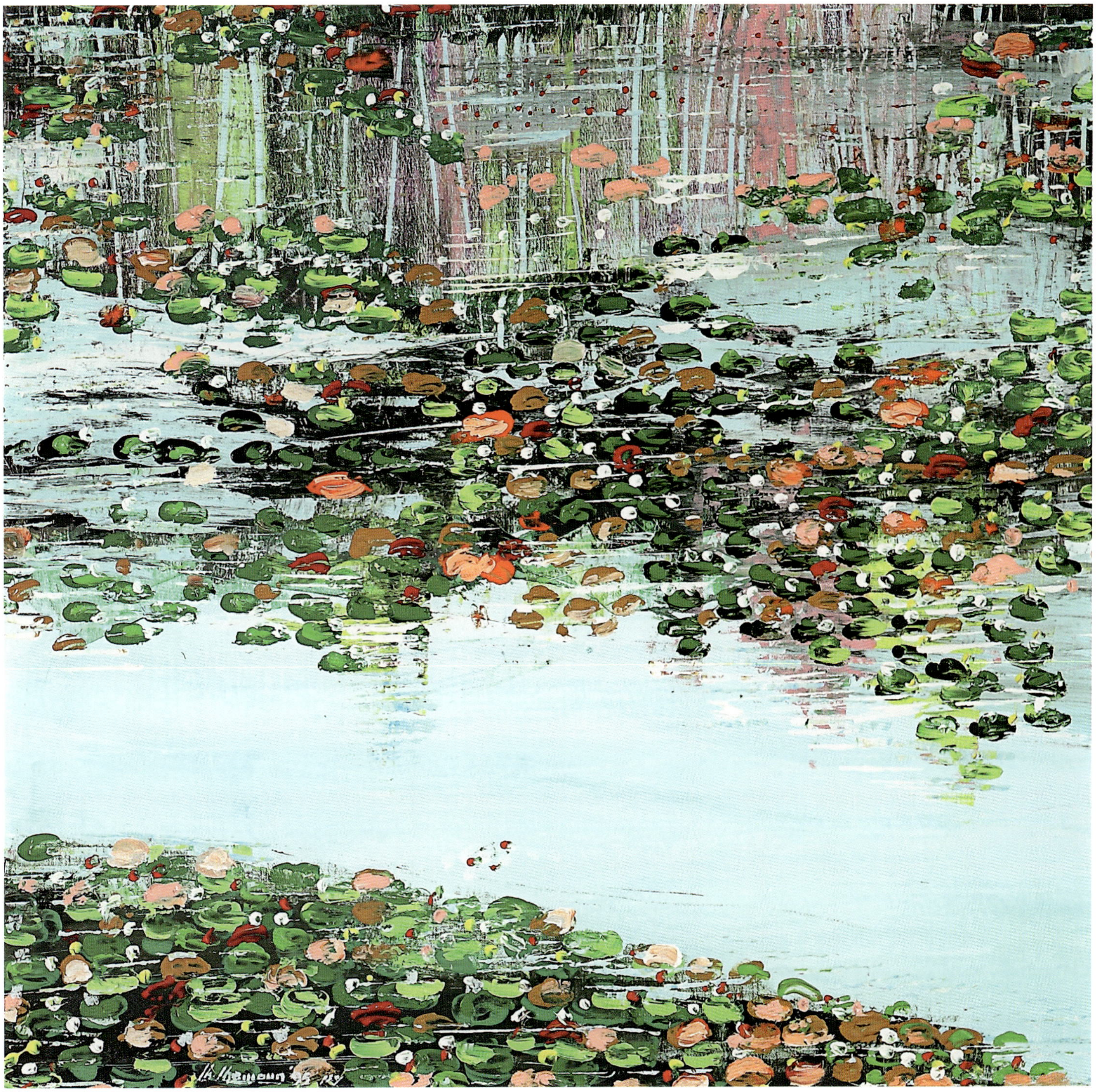

158
LILIES OF HARRIMAN PARK XII, 1995
Acrylic on canvas
82 x 82 cm
(Grand Serail collection)

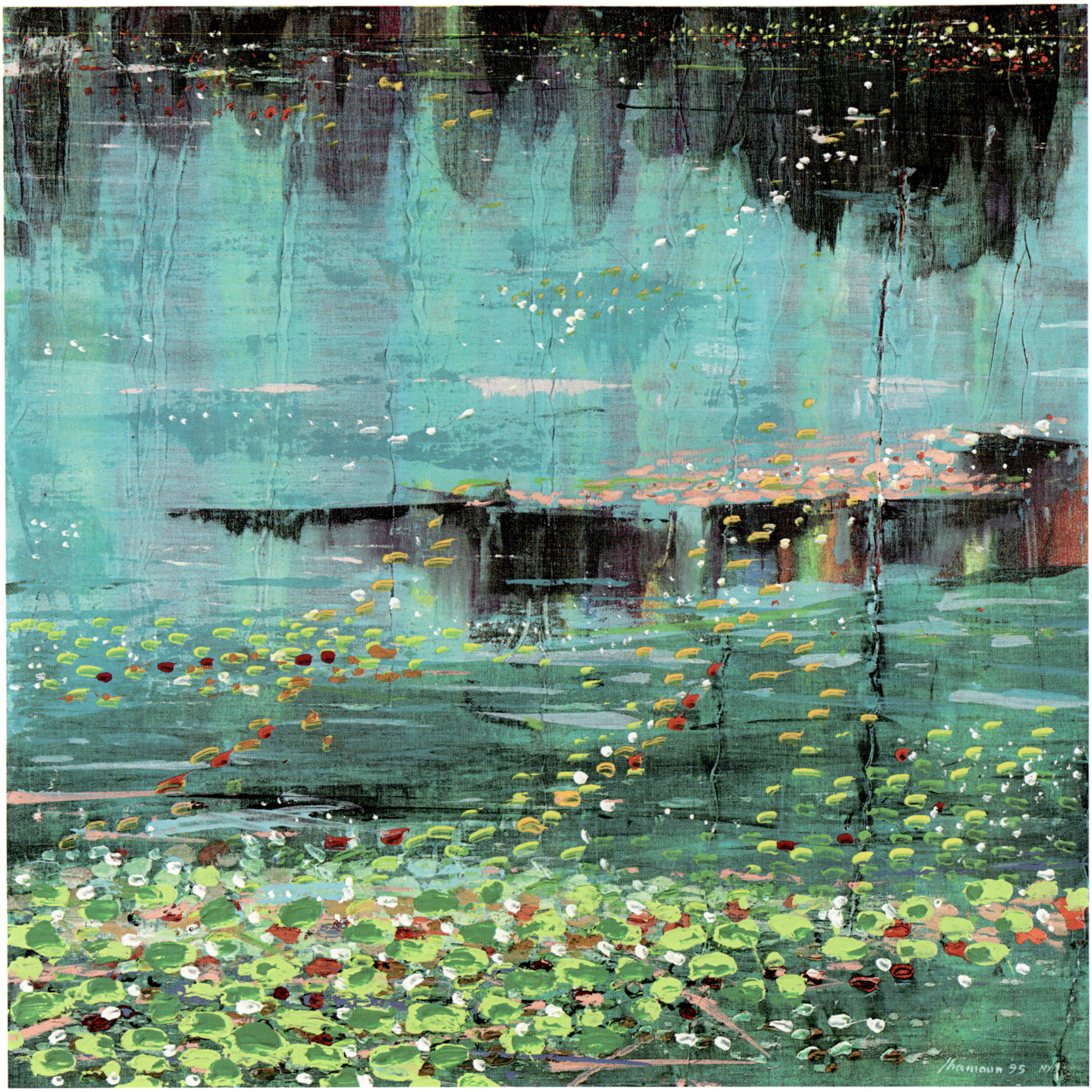

159
LILIES OF HARRIMAN PARK LAKES VI, 1995
Acrylic on canvas
81.5 x 81.5 cm

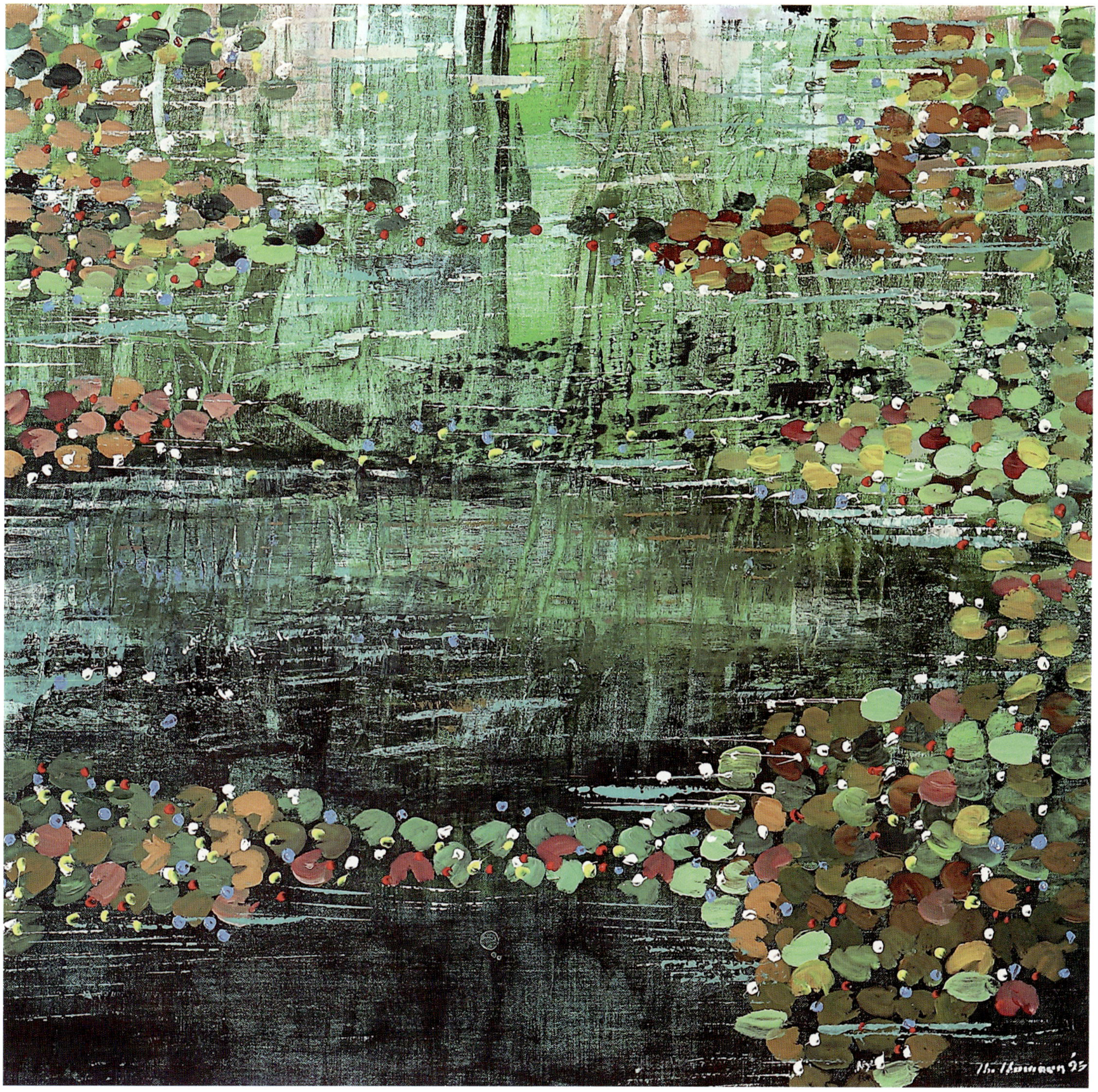

160
LILIES OF HARRIMAN PARK X, 1995
Acrylic on canvas
82 x 82 cm
(Grand Serail collection)

Following spread
161
LAKE WELCH VI, 1995
Acrylic on canvas (detail)
142 x 82 cm

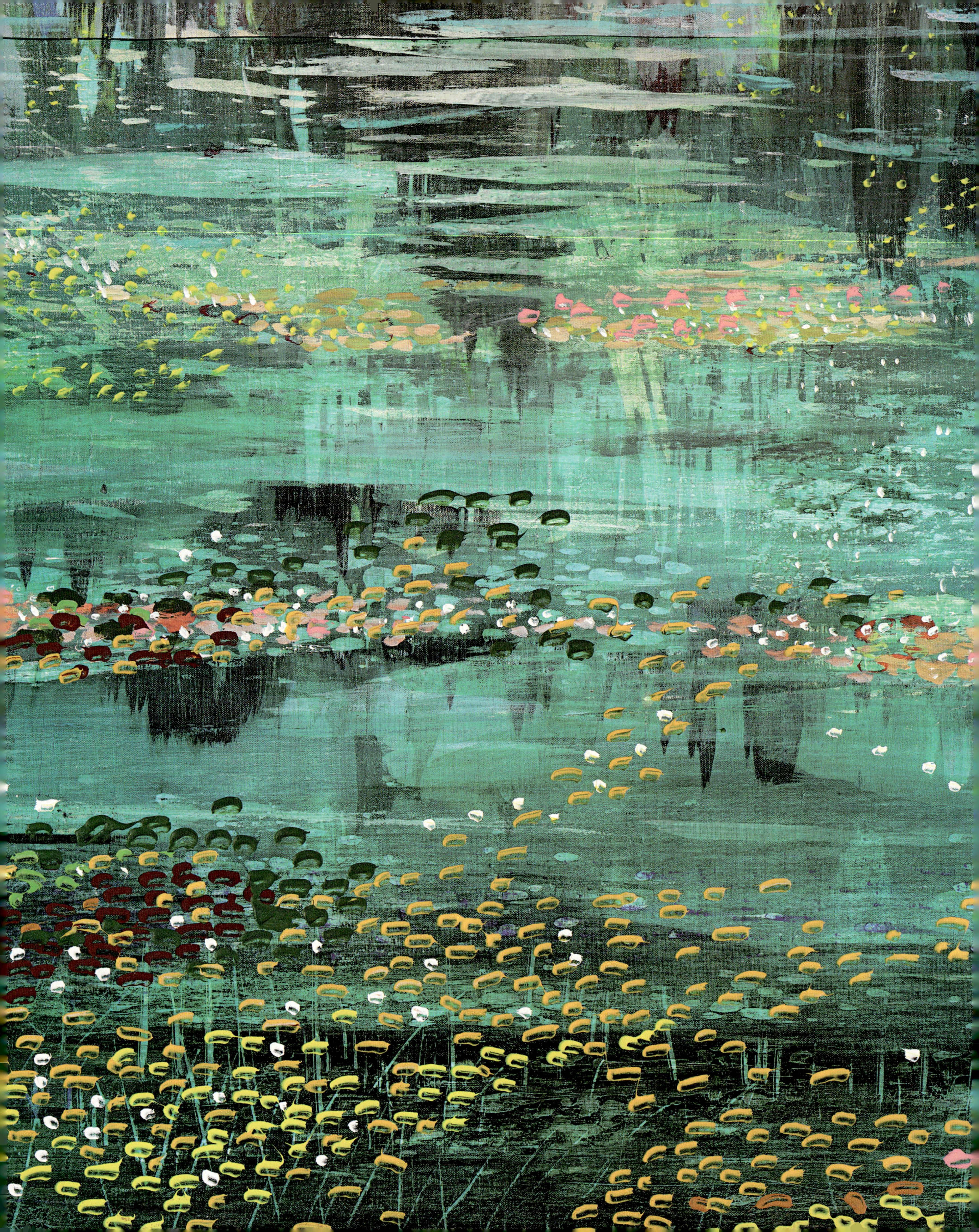

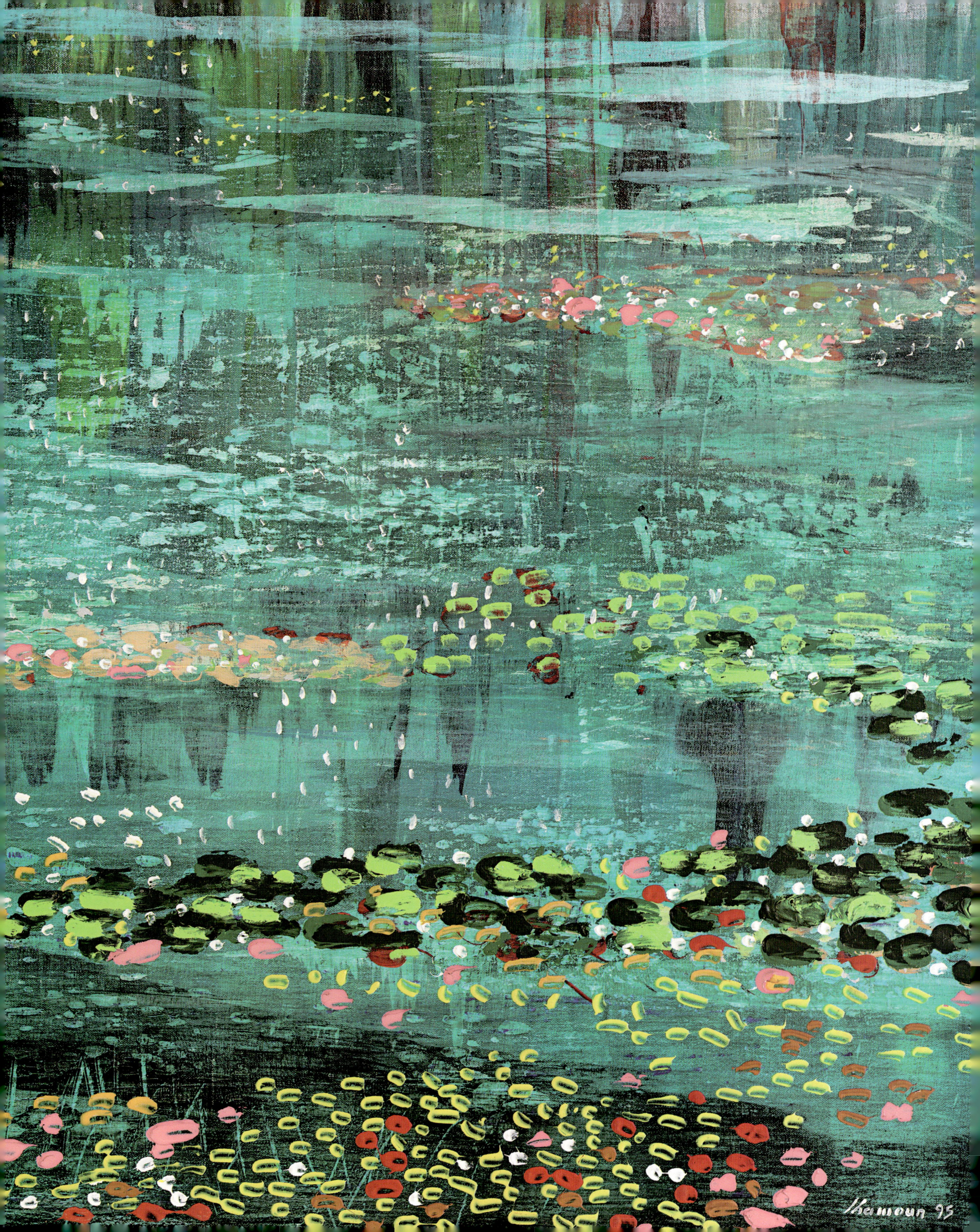
Khamoun 95

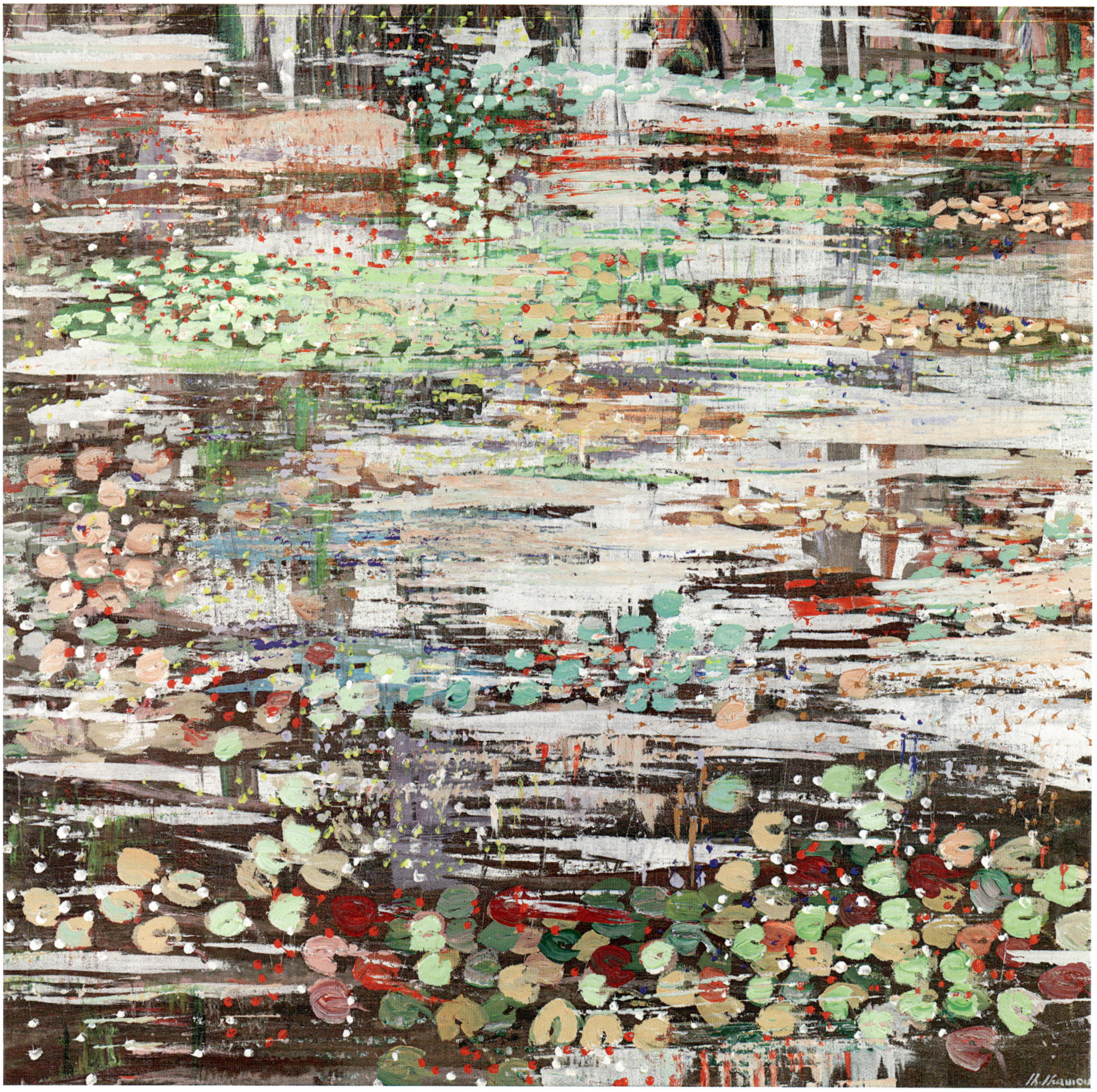

162
LOVE IS FLOWERING, 1995
Acrylic on canvas
82 x 82 cm

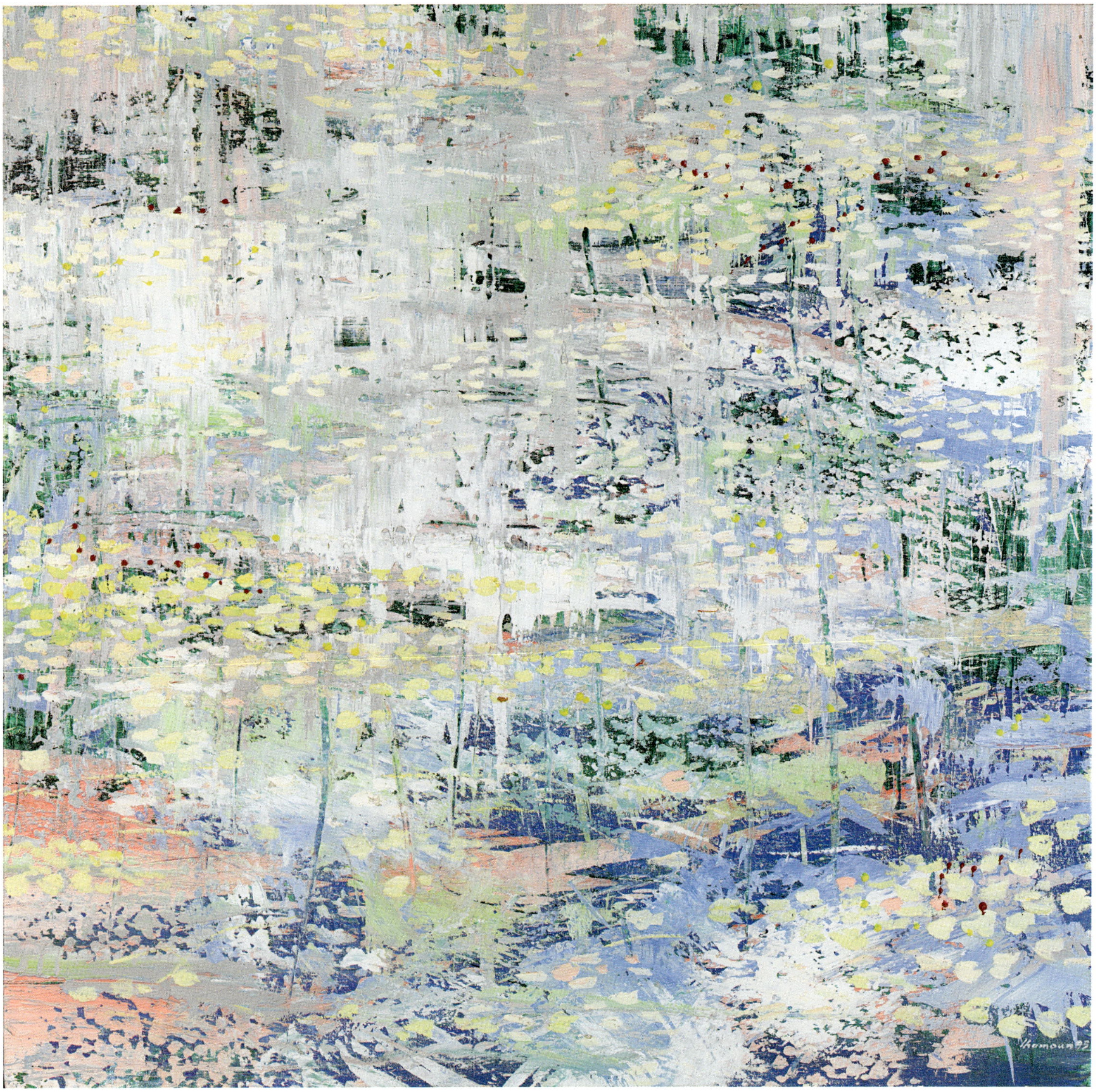

163
MY ONLY LOVE, 1995
Acrylic on canvas
82 x 82 cm

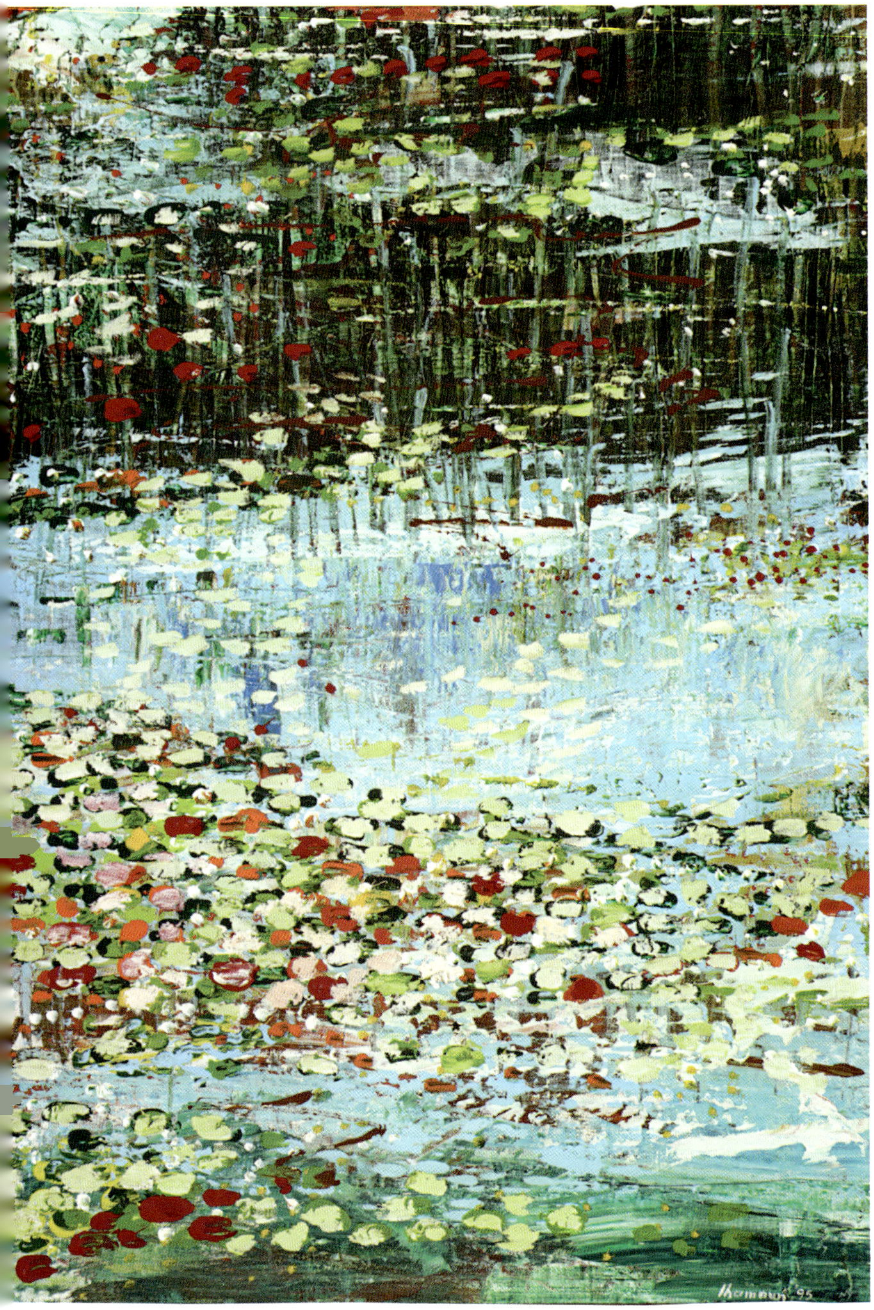

164
FLOWERING SEASON, 1995
Acrylic on canvas (detail)
54 x 82 cm

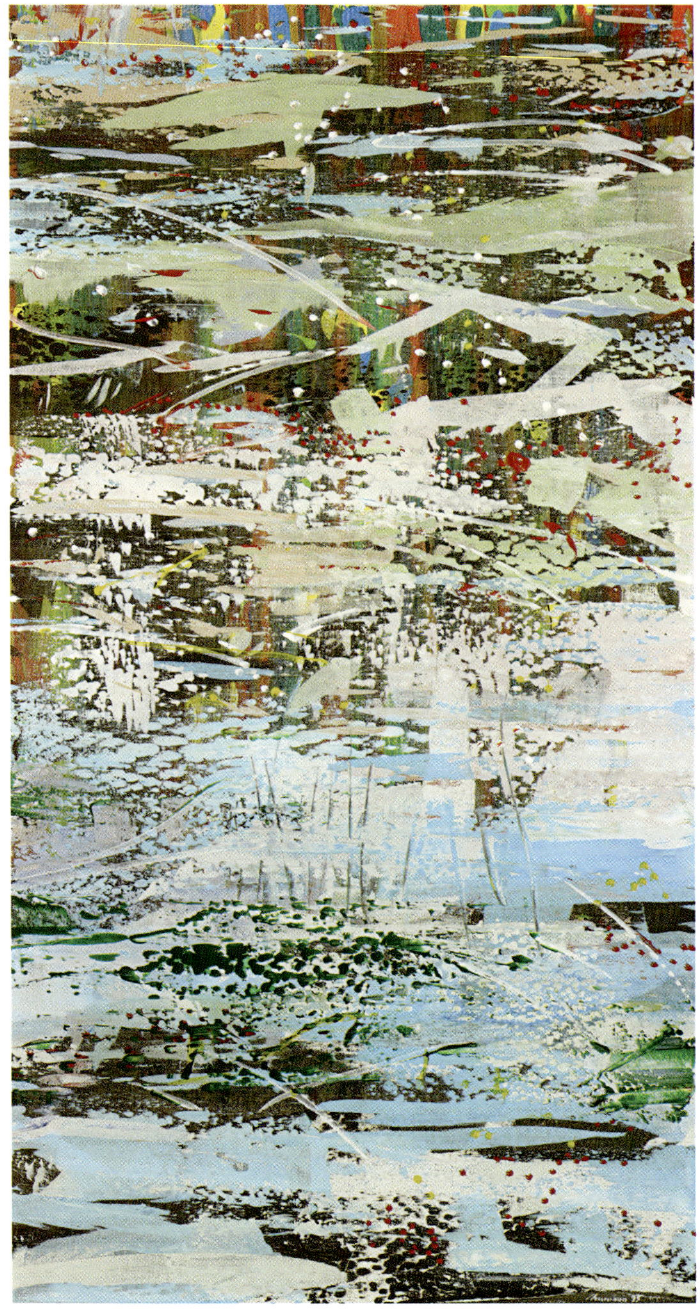

165
FALL AT TUXEDO PARK, 1995
Acrylic on canvas
82 x 142 cm

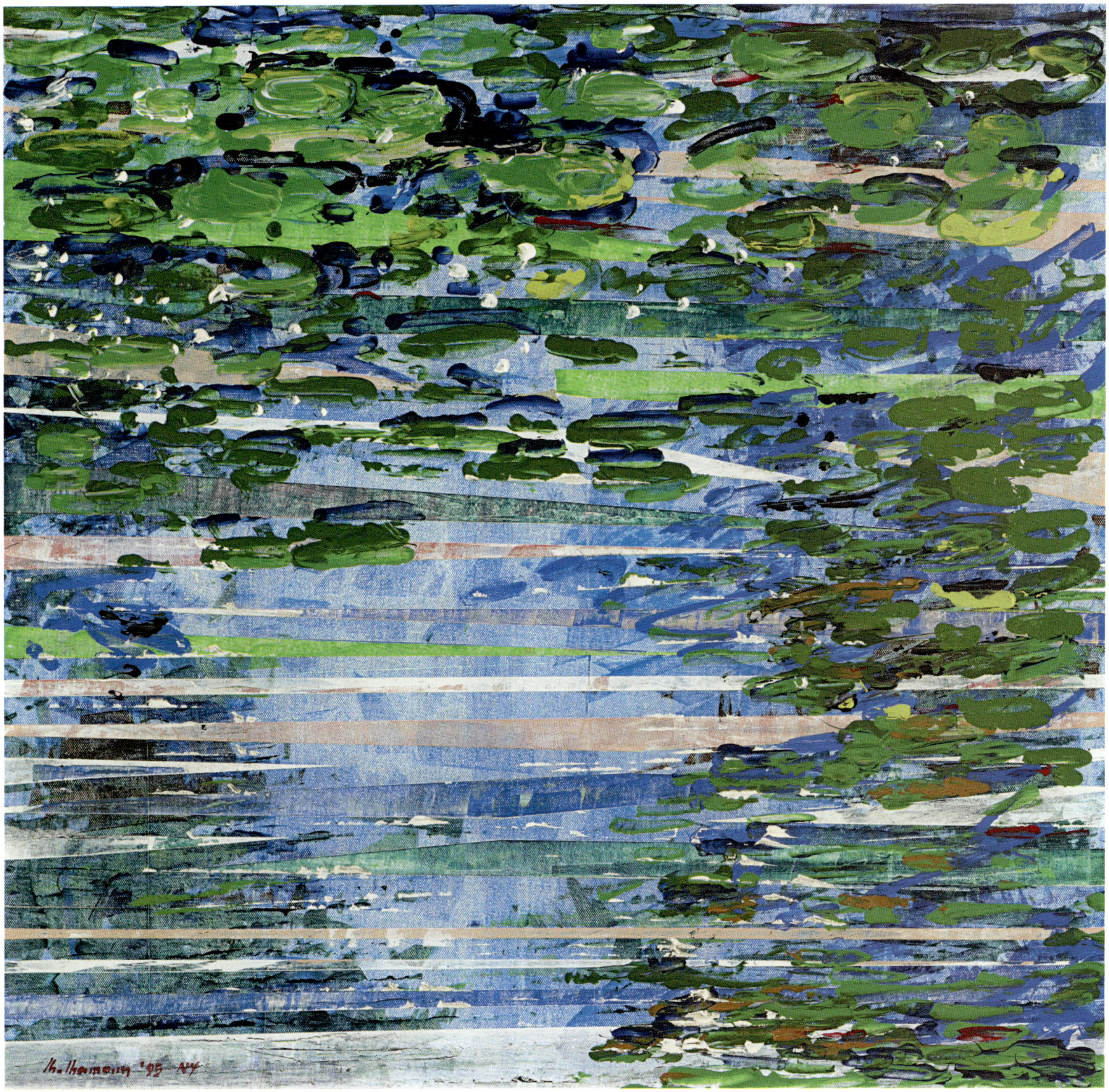

166
GLITTERING HARRIMAN PARK, 1995
Acrylic on canvas
82 x 82 cm

Following spread
167
TUXEDO PARK III, 1995
Acrylic on canvas (detail)
82 x 51 cm

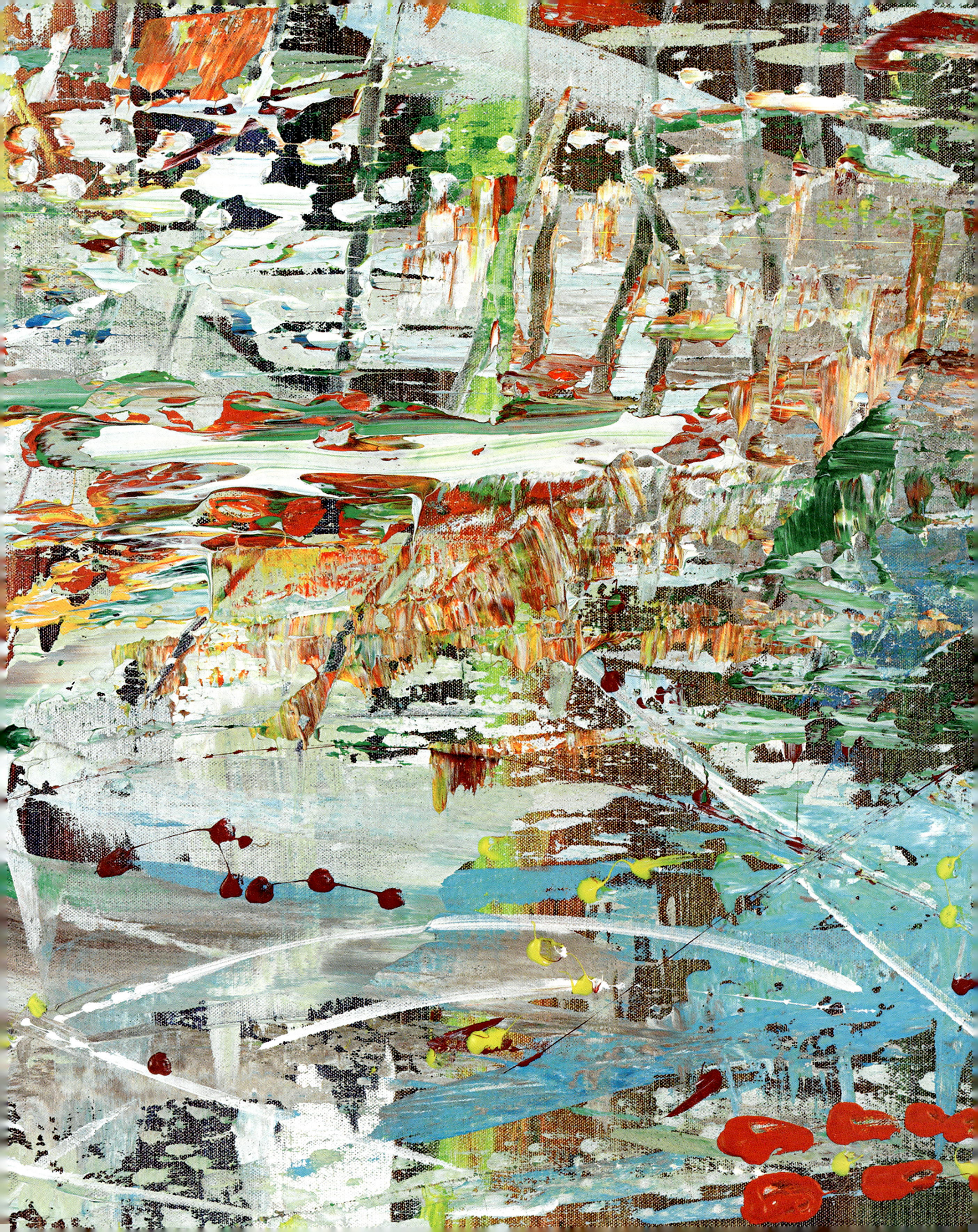

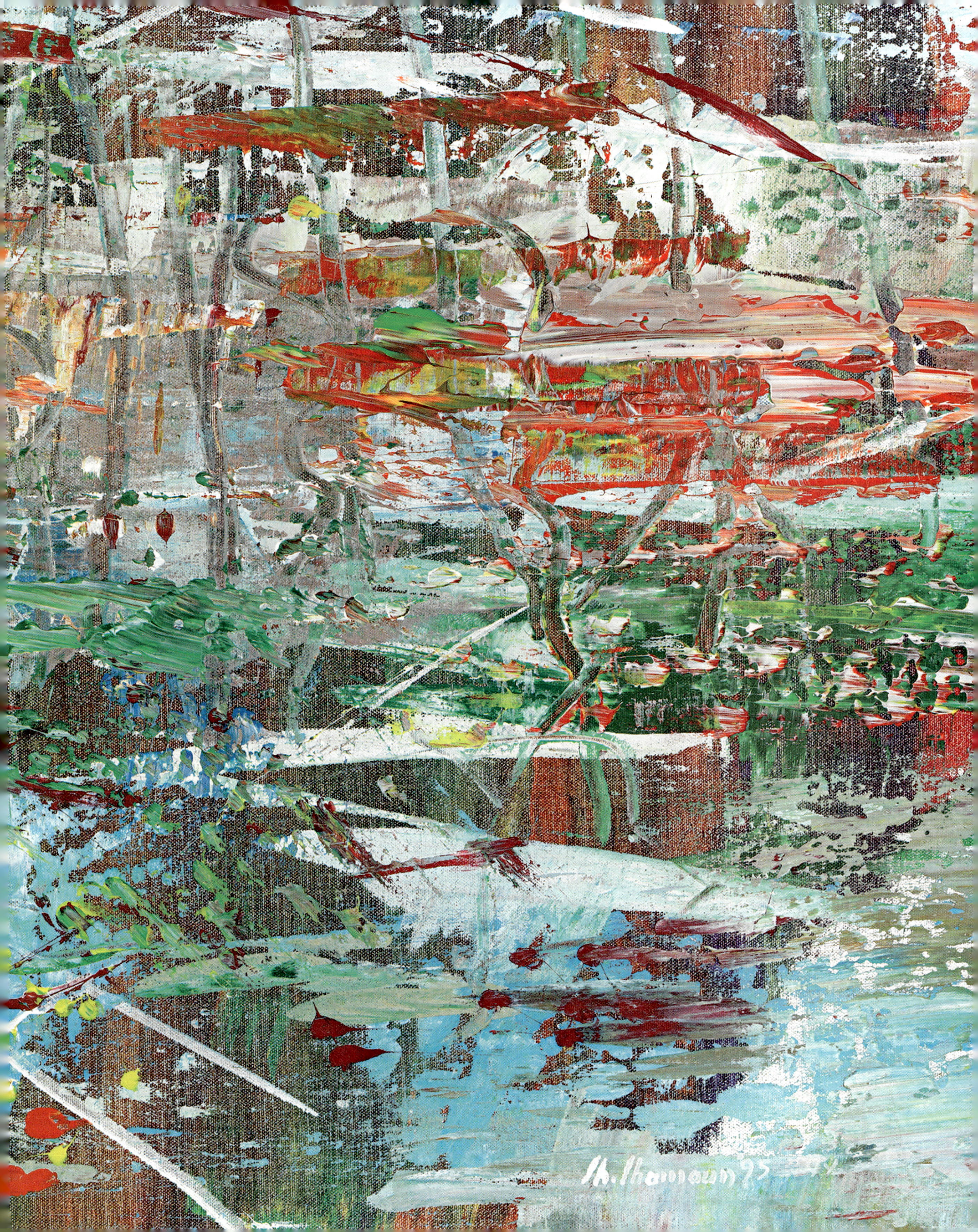

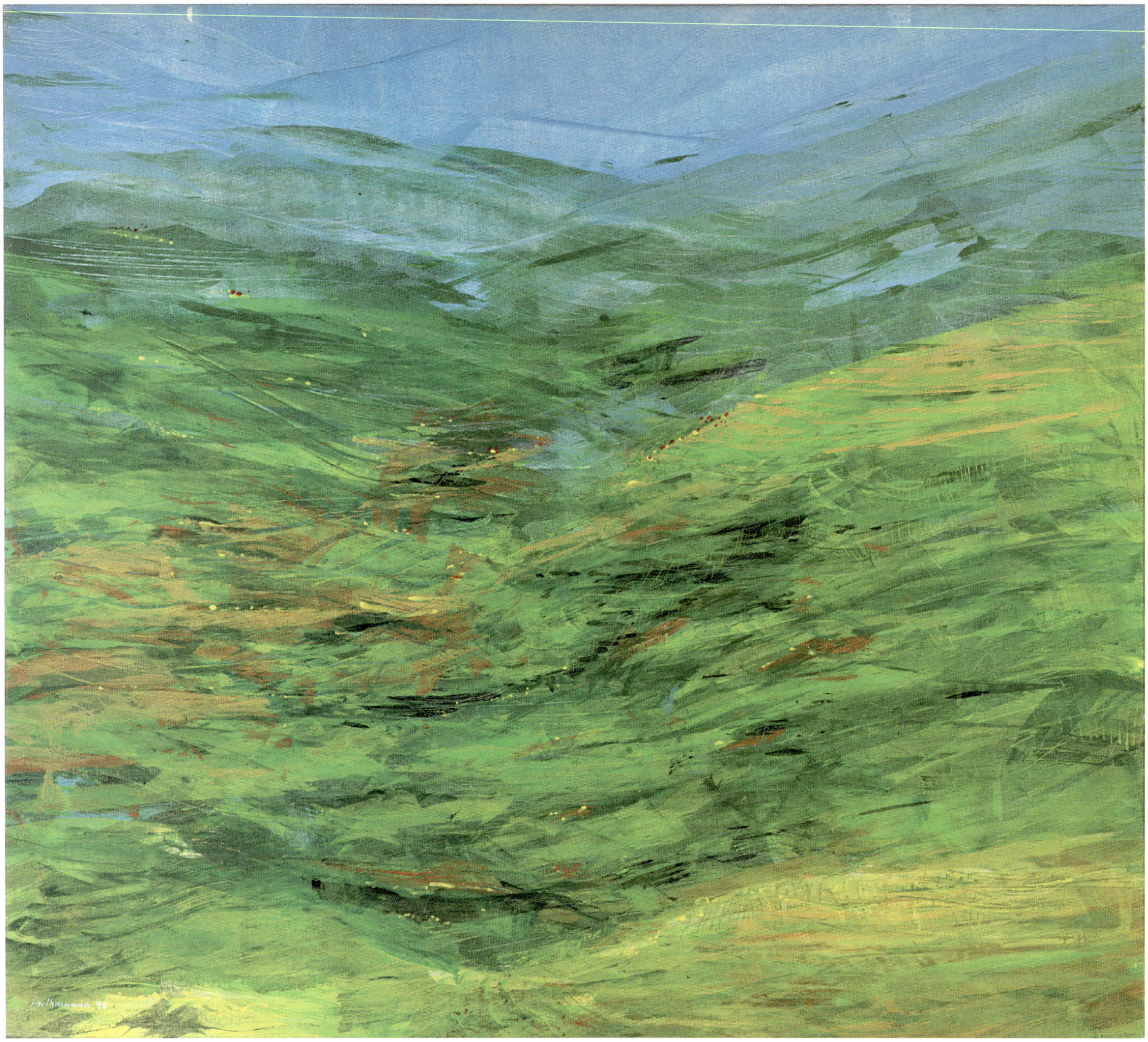

168
SPRING IN AKKAR, 1996
Acrylic on canvas
152 x 138 cm

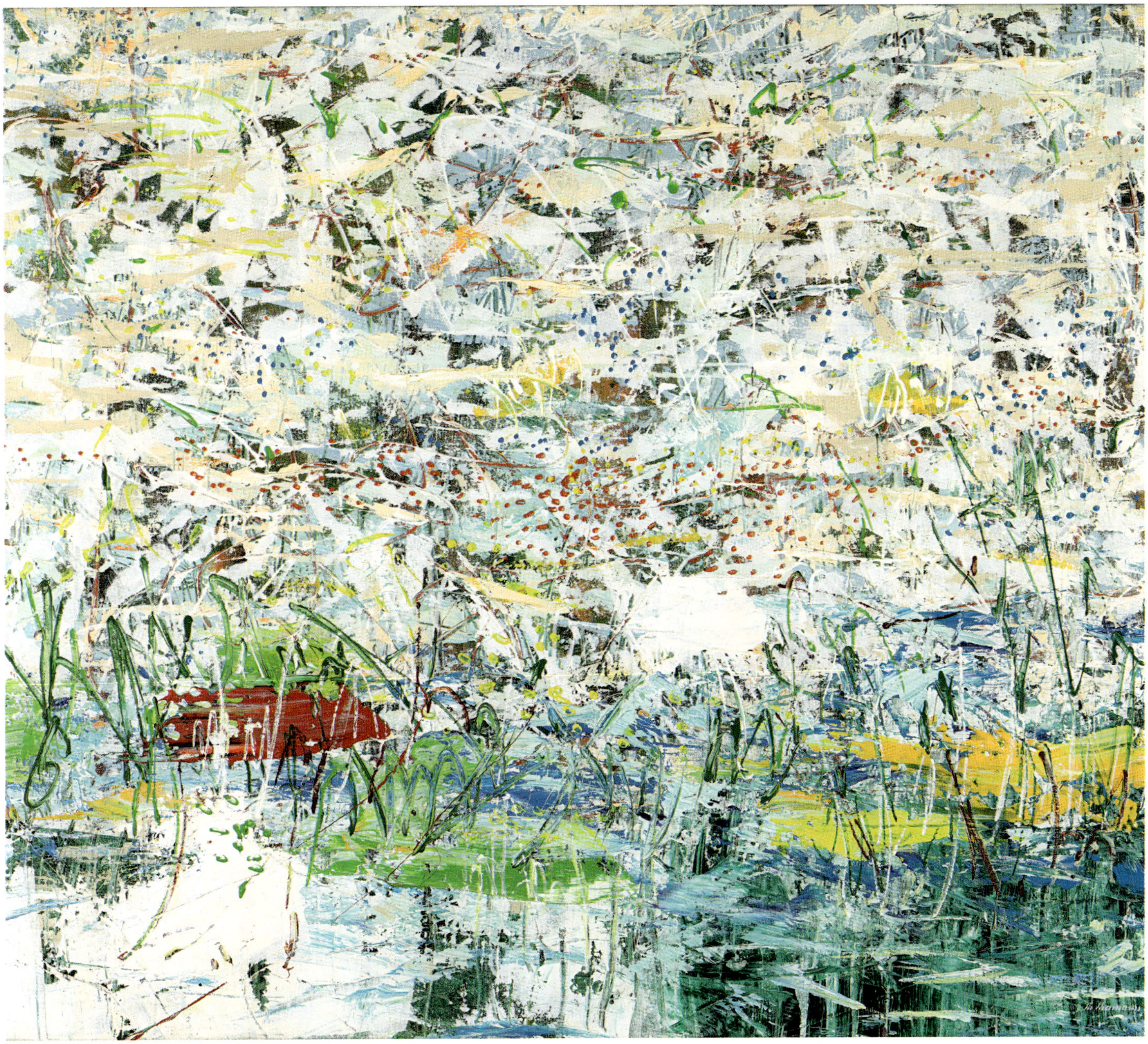

169
TUXEDO PARK II, 1996
Acrylic on canvas
153 x 135 cm

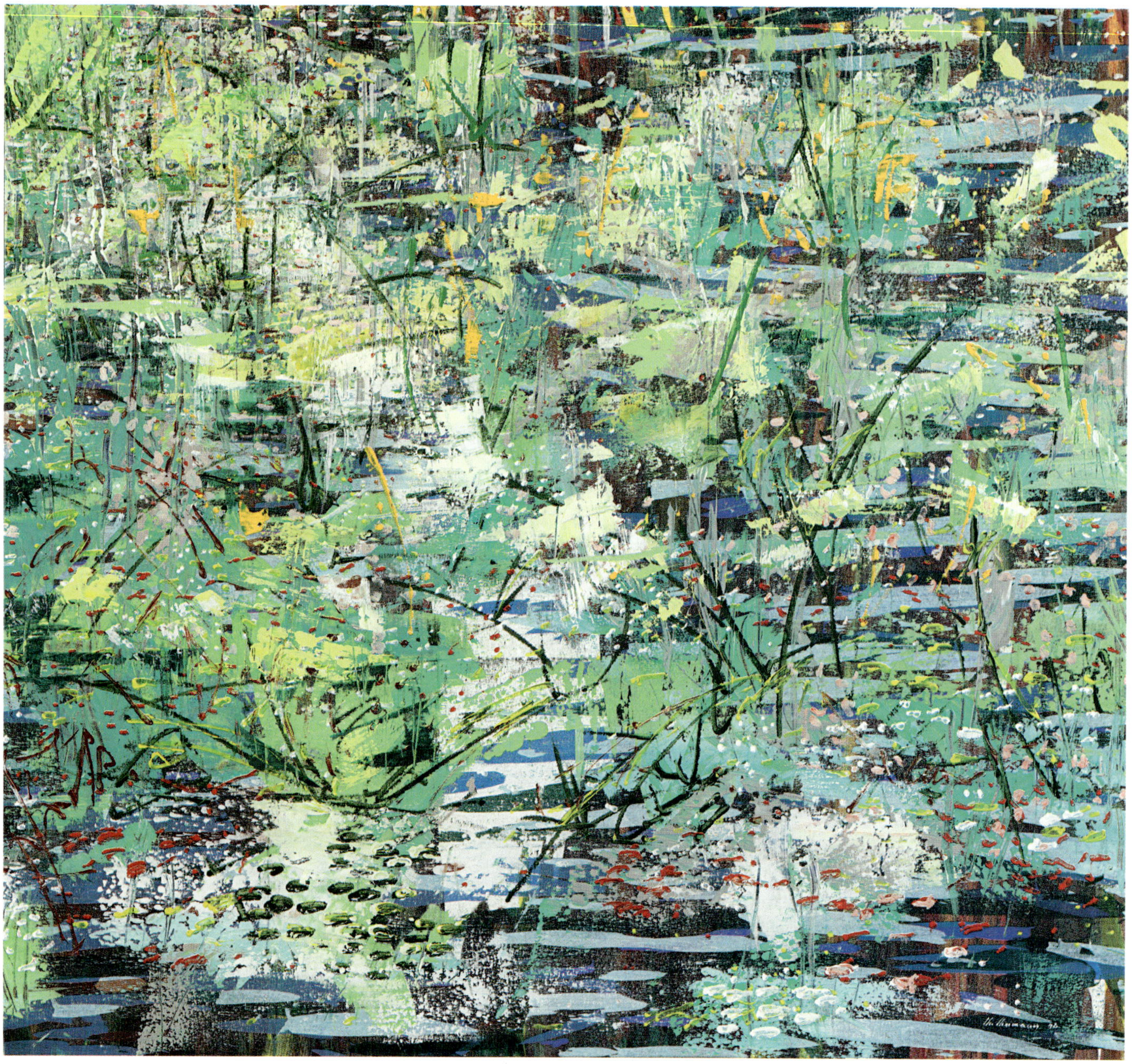

170
NATURE REVISITED, 1996
Acrylic on canvas
154 x 145 cm

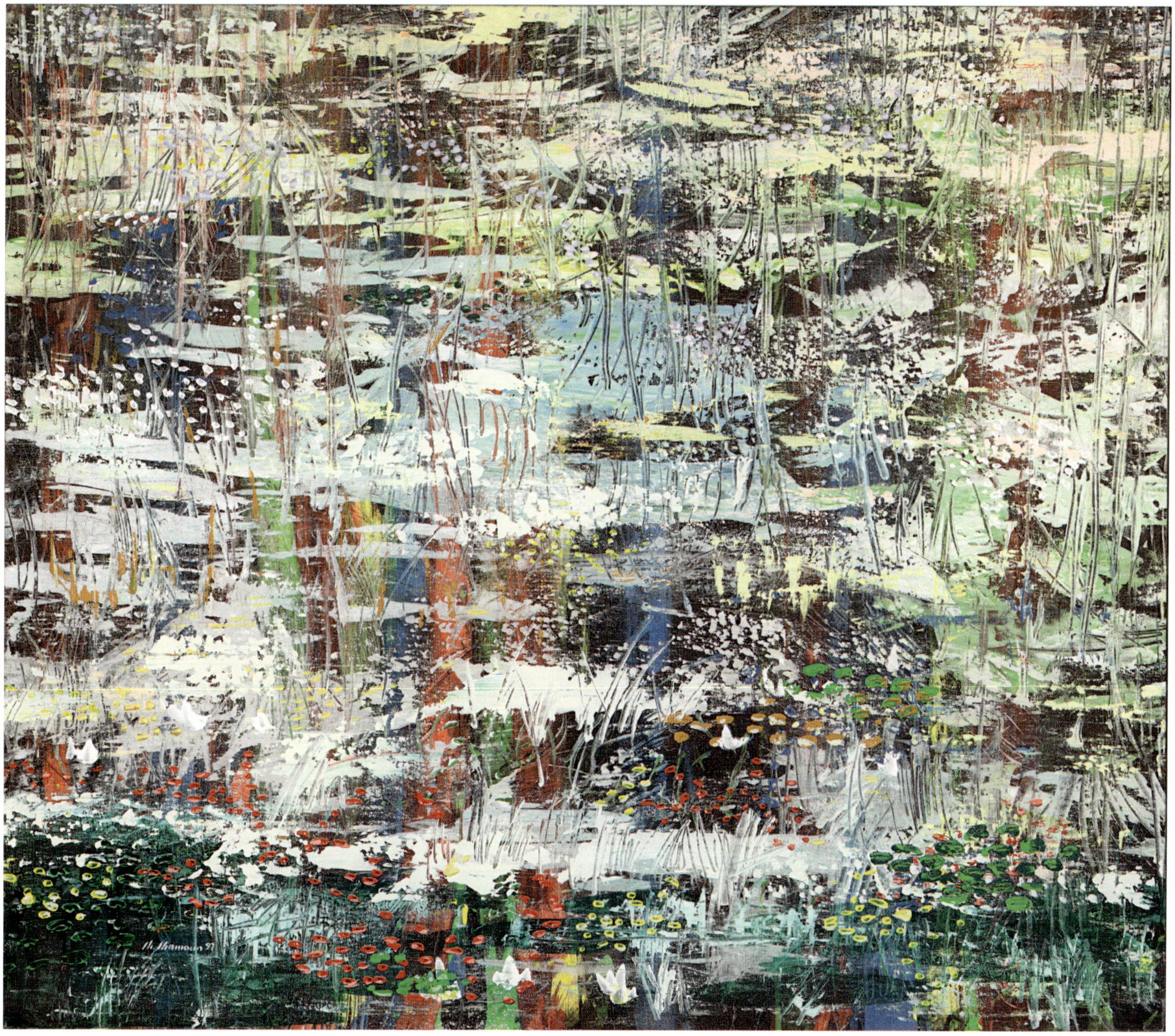

171
NATURE REVISITED #9, 1997
Acrylic on canvas
153 x 135 cm

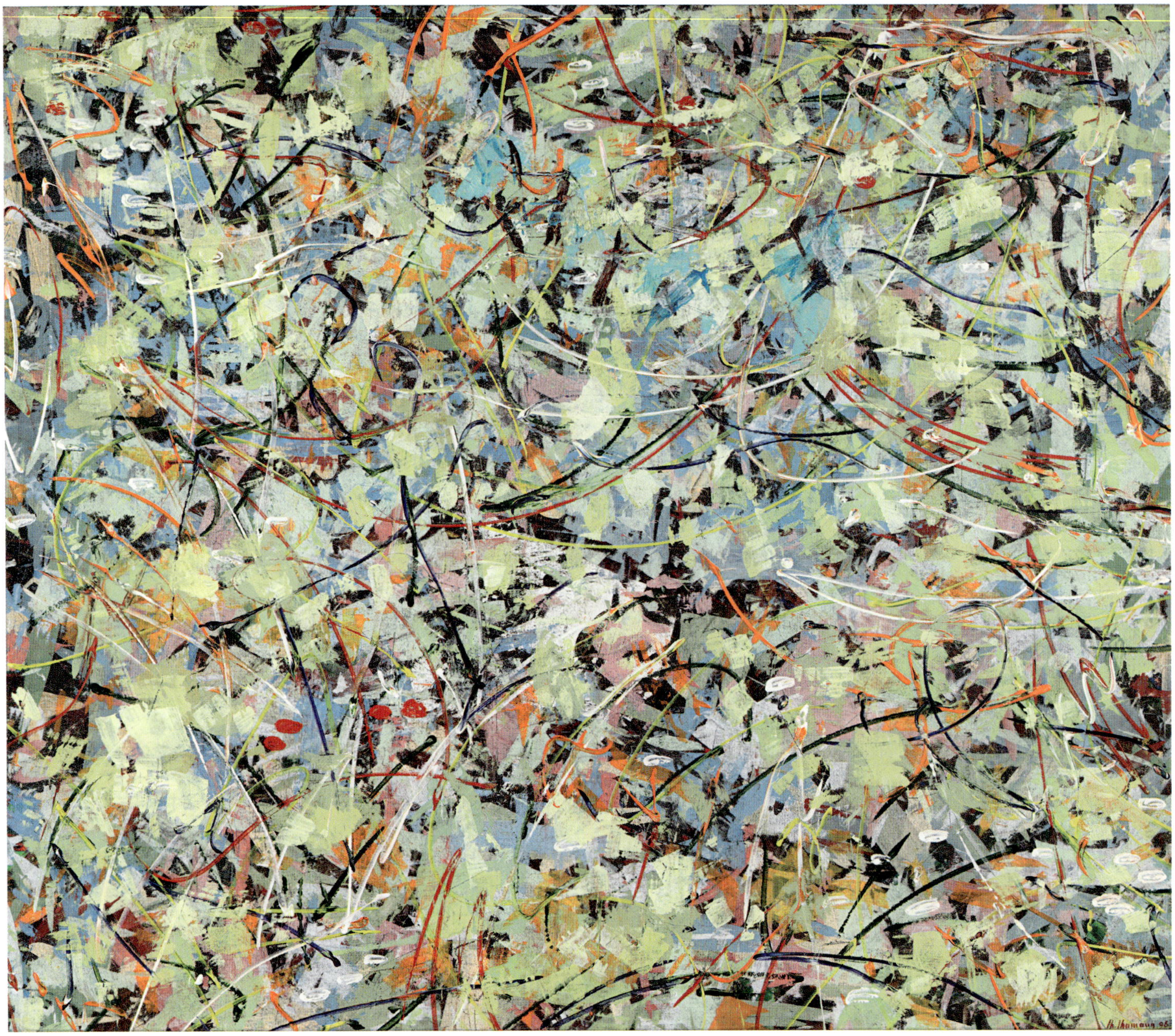

172
ARABESQUE DANCE I, 1996
Acrylic on canvas
153 x 153 cm

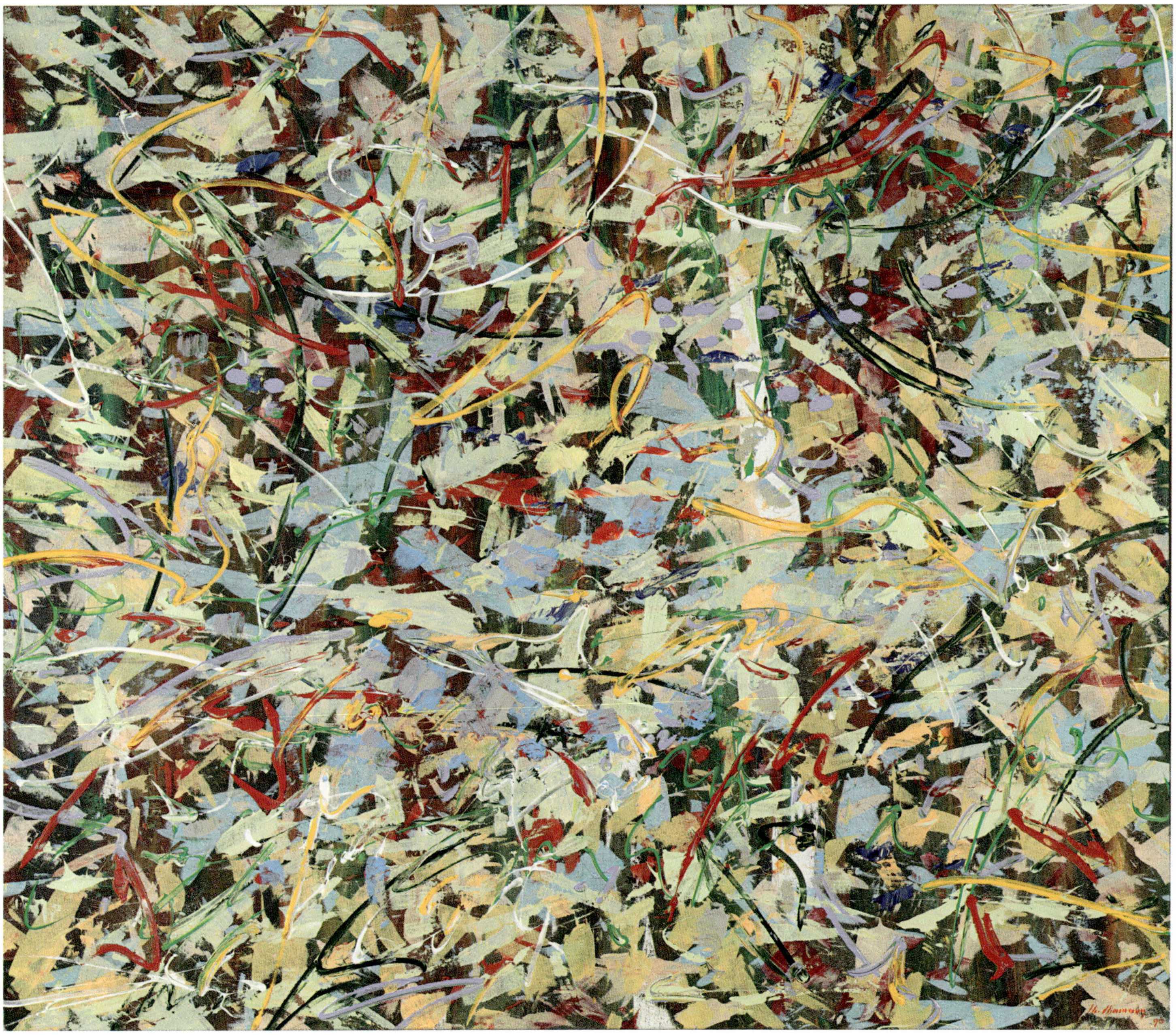

173
ARABESQUE DANCE II, 1996
Acrylic on canvas
153 x 153 cm

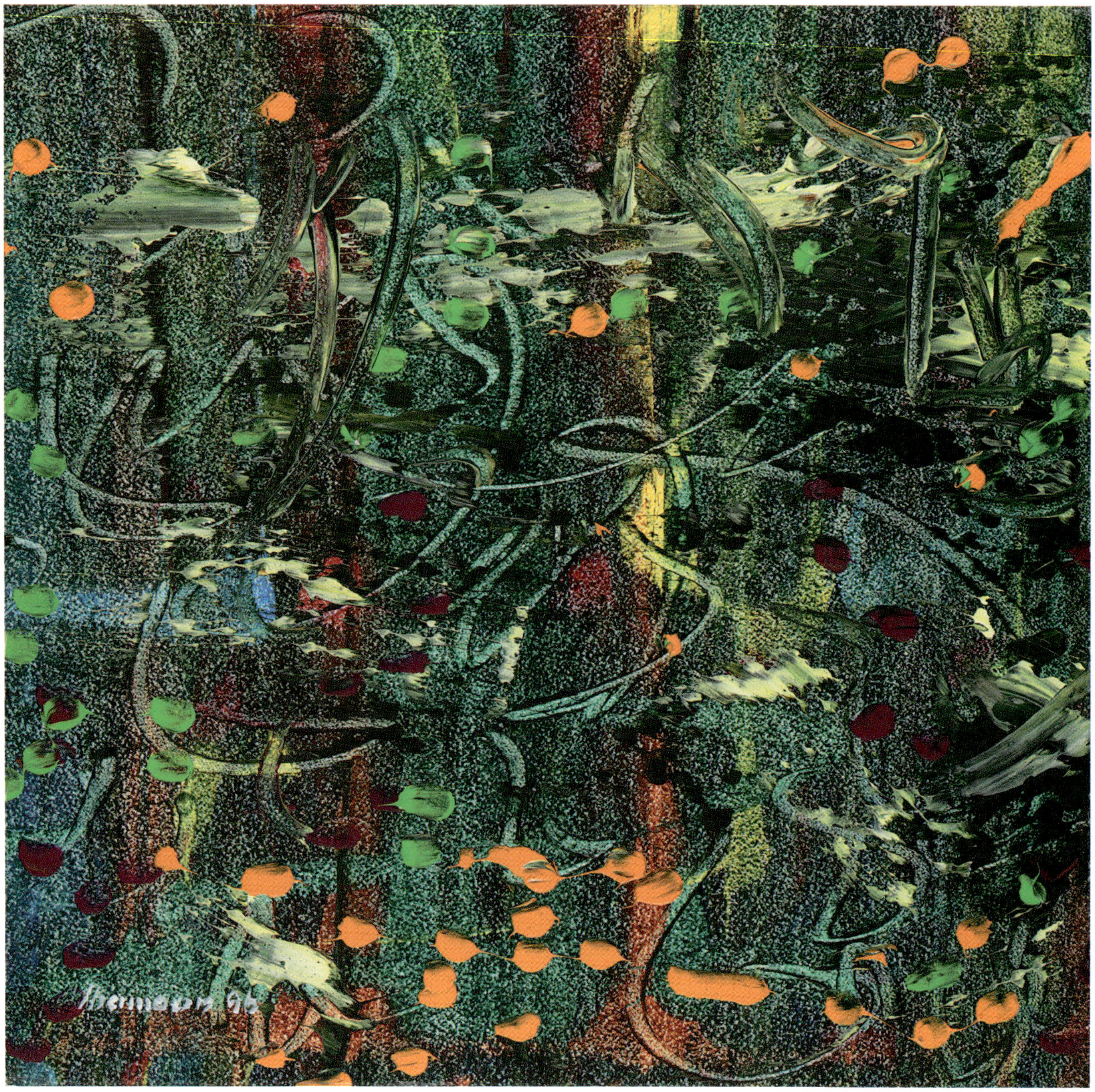

174
WRITING ON WATER, 1996
Acrylic on canvas
35 x 35 cm

Facing page
175
THE FALL IV, 1996
Acrylic on canvas (detail)
35 x 35 cm

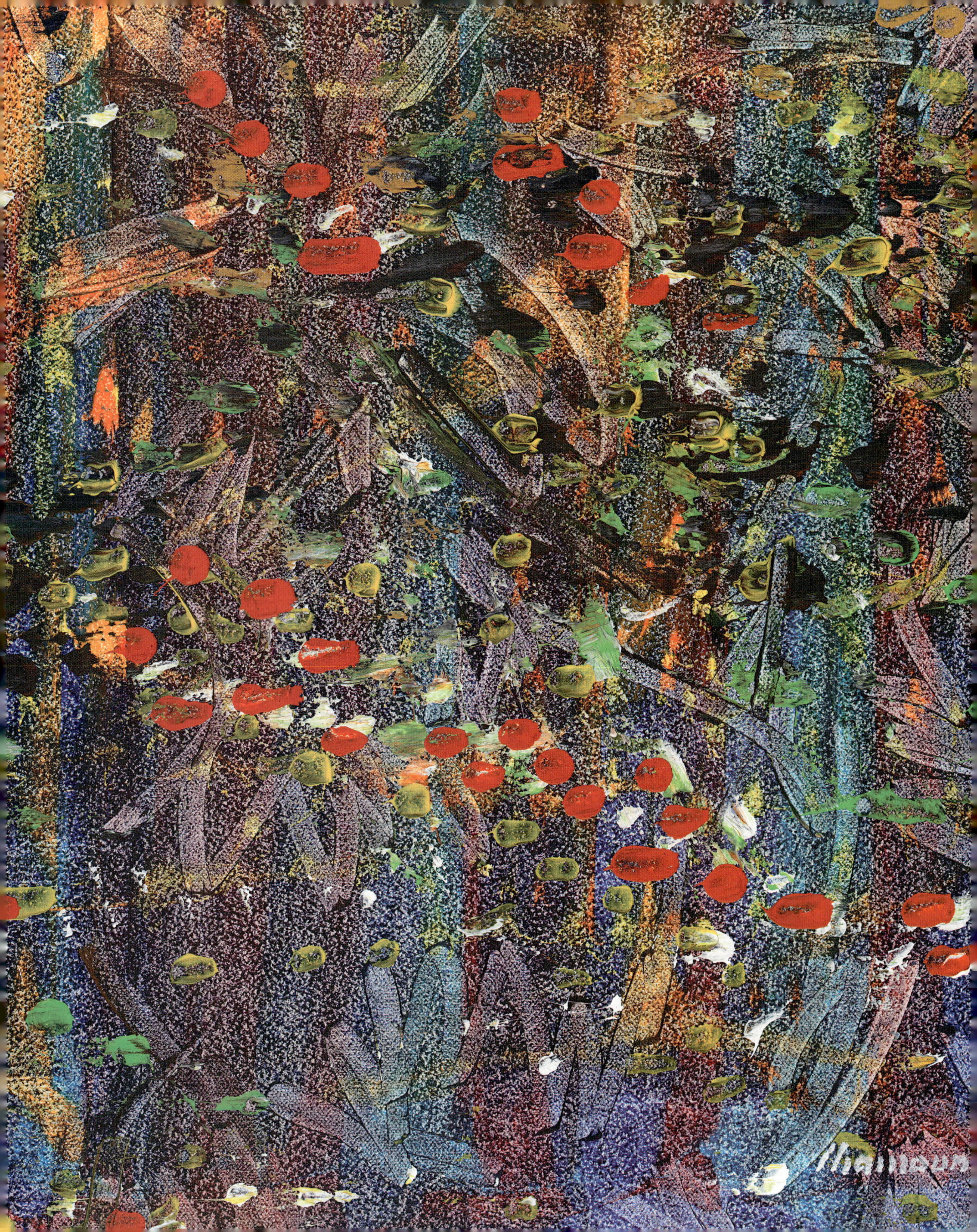

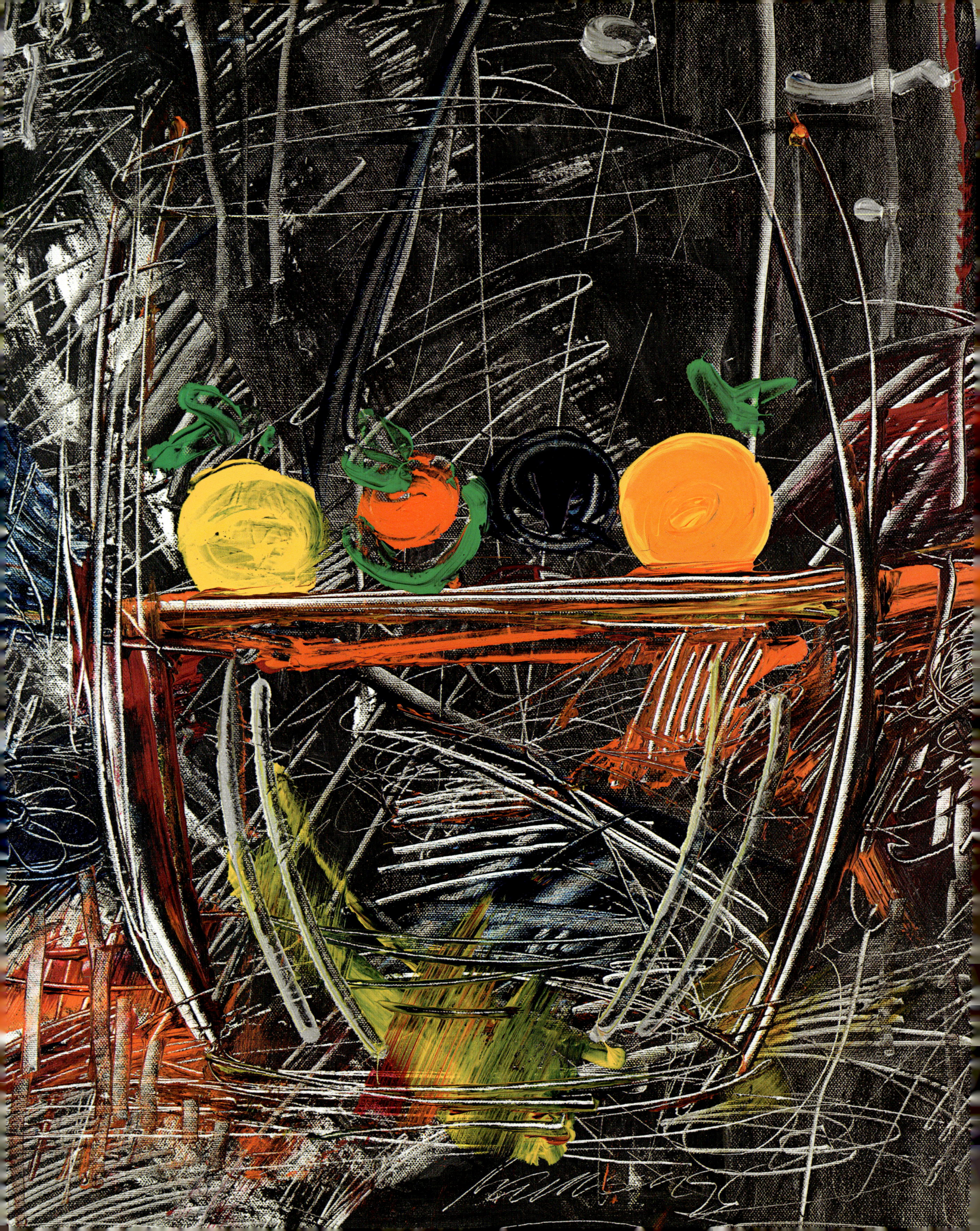

Mostly Black

In the summer of 1996, in my hotel studio in Suffern, I
started the 'Mostly Black' still life and abstract painting
series. It started with a few fruits on a coffee table. I enjoyed
dotting the colours of apples, oranges and prunes in different
176–181 configurations of black, white and grey settings. As the
imagery and the application of paint developed into pure
abstract structural formations of multi-directional gestural
182–186 strokes, I began to envisage different possibilities. The
gestural and abstract works I had painted especially for the
1995 exhibition organised by the Lebanese Artists Association
and curated by Jeoseph Abu Rizk and Nicola Nammar in
187–190 Martyrs' Square, Beirut, were on my mind. What looked
like becoming an endless game of colour-balancing slowly
turned into something akin to a dense child-like scribbling
191–195 on a school blackboard. I did two to three experiments a day.
In due course I rolled fifty small and medium-sized paintings
into a suitcase and brought them back to Lebanon. Several
large paintings followed in my studio in Adonis, where
I benefited from the intense summer activity. I went on
developing this new venture, enjoying playing, child-like, with
196–201 colours, lines and forms. During this period, I also resigned
from my post at the Lebanese University.

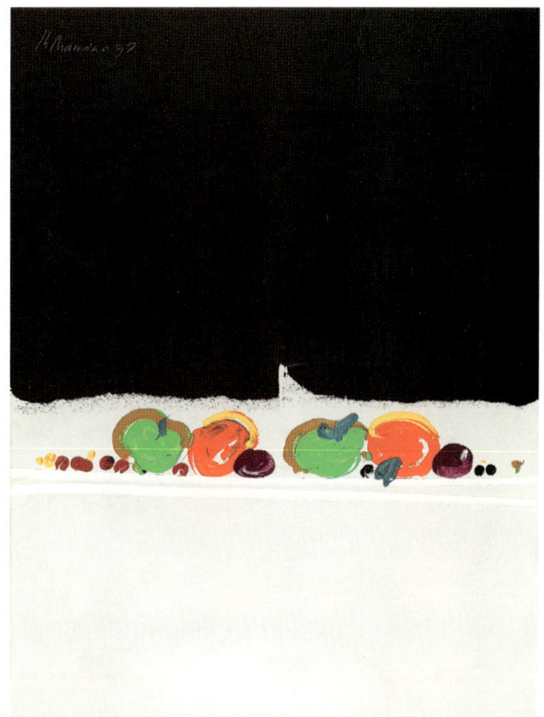

176
STILL LIFE WITH BLACK DROP I, 1997
Acrylic on canvas
52.5 x 72 cm

Facing page
177
STILL LOVE YOU, 1997
Acrylic on canvas (detail)
56 x 56 cm

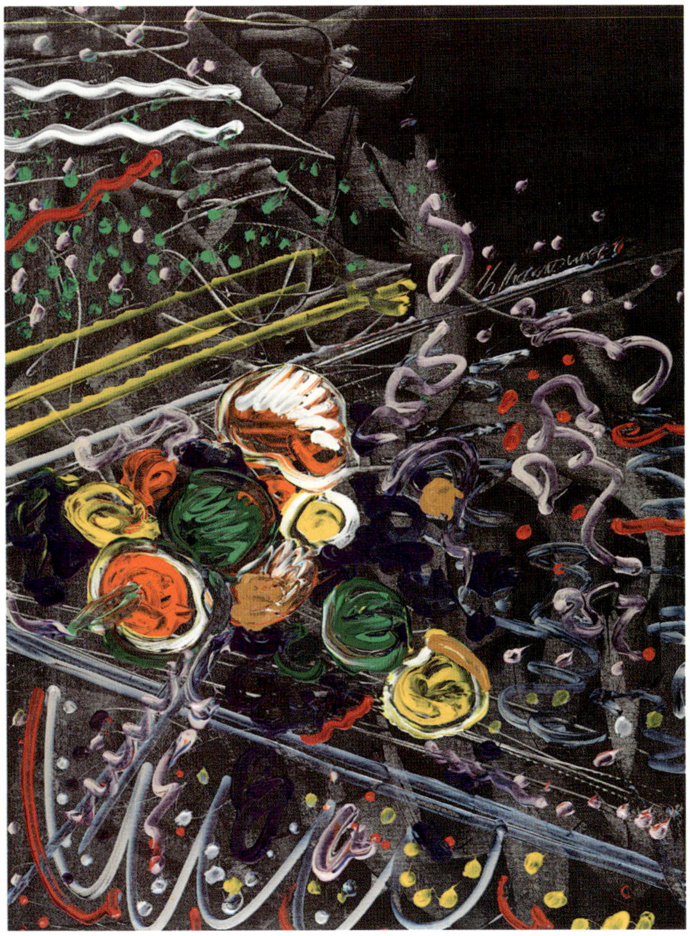

178
STILL LIFE ON BLACK TOP I, 1997
Acrylic on canvas
52.5 x 72 cm

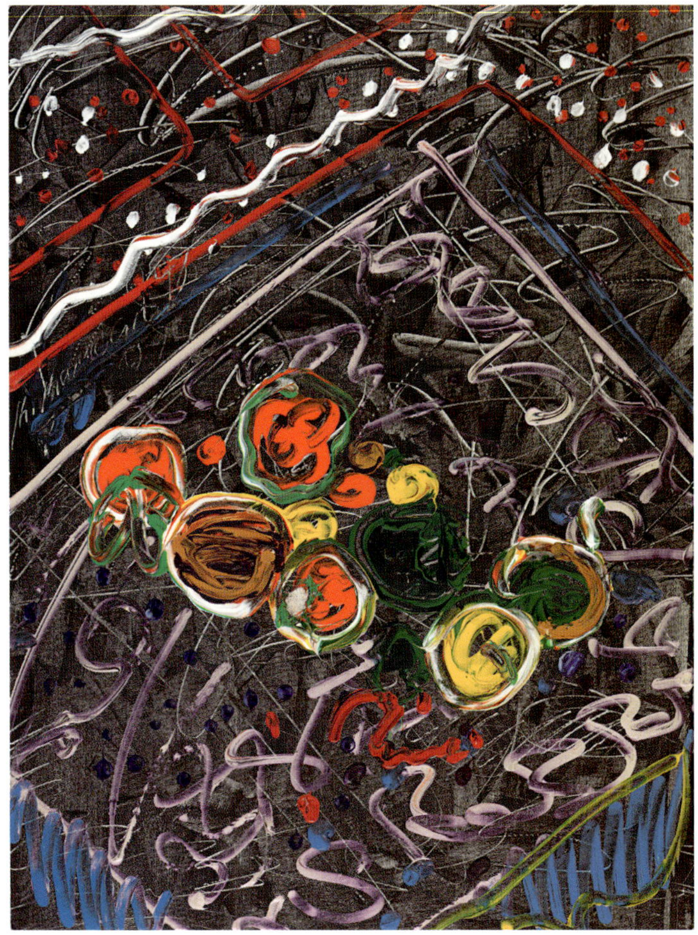

179
STILL LIFE ON BLACK TOP II, 1997
Acrylic on canvas
52.5 x 72 cm

Facing page, top
180
TOP SECRET DINNER, 1997
Acrylic on canvas
103 x 71.5 cm

Facing page, bottom
181
AT HER PLACE, 1997
Acrylic on canvas
113 x 72 cm

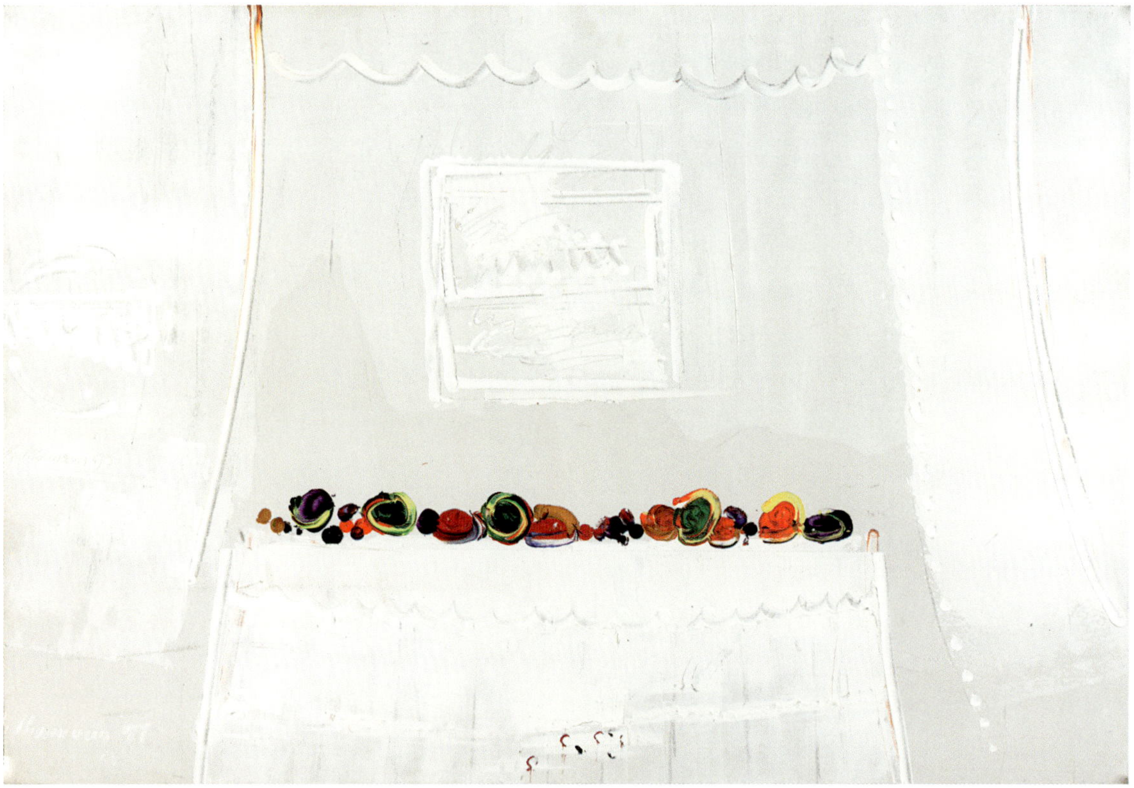

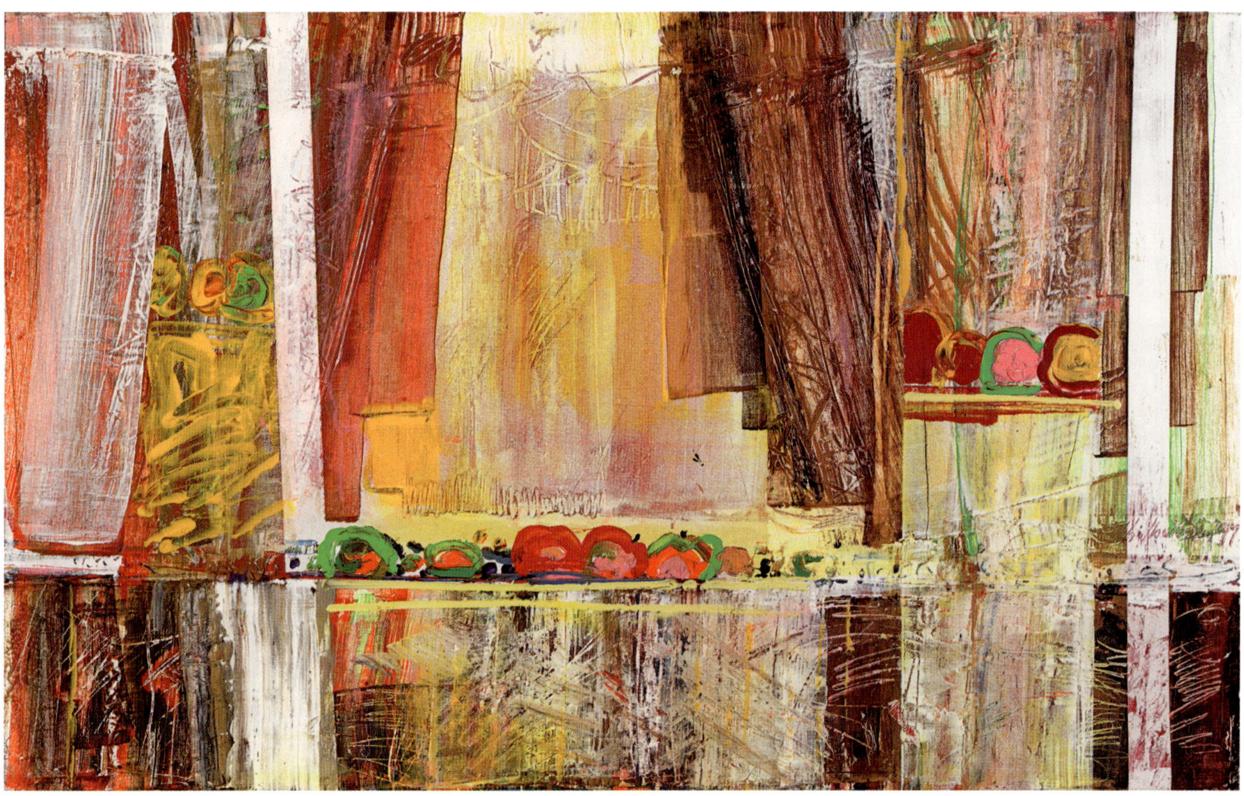

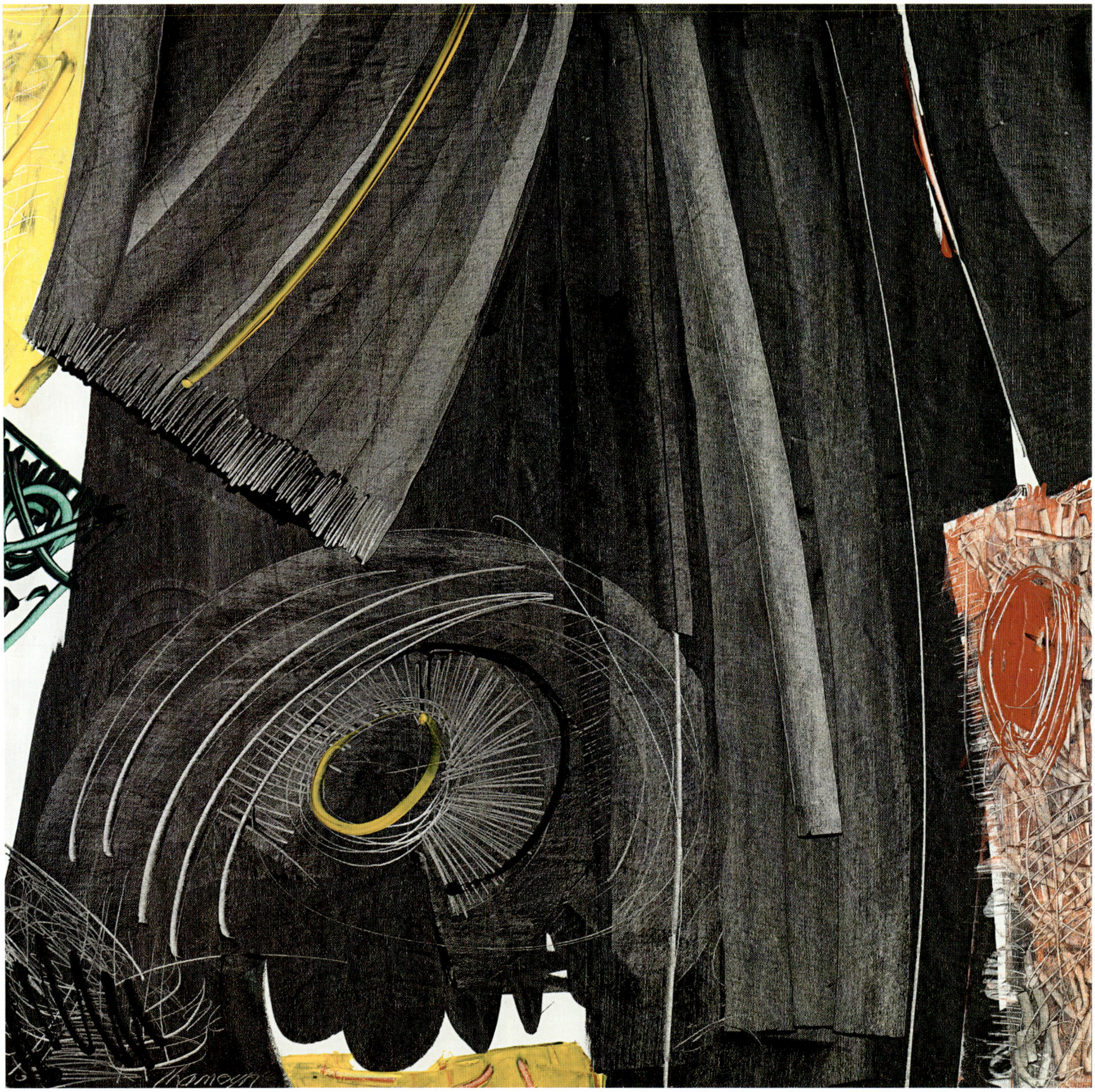

182
THE OTHER DIMENSION #25, 1996
Acrylic on canvas
76 x 76 cm

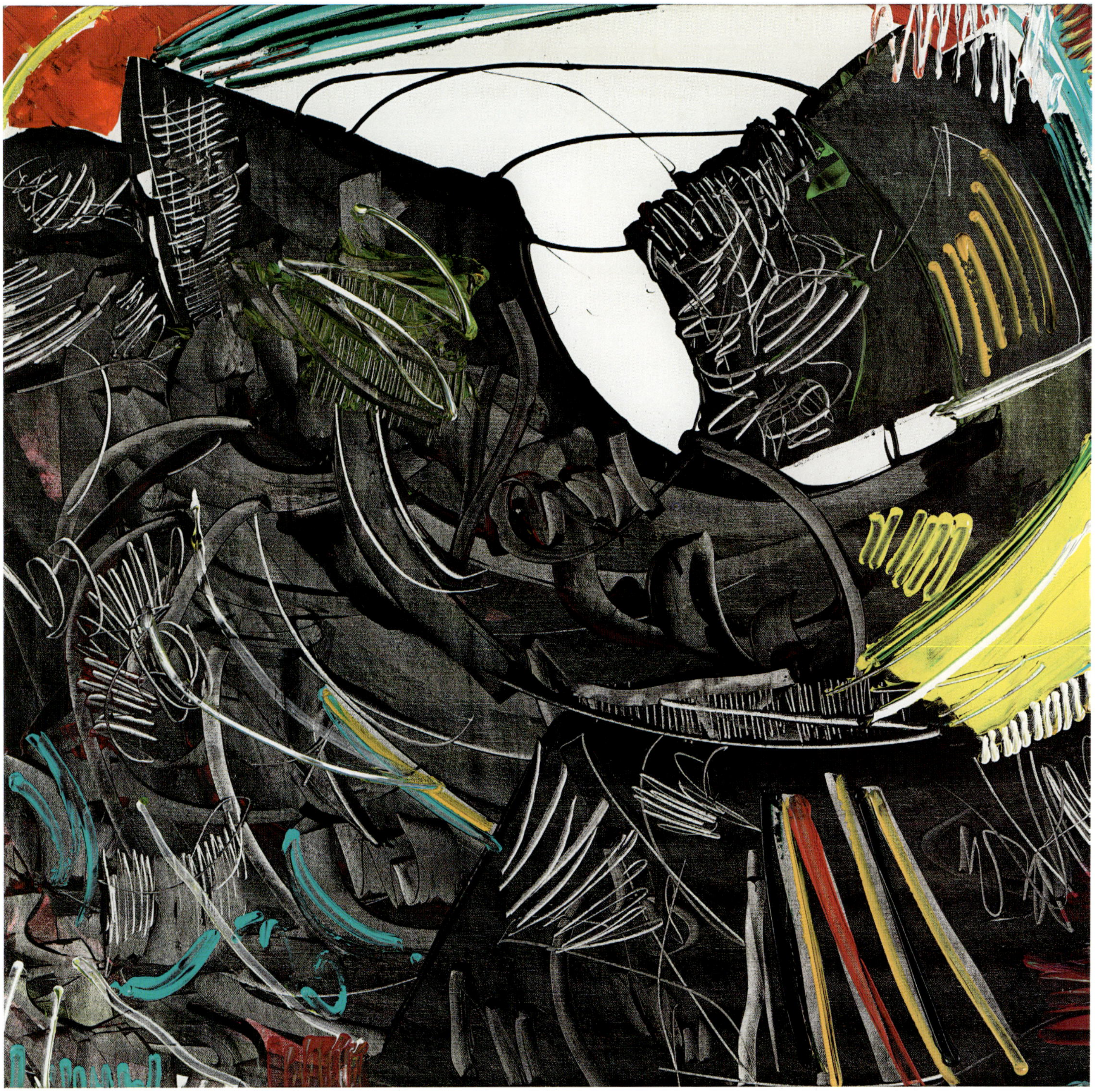

183
THE OTHER DIMENSION #8, 1996
Acrylic on canvas
76 x 76 cm

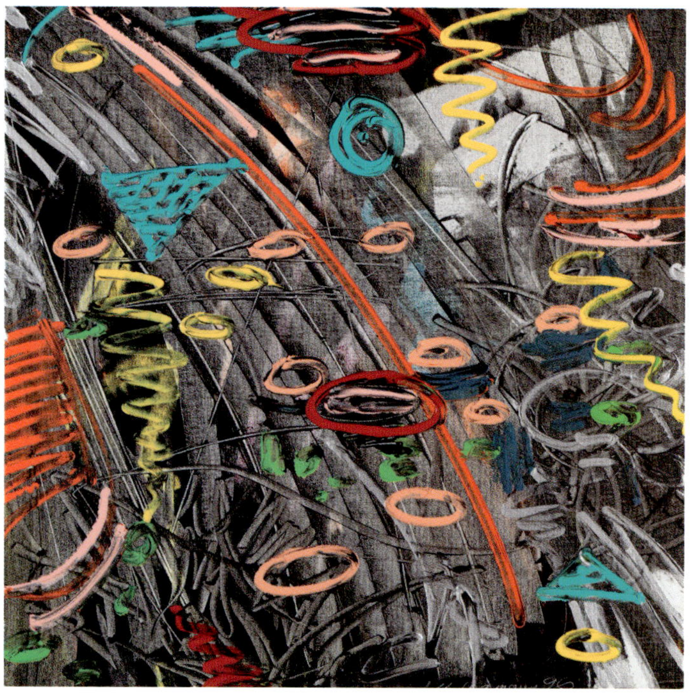

184
THE OTHER DIMENSION #2, 1996
Acrylic on canvas
56 x 56 cm

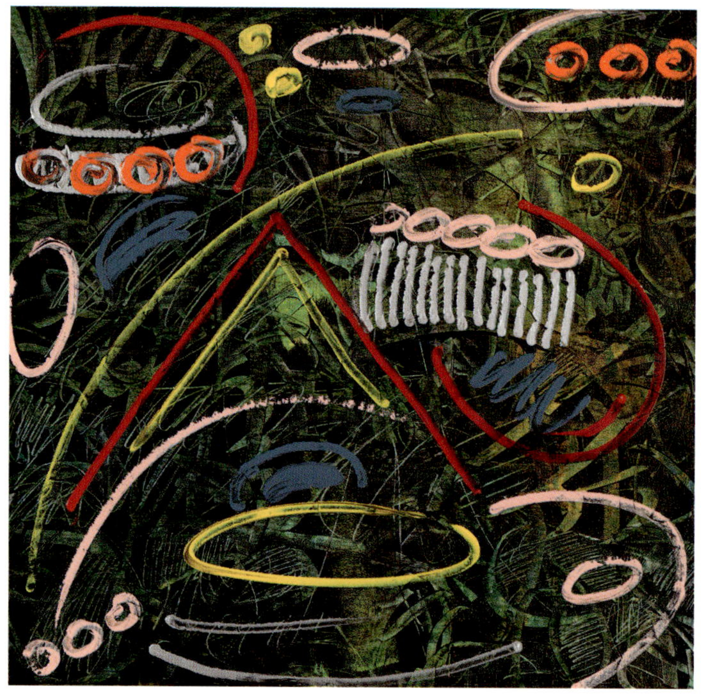

185
THE OTHER GAME, 1996
Acrylic on canvas
56 x 56 cm

Facing page
186
IN THE CROWD, 1996
Acrylic on canvas (detail)
76.5 x 76 cm

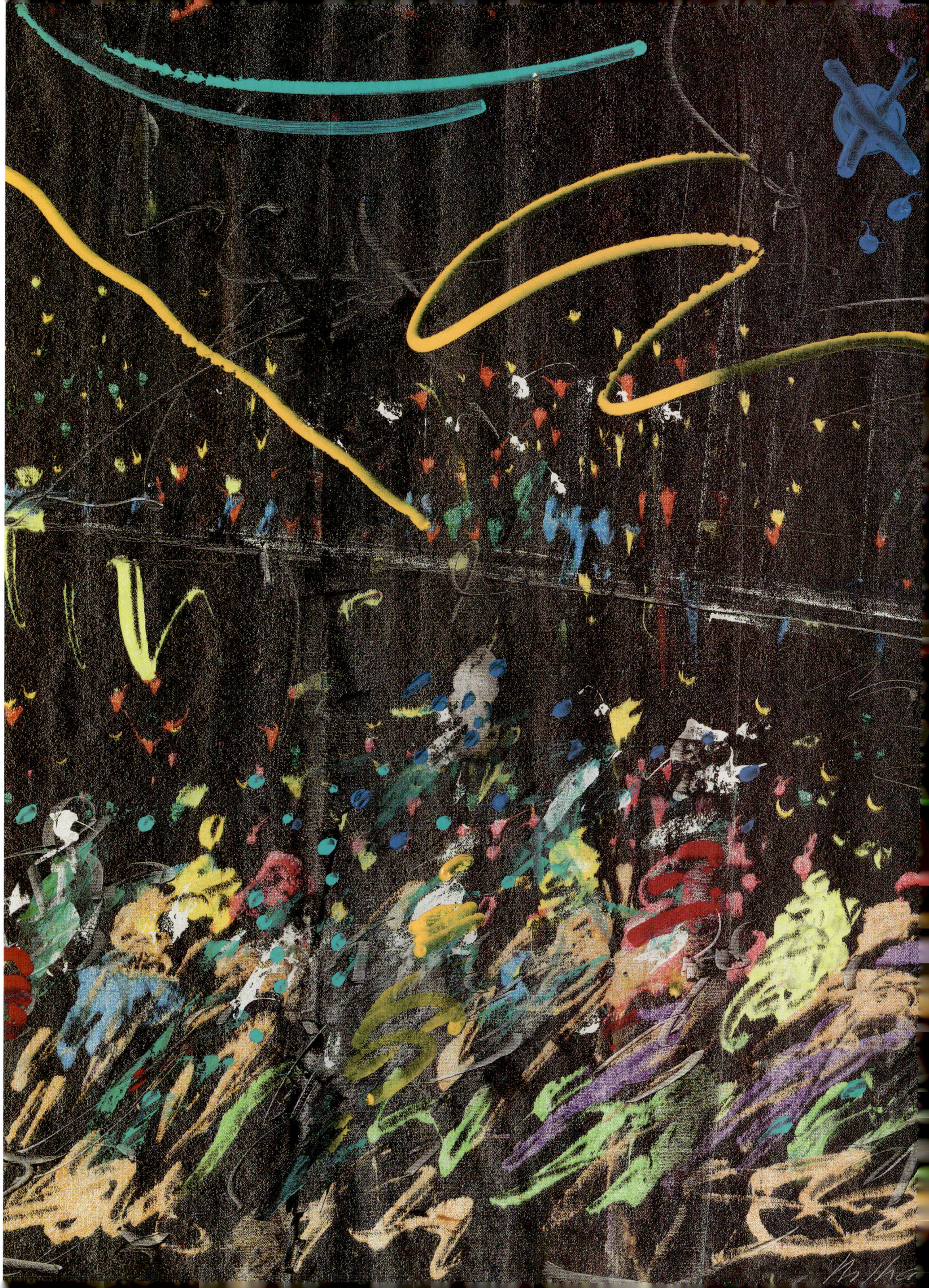

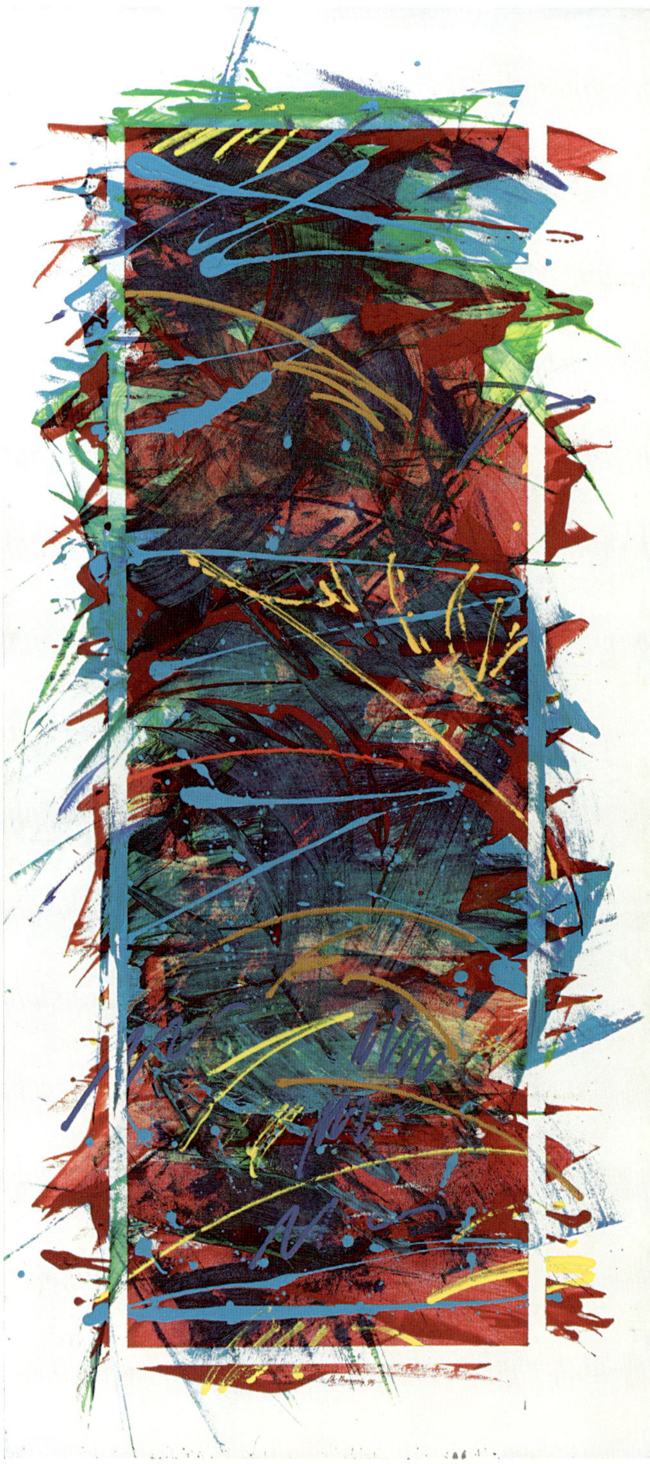

187
ODYSSEY #III, 1995
Acrylic on canvas
90 x 200 cm

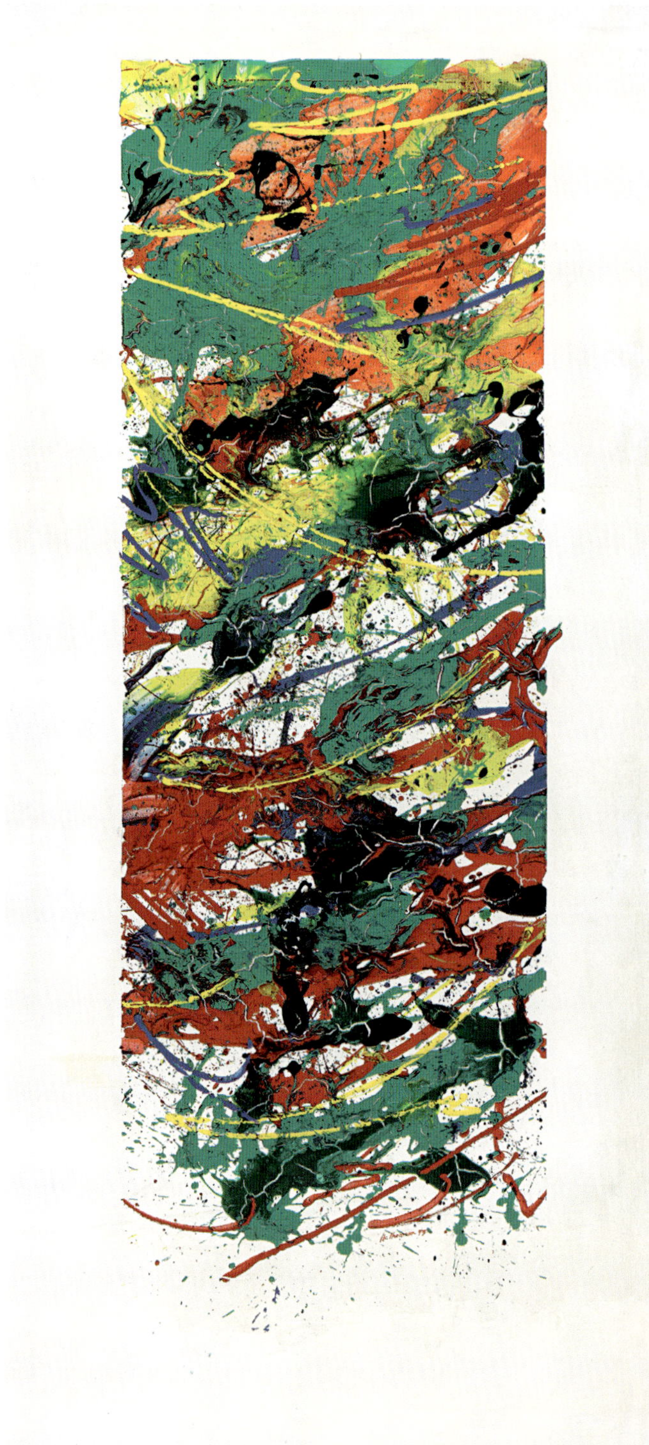

188
TO REMAIN, 1995
Acrylic on canvas
90 x 200 cm

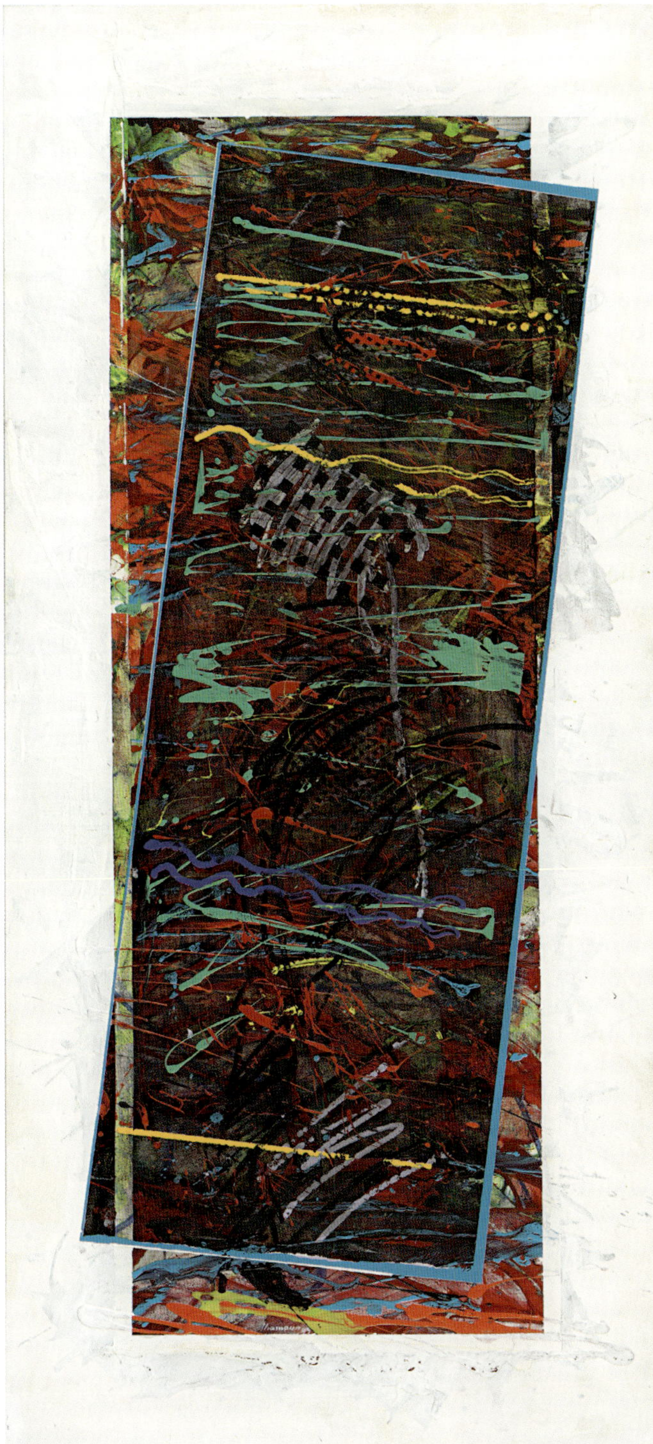

189
ODYSSEY #1, 1995
Acrylic on canvas
90 x 200 cm

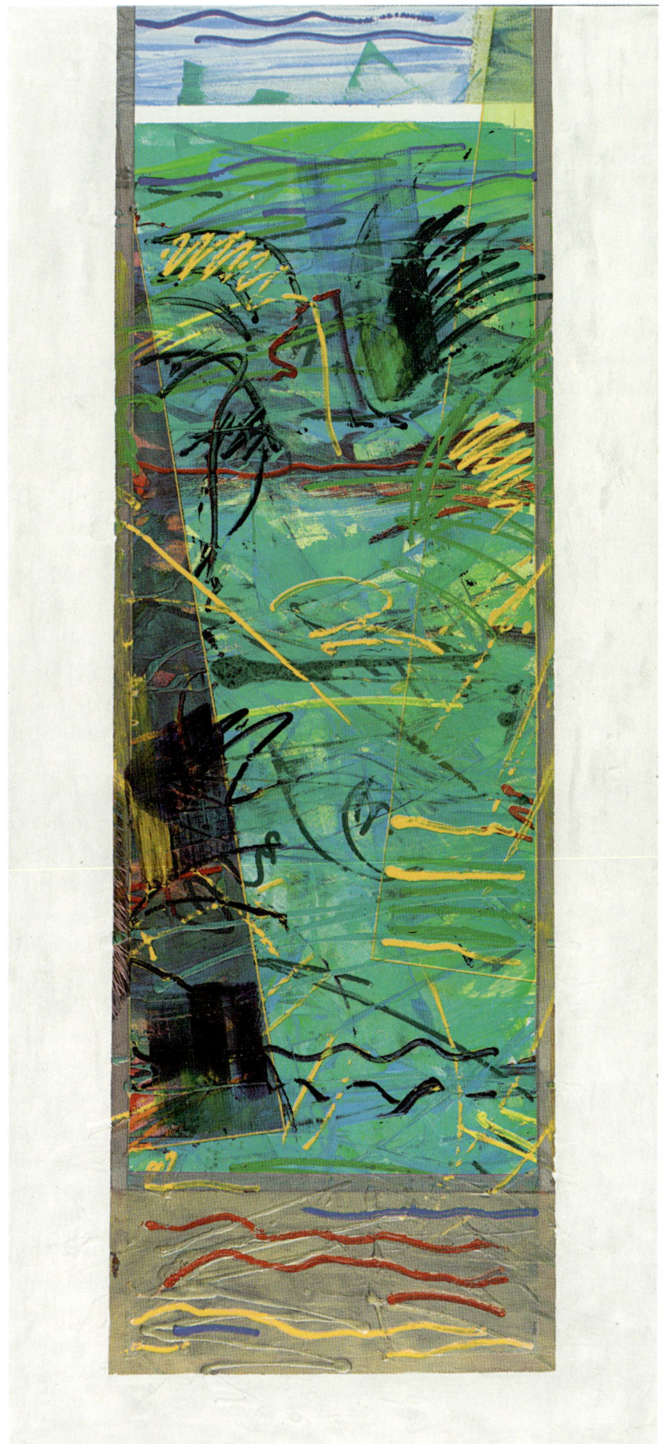

190
ODYSSEY #2, 1995
Acrylic on canvas
90 x 200 cm

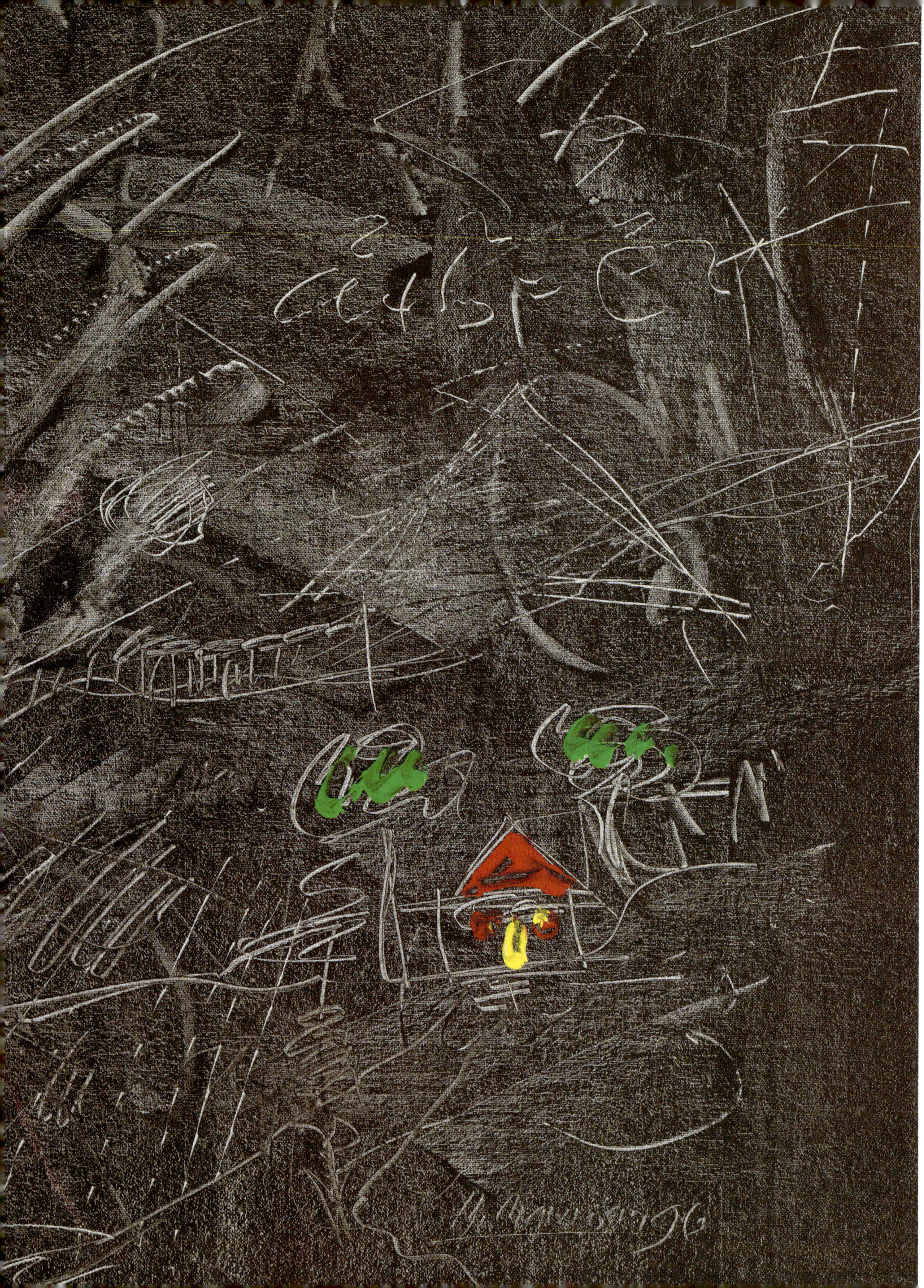

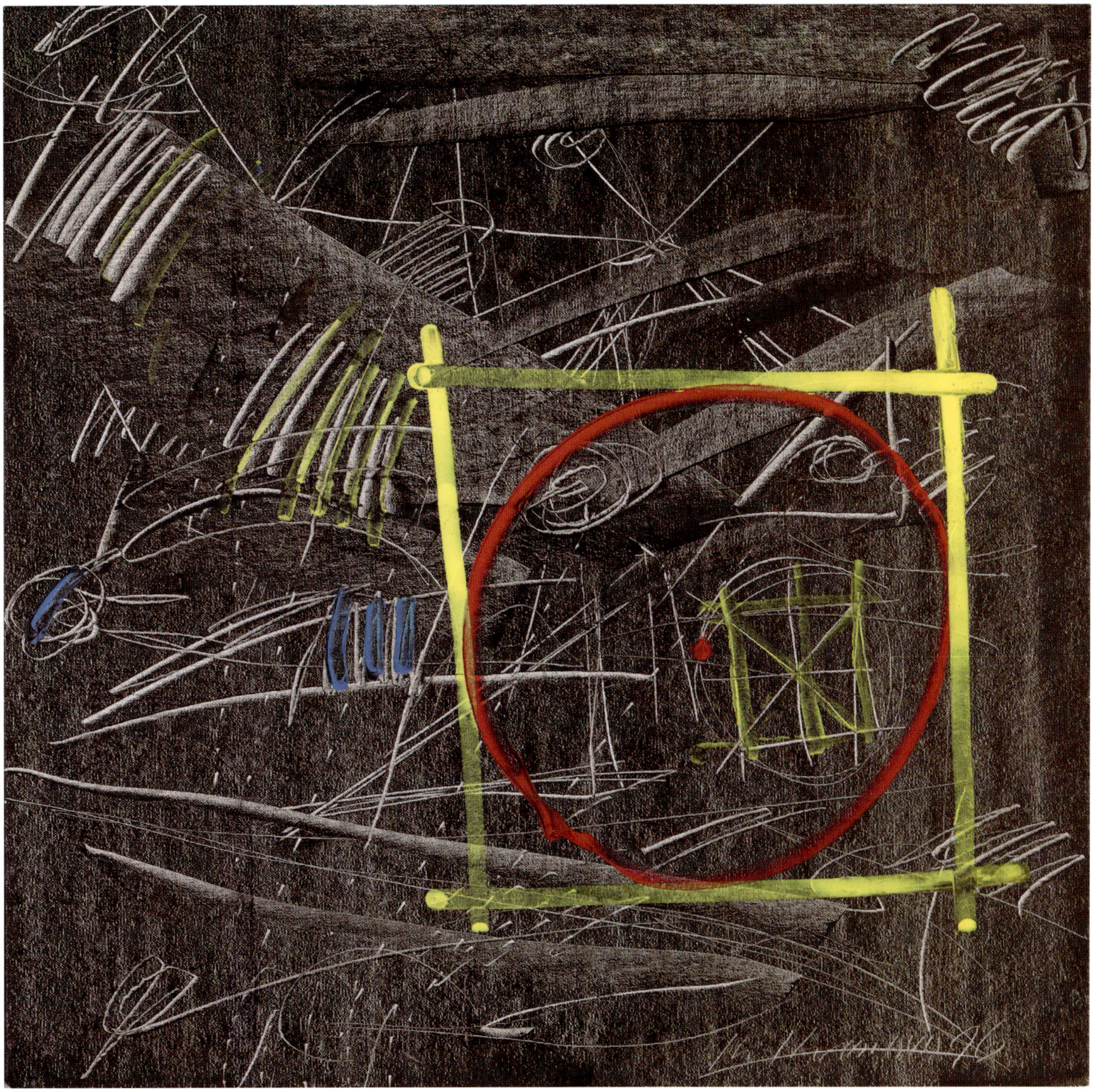

191
ON THE BLACKBOARD IX, 1996
Acrylic on canvas
56 x 56 cm

Facing page
192
ON THE BLACKBOARD VI, 1996
Acrylic on canvas (detail)
56 x 56 cm

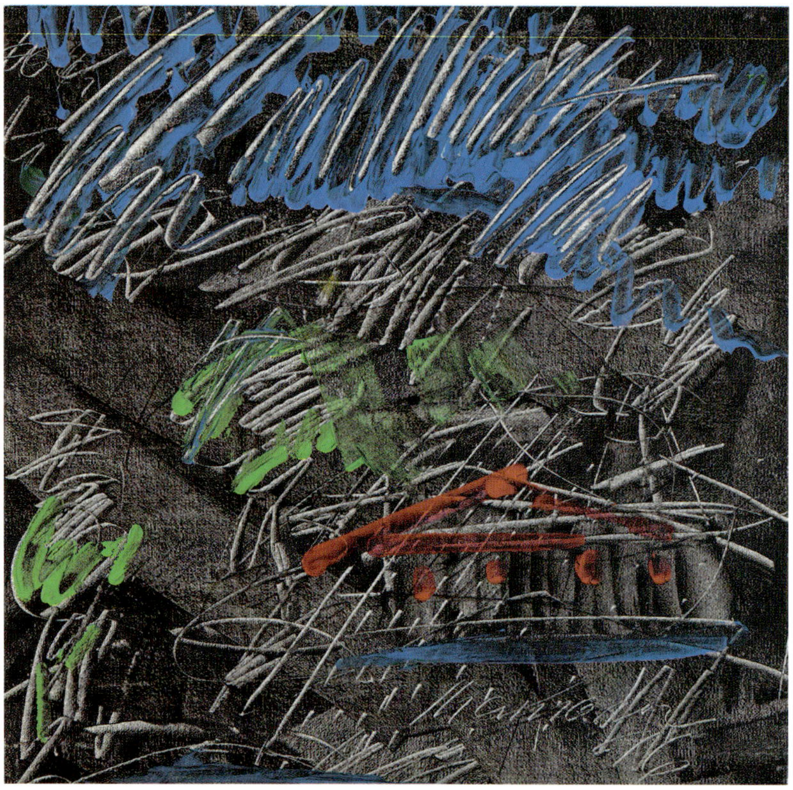

193
ON THE BLACKBOARD II,
1996
Acrylic on canvas
35 x 35 cm

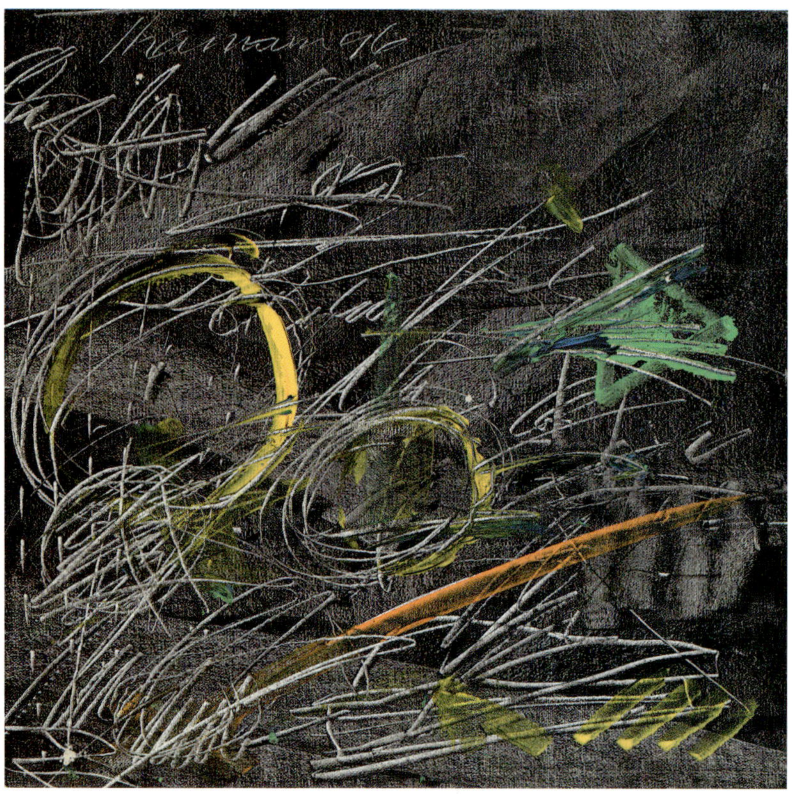

194
ON THE BLACKBOARD III,
1996
Acrylic on canvas
56 x 56 cm

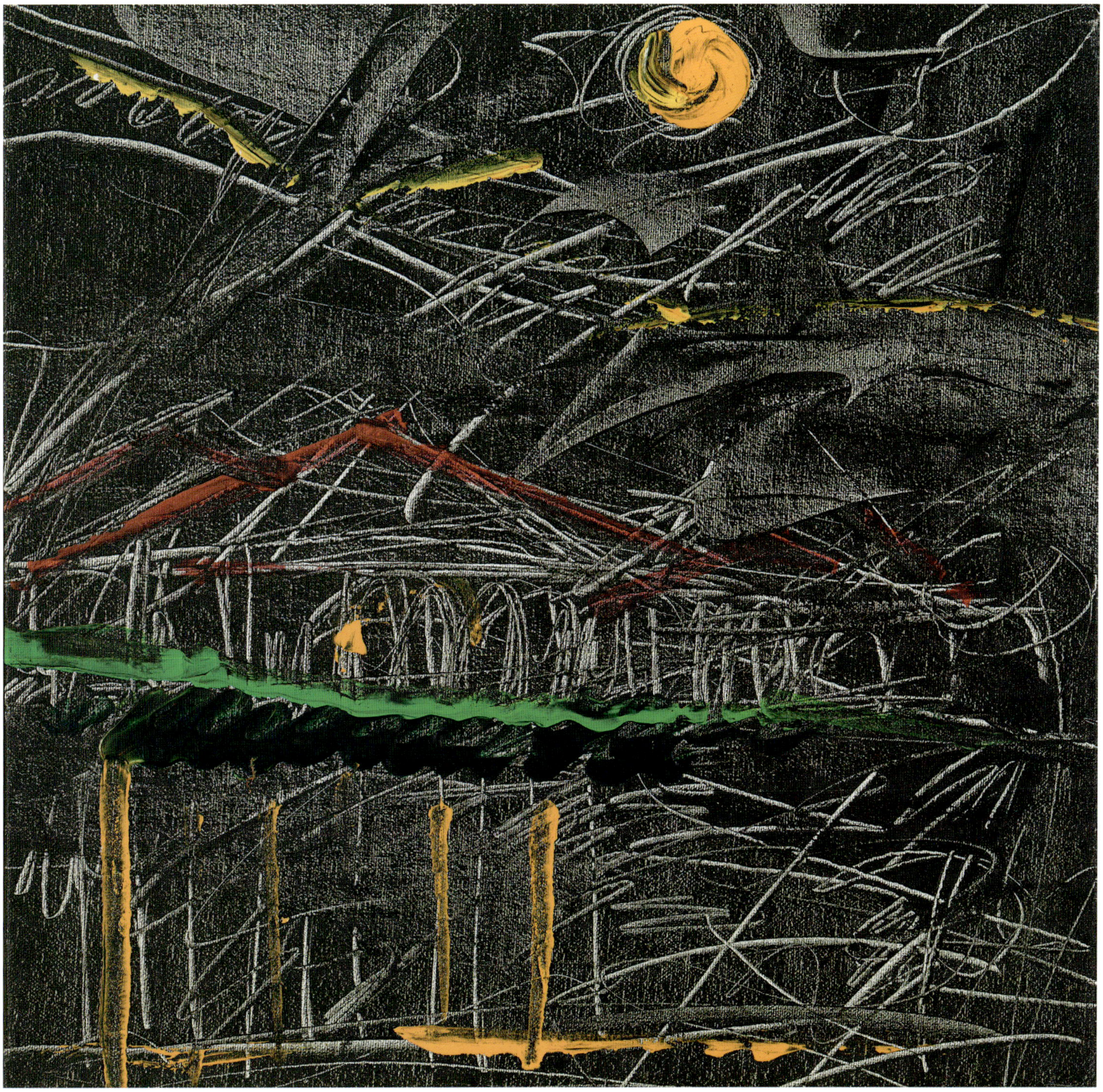

195
ON THE BLACKBOARD V, 1996
Acrylic on canvas
35 x 35 cm

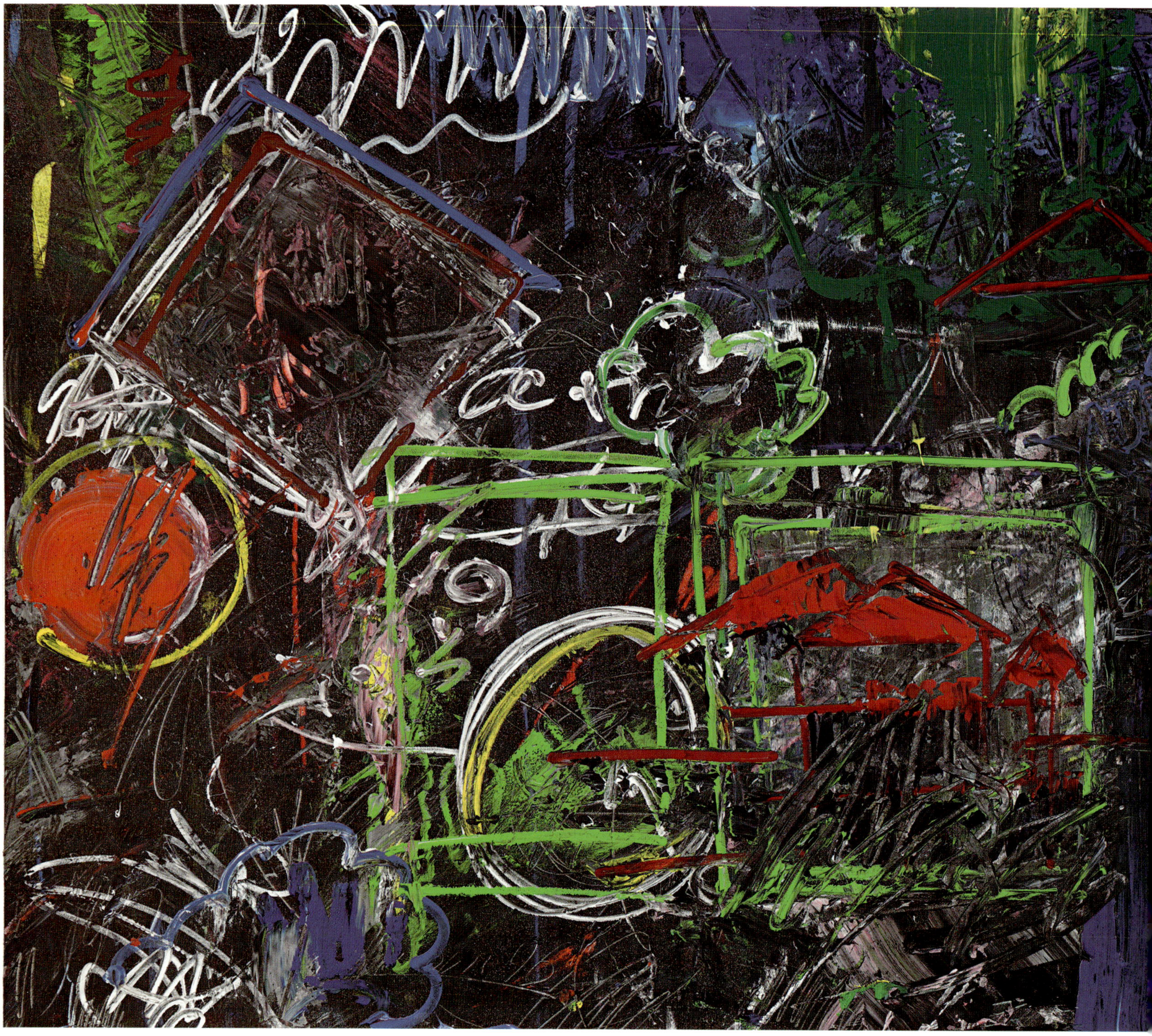

196
RED ROOFS IV, 1996
Acrylic on canvas
223 x 112 cm

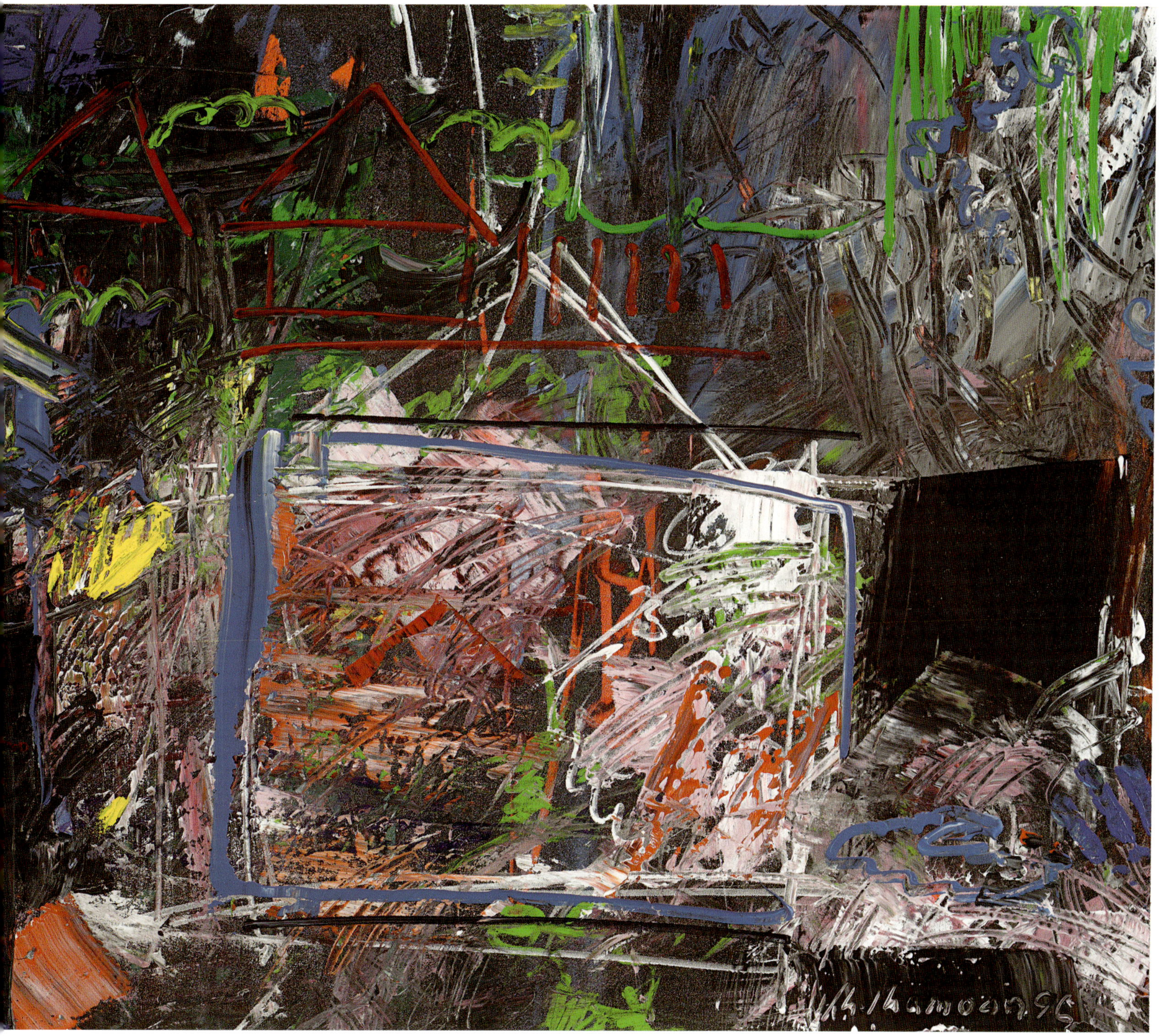

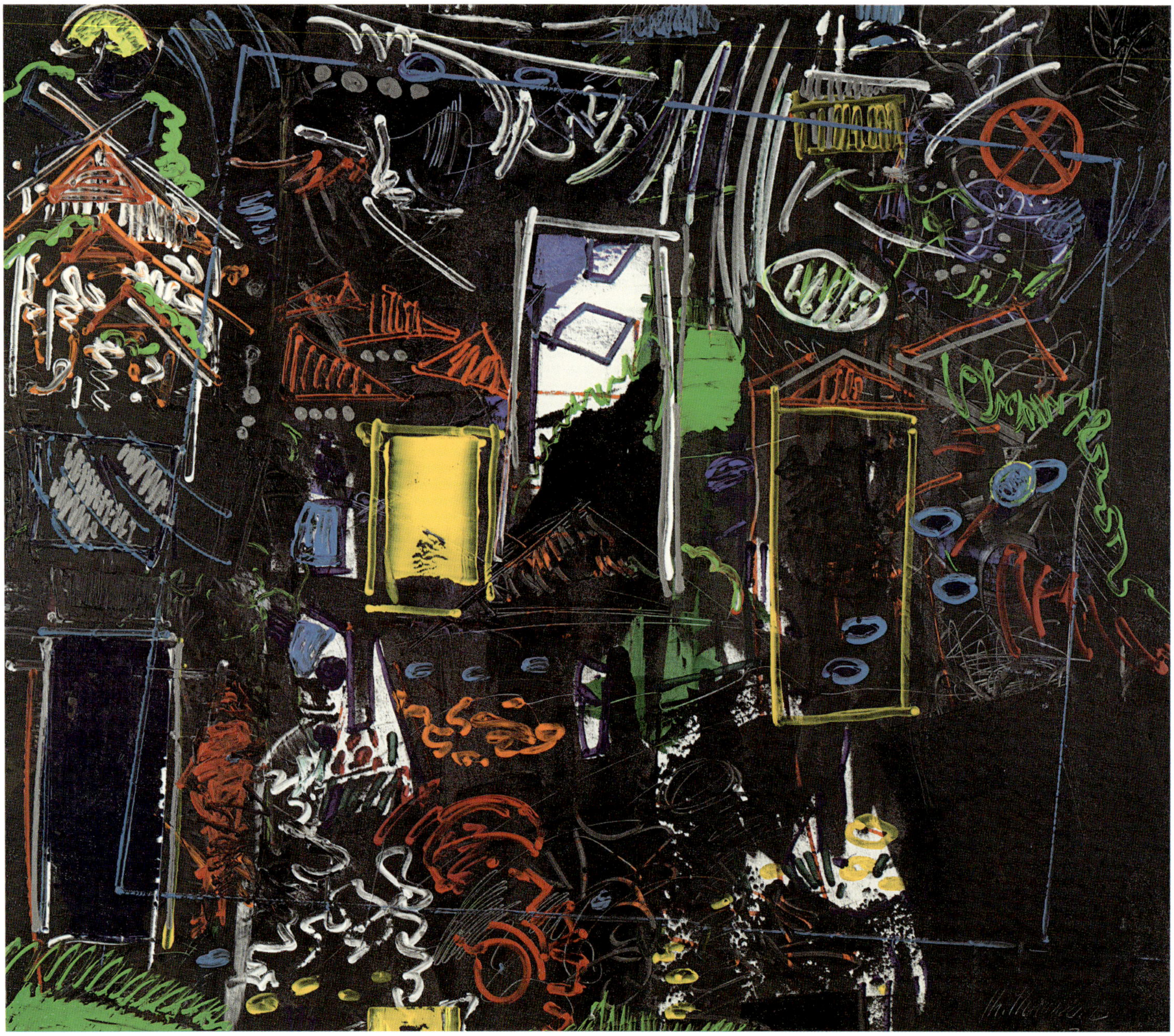

197
WINDOWS, 1997
Acrylic on canvas
158 x 141 cm

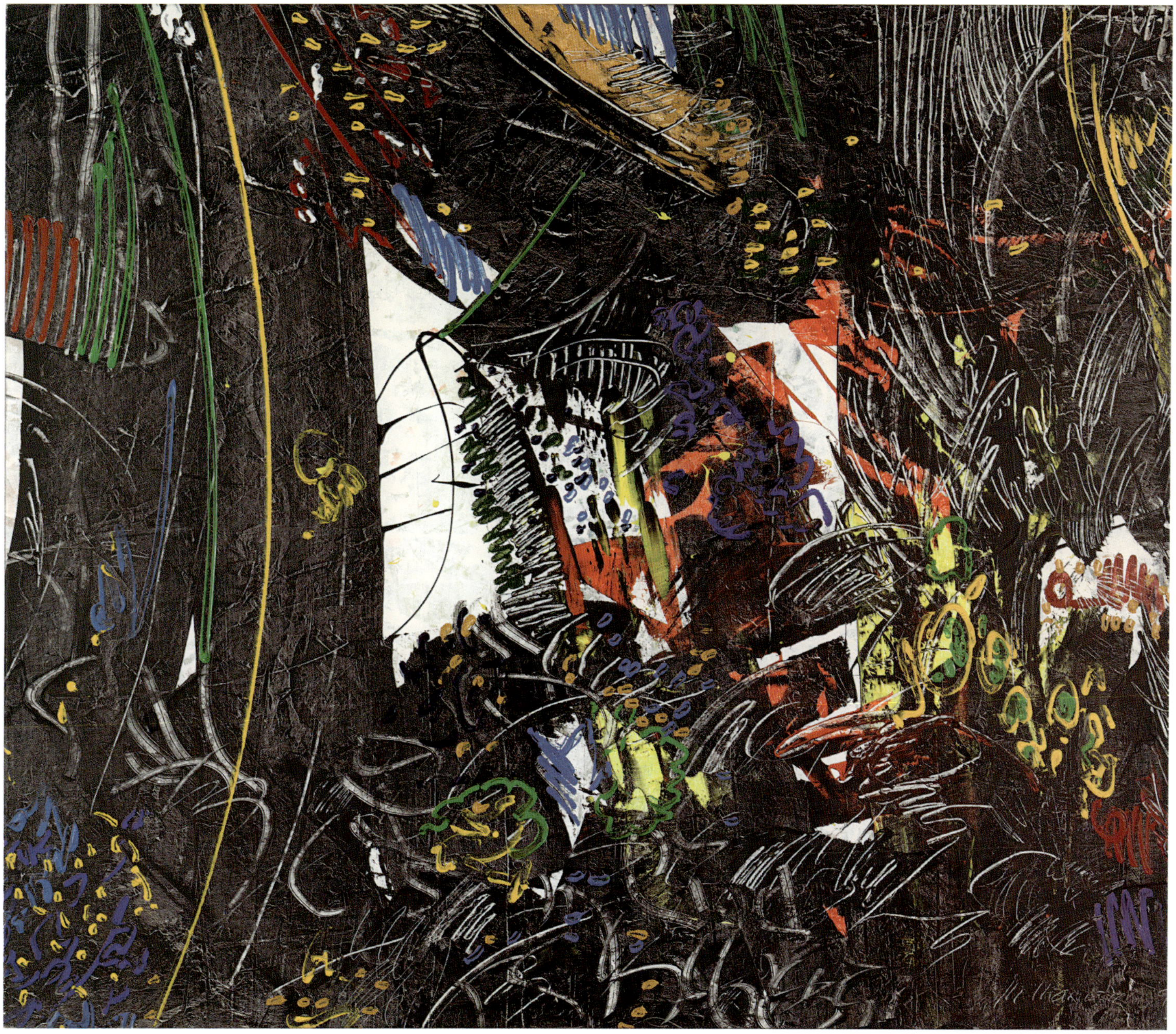

198
GLOWING LINES, 1996
Acrylic on canvas
153 x 135 cm

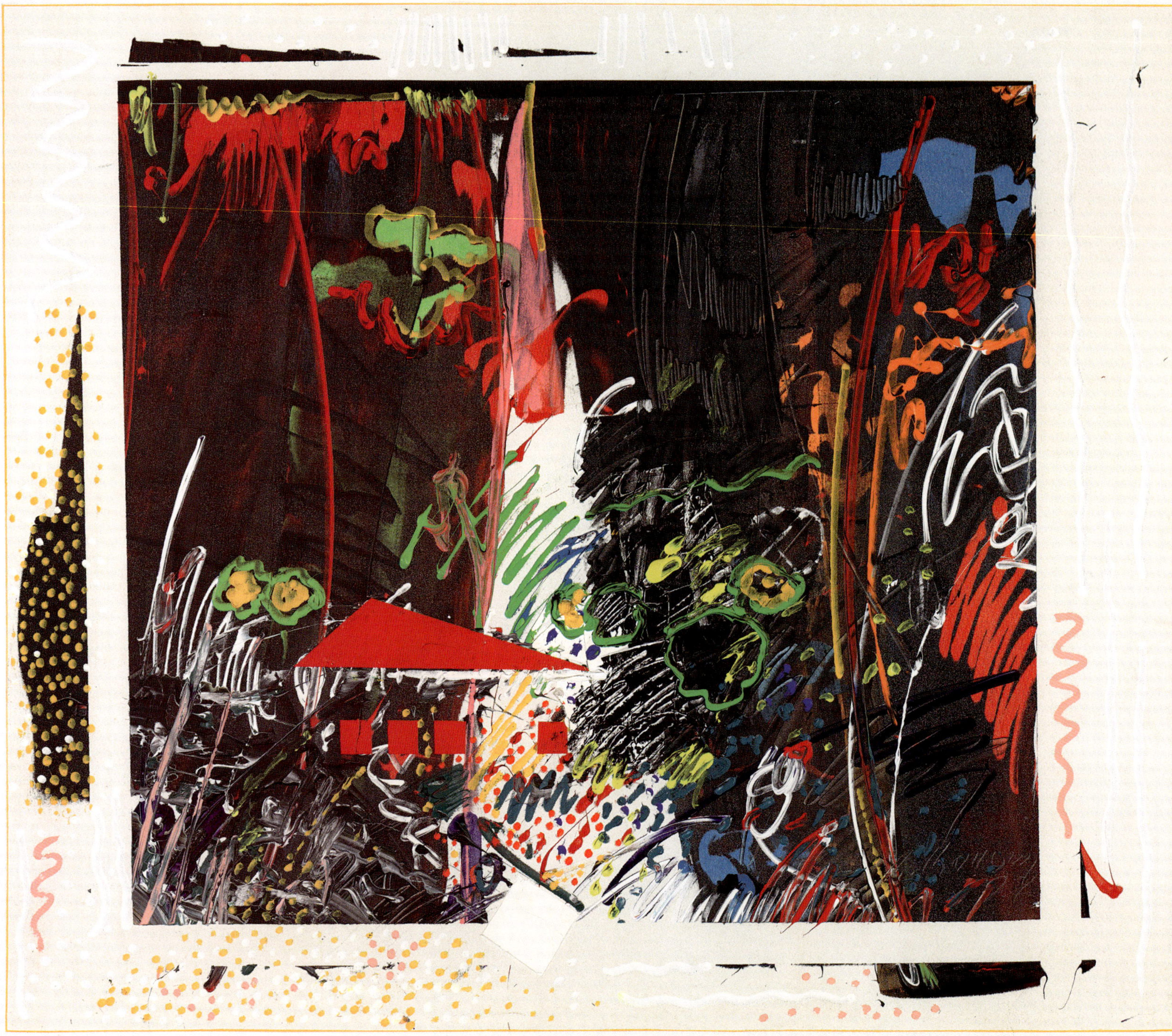

199
THE RED ROOF III, 1996
Acrylic on canvas
158 x 140 cm

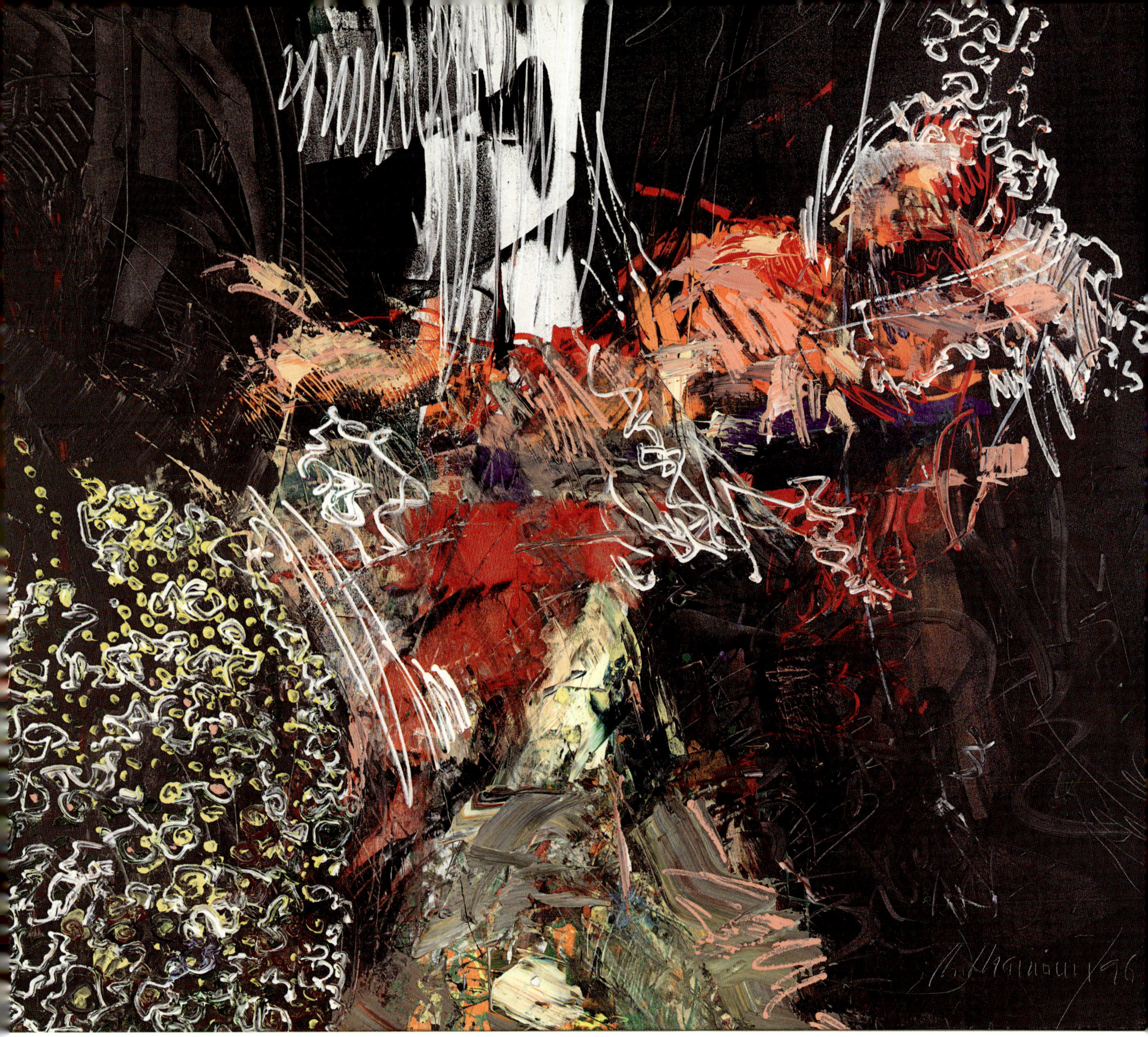

200
LACES OF LIGHT, 1996
Acrylic on canvas
153 x 135 cm

Following spread
201
RED ROOFS V, 1997
Acrylic on canvas (detail)
230 x 112 cm

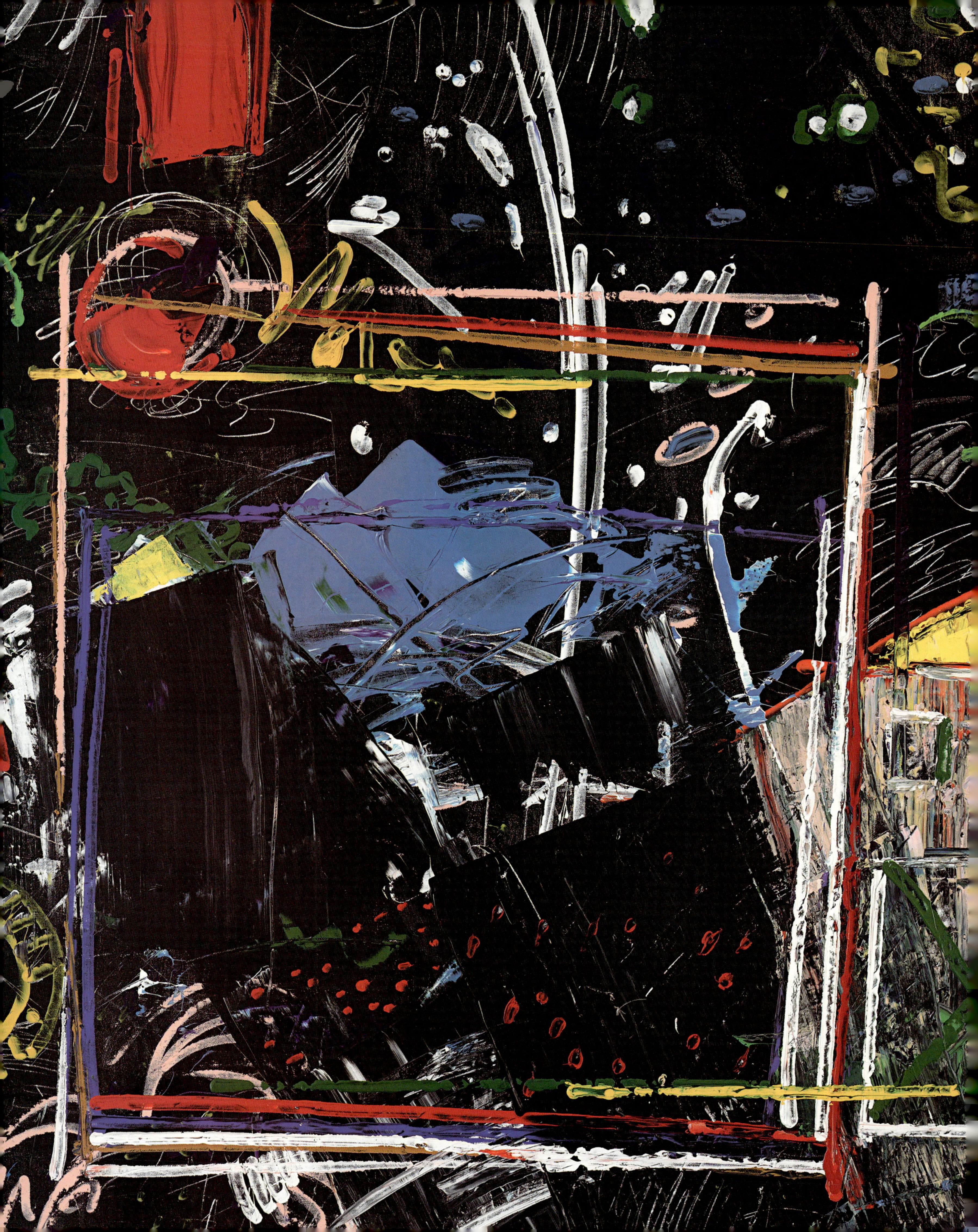

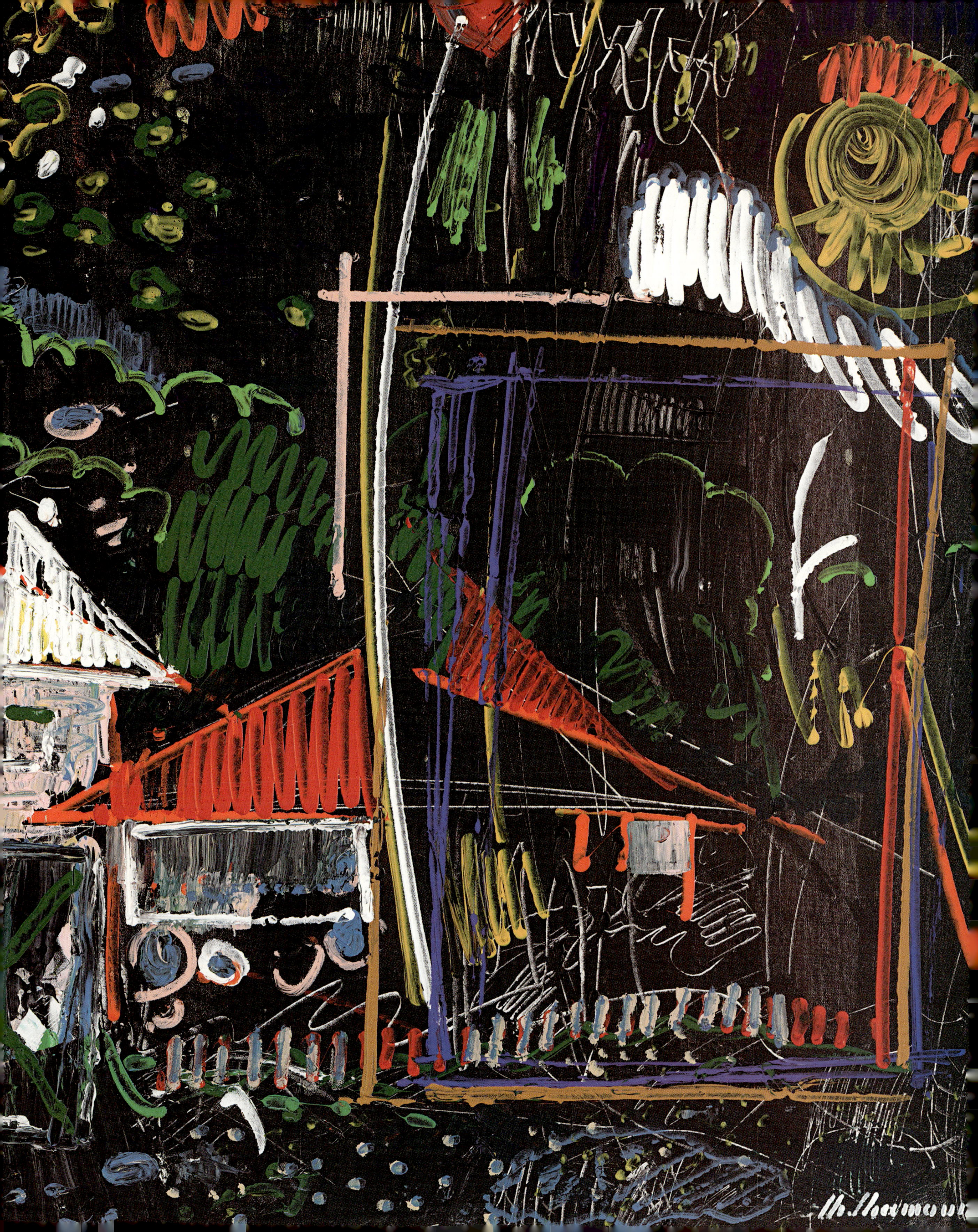

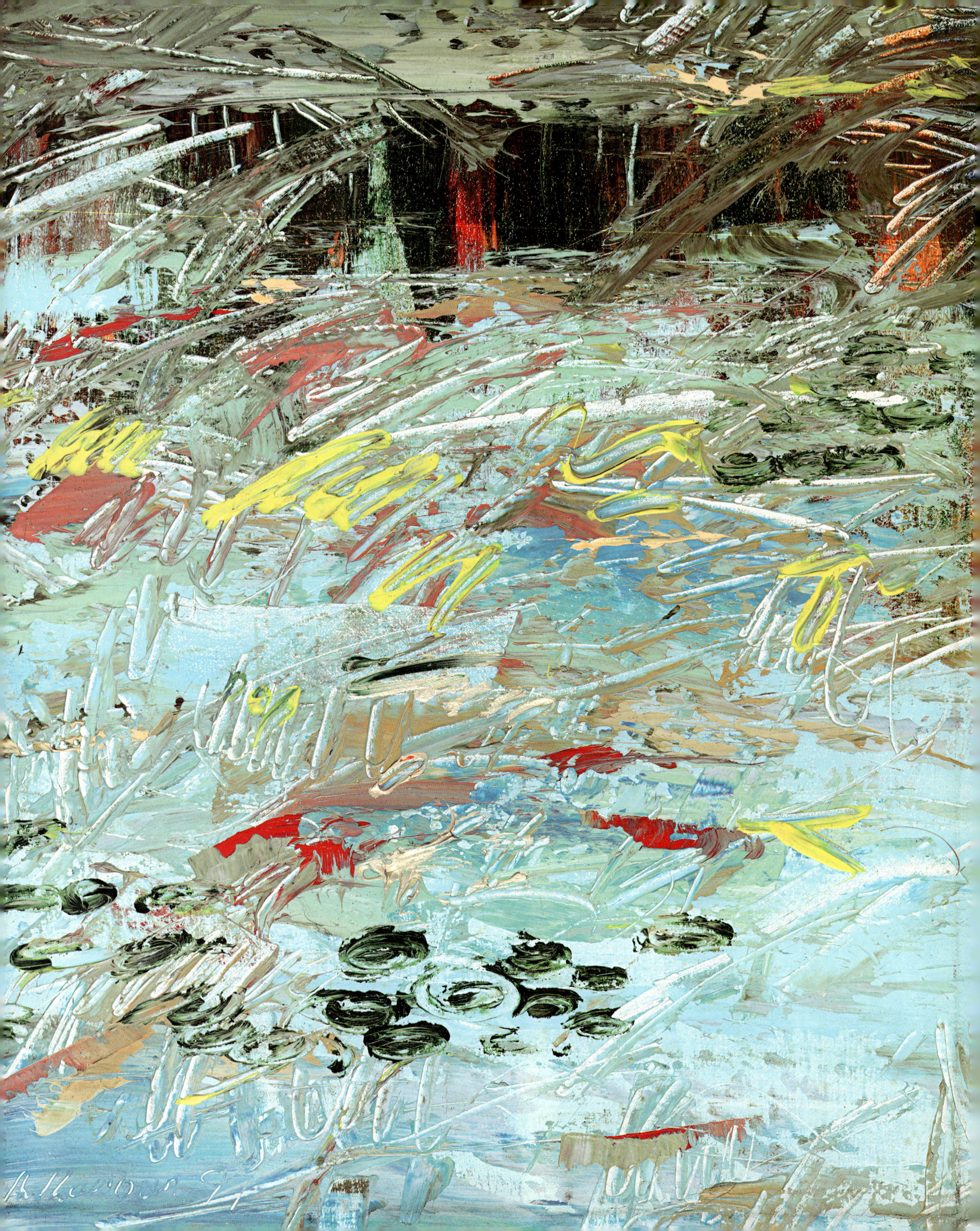

Nature Revisited

I returned to Harriman Park in the summer of 1997 with eyes thirsty for more of that extraordinary natural arrangement of transparent surfaces of water, reflected shades of greenery, and dreamily floating water lilies. The result was a new series of 'Water Reflections' under the spell of 'Nature Revisited', which was finalised and exhibited at the Coffee Art Gallery
202–206 in Kingston, New York, in the autumn of 1997. I missed the opening night because I had to be back in Lebanon in time to take up my new teaching responsibilities at the Lebanese American University. Upon my return to Beirut, I held a large exhibition of the 'Mostly Black' series at the Emmagos Art Gallery.

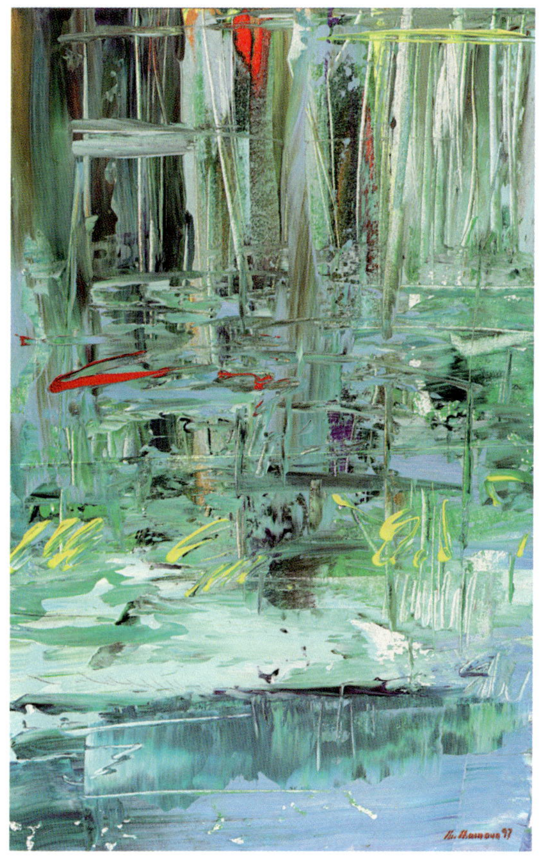

202
REFLECTIONS X, 1997
Acrylic on canvas
50.5 x 79.5 cm

Facing page
203
REFLECTIONS IX, 1997
Acrylic on canvas (detail)
54 x 86 cm

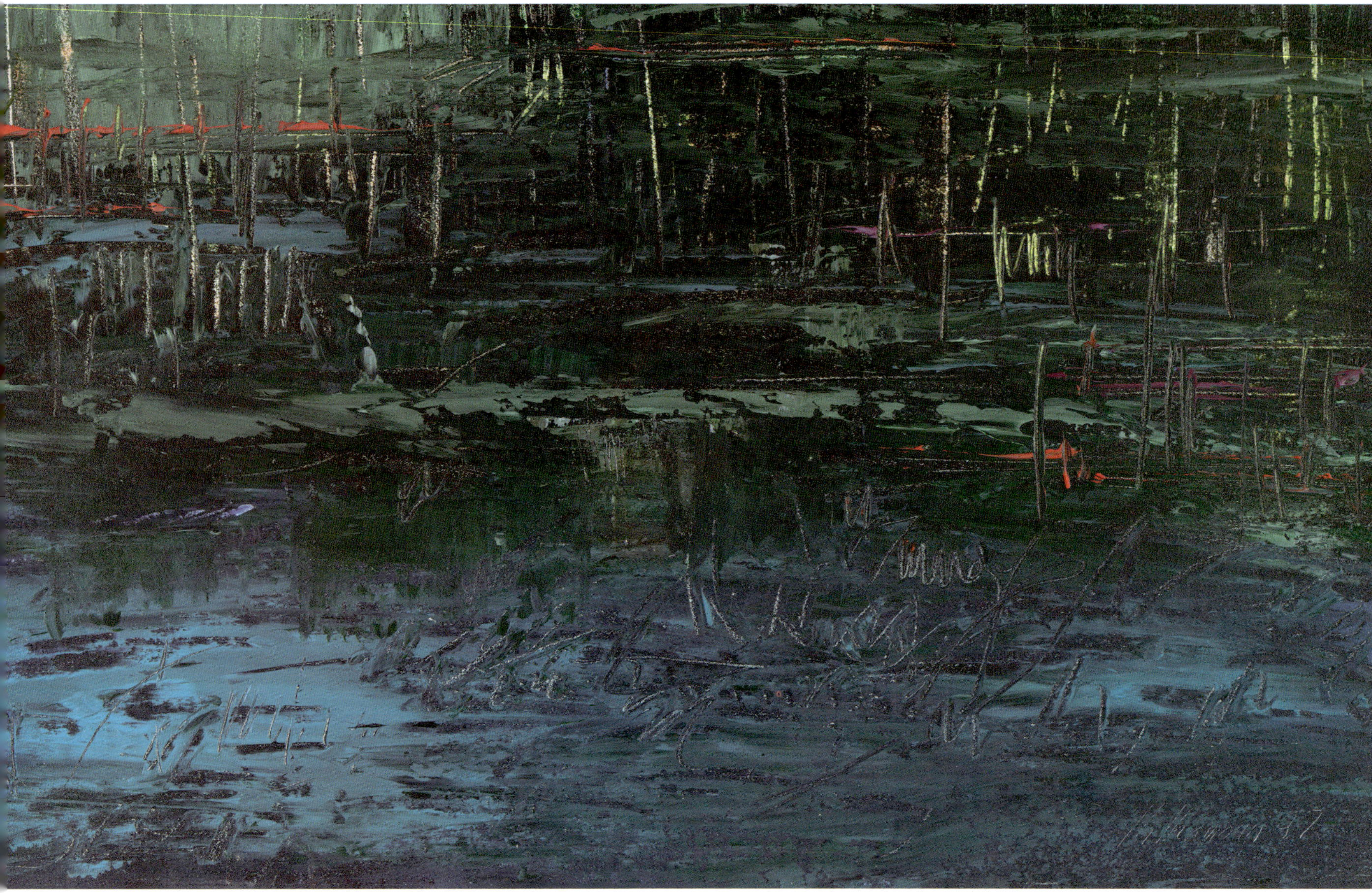

204
REFLECTIONS I, 1997
Acrylic on canvas
86.5 x 54 cm

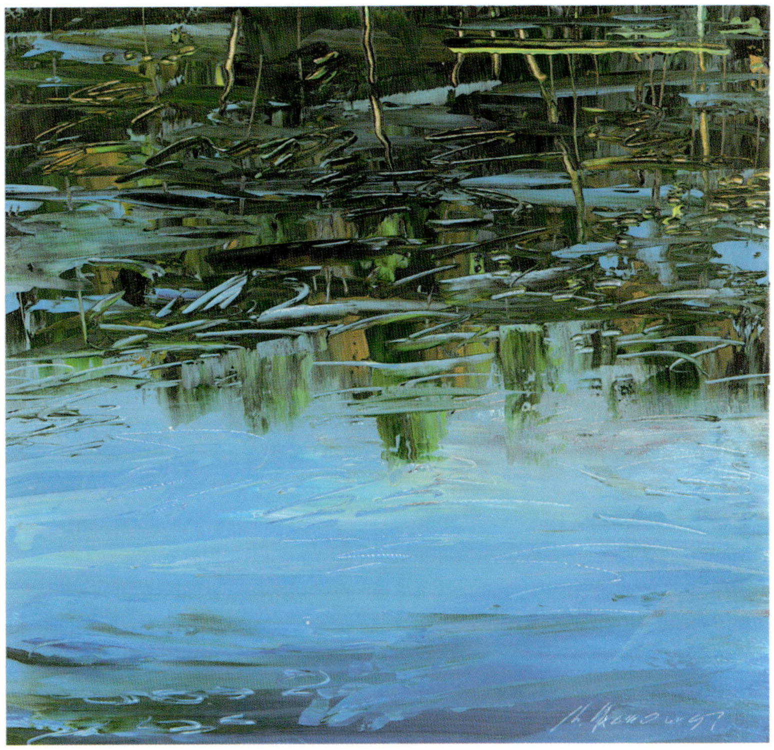

205
REFLECTIONS XXXIII, 1997
Acrylic on canvas
56 x 54.5 cm

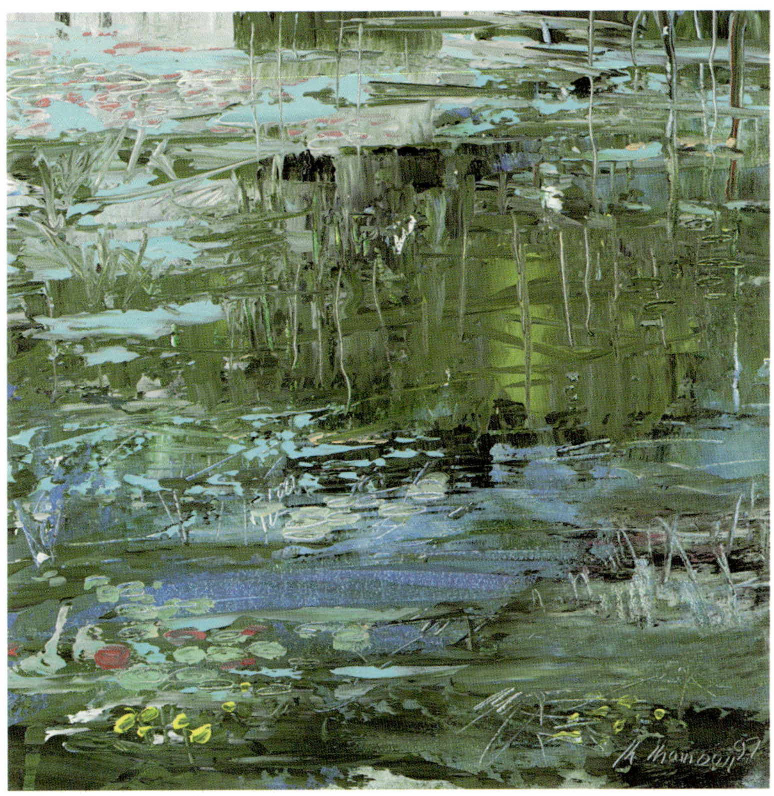

206
REFLECTIONS XXXII, 1997
Acrylic on canvas
54.5 x 56 cm

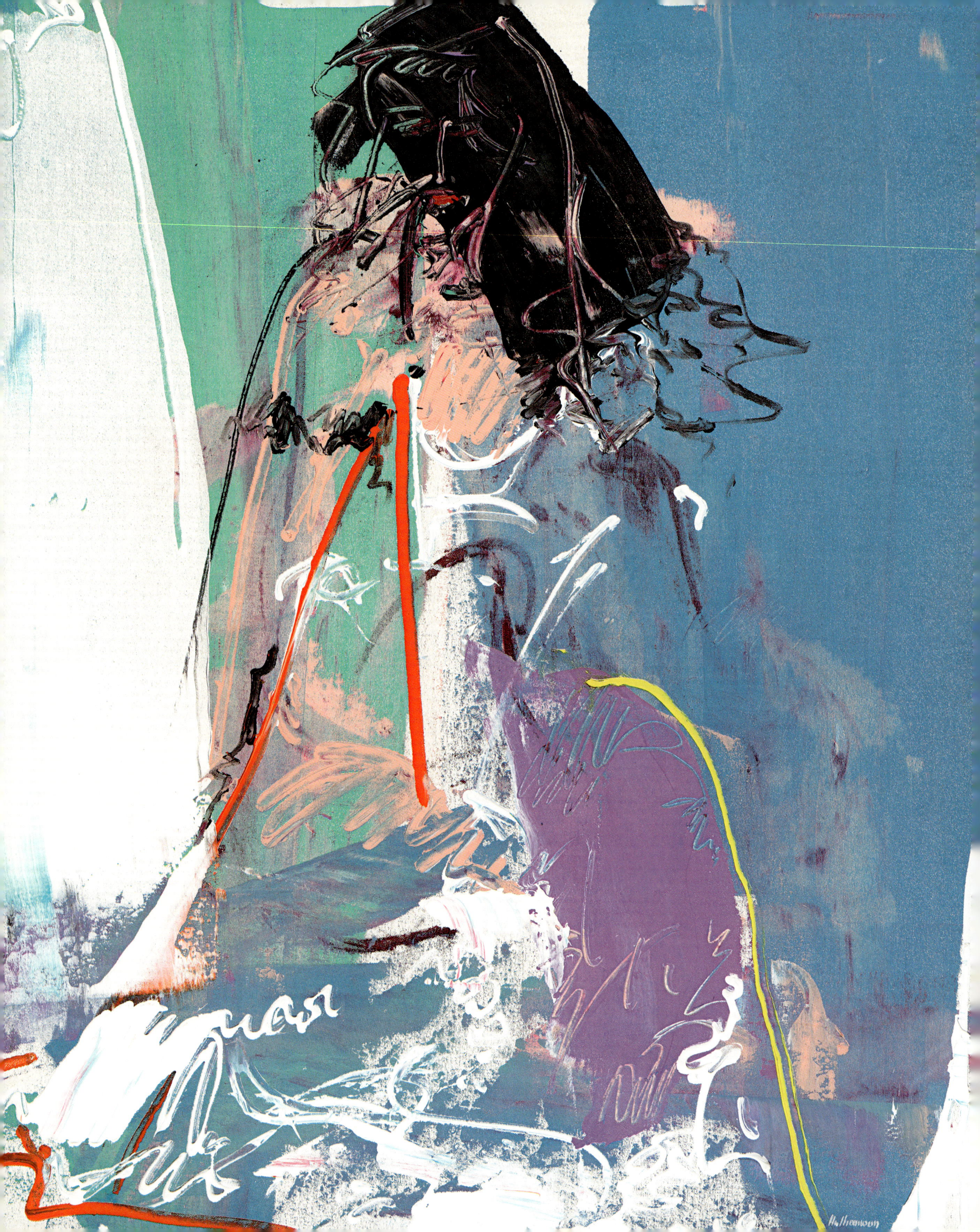

Domestic Inspirations

Leila was sitting for me once again, this time with the children. Aesthetically, this new venture came under the aegis of my preceding work: the theme was one of veiling, as
207–215 developed in the 'Mostly Black' series. It is of interest to note that my love for painting Leila did not diminish through this process; indeed, asking my children to pose for me was both memorable and very special. I used an emphatic combination of abstract and realistic rendering, which begged the question as to how necessary each was to the other. But in making art, I believe, this question subsides. I always do or add what is necessary for the work. Necessity justifies free choices but freedom also justifies necessities. The paintings were exhibited at the Janine Rubeiz Art Gallery in Beirut in 1998.

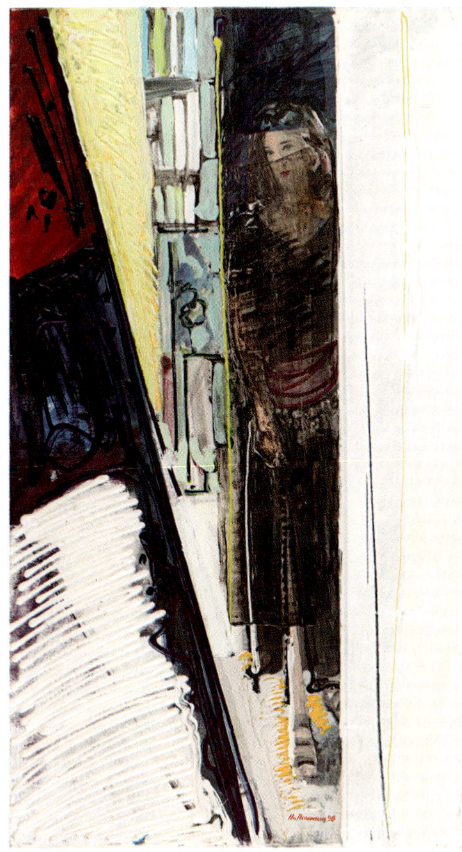

207
AT THE STUDIO DOOR, 1998
Acrylic on canvas
50 x 90.5 cm

Facing page
208
THE OTHER FACE, 1998
Acrylic on canvas
86 x 112 cm

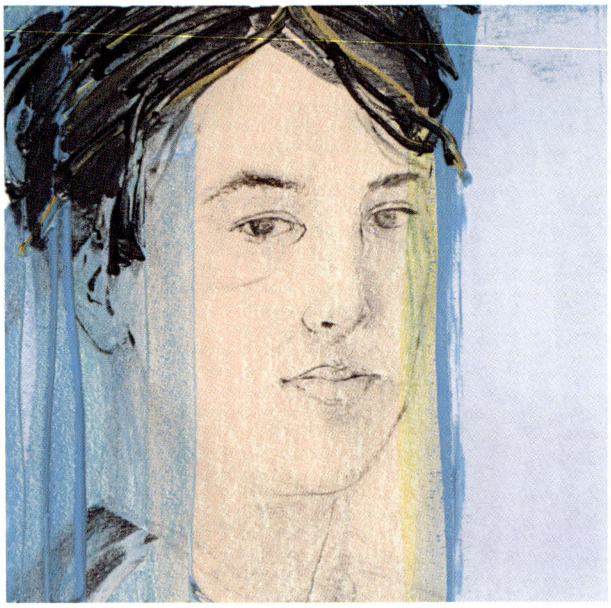

209
GEORGE II, 1998
Acrylic on canvas
60 x 60 cm

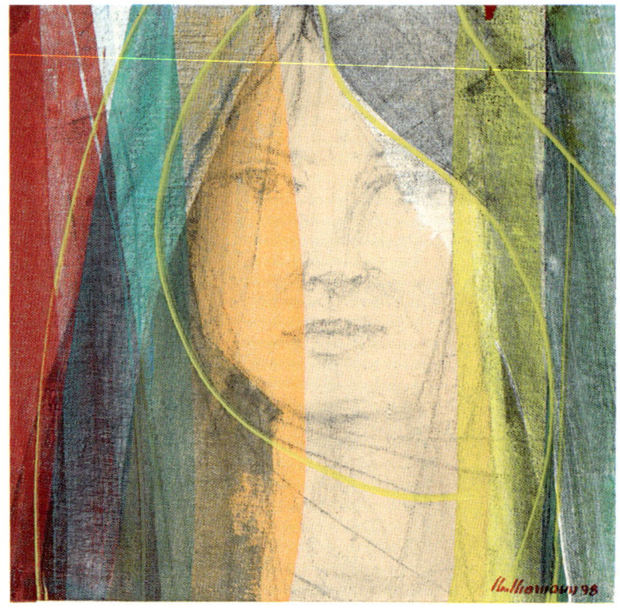

210
VEILING I, 1998
Acrylic on canvas
50 x 50 cm

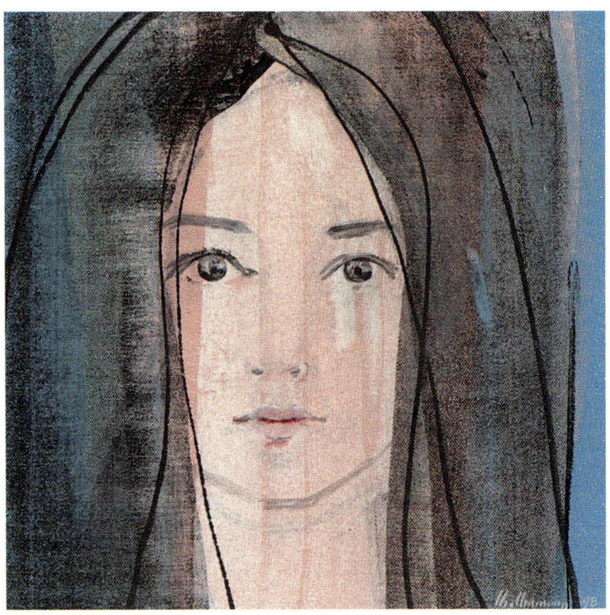

211
ORIANE I, 1998
Acrylic on canvas
50 x 50 cm

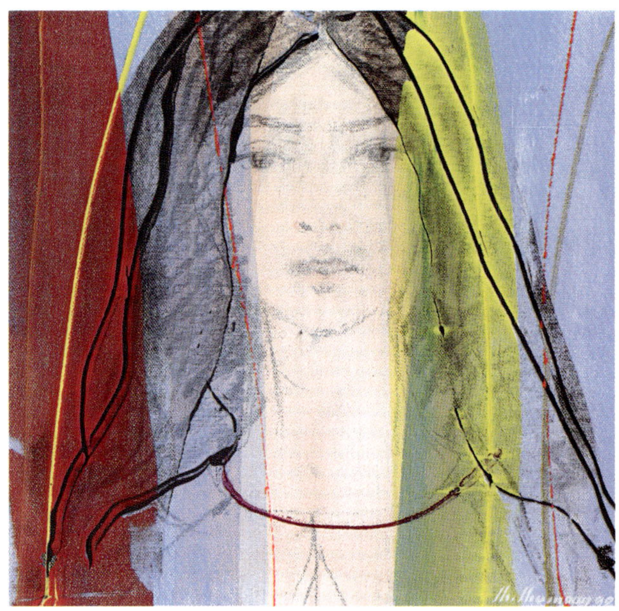

212
OWANA II, 1998
Acrylic on canvas
50 x 50 cm

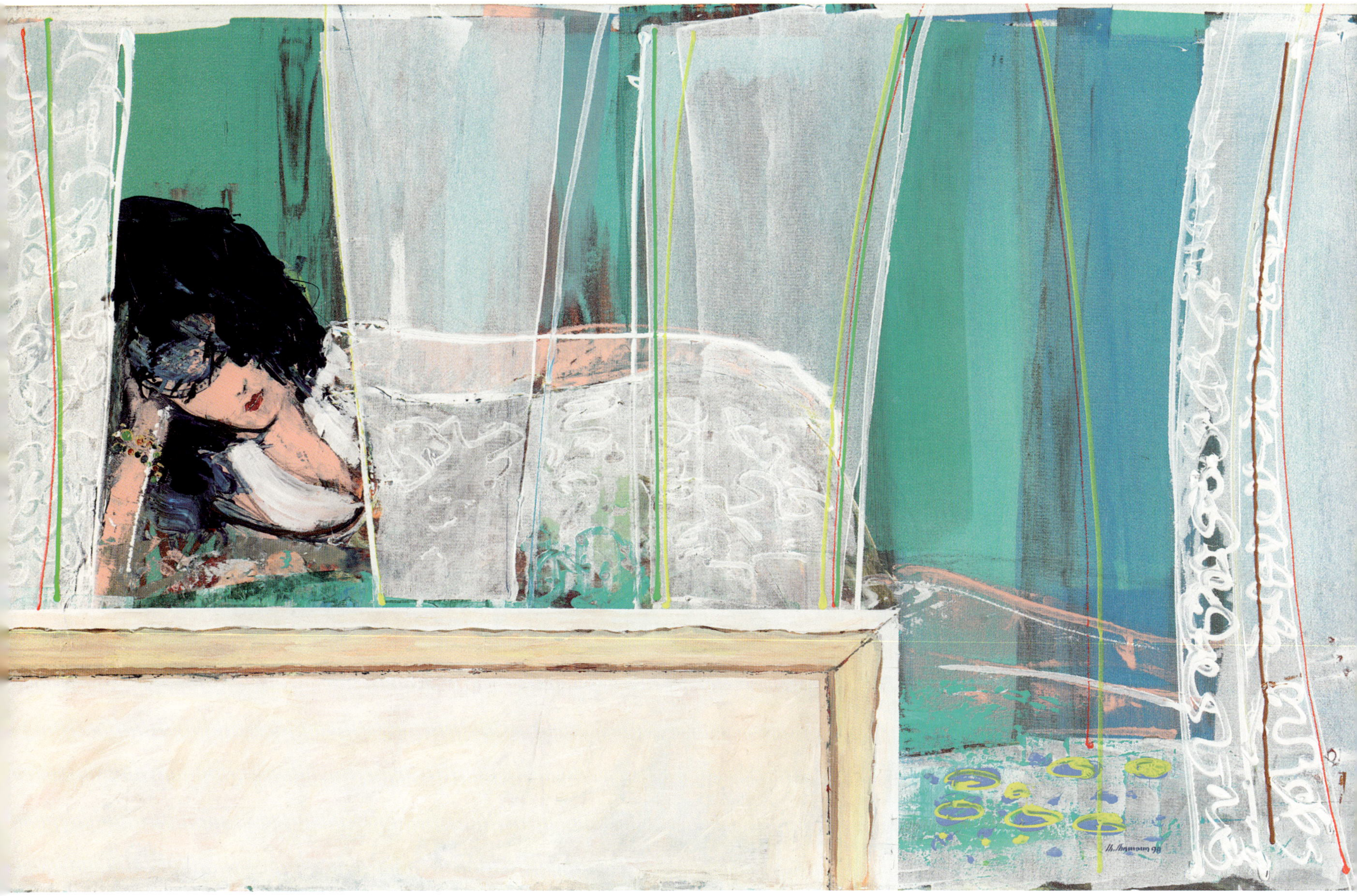

213
A REFLECTION THROUGH THE VEIL, 1998
Acrylic on canvas
142 x 90 cm

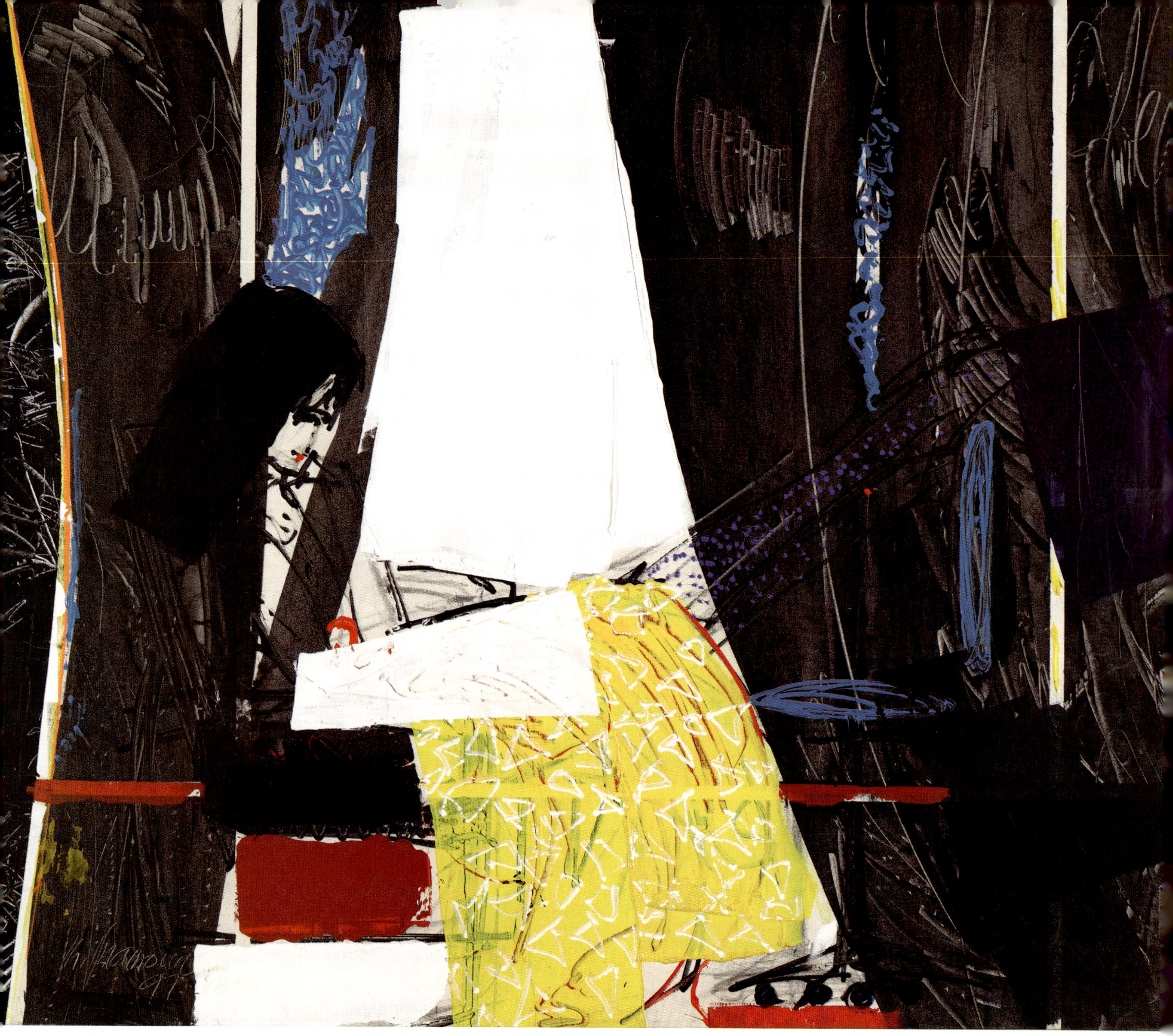

214
IN THE NEWS, 1997
Acrylic on canvas
160 x 145 cm

Facing page
215
WALKING IN HER WHITES, 1998
Acrylic on canvas
86.5 x 190 cm

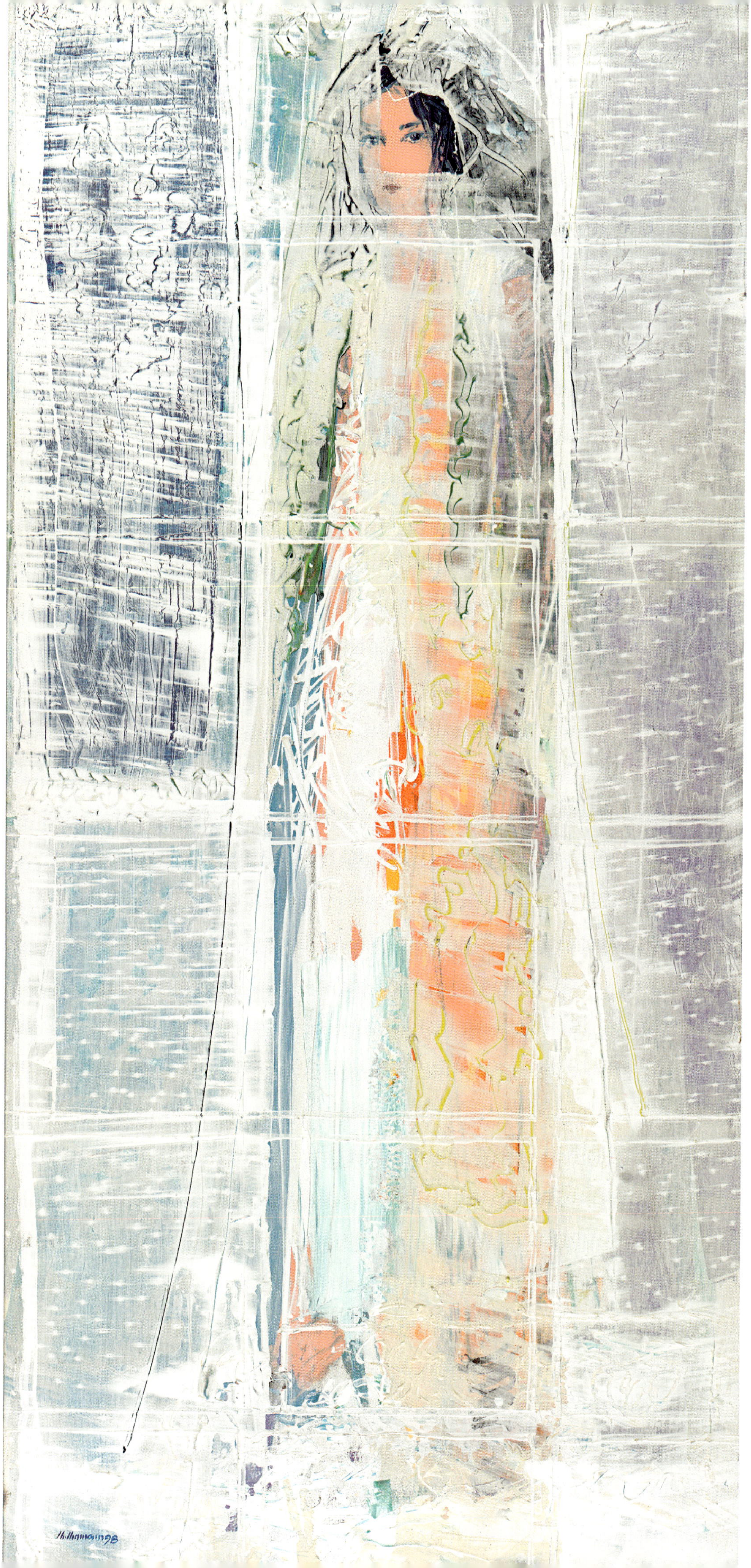

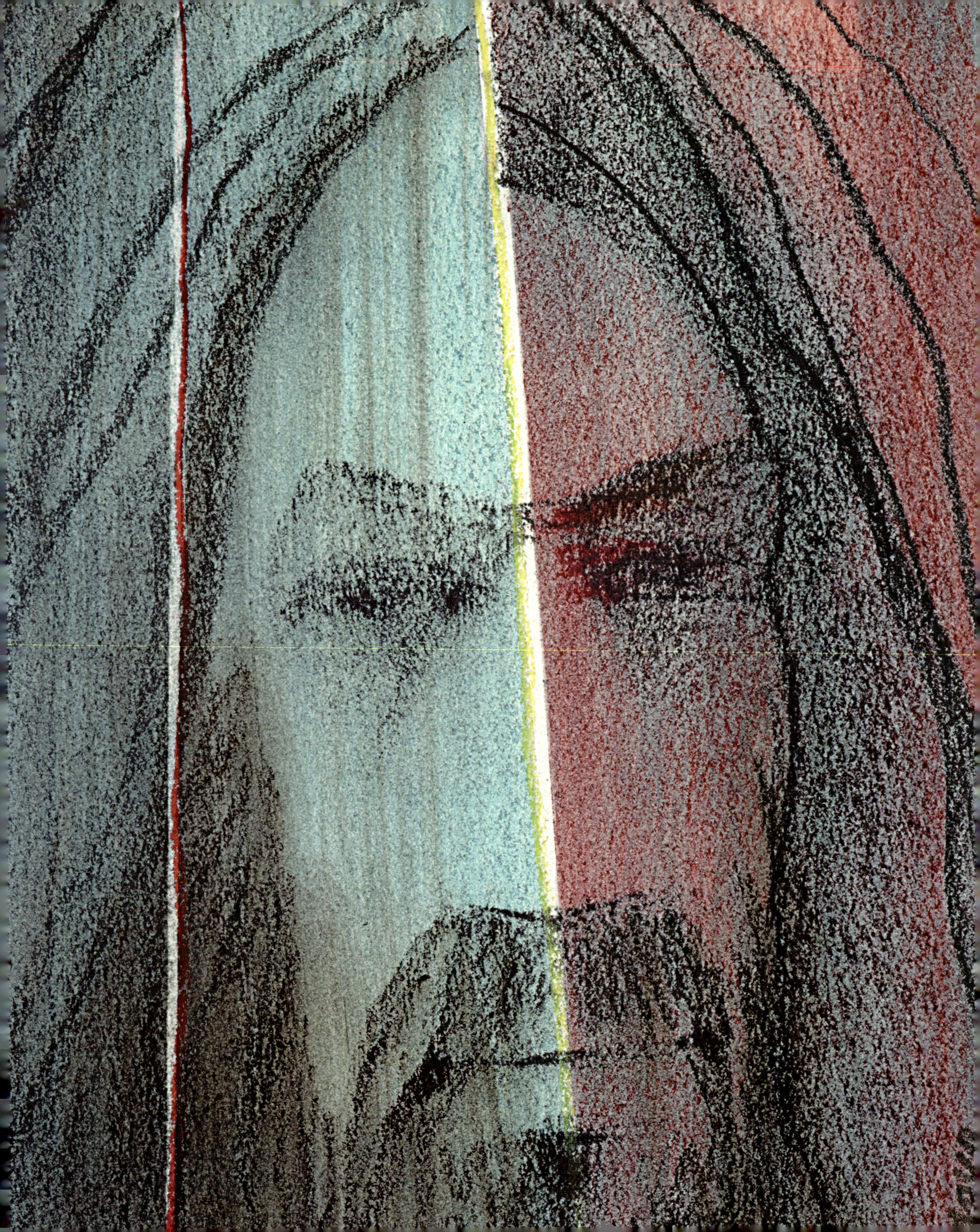

A 2000 Anniversary Homage

As the millennium, two thousand years after the birth of Jesus the Man, approached, I had a sense of graceful expectation of the splendour of the coming event, both as a man and as a believer. I felt a pressing and reverential need to create a tribute to this majestic event and its protagonist. As I travelled
216–219 back and forth, I started drawing His Face. I saw Him in the faces of people I met in planes, hotels, public parks, subways, private homes and streets. I always felt close to Him, and He was the man I strove to be.

At first, I was inspired, even driven, by the icons Leila, my wife, was painting. Somehow I saw The Love Master and Loving Model in every face, regardless of expression, race or colour. I would look at a person and see Him, regardless of whether the person was a man or a woman, Christian or Muslim; black, white or of unspecified colour or ethnic origin. I sketched His face all the time, everywhere: in the subway and on the streets; in buses and on planes; wherever I was. My aim was to make two thousand drawings of Him, commemorating the year 2000, drawings of an ever-living man of love and goodness; the man humanity needed most, I needed most. I drew Him in pencil, pastels, ink pen, watercolour, charcoal and acrylic. Once, on a plane, I

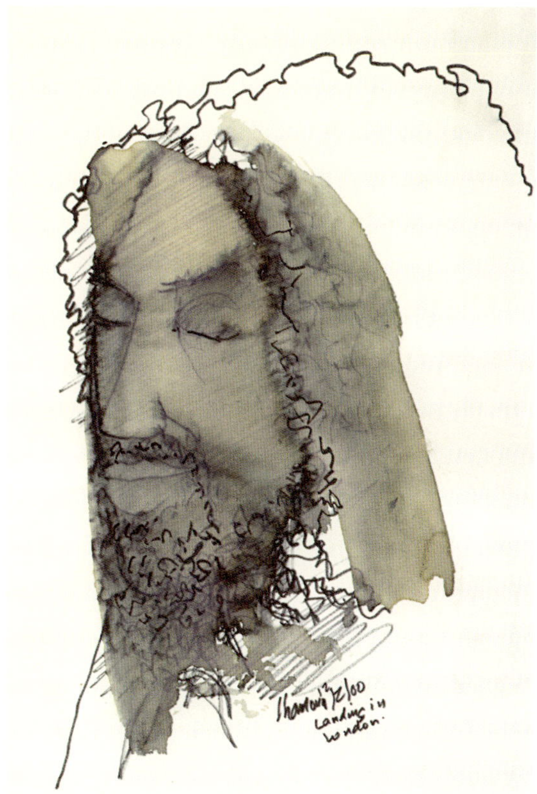

216
ON THE PLANE TO LONDON, 2000
Ink and wine wash
28 x 35 cm

Facing page
217
TWO-NATURE, 2000
Pastel on paper (detail)
28 x 35 cm

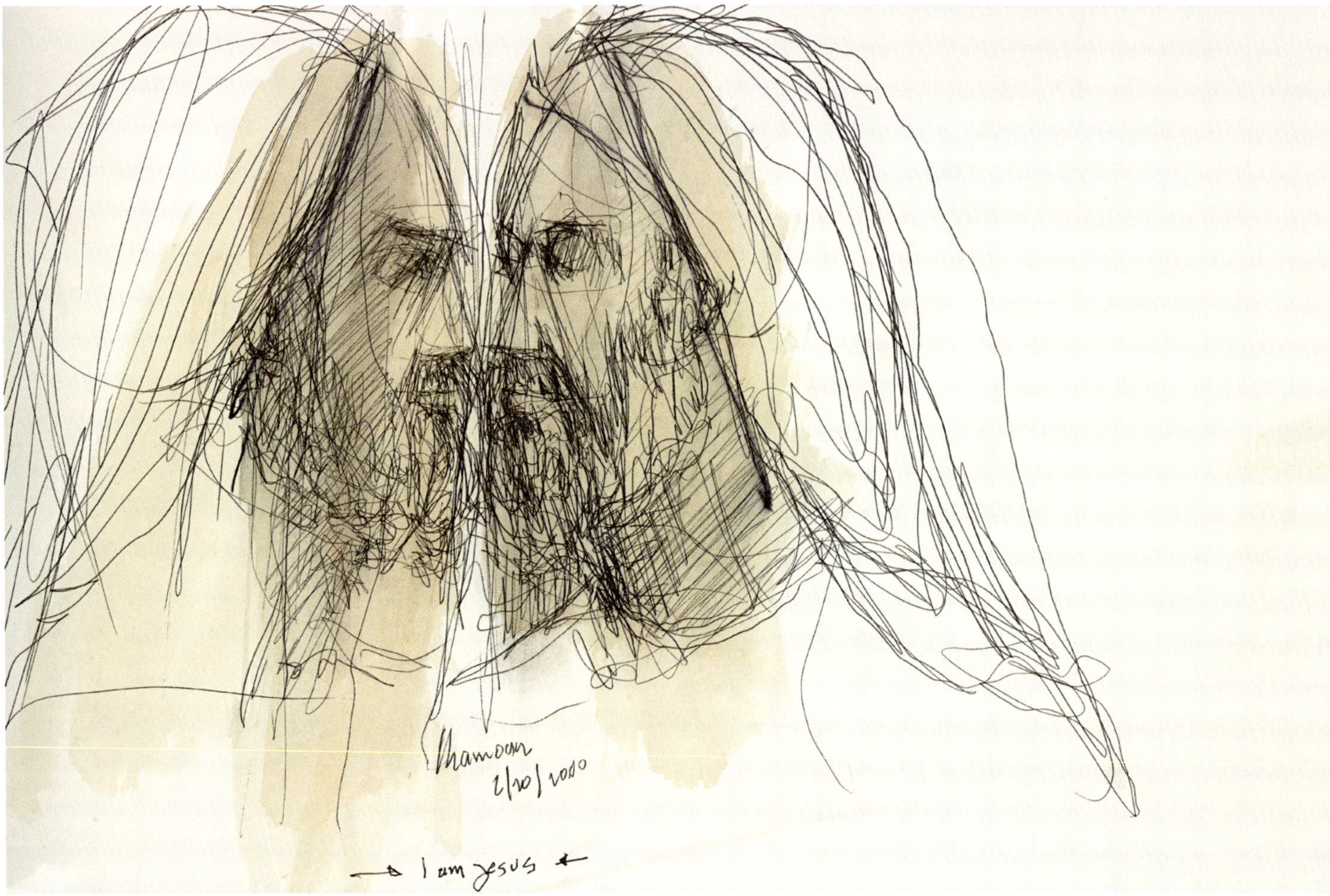

218
I AM JESUS, 2000
Ink and wine wash
28 x 35 cm

Facing page
219
LOOK HIM IN THE EYE, 2000
Pencil on paper
28 x 35 cm

wiped His face with red wine giving the ink pen drawings a watercolour-like wash.

After I had finished about eight hundred drawings, I felt He was getting old in my hands, so I stopped. I know He was crucified at the age of thirty-three: somehow, while drawing Him, I was always drawing my brother who had been abducted and murdered at the age of twenty-six. His face, as the Saviour, the Martyr of mankind, has never aged. Was I in search of him, or of a real story of him in people's faces and eyes? His face never leaves my eyes. After all, to draw faces and nature in all their aspects is a spiritual experience, an iconic creation of the lived world. The drawings and paintings of this revered experience have not been exhibited yet.

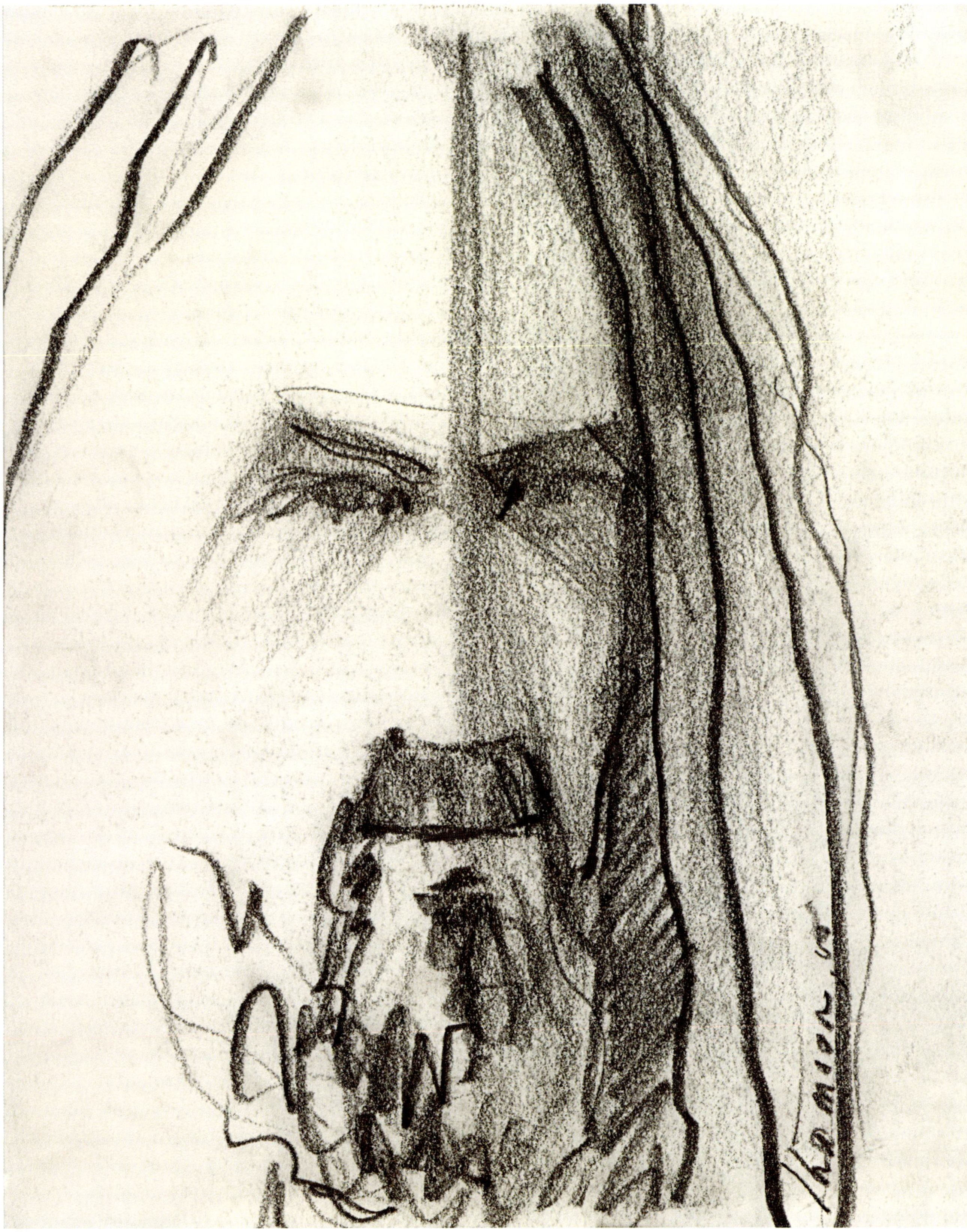

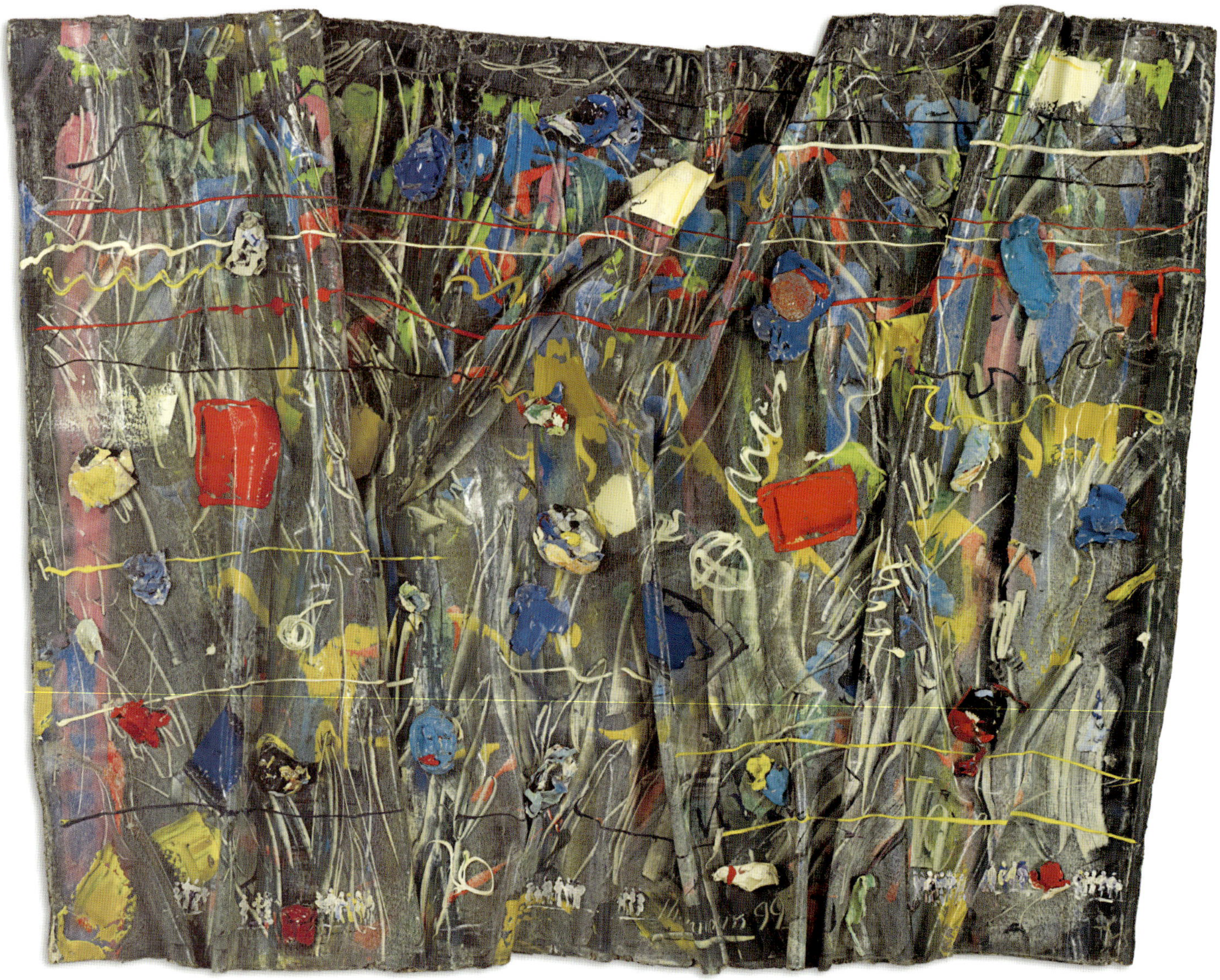

220
CANA I (the painting), 1999
Acrylic on canvas on fibreglass with resin finish
188 x 150 cm

Cana: A Painful Inspiration

'Cana I' is an installation composed of a large crumbled painting commemorating the 1966 Massacre of Cana. It represents the roof of the UN barracks collapsing on the heads of the children, women and elderly people who had sought shelter there from the barbaric Israeli shelling. The painting was hung on a large white canvas representative of the supposedly peaceful territory of the greatest world organisation. The scene was surrounded with barbed wire in the colours of all the nations, symbolising the Arnoon Freedom Demonstration, a challenge to the Israeli occupation. The barbed wire passed over a worn-out old UN chair. Underneath the chair was a waste bucket filled with cast-off UN resolutions, except for Resolution 242, which was caught in the barbed wire. In front of the chair lay an old forgotten torn pair of shoes once worn by whoever ruled for justice in the world and died. On the white part of the canvas, spread on the floor, was written: 'From Cana to Arnoon'. This installation was part of the FIAD 1999
220, 221 exhibition in Beirut.

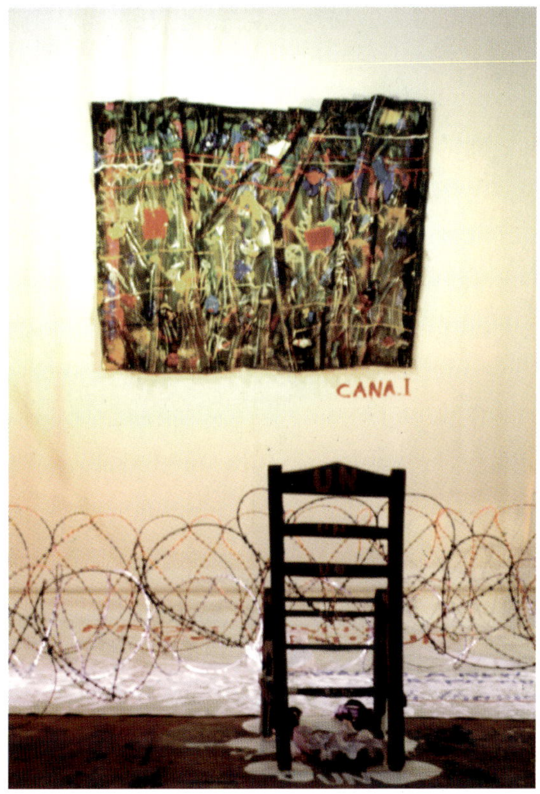

221
CANA I (the Installation), 1999

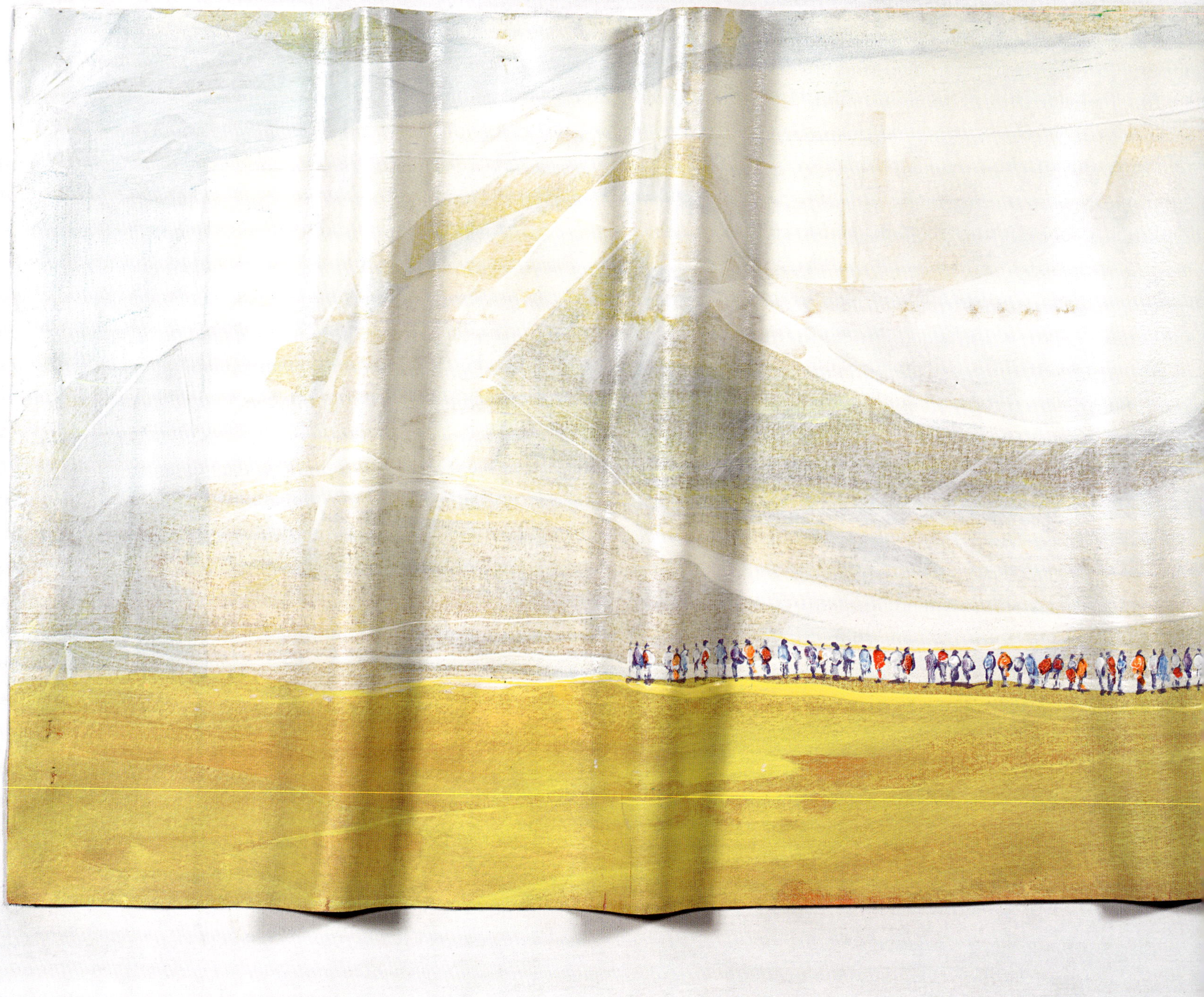

222
IN GOD'S LAND, 2000
Acrylic on shaped canvas with resin and fibre
187.5 x 70 cm

Following spread
223
ELEVATION OF THE BLUE LINE, 2001
Acrylic on shaped canvas with resin and fibre
214 x 85 cm

In 'Cana I', I saw a new aesthetic language taking my art to another venture, to new aesthetic possibilities, using acrylic on canvas moulded onto a bed of resin and fibre in a three-dimensional and frameless artwork. It was exhibited at the gallery Epreuve d'Artiste, in its new location in Achrafieh, in the spring of 2001. 222–228

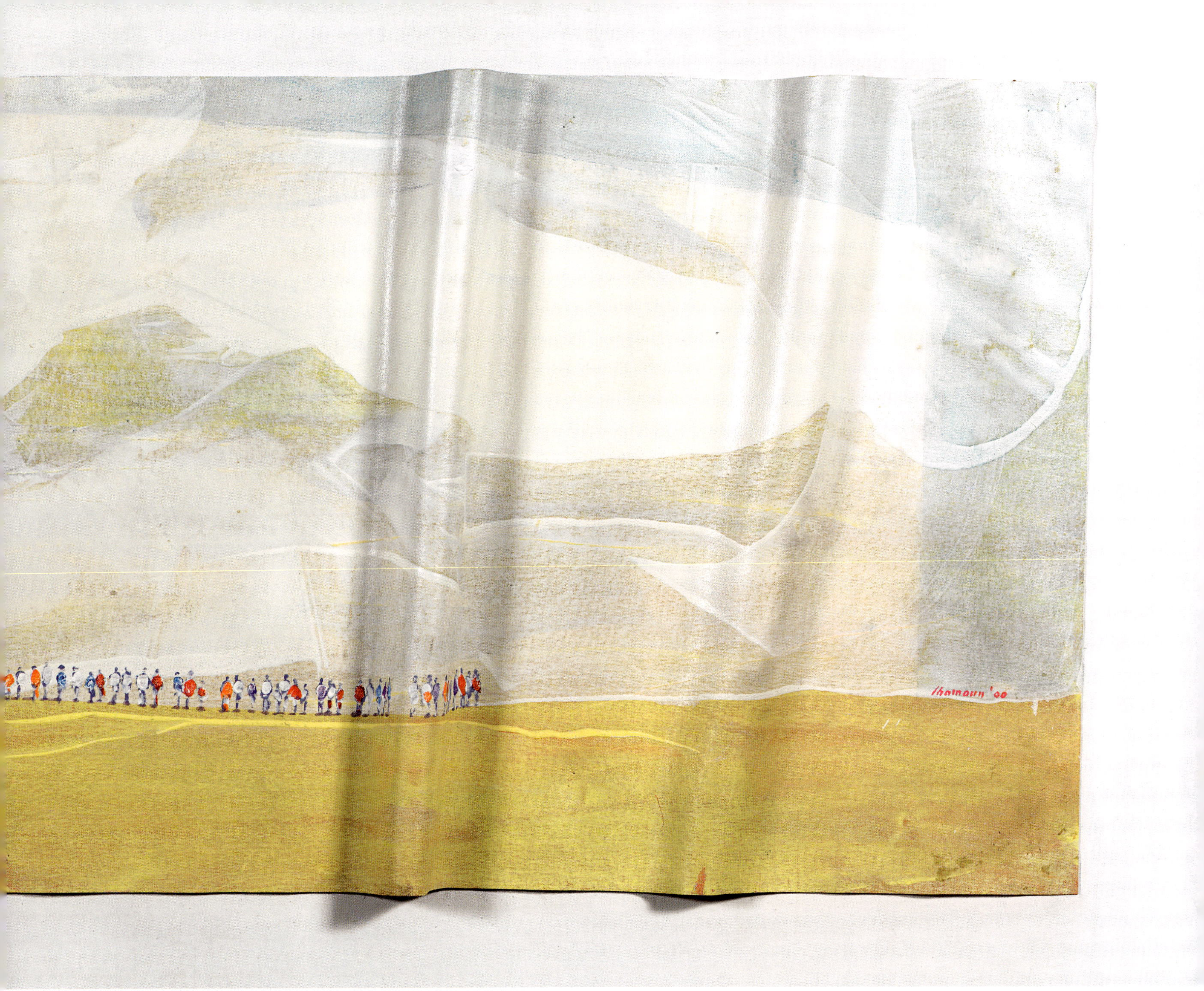

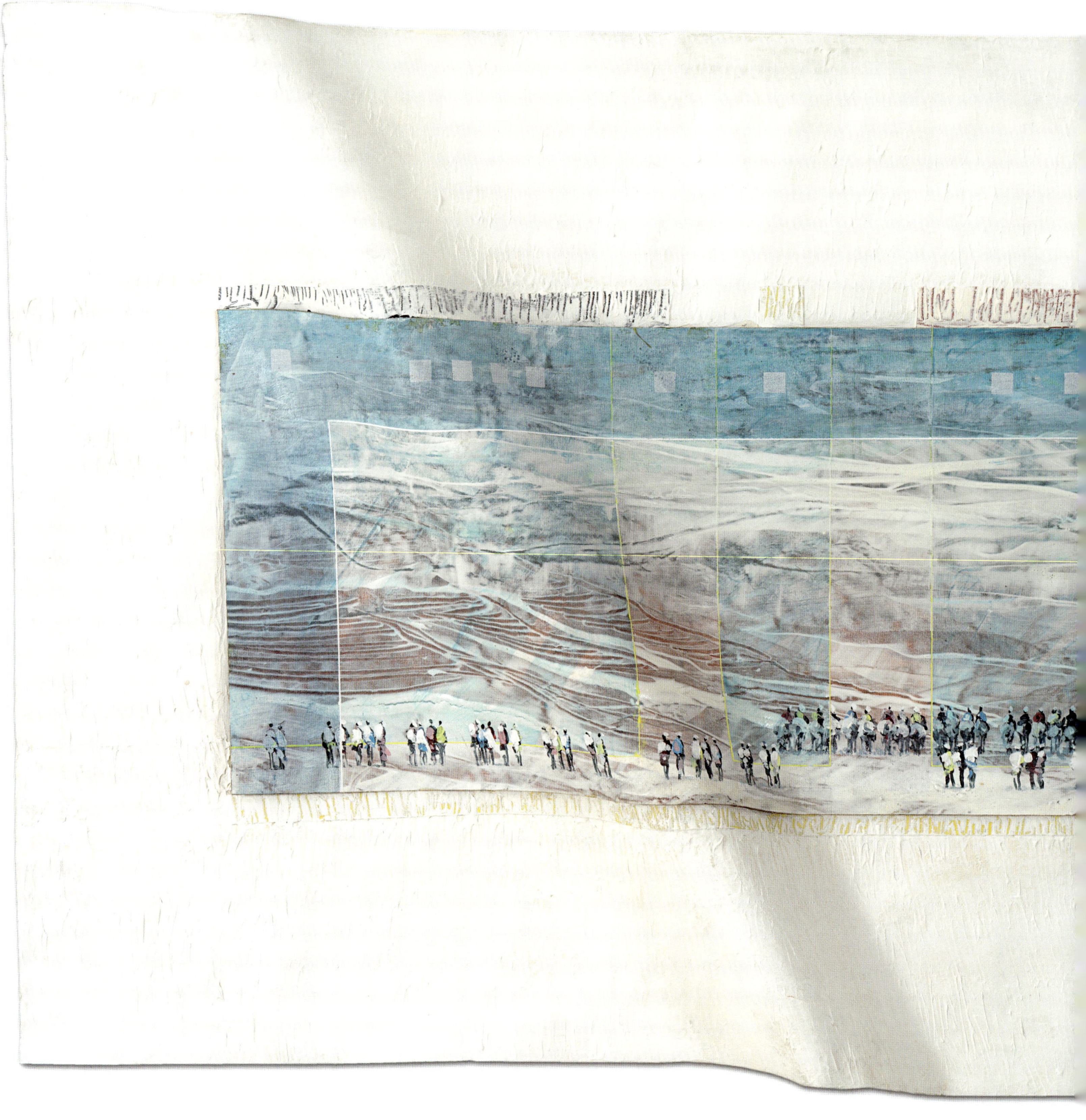

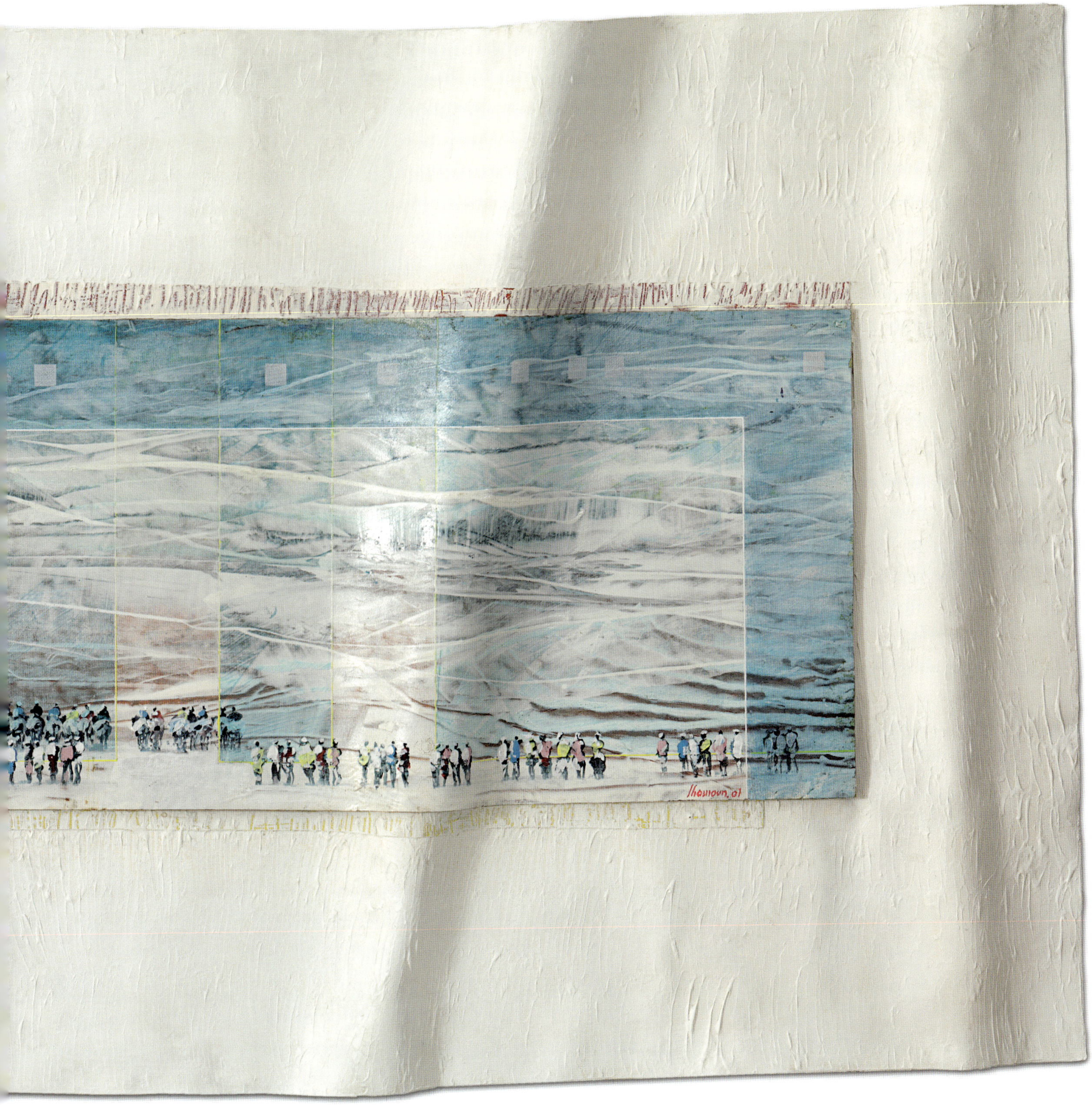

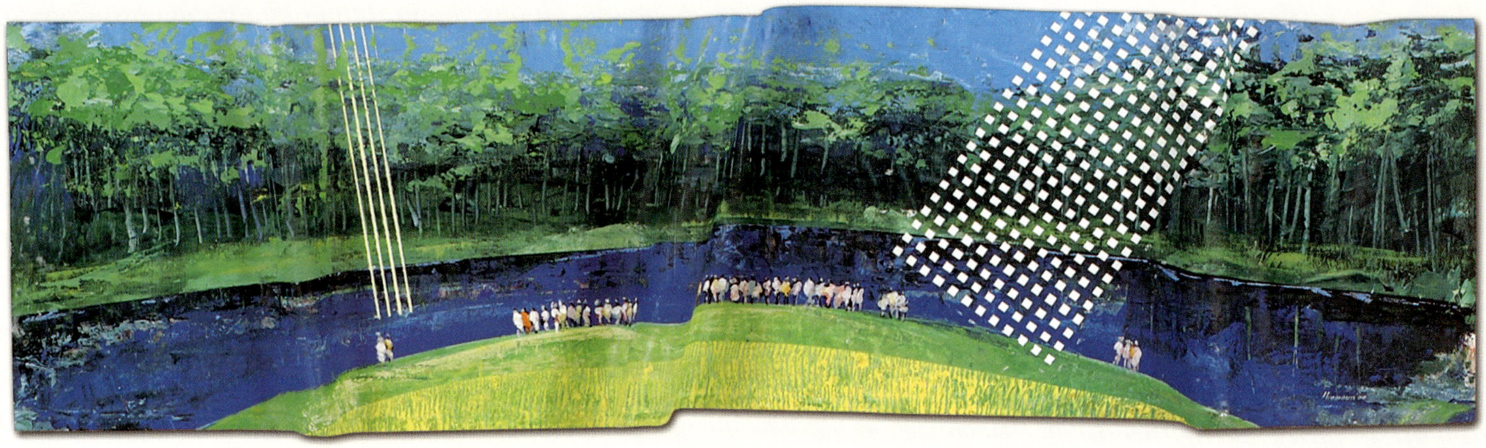

224
BACK TO THE LAKE, 2000
Acrylic fibre
200 x70 cm

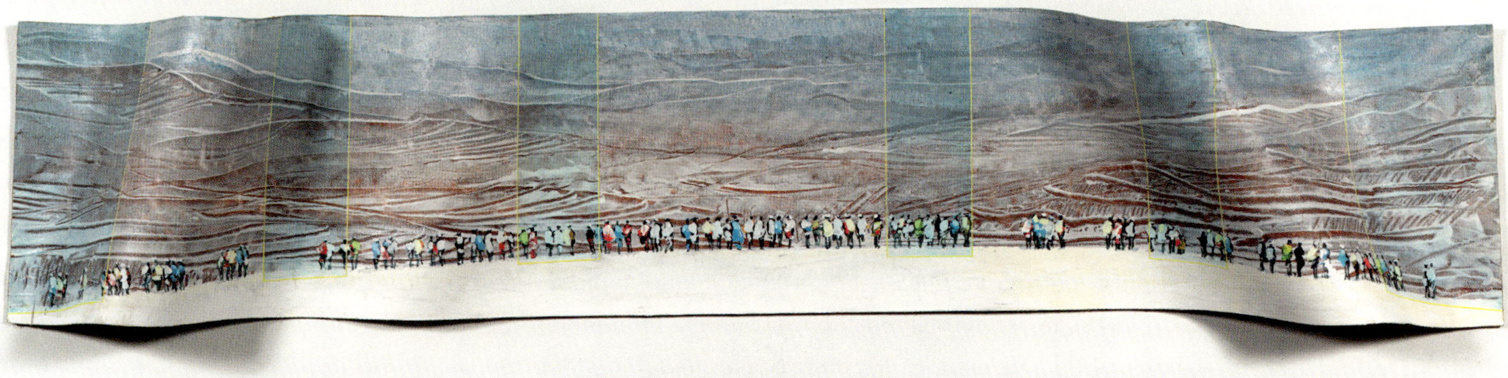

225
MY HOME TOWN, 2001
Acrylic on shaped canvas with resin
and fibre
170 x 50 cm

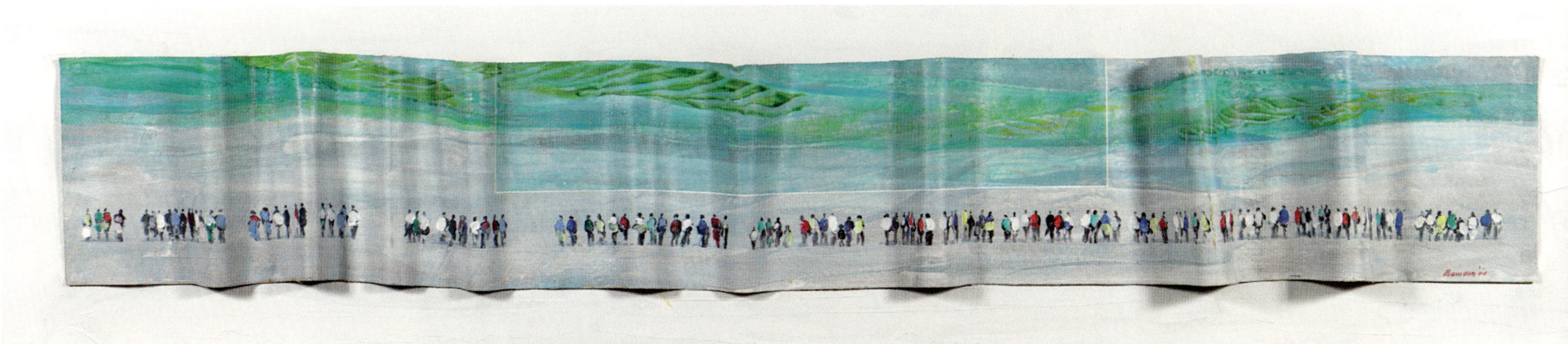

226
A CLOSE ENCOUNTER II, 2000
Acrylic on shaped canvas with resin
and fibre
180 x 50 cm

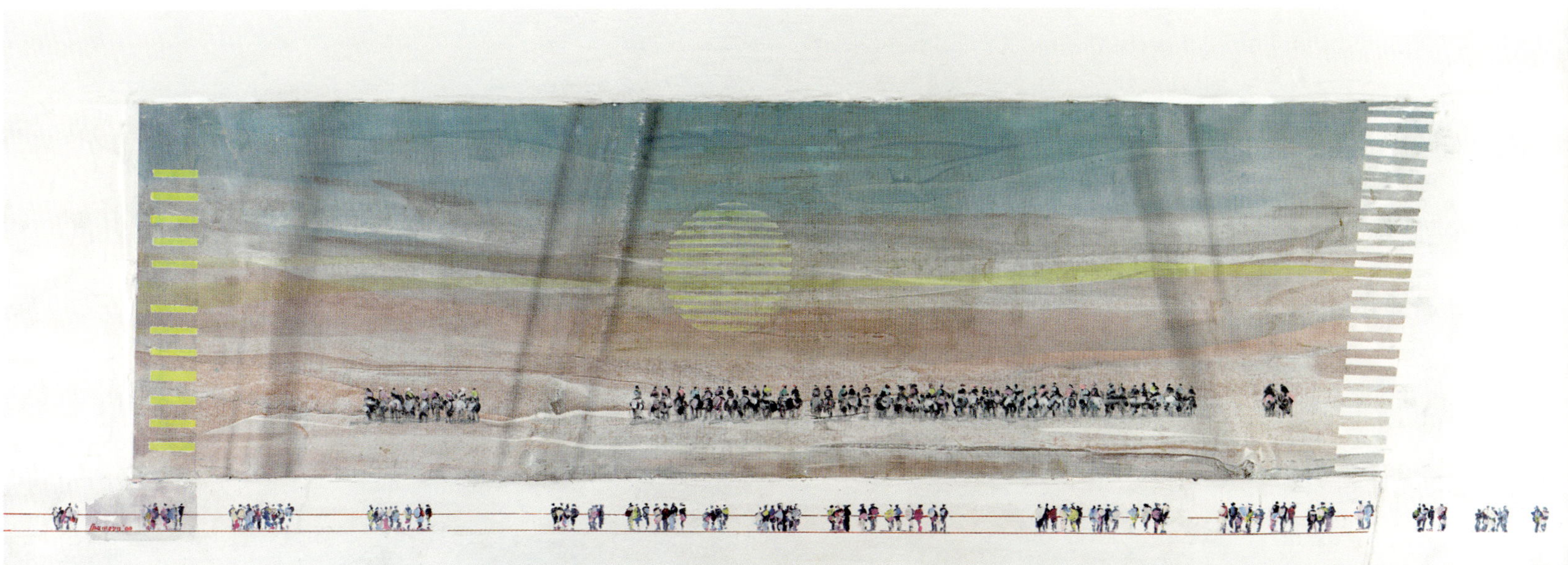

227
SUNRISE, 2000
Acrylic on shaped canvas, with resin
and fibre
200 x 70 cm

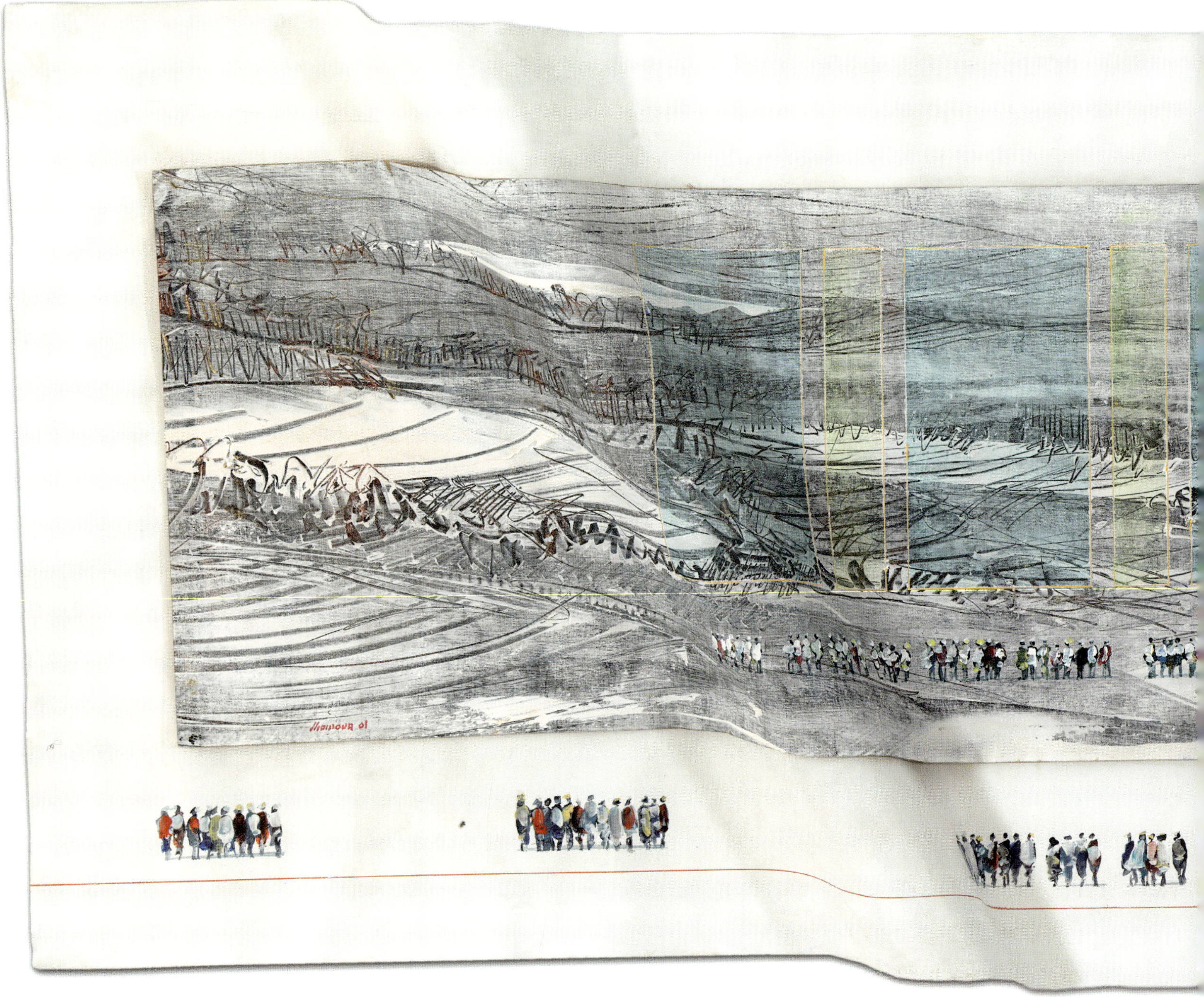

228
SOUTHERN BLUES, 2001
Acrylic on shaped canvas with resin and fibre
191 x 95 cm

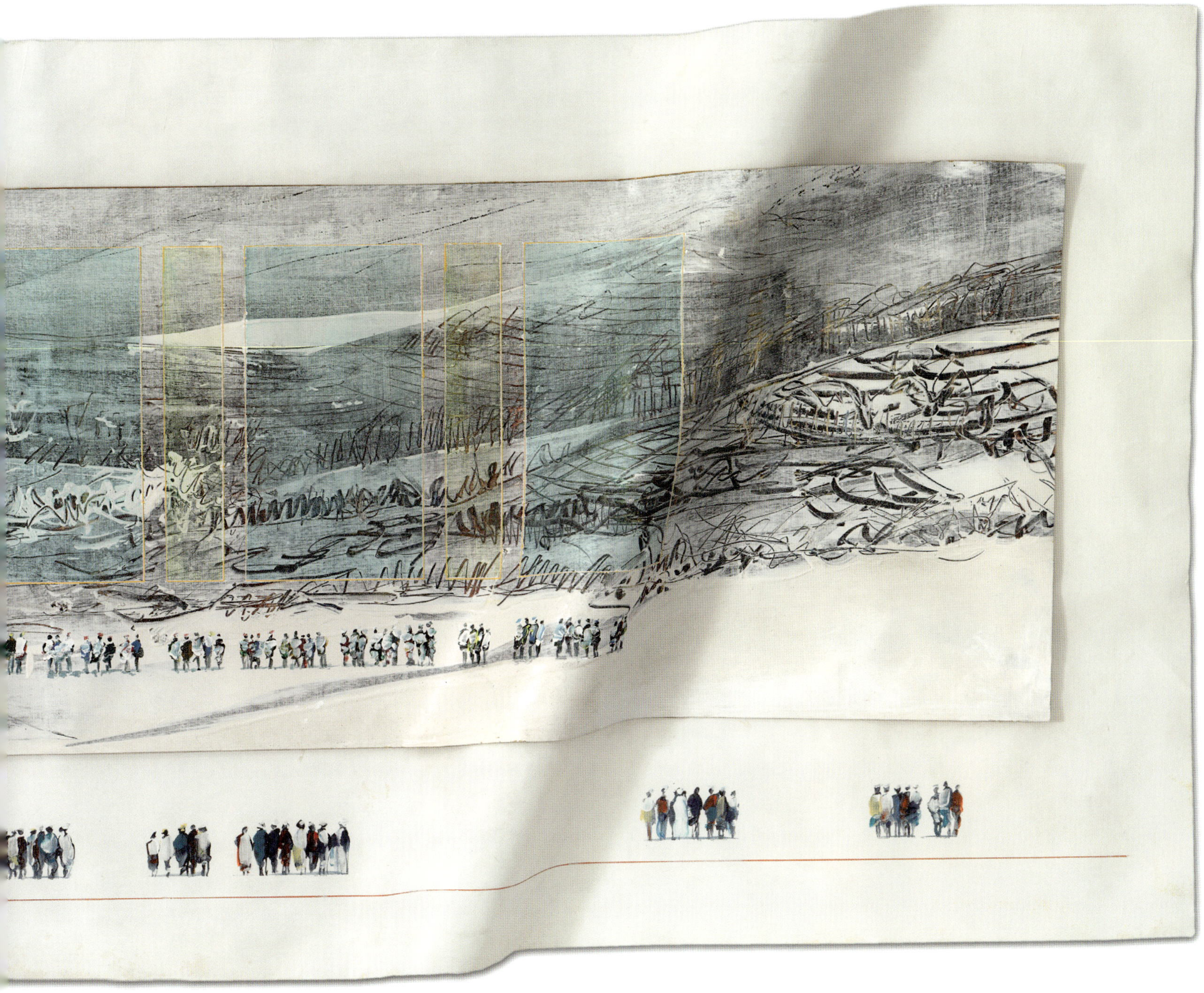

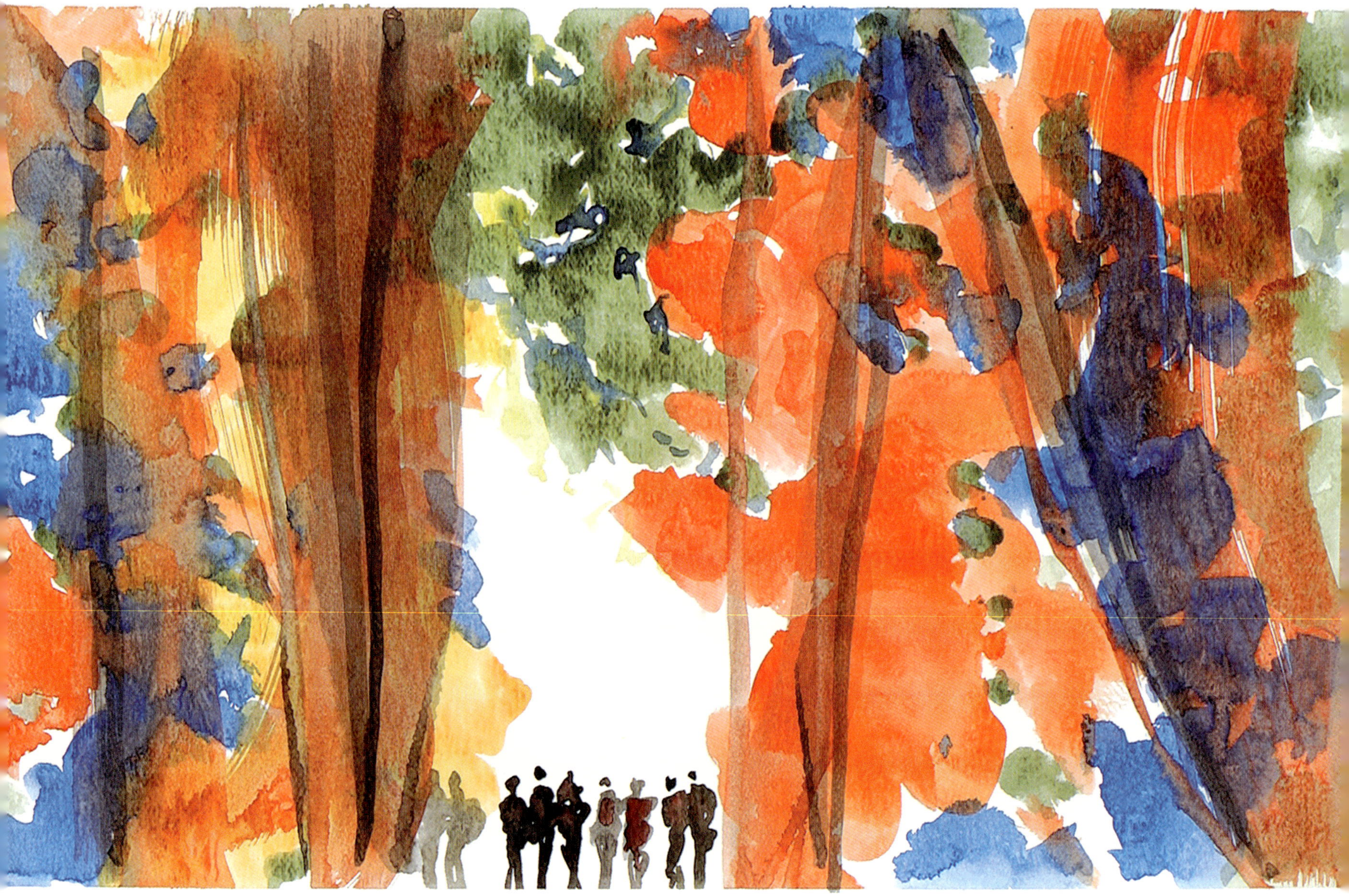

229
LIGHT INFILTRATION, 2003
Watercolour on paper
70 x 70 cm

The Big Fall

At six in the morning on 7 June 2003, I was preparing my car to take my daughter Owana for her SAT exams. I asked her to go and get her mother's cell phone so as to be able to call me when she finished, so she went back to the house. I decided to take my son George's four-wheel drive, as it had not been driven since my son had left for college in the States. I started the car while my feet were still outside it; I had forgotten that this was a stick-shift car whereas my own was an automatic. The car rabbit-hopped and smashed straight through the concrete low wall at the edge of the parking lot, then fell into the other building's parking lot, six metres below. All I remember is asking God to keep the car off me, and then everything went blank.

I woke up when the Red Cross came to remove me, feeling intolerable pain. I screamed and realised that my right leg was broken and my head badly hurt, bleeding and swollen. In the hospital they discovered at least sixteen fractures in my head, with fractures and torn ligaments in the shoulders. My skin turned black all over my body. They had to wait several days before operating to make sure there was no internal bleeding. But I never complained, feeling that complaining would hurt my loved ones who came to see me, especially my

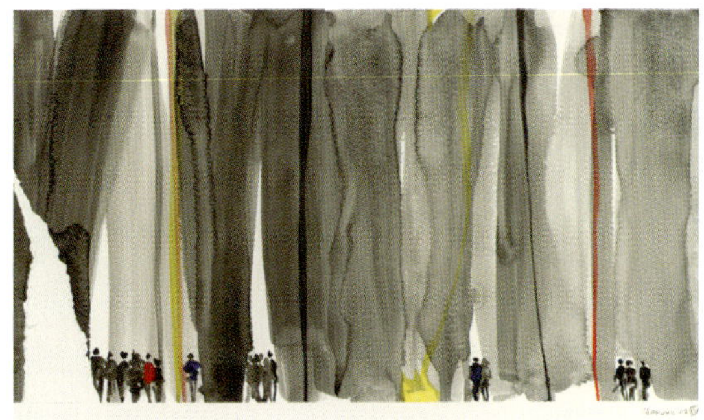

230
03 XV, 2003
Watercolour on paper
60.9 x 47.7 cm

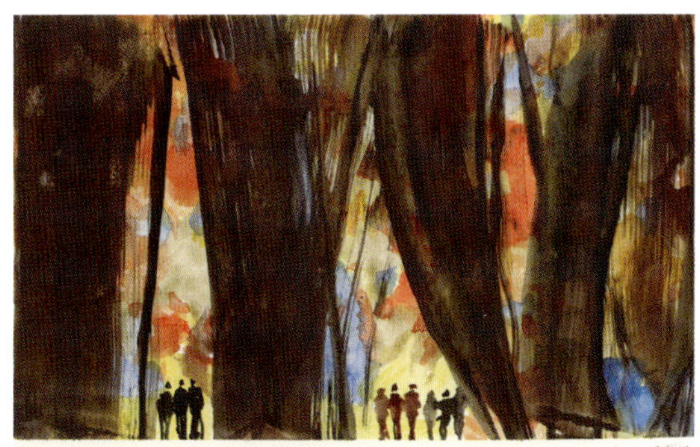

231
03 XXXVII, 2003
Watercolour on paper
60.9 x 47.7 cm

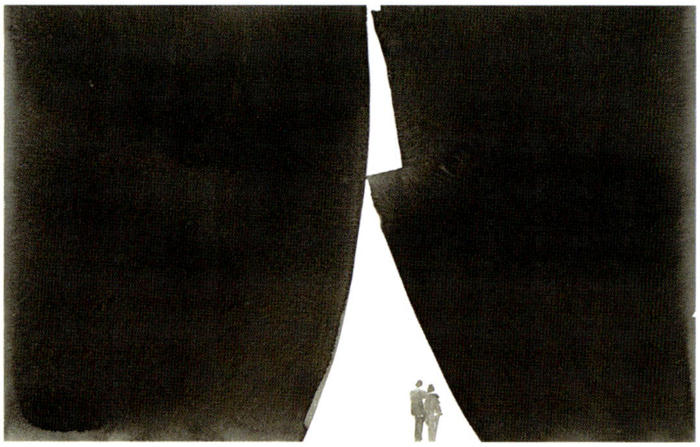

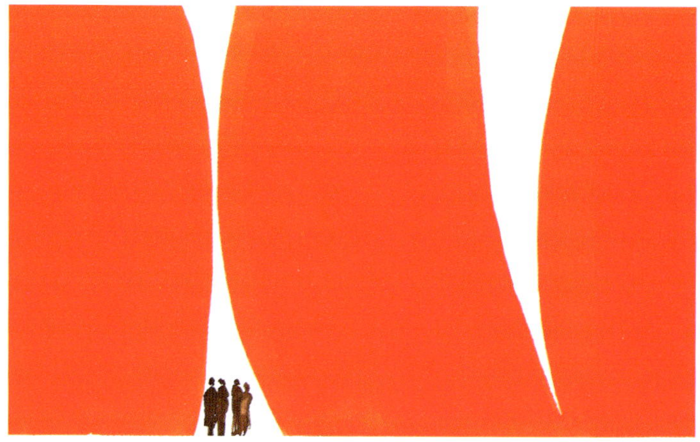

232
UNTITLED 12, 2003
Watercolour on paper
70 x 70 cm

Right
233
UNTILTLED 21, 2003
Watercolour on paper
70 x 70 cm

children who were severely traumatised; nor would it alleviate my own pain. 'Sorry, I forgot to fly,' I told my scared children when they showed up at my hospital room door.

Within two months I was back on my feet and back to my normal life. Luckily, my brain was unaffected by the fractures! Although I had to use a cane, I went back to the US to finalise a project with Dress Barn. While I was in hospital I had started thinking that life cannot be taken for granted. I asked God not to make me lose my humanity or my art; I felt that I had not done all He had 'assigned' me to do. On the way to the US I asked myself what would have happened had I died in that accident without having achieved as much as I wanted to. While I was there, I tried to do as much work as possible, on top of the designs I was paid to do; I came back to Lebanon with eighty watercolours and ink drawings. 229–238

234
03-XXXIX, 2003
Watercolour on paper
60.9 x 47.7 cm

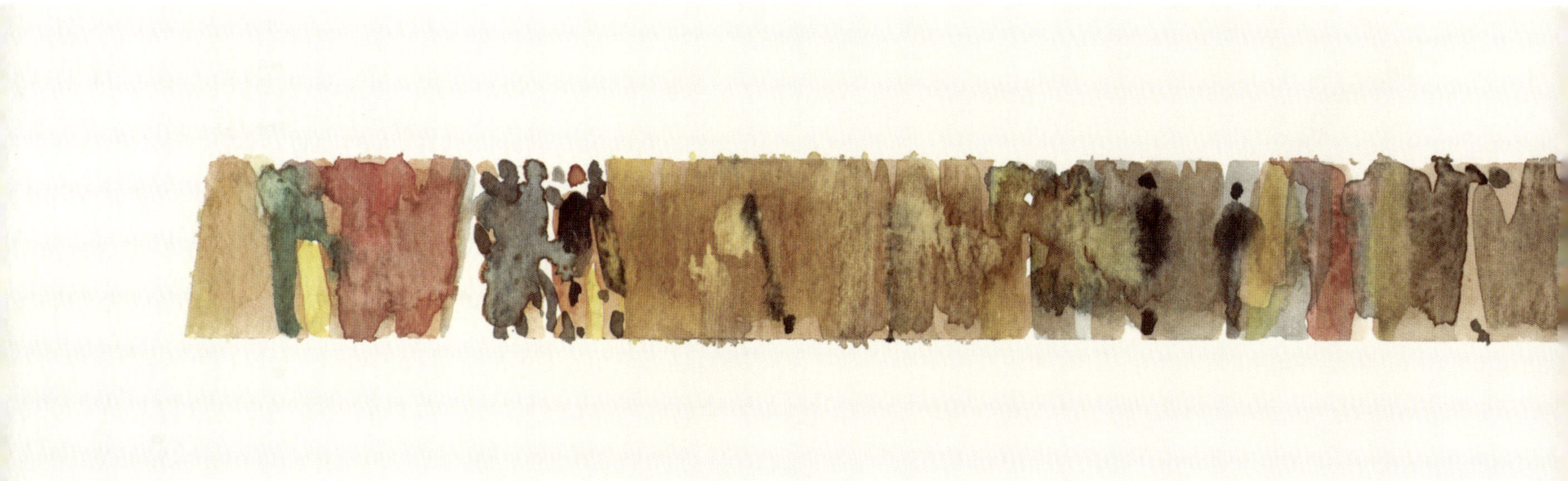

235
03 IX, 2003
Watercolour on paper
60.9 x 47.7 cm

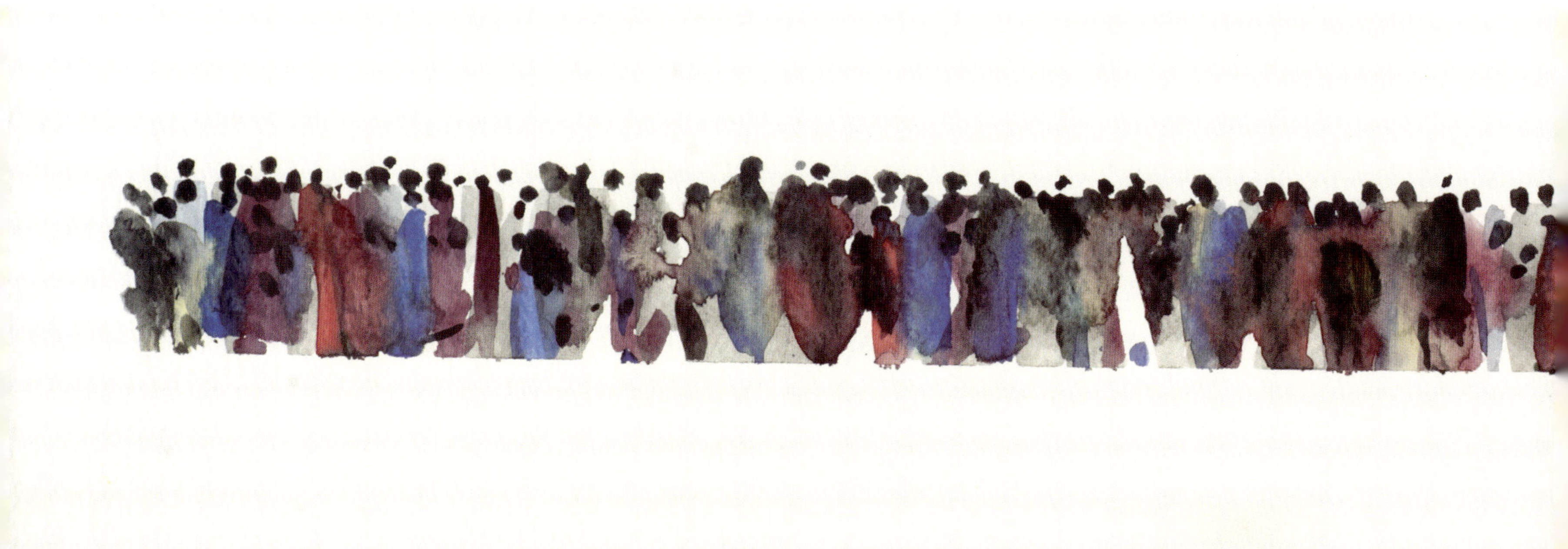

236
03 V, 2003
Watercolour on paper
60.9 x 47.7 cm

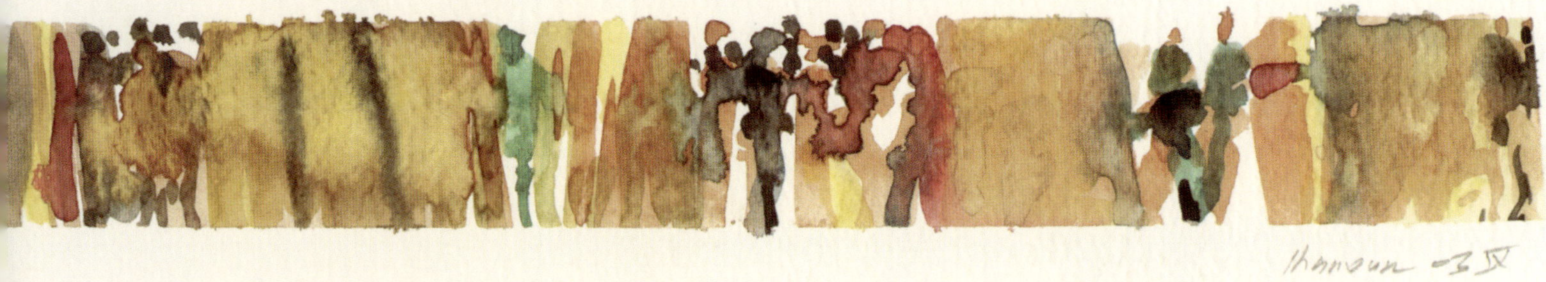

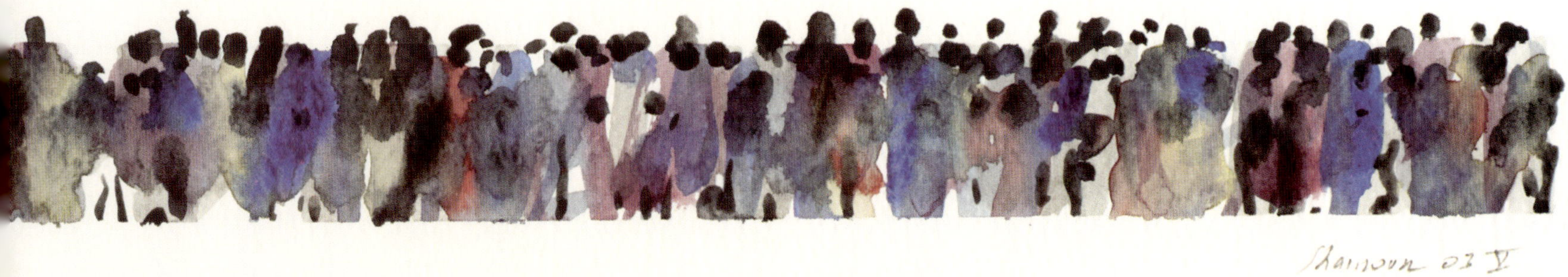

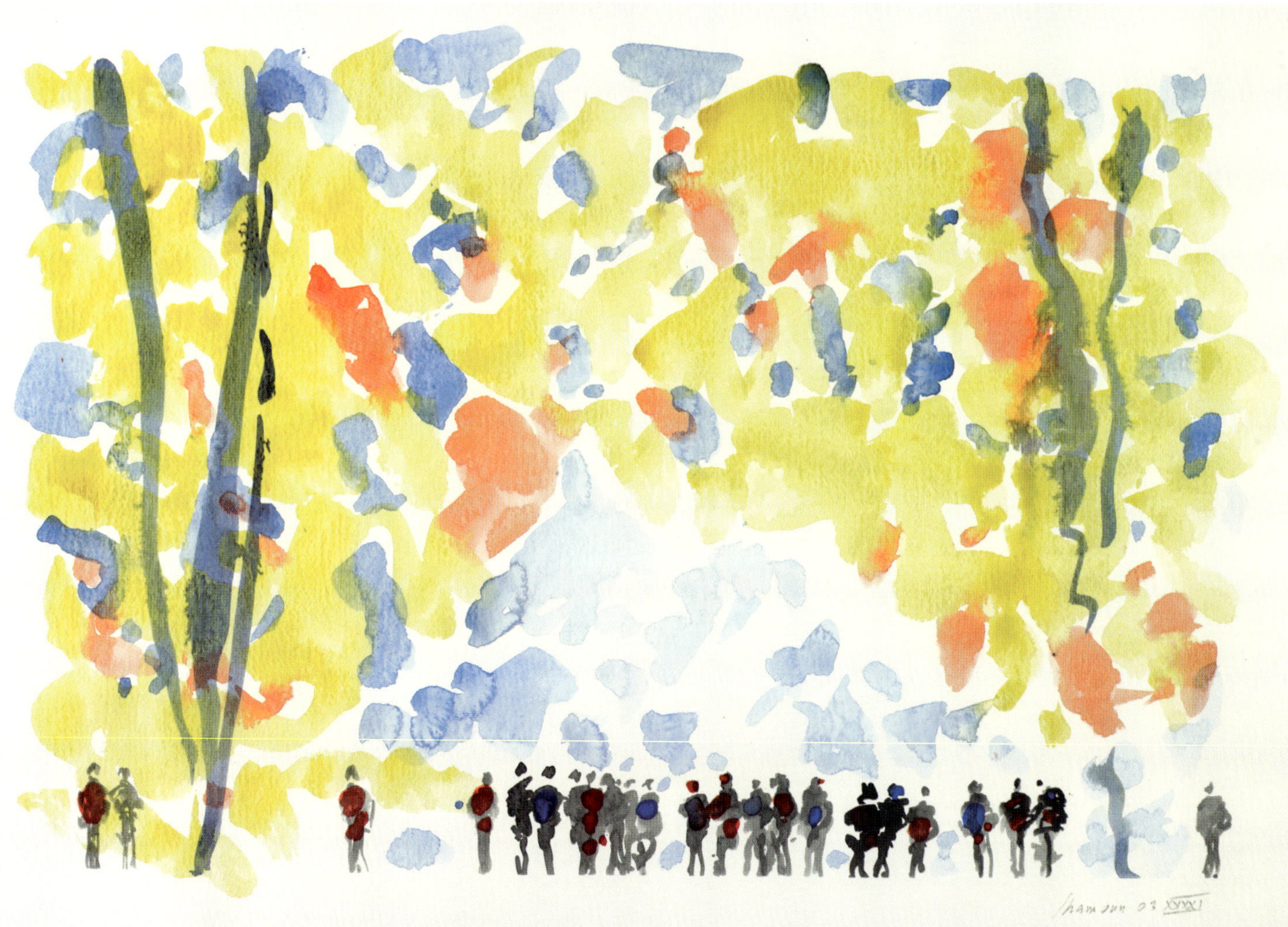

237
03, 2003
Watercolour on paper
60.9 x 47.7 cm

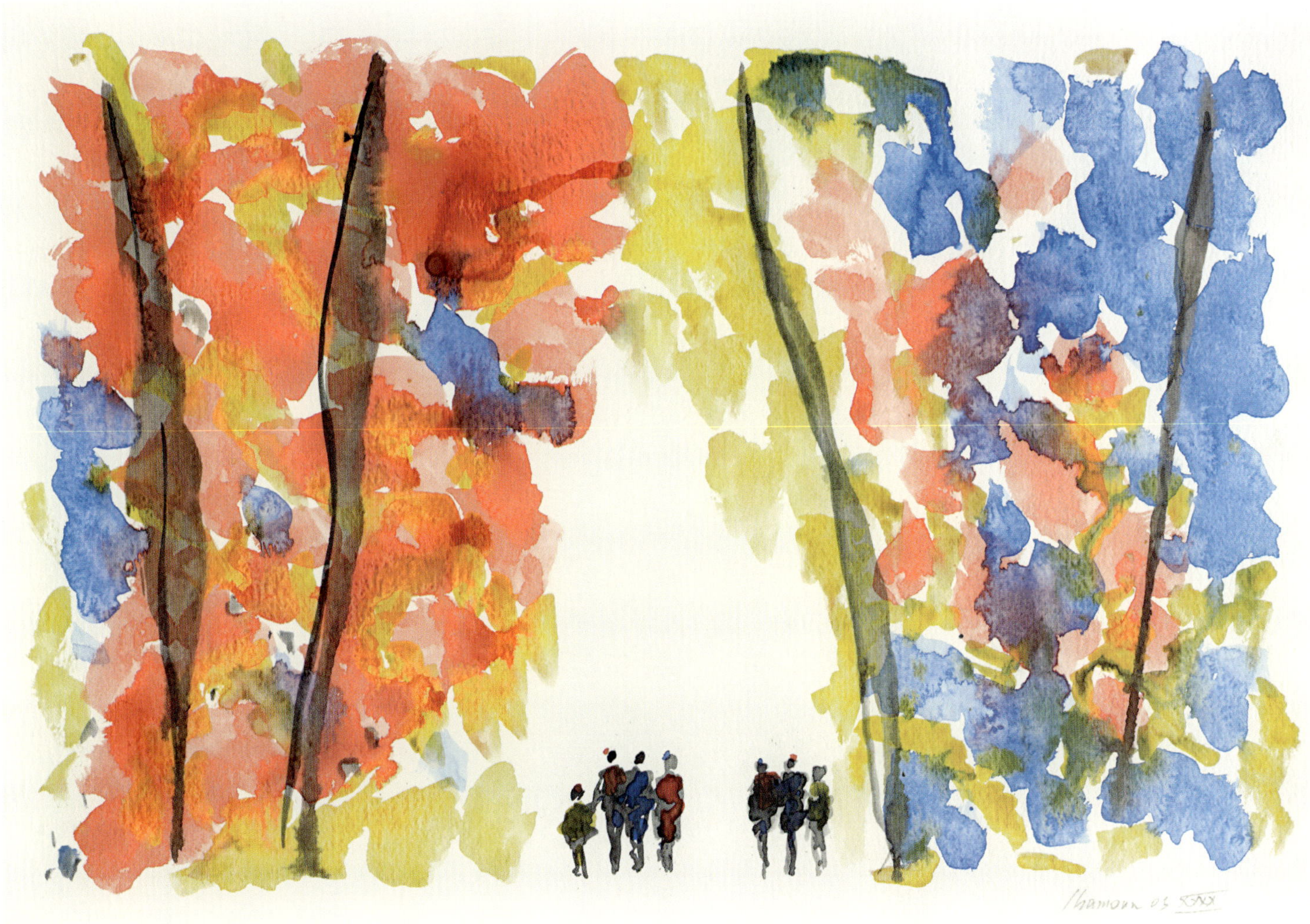

238
03, 2003 - 1
Watercolour on paper
60.9 x 47.7 cm

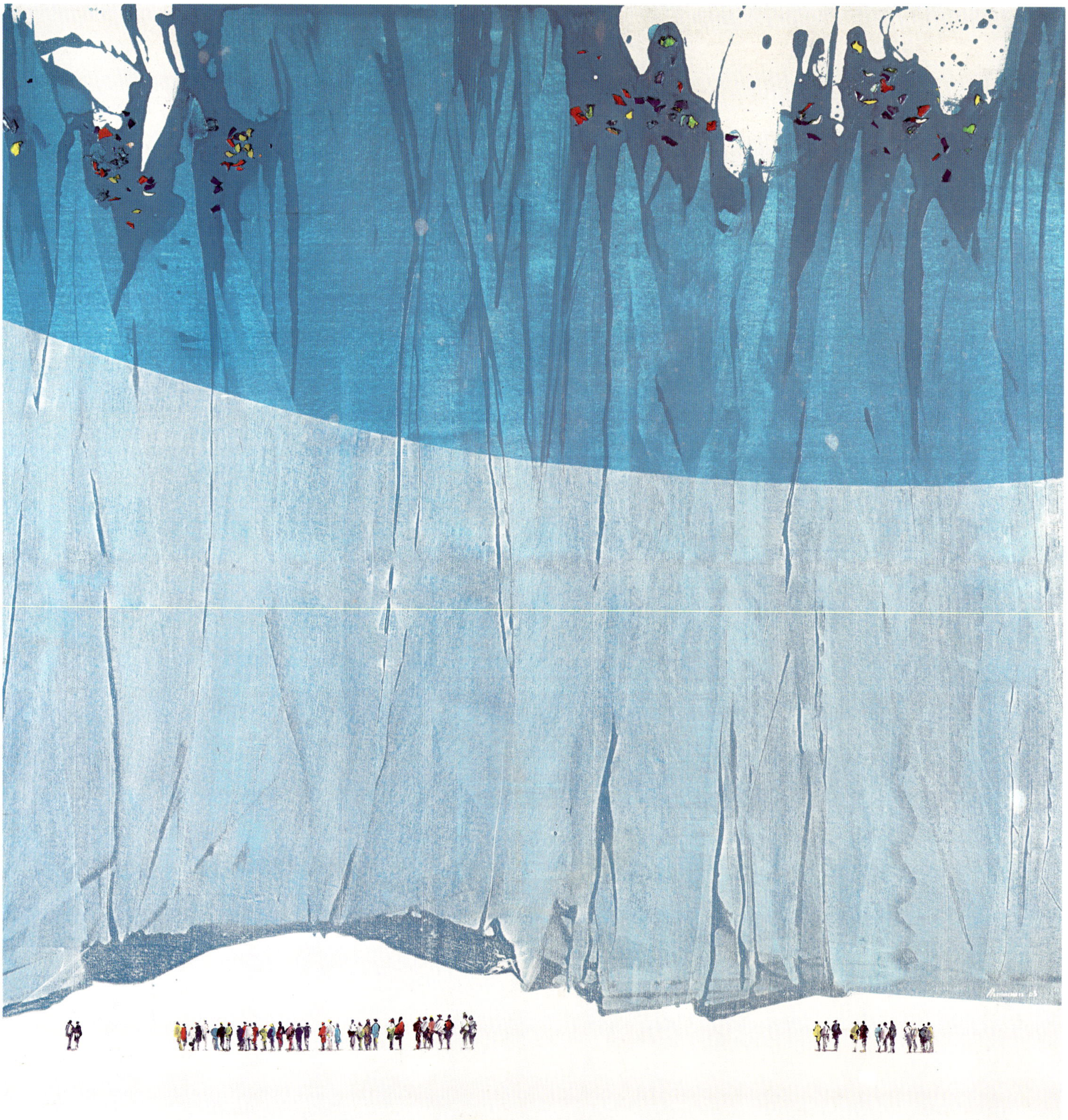

A New Journey

Back in Lebanon, I built platforms on my studio floor, tacked large canvases to them and started implementing my watercolour and ink drawings in acrylic on large canvases. I felt that life had given me a second chance after I survived my accident, and I wanted to realise whatever I could before it was too late.

I devoted all my time to painting and teaching, doing away with design. Teaching never got in the way. I loved teaching and gave my students all I knew, while getting back from them young and fresh insights which kept me up to date. In fact, I was the only person who was getting older in my university studio. My students' age was stable: eighteen to twenty-two. Only the faces changed. Thus I put myself into a 'full-time art mood', and any day when I did not paint was a day I felt I was not a painter.

My painting started to take different directions subject-wise, technique-wise and even size-wise. In the past, when I encountered something different from the style or techniques I happened to be pursuing at the time, I would put it temporarily aside, but rarely came back to it because new findings would take over. Now, though, I would pursue and develop whatever potential aesthetic stimulation arose.

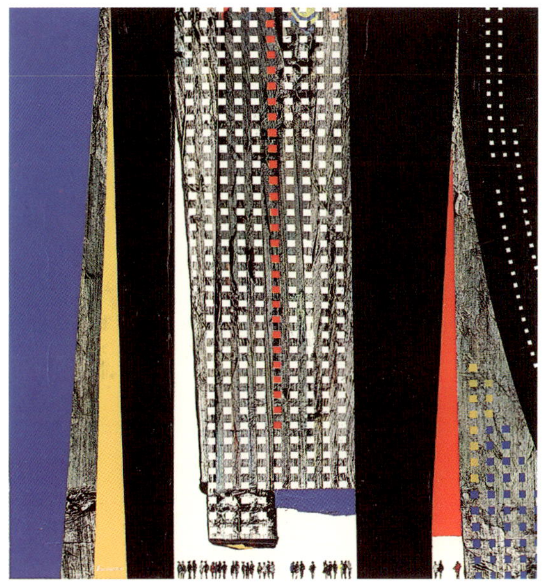

239
AN URBAN ENCOUNTER, 2003
Acrylic on canvas
150 x 160 cm

Facing page
240
THE NIGHT OF THE BIG FALL, 2003
Acrylic on canvas
145 x 154 cm

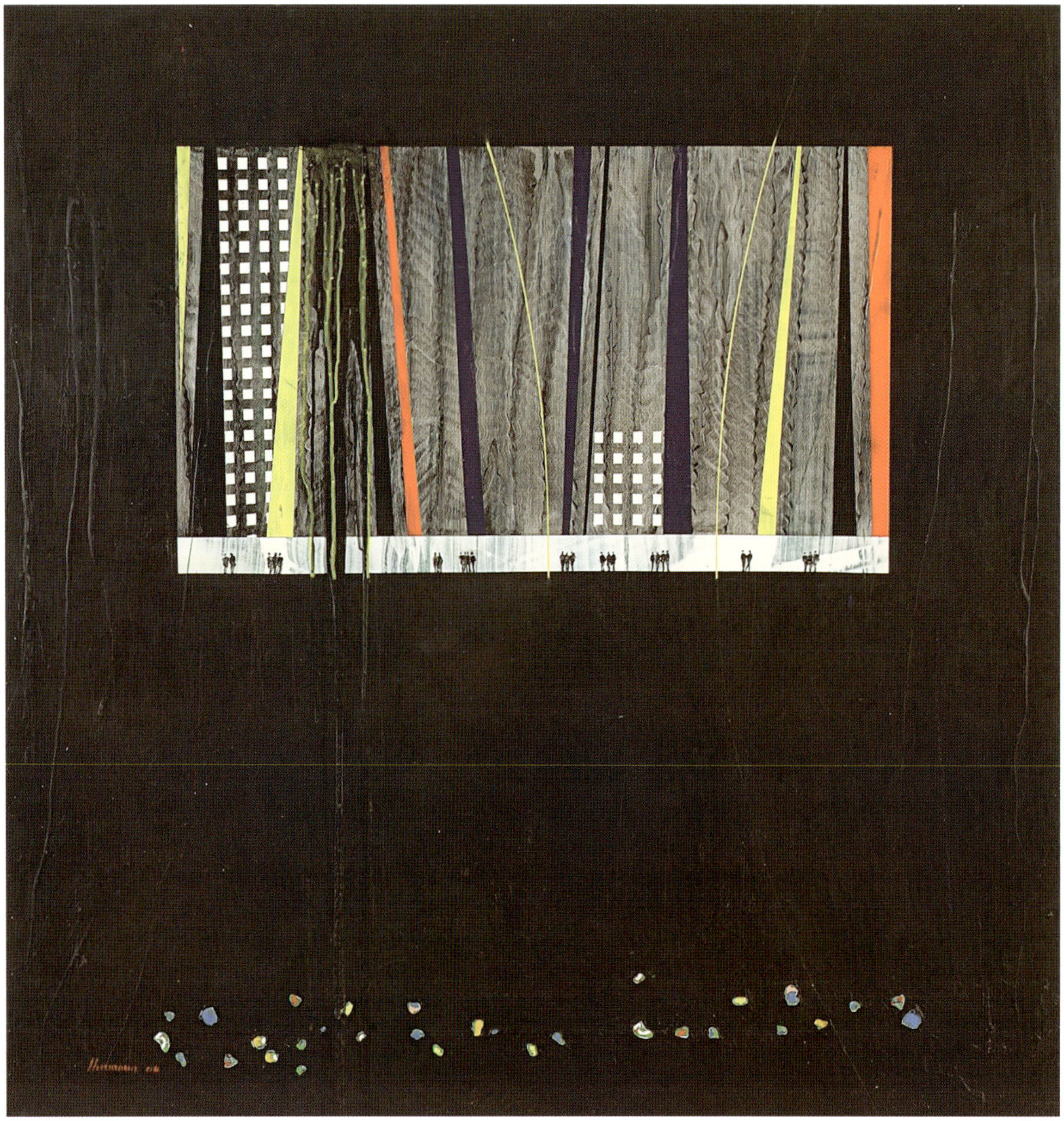

241
AN URBAN ENCOUNTER 2, 2003
Acrylic on canvas
150 x 160 cm

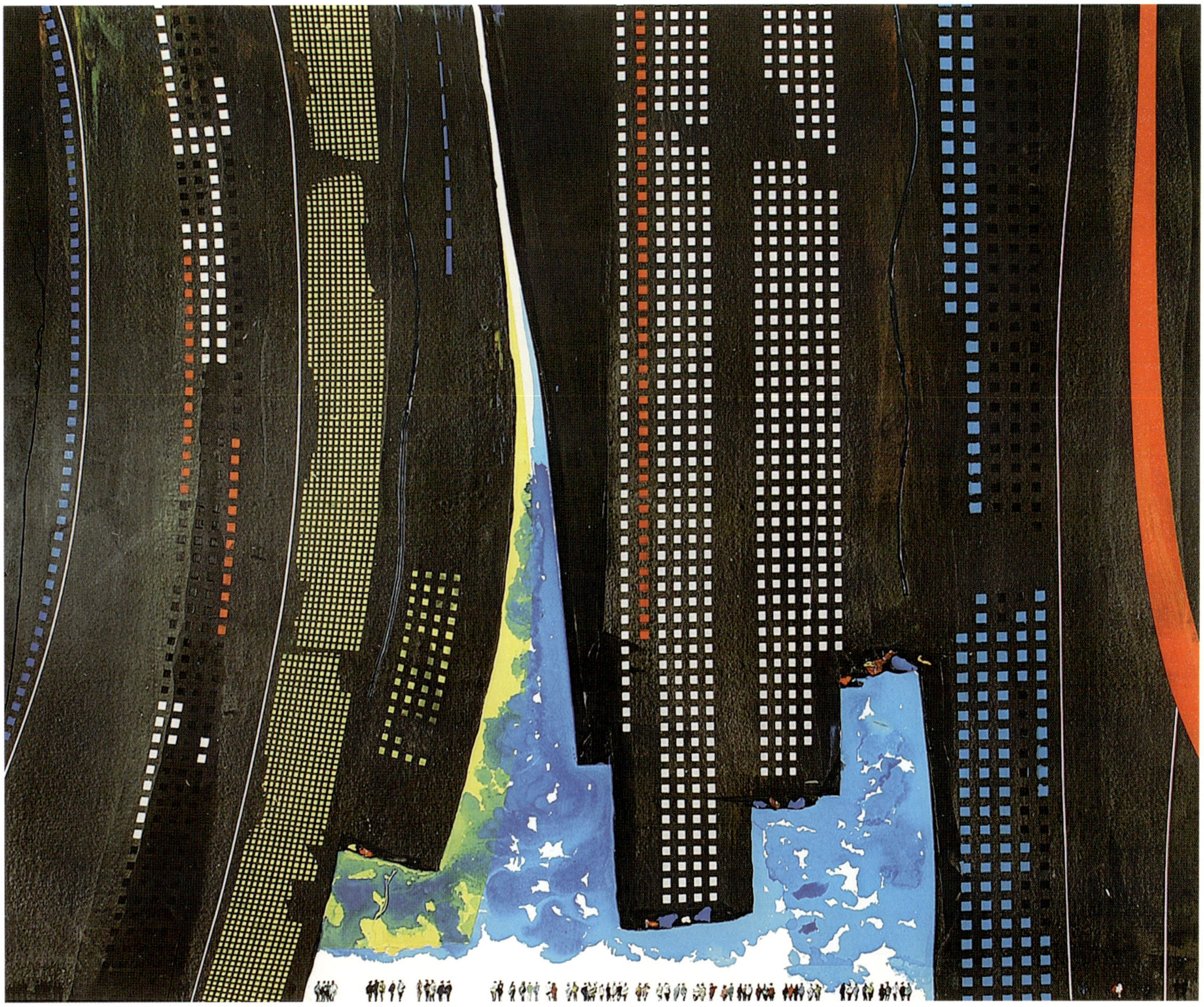

242
TOPPLED CITY, 2004
Acrylic on canvas
290 x 250 cm
(Sold through Christie's auction, Dubai, 2007, for a record price for a living Lebanese artist)

Following spread
243
THE SPLIT, 2003
Acrylic on canvas
236 x 114 cm

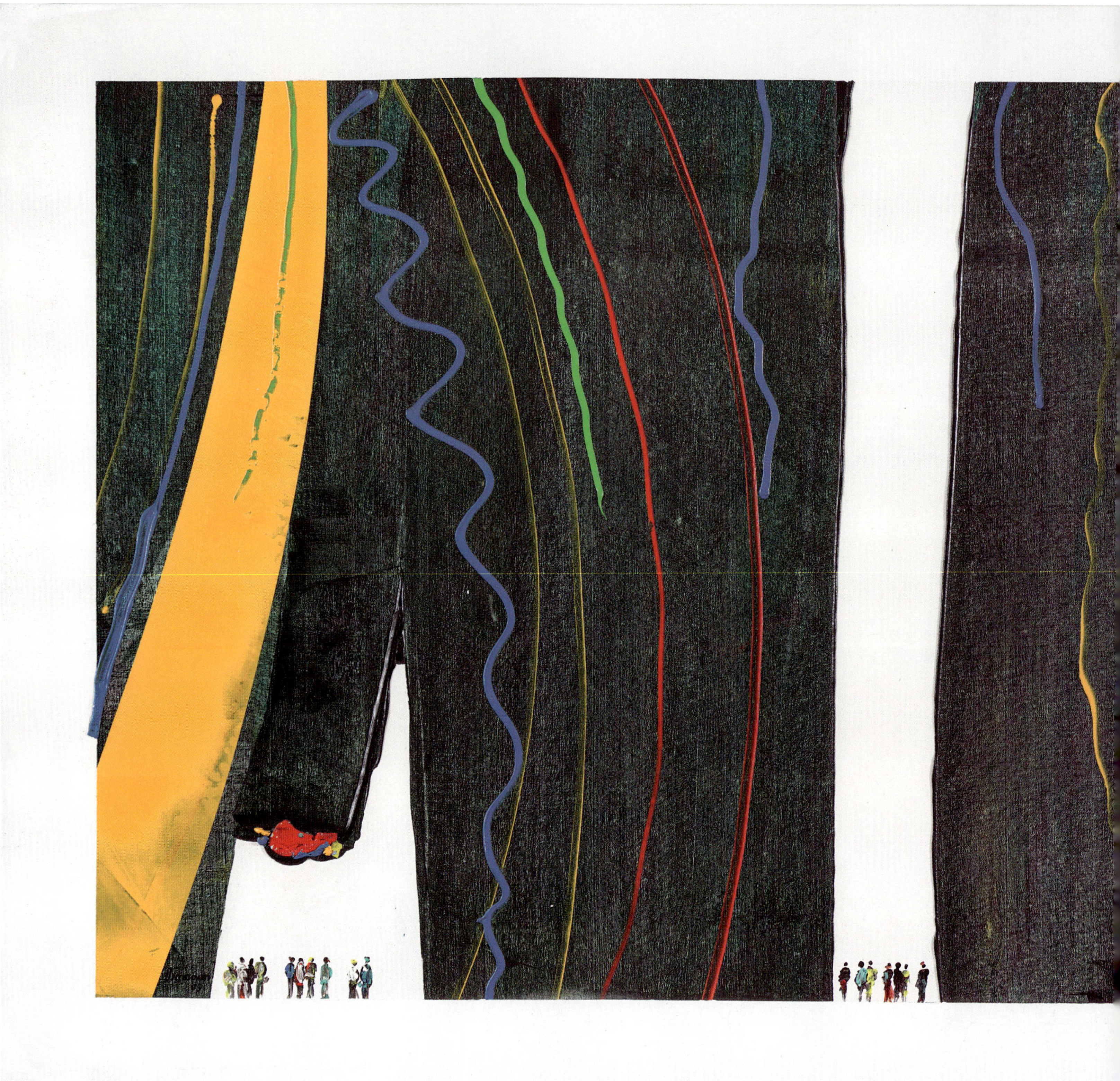

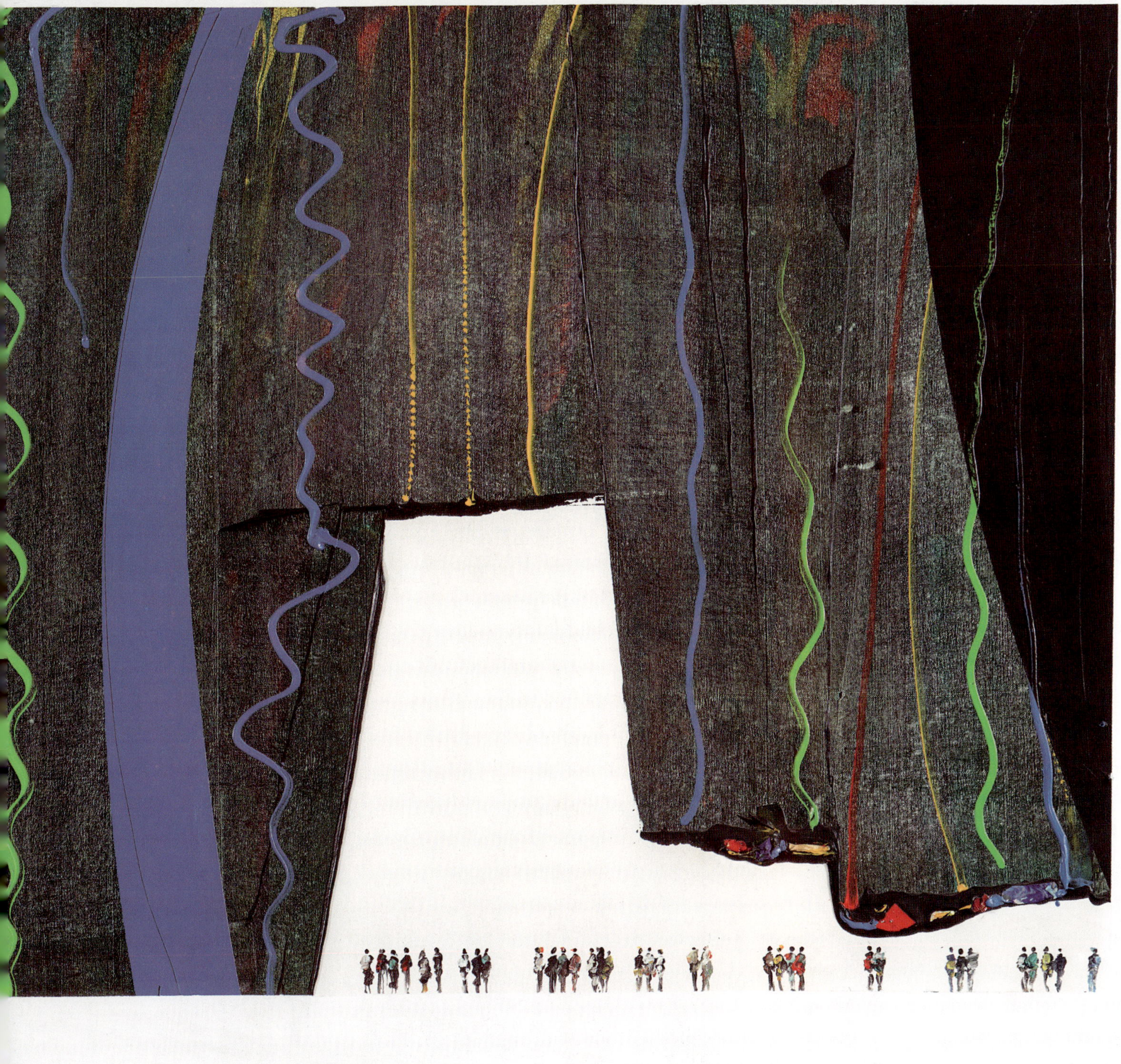

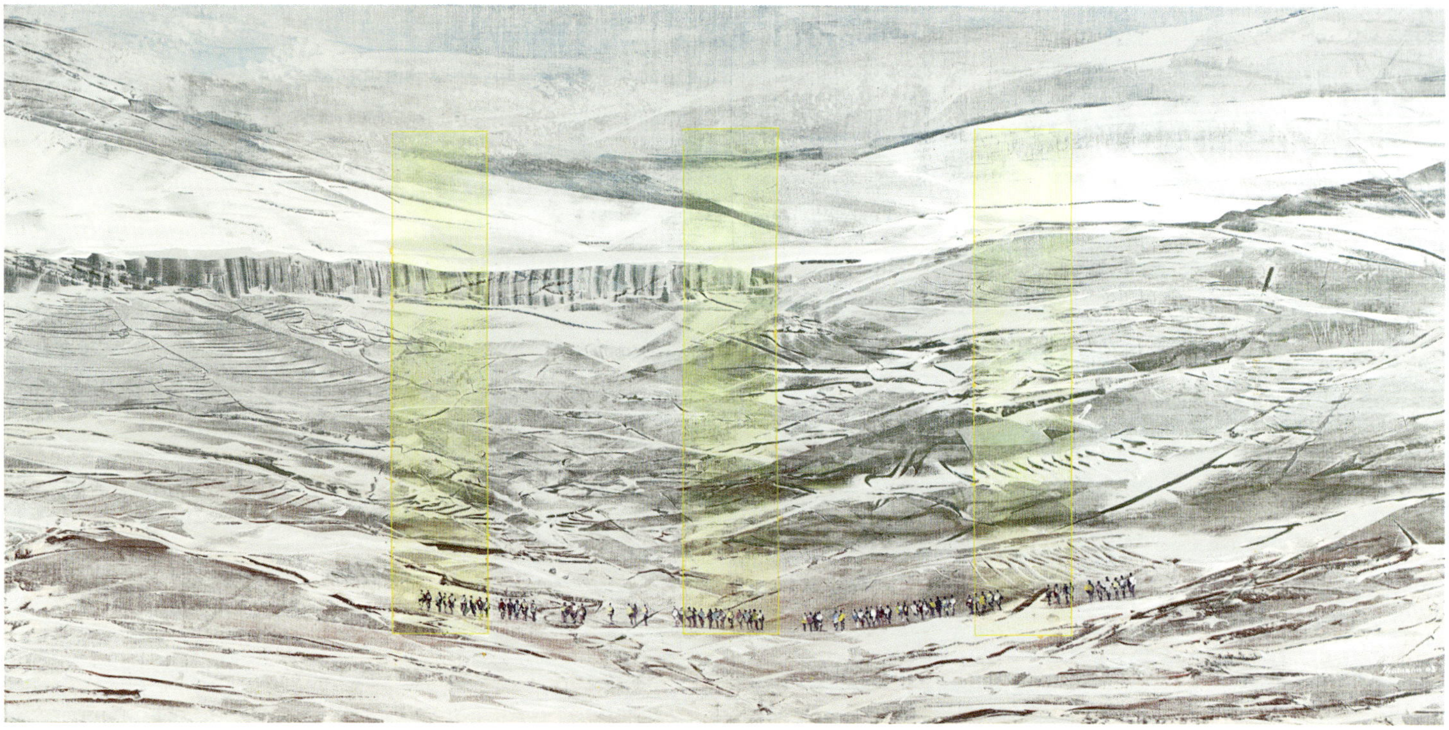

244
ON A WHITE DAY, 2003
Acrylic on canvas
236 x 114 cm

Facing page
245
ON A WHITE DAY, 2004
Acrylic on canvas (detail)
290 x 250 cm
(Auctioned and sold at Christie's, Dubai, 2008)

Before my accident, I considered it a necessity to sustain one single aesthetic problem and one subject for a long period of time in search of deeper aesthetic meaning and a more revealing essence of its existential properties. Developing one single issue required me to shelve any irrelevant thoughts. This was no longer the case. I felt that I had to develop whatever the moment allowed me to do and whatever my emotions, feelings and intellectual engagement led me to.

My painting became the echo of everything I experienced in my daily life, both on the technical and the emotional levels. Nothing had to wait. I never, however, really believed in a single style or one working method for life; experimental in principle and in practice, I developed and pursued different goals and working methods as I deemed necessary. In the end, I can only sign off on the realisation of aesthetically qualitative convictions.

The line of distant people I had painted at the bottom of many of my paintings in the past now became central

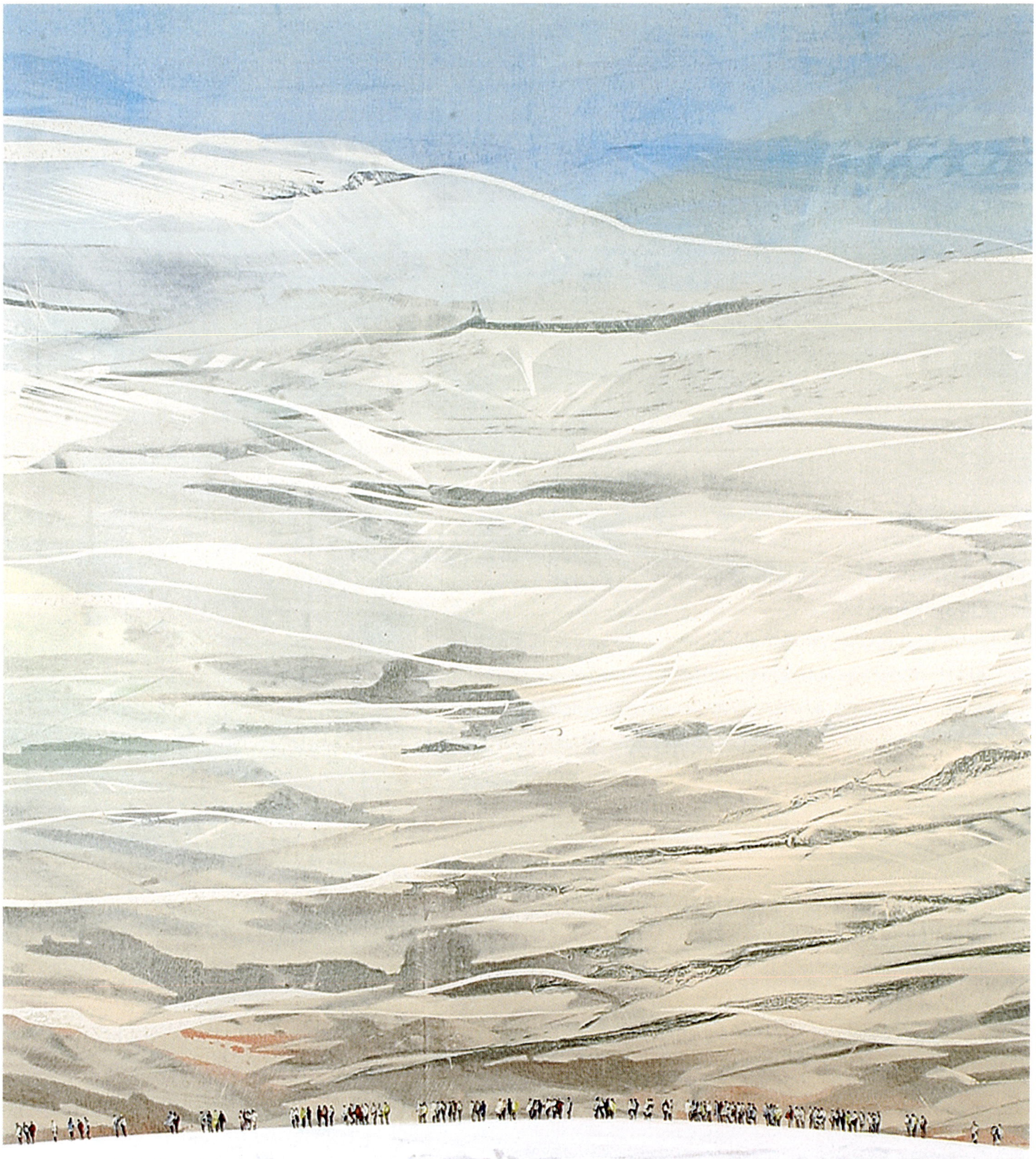

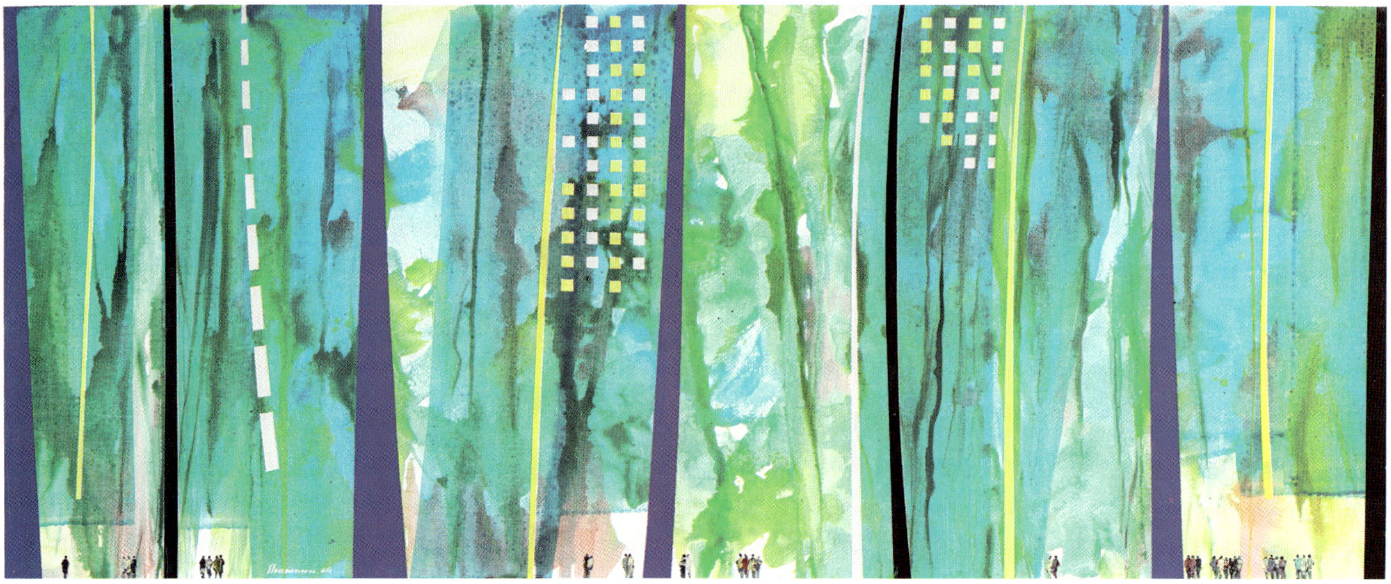

246
AN AESTHETIC STATEMENT, 2004
Acrylic on canvas
236 x 114 cm

to them all. In many cases, this line became the painting itself. Through them, I expressed a waiting mood, or people in tense juxtaposition, or people as walls. In many ways this line of people became my personal line of people. With them I painted, and with them I saw the world. I could not see a painting, whether in a natural setting or in an abstract conceptual composition, without that line of people appearing to be first to witness the experience itself. Sometimes I painted them all by themselves, so that they were the painting, and sometimes they were the visitors in the scenery, whether abstract or realistic. They were men, women and children in different settings, natural or conceptual. For some reason they became my signature; I could not see the painting without them. If they did not come into the painting, I would feel guilty about leaving them out.

In summer 2002 I went to visit Ground Zero at the World Trade Center. I had loved those two towers, which had housed my first major store design. They were the most elegant buildings an architect ever shaped. It was sad to find myself looking down into a huge hole in the ground instead of scanning up the graceful structures which had guided my

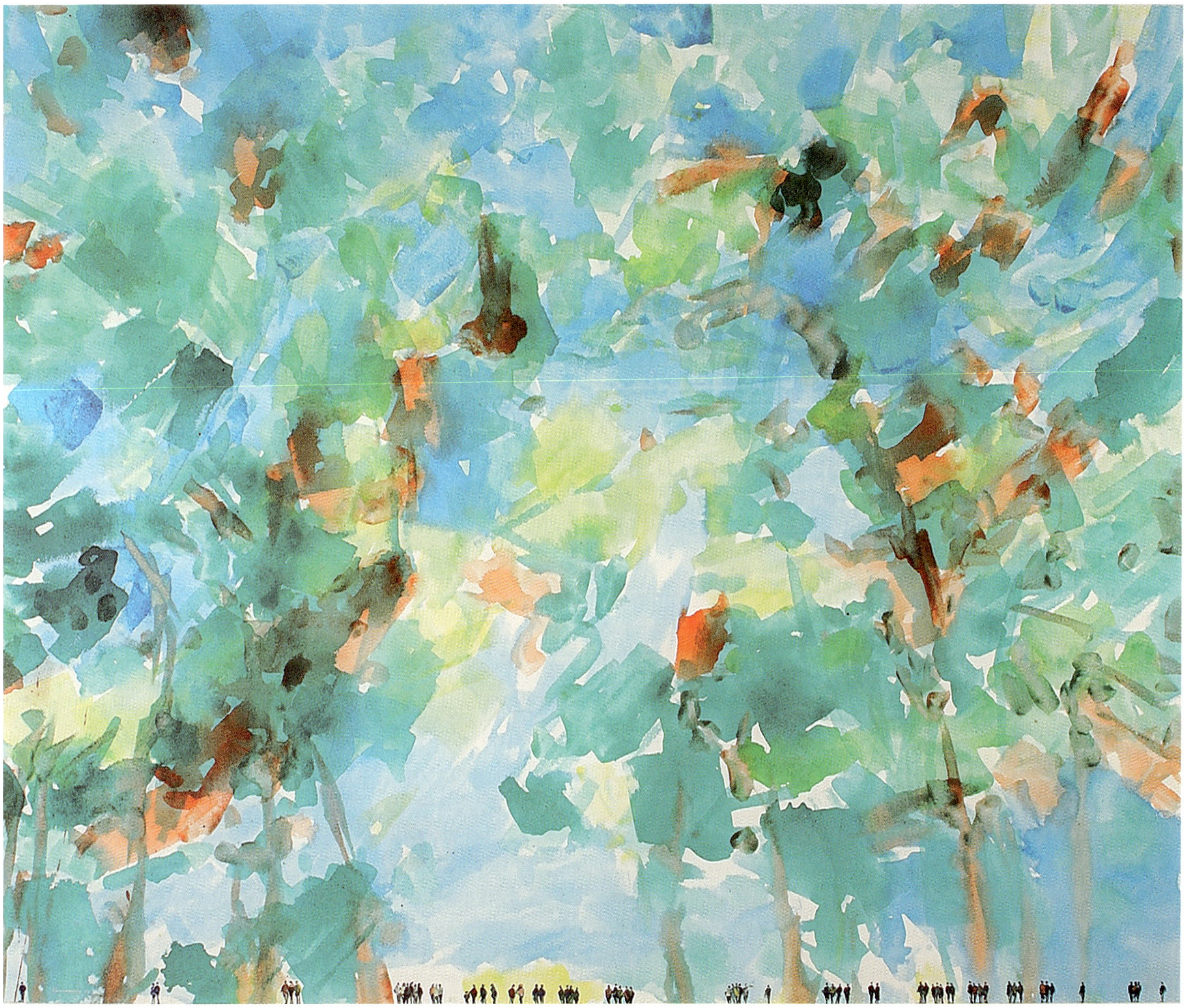

247
BLUE AND GREEN SYMPHONY, 2004
Acrylic on canvas (detail)
290 x 250 cm
(LAU Library Collection)

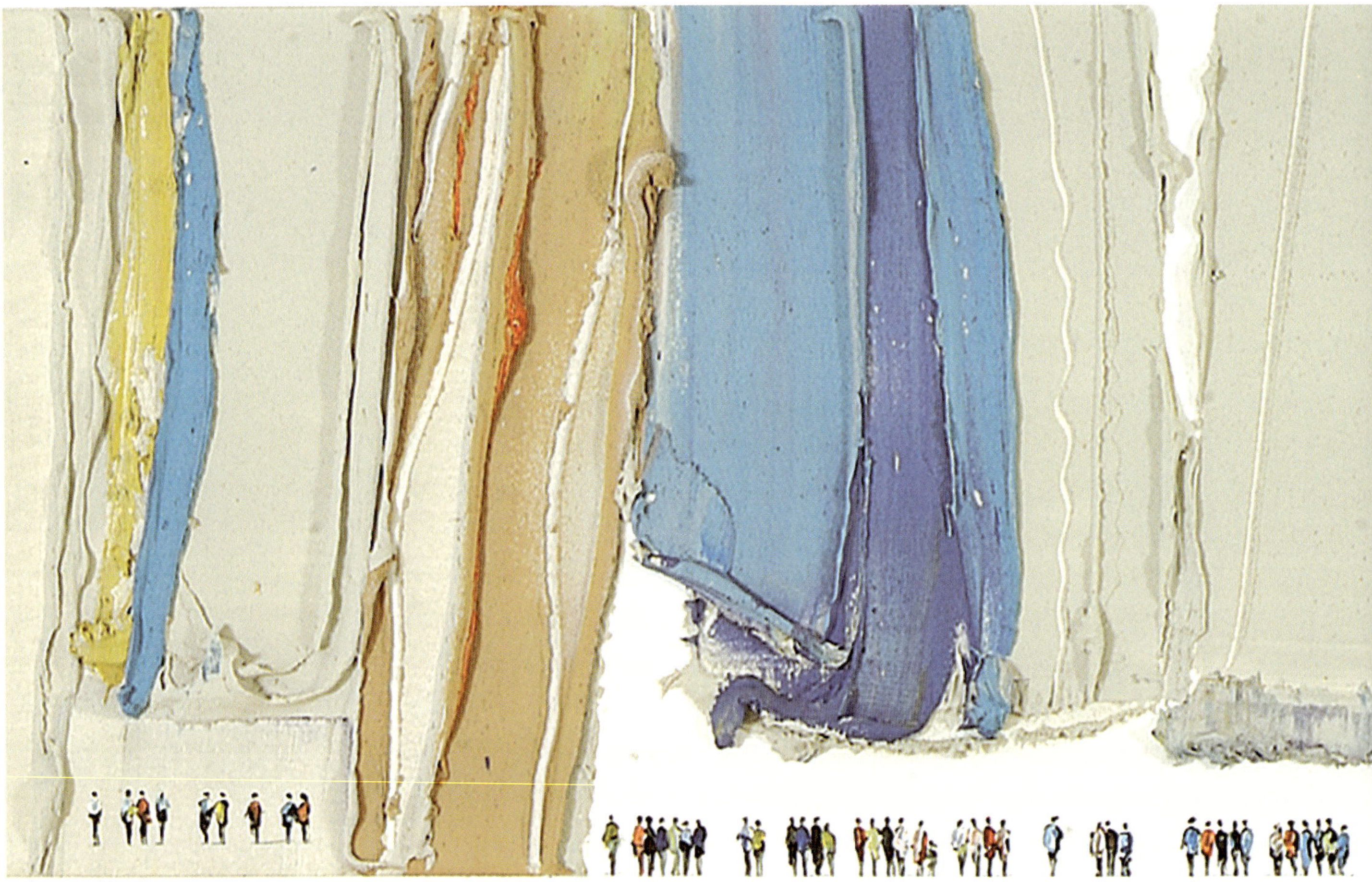

248
WAITING AND WALLS I,
2003
Mixed media
196 x 85 cm

eye to the skies, so I created a eulogy, 'Toppled City'. The 242
painting was auctioned in October 2007 at Christie's in Dubai, bringing the highest price ever for a work by a living Lebanese artist.

The earliest painting I remember doing with this line of distant people at the bottom was made in New York in 1990 when I went with my family to the US, thinking I would never go home to Lebanon. I was always in this line of waiting people. I was waiting with them for the same reason, and I was waiting with them for my own reason.

I reconciled with the world after my close brush with death. I felt that nothing could be taken for granted. Whatever we do or whatever happens to us seems to have some positive effect on our lives. It reflects the qualities that life has given

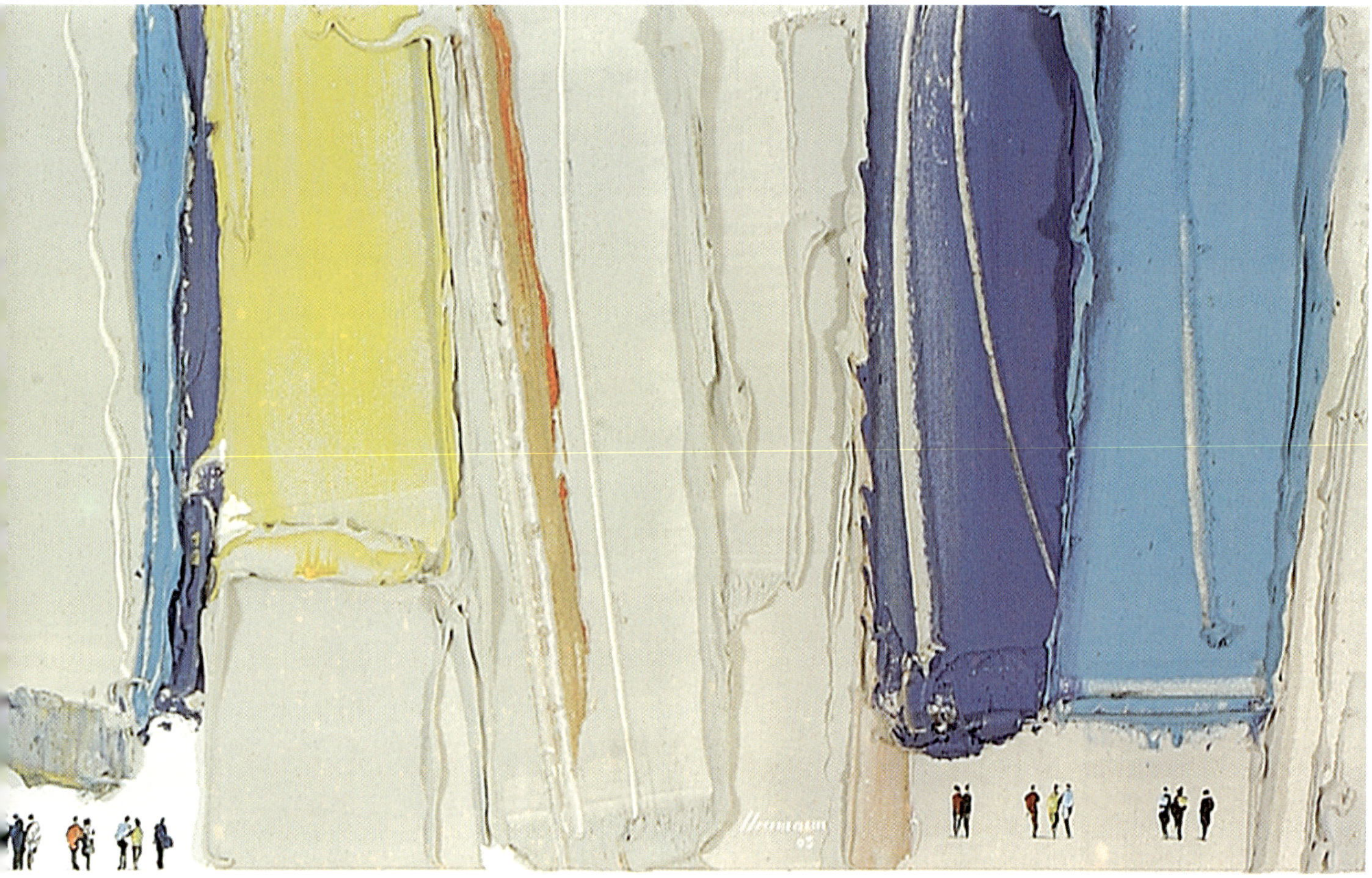

us. I started producing large paintings the size of the floor of my studio. A painting became a playground for me. In the beginning I felt lots of pain kneeling and moving around with all the screws that had been inserted into my body after the accident. But when one has a brush with death one feels and understands that there must be more to life.

I moved on to using industrial and architectural materials, epoxy mixed with sand, gypsum and metals, to form sturdy three-dimensional surfaces. I called the series 'Beyond Walls', thinking of the walls separating people, the walls we have within us. The walls stand high between us and our ambitions and hopes. We are always trying to break through walls, creating openings through which we regain hope and faith in the future. The potential of this new medium

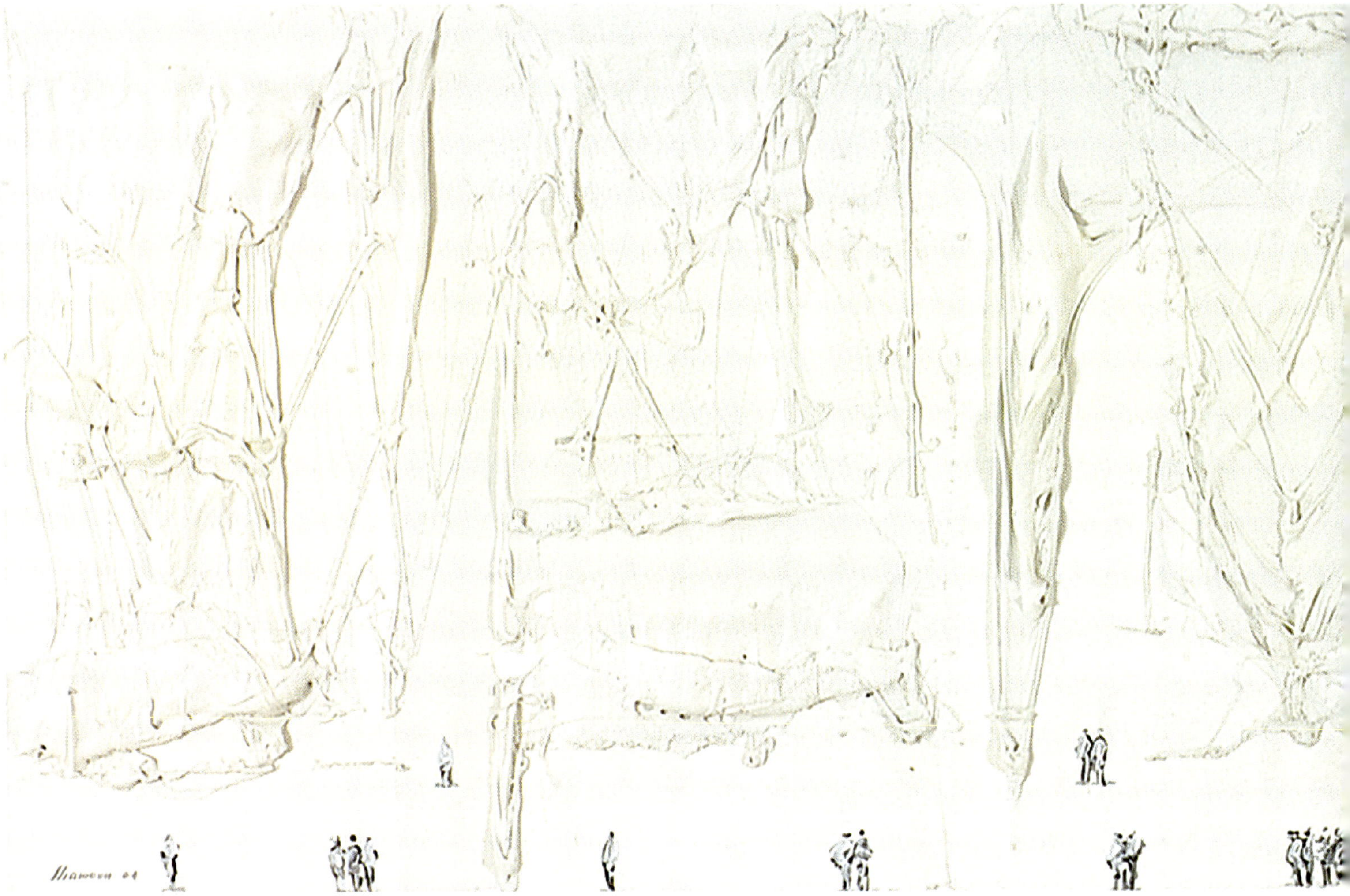

249
WAITING AND WALLS VI, 2004
Mixed media on canvas
196 x 85 cm
(Auctioned and sold at Sotheby's, London, autumn 2007)

was beyond any limits, and I strongly considered exploring its aesthetic horizons. All my paintings between 2003 and 2005 were included in a ten-year retrospective highlighting paintings of the previous decade. 239–253

I suspected that epoxy resin fumes were hurting my eyes despite the fact that I wore protective glasses most of the time. Yes 'most', not all. I could not get into the habit of working safely: I go to work without thinking of health hazards or considering consequences. Working with resin and fibre requires special concentration and adequate time management: the medium has no tolerance for mistakes once drying has begun. I began experiencing distortion of my

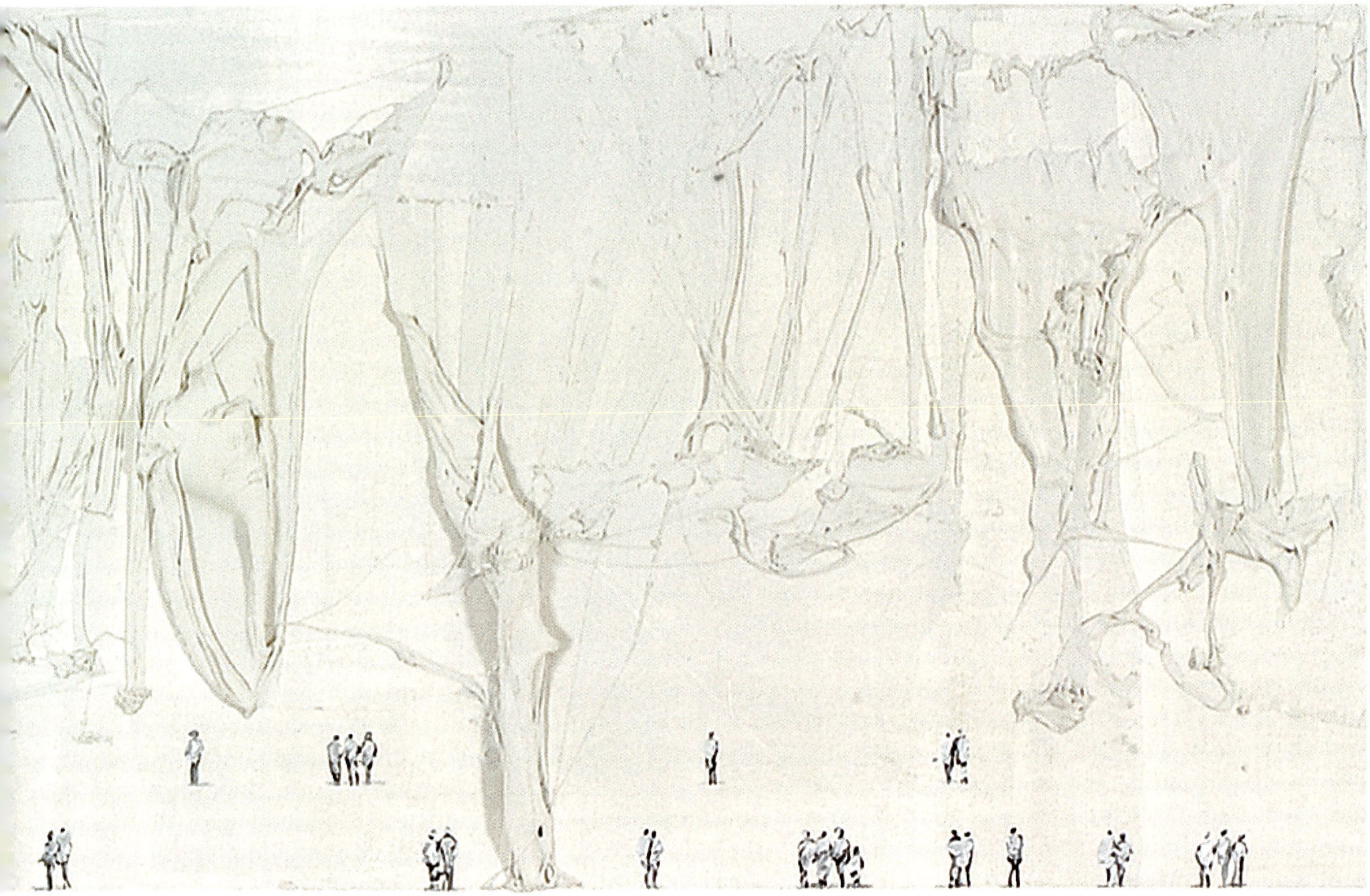

vision. For over a year, I went to see one doctor after another without improvement. Finally, on the recommendation of the artist Yousef Aoun, a former student and colleague, I visited Dr George Cherfan. Dr Cherfan quickly identified the problem and recommended a laser operation, which helped limit the damage and stop the spread of the problem.

Prior to, during and after the barbaric July War of 2006, and up to my Desert Experience, I undertook several experiments in my painting. Some were a scream against the
254–258 savage Israeli bombardment; these would be followed by
259–264 another series of 'Nature Revisited' and a series of calligraphy
265–267 and culturally inspired abstract works.

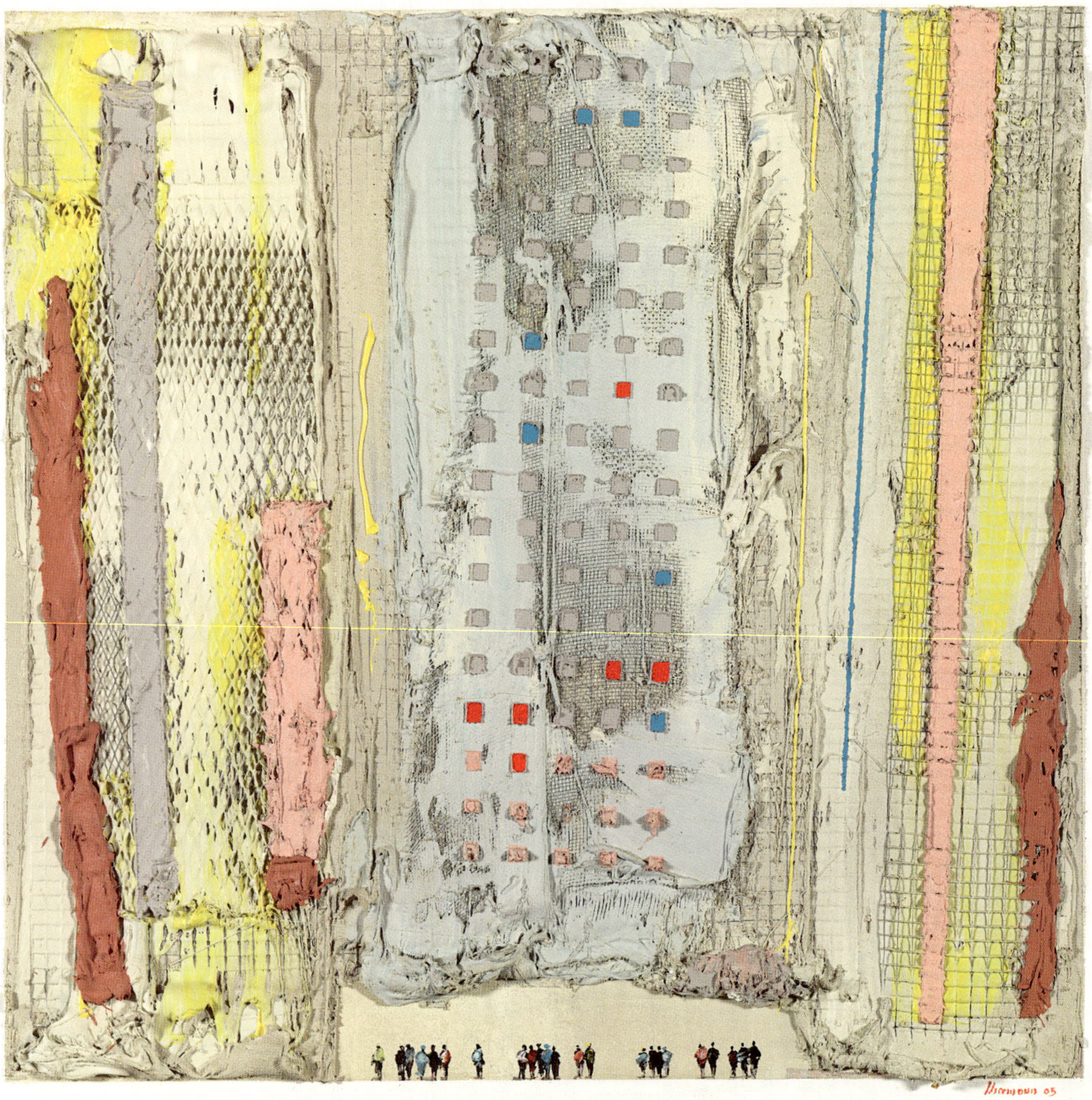

250
DREAM CITY, 2005
Mixed media
112 x 112 cm

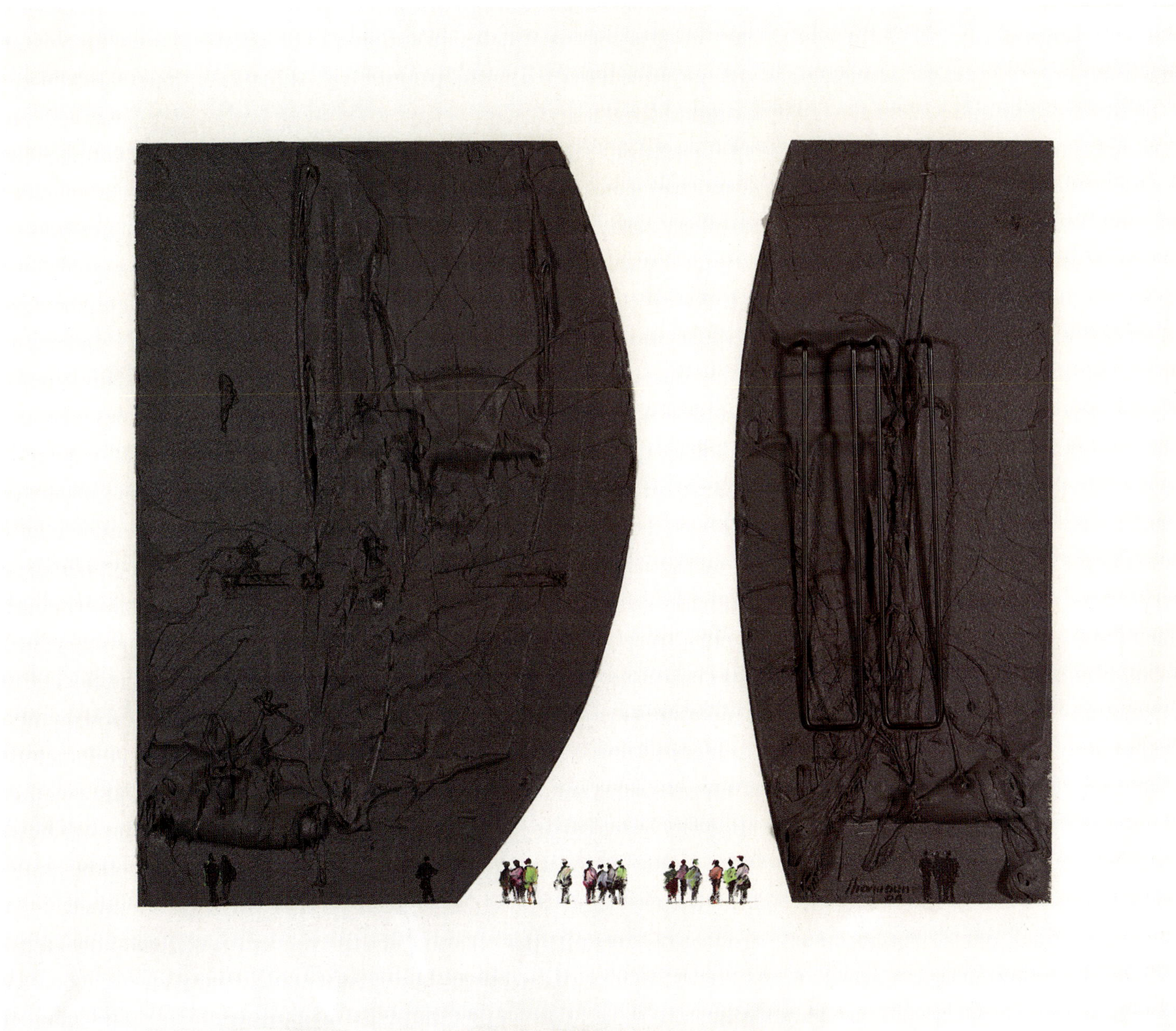

251
MAN AND MANMADE WALLS, 2005
Mixed media
142 x 82 cm

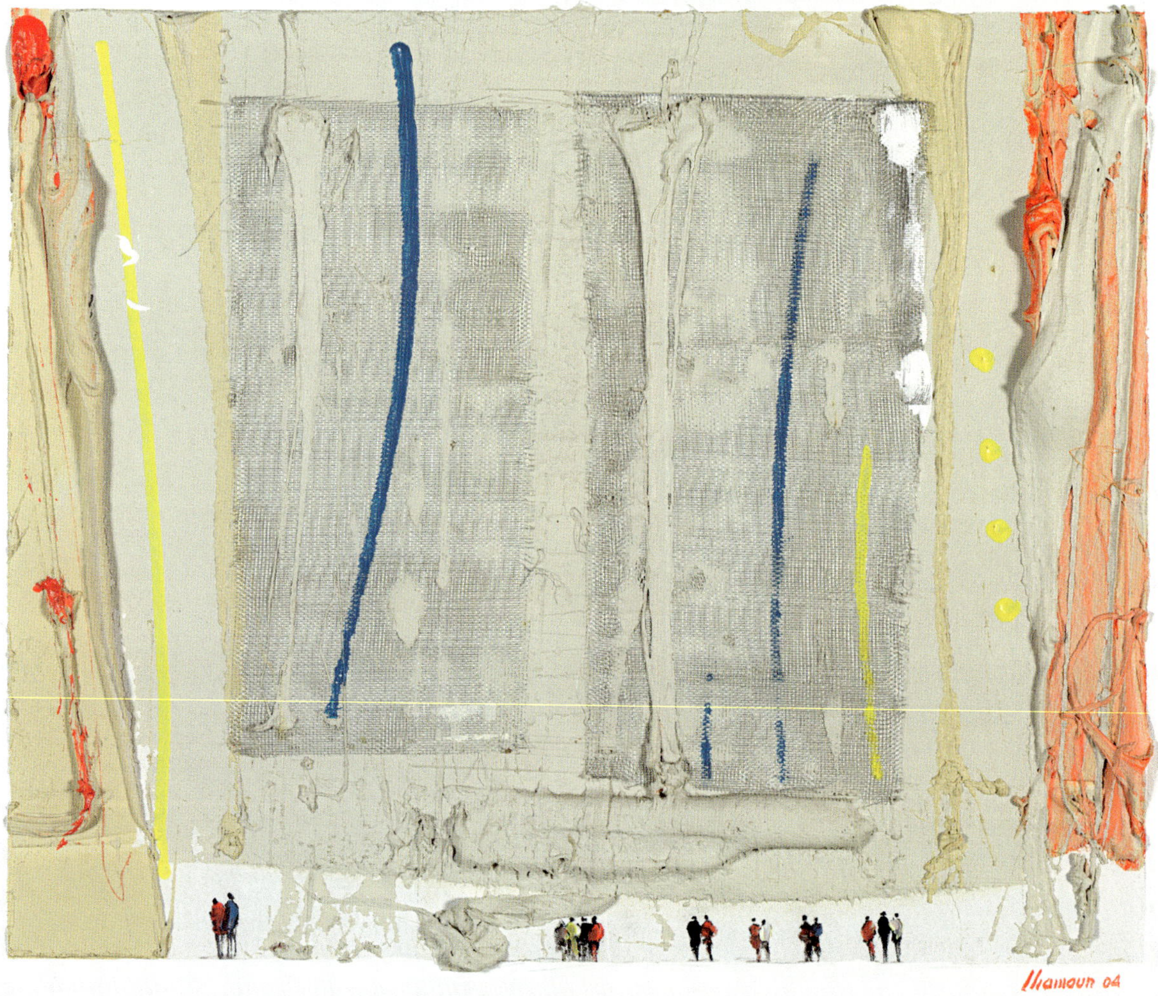

252
BEYOND WALLS VIII, 2004
Mixed media
86 x 73 cm

Facing page
253
BEYOND WALLS XIV, 2005
Mixed media
112 x 112 cm

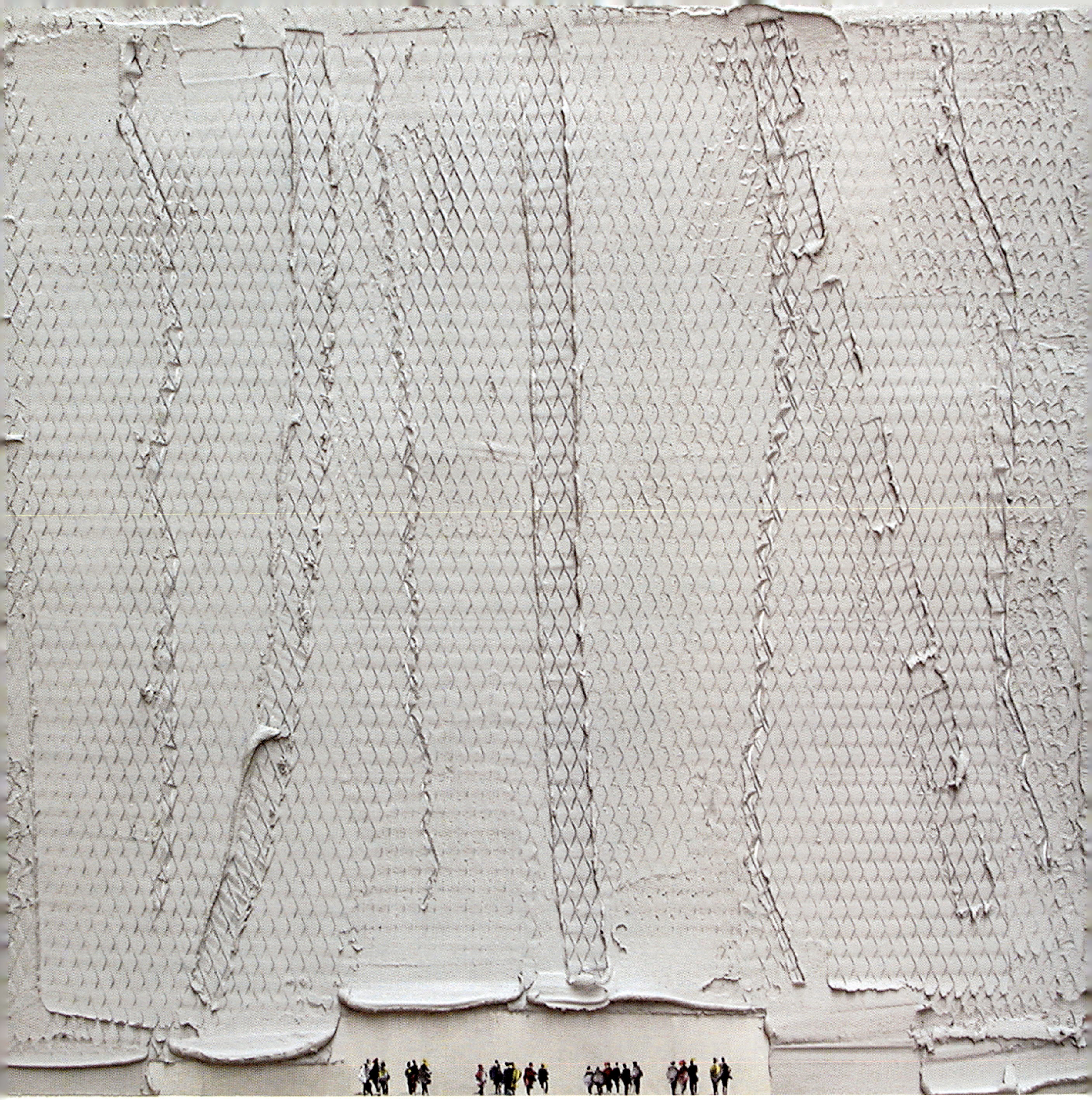

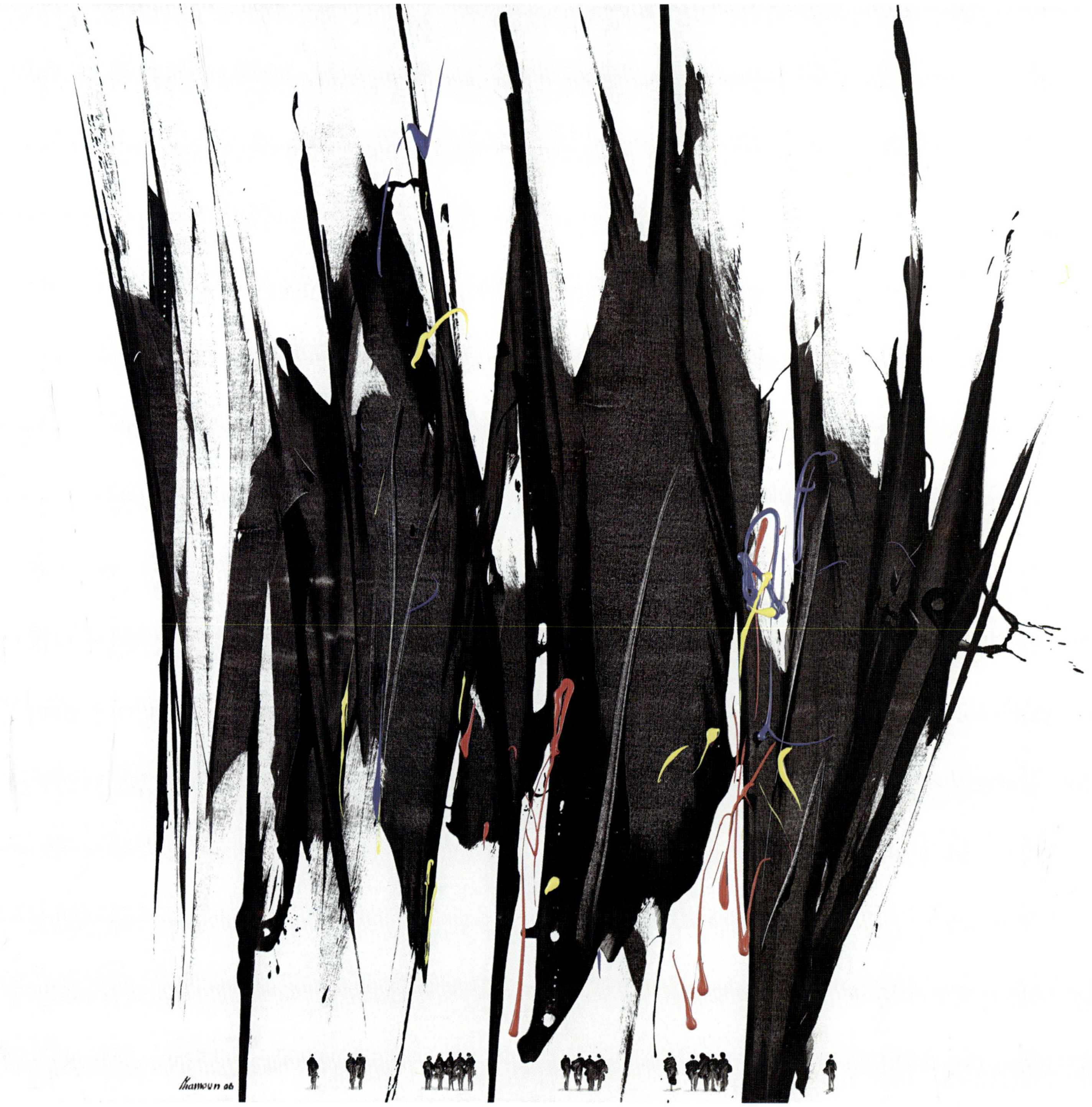

254
JULY 06, 2006
Acrylic on canvas
112 x 112 cm

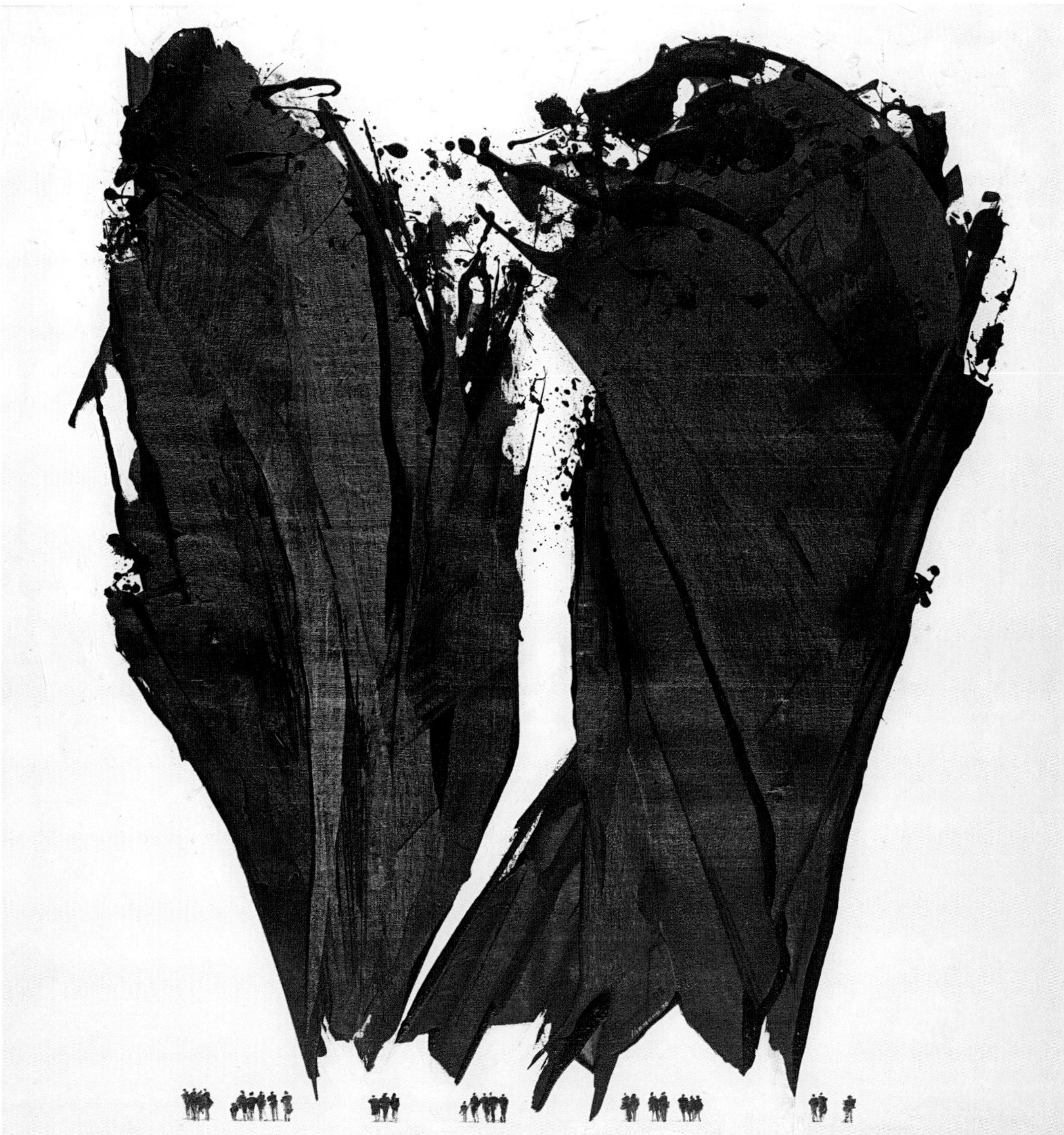

255
THE EIGHTH REBIRTH OF THE PHOENIX, 2006
Acrylic on canvas
150 x 160 cm

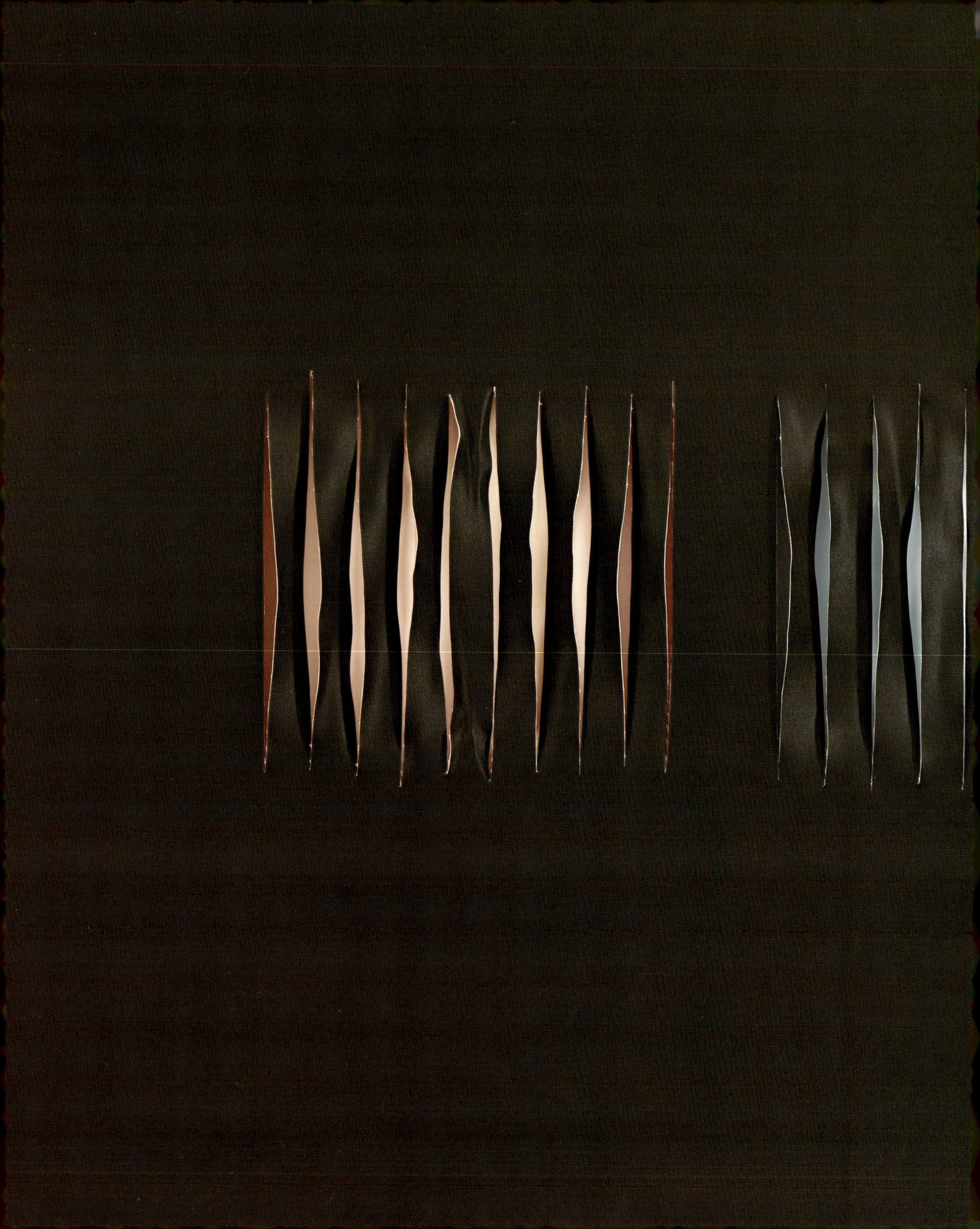

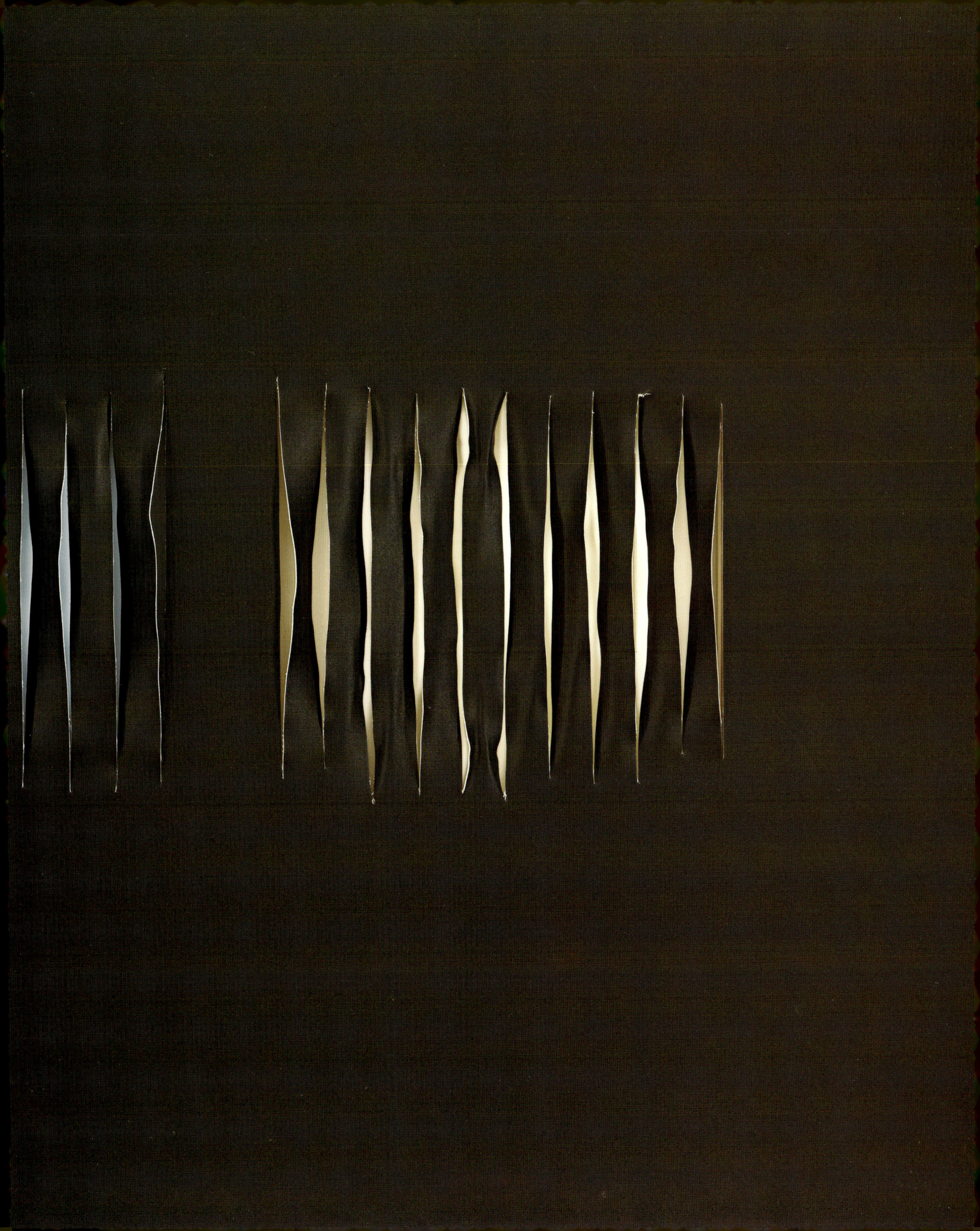

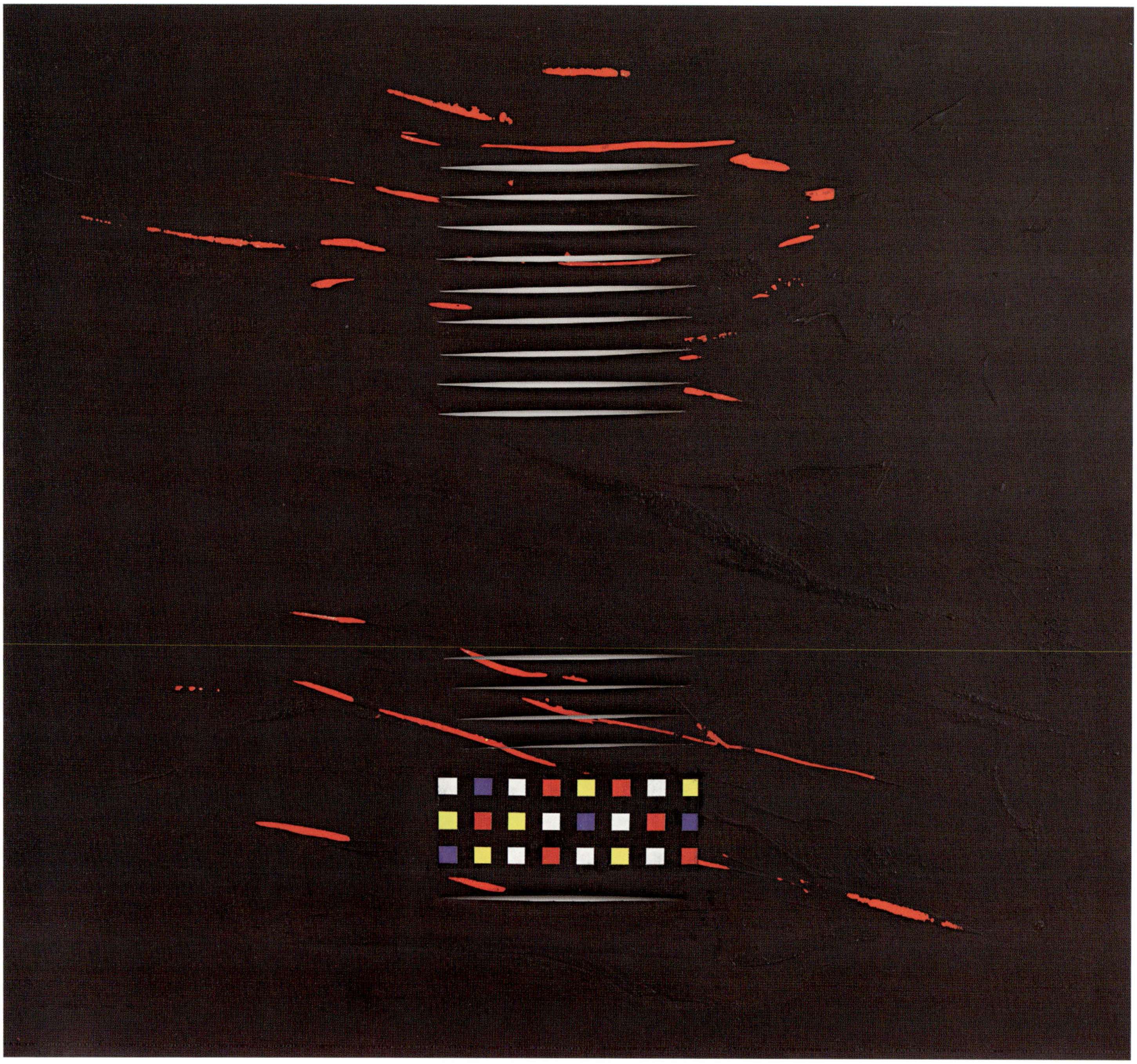

256
SONATA #7 OR THE CONFESSION WALL, 2006
Acrylic and cuts on canvas
160 x 150 cm

Previous spread
257
AESTHETIC OF THE BLACK, 2006
Acrylic and cuts on canvas (detail)
236 x 114 cm

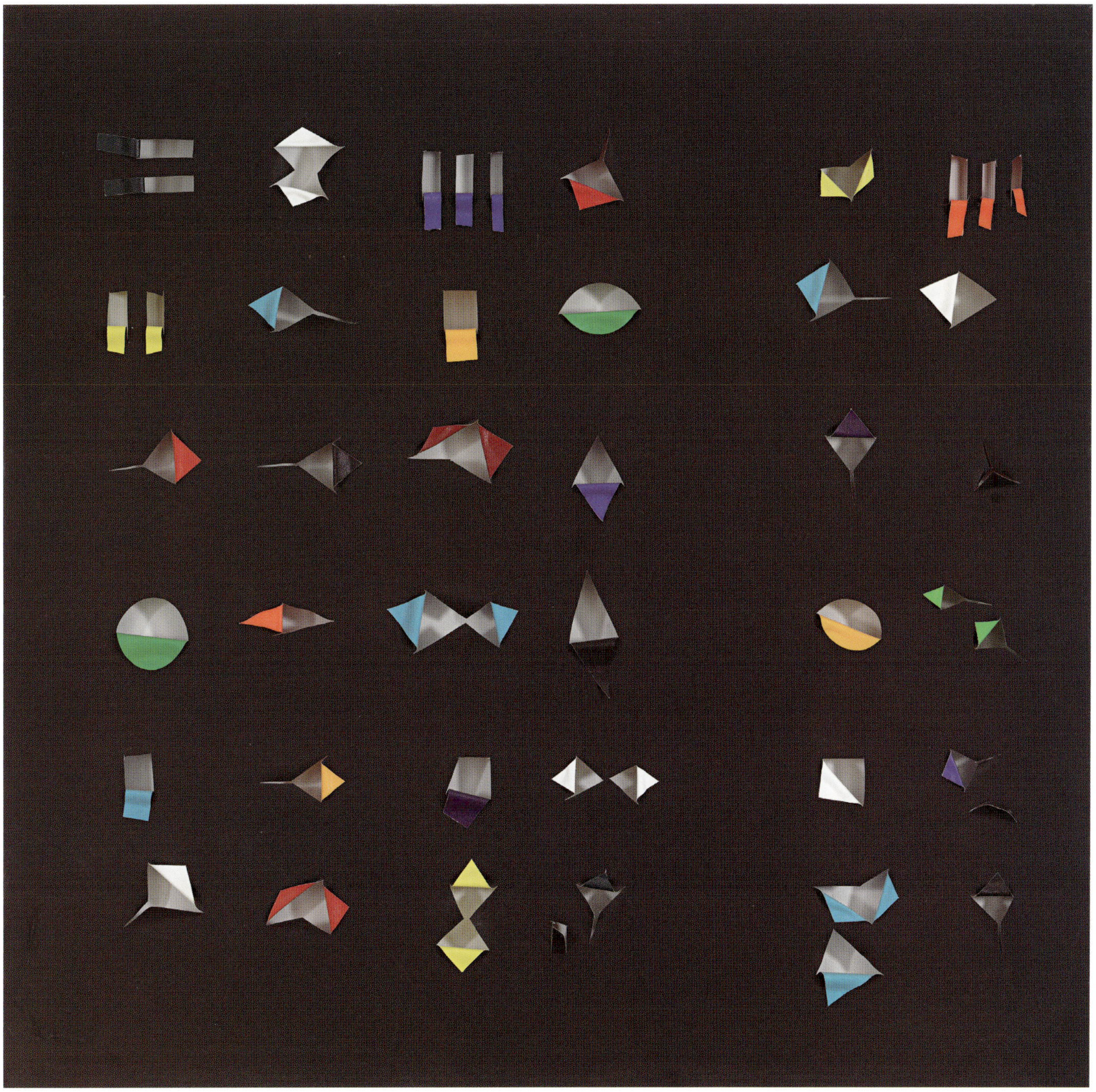

258
UNIDENTIFIED SIGNS, 2007
Acrylic and cuts on canvas
144 x 144 cm

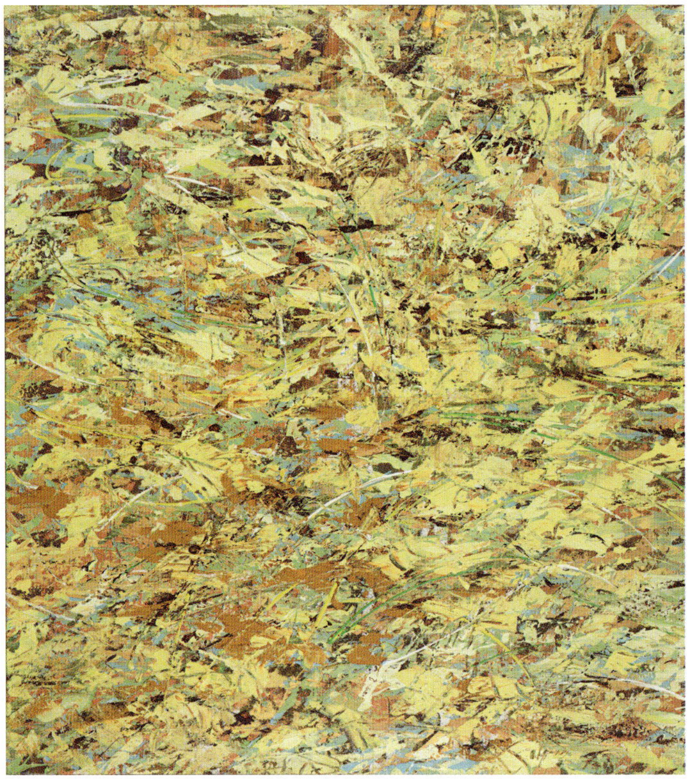

259
TUXEDO PARK REVISITED XIII, 2007
Acrylic on canvas
135 x 153 cm

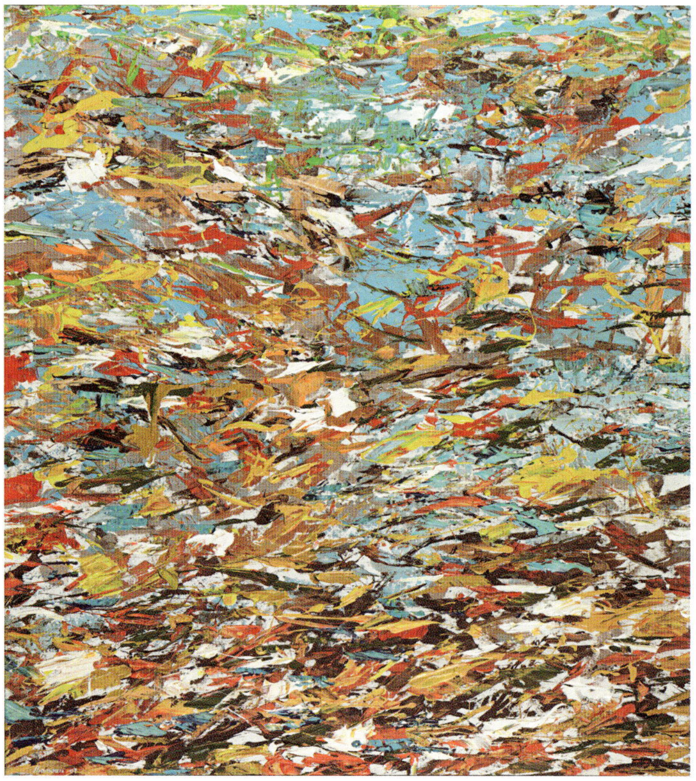

260
TUXEDO PARK REVISITED XXVII, 2007
Acrylic on canvas
135 x 153 cm

Facing page
261
ANOTHER WHITE DAY, 2008
Acrylic on canvas
290 x 230 cm

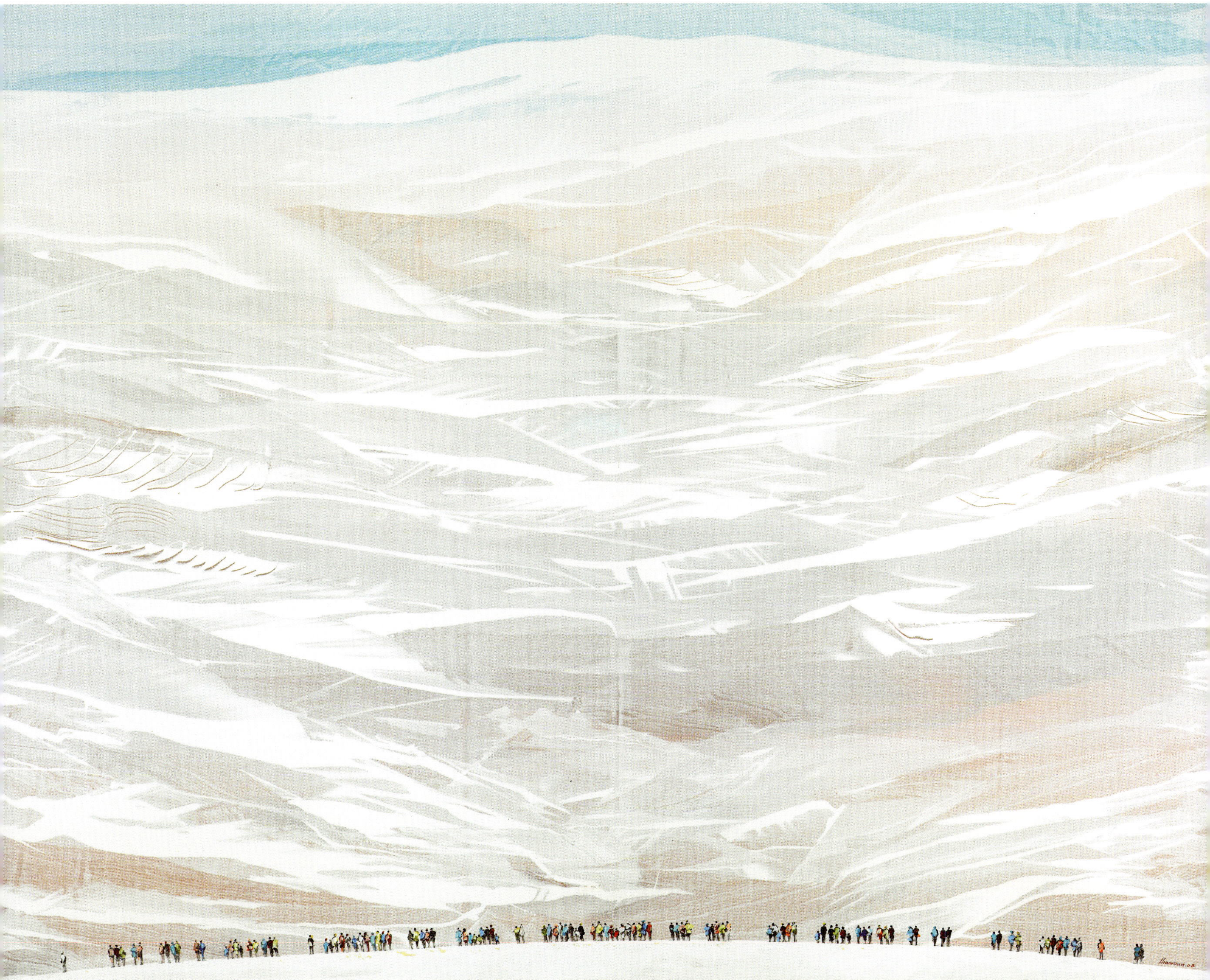

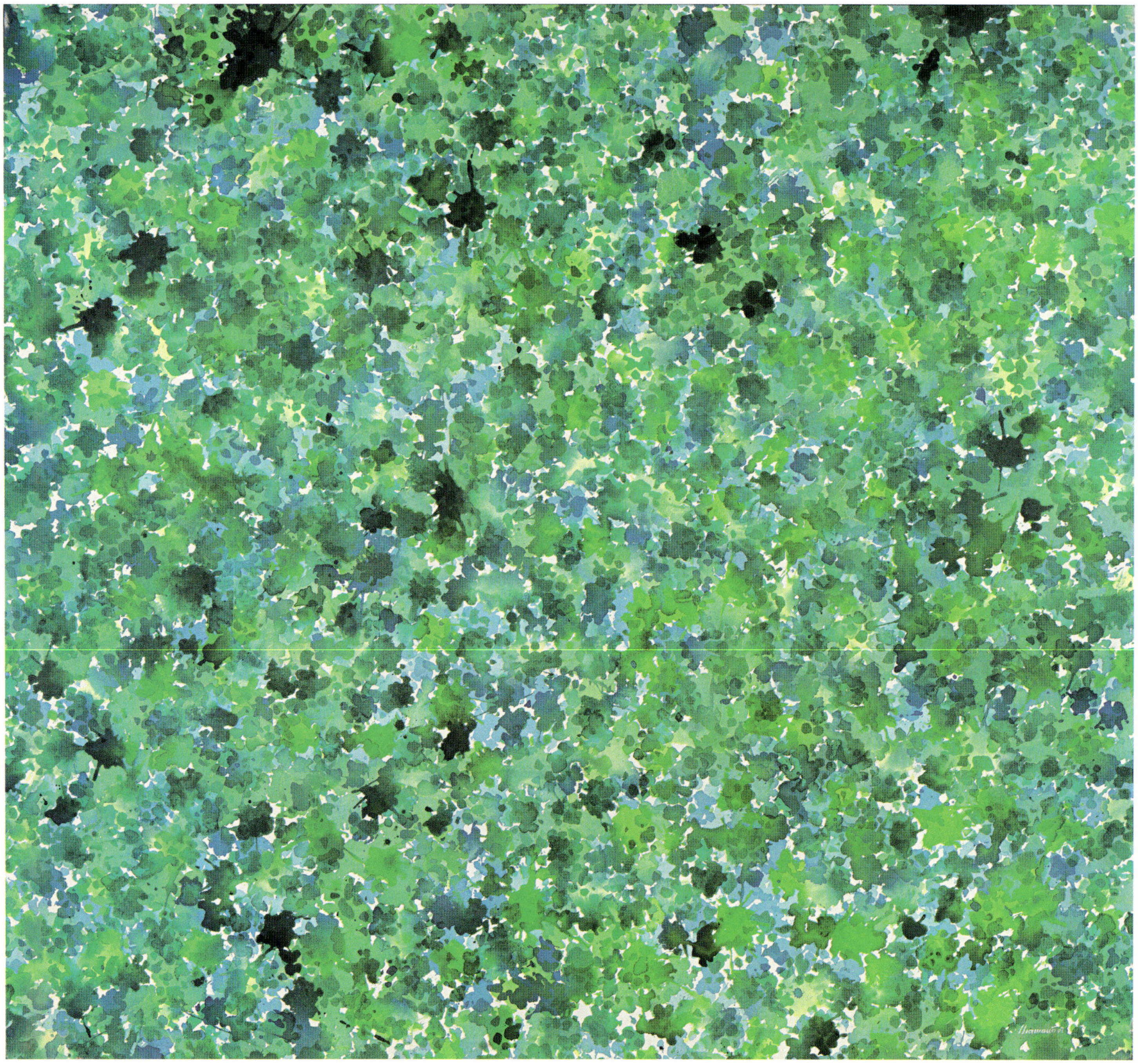

262
FOLIAGE II, 2007
Acrylic on canvas
160 x 150 cm

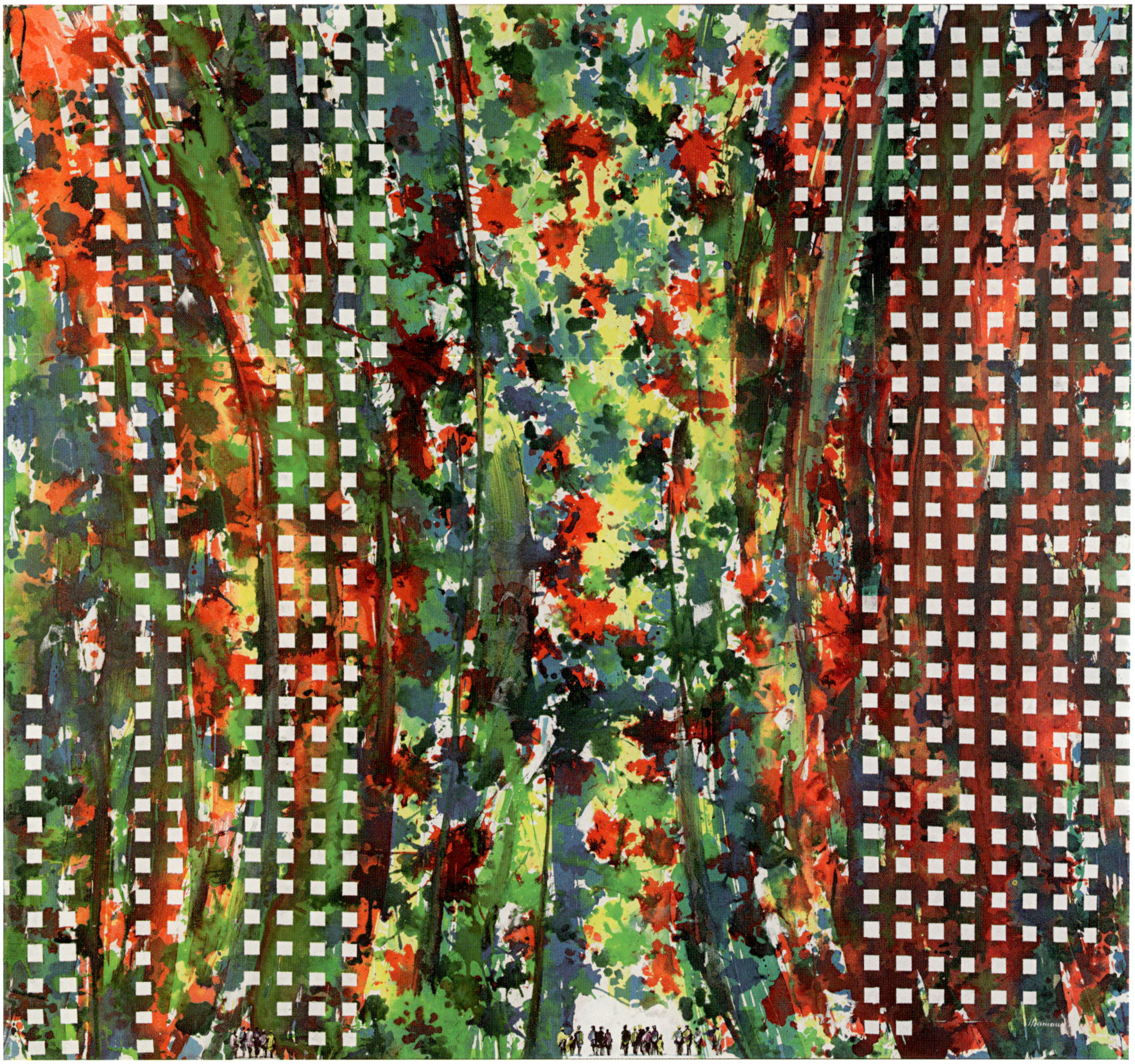

263
FOLIAGE IV, 2007
Acrylic on canvas
160 x 150 cm

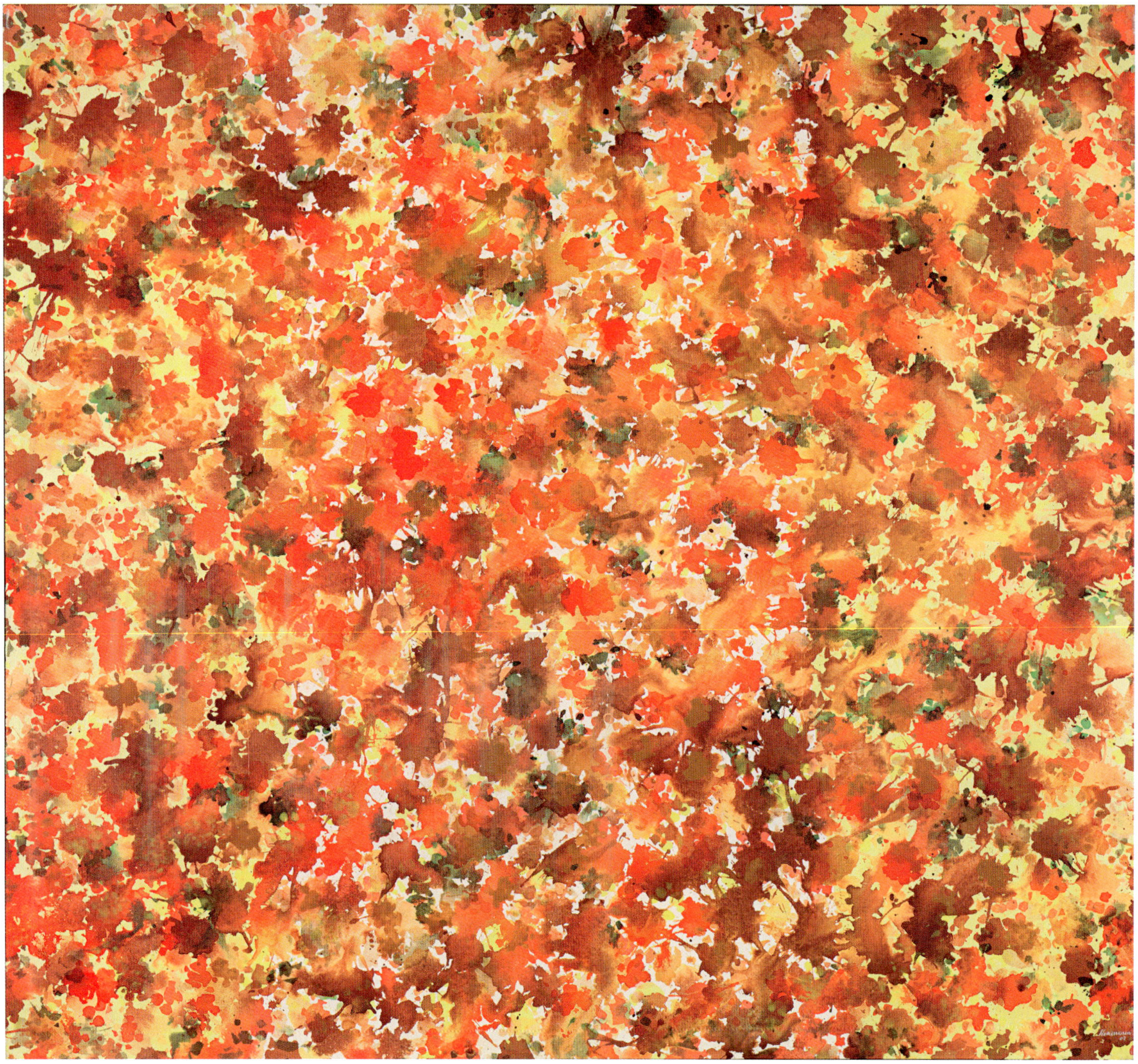

264
FOLIAGE I, 2007
Acrylic on canvas
160 x 150 cm

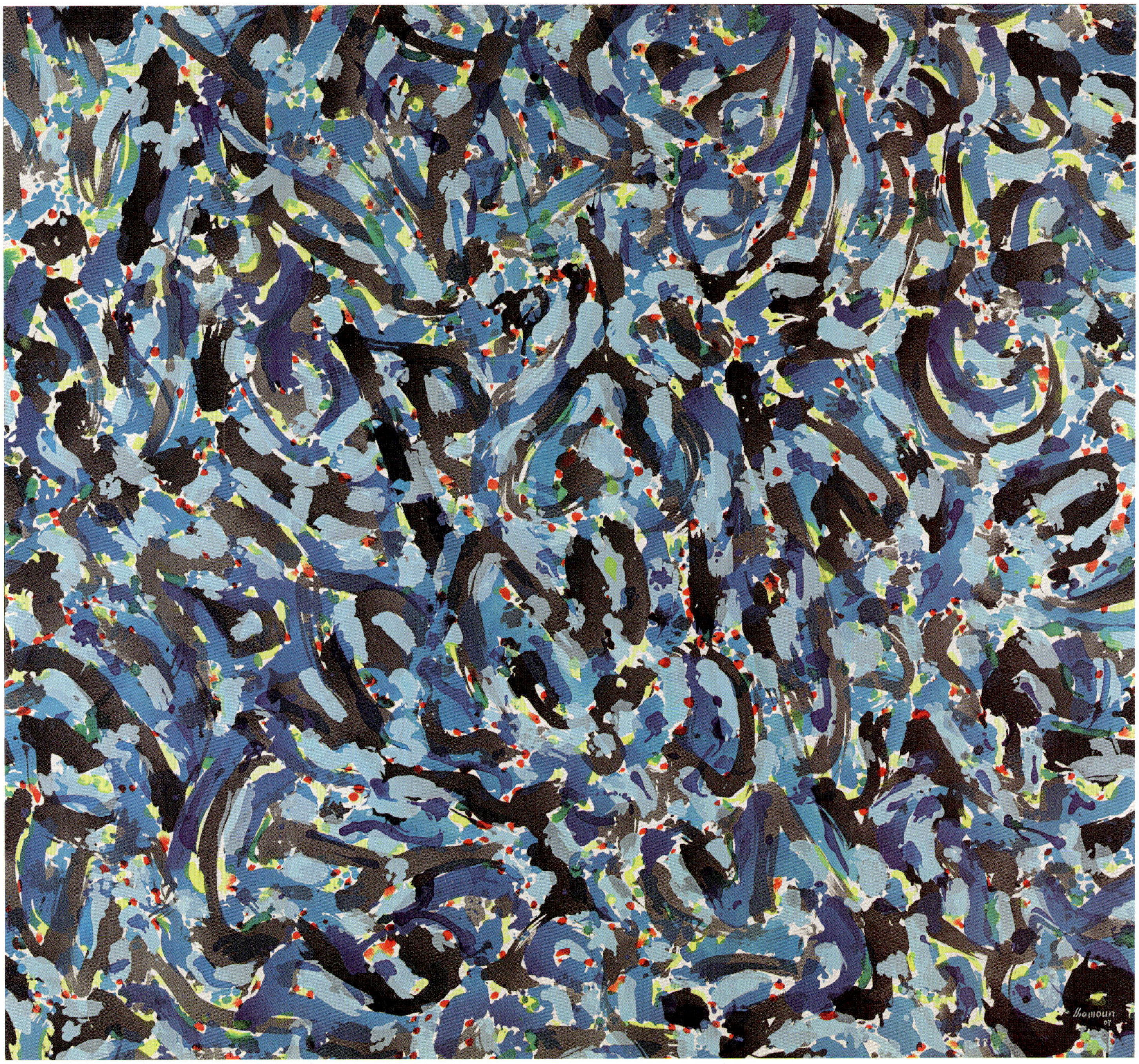

265
SPELLING LOVE I, 2007
Acrylic on canvas
160 x 150 cm

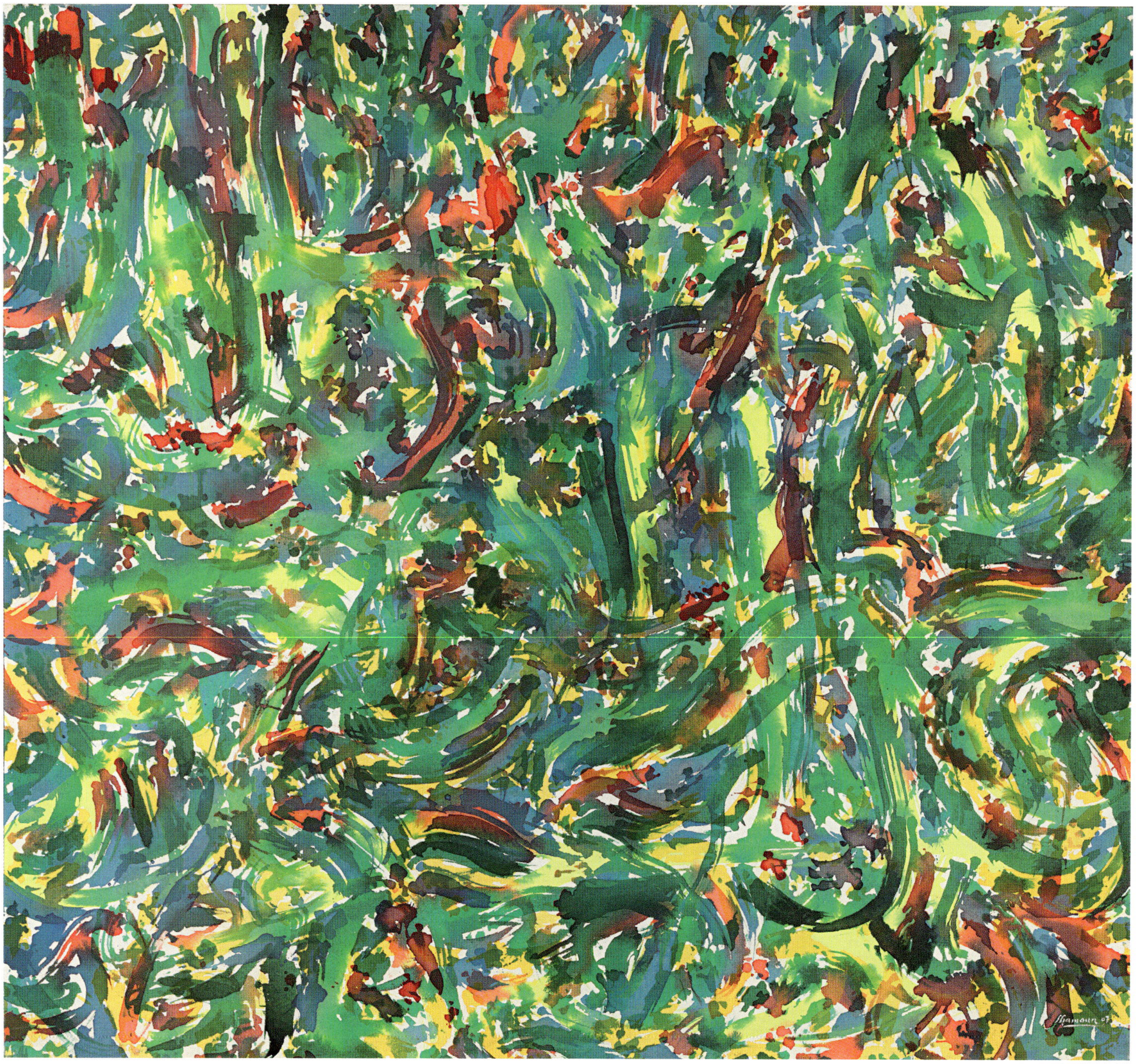

266
SPELLING LOVE IV, 2007
Acrylic on canvas
160 x 150 cm

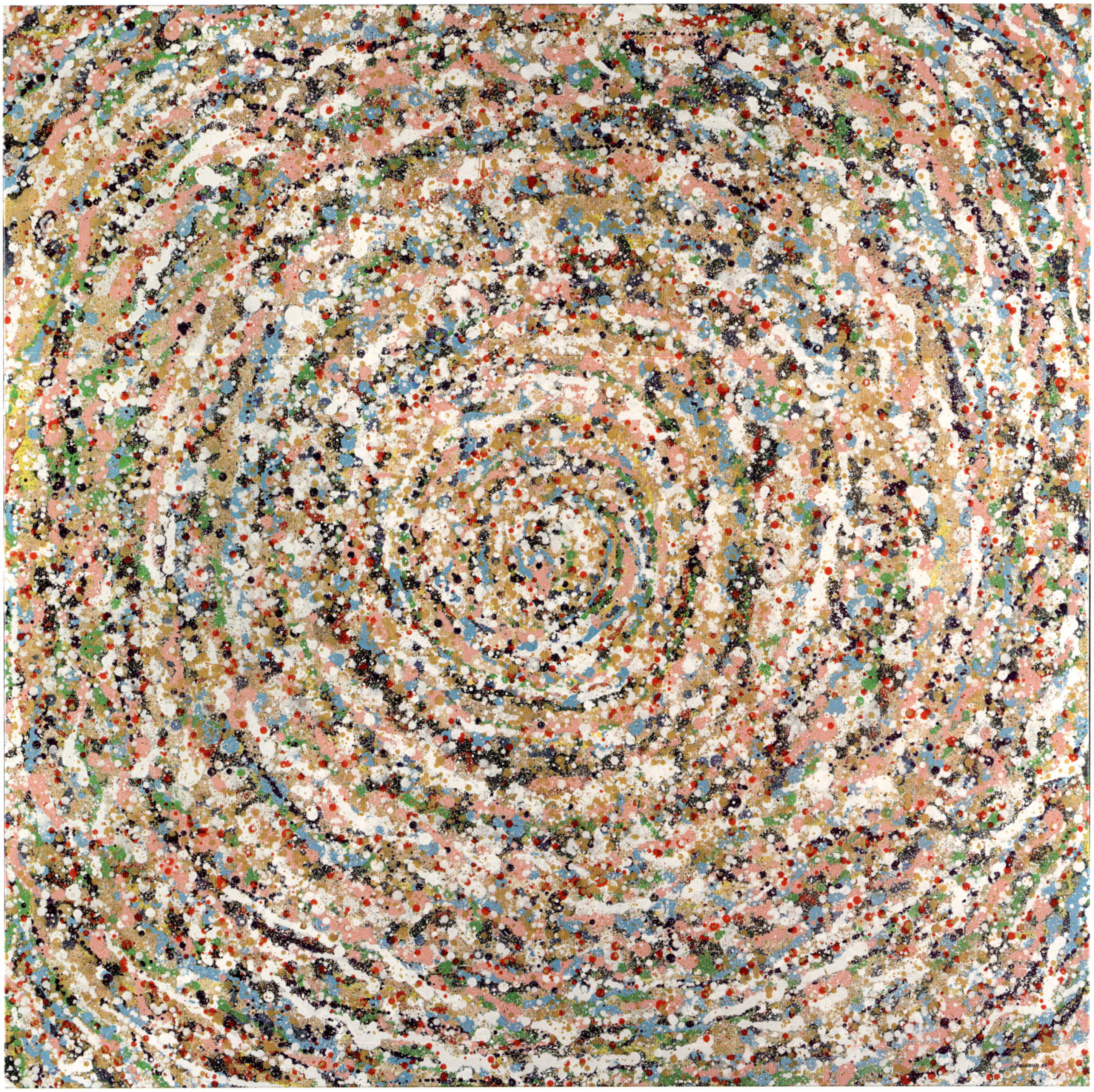

267
DARVISHES SPIRAL LABYRINTH II, 2008
Acrylic on canvas
232 x 232 cm

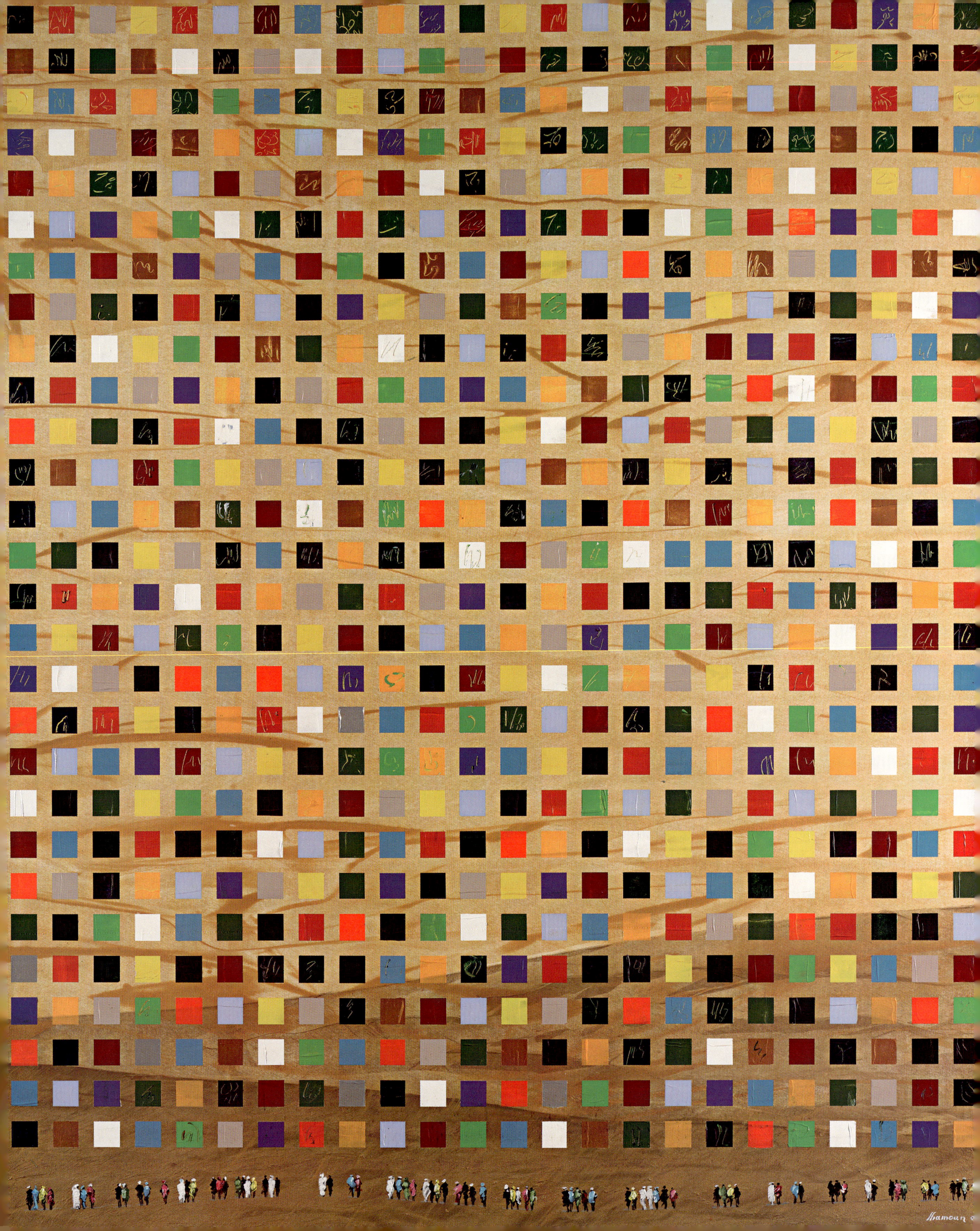

The Desert Experience

Accompanying my paintings to the Art Paris Art Fair in Abu Dhabi in the autumn of 2008 with the Epreuve d'Artiste Art Gallery, we were invited to a dinner in a tent in the desert. As I stepped out of the bus onto the sand I got a chill. 'Amal!' I shouted. 'Thank you for bringing me back to my roots; here are my roots.'

I had visited the city of Dubai several times, admiring and responding artistically to its impressive race with the modern civilised world. I was happy to see real competition with the pride, elegance and dignity of New York and other comparable cities. I gave the title 'Sprouting Sand' to several murals inspired by the fast-growing built-up environment
270–273 in Dubai and Abu Dhabi. Yet I had never been to the desert proper, never walked on its silky sands. I had been brought up looking towards the West: I had learnt Western art and Western science; I had seen Western movies and I had driven Western cars. The East was only a *desert*, nothingness, empty except for poetry and archaic heroism and past glories. I could not share even poetry, my beloved Arabic poetry, when I went West.

126 When I painted 'A Window to the Desert' and others in that series in 1991 I had no sense of the natural texture or

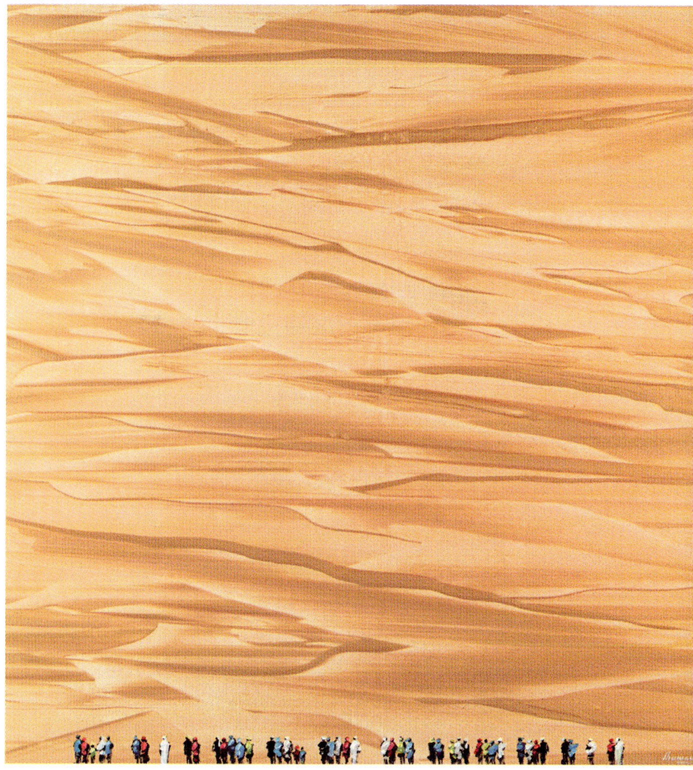

269
TRANSFORMING SAND, 2009
Acrylic on canvas
135 x 135 cm

Previous page
268
MULTIPLICITY OF SAND, 2007
Acrylic on canvas (detail)
290 x 250 cm

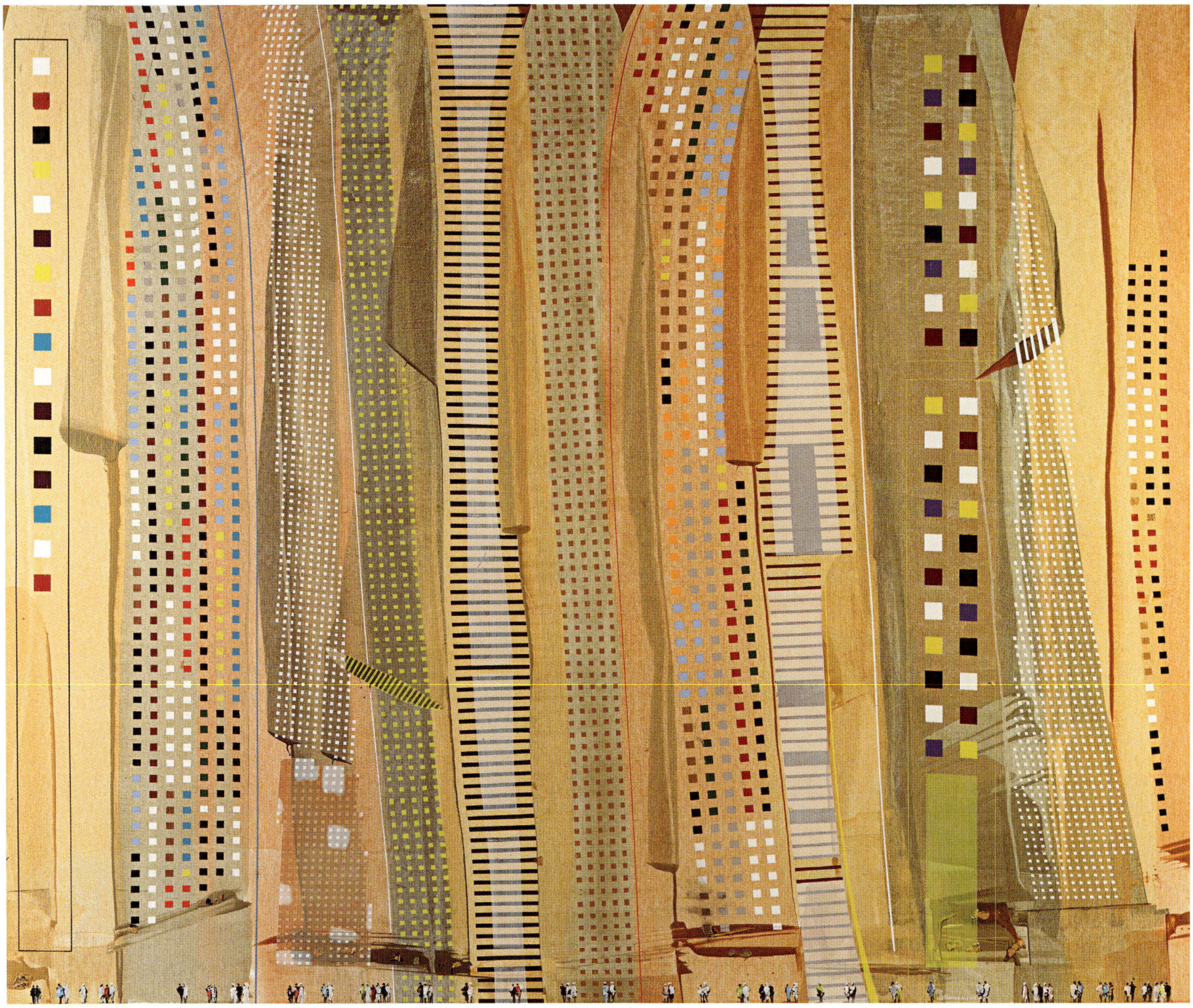

270
SPROUTING SAND, 2007
Acrylic on canvas
290 x 250 cm

feel of the desert. I was dealing with the political, military and economic complexities of 'Desert Storm,' in which I saw an expansion of the blood flooding from Lebanon.

My father proudly identified himself as Ghassanid, a descendant of the Arab Ghassasina tribe. He even named my younger brother Ghassan. When it came to boasting about his Arab roots in the Arabian Desert, he needed to show no historical evidence: when I questioned his belief, he always

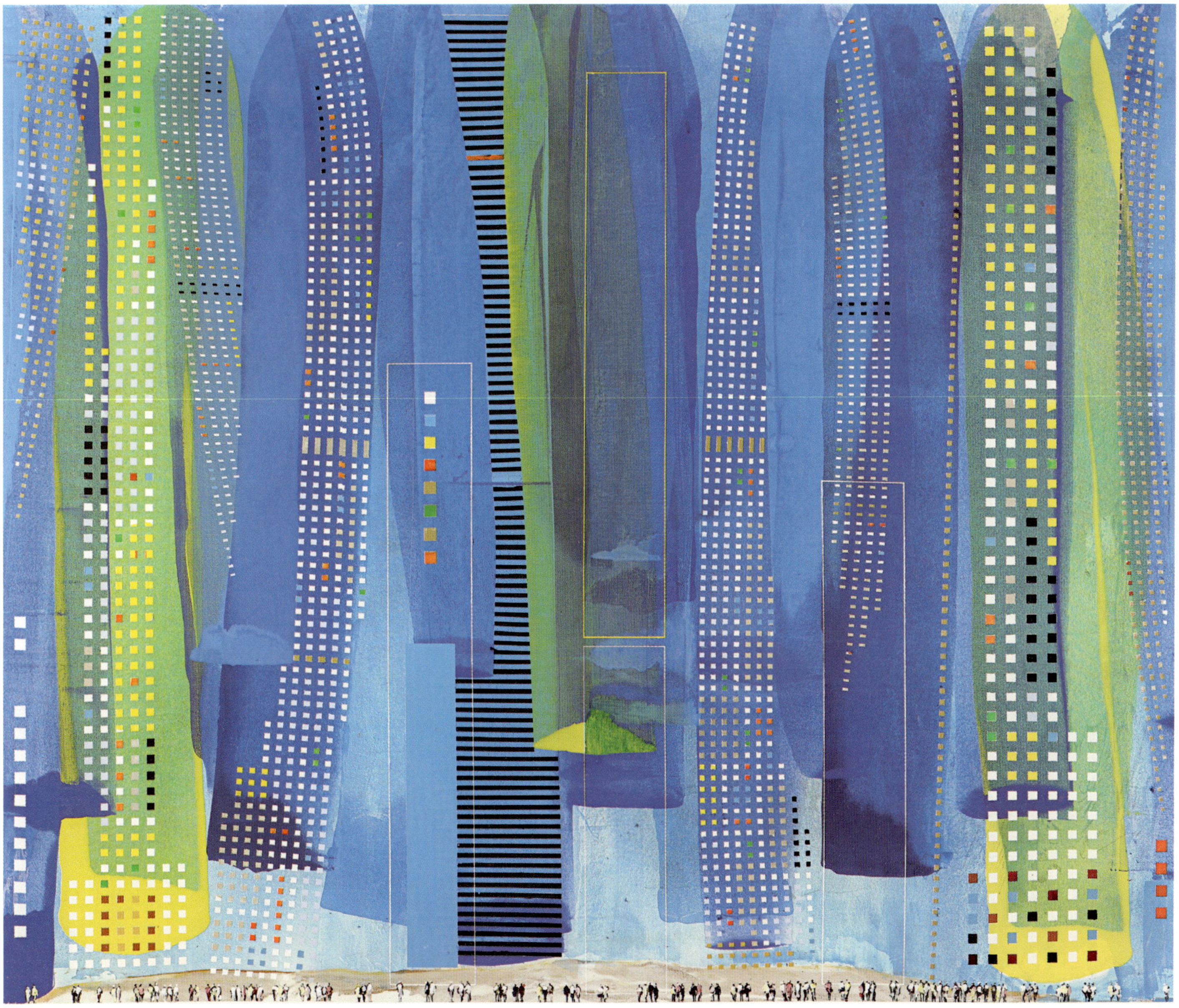

told me that he simply knew. I did not really understand what he meant or felt until I felt at home walking on the cool sand that cool starry night.

Ever since I could remember, I had been hoping to visit the desert. I wanted so much to take the sand into my hands; to run barefoot and roll over the dunes; to feel the wind-rippled furrows and time-wrinkled face of the desert, the most beautiful on earth. That night, I knew deep in my

271
SPROUTING SAND II, 2007
Acrylic on canvas
290 x 250 cm

Following spread
272
SPROUTING SAND III, 2008
Acrylic on canvas (detail)
236 x 214 cm

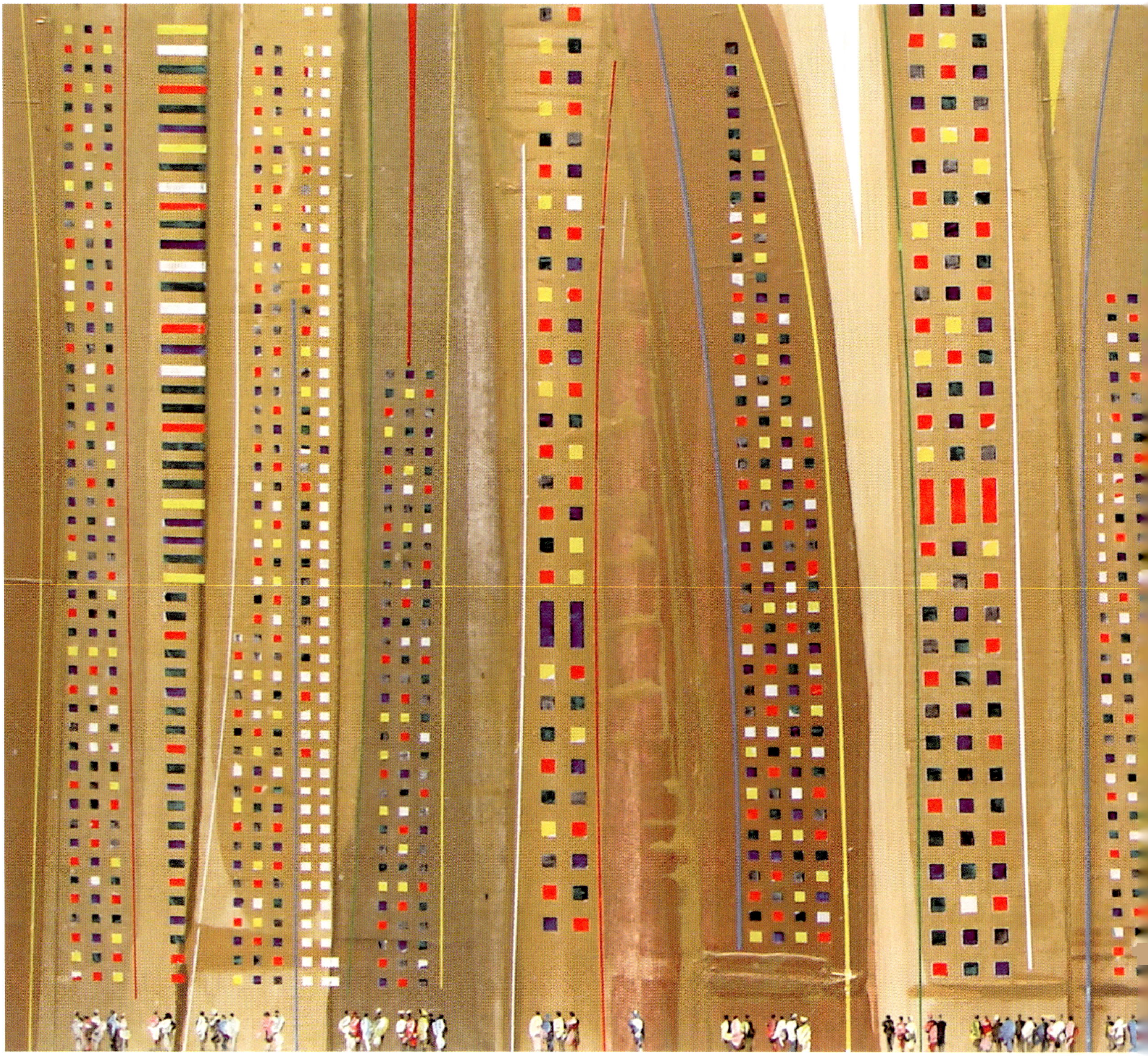

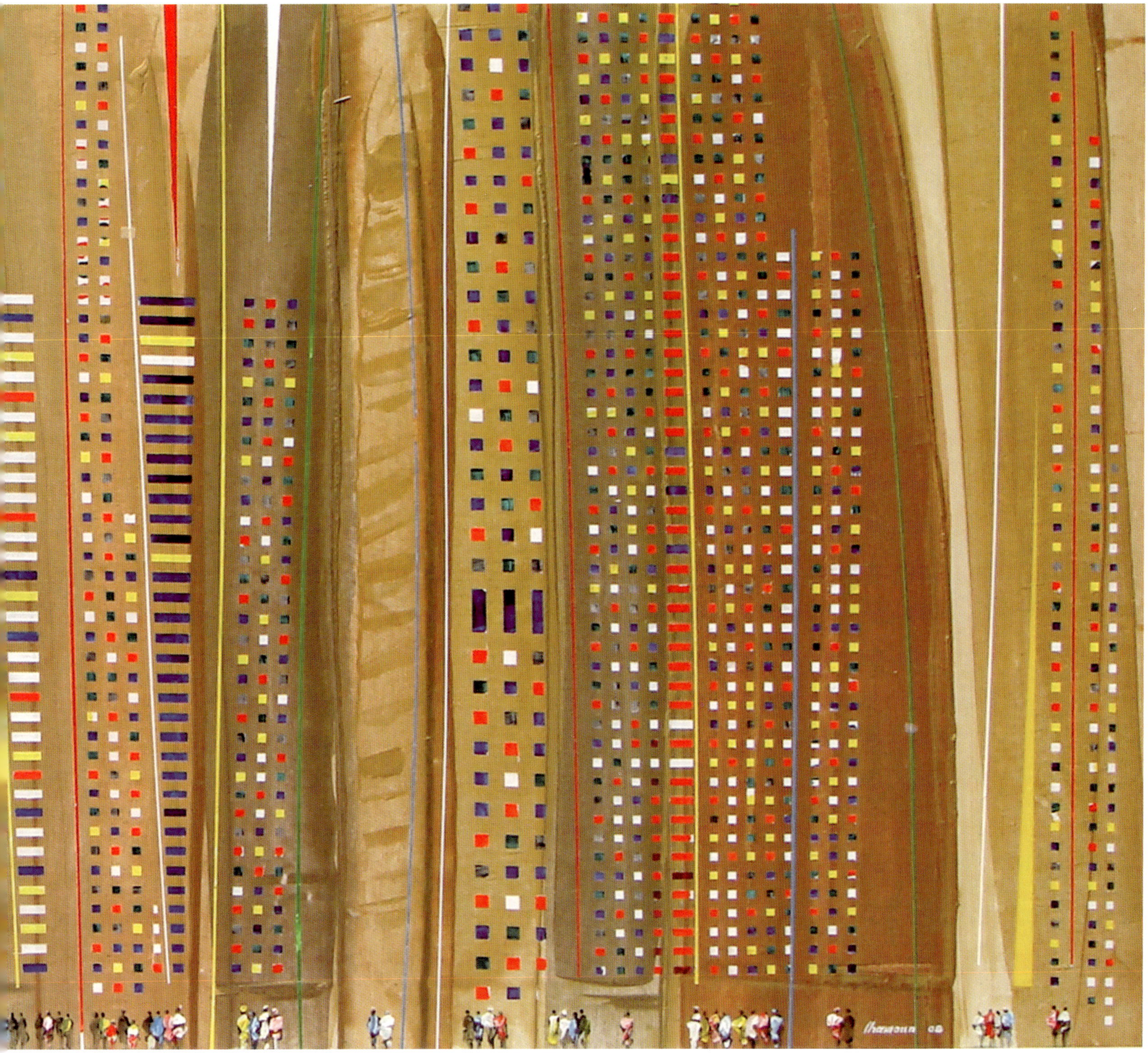

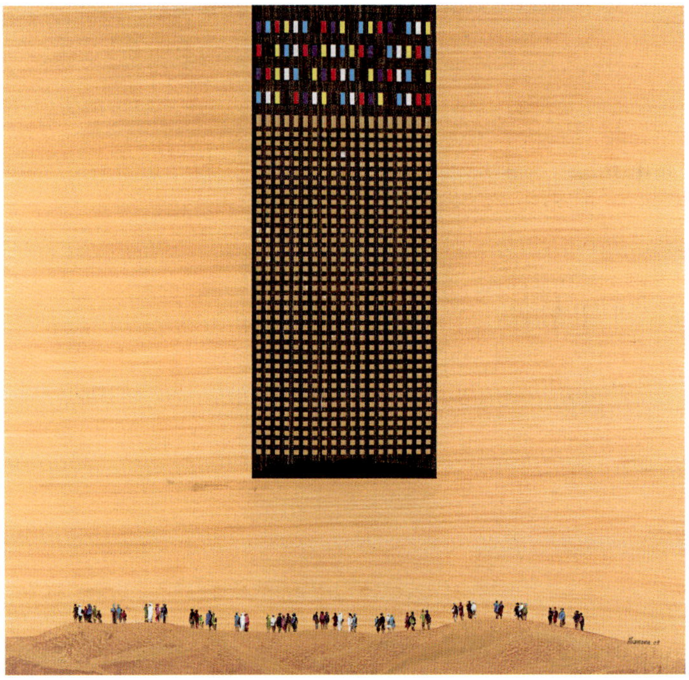

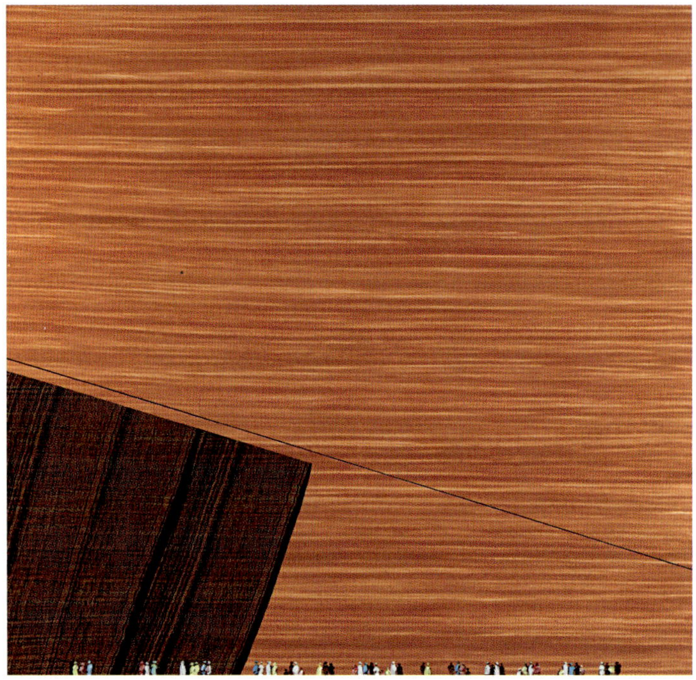

273
ELEVATION OF THE GOLDEN SAND I, 2009
Acrylic on canvas
135 x 135 cm

Right
274
ELEVATION OF THE BLACK TENT II, 2009
Acrylic on canvas
140 x 140 cm

Facing page
275
ELEVATIONS OF DREAMS, 2008
Acrylic on canvas (detail)
290 x 230 cm

heart that I was meeting a three thousand-year-old date, a promise that I would be back. I felt I was home again, and it is always nice to know as you travel into the future that you are home again. My feet had left no traces in the sand, but the last words I murmured as I was leaving were a promise to meet again with the same crisp, cold wind. I collected samples of sand, looking deep into the horizon in search of something I did not know exactly. That night, as I stepped away from the crowd and looked all around me, there was nothing but an endless horizon in every direction. I became the centre of the desert, and the sky was a beautiful deep blue hemispheric tent, lit with eternally shining stars closing on the horizon, imprisoning me forever. That night will always be part of my home-coming party on the golden sand. All that I murmured, thought, felt, and said and did not say will always be there. I trust the wind will only blow my traces away again as it re-draws and re-sculpts the face of the ever-waiting sand.

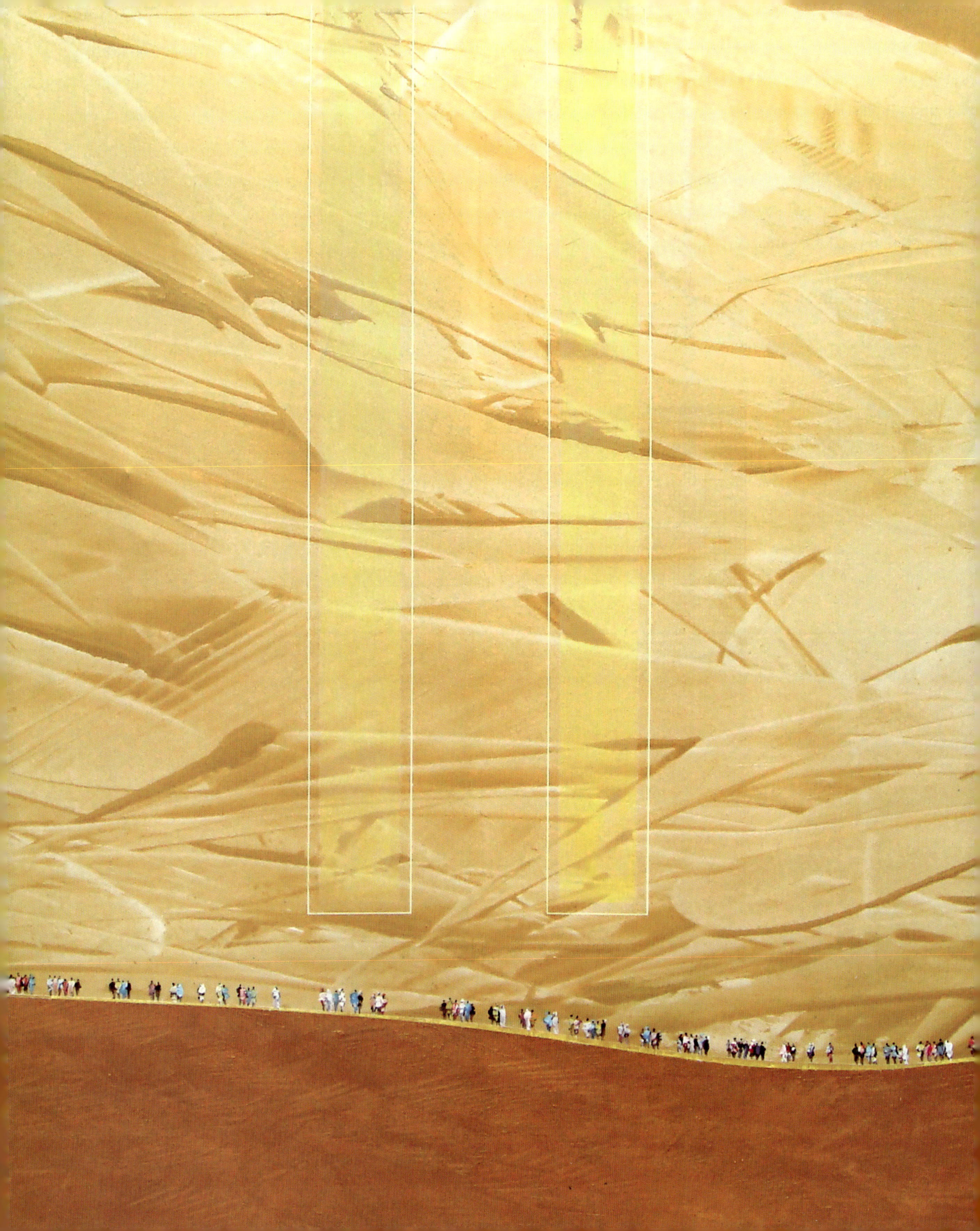

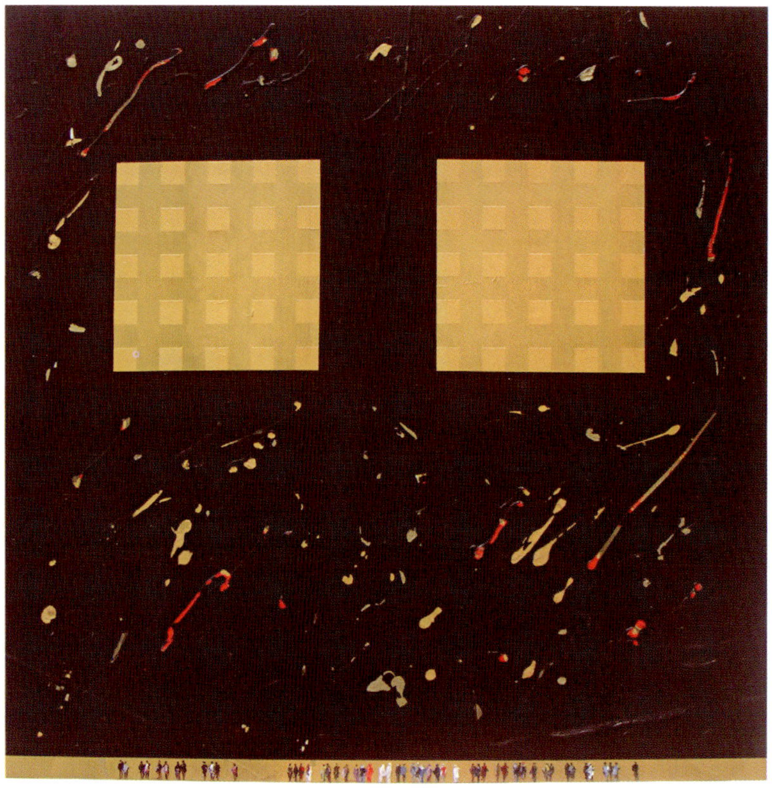

276
NOTHING WAS SAID THAT NIGHT, 2008
Acrylic on canvas
153 x 153 cm

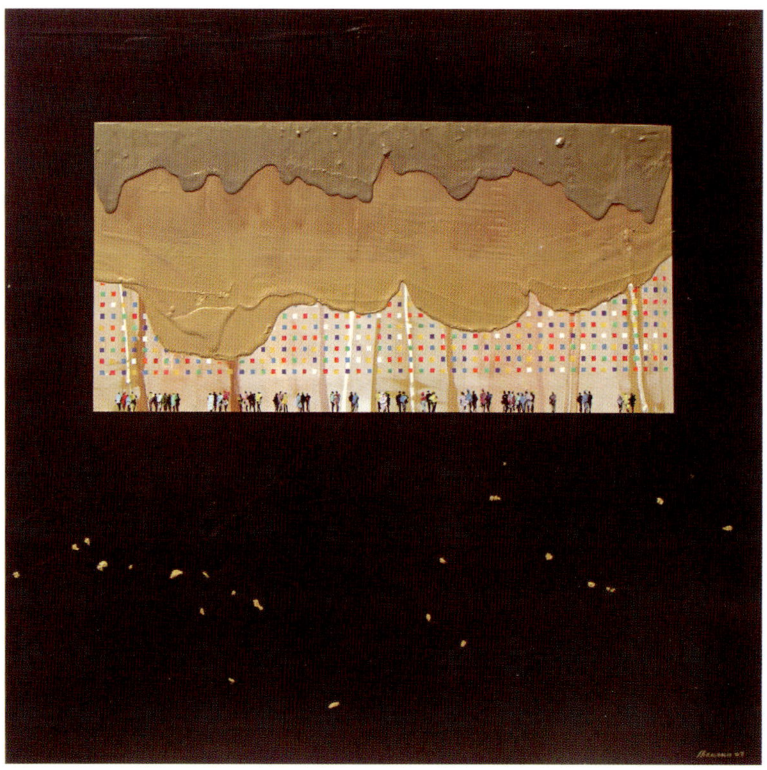

277
TRANSFORMATION I, 2008
Acrylic on canvas
153 x 153 cm

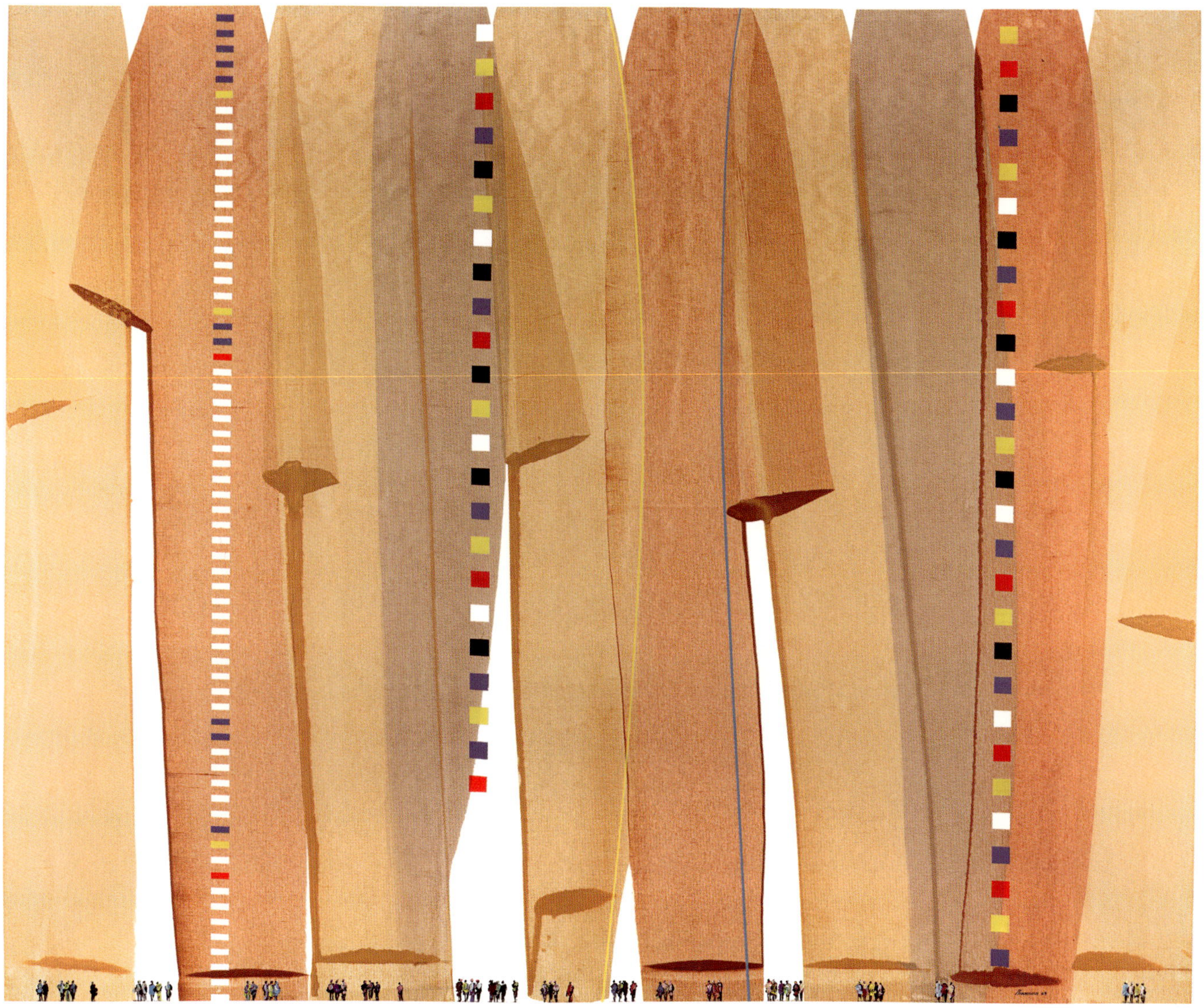

278
SCULPTING THE DESERT, 2007
Acrylic on canvas
290 x 250 cm

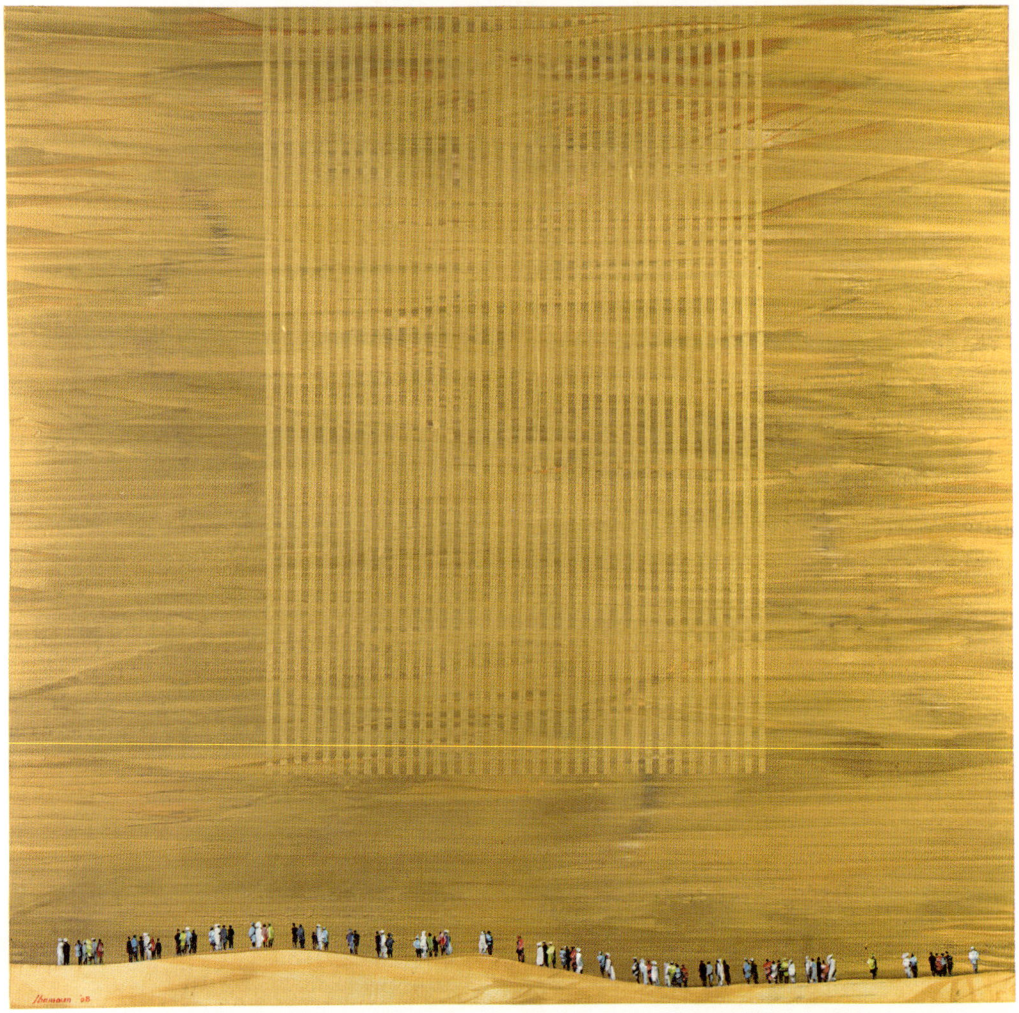

279
ELEVATION OF THE GOLDEN SAND, 2010
Acrylic on canvas
150 x 150 cm

When you are in the open desert, in the middle of the night or beyond, when everyone goes to sleep, you lie down on the crisp sand facing the stars. Nothing on earth looks like that overwhelming hemispherical dome. It is distant, limitless and invites you to invade an unknown depth beyond.

I cannot help being poetic whenever I paint or talk about the desert. Although my painting style and subject bore no relation to the desert or its culture when it successfully hit an international standard with Christie's Dubai and Sotheby's

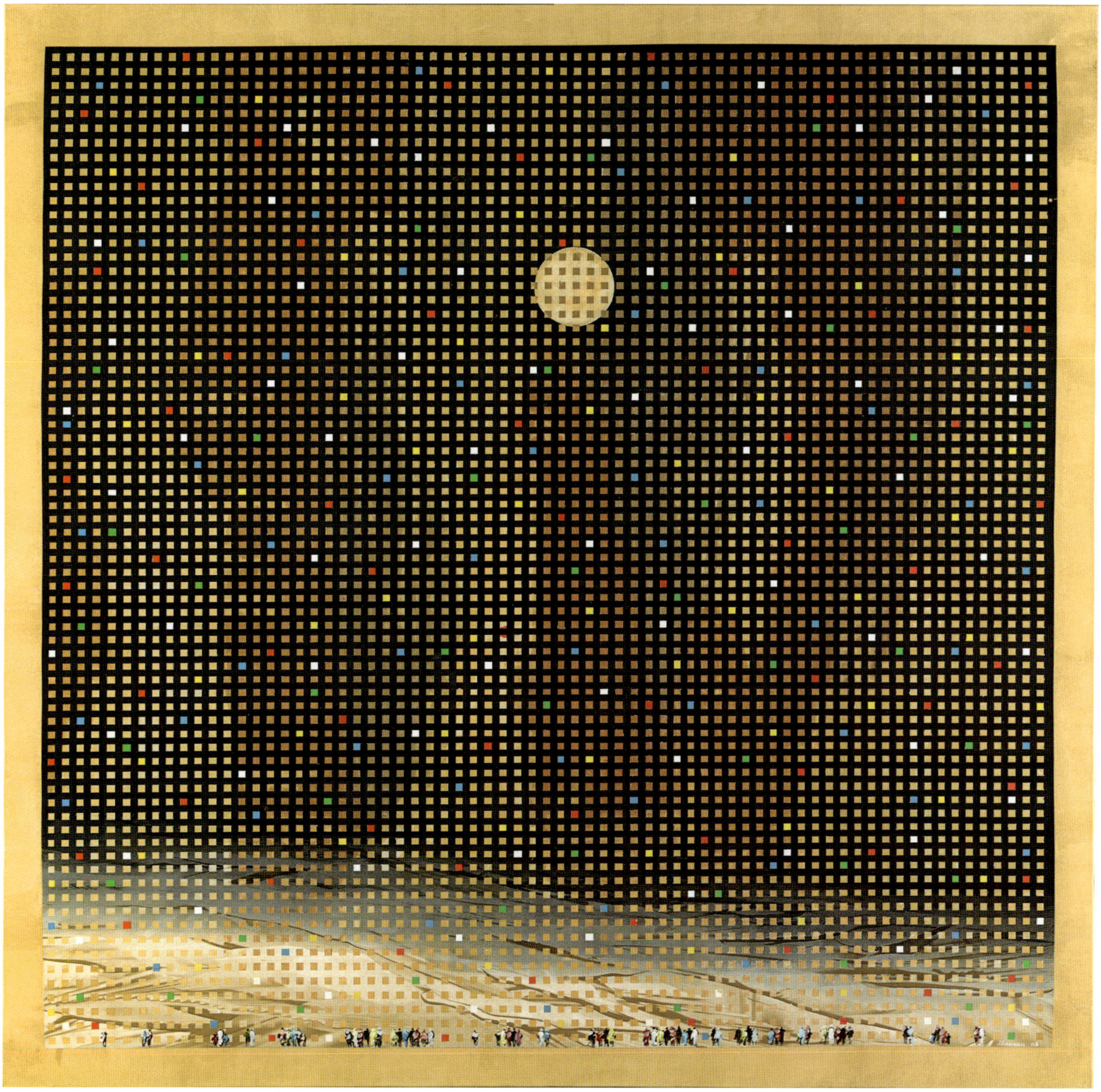

280
THE NIGHT OF THE GOLDEN MOON, 2008
Acrylic on canvas
232 x 232 cm

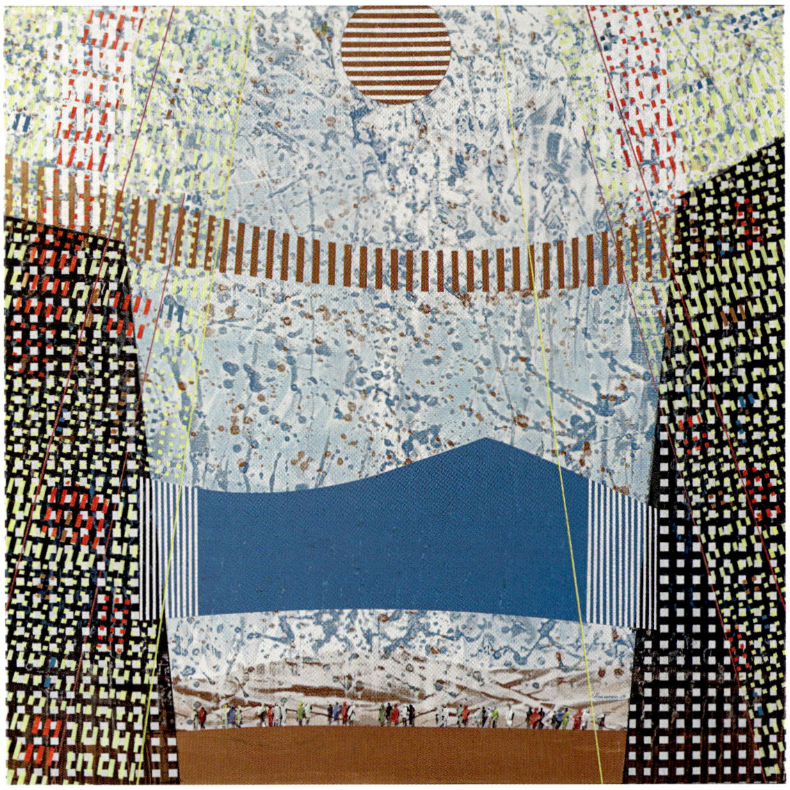

281
THE SIDE OF THE BLUE TENT, 2009
Acrylic on canvas
140 x 140 cm

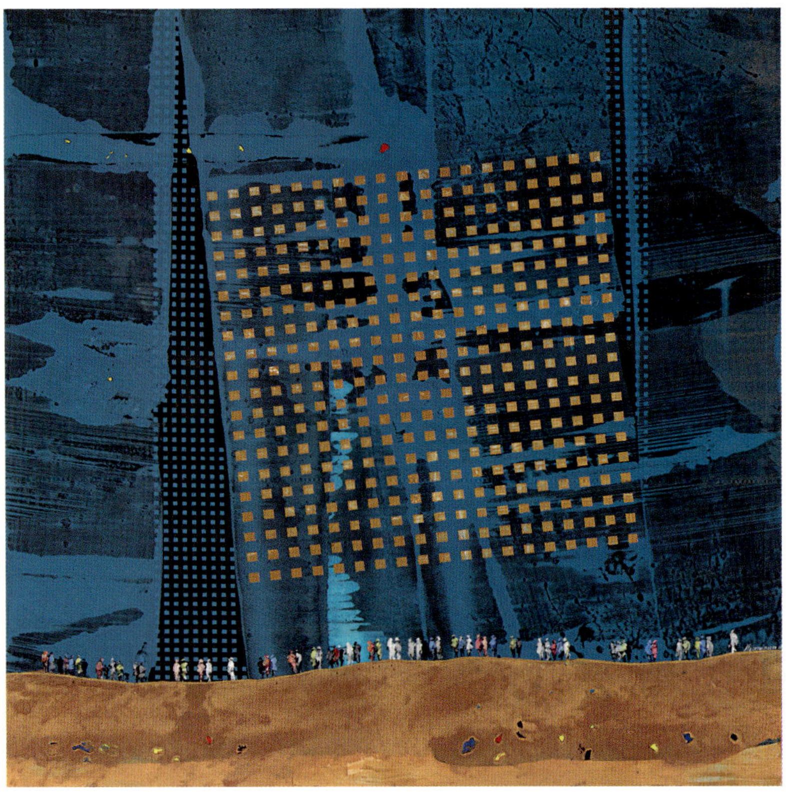

282
SHADOWS OF THE BLACK TENT IV, 2008
Acrylic on canvas
150 x 150 cm

Facing page
283
SKIES ARE NOT THE LIMIT, 2008
Acrylic on canvas
290 x 250 cm

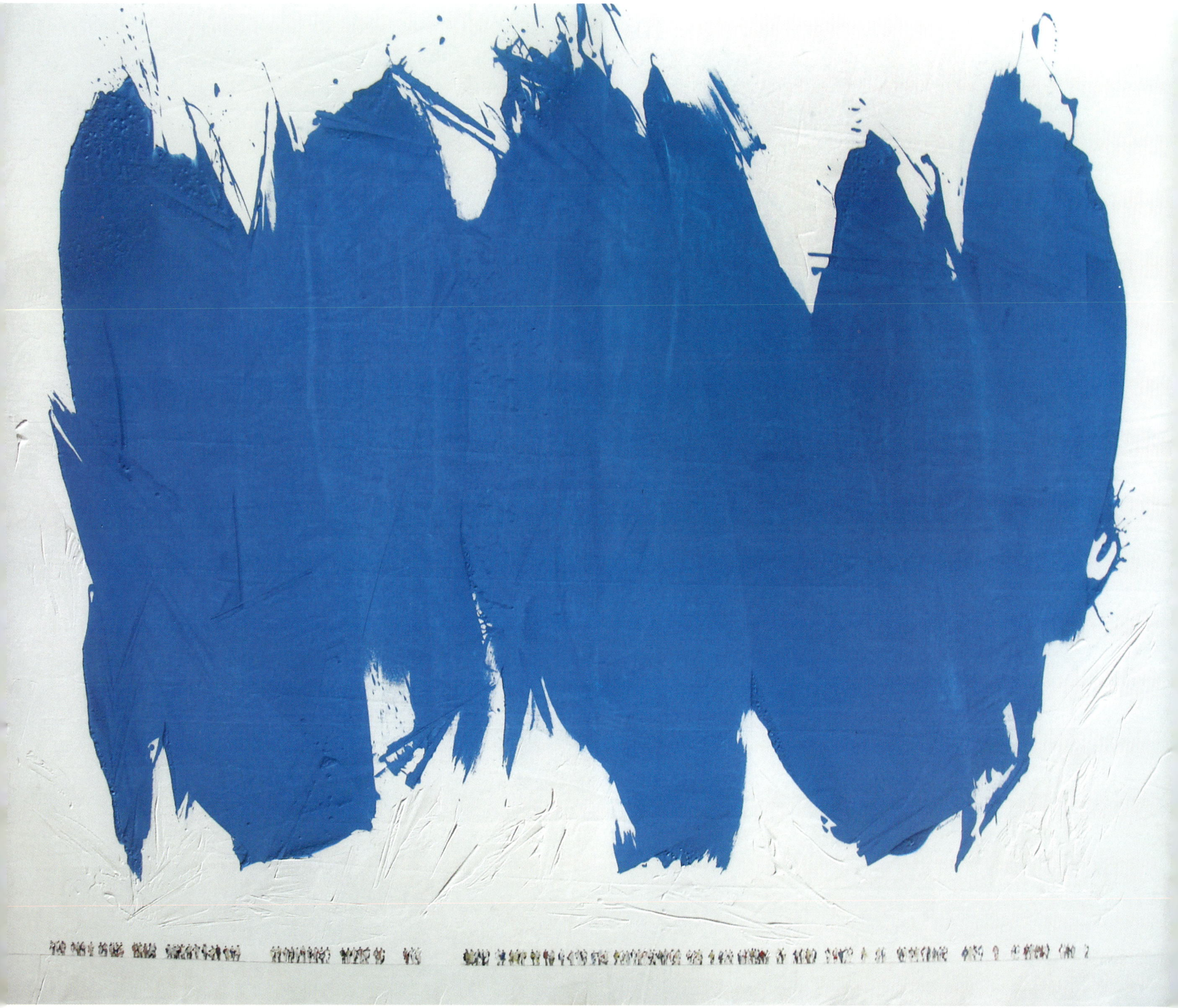

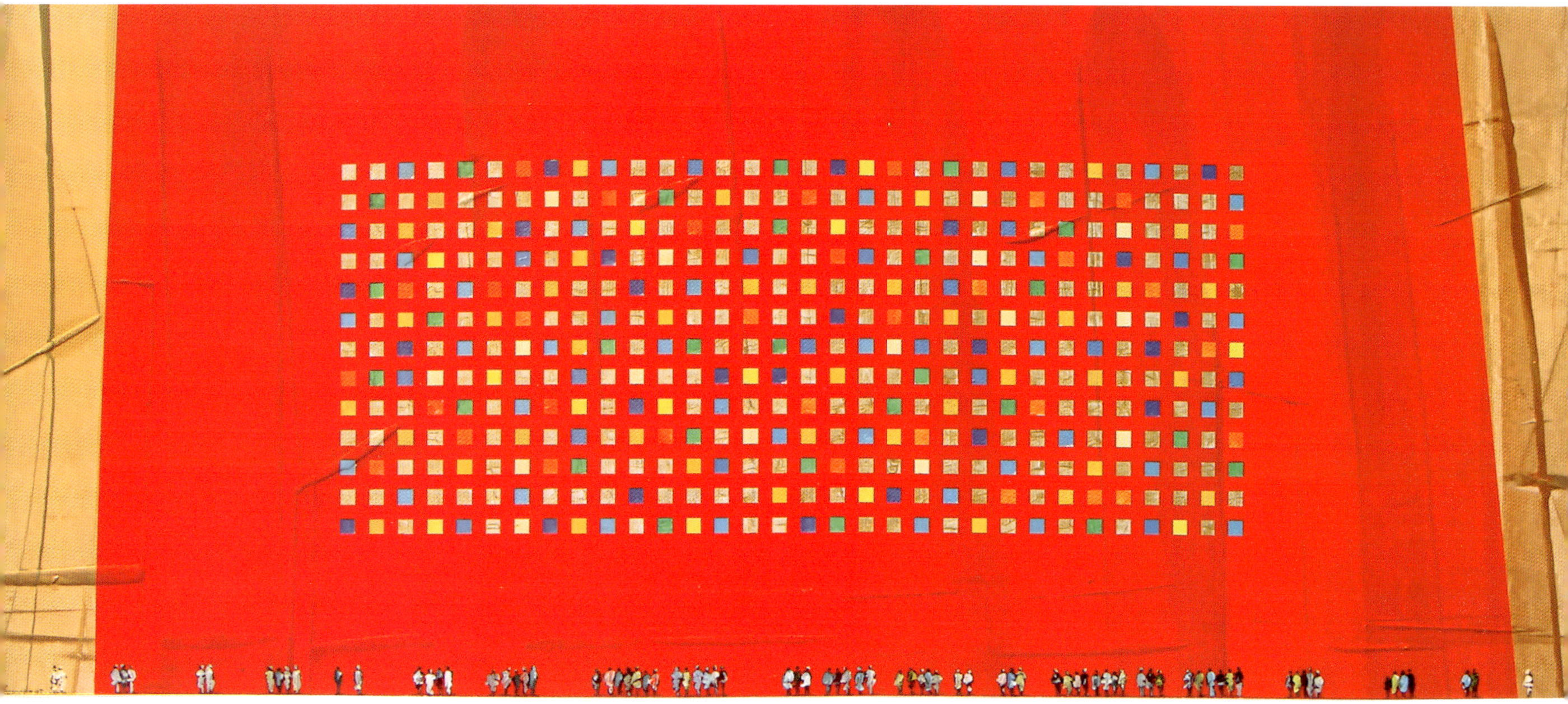

284
THE SIDE OF A RED TENT, 2008
Acrylic on canvas
236 x 114 cm

London in 2007 and 2008, my art shifted to where my love fell. The desert and its culture, past and present, strongly influenced my eye and my mind. I felt a strong energy empowering me, bringing new images of unprecedented artistic writing to my painting. The desert stole me away from my previous aesthetic worries, my attempts to try to refine or redefine my aesthetic values and goals. It offered me an extended stay in a world of unmatched purity in its simplest and most refined revelations. Painting had rarely felt so pleasurable, satisfying and thirst quenching. I felt an urgent creative need to paint day and night. In full harmony with my environment, my past, my present, my future, and myself, I went painting every day.

Amal Traboulsi shipped several of my paintings to Art Paris 2010 in Abu Dhabi as part of a special stand she had commissioned titled, 'The Desert and the Sea'. It was a

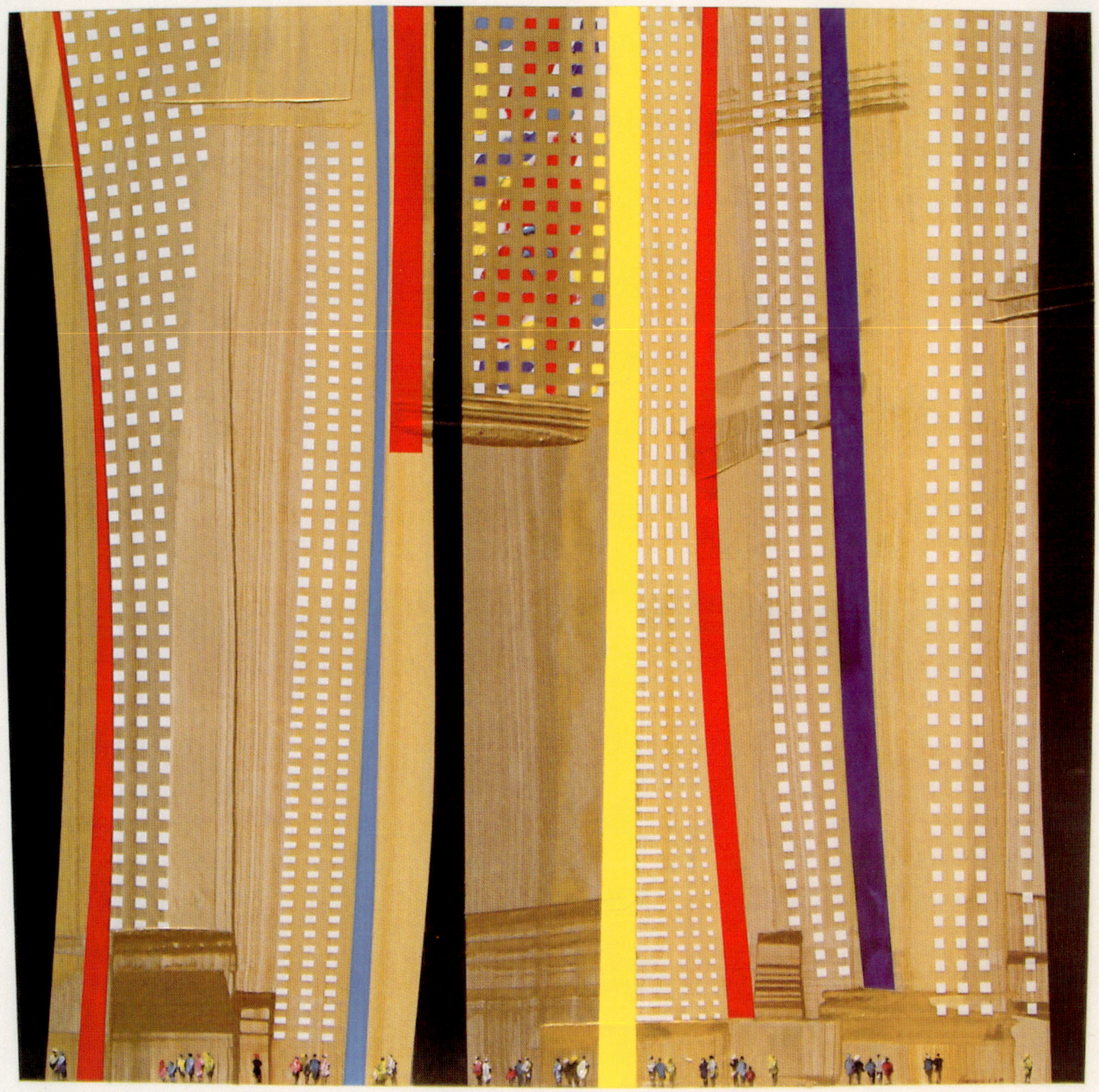

285
SAND URBANIZATION I, 2008
Acrylic on canvas
153 x 153 cm

stunning success. Nine of my large paintings were acquired during the first hour of the VIP reception. I was proud to receive a note saying 'Bravo!' from Amal.

The years 2007–2009 and beyond were to a certain extent the years of the desert *par excellence.* The wholeness of 268–292
the experience matters most to me. The desert was not only the sand I carried back with me to spray on my wet canvas, or mix with my colours for texture or for the semblance of reality. The desert is the story of its men, past, present, and future. The desert is the tent, and the desert is a dream; a futuristic civilisation in the process of becoming. My painting is about capturing the essence of the wholeness of the desert's cultural components and their influences on my eye, mind and feelings. *Bridging the world, Shadows of the Black Tent, Elevation of the Golden Sand, Elevation of the Black Tent, The Return of the Nights, Liquid Sand, Distant Blue,* and *Installation of Proximities* are not only titles of cultural and naturalistic values, they are portraits of cultural and natural realities that inspired new painting of new aesthetic values.

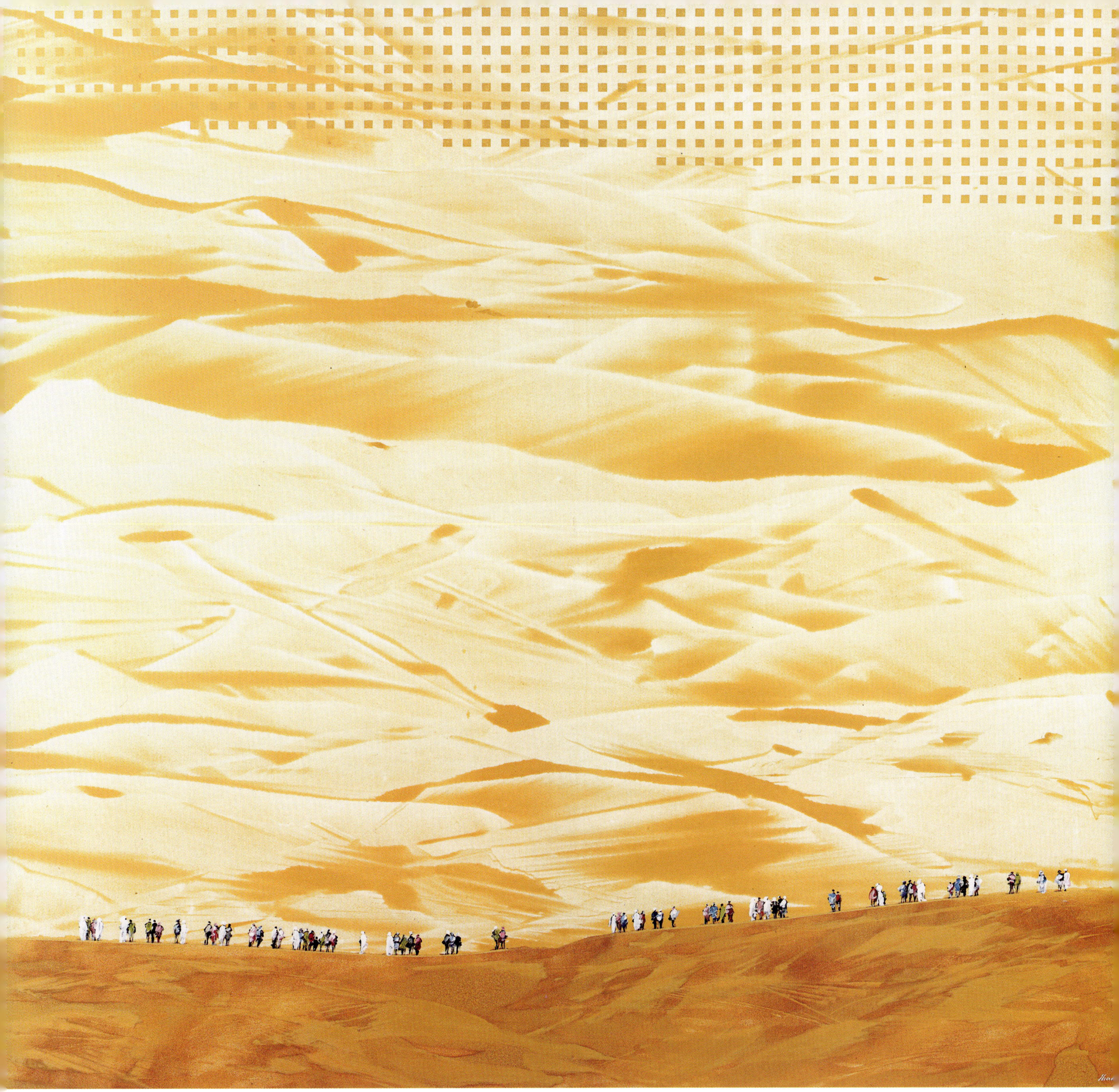

286
PRIOR TO TRANSFORMATION, 2008
Acrylic on canvas
232 x 232 cm

Facing page
287
THE GOLDEN PASSAGE, 2012
Acrylic on canvas (detail)
140 x 180 cm

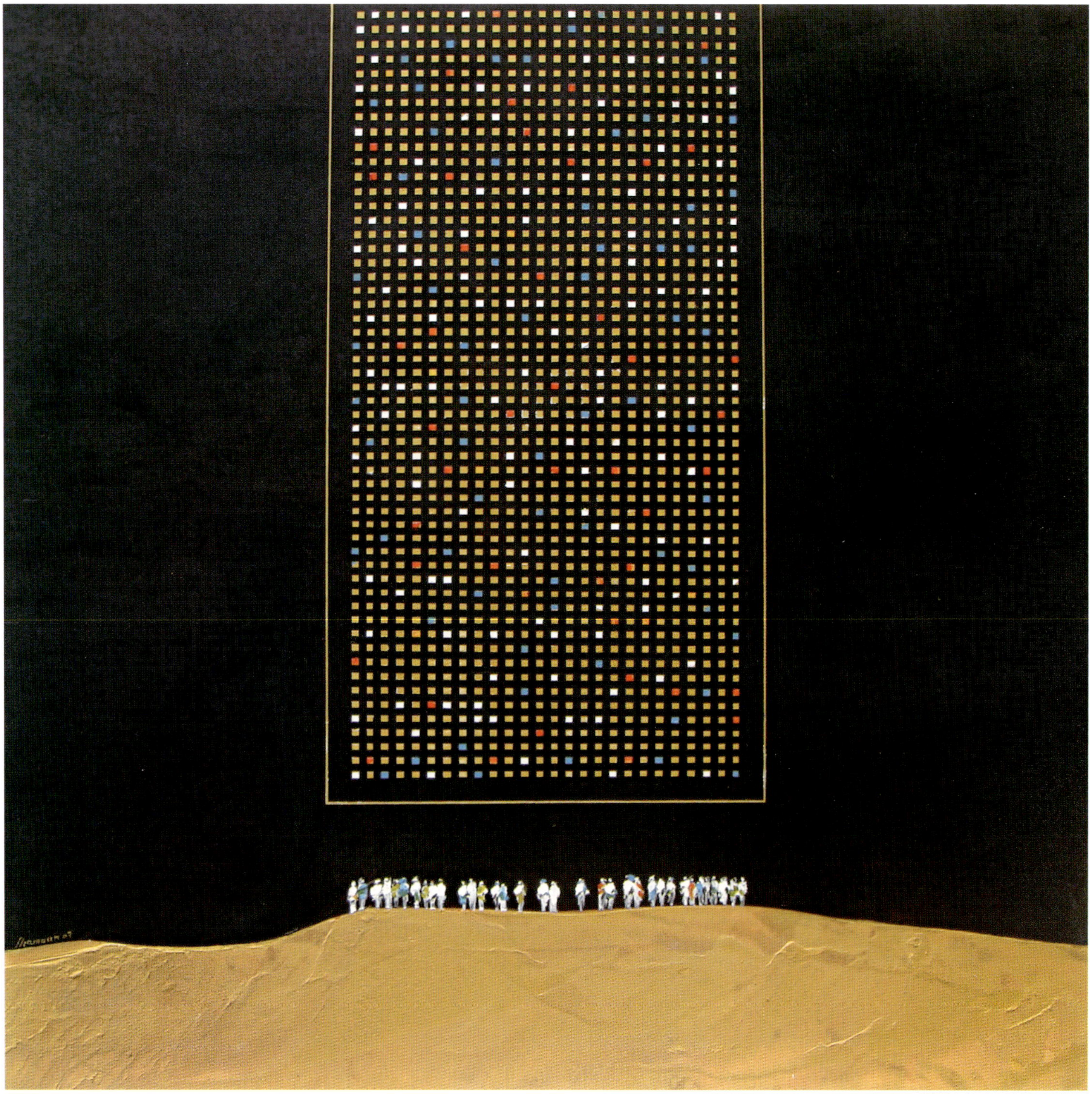

288
THE NIGHT OF THE CONVENING STARS, 2008
Acrylic on canvas
153 x 153 cm

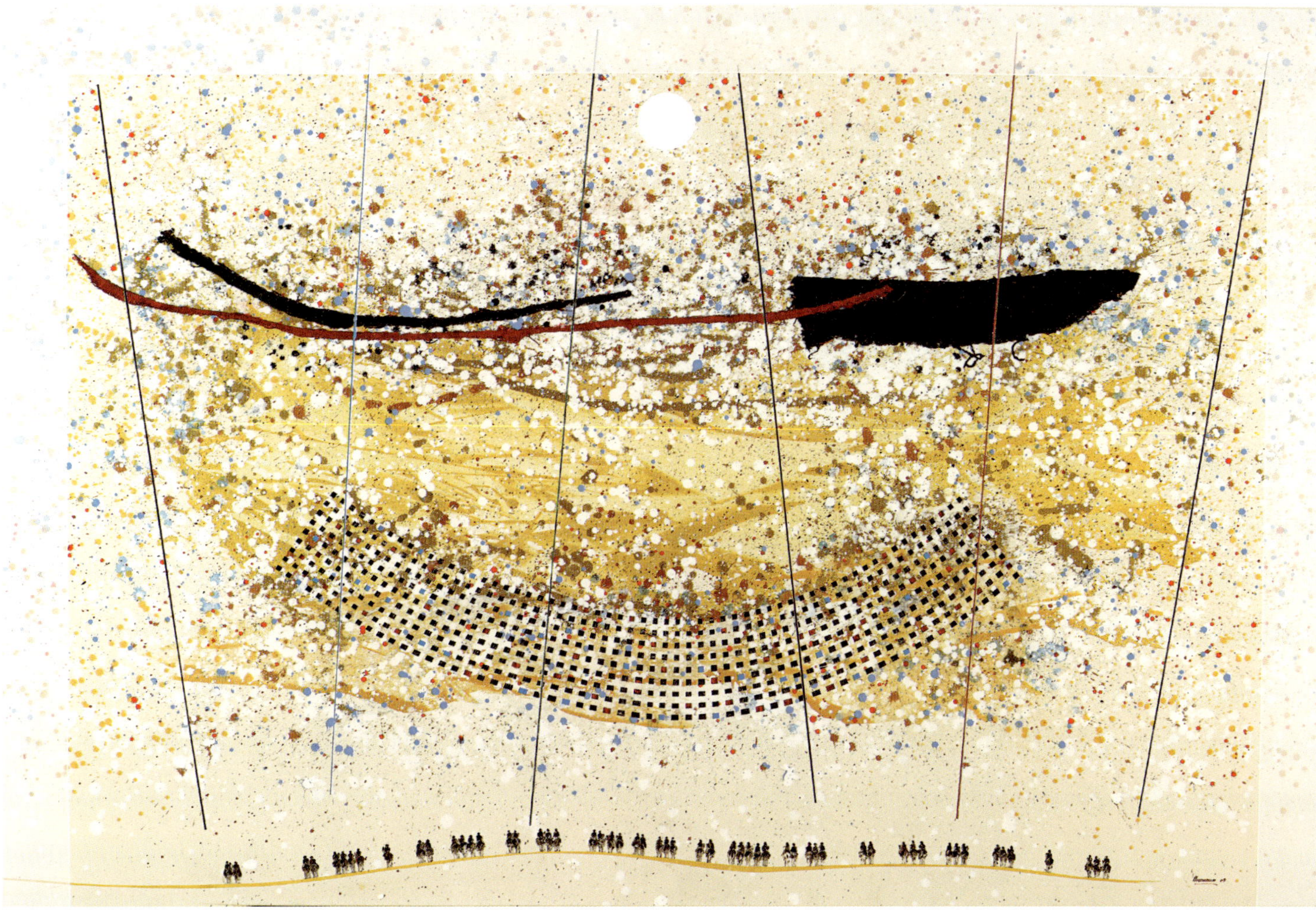

289
INSTALLATION OF PROXIMITIES, 2009
Acrylic and collage on canvas
295 x 200 cm

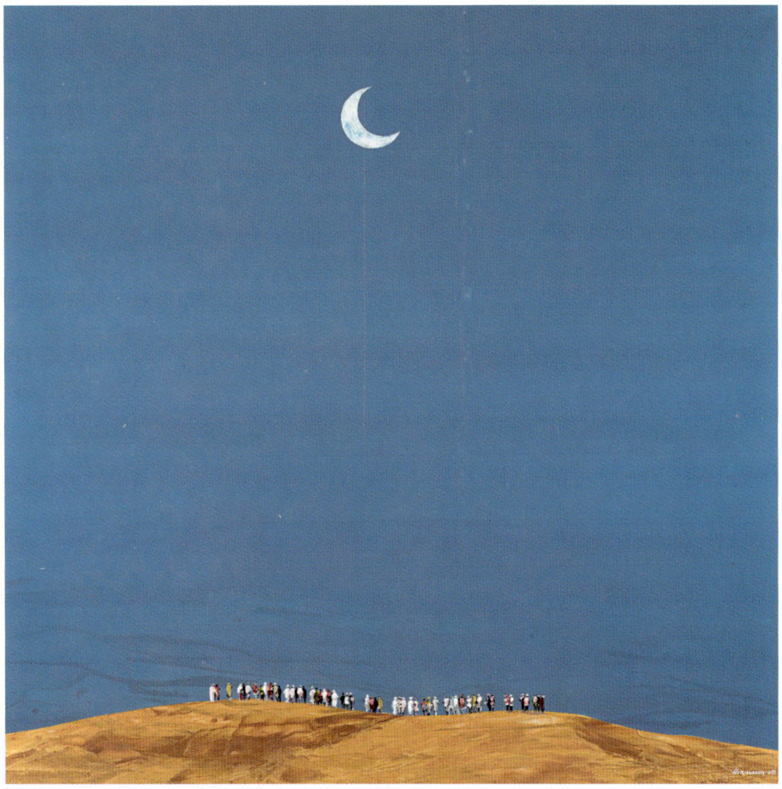

290
NOON PRAYER, 2008
Acrylic on canvas
153 x 153 cm

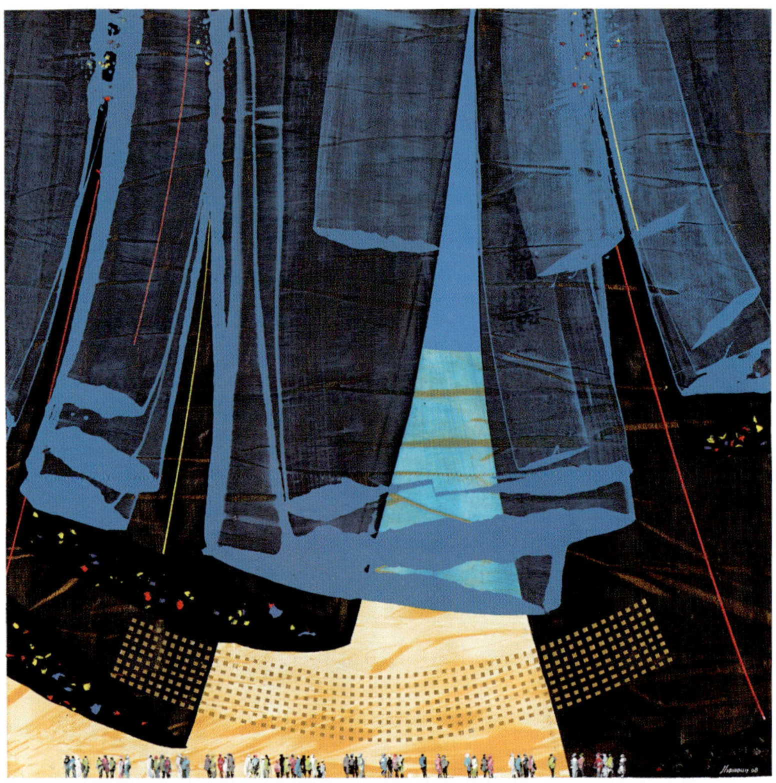

291
SHADOWS OF THE BLACK TENT V, 2008
Acrylic on canvas
150 x 150 cm

Facing page
292
BRIDGING THE WORLD 1+2, 2009
Acrylic on canvas
280 x 250 cm

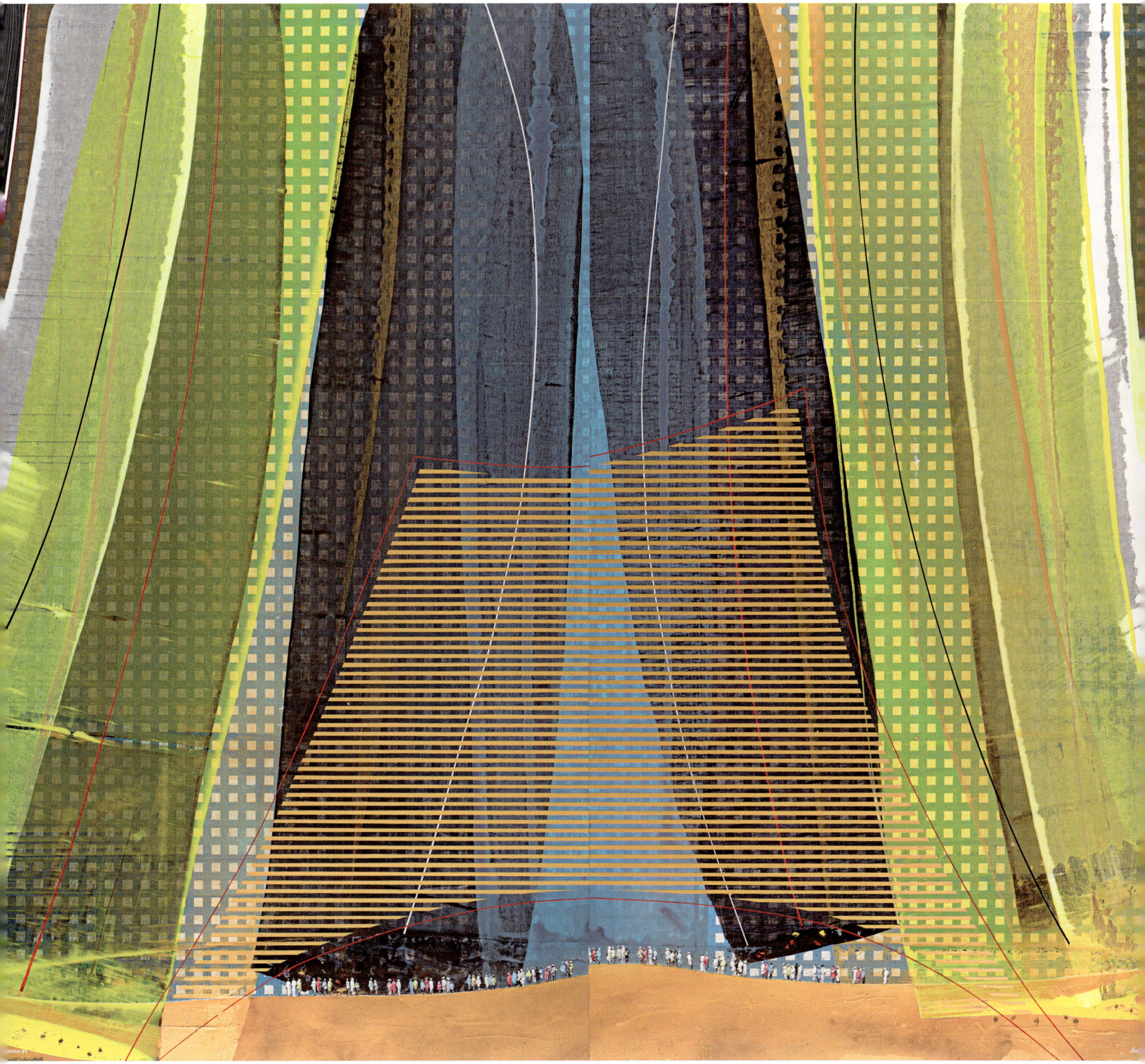

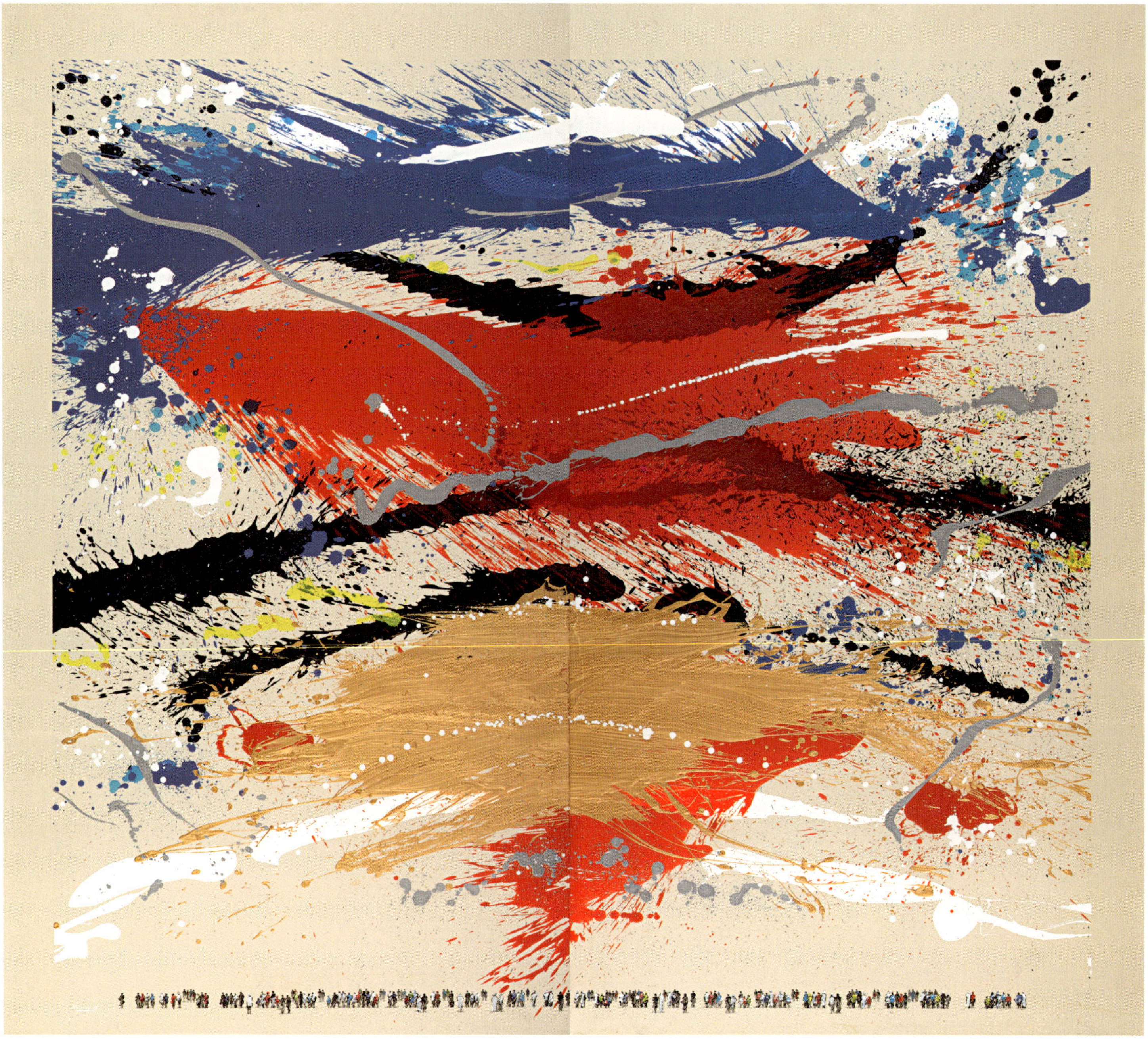

293
THE SUNSET ON THE VIRGIN SAND 1+2, 2009
Acrylic on canvas
280 x 250 cm
(Diptych)

Facing page
294
LAND OF THE KNIGHTS, 2011
Acrylic on canvas
233 x 276 cm

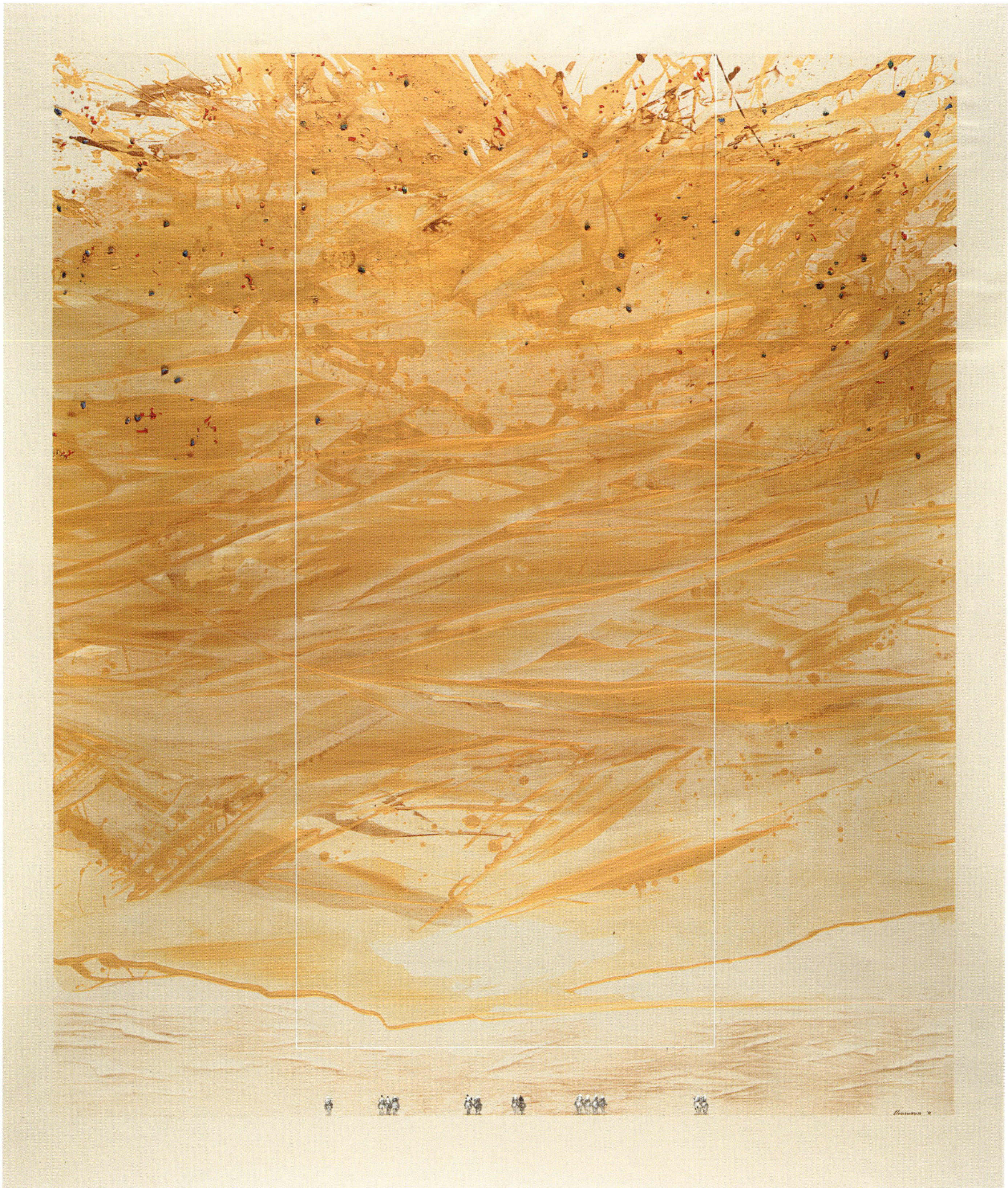

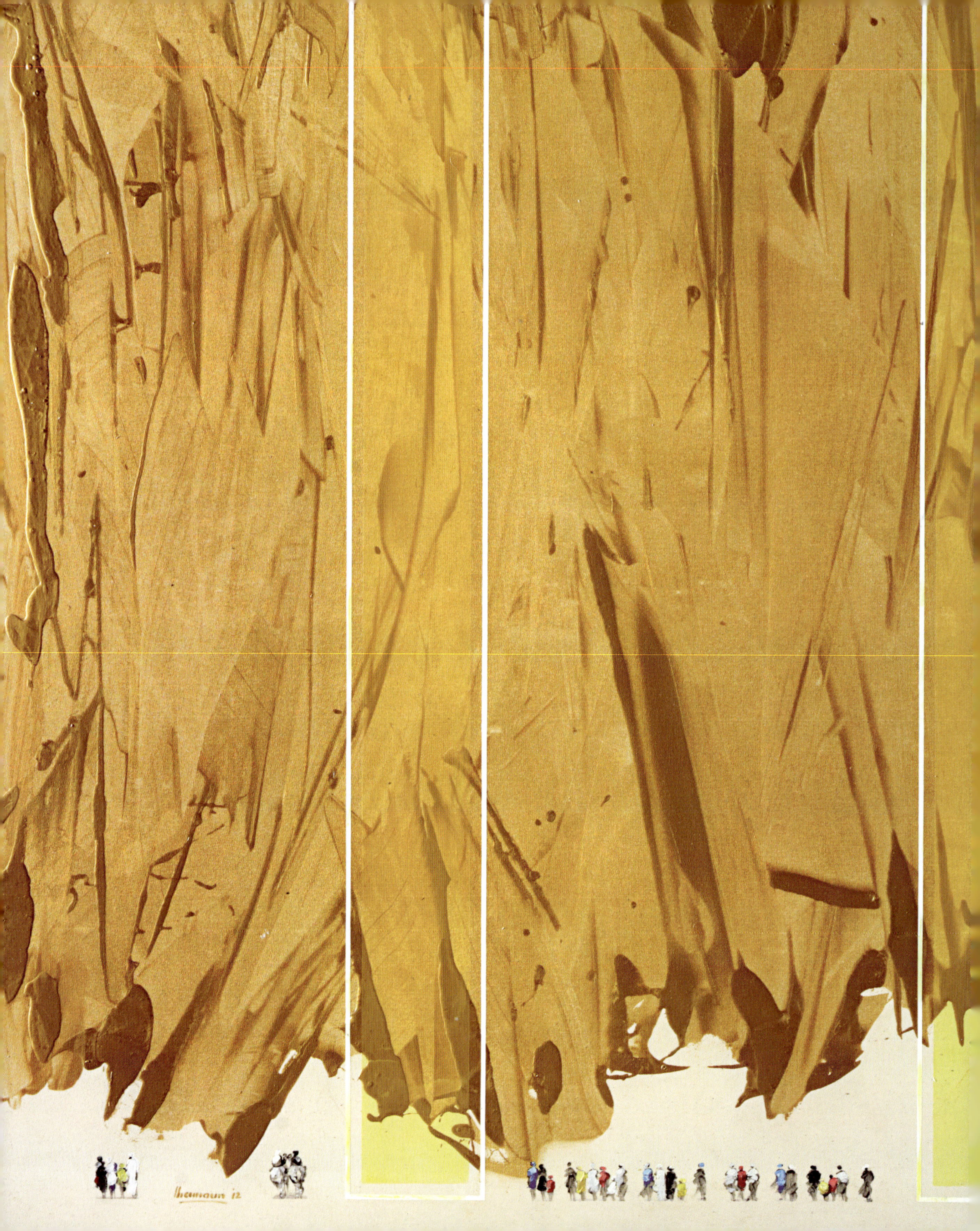

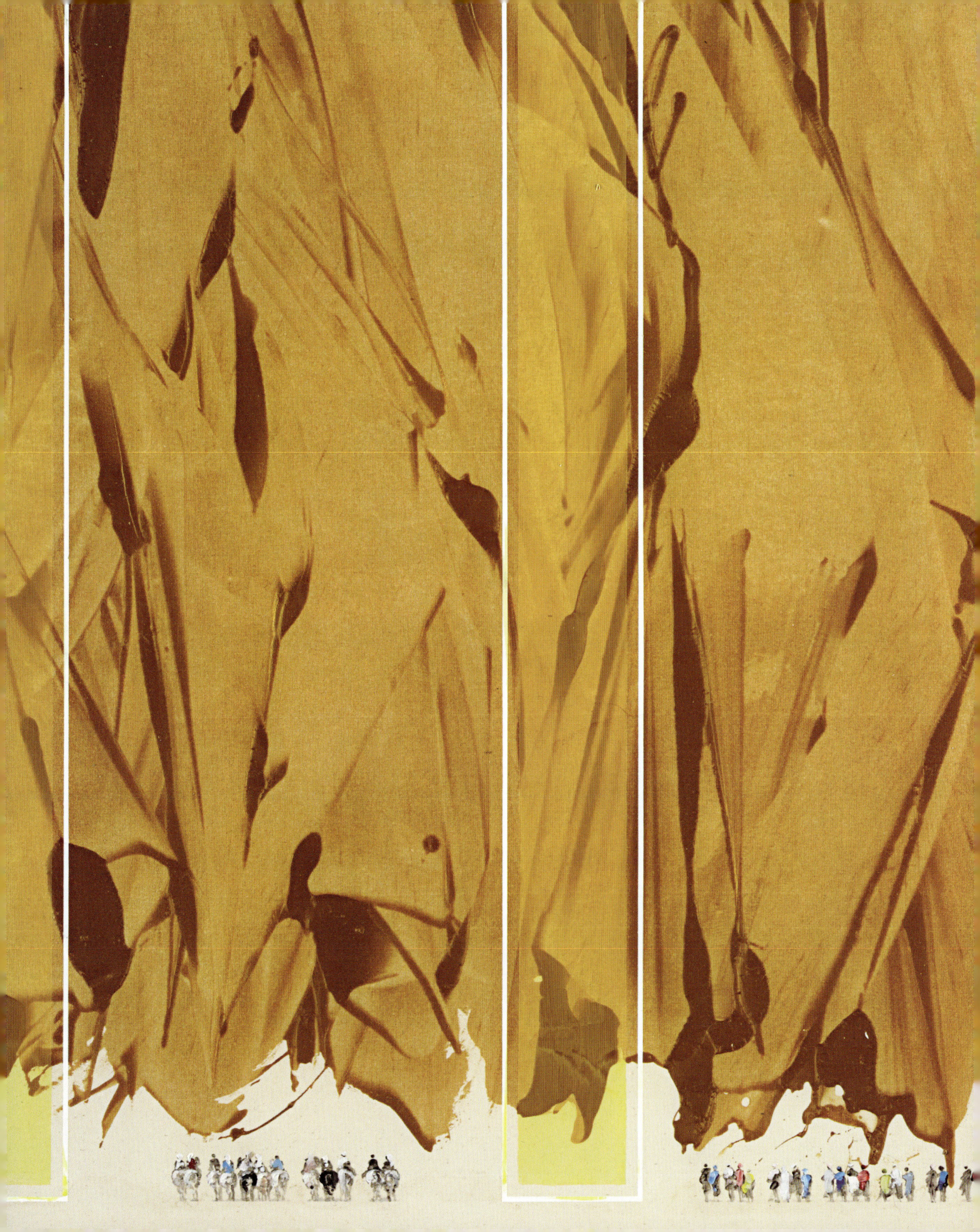

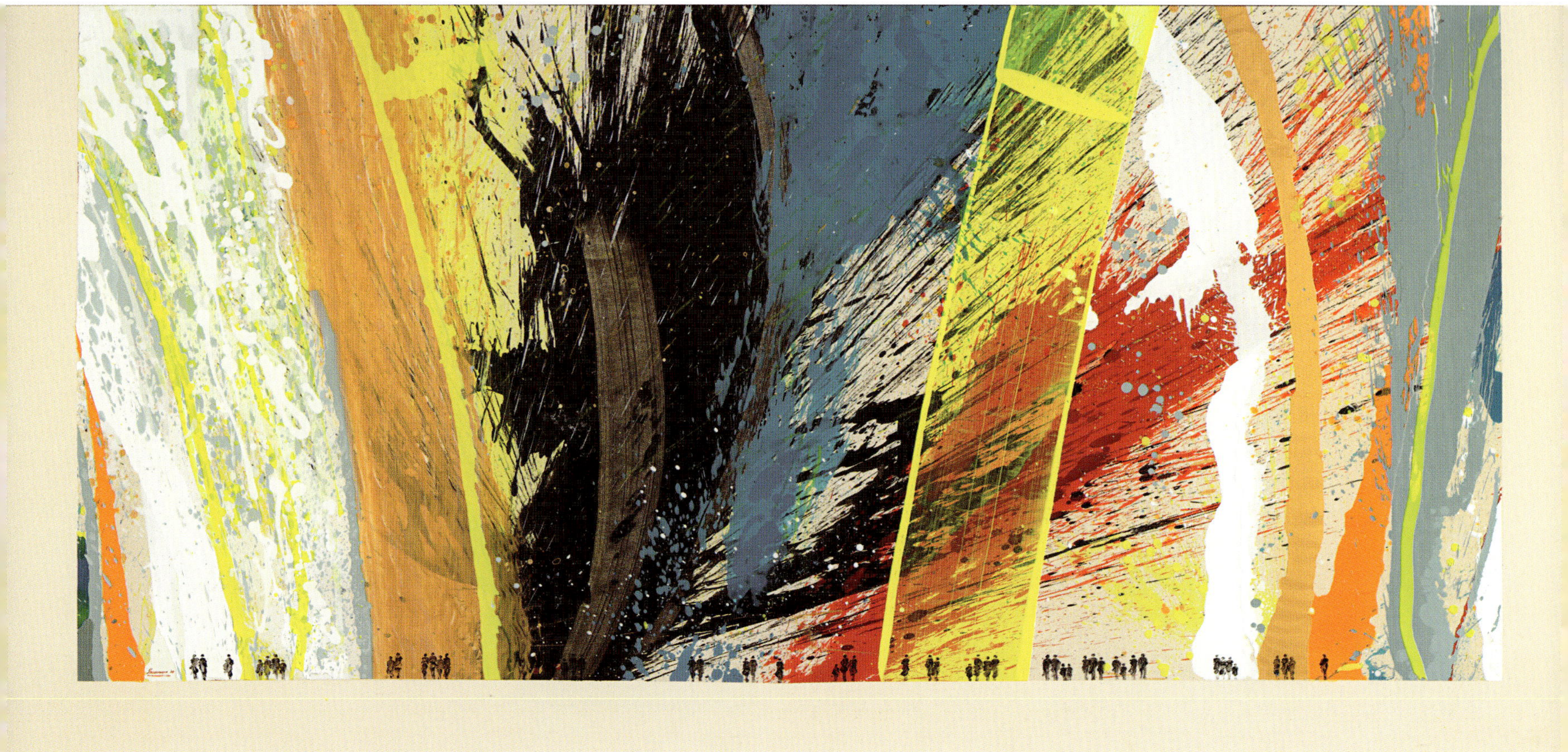

295
STORMING COLOURS, 2010
Acrylic on canvas
236 x 114 cm

Previous spread
296
WAITING FOR THE HERO, 2012
Acrylic on canvas (detail)
315 x 160 cm

Facing page, top
297
ON A GREY DAY, 2009
Acrylic on canvas
140 x 140 cm

Facing page, bottom
298
EARTH WORK, 2010
Acrylic on canvas
160 x 140 cm

Approaching Seventy

The last three years have been years of heightened energy in my race with time. I strongly but humbly believe that they have been years of unlimited freedom, unfettered even from my own teachings and limitations ... I am fortunate indeed to have lived to have a creative experience I always aspired and
293–308 hoped to have.

In parallel, my experiments in expressionist written
309–311 images in ink on gloss paper, started in 1991, found their way onto canvas in 2009. I had now resolved the technical issues, which allowed for a workable surface with the right acrylic emulsion. My creative venture, however, went beyond image writing in the calligraphic sense into a search for a new
312–319 aesthetic alphabet. This series was first featured with Epreuve d'Artiste Gallery in 2011 and in 2012 at the MENESA Beirut Art Fair and was part of a touring exhibition by twelve major Arab and Middle Eastern artists titled 'Written Images' curated by Karin Adrian van Roques with Sundaram Tagore Gallery in New York, Beverly Hills and Hong Kong.

Is it the inherited complex of alphabet discovery that we pride ourselves on having, or the mere calligraphic liberation in search of spiritual exoticism that we are also honoured to retain? The cultural schism which I have witnessed since

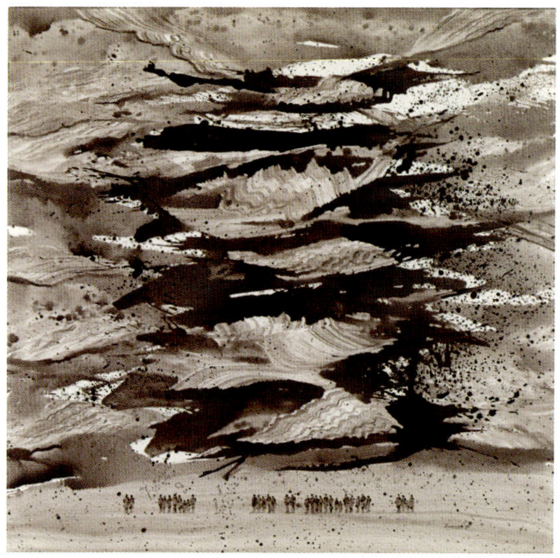

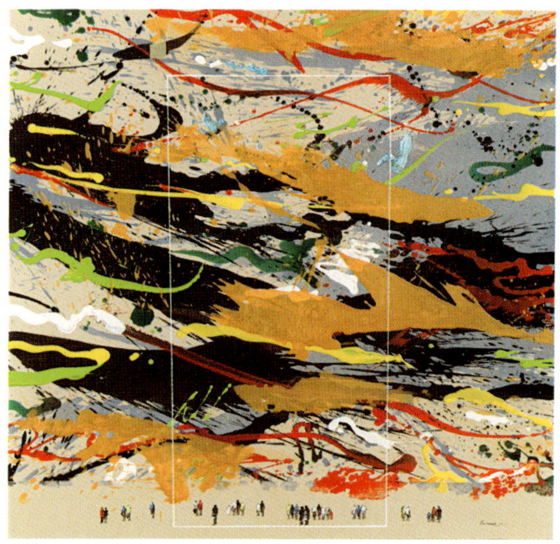

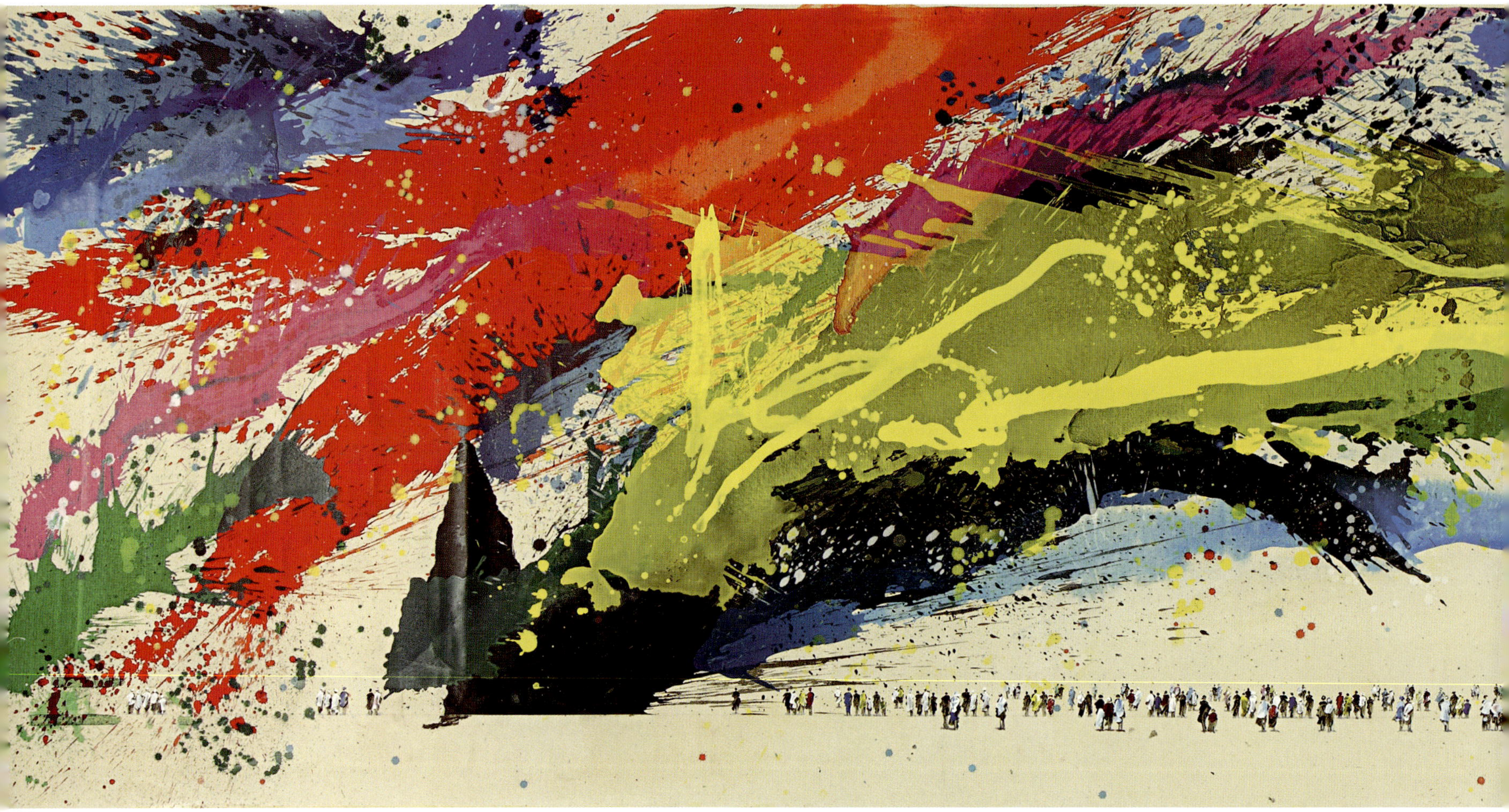

299
UNTITLED III, 2010
Acrylic on canvas
590 x 140 cm

my early formative years among artists and intellectuals as a reflection of the varying cultural affiliations has posed unanswered questions, and left artists looking in many different directions.

Does art have to be this or that particular direction or affiliation? I have never chosen to shy away from pressing aesthetic calls and needs. Like scientists, I have always believed artists must have the freedom to probe into every aesthetic question, to help galvanise and deepen our appreciation of it; for art, like science, must not be confined to one area of inquiry, to one man or one culture. Particularly, I make no attempt to free my art from its alignment with the past, from its place in a heritage, which never ceases to contribute to

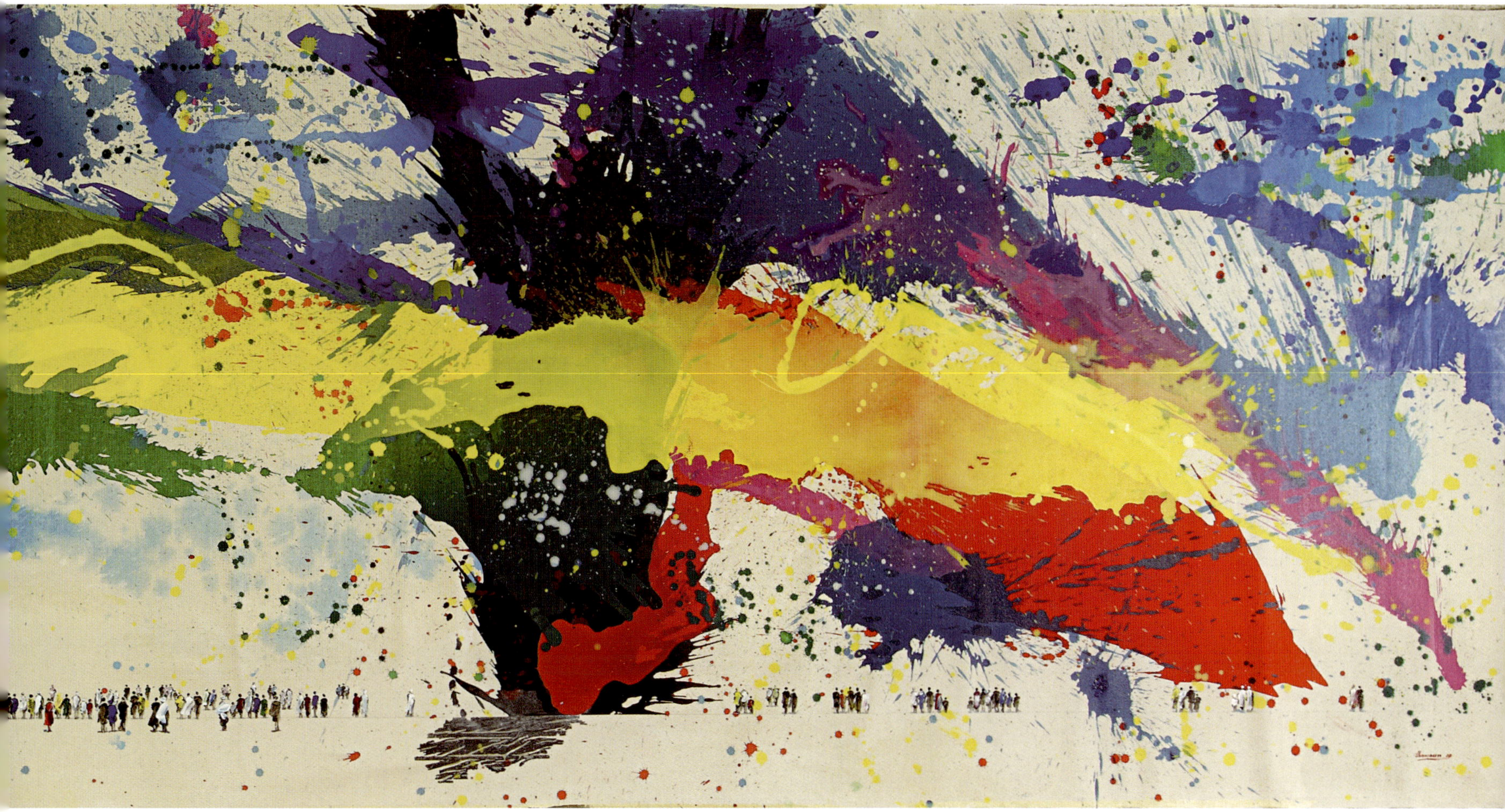

world art. The freedom I have enjoyed in the making of these images has matched every other in-depth quest into creative undertaking that I have ever tackled or that may still be waiting for me to unveil.

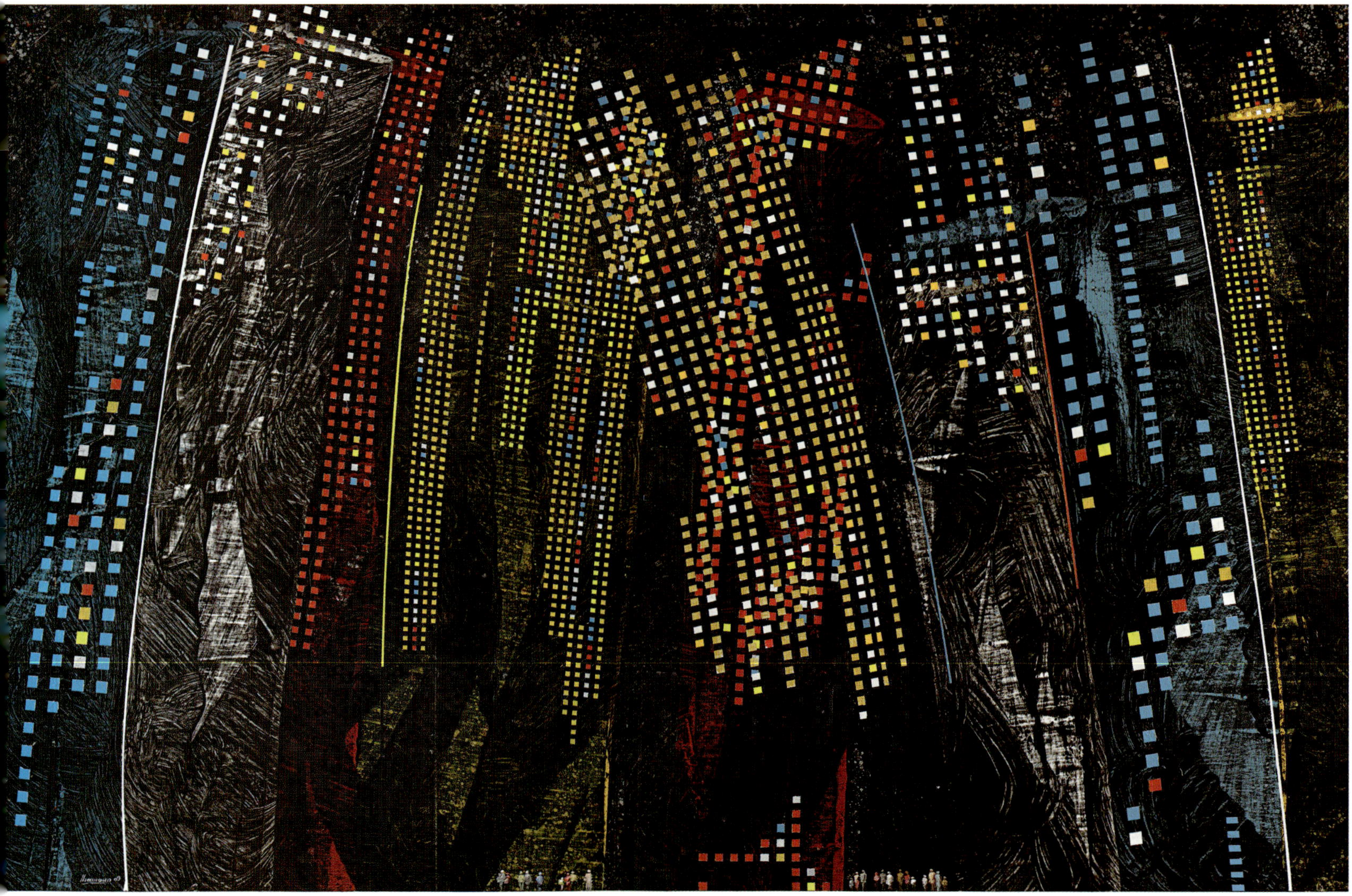

300
SLEEPLESS CITY, 2009
Acrylic on canvas
295 x 200 cm

301
I AM NOT ALONE, 2010
Acrylic on canvas
295 x 200 cm

Following spread
302
BLASTING MEMORIES, 2009
Acrylic on canvas
295 x 200 cm

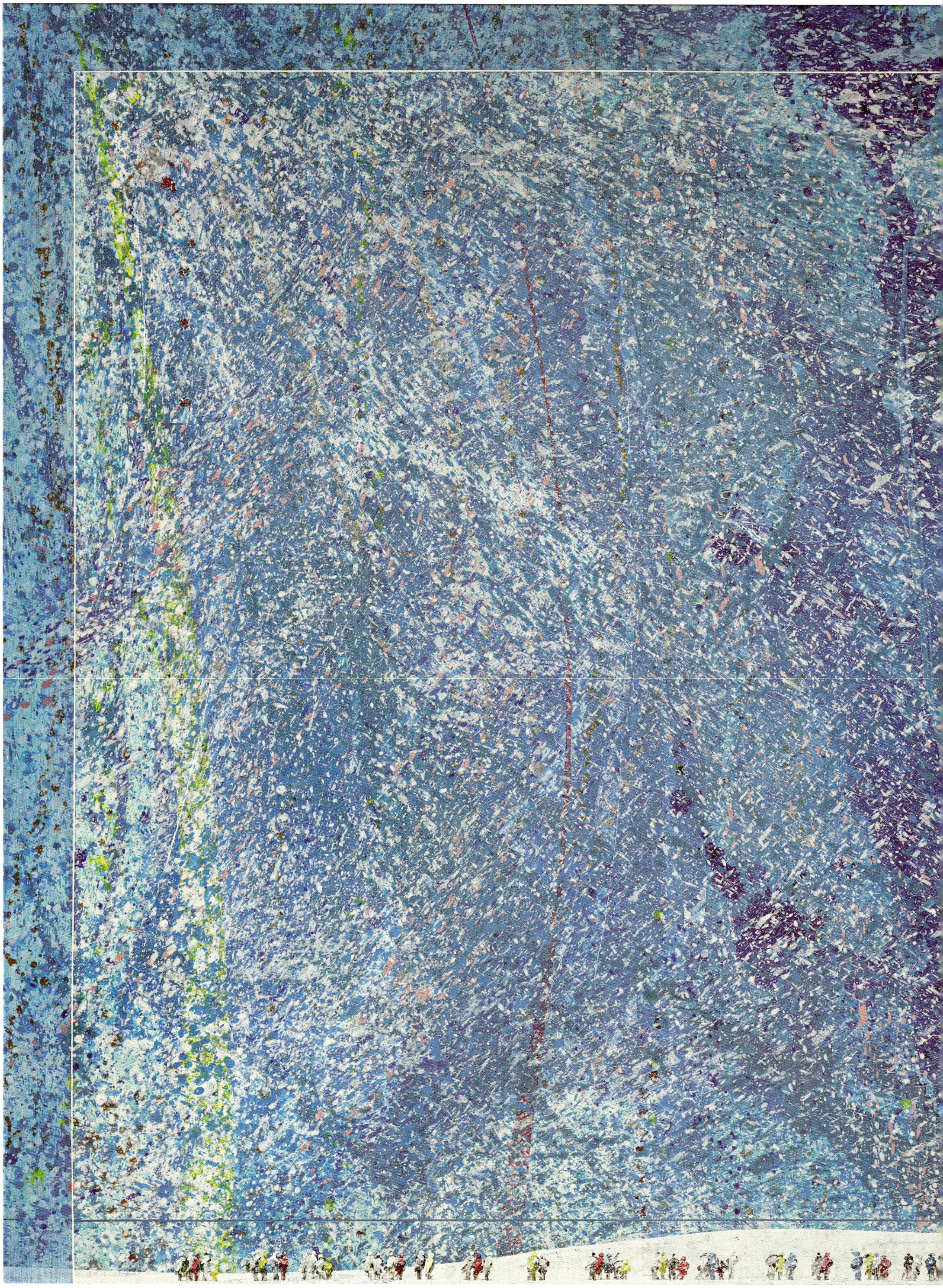

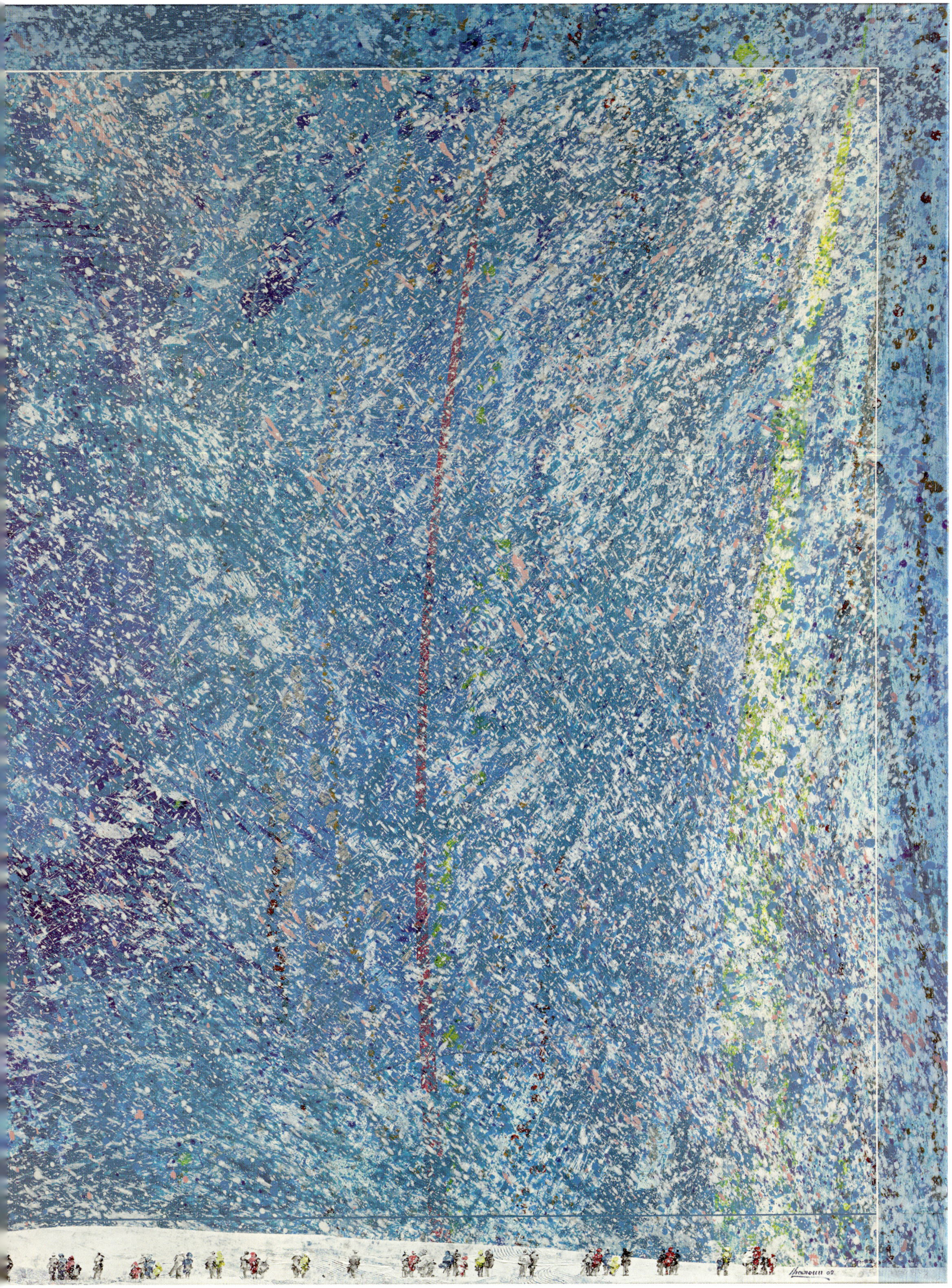

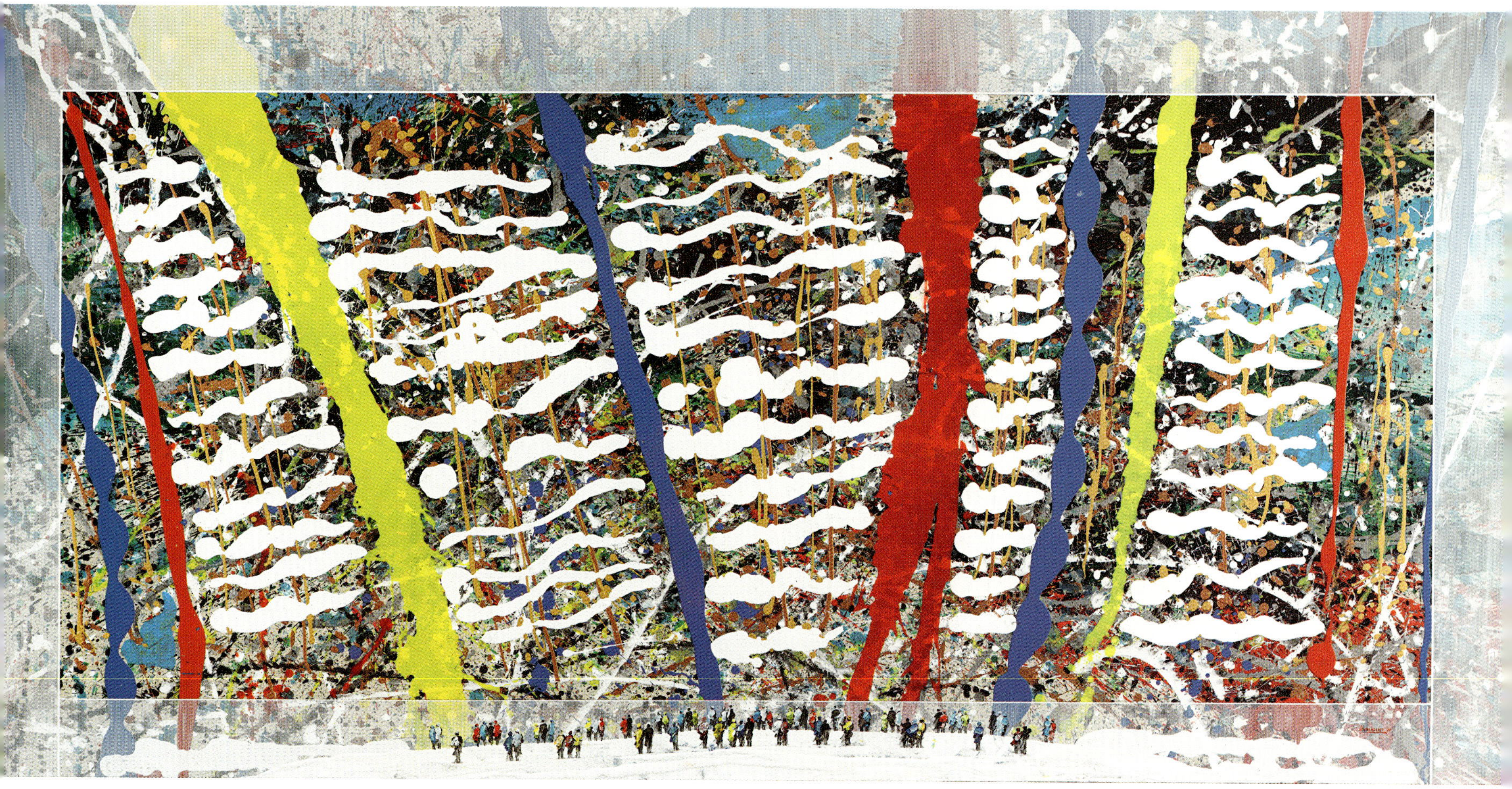

303
VIBRATIONS OF ANOTHER KIND, 2010
Acrylic on canvas
236 x 114 cm

304
GOLDEN WINDOW, 2010
Acrylic on canvas
236 x 114 cm

Following spread
305
ONE EARTH, ONE MAN, ONE DESTINY 1+2+3, 2009
Acrylic on canvas
420 x 250 cm
(Triptych)

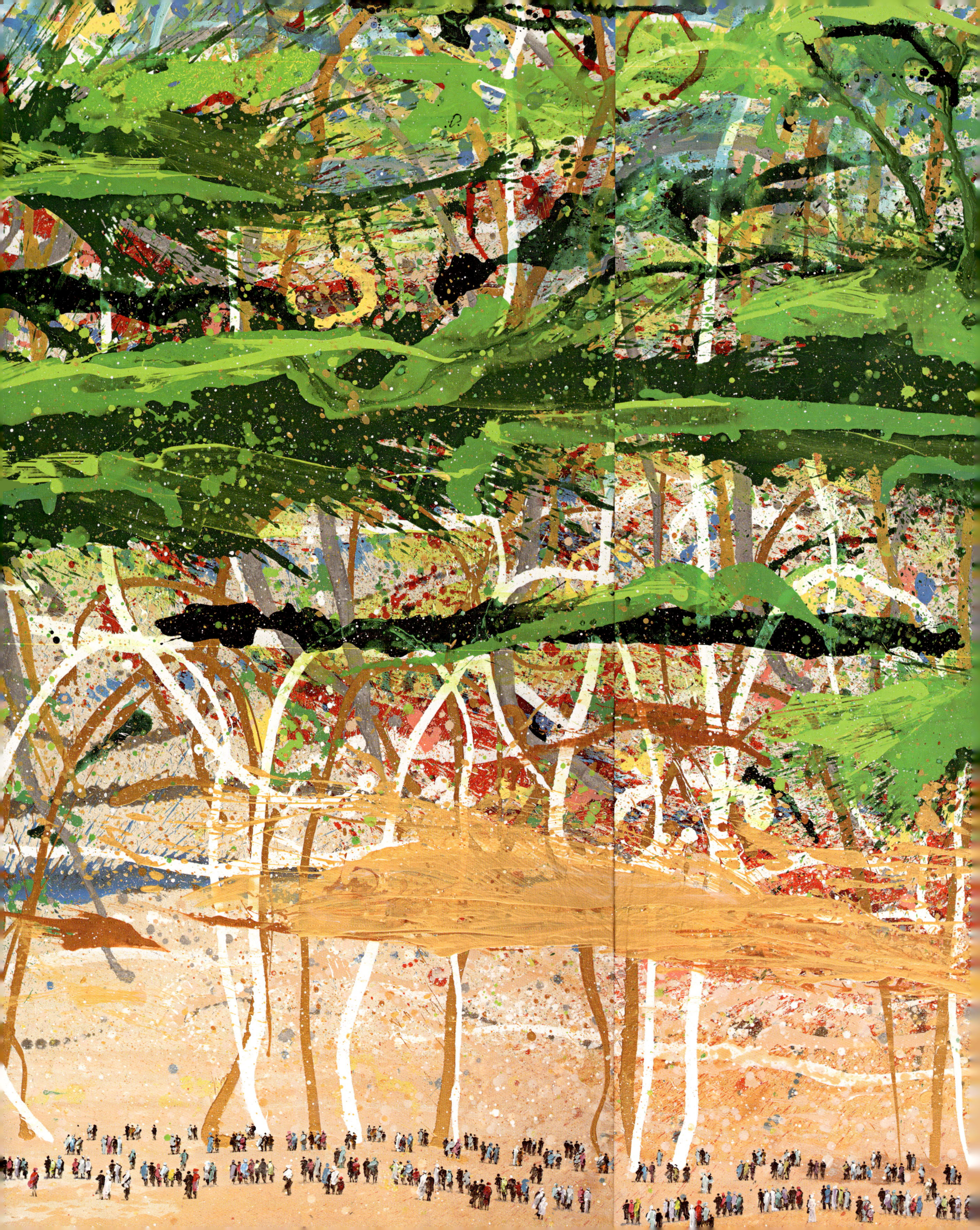

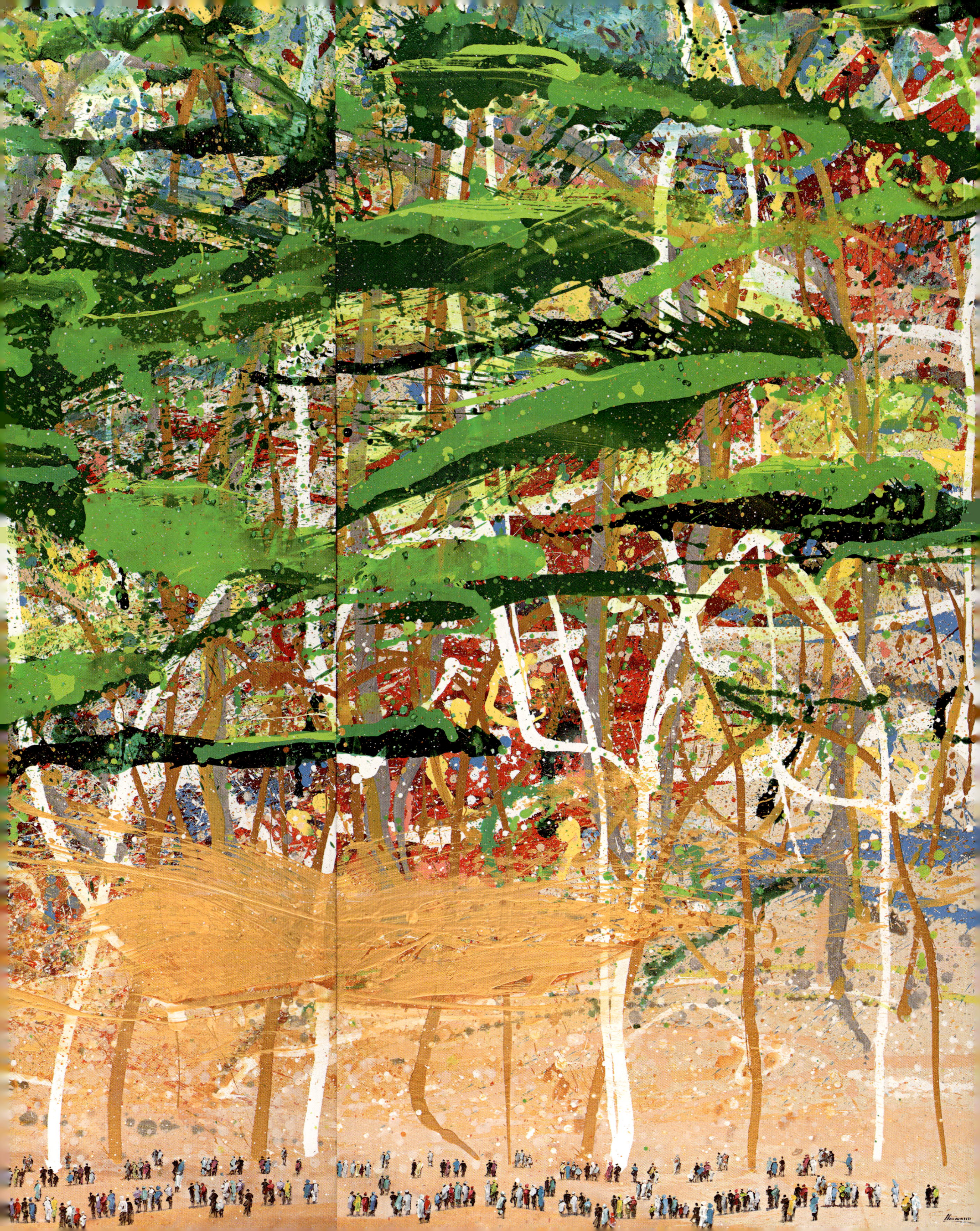

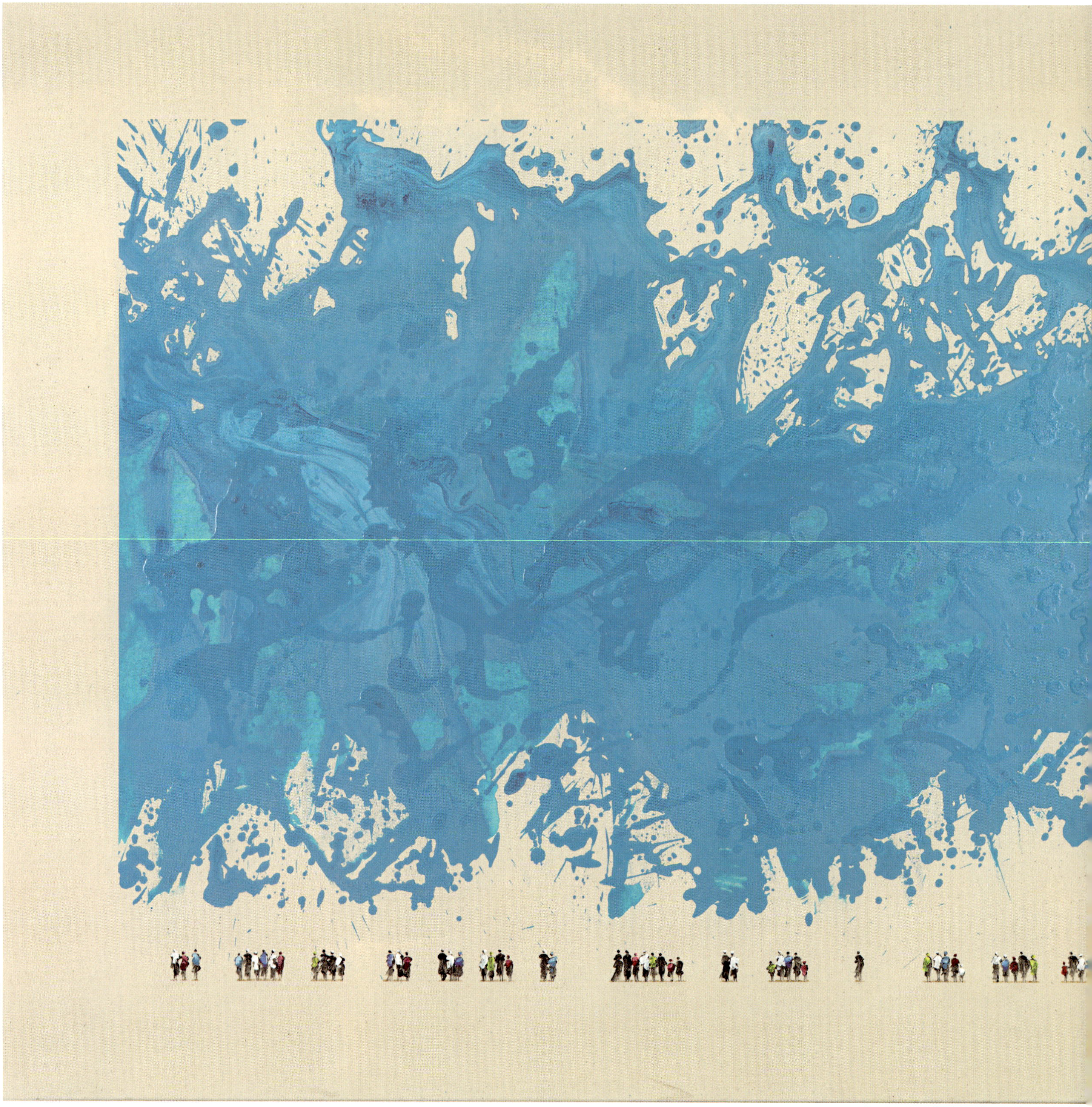

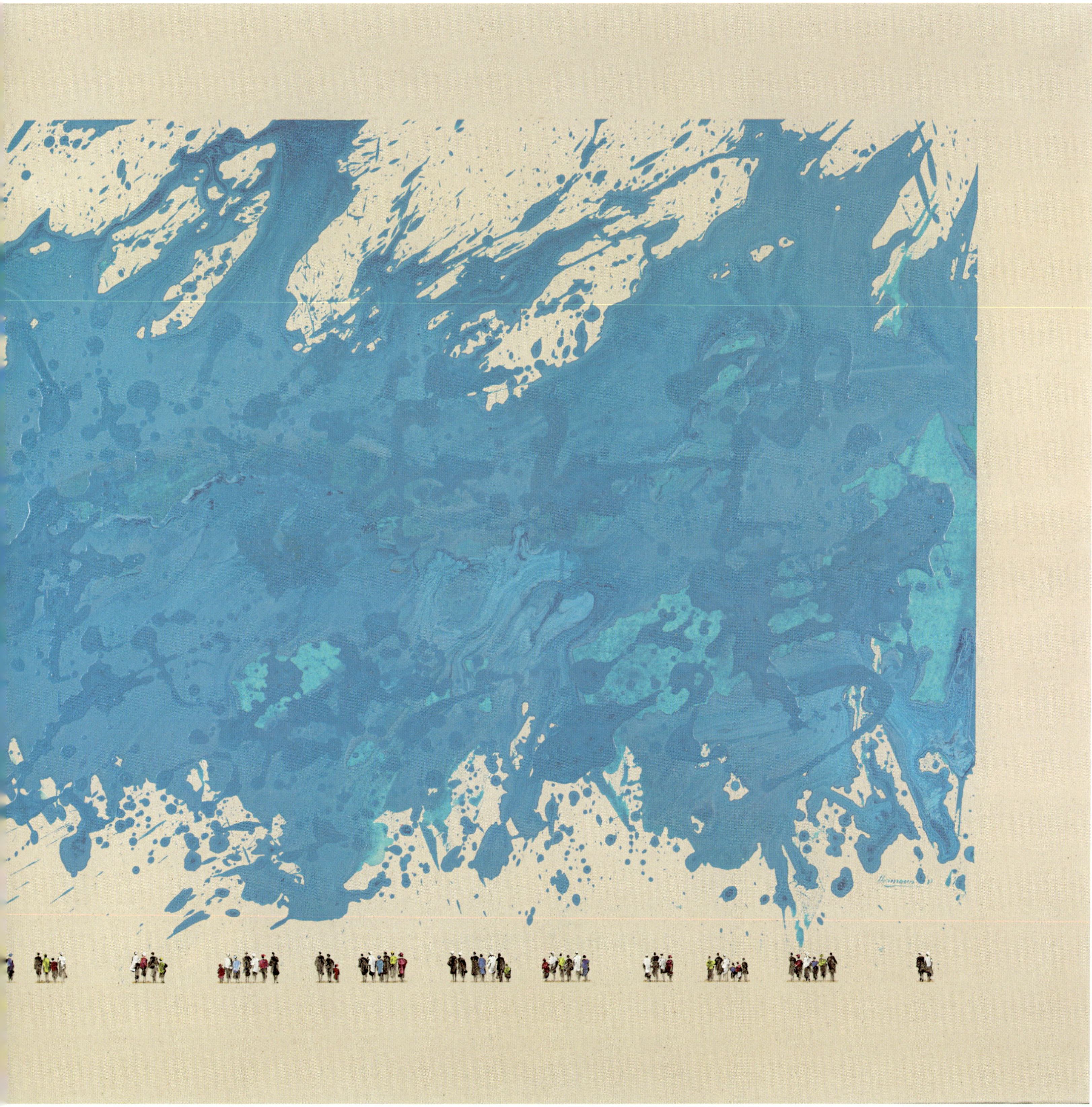

306
REDRAWING THE SKIES 1+2, 2009
Acrylic on canvas
280 x 250 cm
(Diptych)

Previous spread
307
ETERNAL BLUE I+II, 2011
Acrylic on canvas
135 x 135 cm
(Diptych)

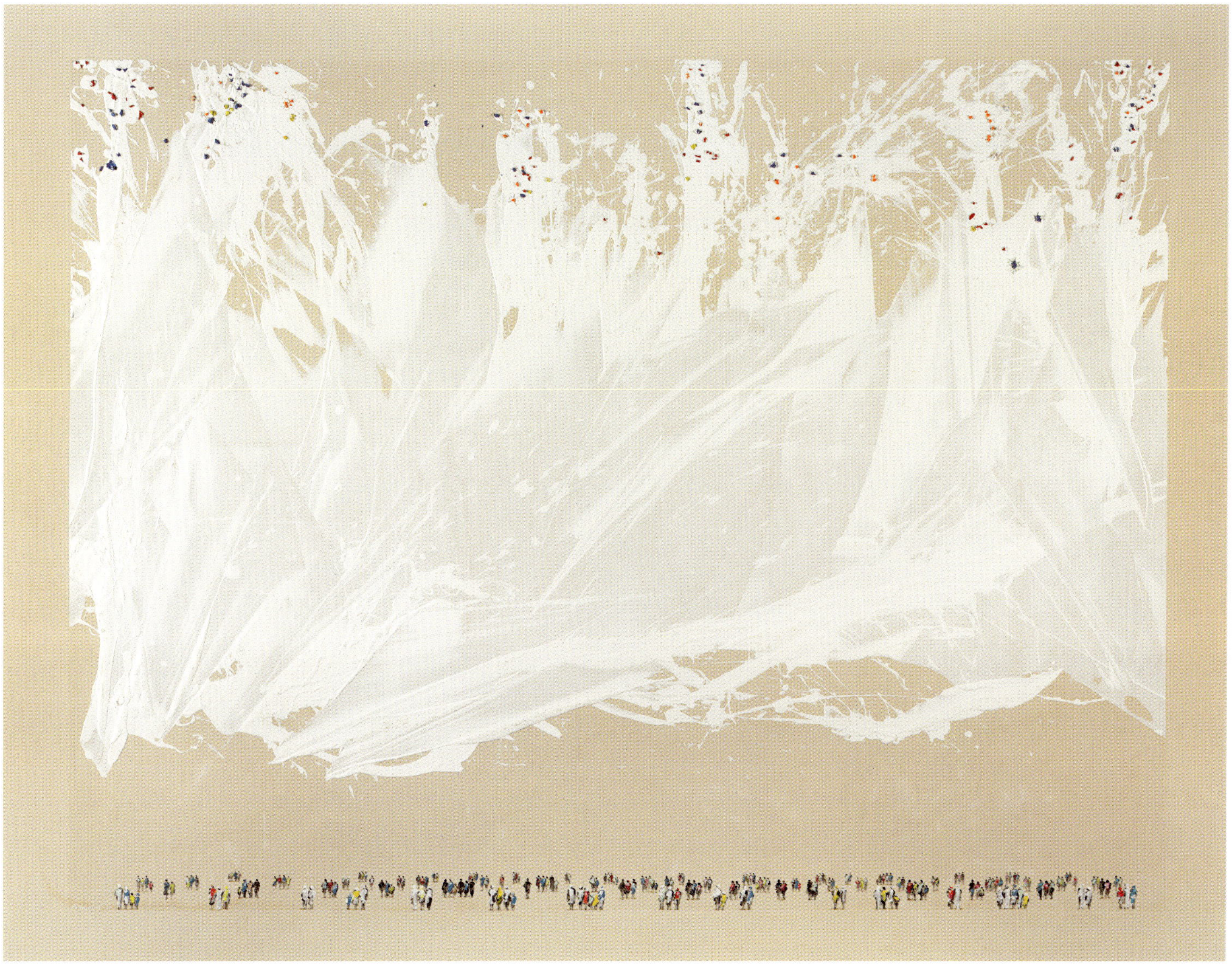

308
STORMING WHITE, 2011
Acrylic on canvas
290 x 230 cm

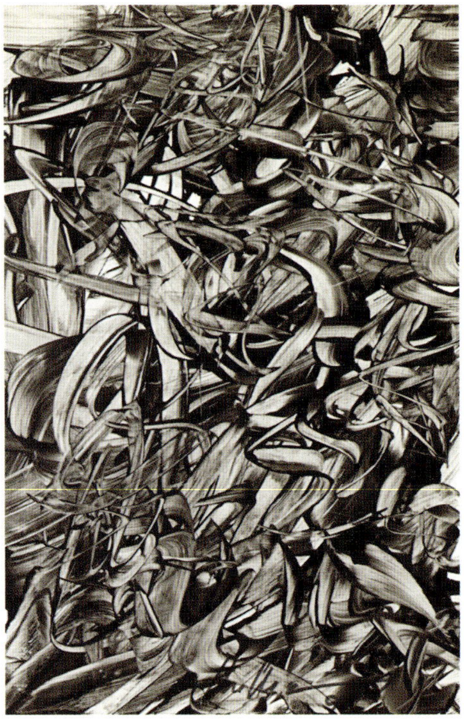

309
LOVE LETTER P4, 1991
Ink on gloss paper
16.5 x 25 cm

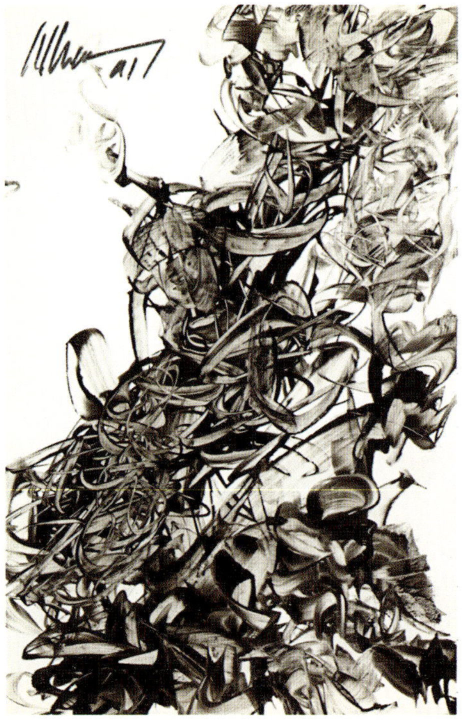

310
LOVE LETTER P5, 1991
Ink on gloss paper
16.5 x 25 cm

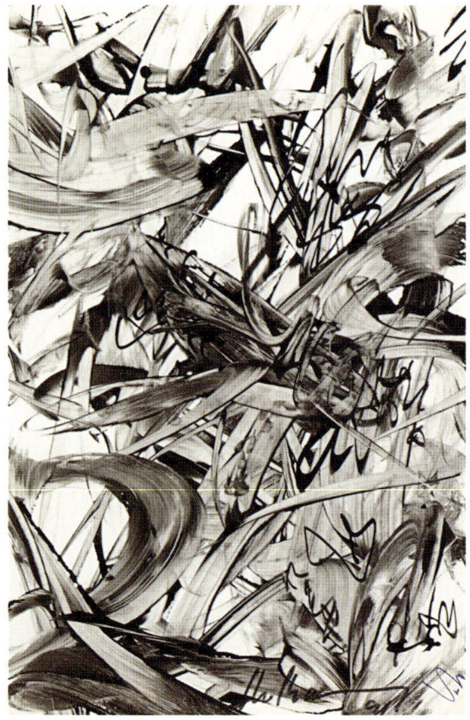

311
LOVE LETTER P6, 1991
Ink on gloss paper
16.5 x 25 cm

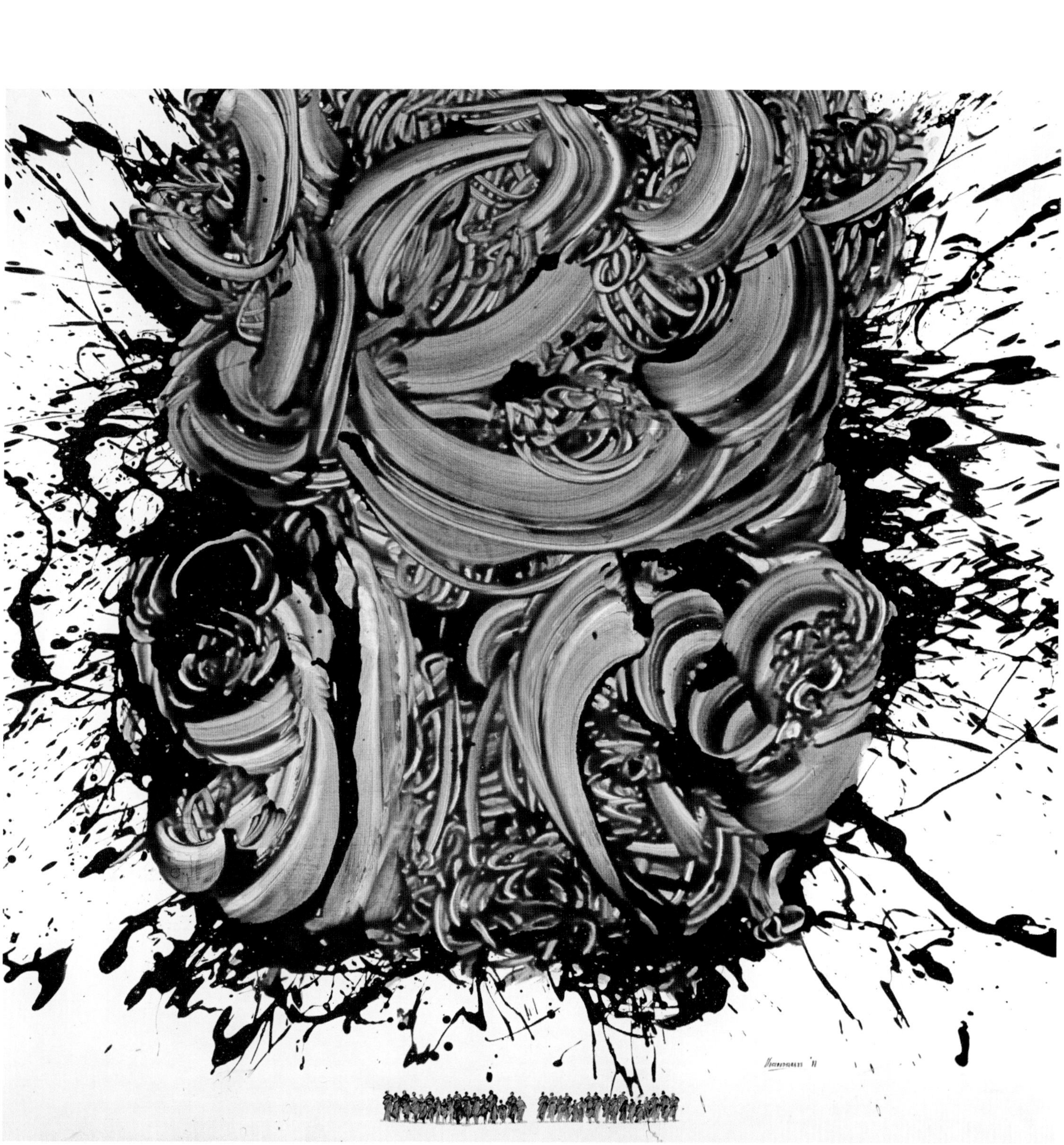

312
REVELATIONS AT NOON TIME, 2011
Acrylic on canvas
140 x 140 cm

Following spread
313
NEW ALPHABET, 2011
Acrylic on canvas
295 x 200 cm

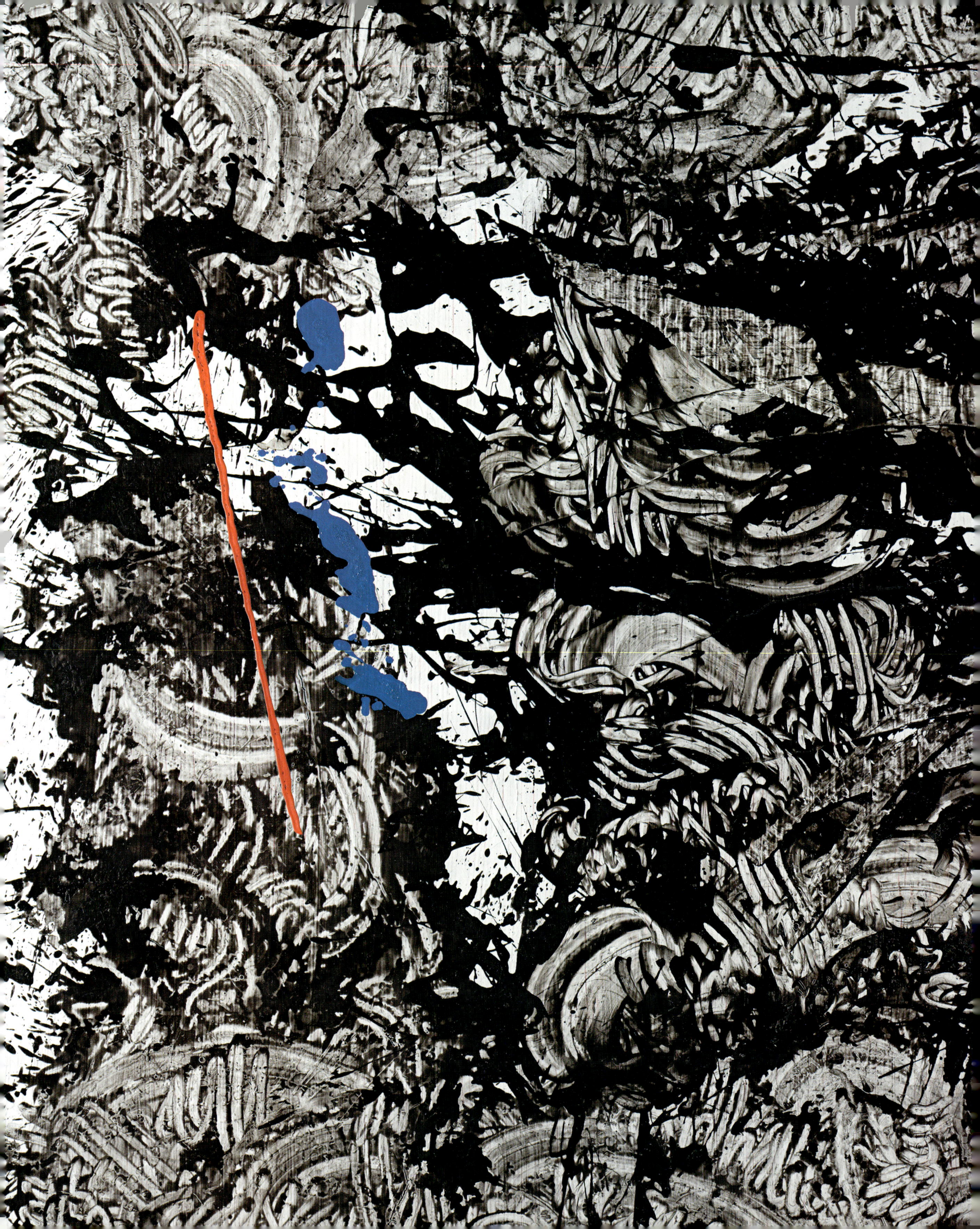

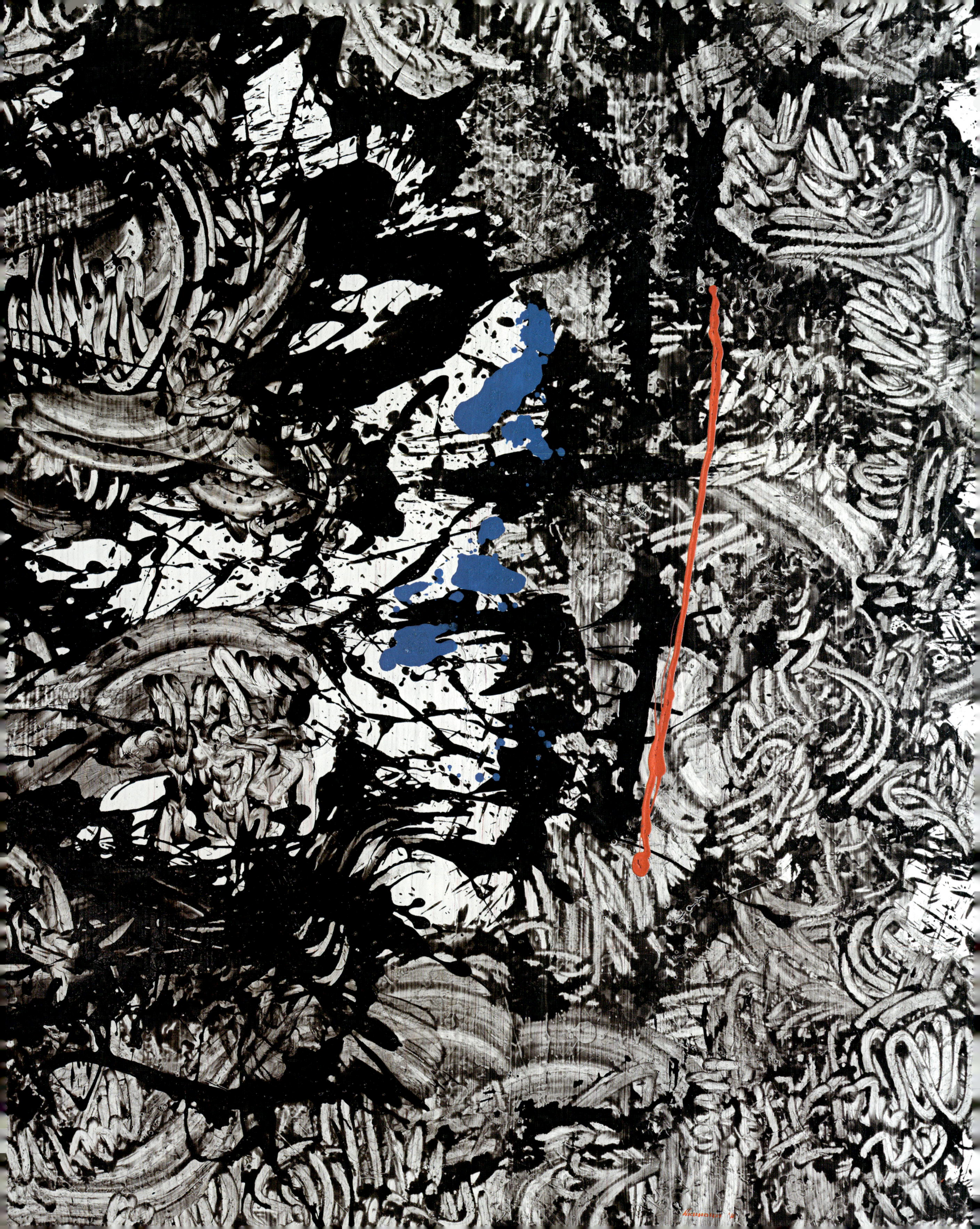

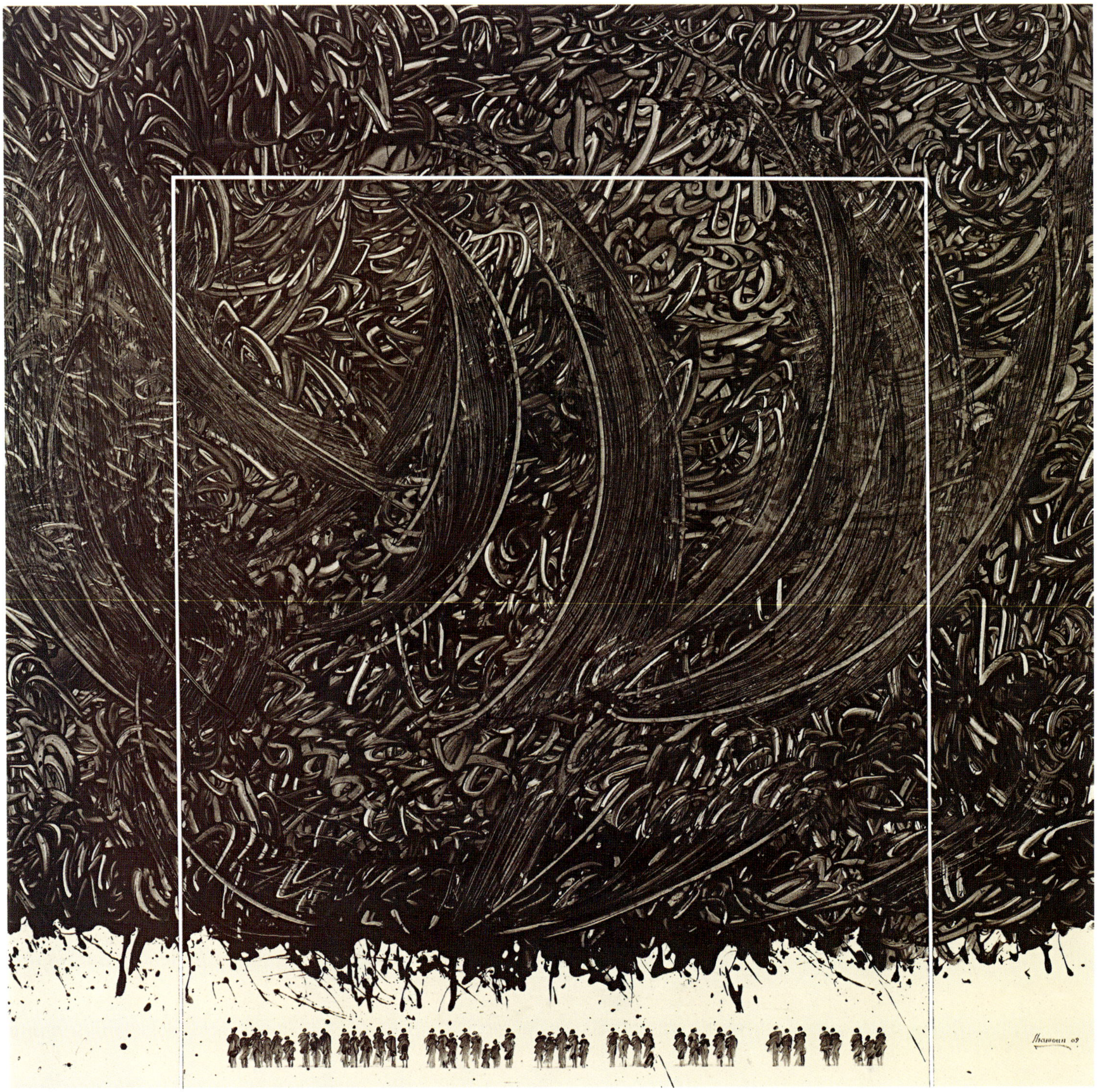

314
WRITING LOVE, 2009
Acrylic on canvas
140 x 140 cm

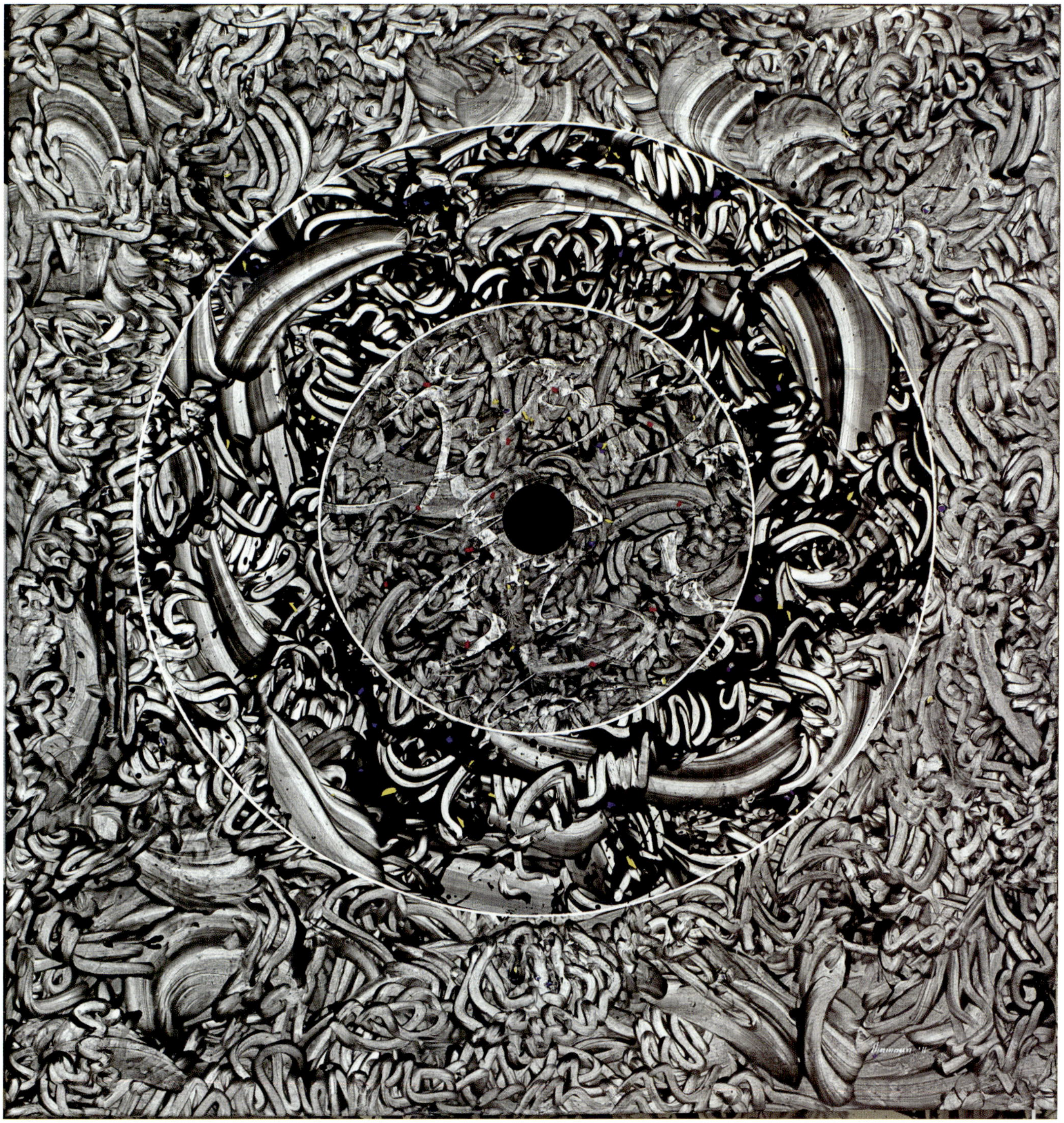

315
SEARCHING FOR LOVE WORDS, 2011
Acrylic on canvas
160 x 150 cm

Following page
316
SOME LOVE WRITINGS, 2011
Acrylic on canvas
140 x 180 cm

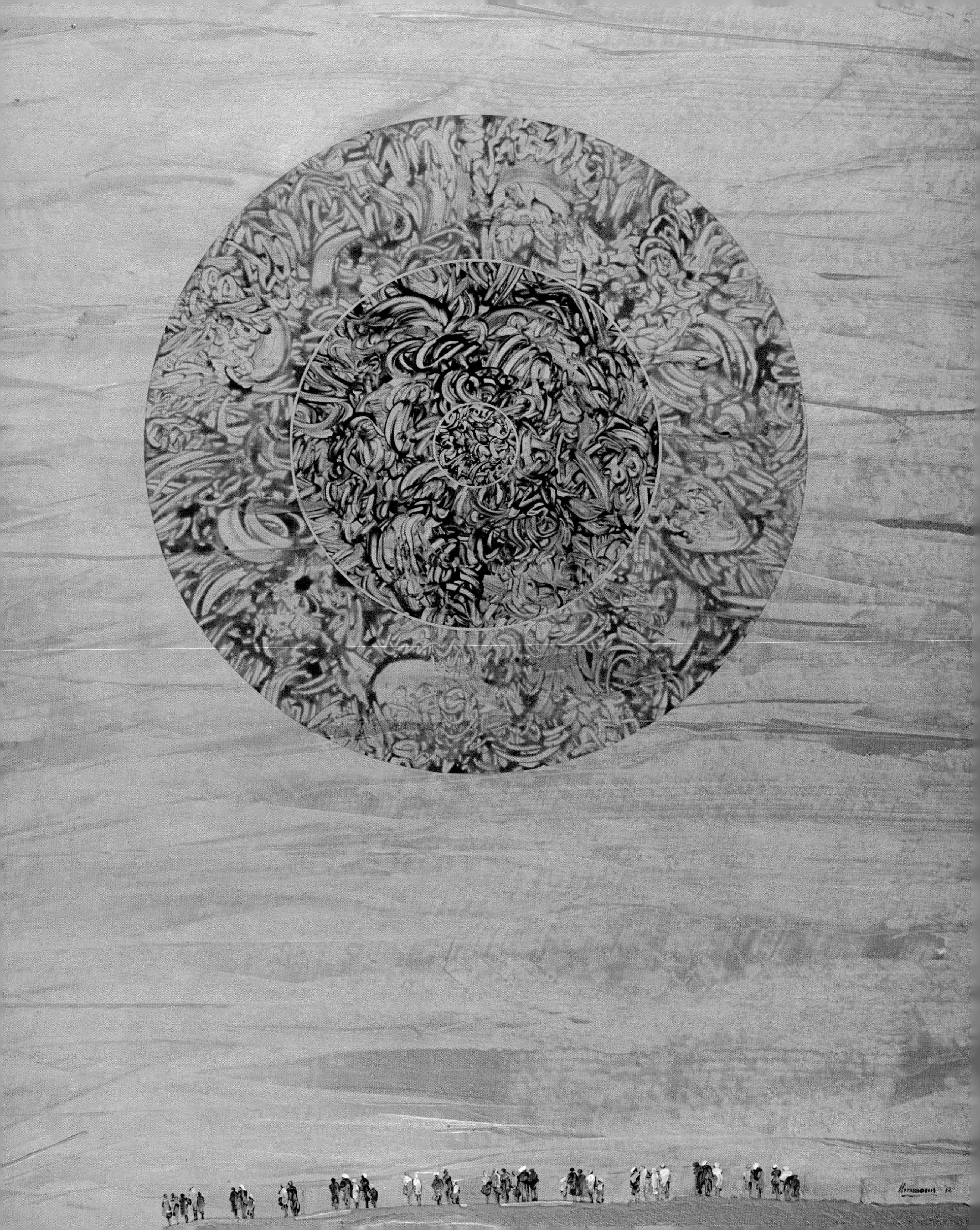

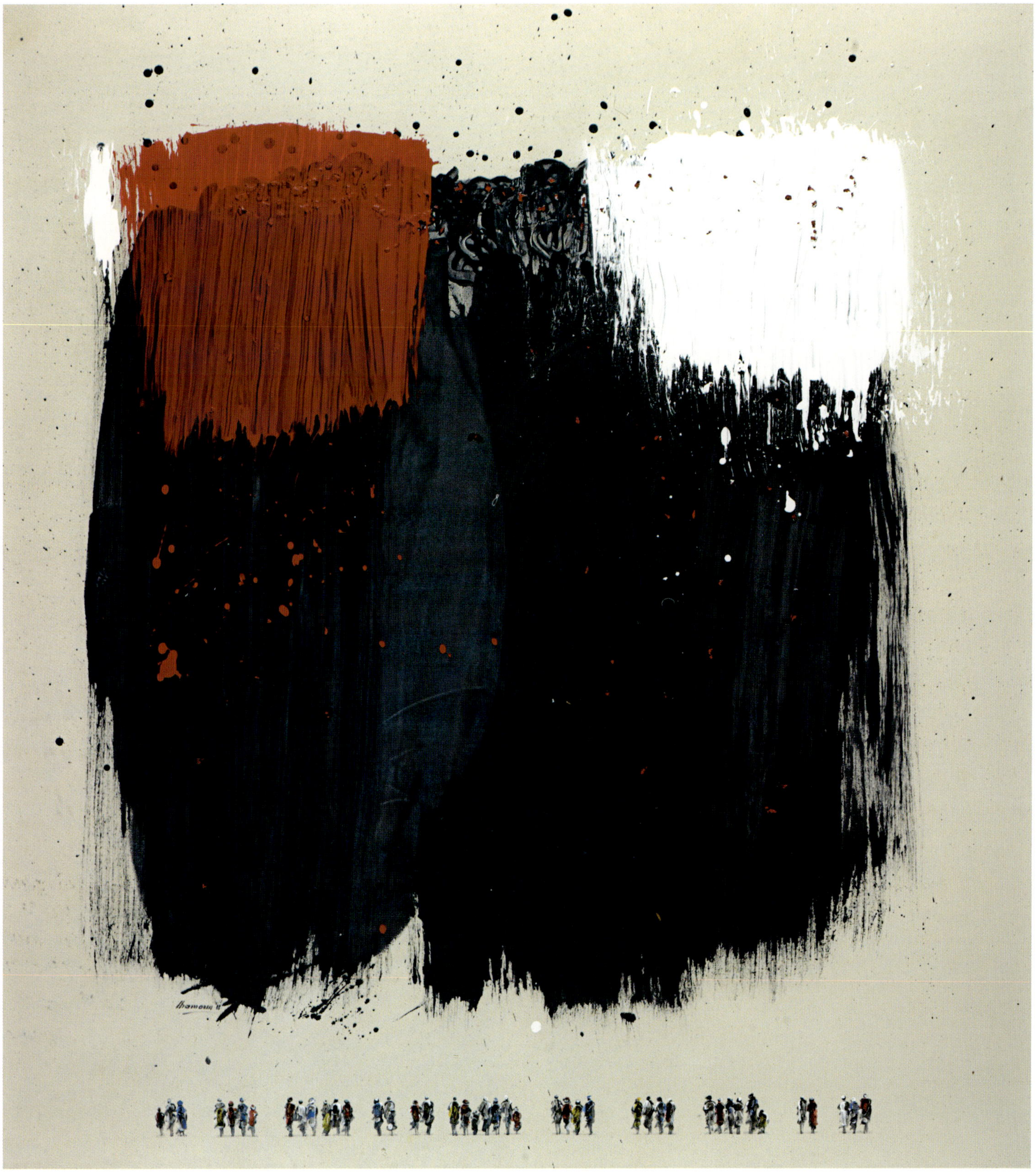

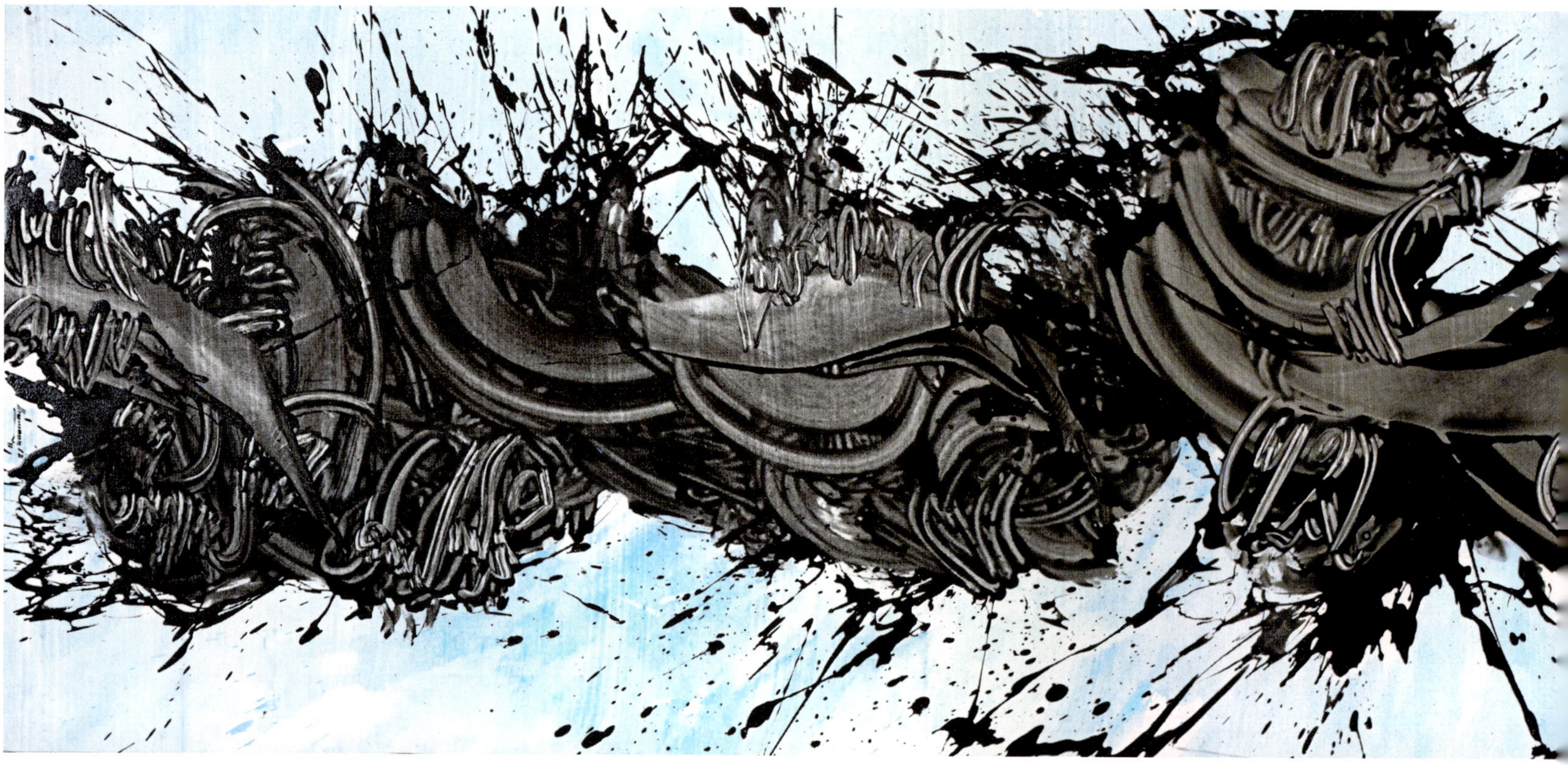

318
LOVE STORIES IN THE SKIES, 2011
Acrylic on canvas
500 x 120 cm

Previous page
317
LOVE IN THE PROCESS, 2011
Acrylic on canvas
150 x 160 cm

Following spread
319
THINKING OF HER, 2012
Acrylic on canvas
450 x 180 cm

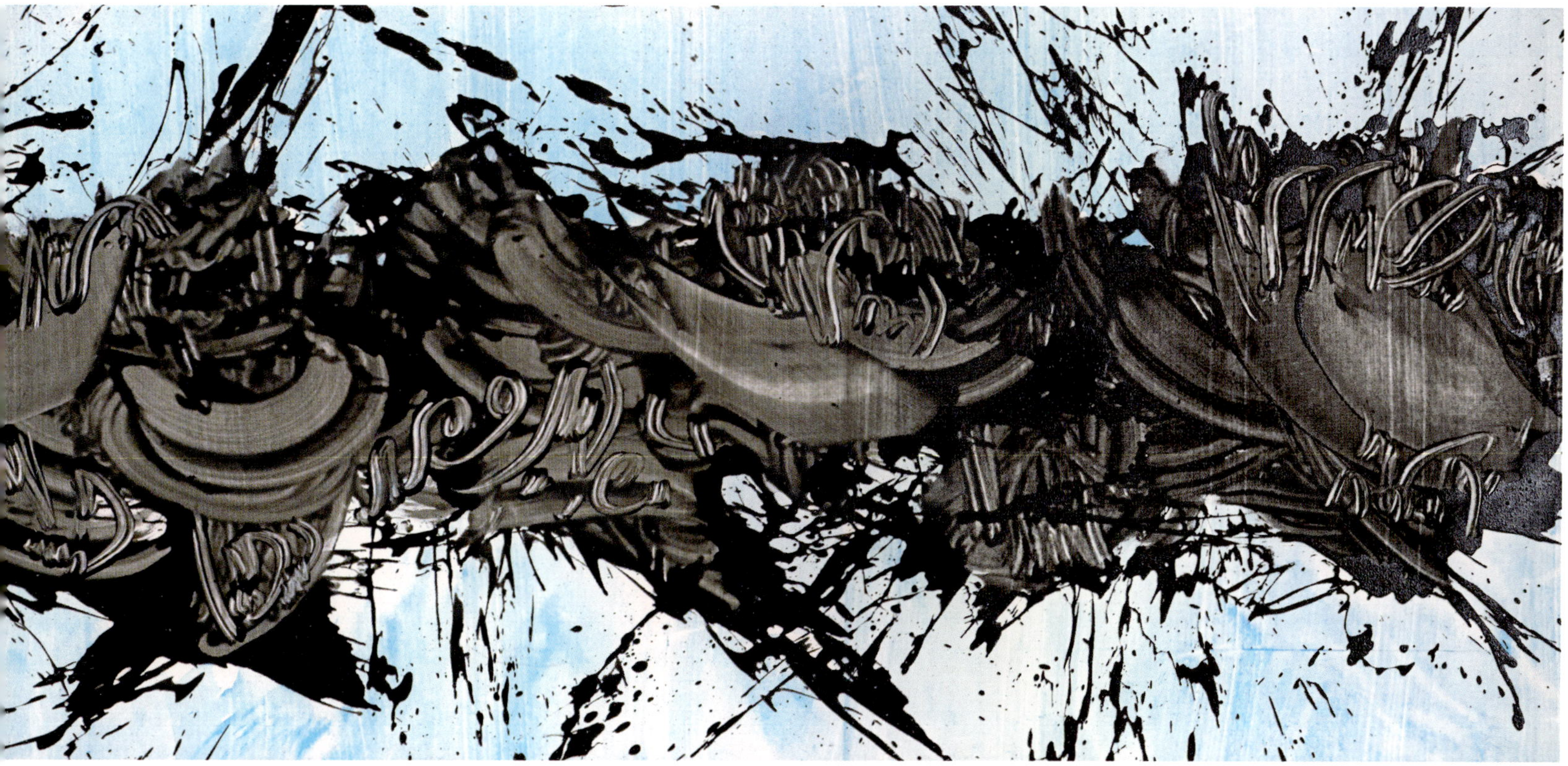

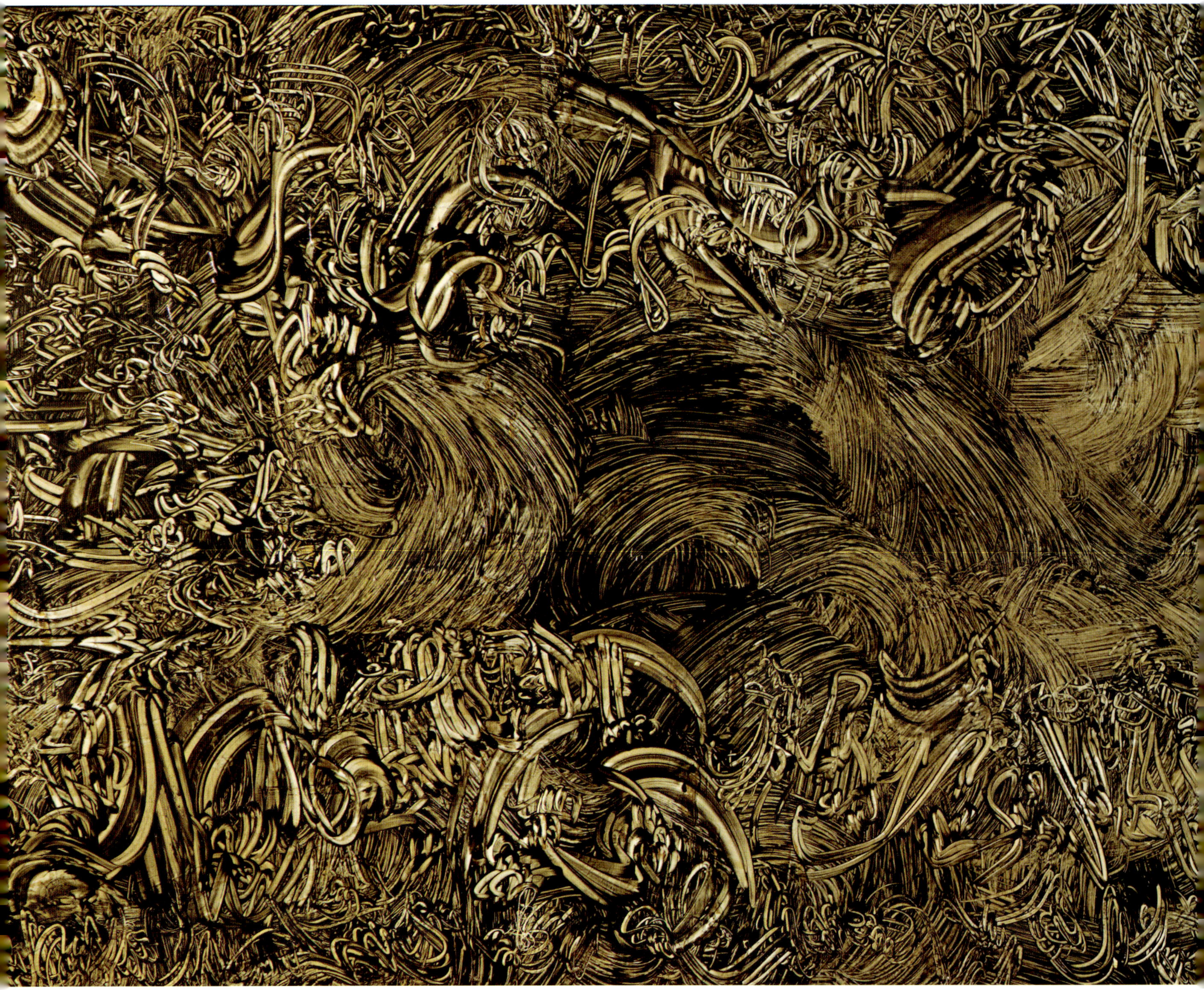

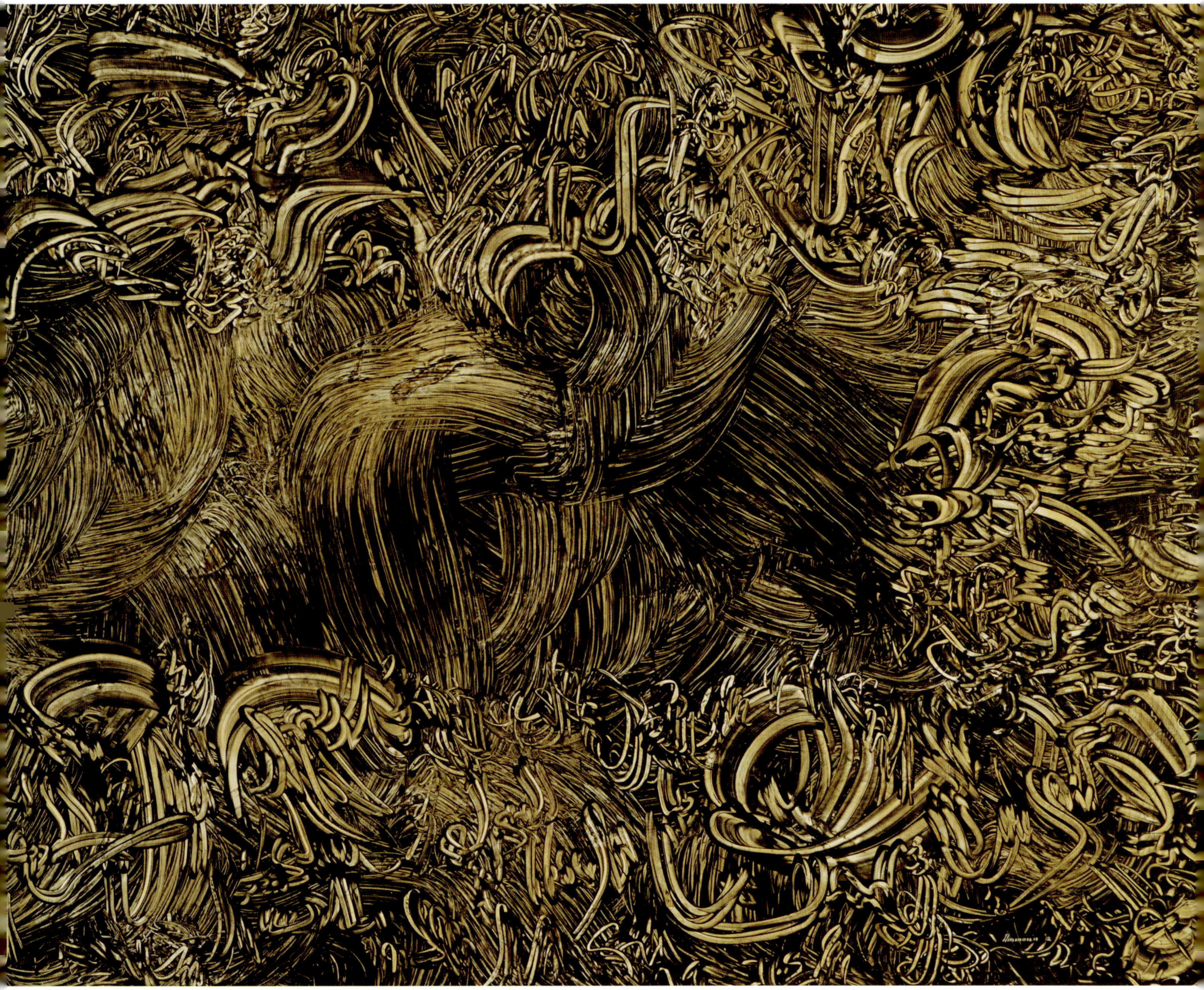

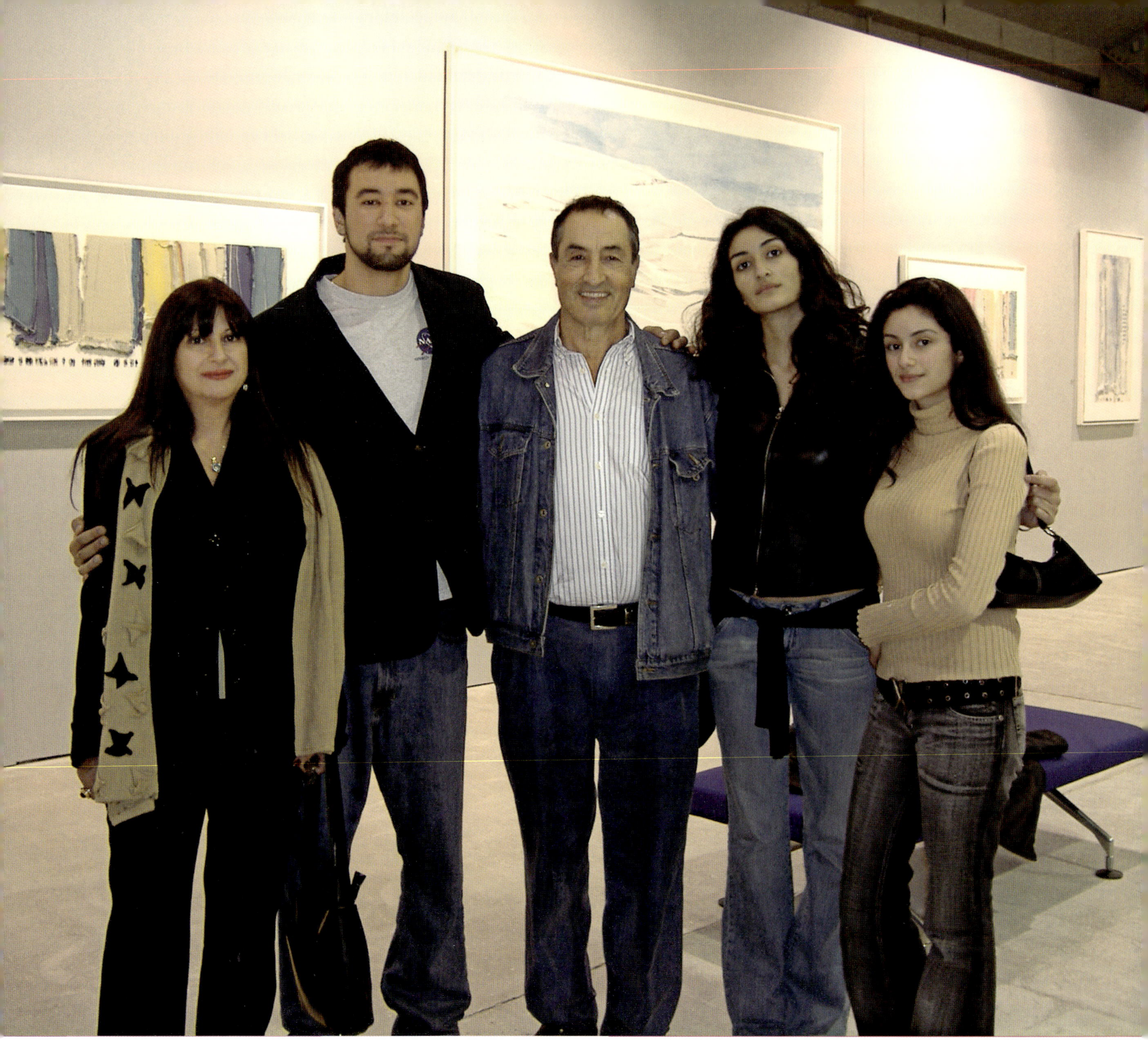

At the 2005 retrospective, Beirut Exhibition Center, Beirut
Left to right: my wife Leila, my son George, myself and my daughters Oriane and Owana

Photo on page 320
SHELTERING, 2011
Acrylic on canvas
200 x 550 cm
Inaugural ceremony for Bkher Development, Lebanon

Biography

1942	Born in Sariine Tahta, Bekaa Valley, Lebanon

Education

1968–1972	Fine Arts Institute, Lebanese University, Beirut, Lebanon
	Diploma of Higher Studies, Painting
1972–1975	College of Visual and Performing Arts, Syracuse University, Syracuse, NY, USA
	Master of Fine Arts, Painting
1975–1979	Department of Art and Art Education, New York University, NY, USA
	Studies in Studio Art and Aesthetics

One Man Show

1975	International Living Center, Syracuse, NY, USA
1976	Anti-War Manifestation, UN, Plaza, NY, USA
1977	New York University, NY, USA
1985	La Toile Gallery, Zouk Mosbeh, Lebanon
1986	Woodex Gallery, New York, NY, USA
1987	La Toile Gallery, Zouk Mosbeh, Lebanon
	Woodex Gallery, New York, NY, USA
1988	Epreuve d'Artiste Gallery, Kaslik, Lebanon
	Woodex Gallery, New York, NY, USA
1989	Epreuve d'Artiste Gallery, Kaslik, Lebanon
	Fakra Club, Fakra, Lebanon
	Opus Gallery, Nicosia, Cyprus
	Woodex Gallery, New York, NY, USA
1990	Epreuve d'Artiste Gallery, Kaslik, Lebanon
	Woodex Gallery, New York, NY, USA
1991	Epreuve d'Artiste Gallery, Kaslik, Lebanon
	Hotel Carlton, Beirut, Lebanon
	Woodex Gallery, New York, NY, USA
1992	Epreuve d'Artiste Gallery, Kaslik, Lebanon
	Marriott Hotel, New York, NY, USA
1994	French Cultural Center, Beirut, Lebanon
1995	Epreuve d'Artiste Gallery, Beirut, Lebanon
1996	Hariri Foundation, Saida, Lebanon
1997	50x70 Art Gallery, Beirut, Lebanon
	Coffey Art Gallery, Kingston, NY, USA
	Emagoss Art Gallery, Zalka, Lebanon

1998	Janine Rubeiz Gallery, Beirut, Lebanon
1999	Beirut Hall, Beirut, Lebanon (Installation 'Cana')
2001	Epreuve d'Artiste Gallery, Beirut, Lebanon
2005	Epreuve d'Artiste Gallery, Beirut, Lebanon
	Beirut Exhibition Center, Solidere, Beirut, Lebanon
2006	Experimental Studio, Saifi Village, Beirut, Lebanon
2008	Experimental Studio, Saifi Village, Beirut, Lebanon
2011	Emile Lahoud Cultural Center, Dbayeh, Lebanon

Group Show

1968–1973	Spring Salon, Beirut, Lebanon
1974	Rochester Museum, Rochester, NY, USA
	Syracuse University, Syracuse, NY, USA
1975	Low Art Center, Syracuse, NY, USA
	Syracuse University, Syracuse, NY, USA
	New York University, New York, NY, USA
1976	Fall Salon, Zouk, Lebanon
1979	New York University, New York, NY, USA
1984	Sursock Museum, Beirut, Lebanon
1991	Platform International Gallery, Washington, DC, USA
1995	Ministry of Art Gallery, Beirut, Lebanon
	World of Art Gallery, Beirut, Lebanon
	Aquarella Gallery, Collina Club, Rabieh, Lebanon
	Martyrs' Square Exhibition Hall, Beirut, Lebanon
	Contemporary Lebanese Art, National Museum, Kuwait
1996	Parliament Hall, Beirut, Lebanon
	World of Art Gallery, Beirut, Lebanon
	Art Museum, Sharjah, UAE
1997	Cultural Center, Tripoli, Lebanon
	Alwan Art Gallery, Kaslik, Lebanon
	Martyrs' Square Exhibition Hall, Beirut, Lebanon
	Biennale, Kaslik University, Kaslik, Lebanon
	Cultural Center, Tripoli, Lebanon
	Art Deco/La Fiad, Beirut Hall, Beirut, Lebanon
	Graphic Art, LAU, Beirut, Lebanon
	Graphic Art, Amman, Jordan
	International Art Exhibition, Vienna, Austria
	Aspects of Lebanese Art, Museum of Modern Art, Cairo, Egypt
1998	Lebanese Plastic Art, Cairo, Egypt
	Lebanese Painting, Dubai, UAE
	Unesco Palace, Arab Art, Beirut, Lebanon

1999	Unesco Palace, Collectors Exhibition, Beirut, Lebanon
2000	National Council of Culture and Art, Kuwait
	Lebanese Art, Sursock Museum, Beirut, Lebanon
2001	Karami International Exhibition Hall, Tripoli, Lebanon
2002	Lebanese Artists Association, Verdun, Beirut, Lebanon
2005	Lebanese Artists Association, (small work), Beirut, Lebanon
2006	Lebanese Artists Association, Verdun, Beirut, Lebanon
	Emile Lahoud Cultural Center, Dbayeh, Lebanon
	Tripoli 1st Sculpture Symposium, Tripoli, Lebanon
	Lebanese Museum, Beirut, Lebanon
	Al-Khorafi Arabic Biennale, Kuwait (prize winner)
2007	Lebanese Artists Association (50 years of the Lebanese Art Movement), UNESCO, Beirut, Lebanon
	Pan-Arab Art Exhibition, Algiers, Algeria (representing Lebanon)
	Sotheby's, Exhibition and Auction, London, UK (work sold)
	Christie's, Exhibition and Auction, Dubai, UAE (record sale for a living Lebanese artist)
	Art Paris, Abu Dhabi, UAE
2008	Christie's , Exhibition and Auction, Dubai, UAE
	Alexandria Biennale, Alexandria, Egypt (representing Lebanon)
	Pan-Arab Art Exhibition, Sanaa, Yemen (representing Lebanon)
	Sursock Museum, Beirut, Lebanon
	Art Paris, Abu Dhabi, UAE (Epreuve d'Artiste)
2009	UNESCO Palace, Beirut, Lebanon (presentation and tribute by the Lions Club)
2010	Katzen Museum, AU, Washington, USA (Convergence: New Art from Lebanon)
	Menasa Art Fair, Biel, Beirut, Lebanon (Epreuve d'Artiste)
	Old Beirut City Center, Beirut, Lebanon
	Abu Dhabi Art , Abu Dhabi, UAE (Epreuve d'Artiste)
2011	Rebirth, Beirut Exhibition Center, Beirut, Lebanon
	Menasa Art Fair, Biel, Beirut, Lebanon (Epreuve d'Artiste)
	Sandaram Tagore Gallery, New York and Los Angeles, USA ('The Written Image')
2012	Sandaram Tagore Gallery, Hong Kong ('The Written Image')
	MENASA Art Fair, Biel, Beirut, Lebanon (Epreuve d'Artiste)
	Epreuve d'Artiste Thirtieth Anniversary Show, Beirut, Lebanon

Teaching

1974–1975	Syracuse University, New York University, USA (T.A.)
1979–1980	New York University, USA (TA with Dr Bob Kapelus)
1982–1984	Holy Spirit University, Kaslik, Lebanon
1982–1989; 1994–1997	Lebanese University, INBA II, Beirut, Lebanon (Chairman, Art Department)
2007–2008	American University of Beirut, Beirut, Lebanon
1997–	Lebanese American University, Beirut, Lebanon

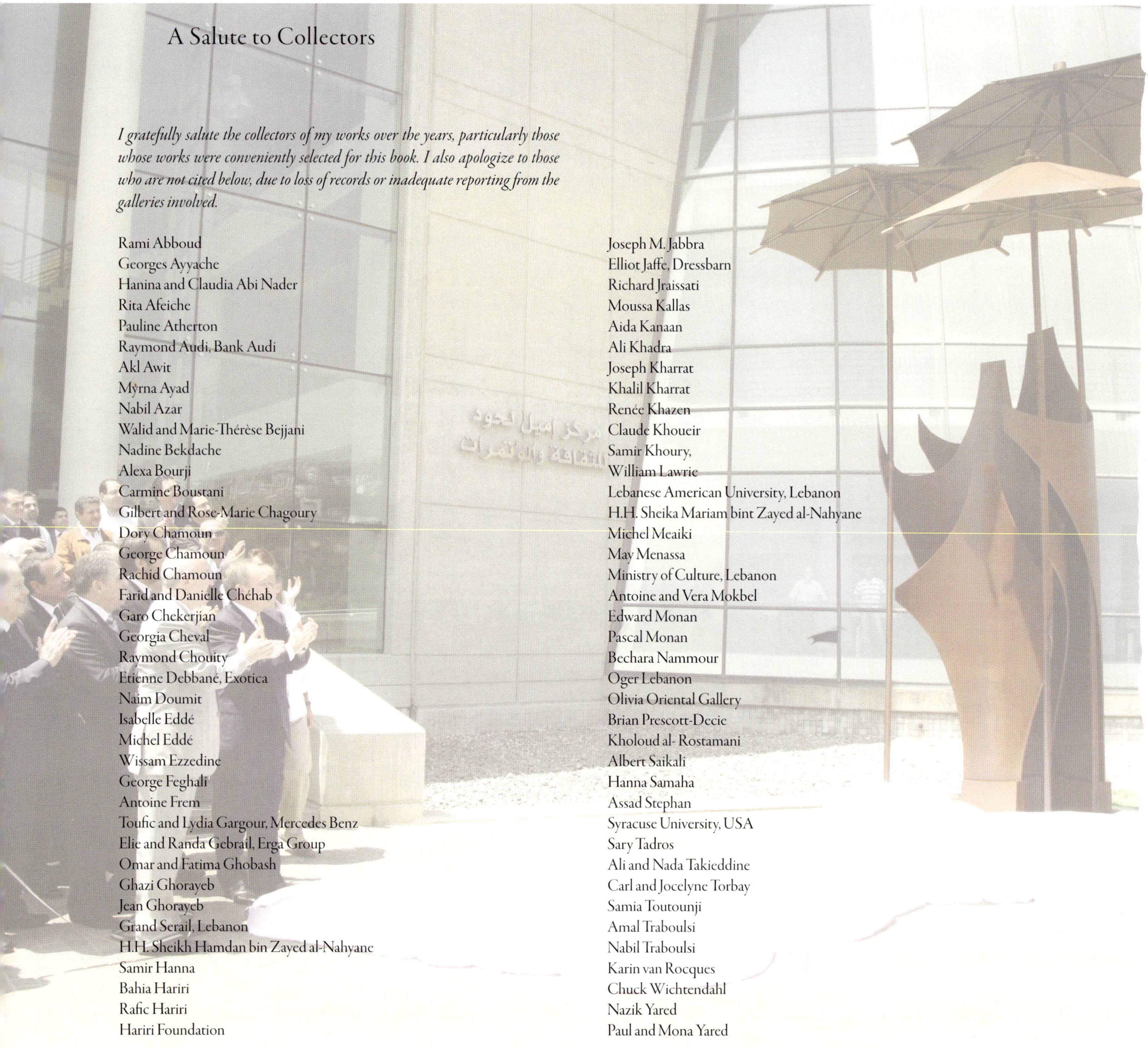

A Salute to Collectors

I gratefully salute the collectors of my works over the years, particularly those whose works were conveniently selected for this book. I also apologize to those who are not cited below, due to loss of records or inadequate reporting from the galleries involved.

Rami Abboud
Georges Ayyache
Hanina and Claudia Abi Nader
Rita Afeiche
Pauline Atherton
Raymond Audi, Bank Audi
Akl Awit
Myrna Ayad
Nabil Azar
Walid and Marie-Thérèse Bejjani
Nadine Bekdache
Alexa Bourji
Carmine Boustani
Gilbert and Rose-Marie Chagoury
Dory Chamoun
George Chamoun
Rachid Chamoun
Farid and Danielle Chéhab
Garo Chekerjian
Georgia Cheval
Raymond Chouity
Etienne Debbané, Exotica
Naim Doumit
Isabelle Eddé
Michel Eddé
Wissam Ezzedine
George Feghali
Antoine Frem
Toufic and Lydia Gargour, Mercedes Benz
Elie and Randa Gebrail, Erga Group
Omar and Fatima Ghobash
Ghazi Ghorayeb
Jean Ghorayeb
Grand Serail, Lebanon
H.H. Sheikh Hamdan bin Zayed al-Nahyane
Samir Hanna
Bahia Hariri
Rafic Hariri
Hariri Foundation
Joseph M. Jabbra
Elliot Jaffe, Dressbarn
Richard Jraissati
Moussa Kallas
Aida Kanaan
Ali Khadra
Joseph Kharrat
Khalil Kharrat
Renée Khazen
Claude Khoueir
Samir Khoury,
William Lawrie
Lebanese American University, Lebanon
H.H. Sheika Mariam bint Zayed al-Nahyane
Michel Meaiki
May Menassa
Ministry of Culture, Lebanon
Antoine and Vera Mokbel
Edward Monan
Pascal Monan
Bechara Nammour
Oger Lebanon
Olivia Oriental Gallery
Brian Prescott-Decie
Kholoud al- Rostamani
Albert Saikali
Hanna Samaha
Assad Stephan
Syracuse University, USA
Sary Tadros
Ali and Nada Takieddine
Carl and Jocelyne Torbay
Samia Toutounji
Amal Traboulsi
Nabil Traboulsi
Karin van Rocques
Chuck Wichtendahl
Nazik Yared
Paul and Mona Yared